Expert Guide to Visual Basic 6

D1609382

Expert Guide™ to Visual Basic® 6

Wayne S. Freeze

SYBEX®

San Francisco • Paris • Düsseldorf • Soest

Associate Publisher: Gary Masters
Contracts and Licensing Manager: Kristine Plachy
Acquisitions & Developmental Editor: Peter Kuhns
Editor: Marilyn Smith
Project Editor: Diane Lowery
Technical Editor: Tyler Regas
Book Designer: Kris Warrenburg
Graphic Illustrator: Tony Jonick
Electronic Publishing Specialist: Kris Warrenburg
Production Coordinator: Blythe Woolston
Indexer: Ted Laux
Companion CD: Ginger Warner
Cover Designer: Ingalls + Associates
Cover Illustrator/Photographer: Mark Johann

Screen reproductions produced with Collage Complete.

Collage Complete is a trademark of Inner Media Inc.

SYBEX is a registered trademark of SYBEX Inc.

Expert Guide is a trademark of SYBEX Inc.

TRADEMARKS: SYBEX has attempted throughout this book to
distinguish proprietary trademarks from descriptive terms by following the capitalization style used by the manufacturer.

The CD Interface music is from GIRA Sound AURIA Music
Library © GIRA Sound 1996.

Library of Congress Card Number: 98-86637
ISBN: 0-7821-2349-X

Manufactured in the United States of America

10 9 8 7 6 5 4 3 2

*To my mother, who made me work
on this book rather than visit her
when she needed me the most*

ACKNOWLEDGMENTS

Nearly everyone thinks being an author is a wonderful job. You get to work at home, set your own hours, and have the freedom to do what you please. The only people who don't believe this are the authors, their families, and the people who take the manuscripts and make them magically appear in books. They know that writing is hard work, and the few minutes of joy don't always make up for the months of 16-hour days.

I want to thank Laura Belt for all her hard work. Maybe someday we'll be able to make a real living from writing! When can Koko come over and play with Freddie?

I also want to say thanks to my new friends at Sybex: Pete Kuhns (the first editor I met in person before I started writing for him); Diane Lowery (who tried to keep me on schedule and couldn't); Marilyn Smith (who rewrote the few lines my wife didn't rewrite and made a good book even better); Michael Lee (who wrote Appendix A when I ran out of time); Tyler Regas (who checked the book for technical accuracy); Ginger Warner (who made sense of all those Visual Basic files on the CD-ROM); Kris Warrenburg (who transformed the word processor files into the printed pages); Tony Jonick (for the artwork); and Blythe Woolston (for her comments in the galleys—I'm glad you found the book fun to read). Without your efforts and patience, this book wouldn't be worth reading. Now, when can I start on the next one?

One other aspect of writing is that it occupies so much time, I don't always find time to visit or even talk to my friends. Shaun, Elwyn, Rick, Bob W., Veronica, Scott, Bob K., and Ian, I'll be in touch soon. I promise. Thanks for your support.

Family is also very important to me. I thought writing would let me have more time for them. Wrong! However, I want to say that Bucky and Goose are two of the best in-laws you could ask for. Life around you is never boring!

I feel badly about not being able to go visit my Mom and Dad as often as I'd like. I'm sorry I couldn't be there a few weeks ago. I'm coming up to visit as soon as I can finish writing this book. (By the way, would you mind watching the kids while Jill and I run a few errands?)

If you read this book carefully, you will find several references to Christopher, Samantha, and Jill. Chris is just five years old and knows more about computers than some well-paid people I used to work with! And Samantha is only four, but she's not that far behind Chris in her ability to crash Windows on demand. I love both of you a whole lot. Now who wants to take a ride in the Porsche?

My lovely wife Jill is a respected writer in her own right, having written books on Microsoft Office, Internet Explorer, and WebTV. I just want to say that if you believe in yourself, anything is possible, and that I love you.

CONTENTS AT A GLANCE

Introduction   *xxvii*

PART I   Visual Basic Fundamentals

    Chapter 1: Introducing Visual Basic 6   3

    Chapter 2: Preparing the Visual Basic Environment   33

    Chapter 3: Debugging Visual Basic Programs   65

    Chapter 4: Using Disk Files   89

    Chapter 5: Using Virtual Basic Functions   127

    Chapter 6: Helping Your Users   161

PART II   Useful Visual Basic Objects and ActiveX Controls

    Chapter 7: Displaying Information with the Big Controls   207

    Chapter 8: Reading and Sending E-Mail Messages   251

    Chapter 9: Printing with Visual Basic   295

    Chapter 10: Providing Useful Controls for Your Users   329

PART III   Internet Applications

    Chapter 11: Transferring Files over the Internet   391

    Chapter 12: Building Client/Server Programs with Winsock   421

PART IV   **Advanced Programming Techniques**

Chapter 13: Adding Scripting Support to Your Application   463

Chapter 14: Incorporating Animated Agents into Your Programs   503

Chapter 15: Communicating with Other Programs   557

Chapter 16: Writing Win32 API Programs   593

Chapter 17: Making Visual Basic Do What You Want   651

Chapter 18: Dynamically Adding Controls at Runtime   697

PART V   **Application Optimization**

Chapter 19: Optimizing Your Application   727

Chapter 20: Handling Errors in Visual Basic   759

Appendixes

Appendix A: Using Microsoft Transaction Server with Visual Basic   785

Appendix B: About the Sample Programs   821

Index   *863*

TABLE OF CONTENTS

Introduction   *xxvii*

PART I   **Visual Basic Fundamentals**

   1   **Introducing Visual Basic 6**   **3**

From Visual Basic 3 to Visual Basic 6   4
The Different Editions of Visual Basic   5
   The Learning Edition   6
   The Professional Edition   6
   The Enterprise Edition   6
System Requirements for Visual Basic 6   7
New Features in Visual Basic 6   8
   New Data-Access Features   8
   New Internet Access   9
   New Language Features   10
   New Wizards   11
   New Controls   11
   New Help Facility   13
How Visual Basic Works   14
   Windows Programming Concepts   15
   How Visual Basic Runs a Program   17
   Types of Visual Basic Programs   18
   Files Associated with a Visual Basic Project   19
Migration from Previous Versions of Visual Basic   21
   General Migration Issues   21
   Migration of Controls   22
   Database Issues   27
Final Thoughts   30

   2   **Preparing the Visual Basic Environment**   **33**

Tweaking the IDE   34

Setting IDE Options   34
Using Templates   38
Adding Objects and ActiveX Controls   39
Setting Project Properties   42
Requiring a License Key   43
Choosing a Threading Model   44
Adding Copyright and Version Information   45
Adding Command-Line Arguments   47
Using Conditional Compilation   48
Using the Object Browser   48
Using the Package and Deployment Wizard   50
Packaging Your Application   51
Deploying Your Application   61
Customizing Your Setup Program   61
Final Thoughts   62

3   Debugging Visual Basic Programs   65
Preventing Bugs Before They Occur   66
Using Option Explicit   67
Applying the KISS Principle   68
Applying the SMILE Principle   68
Taking Advantage of Object-Oriented Programming   69
Using Comments and Coding Conventions   70
Being a Lazy Programmer   74
Isolating Bugs the Easy Way   75
Displaying Information with MsgBox   76
Using Ctrl+Break and the Immediate Window   77
Adding Debug.Assert   78
Adding Debug.Print   79
Using the Visual Basic Debugger   79
Debugging with Breakpoints   79
Watching Expressions   82
Tracking Down the Problem   84
Finding Array Problems   85
Checking Parameter Ranges   85
Watching for Error Object Problems   86
Final Thoughts   86

4   Using Disk Files   **89**

Using the Traditional File-Access Approach   90
   Making Statements   90
   Using Functions to Process Files   92
   Displaying File Information with Controls   94
   Selecting a File   94
   Accessing Files Sequentially   99
   Accessing Files Randomly   103
Introducing File System Objects   108
   Working with Drives   111
   Working with Folders   114
   Working with Files   117
   Reading and Writing a File Sequentially   120
Final Thoughts   124

5   Using Virtual Basic Functions   **127**

Using Date Functions   128
   Dealing with Year 2000 Issues   130
   Converting Strings to Dates and Back Again   132
   Creating Your Own Date Formats   134
   Getting Date and Time Information   138
   Performing Date Arithmetic   139
Using Financial Functions   141
   Calculating Depreciation and Rate of Return   142
   Computing Annuities   143
Using String Functions   144
   Formatting Data for Presentation   147
   Searching and Editing Strings   149
Using Resource Files   150
   Working with Multiple Foreign Languages   151
   Creating a Resource File   151
   Accessing a Resource File   157
   Making International Programs   158
Final Thoughts   159

6   Helping Your Users   **161**

Handling Forms   162
   Centering a Form   162

Remembering Where You Put a Form   164
Resizing a Form   167
Loading Your Form Faster   171
Processing the Tab and Access Keys   172
Handling Tabs   172
Creating Access Keys   174
Checking User-Input Values   176
Using the KeyPress Event to Check Data   177
Using the Change Event to Check Data   178
Using the LostFocus Event to Check Data   179
Using the Validate Event to Check Data   180
Using Combo Boxes to Enter Data   180
Handling Long Processing Waits   184
Getting Information about the User's System   187
Getting Operating System Information   187
Getting Power and Battery Information   188
Getting Screen Information   191
Getting Application Information   194
Tracking System Events   196
Saving the System Information   200
Final Thoughts   202

PART II   Useful Visual Basic Objects and ActiveX Controls

7   Displaying Information with the Big Controls   207

Using TreeView and ListView   208
Managing Hierarchies with the TreeView Control   209
Listing Items with the ListView Control   215
Using MSFlexGrid and MSChart   221
Displaying Data with the MSFlexGrid Control   222
Displaying Charts with the MSChart Control   237
Final Thoughts   247

8   Reading and Sending E-Mail Messages   251

Using Simple MAPI   252
Establishing a MAPI Session   253
Fetching MAPI Messages   255
Reading a MAPI Message   256

Sending a MAPI Message   256
Sending a MAPI Message Revisited   257
Introducing Collaboration Data Objects   259
Adding CDO to Your Program   260
Using the Session Object   264
Working with InfoStores   267
Working with Folders   267
Working with Messages   268
Working with Attachments   272
Working with Recipients   274
Working with Address Lists   276
Working with Address Entries   276
Programming with CDO   278
Initializing the MAPI Session   279
Loading InfoStore Information   280
Loading the MAPI Folders   281
Displaying the Contents of a Folder   283
Displaying a Message   286
Processing a Message   287
Final Thoughts   292

9   **Printing with Visual Basic**   **295**
Introducing the Printer Object   296
Printing in Windows   298
Printing from Applications   299
Selecting a Printer   299
Loading Device Names into a Combo Box   299
Showing the Printer Dialog Box   300
Creating Output for the Printer   302
Printing Text   303
Generating Simple Graphics   312
Including Images   314
Pulling It Together   315
Building a Print Preview Window   318
Creating Output for a Particular Page   318
Using Common Routines   319
A Simple Print Preview Example   323
A More Complex Print Preview Example   324
Final Thoughts   326

10   Providing Useful Controls for Your Users   329

Adding Menus   330
  Designing Your Menu Structure   331
  Creating Menu Arrays   336
  Building Pop-Up Menus   338
Adding Status Bars   340
  Defining Panels in the Status Bar   342
  Displaying Information in a Status Bar   345
  Responding to Click Events in a Status Bar   346
Adding Toolbars   348
  Creating a Toolbar   348
  Adding Buttons to a Toolbar   352
  Handling a Toolbar's Events   354
  Customizing Your Toolbar   357
Adding CoolBars   358
  Creating a CoolBar   359
  Adding Controls to a Band   361
  Programming Your CoolBar   362
Using Controls to Aid Data Entry   366
  Using the MonthView Control   367
  Using the DateTimePicker Control   372
  Using the ImageCombo Control   377
  Using the MaskedEdit Control   381
Final Thoughts   385

PART III   Internet Applications

11   Transferring Files over the Internet   391

Reviewing Internet Requirements   392
  Assigning IP Addresses and Domain Names   393
  Using Port Numbers and Protocols   394
  Using Universal Resource Locators   396
Reviewing the Protocols Supported by the Internet Transfer Control   397
  Using the File Transfer Protocol   397
  Using the HyperText Transport Protocol   399
Using the Internet Transfer Control   400
  Adding an Internet Transfer Control   400
  Using Internet Transfer Control Methods   402

Issuing FTP Commands   404
Issuing HTTP Commands   406
Programming with the Internet Transfer Control   407
Final Thoughts   418

12 Building Client/Server Programs with Winsock   421

Reviewing the Network Service Protocols   422
Using the Winsock Control   423
Adding a Winsock Control   423
Using Winsock Control Methods   426
Using Winsock Control Events   427
Building an Internet Client Program   428
Requesting the Quote   430
Receiving the Quote   431
Building an Internet Server Program   432
Starting the Server   433
Handing Multiple Connection Requests   434
Running the Telnet Session   435
Processing a Line of Input   437
Processing a Command   440
Building a Client/Server Application   442
Playing the Game   443
Developing the Protocol   445
Requesting a Connection   448
Making a Connection   449
Receiving Data   450
Processing Protocol Statements   451
Building the Game Board   455
Attacking an Opponent   456
Final Thoughts   458

PART IV   Advanced Programming Techniques

13 Adding Scripting Support to Your Application   463

Using the ScriptControl   464
Adding a ScriptControl   465
Using ScriptControl Methods   466
Using ScriptControl Events   468
Getting Error Information   468

Programming with VBScript   469
    Following Data Type Rules   470
    Using VBScript Statements   470
    Using VBScript Functions   471
    Using VBScript Objects   474
Building a Simple MSScript Program   474
    Adding Code to the Scripting Engine   475
    Evaluating an Expression   477
    Executing a Statement   479
    Running a Program   480
    Handling Errors   481
Designing a Calculator   483
    Handling KeyButton Events   485
    Updating the VBScript Routine   486
    Trapping Script Errors   487
    Defining Objects for the VBScript Program   489
    Loading the VBScript Program   490
    Writing the Calculator Script Program   492
Calculating Equations in a Spreadsheet   494
    Initializing the ScriptControl   495
    Entering an Equation into a Cell   496
    Computing the Value of a Cell   497
    Recalculating the Grid   498
Using the ScriptControl in Your Own Programs   499
Final Thoughts   499

14   Incorporating Animated Agents into Your Programs   503
Introducing Microsoft Agent   504
Installing and Configuring Microsoft Agent   506
    Installing the Software   507
    Installing the Characters   509
    Configuring the Agent Server   510
Using the MSAgent Control   513
    Adding the MSAgent Control to Your Program   514
    Using MSAgent Control Events   515
    Working with Characters   518
    Working with Commands   527
    Working with Balloons   531

Working with Requests   532
Using Other Agent Objects   533
Building a Simple MSAgent Program   534
Making Global Declarations for Hello Jill   535
Initializing the MSAgent Control   535
Speaking the Message   536
Using the Speech Recognition Engine   536
Making Global Declarations for Agent Demo   537
Initializing the Commands Collection   537
Processing Spoken Commands   539
Waiting for a Request to Complete   541
Stopping the Character   542
Developing an Animated Game   542
Making Global Declarations for I'm Thinking of a Color   544
Getting Started   544
Running the Game   545
Initializing the Characters   547
Adding the Commands   548
Receiving Commands   549
Beginning the Game   550
Final Thoughts   553

15 Communicating with Other Programs   557
Running Another Program   558
Starting a Program with the Shell Function   559
Transferring Focus with the AppActivate Statement   560
Sending Keystrokes with the SendKeys Statement   560
Programming with Shell, AppActivate, and SendKeys   563
Using an Application's Objects   565
Creating and Getting Objects   567
Creating a Workbook and Worksheet   570
Adding Data to the Worksheet   571
Formatting Cells   572
Charting the Results   574
Copying the Chart   575
Saving the Workbook   576
Closing the Workbook   577
Exiting Excel   577

Writing ActiveX Programs 578
Using ActiveX 578
Introducing Honest Wayne's Used Airplane Lot 579
Creating the Airplane and Airplanes Objects 579
Starting the Server 581
Getting Information about an Airplane 583
Placing an Order 586
Final Thoughts 588

16   Writing Win32 API Programs   593

Introducing the Win32 API 594
Win32 API Character Sets 595
Win32 API Data Types 596
Calling a Win32 API Routine 599
Declaring a Win32 API Call 599
Defining Win32 API Structures and Constants 601
Using the API Text Viewer 601
Pulling It All Together 602
Using Some Interesting Win32 API Functions 606
Getting Windows Information 608
Getting and Setting Environment Information 612
Getting Process Information 614
Sleeping for a While 620
Playing with System Colors 624
Running a Program 628
Running a File 634
Grabbing an Icon 637
Using New Functions for Text Boxes 641
Shutting Down Windows 646
Final Thoughts 648

17   Making Visual Basic Do What You Want   651

Building Screen Savers 652
Creating the Display Portion 653
Displaying the Form in Full-Screen Mode 657
Unloading the Form on User-Initiated Events 658
Adding a Configuration Form 659
Adding a Module and a Sub Main Routine 660

Adjusting the Program's Properties   661
Installing and Configuring Your Screen Saver   661
Displaying an Icon in the System Tray   664
Adding the Systray Control   664
Programming the Systray Control   666
Accessing the Windows Registry   671
Back Up Your Windows Registry   672
Understanding the Registry Structure   674
Using the Registry Editor   678
Accessing the Registry from Visual Basic   680
Writing Registry Programs   689
Final Thoughts   693

18   Dynamically Adding Controls at Runtime   697

Creating Forms Dynamically   698
Creating a Form   699
Listing Forms   700
Deleting a Form   701
Adding New Controls Dynamically   701
Using Control Arrays   702
Creating Controls without Events   706
Creating Controls with Normal Events   712
Creating Controls with ObjectEvent   714
Using Functions with Dynamically Created Controls   717
Using the CallByName Function   718
Determining Object Type with TypeOf   719
Getting Variable or Expression Type with TypeName   719
Final Thoughts   722

PART V   Application Optimization

19   Optimizing Your Application   727

Defining Your Goals and Constraints   728
Setting Goals   729
Defining Constraints   729
Understanding the Costs   729
Following the General Rules   730
Getting It Right   731

Waiting Until Tomorrow 731

Building Modularly 731

Speeding Up Your Code 732

Using Integers and Longs 732

Avoiding Variants 733

Limiting Property Accesses 733

Setting AutoRedraw and ClipControls to False 734

Hiding Controls and Forms 735

Using Collections 735

Using Lightweight Controls 736

Avoiding Anything Unnecessary 737

Using Early Binding 738

Unrolling Your Loops 738

Sending Multiple Requests to a Server 739

Replacing Calls with Inline Code 739

Reducing the Dots in an Object Reference 741

Testing for Empty Strings 741

Moving Controls with Move 742

Forgetting the Next Variable 743

Tricking the User 743

Handling Long Tasks 743

Performing Background Processing 744

Displaying a Splash Panel 745

Loading Modules and Libraries 746

Being Frugal with Memory 746

Choosing the Optimal Program Type 748

Using an ActiveX Control 750

Using an ActiveX EXE 751

Using an ActiveX DLL 752

Choosing Optimizations 752

Setting Basic Optimizations 754

Setting Advanced Optimizations 754

Final Thoughts 756

20 Handling Errors in Visual Basic   759

Using Visual Basic's Error-Handling Features 760

Getting Error Information with the Err Object 760

Handling Errors with the On Error Statement 762

Continuing with the Resume Statement 762

Programming Error Traps   763
    Using the On Error GoTo Statement   764
    Using the On Error Resume Next Statement   766
    Raising Your Own Errors   767
Adding Your Own Help File   770
    Creating the Topic File   770
    Building the Help File   773
Final Thoughts   783

Appendixes

A   Using Microsoft Transaction Server with Visual Basic   785

Understanding Distributed Application Architecture   786
    Defining Client/Server Architecture   786
    Dividing Tasks into Services   788
    Implementing a Multiple-Tier Architecture   793
Introducing Microsoft Transaction Server   799
    Providing Scalability   800
    Adding Security   801
    Supporting Transactions across Objects   802
Creating MTS-Enabled Components with Visual Basic   805
    Creating the Services   805
    Adding Transaction Support   809
Deploying Components through MTS   811
    Creating an MTS Package   812
    Installing Components into a Package   815
Looking to the Future   818

B   About the Sample Programs   821

Agent Demo   822
CDO Demo   823
Charter   824
Control Tabs   826
Date/Time Demo   827
DateControl   828
DoEvents   828
Dynamic Controls   829
Excel Demo   830

File Viewer   832
Financial Function Demo   833
Forms Collection Demo   834
Hello Jill   834
Honest Wayne's Used Airplane Lot   835
I'm Thinking of a Color   836
Internet Updater   838
Make Errors   839
MAPI Demo   840
MSScript Demo   841
Notepad Writer   841
Package   842
Print   843
Printer   844
Quote of the Day   845
Random File Access   845
Really Programmable Calculator   846
RegTool   847
Resource File Demo   848
Scheduler   849
Screen Saver   849
Sea Wars   851
Sequential File Access   852
Slide Show   852
StarSX   853
String Demo   854
System Information   855
Telnet Server   856
Tips and Tricks Demo   857
VB4 Sample   858
Weather Maker   858
Win32 API Demo   859

Index   *863*

INTRODUCTION

Over the years, the Microsoft developers have invested a lot of time and effort into making Visual Basic easy to use. However, there is always a tradeoff between making something easy to use and making it powerful and flexible. While Microsoft has done an excellent job placing the tradeoff line, there will always be a group of people who wished Microsoft had moved the line closer to the powerful-and-flexible side than to the easy-to-use side. Since you're reading this book, I'm assuming that you are a member of that group. I'm a member of that group also, so I decided to write this book for people like myself.

Where Is Visual Basic Headed?

Visual Basic is Microsoft's strategic language for Rapid Application Development (RAD). It is targeted at programmers who need to build enterprise applications quickly and without a lot of fuss. Visual Basic takes care of most of the grungy details of programming in Windows, leaving you free to concentrate on your application.

You can build a meaningful program in Visual Basic without a single line of code. Don't believe me? Start a new program and put a Data control on it. In the Data control's properties, specify the name of the database and the name of the table you wish to access. Then put some Textbox and Label controls on the form. Set the `DataSource` property to the Data control and set the `DataField` property to the name of a column in your database. When you're finished, click Run. You now have a program without a single line of code that can scroll through a database table.

To create this type of program in Visual C++ would take a lot of code and a lot more time to put all of the pieces together. While the C++ program might be faster, the average user wouldn't notice the difference in speed between the two programs. So why write in Visual C++? Well, there will always be a need for a programming language like C++. Visual Basic is a little too far removed from the hardware to build efficient operating systems and compilers. But when was the last time you wrote an operating system or compiler?

Visual Basic is also Microsoft's choice for a macro language. You saw it first in Excel 5 and then again in the entire suite of Office 97 products. It's buried inside Internet Explorer to give web site developers an alternative to JavaScript. Microsoft has just included a replacement for the .BAT files in Windows 98 and Windows NT 5 called Windows Scripting Host. What's it based on? You guessed it—Visual Basic.

What will the future bring for Visual Basic? If the current version is any indication, you'll see more controls that make it easier and faster to build application programs. You'll also see integration into more tools like Windows Scripting Host and Internet Explorer, as well as the ability to work with other operating system components like the Internet Information Server (IIS) and Microsoft Transaction Server (MTS). Visual Basic already includes support for the Component Object Model (COM) and Distributed Component Object Model (DCOM), so when COM+ is made available, you can bet that Visual Basic will be there too.

Why Not Use Third-Party Visual Basic Tools?

Since I started using Visual Basic years ago, I kept running into limitations that I didn't like. I was faced with two choices: I could either buy someone else's solution or build my own.

There are two major problems with buying a third-party software package. First, these software packages cost money. The costs vary from a few dollars to register your favorite shareware utility to hundreds of thousands of dollars or more for complicated utilities that run on large-scale servers and networks.

Second, as Microsoft changes Visual Basic, these software packages must change as well. Microsoft frequently introduces a new feature that makes the third-party package obsolete or changes the way Visual Basic works so that you need to upgrade to the latest and greatest Microsoft product. This costs still more money indirectly, either in time needed to convert your program to the new standard or to upgrade your third-party software package.

I've been programming for more than 25 years. I've used more programming languages and operating systems than I can remember, so this isn't really a new issue. It's been a problem in the mainframe world for a long time. Using third-party tools often solves your immediate problems, but over time, upgrades will lag, the technology will become obsolete, and you're still stuck with the product. Eventually, the vendors will stabilize the product, which means that they won't even fix bugs anymore.

You can avoid these problems by trying to exploit every last little capability that comes on those CD-ROMs you bought from Microsoft. The Microsoft developers put all that stuff there for a reason, and they don't plan on abandoning support for it—at least not in the short run.

Who Should Read This Book?

This book is aimed at intermediate to advanced programmers who already have a good working knowledge of Visual Basic. This means that you should know how to build programs, be comfortable with the development environment, and know how to use most of the common controls, such as Textbox, Label, and Command-Button. I also assume that you know how to use Windows and understand concepts such as files, directories, and overlapping windows.

If you don't know this material, then I suggest reading *Mastering Visual Basic* (published by Sybex). Then you can return to this book and become an expert.

What Does This Book Cover?

This book tries to cover many of the "Gee-Whiz" features that are in Visual Basic 6, plus all that other stuff you need to help you build fast and stable programs quickly and efficiently. It is written from the point of view of someone who has a deadline and doesn't want to go down an alley that seems promising at first but then turns out to be a dead end. This book will help you avoid those pitfalls.

Visual Basic has so many interesting features that no single person can be an expert on all of them. However, you don't need to be an expert on all of the features to use them in your programs. You can learn just enough information about a particular feature or technique so that you can begin using it immediately. If you find it useful, you can pursue more detailed information in other, more specialized books.

The Book's Organization

This book is organized into five parts. The first part, "Visual Basic Fundamentals," covers some of the new features of Visual Basic 6, as well as the features that have been around for a while but you might not have considered using. I get you started with some tips on setting up the Visual Basic environment, debugging your programs, using disk files, and programming with Visual Basic functions. The last chapter in the part offers some tips and tricks that make your applications easier to use, such as remembering the last location where a form was displayed and how to build a resizable form.

The title of the second part, "Useful Visual Basic Objects and ActiveX Controls," says it all. In those chapters, I talk about the controls that make Visual Basic so easy to use. I begin with what I call the "big controls," which include TreeView, ListView, MSGrid, and MSChart. The next chapters discuss the controls for e-mail programs and the controls for printing. The final chapter in Part II is a long one, because it covers all those controls that make your programs easy for your users to use—toolbars, status bars, menus, and the new MonthView and DateTimePicker controls.

The third part, "Internet Applications" is short, with only two chapters, but crucial to programmers who want their applications to access the Internet (and who doesn't?). The first chapter describes how to use the Internet Transfer control, which supports FTP and HTTP file transfers. The other chapter is about using the Winsock control to implement standard Internet protocols and the techniques to use it to build your own Internet-based client/server programs.

In the fourth part, "Advanced Programming Techniques," I cover a variety of techniques that allow you to get the most from Visual Basic. Here, you'll read about adding scripting support, including Office-Assistant type animations using Microsoft Agent, and communicating with other programs using COM and DCOM. I also describe how to make Win32 API calls to take advantage of many useful functions that aren't available in Visual Basic and how to do some things in Visual Basic that you thought you couldn't. Finally, I explain how to add controls to your form dynamically.

The final part, "Application Optimization," contains two chapters with information that every programmer should know. One of these chapters contains some tips and tricks for optimizing your applications, and the other covers error handling in your Visual Basic programs.

The book also has two appendices. Appendix A is about using Microsoft Transaction Server (MTS)—a big topic that is just touched upon here to give you an idea of how you can program MTS-enabled components. Appendix B is a reference to all the sample programs that are discussed in the book and included on the CD-ROM that accompanies this book.

The CD-ROM

Nearly as important as the book is the CD-ROM. Every program discussed in this book is on the CD-ROM. You should take the time to try the programs on the CD-ROM or at least look at the source code. If you wish, you can copy parts of these programs into your own programs. That's why the book has a CD-ROM. In Appendix B, you can find a list of all the programs, which chapters contain listings from which programs, and where the programs are located on the CD-ROM.

While you can run all of the programs I wrote for this book (can you believe there are 40 of them?), most need additional work if they are to be used by a non-programmer. This is intentional. My goal is to communicate how to use specific features of Visual Basic, not necessarily how to build polished applications. If I can accomplish that by leaving out such nice features as an Exit button, then so be it.

The CD-ROM also contains some other goodies, including some third-party Visual Basic software, such as Applet Designer 1.7, InstallShield, and RoboHelp. See the last page of this book for a complete list.

What Isn't Covered in This Book?

This book doesn't attempt to teach you the fundamentals of programming. If you don't know the difference between an event and a text box, come back after you've read *Mastering Visual Basic 6* (Petroutsos, Sybex, 1998) and have worked with Visual Basic for a few months. You'll feel a lot more comfortable with the subject matter.

This book also doesn't cover database programming. A good introduction to Visual Basic database programming would have doubled the size of the book. The *Visual Basic Developer's Handbook* (Petroutsos and Hough, Sybex, 1999) covers database programming and a number of other more advanced Visual Basic programming techniques. It would be a good book to read after finishing this one.

What About the Author?

In case you're wondering, I'm a full-time computer book author and computer technology consultant, and this is my fifth computer book. My previous books discuss programming in Visual Basic, SQL, and the Internet. I'm also the author of a popular shareware program called *Car Collector*, which is written in Visual Basic.

My experience with personal computers began in 1977 when I built one of the original personal computer systems, the Altair 8800, from a kit. With 4KB BASIC in ROM and 1KB of RAM, it wasn't very practical, but it was a lot of fun. Since then, I have used nearly every major type of personal computer made and many different medium and large-scale computers. I currently have six or seven computers scattered around the house, but my Gateway 9100 laptop is currently my computer of choice.

If you look closely, you'll see evidence of my hobbies throughout this book. I collect cars ranging in size from a 1:144 Dodge Viper to a 1:1 Porsche Turbo, driven only when there is no rain in sight. I can also be found at air shows photographing World War II fighters. I hope to get my pilot's license someday and then get certified to fly a P-51 Mustang.

I currently reside in Beltsville, Maryland, with my lovely wife, Jill, who helps me with my writing by deleting all those unnecessary commas and making sure that everything I say makes sense. Jill is also a full-time author with her fourth computer book due out shortly. My son Christopher is five and was the youngest unofficial beta tester for Microsoft Windows 98, using it for over two months before it was officially released. My four-year-old daughter Samantha specializes in being cute and practicing her cartwheels at the least convenient times. My family also includes three cats (Pixel, Terry, and Cali), a brand new golden retriever puppy named Lady Kokomo, and an aquarium with some beautiful veiled angelfish and a neon-blue shrimp.

I maintain a web site at `http://www.JustPC.com` with additional information about the books that my wife and I have written. I try to answer frequently asked questions about the books and will try to point you to other resources you may find interesting.

You're also welcome to send me e-mail at `WFreeze@JustPC.com`. I'll try to respond to your questions and comments as best as I can. However, please understand that I make my living from writing, so you may not necessarily get as prompt or as complete an answer as you may desire. A question I can answer off the top of my head, I'm likely to answer quickly. Likewise, if I can point you in the right direction to help you solve your own problem, I'll do that. If you find a bug or have an idea to improve any of the sample projects, please let me know. With your permission, I'll add any good information to my web site so others can benefit from it.

PART I

Visual Basic Fundamentals

CHAPTER
ONE

1

Introducing Visual Basic 6

- Some Visual Basic history

- Editions of Visual Basic 6

- Visual Basic 6 system requirements

- Visual Basic 6 features and enhancements

- The Visual Basic programming environment

- Visual Basic version migration issues

Unlike the change from Visual Basic 3 to Visual Basic 4, which introduced us to the 32-bit world, and from Visual Basic 4 to Visual Basic 5, which let us build our own ActiveX objects, the change from Visual Basic 5 to Visual Basic 6 is more evolutionary than revolutionary. The changes mainly involve new controls, objects, and wizards that will make your life easier. This doesn't mean that upgrading to Visual Basic 6 is not worthwhile; it merely means that the transition will be easier than in the past. (If you're like me, you still have some 16-bit code lying around that you never got around to upgrading to 32-bit because it wasn't worth the headaches.)

In this chapter, I'll start with some background information that may or may not be familiar to you. Then I'll cover the various editions of Visual Basic, the new features of Visual Basic, and an overview of how Visual Basic works. I'll also talk about some of the problems you may encounter when migrating from a previous version of Visual Basic to Visual Basic 6.

From Visual Basic 3 to Visual Basic 6

Visual Basic version 3 (released in May 1993) was the first version of Visual Basic to give developers the ability to easily create their own Windows database applications. The database system used in Visual Basic 3 was Microsoft Jet 1.1, which was an enhanced version of the database engine used in Access 1.0.

Visual Basic version 4 was the first version of Visual Basic that could develop 32-bit Windows programs. However, due to the popularity of Windows 3.x, a 16-bit version of Visual Basic was also included. The 16-bit version offered many new features beyond what had been available in Visual Basic 3, while making it relatively easy to upgrade. It also featured Jet 2.5, which was an improved Access 2.0 database engine.

The 32-bit version of Visual Basic 4, however, wasn't as compatible with Visual Basic 3 as the 16-bit version of Visual Basic 4. Many new controls existed, some of which replaced older controls. The database engine was also different since it was based on the Jet 3.0 database engine used for Access 95.

In Visual Basic version 5, the 16-bit support was completely dropped. This caused developers some grief, and many developers didn't bother to migrate since they couldn't use it to develop for Windows 3.x platforms. Visual Basic 5 featured the Jet 3.5 database also used in Access 97.

Visual Basic 5 also introduced the capability to build your own controls. Previously, if you wanted to create your own controls, you needed to write them in C++, which was time-consuming and complicated, because they had to be written to OLE 2 specifications rather than today's lighter weight ActiveX specifications.

Visual Basic 6 is based heavily on Visual Basic 5. In fact, I think of Visual Basic 6 as Visual Basic 5 plus every available factory option. While version 6 adds a lot of new features, it doesn't change any of the existing features. So, where Visual Basic 5 had an AM/FM radio with cassette player, Visual Basic 6 adds the multi-disk CD changer that is controlled from the AM/FM radio.

From a compatibility point of view, if it ran in Visual Basic 5, it should run in Visual Basic 6 without modification. Please don't take this to mean that there are no changes to the Visual Basic programming environment, or that if you happened to name one of your user controls ImageCombo (a new control in version 6) you won't see the difference. However, there are no significant changes that need to be made to your source code to make it run under Visual Basic 6. I'll talk about Visual Basic migration issues in more detail later in this chapter.

The Different Editions of Visual Basic

Visual Basic comes in three different flavors: the Learning edition, the Professional edition, and the Enterprise edition. All three editions are based on the same technology and differ only in the controls and tools provided.

The Microsoft Developer's Network CD-ROMs are included with each of the Visual Basic editions. These CD-ROMs contain the documentation for Visual Basic plus many sample programs, questions and answers, and other relevant information.

Visual Basic is also included as part of the Visual Studio package, along with Visual C++, Visual InterDev, Visual J++, and Visual FoxPro. Visual Studio is available in two editions: the Professional edition and the Enterprise edition. They offer the same features as the Visual Basic Professional and Enterprise editions (which I'll describe in a moment).

TIP
Visual Studio versus Visual Basic: If you program in more than one language, consider purchasing Visual Studio. For about 50 percent more than the cost of Visual Basic, you can purchase all five of Microsoft's programming languages. Even if you aren't currently working with any of the other languages, having them available in Visual Studio provides an excellent opportunity to learn them.

Since you already know Visual Basic, I'm going to assume that you are using either the Professional or Enterprise edition of Visual Basic. This doesn't mean that what I'm talking about won't work on the Learning edition. It just means that I haven't tried it.

The Learning Edition

The Learning edition of Visual Basic is targeted at students and other individuals who wish to learn how to program in Visual Basic. It includes a multimedia CD-ROM called "Learn VB Now," which teaches the user the fundamentals of programming with Visual Basic.

As you might expect, the Learning edition of Visual Basic is the least functional of the trio. It contains all of the intrinsic controls and the Grid, Tab, and data-bound ActiveX controls, but the other ActiveX controls are missing.

The Professional Edition

The Professional edition of Visual Basic is targeted at programmers who need the full range of capabilities of Visual Basic but don't need the Microsoft BackOffice features included in the Enterprise edition.

The rest of the ActiveX controls (those missing from the Learning edition) are included in the Professional edition, plus the Internet Server Application Designer, the Dynamic HTML Page Designer, the Data Environment, the Integrated Data Tools, and the ActiveX Data Objects.

The Enterprise Edition

The Enterprise edition of Visual Basic is targeted at groups of people developing applications jointly. It includes special versions of Microsoft SQL Server, Transaction Server, Internet Information Server, and SNA Server from the Microsoft BackOffice suite.

Besides the BackOffice tools, the Enterprise edition also includes a number of useful tools, such as:

- Application Performance Explorer, to examine your program for bottlenecks

- Visual Component Manager, to access and organize reusable components

- Visual Modeler, to create diagrams of an application's architecture

- Visual Source Safe, to manage your source code

- Data Environment Designer, to create ActiveX Data Objects

- OLE-DB, for use as a lower-level database-access method

- Remote Data Objects (RDO), the RemoteData control, and a SQL Editor that can edit stored procedures in SQL Server and Oracle databases

System Requirements for Visual Basic 6

Microsoft states that Visual Basic requires a Pentium 90 with at least 24MB of main memory running Windows 95 or 98, or 32MB of memory when running Windows NT. It will not run on Windows 3.1 or earlier systems.

Based on personal experience, 32MB of memory is fine for Windows 95 and 98, but Windows NT requires a minimum of 64MB for acceptable performance. (Of course, Windows NT really needs 64MB to run anything more complicated than Solitaire.)

Obviously, Visual Basic requires a CD-ROM for installation, but unless you have lots of disk space, you'll probably be using the CD-ROM to hold the documentation. Disk space required for the core product ranges from 48MB to 147MB.

Also, Visual Basic will require the latest version of Internet Explorer (4.01) and the Microsoft Developer's Network (MSDN) library to display help information. These will take anywhere from an additional 133MB to more than 550MB of disk space.

Bigger Is Better

Visual Basic 6 uses Microsoft Developer's Network (MSDN) as its help engine. MSDN now uses the latest HTML technology to store its information. This requires loading Internet Explorer 4 when you want to display help information.

If you want to have instant access to the help files, plan on loading at least part of the MSDN library to your hard disk. Additional main memory is also a good idea, since it will help to minimize the amount of swapping when you are using both Visual Basic and Internet Explorer.

Also note that the speed of the processor is not as critical as main memory. If you can't afford the fastest processor available and lots of memory, buy a slightly slower processor and put your money into more memory. You'll get better performance in the long run.

New Features in Visual Basic 6

In its latest version, Visual Basic has been enhanced in a number of different areas. The main focus has been improving Visual Basic's ability to access data, both from databases and over the Internet. Some new ActiveX controls are also included, and some enhancements have been made in the Visual Basic language itself.

New Data-Access Features

Microsoft has superceded both Data Access Objects (DAO) and Remote Data Objects (RDO) with a new technology called ActiveX Data Objects (ADO). ADO uses a much simpler object model than either DAO or RDO, while providing a more uniform method to access data stored in both databases and non-database data stores (such as Outlook).

Many of the old database programming techniques remain the same. For instance, there is a new ADO Data control that corresponds to the Data control used by DAO. The Data Environment allows you to encapsulate the ADO Recordsets and Connections into a dynamic object, where you can write code that handles the ADO events and create methods to perform functions in the new object. Later in this chapter, we'll look at how Visual Basic's new data-access technology affects migration from previous Visual Basic versions.

Enhanced data binding is another new feature. It provides functions similar to bound data controls, but allows you to bind any data source to any data consumer. Thus, you are no longer limited to a Data control as your data source.

The Data Repeater control makes it easier to build forms with repeating fields. Previously, you needed to manually handle the number of times a set of fields was displayed in a hierarchical form. Imagine the code required to display an order form with the customer information at the top of the form and a variable number of items in the order. The Data Repeater control simplifies this by treating a single item in the order and repeating it as many times as necessary.

A new Hierarchical FlexGrid control is available to display hierarchical data sets created from multiple data sources. Format objects are provided to format data as it is moved from a database to your program and back again.

Data Report replaces Crystal Reports as the primary tool used to generate reports in Visual Basic. This new tool offers you much more flexibility and provides better integration with Visual Basic than Crystal Reports.

The Enterprise edition also includes a Database Designer and Query Designer, which simplify building databases and queries, and the SQL Editor, which allows you to build stored procedures in SQL Server and Oracle databases.

Also new to Visual Basic 6 is the File System Objects approach to managing and accessing files. You'll see how this works in Chapter 4, where I talk about using disk files with your Visual Basic programs.

New Internet Access

Besides overhauling the data-access strategy, Microsoft has added new support for Internet programming. Two new features are available: IIS Applications and DHTML Applications.

With previous versions, if you wanted to take advantage of the improved performance offered by the Internet Server Applications Programming Interface (ISAPI) available on the Internet Information Server (IIS), you had to either write your programs in C++ or use a kludge called OLEISAPI. OLEISAPI translated ISAPI calls into OLE calls, which permitted you to build your own ActiveX program that would be called from IIS and would return an HTML document. Now, Visual Basic includes a feature called IIS Applications, which allows you to write Visual Basic programs that hook directly into IIS.

DHTML Applications allows you to take advantage of Internet Explorer 4's capabilities to process Dynamic HTML. Thus, you can build routines that respond to the events in a DHMTL web page and manipulate the properties and use the methods accordingly.

The `AsyncRead` method has been enhanced to provide more information about the state of action while the process is still active. Internet Explorer now handles downloading ActiveX documents in the same fashion as ActiveX controls. State information may now be saved across pages and frames to a global Property Bag when using Internet Explorer 3 or 4.

I'll go into details about using these features in the chapters in Part 3, which cover building Internet applications.

New Language Features

How can you improve a language like Visual Basic? If you're smart, you make only minor changes to the language's syntax and add bunches of new routines. Well, I guess the Microsoft developers are very smart, since they did exactly that.

In terms of syntax, user-defined types can now be used in public methods, functions can return arrays, and resizable arrays may now be on the left side of an assignment statement. (Fixed-sized arrays still may appear only on the right side of an assignment.)

New and improved functions include:

- `CallByName` permits you to call a method or access a property by specifying the appropriate names as a set of strings.

- `CreateObject` now lets you create an object on a remote machine.

- `StrConv` lets you specify a local ID to be used during the conversion process.

Also, a bunch of new string functions are available in Visual Basic 6: `Filter`, `FormatCurrency`, `FormatDateTime`, `FormatNumber`, `FormatPercent`, `InStrRev`, `Join`, `MonthName`, `Replace`, `Found`, `Split`, `StrReverse`, and `WeekdayName`.

New Wizards

A new Package and Deployment Wizard replaces the old Setup Wizard. It allows you to package your finished application and create a .CAB file. Then you can post the package to a web site for downloading or put it in a public folder for distribution. Figure 1.1 shows the Package and Deployment Wizard window. You'll learn more about this wizard in Chapter 2.

FIGURE 1.1:

The new Package and Deployment Wizard

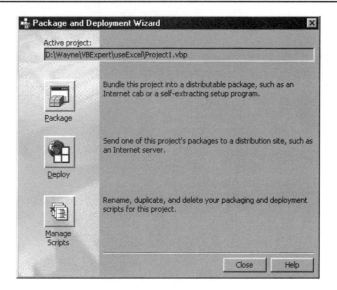

The Application Wizard has been enhanced to make it easier to develop your next application using the values from the last application. Wizards are also available to create Data objects and Data forms. A new Toolbar Wizard helps you build customizable toolbars.

New Controls

Okay, now for the real fun. Of all the new features included in Visual Basic, the new controls are the ones you probably want to try first (at least, they were the first things I played with). Since I already talked about the data-access controls, I'll cover the rest here.

Do you wish you could build toolbars like those on Internet Explorer? Well, the CoolBar control is just waiting for you. You can also add flat scroll bars to your program with the FlatScrollbar control. Figure 1.2 shows a window with both a CoolBar control and a FlatScrollbar control.

FIGURE 1.2:

The cool new CoolBar and FlatScrollbar controls

Do your users get confused when entering dates or ranges of dates? There are two new controls that address this problem. The DateTimePicker and the MonthView controls allow users to enter date information from drop-down calendars. Figure 1.3 shows an example of the new MonthView control.

FIGURE 1.3:

The new MonthView control

Of all the new controls, perhaps the most interesting is the ImageCombo control. It works just like a regular combo box, but now you can put your own icons next to each entry in the combo box. Figure 1.4 shows an example with weather icons.

FIGURE 1.4:

The new ImageCombo
control

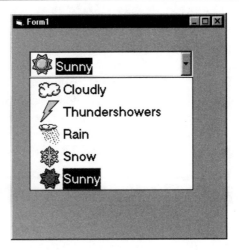

The CoolBar, DateTimePicker, MonthView, and ImageCombo controls are covered in Chapter 10.

New Help Facility

Microsoft has switched to the new HTML-based help facility for Visual Basic 6. You now access help through the MSDN information screens. This is both good and bad. All of the information for Visual Basic and the rest of the Visual Studio products is centralized into one big index. However, because all of this information is combined, you often will run across keywords that differ in capitalization or punctuation—what you think may be a Visual Basic feature may turn out to be Visual FoxPro feature. Also, the sheer size of the MSDN library requires Microsoft to ship it on two CD-ROMs.

TIP

CD-ROMs are fast, but hard disks are faster: When you install Visual Basic (or Visual Studio), you can choose which documentation libraries to load onto your hard disk. You should always load the Visual Basic documentation libraries (about 13MB). If you have the space, you should also load the Full Text Search Index (nearly 100MB). Loading both will save you much time and grief when you search for information in the new library. Plus, it will free up your CD-ROM drive for other tasks.

How Visual Basic Works

Years ago, it was possible to think of BASIC as a programming language. Visual Basic is more of a programming environment than simply a language, since you can't just write a Visual Basic program and run it. You need to create a project, add forms and controls, process events, set properties, and invoke methods. Gone are the days when you could simply type some code. On the other hand, gone are the days whern you had to develop your own screen handler, write your own database routines, and build your own utilities.

The Visual Basic Integrated Development Environment (IDE) ties all of this together, providing visual tools that allow you to quickly build Windows programs. You create a Visual Basic program by dragging and dropping ActiveX controls onto a form that creates windows with all of the graphical user interface (GUI) features that Windows users have become accustomed to. Figure 1.5 shows the New Project window in the Visual Basic IDE.

FIGURE 1.5:

The Visual Basic Integrated Development Environment (IDE)

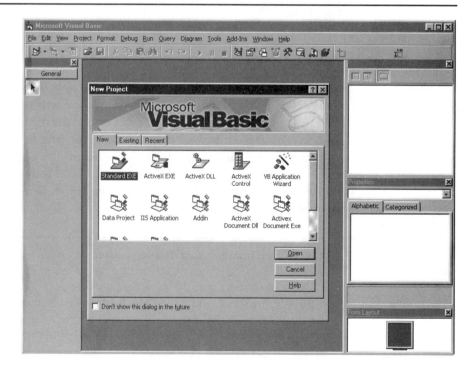

Windows Programming Concepts

Let's begin our discussion by quickly reviewing how Windows programs work. In the following discussion, I greatly oversimplify many of the concepts. If you are interested in the details, you may want to dig into an advanced Windows programming book. However, the information presented here is more than sufficient if you just want to understand how Visual Basic works.

Forms, Objects, and Controls

The fundamental unit in a Visual Basic program is the *form*. A form is really a window on which objects called *controls* are placed. A *window* is simply a rectangular area on your screen where information and images are displayed.

A control is an object that usually has a graphical representation that the user can interact with, such as a button, a scroll bar, a toolbar, or a text box. A control can also simply convey information or images to a user. A control may be a shape, a line, a label box, or a picture box.

Some controls can contain other controls. For instance, a picture control can contain buttons, scroll bars, and nearly any other control you can place on a form. In fact, a form is treated as just another control.

Visual Basic also contains objects that do not have a graphical representation. These are often used for managing data access or building collections of similar items. Each item is declared to be a specific object with standardized ways to access the information it contains.

Messages and Message Processing

Windows programs work by sending information from one object to another. This information is called a *message*, which is created by an *event*. When a message arrives at an object, it must be processed. The object will then read the message and then usually take some action—send a message to another object or perform some processing—but sometimes it simply does nothing.

For instance, each time a key is pressed on the keyboard, Windows determines what is the currently active window and sends it a message containing the key that was pressed. This code associated with that window will receive the message and, in turn, may pass the message onto another object or window.

Events, Methods, and Properties

Each object in Visual Basic contains two basic parts: a public interface and a private part. The public part consists of an interface, through which other objects can interact. The private part consists of code and data, which can be used only inside the object.

The interface consists of three parts:

- Events, which are subroutines that are called when a message has been received from another object

- Methods, which are a way to send a message to another object

- Properties, which are a way of setting and retrieving public values from the object

One of the most difficult aspects of writing Windows programs in C is that you need to provide code to respond to every message. In many cases, all you want to do is pass the message onto another object or take some standard default action. By providing reasonable default handling for most events, Visual Basic makes writing Windows programs easy.

A Simple Program

A Visual Basic program consists of one or more forms, plus a series of zero or more controls on each form, plus code placed in the events of the form and controls. In the simplest case, a Visual Basic program has a blank form and no programmer-supplied code. In this case, all you can do is minimize, maximize, or close the form. The default code supplied by Visual Basic is sufficient to handle all of the standard processing required. For instance, you can close the form by clicking the close button in the upper-right side of the title bar, or you can press Alt+F4 to get the same result. This processing is handled totally by Visual Basic.

In a more complicated example, characters typed on the keyboard will appear in the text box displayed on the form—again, without any programmer-written code.

The equivalent C program to accomplish the same task would be several hundred lines long, and it could be even longer if the same level of error handling as used by Visual Basic were included. Using Microsoft Foundation Classes (MFC) in C++ programs saves a lot of the C code, but these programs will still be longer than the equivalent Visual Basic programs.

How Visual Basic Runs a Program

Unlike most programming languages, BASIC was designed to be an interpreted language. In a traditional programming language like C, the source code is typed into the computer, then compiled into a binary file, which is then linked with other binary files containing the runtime library, and finally loaded into memory and executed.

The Interpreter

In BASIC, the first statement is decoded into its component parts, and then each of the parts is executed. Then the next statement is decoded and executed. IF statements and loops merely move the pointer to the appropriate statement and the processing continues. This technique is called *interpreted execution*, and the program that does this is called an *interpreter*.

While this is not the most efficient way to execute a program (for example, you decode the same statement inside the loop each time the loop is executed), it does allow you to build an environment that can run a BASIC program in a relatively small package. (Microsoft's Visual Basic traces it roots back to the mid-1970s, when Bill Gates wrote a BASIC interpreter in less then 4096 bytes of memory.)

Another advantage of this approach is that when a statement has an error, the interpreter can stop the program and allow the programmer to correct the statement. Debugging is also easier because the programmer can interrupt the program and look at the various variables, change their values, and resume execution.

Visual Basic maintains this concept and improves on it. To speed up processing, Visual Basic checks the syntax of each statement as it is typed into the computer and stores the state in memory in its decoded form. When the statement is displayed on the screen, it is reassembled from its decoded form. (This is why the statements always look slightly different than when you typed them.)

The Compiler

While it is extremely useful to a programmer to develop a program using an interpreter, it causes problems for anyone else using the program. First, you must have the entire BASIC environment available, and second, the program will still run slower compared to compiled programs. Thus, Visual Basic allows you to compile the program into a traditional .EXE file and run it just like any other Windows program.

Prior to Visual Basic 5, the compiler simply stored the decoded form of each statement in the .EXE file and used a runtime library to execute the decoded statements. This type of program is called a *semi-compiled* program. There are two main drawbacks to the semi-compiled program. First, the programs are still slower than compiled programs. Second, the program still needs most of the BASIC environment; it's just stored in the runtime library.

Starting with Visual Basic 5, a true compiler was used to create the .EXE file. In addition, it can create .OCX files and .DLL files to handle your own ActiveX controls. This approach allows Visual Basic programs to run nearly as fast as C programs.

Types of Visual Basic Programs

Visual Basic can build many different types of programs:

Standard Windows application This type of application is built from a series of one or more forms, modules, and classes. A form is a visual window that contains controls and interacts with the user. A module is a collection of Visual Basic subroutines that can be called from other subroutines. Classes correspond to objects that can be created in your program. Each time a class object is created, an independent area is reserved for the information associated with the class.

ActiveX control This type of control is similar to the controls supplied with Visual Basic, but with one major difference: You build it yourself, without waiting for Microsoft to write it for you. Many people associate this feature with web browsing, because Microsoft originally positioned ActiveX as a way to compete with Java. However, building your own ActiveX controls allows you to isolate data and the methods that can manipulate the data, and you might want to include such custom controls in most of your application programs.

ActiveX document This is a form that can appear in a web browser. ActiveX documents are very similar to regular Visual Basic forms and are designed in the same way. They also can be included in the Microsoft Office Binder in the same way that Word and Excel documents can be included.

IIS application This type of application uses the Internet Information Server's (IIS) ISAPI interface to write server-side Visual Basic programs.

These programs are far more efficient than the typical CGI-BIN, PERL scripts and let you exploit you Visual Basic programming skills.

DHTML application This is another type of web browser application. It works with the web browser to change how the web page is displayed after it is downloaded. DHTML applications require Internet Explorer 4 and exploit the new Dynamic HTML features of the browser.

A Visual Basic project can create any one of these types of programs. If you want to build more than one of these types of programs, you can create a Visual Basic project group, which lets you manage multiple projects in a single development session.

Files Associated with a Visual Basic Project

Several files are associated with a Visual Basic project. Originally, the only file associated with a BASIC program was a .BAS file. Today, your Visual Basic program is stored in a number of different files depending on the type of component. Table 1.1 lists the file types used by Visual Basic with a short description of their contents.

TABLE 1.1: Visual Basic File Types

File Type	Description
.BAS	A module file, containing the Visual Basic code that is not associated with a class or a form
.CLS	A class file, containing the Visual Basic code associated with a user class
.CTL	A control file, containing the Visual Basic code associated with a user control
.CTX	A control extension file, containing the binary elements for a .CTL file
.DCA	An Active Designer cache file
.DDF	A Package and Deployment Wizard .CAB information file
.DEP	A Package and Deployment Wizard dependency file
.DLL	An object code file containing an in-process ActiveX component
.DOB	An ActiveX document form file, containing the Visual Basic code associated with an ActiveX document
.DOX	An ActiveX document extension file, containing the binary elements for a .DOB file

TABLE 1.1 (CONTINUED): Visual Basic File Types

File Type	Description
.DSR	An ActiveX Designer file
.DSX	An ActiveX Designer extension file, containing the binary elements for a .DSR file
.DWS	A Package and Deployment Wizard script file
.EXE	An object code file containing either the executable program or an ActiveX control
.FRM	A form file, containing the Visual Basic code associated with a form
.FRX	A form extension file, containing the binary elements for an .FRM file
.LOG	A log file containing errors that were encountered when loading a particular form or object
.MAK	An obsolete Visual Basic project file (if loaded, this file will be upgraded to a .VBP file)
.OCA	A Control TypeLib cache file
.OCX	An object code file containing an ActiveX control
.PAG	A Property Page file
.PGX	A Property Page extension file, containing the binary elements for a .PAG file
.RES	A Resource file
.TLB	A Remote Automation TypeLib file
.VBD	A runtime ActiveX document state file
.VBG	A Visual Basic group project file, containing information about the individual projects in a Visual Basic project group
.VBL	A Visual Basic control licensing file
.VBP	A Visual Basic project file
.VBR	A Visual Basic Remote Automation registration file
.VBW	A Visual Basic workspace file
.VBX	An obsolete Visual Basic extension, similar in function to an .OCX file, but limited to 16-bit code
.VBZ	A Visual Basic wizard launch file
.WCT	A WebClass HTML file

You may want to look at some of these files. Many of the files, such as the .FRM and .BAS files, are stored as simple ASCII text. This means you can view them with Notepad, Write, or even the plain, old DOS Edit command. This can be useful if you need to take a quick look at the code without starting the entire Visual Basic development environment.

WARNING   **Change these files with care:** Since you can view the Visual Basic files with an editor, you can also change these files with an editor. If you want to do this, use extreme caution! Make sure that none of the files are open in Visual Basic. Then make a backup copy of the file before making your changes. This way, if Visual Basic can't load the changed file, you can always restore the old one.

Migration from Previous Versions of Visual Basic

As mentioned earlier in the chapter, migrating from Visual Basic 5 to Visual Basic 6 is no big deal. In most cases, you can migrate your application by simply loading it into the new version and saving it. However, there is some information you should consider before you make your decision.

General Migration Issues

There are two basic issues you need to consider when you migrate from one version of Visual Basic to another:

- What should I do about the obsolete features?
- What should I do about the new features?

You have three different options: don't bother migrating; migrate, but don't take advantage of any new features; or migrate and take advantage of the new features.

Not Migrating

You probably don't want to migrate if:

- Your customers are using Windows 3.x and can't upgrade to Windows 95 or 98.

- You're using third-party controls that won't work with Visual Basic 6.

Migrating but Not Using New Features

You may want to consider migrating but not taking advantage of the new features if:

- Your customers are using Windows 95 or 98 or Windows NT.

- Your customers are satisfied with their current version of the application.

- You are looking for improved performance in your application.

- You want to position yourself to take advantage of future enhancements in Visual Basic.

Migrating and Using New Features

You may want to consider migrating and taking advantage of the new features in Visual Basic if:

- You need to make significant enhancements to your application, and the conversion process wouldn't add that much effort.

- One or more of the new features will add significant value to your application.

For the most part, Microsoft has made the upgrade process very easy. The Visual Basic language has always been upward-compatible between versions. The primary issues relate to migrating controls and migrating database technology.

Migration of Controls

Probably the most visible problem area you will encounter when migrating from one version of Visual Basic to another is that of missing controls. This is especially true when migrating from Visual Basic 3 and the 16-bit version of Visual Basic 4. However, there are even problems when migrating from Visual Basic 4 or 5 to Visual Basic 6, because not all of the 32-bit controls were carried forward.

Migrating 16-Bit Controls

Most of the 16-bit controls in Visual Basic have 32-bit equivalents. However, most of these 32-bit equivalent controls themselves have become obsolete (see the next topic). Just remember that your .VBX controls are 16-bit only and can't be used by any of the 32-bit flavors of Visual Basic.

Migrating Visual Basic 4 32-Bit Controls

The following controls existed in Visual Basic 4 and were removed from Visual Basic 5 and 6. In most cases, the same function exists in a different control.

AniButton This control allowed you to display a picture (icon, bitmap, or metafile) on a command button. You can now do this with the intrinsic CommandButton control. You can set the `Picture`, `DownPicture`, and `DisabledPicture` properties to show any image (icon, bitmap, GIF, or JPEG).

Gauge This control allowed you to display the progress of a long-running function. You can now use the ProgressBar control from the Windows Common Controls library. Note that the needle display from Gauge is no longer supported.

Graph This control allowed you to display your own charts and graphs. You can use the MSChart ActiveX control to perform these tasks. Note that while the MSChart control is much more powerful, it is also more complicated to use.

Grid This control allowed you to display information in a spreadsheet-like format. Visual Basic 5 offered the MSFlexGrid ActiveX control as a more functional replacement. Visual Basic 6 adds the MSHFlexGrid ActiveX control, which can display hierarchical grids.

KeyState This control allowed you to read or set the values of the Caps Lock, Num Lock, Ins, and Scroll Lock keys. There is no direct replacement for this control. You can use the Windows API to perform these functions (which I'll discuss in Chapter 16), or you can display this information to the user with the StatusBar control.

Outine This control allowed you to display a hierarchical list of items. You can use the TreeView control to provide the same function.

Spin This control allowed you to place a small control that would increment or decrement a value. You can use the UpDown control in the Microsoft Windows Common Controls library 2 to provide the same function.

ThreeD This control allowed you to display three-dimensional versions of several intrinsic controls such as the CommandButton and the CheckBox controls. This functionality has been included with the intrinsic controls via the Appearance property.

Migrating Visual Basic 5 Controls

Microsoft has effectively replaced Crystal Reports with the new Data Report tool. You can obtain Crystal Reports in two ways:

- Buy the latest version of Crystal Reports from a software vendor.

- Install the old Visual Basic 5 version. Microsoft included it on the CD-ROM, in \Common\Tools\VB\CrysRept.

Testing Migration

The best way to determine if you are going to have problems when you try to migrate your application is to try to load it into Visual Basic 6. Visual Basic will attempt to update your control references and will let you know if it encounters any problems on a particular form. These problems will be written to a log file in the same folder as the form. The log file will have the form's name followed by the extension .LOG. You can examine this file to see what the actual problems are. Here is a sample log file:

```
Line 15: Class Threed.SSCommand of control SSCommand1 was not a loaded
control class.
```

This log file shows that the control Threed.SSCommand was not installed on the system. So when the load process is finished, this control will be converted to a PictureBox control.

Handling Problem Controls

Suppose that you've analyzed the problem and decided that you can easily migrate all of your controls but one. What can you do?

The first step is to understand exactly which control is causing the problem. Chances are that there is a third-party replacement control that maintains the same interfaces and provides the same function.

I can't live without it: Check the \Common\Tools\VB\Controls directory on your Visual Studio CD-ROM for copies of some obsolete controls from Visual Basic 4. Included with the controls are their documentation and installation instructions. Note that while these controls have been fixed to work with Visual Basic 6, Microsoft does not support them.

If buying a third-party control is not acceptable or you can't locate one, consider writing the control yourself. Some controls, such as a TabbedDialog or MaskedEdit control, can be easily duplicated from scratch. Other controls, like the Grid control, are much more difficult, but you might be able to build a wrapper that converts the interface from one control to another.

You can also consider building a simple program (or editor macro) that scans through the raw Visual Basic form file and replaces references to obsolete controls with references to replacement controls (like Threed.SSCommand with VB.CommandButton) and then try loading the file again. While the results may not be exactly what you want, it's better than converting each PictureBox by hand.

The form file that generated the error we saw in the sample log file in the previous section is shown below.

```
VERSION 4.00
Begin VB.Form Form1
Caption         =    "Form1"
ClientHeight    =    3105
ClientLeft      =    1140
ClientTop       =    1515
ClientWidth     =    4155
Height          =    3510
Left            =    1080
   LinkTopic        =    "Form1"
   ScaleHeight      =    3105
   ScaleWidth       =    4155
   Top              =    1170
   Width            =    4275
   Begin Threed.SSCommand SSCommand1
      Height              =    735
```

```
            Left           =    600
            TabIndex       =    0
            Top            =    840
            Width          =    1215
            _version       =    65536
            _extentx       =    2143
            _extenty       =    1296
            _stockprops    =    78
            caption        =    "Hello"
        End
    End
Attribute VB_Name = "Form1"
Attribute VB_Creatable = False
Attribute VB_Exposed = False
Private Sub SSCommand1_Click()

MsgBox "Hello Jill"

End Sub
```

To make this form load properly, I changed the line that reads

```
Begin Threed.SSCommand SSCommand1
```

to read

```
Begin VB.CommandButton SSCommand1
```

and loaded the project again. Note that I left the name of the control as SSCommand1. Otherwise, I would have needed to change every occurrence of SSCommand1 to the new name.

When I loaded the program in Visual Basic a second time, I still got some errors, as shown in this log file:

```
Line 21: The property name _version in SSCommand1 is invalid.
Line 22: The property name _extentx in SSCommand1 is invalid.
Line 23: The property name _extenty in SSCommand1 is invalid.
Line 24: The property name _stockprops in SSCommand1 is invalid.
```

However, the control is now recognized as an intrinsic CommandButton control.

I could have fixed these errors by simply deleting the invalid properties from the form file. I didn't bother because they don't cause any problems and will disappear when I save the form file.

While the technique of editing form files can be used to correct a lot of problems you may encounter when upgrading from Visual Basic 3 and Visual Basic 4 applications, you should use extreme caution when editing these files. You should never edit your only copy of your source code. Copy the file and edit the copy. When you are certain that your changes are acceptable, you can switch the copies. Better yet, copy your entire Visual Basic project first, so that your original project remains untouched.

Also, don't use a word processor such as Microsoft Word to edit the file. Use Notepad or the DOS Edit command to ensure that no extraneous characters are inserted into the file. We all know what havoc some of Word 97's AutoCorrect features can wreak!

Database Issues

Visual Basic has been using the Microsoft Jet database engine since Visual Basic 3 was first released in 1993. The technology used to access the database was called Data Access Objects (DAO). This technology was extended over time to support access to ODBC (Open Database Connectivity) databases by passing through the Jet database engine.

When Visual Basic 5 was released, Microsoft introduced a new technology called Remote Data Objects (RDO) that provided better performance and functionality than DAO for databases like SQL Server. RDO is a low-overhead interface to an ODBC database, much like DAO is a low-overhead interface to a Jet database.

As mentioned earlier in the chapter, in Visual Basic 6, Microsoft has introduced a new data-access technology called ActiveX Data Objects (ADO). This technology is based on the assumption that you can't store everything in a relational database. Therefore, you need a Universal Data Access model that can access anything from a SQL Server relational database to an Outlook contact list. It will talk to any data store that speaks OLE-DB.

Migrating Data Access Objects

As DAO evolved, there was a major change to the object library in order to maintain backward-compatibility (so programs that used the older objects would continue to run unchanged); however, new programs could take advantage of the new features offered by the new objects.

In Visual Basic 6, there are two versions of the DAO runtime libraries: the 2.5/3.5 compatibility library and the 3.5 object library. The 2.5/3.5 library maintains all of the old objects so that the older programs can continue unchanged. The 3.5 library removes these obsolete objects. By selecting the 3.5 object library, you can quickly identify the old objects and correct the references in your program.

NOTE   My library is missing: While Microsoft is not saying that future versions of Visual Basic will not support the 2.5 object references, the handwriting is on the wall. You should either convert to the 3.5 object library or consider upgrading to the new ADO libraries.

DAO 2.5 and prior allowed you to manipulate three basic types of database data: Dynasets, Snapshots, and Tables. These three types were combined into the Recordset concept used in DAO 3.0 and later. (This concept is also used in RDO and ADO.) All DAO objects that directly manipulated these objects have been mapped into corresponding Recordset objects. Also, many methods that were used to extract information about a database object were replaced with collections containing the same information, such as the Tabledefs collection and the Fields collection. Table 1.2 lists the obsolete DAO objects, methods, statements, and properties, and their replacements.

TABLE 1.2:   Obsolete DAO Items and Their Replacements

Obsolete Item	Replacement Item
CreateDynaset method	OpenRecordset method
CreateSnapshot method	OpenRecordset method
CompactDatabase statement	DBEngine.CompactDatabase method
CreateDatabase statement	DBEngine.CreateDatabase method
DBEngine.Freelocks method	DBEngine.Idle method
DBEngine.SetDefaultWorkspace method	DBEngine.DefaultUser method DBEngine.DefaultPassword property
DBENfine.SetDataAccessOption method	DBEngine.IniPath property
Database.BeginTrans method	Workspace.BeginTrans method

Continued on next page

TABLE 1.2 (CONTINUED): Obsolete DAO Items and Their Replacements

Obsolete Item	Replacement Item
Database.CommitTrans method	Workspace.CommitTrans method
Database.DeleteQuerydef method	Delete method
Database.ExecuteSQL method	Execute method
Database.ListTables method	Tabledefs collection
Database.OpenQuerydef method	Querydefs collection
Database.OpenTable method	OpenRecordset method
Database.Rollback method	Workspace.Rollback method
Dynaset object	Recordset object
Fieldsize method	Fieldsize property
Index.Fields property	IndexFields collection
ListFields method	Fields collection
ListIndexes method	Indexes collection
OpenDatabase statement	DBEngine.OpenDatabase method
Querydef.ListParameters method	Parameters collection
Snapshot object	Recordset object
Table object	Recordset object

Migrating Remote Data Objects

In the Enterprise edition of Visual Basic 5, Microsoft released the RDO database object library, with the idea that the RDO library could provide more efficient access to enterprise databases like SQL Server and Oracle 7. The RDO library is similar to the DAO 3.0 library, but it offers a much simpler interface. Its capabilities correspond closely to those of the underlying ODBC interface.

There haven't been any major changes to RDO in Visual Basic 6, so there should be no issues related to migrating RDO applications.

Final Thoughts

Visual Basic 6 brings many new features to the table, but it's still based on the Visual Basic 5 core that we've grown to know and love. New controls are always a treat, and the new database-access structure is definitely the way to go for new applications. Probably the most noticeable change is the new help facility. The switch to HTML help is certainly dramatic, and it's full of information that no one can find.

Migrating Visual Basic applications is relatively easy. In fact, in most cases, it's transparent—unless you happened to use an obsolete control. Hidden away on the installation CD-ROMs are versions of many of these controls that have been updated to be compatible with Visual Basic 6. While you can use them, you might want to bite the bullet and upgrade to the newer controls, especially if the new controls have the word Microsoft somewhere in their name.

CHAPTER

TWO

2

Preparing the Visual Basic Environment

- Visual Basic IDE options

- Templates for Visual Basic

- Objects and ActiveX control add-ins

- Visual Basic program properties

- The Object Browser

- The Package and Deployment Wizard

In this chapter, I'll talk about some things you should take care of before you start building Visual Basic programs. First, you can set various Visual Basic Integrated Development Environment (IDE) options to make your programming life easier, as well as add objects and controls to your program.

Next, you can use templates. Since I'm a rather lazy programmer (more on that in the next chapter), I rarely write a program from scratch. Instead, I start from a template. By creating your own templates, you can gain many of the same advantages of starting with an existing program without needing to strip out any old code.

Then I'll go over some of the important program properties you can select. There is a wide range of properties available, such as those that allow you to protect your custom ActiveX controls, add version and copyright information, and set various types of optimizations.

I'll also discuss one of the most useful tools I've found in Visual Basic—the Object Browser. This tool lets you look at any ActiveX control or Visual Basic object and determine its properties, methods, and events. The Object Browser is especially useful when you are using ActiveX controls with minimal documentation.

Finally, I'll cover the Package and Deployment Wizard, which is new with Visual Basic 6. This tool is particularly helpful for packaging applications for distribution.

Tweaking the IDE

The Visual Basic IDE is one of the most flexible tools Microsoft has developed. There are three major ways to change the IDE:

- Select options from the Options dialog box.
- Include add-in components.
- Use templates.

Setting IDE Options

To access the Options dialog box for the Visual Basic IDE, select Tools ➢ Options. As shown in Figure 2.1, this dialog box contains six tabs: Editor, Editor Format, General, Docking, Environment, and Advanced. Many of these options can be used to tweak the user interface to make it more convenient for you to use. Some of the options directly affect how your Visual Basic program is written and how it runs. You can look over the options and experiment with the ones that interest you. Here, I'll talk about some of the options that I've found most useful.

FIGURE 2.1:

The Editor tab of the Options dialog box

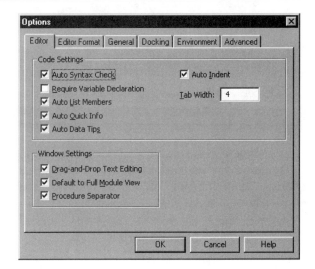

FIGURE 2.1:

The Editor tab of the Options dialog box

Requiring Variable Declarations

One of the most important things you can do in any Visual Basic program to improve its reliability is to check the Require Variable Declaration box on the Editor tab of the Options dialog box. Choosing this option ensures that every new module you create in Visual Basic includes an Option Explicit statement. (It only works for modules you create after setting the option; you will need to manually enter Option Explicit into any existing modules.)

Why is this one statement so important? By requiring variables to be declared before they can be used, you prevent problems like the one in the following code.

```
Dim Counter As Integer
Dim I As Integer
Dim MyArray(15) As Integer

' Initialize MyArray to contain a 1 in each element
```

```
For I = 0 to 15
   MyArray(I)= 1
Next I

' Count the number of elements in MyArray whose
' value is greater than zero.
Counter = 0
For I = 0 to 15
   If MyArray(I) > 0 Then Counter = Countor + 1
Next I
```

When you first glance at this code fragment, nothing obviously wrong jumps out at you. But the variable Counter at the end of the second loop contains a problem. Why?

On the second pass through the code, notice that Counter was called Countor inside the expression. Since Countor doesn't exist, Visual Basic will automatically create a new variable with that name. Since Countor doesn't have a value, a value of zero will be assumed. So each time through the loop, Counter would be assigned a value of one, rather than be incremented. Option Explicit prevents this from happening, since Countor was not declared.

NOTE   **This can happen to you:** I guarantee that a similar type of variable name problem will happen to you sooner or later if you don't use Option Explicit. This is especially true if you use Microsoft's naming conventions for variables. These conventions can result in rather long prefixes on occasion, which can easily lead to misspelled variables.

Saving Your Program

Another option I highly recommend changing is how your changes are saved. The Environment tab of the Options dialog box, shown in Figure 2.2, includes three choices for saving, under the heading When a Program Starts. The default setting for this option is Don't Save Changes.

Over the years, I've learned not to trust a computer when testing a new program. All too often, the computer or Visual Basic will lock up or generate a runtime error, and you've lost all your changes.

The Environment tab of the
Options dialog box

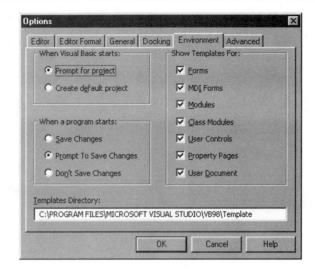

I recommend choosing the Prompt To Save Changes option rather than the Save Changes option for two reasons. First, you can be certain that the changes actually were saved. Second, there are times when you may not want to keep the changes. You may be debugging a program and have deleted a large chunk of code trying to locate a problem, or you may be testing a new feature and you don't want to overlay a working program. In either case, having the option to save is a big improvement over automatically saving or not saving at all.

Switching to the SDI Development Environment

The Multi-Document Interface (MDI) development environment is the default Visual Basic development environment. Similar to all of Microsoft's other products, like Word and Excel, all of the windows related to the current project are displayed inside the IDE's main window.

As an alternative, you can also select the Single Document Interface (SDI) development environment. This setting is on the Advanced tab of the Options dialog box, as shown in Figure 2.3.

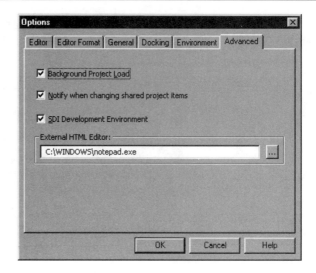

For the most part, the two interfaces operate in the same way. However, the big difference for me is that with the SDI, I can see through the Visual Basic IDE to the Windows Desktop. The MDI is like working inside a box; the SDI is like working on a desktop. This makes it easier to see all the other open windows, like the Help or Word window. And you will have multiple open windows because, as the old saying goes, "A cluttered desk[top] is a sign of genius."

TIP

SDI versus MDI: I suppose everyone has a preference for one over the other. I personally find the MDI environment too constraining, so the first thing I do after installing Visual Basic is to switch to the SDI environment. I usually have at least six applications started at any time, and the SDI environment is natural to me. However, if you usually run only one application at a time, you might prefer the MDI environment. The best advice I can give you is to try both and see which environment works better for you.

Using Templates

Another powerful concept used in Visual Basic comes from the Microsoft Office family of programs. Rather than creating documents from scratch each time one is needed, you can create a skeleton document known as a *template*. The template contains the bare essentials for a particular type of document. For instance, you may create a standard business letter with your company's logo or a standard spreadsheet for reporting business expenses.

You can also build templates in Visual Basic. You can create templates for a variety of items:

- A project
- A form
- An MDI form
- A module
- A class module
- A property page
- A user control
- A user document

To create a template, simply create the object with all of your customizations and save it into the appropriate template folder.

Visual Basic ships with a lot of templates for forms, ranging from splash screens to tip boxes. Other objects also have some templates (though not nearly as many) or wizards that will help you build objects.

What kind of templates should you create? You could start by creating your own standard form with code for resizing the form, set up menu options and toolbars, and add any other code you might find useful. You could also create your own project that contains the version and copyright information you want to include. (I'll cover including version and copyright information later in this chapter, in the "Setting Project Properties" section.) You might want to include some standardized forms, such as an About dialog box and an Options window.

Adding Objects and ActiveX Controls

Visual Basic ships with a large number of ActiveX controls and other objects. However, most of the default projects are not set up to take immediate advantage of these controls. Through the Visual Basic IDE's Components dialog box, you can add ActiveX controls to your Visual Basic program. The References dialog box lets you add other objects.

Adding ActiveX Components

To display the Components dialog box, select Project ➤ Components or right-click on the toolbox and select Components. This dialog box displays all of the available ActiveX controls on your system, as shown in Figure 2.4. The controls that have a checkmark beside them are already in the toolbox.

FIGURE 2.4:

The Controls tab of the Components dialog box

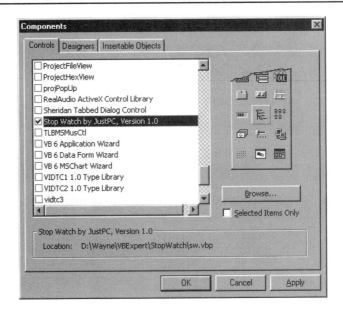

Looking for something new? Look carefully through your Visual Basic CD-ROM installation disk. You'll find many interesting, undocumented tools (some of which I'll cover later in the book). Try the \Common\Tools\VB folder as a starting point. Also check any folder labeled Unsupprt or Unsupported—you might be surprised at what you find.

There are three tabs in this Components dialog box:

- The Controls tab lists all of the ActiveX controls registered in the Windows Registry on your system.

- The Designers tab lists all of the designers available for you to use to help you build complex parts of your application.

- The Insertable Objects tab lists the objects you can include in your program that will function like ActiveX controls.

To add a control to your toolbox, simply put a checkmark by the desired control, then click the OK or Apply button to make the changes. (You can delete unnecessary controls by removing the checkmark next to them.) Note that none of the intrinsic controls are listed; these are part of the Visual Basic system and cannot be removed or replaced.

TIP

Too many controls? You can always make the toolbox bigger, but you can also use multiple tabs to group the controls into more manageable groups. Right-click on the toolbox and select Add Tab to add a new tab to the toolbox. Then you can put your extra controls on that tab.

Adding Object References

Unlike ActiveX controls, objects are not always visible. Often they provide access methods or data types and objects used by other ActiveX controls.

The References dialog box lists all of the available objects and type libraries on your system, as shown in Figure 2.5. To display this dialog box, select Project ➤ References. The object references that are already available to you are checked.

Selecting an ActiveX control or insertable object from the Components dialog box (discussed in the previous section) causes the necessary objects and type libraries to be automatically selected in the References dialog box. Even through the References dialog box lists the same insertable objects as appear in the Components dialog box, there is no need to select them again.

FIGURE 2.5:

The References dialog box

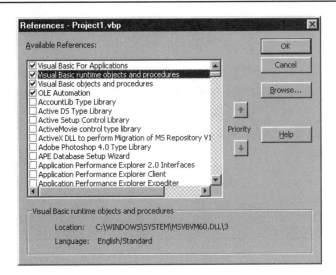

> **NOTE**
>
> **You can't delete them:** Some object references are required by Visual Basic and can't be removed. These are Visual Basic for Applications, Visual Basic runtime objects and procedures, Visual Basic objects and procedures, and OLE Automation. You don't need to worry about accidentally removing these object references because Visual Basic will prevent you from deleting them.

Setting Project Properties

By now, you may have written a lot of Visual Basic programs. But how often did you stop to check some of the properties that were set? Did you review the default compiler optimizations? What about version numbers? These types of settings are useful to review from time to time to ensure that your Visual Basic programs are giving you the best results.

You can set properties for your project by selecting Project ➤ *<Project Name>* Properties. The Project Properties dialog box, shown in Figure 2.6, contains five tabs: General, Make, Compile, Component, and Debugging. Many of these properties are self-explanatory, like the startup object and project name; however, some of the others are worth discussing in a bit more detail.

FIGURE 2.6:

The General tab of the
Project Properties dialog box

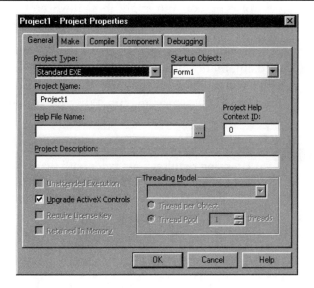

Requiring a License Key

Suppose that you've put a lot of hard work into your Solitaire ActiveX control, and you don't want anyone who gets a copy of the .OCX file to be able to add it to their program without your permission. You can prevent this from happening by requiring a license key.

ActiveX controls normally have no restrictions on their use. If other programmers find an .OCX file on their systems, they can use the Components dialog box (discussed in the previous section) to include the control in their Visual Basic project. Then they can build their application and redistribute your control without you even knowing it.

When you put a checkmark in the Require License Key box on the General tab of the Project Properties dialog box (see Figure 2.6), the control will check to see if it was properly licensed when it is loaded. If the appropriate license information isn't available, the control will return an error code and will not operate.

The license key must be stored either in the Windows Registry or in the program that is using the control. If the license key is stored in the Windows Registry, then any program on that machine can use the control. If you are distributing the control as part of your application, the license key will automatically be included with your program.

If you are building stand-alone ActiveX controls, the license key will be generated automatically and stored in a .VBL file. This information will be included when you use the Package and Deployment Wizard (discussed later in this chapter) to build the setup program. When the user runs the setup program, the license key will be added to the user's Registry.

WARNING   **Licensing requirements work both ways:** If you are building your application or ActiveX control using other ActiveX controls, you must make sure that you have the right to redistribute the other ActiveX controls to your clients.

Choosing a Threading Model

ActiveX control and ActiveX DLL projects have the ability to specify the threading model used. Unfortunately, there are only two threading models available for Visual Basic: apartment and single-threaded. You can choose between these two models in the Threading Model section of the Project Properties dialog box's General tab.

In the apartment model, all of the resources owned by a single instance of the control are separate from all other instances. This includes global data. The upside of this approach is you don't have resource conflicts with other instances of your control. The downside is that you can't keep a single common area that is used by all instances of your controls. This makes it more difficult to communicate between instances of your control. (Assigning a value to a global variable in one instance of the control doesn't assign it in another.)

TIP   **Don't be single-threaded:** If you don't have a good reason for your control to be single-threaded, choose the apartment model. This will yield better performance in the long run.

The single-threaded model is not a true single-threaded model, but simply an apartment model with only a single apartment. This means that your single-threaded control is safe to use with multithreaded clients.

You can also specify the number of threads that an ActiveX EXE project will use. You can specify a pool of threads that will be used on a round-robin basis to satisfy requests, or you can specify that one thread per object be used. These are the Thread per Object and Thread Pool settings, respectively, in the Threading Model section of the Project Properties dialog box.

TIP

More may be less: Although you may think the more threads a control can use, the better, this is not always the case. Start out with two or three threads and see how the application performs in live conditions. Then when you add more threads, you will have a frame of reference to see if that improves performance.

By the way, if you are building an ActiveX EXE project without a user interface, check the Unattended Execution checkbox to the left of the Threading Model section of the Project Properties dialog box. This will prevent your application from having any user interaction, including any message boxes and system error dialog boxes. This information will be saved in the log file specified by the **App** .LogPath property. You can include your own entries in the log file by using the App.LogEvent method.

Adding Copyright and Version Information

If you write and distribute programs, you should include copyright and version information in the object code. This information is useful when you need to identify the piece of object code. Version and copyright information is kept on the Make tab of the Project Properties dialog box, as shown in Figure 2.7.

To include a copyright message, select Legal Copyright from the Type list in the Version Information section. In the Value box, specify a value like "Copyright © 1998 Wayne S. Freeze." You should also select File Description and Product Name and fill in values for them to allow you to identify the contents of the object code file. Other version information fields, such as Legal Trademarks, Company Name, and Comments, are self-explanatory.

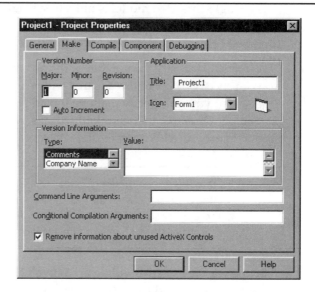

It also is useful to assign a version number to each project by filling in the boxes in the top-left area of the Make tab. This is simple but important. When you begin distributing code, it is useful to be able to identify when a particular component has been revised and tie it back to the appropriate version of the source code.

The Auto Increment feature is extremely useful. When you check this box on the Make tab, each time you make the project, the revision number is incremented by 1, ensuring that every single object file you create has a unique version number. This is how Microsoft generates the build numbers on its various beta projects.

You can see all of this information for an .OCX file or a .DLL file by right-clicking on the file's icon and then displaying the file's properties. Figure 2.8 shows an example of a file's Properties dialog box with copyright and version information.

FIGURE 2.8:

An .OCX file's version and copyright information

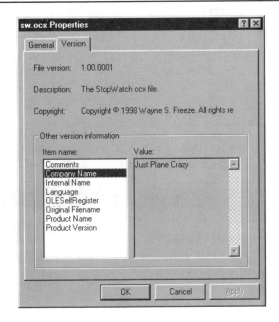

Adding Command-Line Arguments

Contrary to popular belief, command-line arguments didn't disappear with DOS; they just got hidden. When a Windows program starts, the command-line arguments are passed to the program. Traditionally, this is the name of a file that has been dropped on the program file's icon.

However, command-line arguments can be useful when you are debugging a compiled version of the program. They can be used to force alternate default values for application parameters, enable certain application options, or execute a special block of code. For instance, by specifying /Reset, you can cause the program to reinitialize all of its Registry and .INI information before the program starts. You could also use /Delete to remove all of the information. Likewise, you could include /Debug to enable debugging options that you included in the program but didn't make publicly available.

You can add command-line arguments for your program through the Make tab of the Project Properties dialog box (see Figure 2.7, shown earlier).

Using Conditional Compilation

If you need to create programs for more than one machine and don't want to maintain two different programs that are nearly identical, you may want to consider using conditional compilation. Conditional compilation allows you to include two special statements: #CONST and #IF THEN #ELSE #ENDIF. These statements work the same as their C++ counterparts in that the identified parts of code are only included in the final compiled program.

You can specify a conditional compilation constant in the Conditional Compilation Arguments box on the Project Properties dialog box's Make tab (see Figure 2.7). For example, suppose that you have a shareware application and you want to include the following additional code in the shareware version (which does not appear in the registered version):

```
#If Shareware Then
' If the user has performed more than the permitted operations
' remind the user to register their program.

NagCounter = NagCounter + 1
If NagCounter > NagLimit Then
   NagForm.Show 1
   NagCounter = 0
End If
#End If
```

(Note that the End If and the #End If statements serve completely different purposes and both are required, even though it does look a little strange.)

Then to compile the shareware version of the program, all you need to do is to include Shareware=-1 in the Conditional Compilation Arguments box.

Using the Object Browser

The Object Browser is one of the most useful tools in Visual Basic when it comes to understanding how objects and controls are structured. You can start the Object Browser by selecting View ➤ Object Browser or pressing the F2 key. Figure 2.9 shows the Object Browser window.

FIGURE 2.9:

The Object Browser window

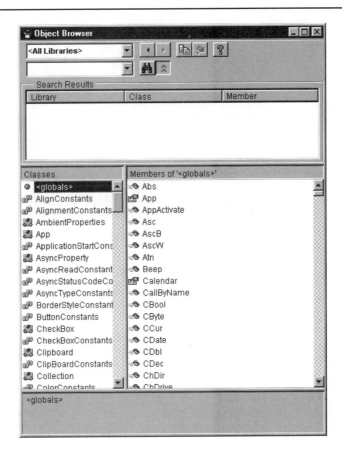

The Object Browser provides a view of all of the objects and controls that are available to your program. The library or libraries that you wish to search for information are displayed at the top in a drop-down box. All Libraries is the default setting. Below that box is another drop-down box for search text. Clicking the drop-down button shows a list of previous searches. The Search Results box displays the libraries, class, and member where the search information was found. The Classes box shows the classes for the selected library in the Search Result box, and the Members box lists the members of the selected class.

Reorder the results: By default, the Object Browser displays information in alphabetical order. By right-clicking on the Object Browser window and selecting Group Members, you can display the information sorted by object type. This can make it easier to find a property or method, because you don't need to search through a large list of irrelevant information.

When you click on a member, you will see a short description of the object at the bottom of the window. Some of the text in the description box is underlined and displayed in green. These bits of text are hyperlinks to the parent object, a link to the list of enumerated data types for a specific data type, or the object itself (if the member is an object).

The Object Browser is very useful when you are using an ActiveX control with little documentation. It will let you see the properties, methods, and events associated with the new control, along with a short explanation of how it works (or at least the parameter and type information).

Another way this tool can be useful is when you need to deal with a control or object that uses other objects, such as the MSChart control (discussed in Chapter 7). You can navigate through the object relationships.

See all that you can see: Right-click on the Object Browser window and then select Show Hidden Members to display all of the elements of the selected object. The hidden member's names will be displayed with gray text, while the nonhidden members will be displayed in black.

Using the Package and Deployment Wizard

Another useful tool that you should know about is the Package and Deployment Wizard. This tool analyzes your application to determine which files need to be distributed with the package and loads them into a standard Microsoft cabinet

(.CAB) file. It also uses the Setup Toolkit to create the program that will install your application.

Obviously, before you use this wizard, you need a program that you're ready to distribute. You also should prepare all of the other files that go along with your program, such as help files, readme files, and database files. You don't need to worry about which Visual Basic files are needed—the wizard can determine that by analyzing your program.

To show you how to use the Package and Deployment Wizard, I built a simple program that plays a wave (.WAV) or MIDI (.MID) file, as shown in Figure 2.10. The user can enter the name of the file into the text box or double-click on the text box to display a file-open dialog box. This program uses the MultiMedia control (MMControl) to play the sounds and the CommonDialog control to help the user select a file to play.

FIGURE 2.10:

The Setup Package
Demo program

Packaging Your Application

Once your application is ready for packaging, start the wizard either from Windows or Visual Basic:

- From the Windows Taskbar, select Start ➤ Programs ➤ Visual Studio 6.0 ➤ Visual Studio 6.0 Tools ➤ Package & Deployment Wizard.

- From Visual Basic, select Add-Ins ➤ Package and Deployment Wizard.

If the Package and Deployment Wizard is not listed, you can use the Add-In Manager to add it, as shown in Figure 2.11. Select Add-Ins ➤ Add-In Manager, choose the Package and Deployment Wizard, and check the Loaded and Load on Startup checkboxes.

FIGURE 2.11:

Including the Package
and Deployment Wizard in
Visual Basic

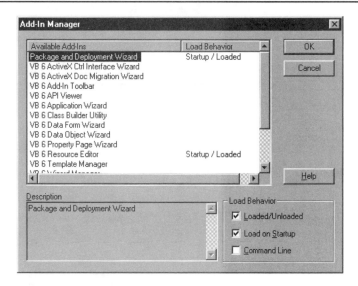

When you start the wizard, it offers three options: Package, Deploy, and Manage Scripts. To build a package, click the Package button. If you start the wizard from the Windows Start menu rather than from Visual Basic, you can automatically select the most recently accessed Visual Basic project, choose any project from the Recent list, or browse to specify your own project.

The first thing the wizard does is to analyze the project's .EXE file. If it can't find it, it will ask you to locate it or recompile it:

If the wizard finds your .EXE file but it isn't current, the wizard will let you know and ask you if you wish to recompile it:

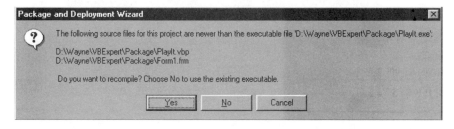

Once the wizard has a valid executable file, it will analyze that file as it prepares to package your application. It will then display the Package Type window, as shown in Figure 2.12. You can choose to build your application package (Standard Setup Package) or merely create a file with all of the dependency information (Dependency File). Creating a dependency file can help you understand which modules your application uses during execution.

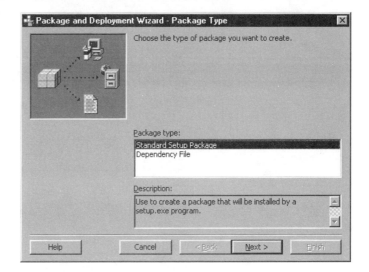

To build the demo program, I chose Standard Setup Package. The next window asks where to create your setup package, as shown in Figure 2.13. By default, a new directory called Package will be created in the project's directory and will hold all of the setup files. Since I usually dedicate a directory to each Visual Basic project, I didn't change the default.

In the next step, the wizard lists all of the dependent files for the application, as shown in Figure 2.14. Table 2.1 lists the files included for my Setup Package Demo program. You can eliminate a file from this list by removing the checkmark next to the file's name. You can also click the Add button and add your own files.

FIGURE 2.13:

Choosing where to place the setup package

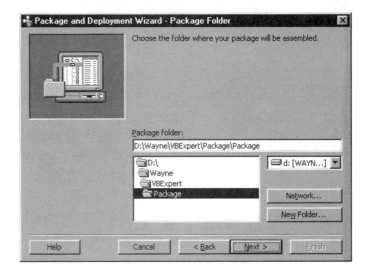

FIGURE 2.14:

Including files in your package

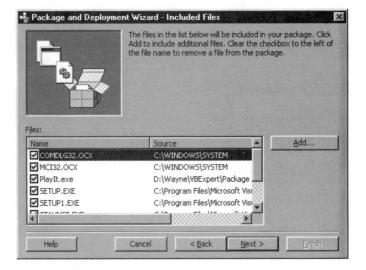

TABLE 2.1: Files Selected by the Package and Deployment Wizard for the Setup Package Demo Program

File	Description
COMDLG32.OCX	Needed by PlayIt.EXE
MCI32.OCX	Needed by PlayIt.EXE
PlayIt.EXE	The application's executable program
SETUP.EXE	Initializes the setup environment and starts SETUP1.EXE
SETUP1.EXE	Installs the application
ST6UNST.EXE	Contains the uninstall program
VB6 Runtime and OLE Automation	Contains the files needed by the SETUP.EXE program
VB6STKIT.DLL	Used by SETUP.EXE and SETUP1.EXE

I have a readme.txt file that contains information that I want to distribute with my application, so I add it here, as shown in Figure 2.15. For your own application, you should add any other files—such as database, image, and help files—that should be installed along with your application.

FIGURE 2.15:

Adding a file to the package

The next step of the wizard allows you to choose the size of the file you wish to distribute, as shown in Figure 2.16. You can choose to distribute everything in a single .CAB file, which is useful for distributing the application on a CD-ROM, the Internet, or a local file server. You can also choose to break the application into chunks that will fit on a diskette.

Don't do a deck of diskettes: I don't recommend distributing applications on diskette. The Visual Basic 6 runtime library is large. If your application uses a bunch of ActiveX controls, you could easily end up with four or five diskettes worth of data. A better way to distribute your application is to use a CD-ROM. You can fit a lot of data on a CD-ROM, and a blank CD-ROM may be cheeper than a bunch of diskettes.

FIGURE 2.16:

Choosing a package size

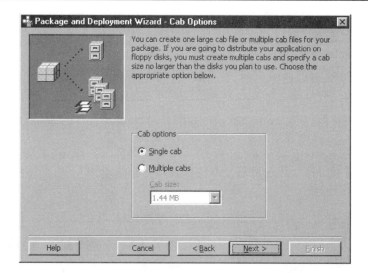

Next, you can specify the title that will be displayed in large letters while the setup program runs. As you can see in Figure 2.17, I picked PlayIt as an installation title.

After you specify the title, the wizard lets you change the items that appear in the Start menu, as shown in Figure 2.18. By default, on a Windows 95 or 98 system, only the main application is displayed. On a Windows NT system, the main application and the uninstall application are included. You can change any of this Start menu information. For my application, I decided to add an entry to display the readme.txt file. I clicked the Add button and filled in the appropriate information, as you can see in Figure 2.19.

FIGURE 2.17:

Specifying the title of your application

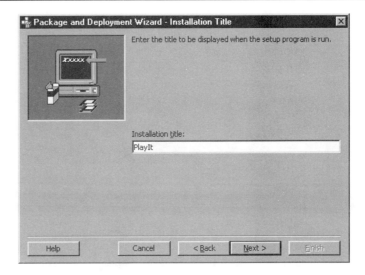

FIGURE 2.18:

Collecting information for the Start menu

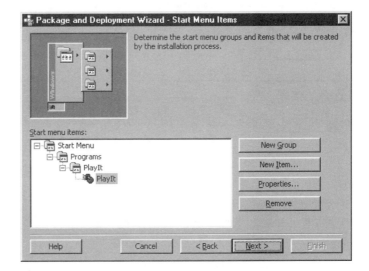

FIGURE 2.19:

Adding ReadMe to the
Start menu

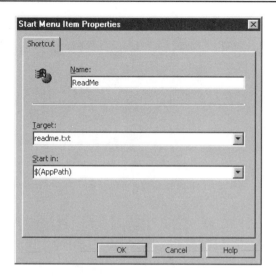

In the next dialog box, you can specify which directory will hold each of the files, as shown in Figure 2.20. Note that the files listed by the wizard are those that were added to the base Setup Toolkit. You can't change the location of the rest of the files and shouldn't change the location of any of the system files, such as COMDLG32.OCX and MCI32.OCX.

FIGURE 2.20:

Specifying file locations

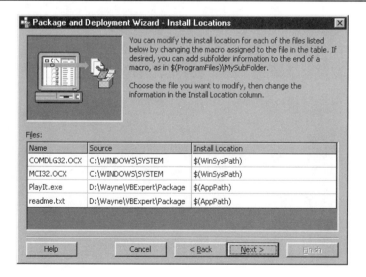

You can mark your own files as shared if it is possible that more than one application will reference them. Figure 2.21 shows this offer for my executable and readme files. You should use this option only if the files are truly shared. Windows will track who installed each shared file and delete it only if every application that installed the file removes it. This is a lot of extra overhead. It also can leave hanging references if the user accidentally deletes the file or its directory, preventing the uninstall program from completing properly.

FIGURE 2.21:

Marking your own files as shared

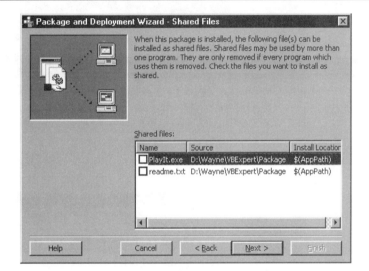

In the final window, the wizard asks for a name under which to store the setup script, as shown in Figure 2.22. Clicking Finish completes the setup process and displays a report such as the one shown in Figure 2.23.

In the Package directory, you'll find three files: PlayIt.CAB, SETUP.EXE, and SETUP.LST. The SETUP.EXE file uses the SETUP.LST and PlayIt.CAB files to install the PlayIt application. You'll also find a directory called Support. The Support directory contains all of the files in PlayIt.CAB, plus a .BAT file that will recreate the .CAB file.

FIGURE 2.22:

Finishing the wizard

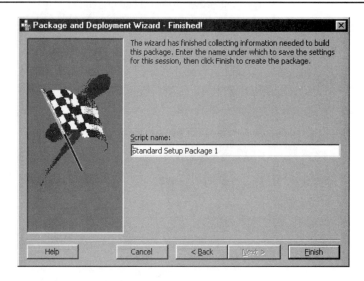

FIGURE 2.23:

The Package and Deployment
Wizard report

Deploying Your Application

After you've created your distribution package, you need to determine how to distribute your application. You can deploy your application to a local file server or to the Internet using the web publishing software. You can also take the files and use them in any fashion you want.

Based on my experience with the "Deployment" part of the Package and Deployment Wizard, I wouldn't bother using it. Basically, all the two supported options do is to copy the files to a file server or upload them to an Internet web or FTP site. Frankly, it's quicker and easier to do this yourself than to use the wizard.

Distributing Shareware over the Internet

Based on my experience with distributing a shareware application over the Internet, you need to put these setup files into a self-extracting .EXE file. This is very easy to do with the WinZip Self-Extractor utility. There are several other programs available that will do the same thing. Basically, all the user needs to do is to download the .EXE file and run it. This eliminates much of the confusion that occurs when someone doesn't download all of the setup files and also when the user doesn't know what to do with a .CAB file.

If you plan to deploy your application on the Internet as shareware, you should consider building some web pages to access it. I suggest that you include web pages that ask the users for information like name and e-mail address before you let them download the application. Then you can follow up with the users sometime in the future. This might be a gentle query asking how they like the software or perhaps a stronger note reminding them that the application is shareware and they should register it if they plan to use it. You also will have an e-mail address to use when you release a new version of the application.

For business applications, you should do something similar but give the users access only if they are properly registered. Then you could download the software using a secure link. This may help to ease the mind of the auditors, who will probably want to closely scrutinize how your application is distributed—especially if it deals with money.

Customizing Your Setup Program

The complete source code to the Setup1 program is supplied as part of the Visual Basic Setup Toolkit. You may want to make changes to this code when you have a more complex setup process that involves allowing the user to select various application options beyond choosing the current directory and the desired location on the Start menu.

You can find the Setup1 project in the Wizards\PDWizard\Setup1 directory in the main Visual Basic directory. This program is well commented and relatively straightforward. Take a look at the Form_Load event in the Setup1.FRM file. This single event contains all of the code necessary to perform the setup process.

After you have made the changes to the Setup1 program, simply copy the newly compiled version of the program to the Package\Support directory and run the .BAT file to create a new copy of the .CAB file. From there, you can deploy your application as you see fit.

Final Thoughts

This chapter covered a lot of issues related to using Visual Basic. Many of these issues may seem minor, but they can affect your program's performance and your productivity. They may even have legal implications.

In my opinion, the most important thing you should do is incorporate your own copyright information in your program. Considering how easy it is to copy programs, establishing your rights may be crucial. Probably the next most important thing to do is to include version information in your program. Over the years, I've found that one of the biggest problems with applications is making sure that you are using the most current version. This is especially true if your application has had several updates and is distributed on many different machines. Without solid version indicators in your program, you may spend a lot of time trying to fix a problem you, or more likely someone else, has already fixed.

Choosing between an MDI development environment and an SDI development environment becomes a matter of personal preference. I prefer SDI over MDI and wish that Microsoft provided that option for all of its tools, especially Word. However, the keyword here is *choice*. Try both and see which you like better—you may be surprised.

The Object Browser may be one of the most underestimated tools in Visual Basic. This tool has the complete syntax for Visual Basic in abbreviated form. It's the first place I look when I can't remember which method I should use to perform a specific function. You can even examine Visual Basic statements and functions by looking at the VB and VBA objects.

Another overlooked tool is Visual Basic templates. Developing your own templates can be a real hassle, but it can be worth it if you have a group of people developing pieces of a large application or developing multiple applications. It makes sense to create a form template that includes your standard menus, toolbars, and their supporting code logic once rather than implement them from scratch each time you need them.

The Package and Deployment Wizard is a new utility in Visual Basic that replaces the old Setup Wizard. It's an improvement, but there are still some problems to be overcome. Until Microsoft allows you to build self-extracting .EXE files, I wouldn't bother with the deployment part of the wizard. All it does is copy the files to a local file server or onto the Internet. You can do the same thing yourself and probably with less effort.

While you have the option do distribute your application on diskettes, forget it. The Visual Basic runtime library (MSVBVM60.DLL) is nearly the size of a diskette before compression. Even the relatively trivial program I used in the example has a .CAB file that was larger than a single diskette. Adding the SETUP.EXE and SETUP.LST files meant that two diskettes were necessary. A more serious application that uses more than two simple ActiveX controls might need three or four diskettes. If you add any kind of graphics, you might need even more diskettes. The best way to distribute applications is to use CD-ROMs or Internet downloads.

CHAPTER

THREE

3

Debugging Visual Basic Programs

- Bug prevention techniques

- Methods for isolating bugs

- Breakpoints and watches

- Visual Basic program problem areas

This chapter is a collection of debugging tips and tricks you can use with Visual Basic. Many of these tricks are those I've learned from experiences I've had writing programs in a wide variety of languages and on a number of different platforms.

I've broken this chapter into three "how-to" parts: preventing bugs, isolating bugs, and using the Visual Basic Debugger. Finally, I'll talk about some problems that you may encounter with your Visual Basic programs.

Preventing Bugs Before They Occur

Perhaps the best way to fix a bug is to keep the bug from happening in the first place. For the most part, the techniques for preventing bugs are common sense things (or would be common sense if common sense were common) that most programmers would do if they took the time to think about it. But let's face it, with increasing demands on our time, we don't always have the time we need to pay such attention to detail!

The Fascinating StarSX Program

For the examples in this chapter, I'm using one of my favorite programs of all time: StarSX. Many years ago, I was learning how to program on a Hewlett Packard 2000 F time-share system that allowed you to program only in BASIC. One of the terminals attached to the system was an old Tektronics 4010 graphic display terminal, and one of my favorite pastimes was creating graphics programs for it.

Someone wrote a few programs for it before I started at the school (Essex Community College). One of these programs was called The Star of Essex, which was shortened to StarSX. I was so fascinated with the program that I rewrote it many times over the years. It was originally written in BASIC, but has been converted into FORTRAN, C, C++, Pascal, SPL (don't ask), and most recently, Visual Basic.

As I rewrote the program, I continued to enhance it by allowing the user to change various parameters to get different results. The version included with this book has the most parameters of any of the versions I've written. However, don't start playing with this program unless you have a lot of time on your hands—it's more addicting than it looks!

Continued on next page

Technically, all this program does is draw a circle, by drawing a series of straight lines between two points on the circle. The closer you choose the points, the more round the circle looks. However, by choosing points fairly far apart on the circle and decreasing the radius of the circle each time you draw a point, you create a picture like the one you see below. My kids love to watch all the bright colors move and swirl across the screen.

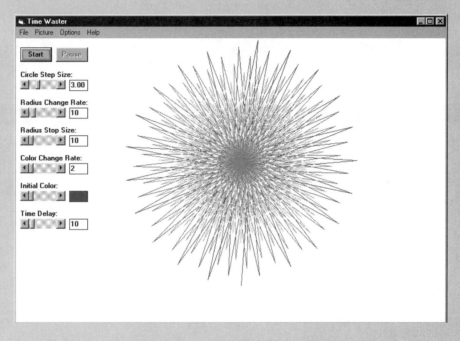

Using Option Explicit

Most programming languages in use today require that you declare a variable before you use it. In some languages, declaring variables is done to make it easier to write the compiler. With other languages, programmers declare variables just for documentation purposes; others do it simply because it was always done that way. But I've found that declaring a variable does two things: it ensures that you get the variable type you want, and it prevents you from misspelling the variable's name. Sometimes, finding a misspelled variable can be very difficult, since Clock and C1ock look the same to you and me, but not to the compiler.

By default, Visual Basic will create a variable automatically the first time you use it. To disable this feature, you need to include `Option Explicit` at the top of each module in your program. For new projects, you can set the Visual Basic IDE option Require Variable Declaration (in the Options dialog box), as explained in Chapter 2. For existing projects, you can simply enter `Option Explicit` into the Global Declarations section of any module.

The big limitation of `Option Explicit` is that it applies only to a given module, not to the entire project. So in a complex project with a lot of forms and classes, you need to ensure that each module has `Option Explicit` included.

Applying the KISS Principle

A long time ago, I learned about the old KISS (Keep It Simple, Stupid) principle. In the case of Visual Basic, the idea is that, in the long run, an overly complex program will cause more problems than a simple program. A simple program is easier to understand, thus making later modifications and debugging a whole lot easier (especially if someone else is doing those modifications). A simple program may even be more efficient, since it is not carrying around a lot of baggage caused by extra features that aren't used.

The simple is better philosophy does not always work, however. A heap sort is more complex than a bubble sort, but the results are often worth it. Yet, true believers in the KISS principle will say that using a prepackaged sort routine will give you even better results with less code to go wrong.

Applying the SMILE Principle

Like very complex programs, large blocks of code can also lead to problems. Someone once told me years ago that if you can't see an entire subroutine or function, then it's too large. I call this the SMILE (Simple Makes It Lots Easier) principle.

I learned about applying the SMILE principle back when I used to compile large programs as a batch job. The compiler would generate a few hundred pages of paper with the program's source code and other diagnostic information. Each subroutine or function would begin on a new page, so this meant that a practical limit was about 50 lines of code per routine.

Today, I find that limit somewhat high in most cases, but a little bit restrictive in a few other cases. Now, I try to use what I can fit on a typical screen—about 30 lines. This means that I can see the entire routine easily. If I can't fit the code into that much space, I'll divide the code into a few private subroutines and call them from the original.

Occasionally, I find that I want to use a large subroutine. This usually happens when I have many assignment statements or subroutine calls, or I have a `Select Case` statement or `If...Then...ElseIf` statement with many individual conditions. In the first situation, I try to group the statements into meaningful chunks. In the second situation, I try to limit myself to less than a dozen statements in each of the individual cases.

Taking Advantage of Object-Oriented Programming

Object-oriented programming means many things to many people (especially those in the marketing department). The answer to the question "Is Visual Basic object-oriented?" doesn't really matter. What matters is that when you break your program into chunks of code with well-defined interfaces between the chunks, your programs become more reliable.

By using well-defined interfaces, you are forced to think about how the chunk will be used. Since you can't cross boundaries and change a particular value inside a chunk even though you think it's safe, you may need to include an additional interface in the future. But at least you will know all of the code that could possibly modify the chunk's data. So if the chunk's data gets corrupted, this approach simplifies the debugging process considerably.

The other advantage of chunks is that they are easy to build and easy to test by themselves. Once they have been tested, you can build other components using these chunks. Since your chunks communicate through well-defined interfaces, you can check for invalid parameters and trap more errors before they occur.

Of course, you also get the fundamental advantage of object-oriented programming. When you need to change an object's architecture, your existing program will continue to work without changes, as long as the interfaces continue to work the same way. Also, you can use the object in more than one place, which will help to reduce your overall programming effort.

TIP

Custom Visual Basic objects: Probably the best way to build your own objects in Visual Basic is to build your own ActiveX controls. You gain the isolation and clear interfaces that I've described here, and the ability to test and debug the object apart from the rest of the program. Also, this gives you the ability to easily change the way the object works, as long as you maintain the existing properties, methods, and events. In Chapter 17, I'll cover how to build an ActiveX .EXE program that allows you to create an object model similar to the one used in Microsoft Word.

Using Comments and Coding Conventions

Comments and coding conventions are also important to minimizing problems in your code. While these things may not prevent bugs per se, they will help the next person who comes along to understand what you did and why you did it. Then if something should go wrong, it will be easier for that next person to rectify the problem.

Adding Comments

There is more to writing comments than simply repeating what is obvious from reading the code. Writing good comments takes a little time and some thought, but the end result should be useful to anyone (including yourself) who may read those comments in the future.

It is important to understand that with comments, more is not always better. Take a look at the following code fragment from the StarSX program. It has one line of comments for each line of code. Note that the comments are particularly uninspired, so while the number of comments is equal to the number of lines of code, no useful information is passed.

```
' Compute new x coordinate
NewX = CenterX + Sin(Theta) * Radius
' Compute new y coordinate
NewY = CenterY + Cos(Theta) * Radius

' Draw a line from the old coordinate to the new coordinate
Form1.Line (OldX, OldY)-(NewX, NewY), RGB(Red, Green, Blue)
' Set the line mode
Form1.DrawMode = vbCopyPen
```

```
' Save the new x coordinate in place of the old x coordinate
OldX = NewX
' Save the new y coordinate in place of the old y coordinate
OldY = NewY

' Add AngleStep to Theta
Theta = Theta + AngleStep
' Subtract RadiusDecrement from Radius
Radius = Radius - RadiusDecrement
```

Now look at the next code fragment from the StarSX program. You see only one comment, but this comment spans five lines. Instead of restating each line of code, this comment tries to explain how this routine works. From reading this, you understand why DrawMode was reset after the line was drawn. Also, you can understand how the arc of the circle is drawn rather than trying to figure out what CenterX + Sin(Theta) * Radius really means.

```
' Draw the arc of a circle from the coordinates (OldX, OldY)
' to the point determined by Theta, Radius with center at
' (CenterX, CenterY). The first time, Form1.DrawMode is set to
' vbWhiteness, so the arc is not drawn. Set it to vbCopyPen so
' subsequent arcs will be visible.

NewX = CenterX + Sin(Theta) * Radius
NewY = CenterY + Cos(Theta) * Radius

Form1.Line (OldX, OldY)-(NewX, NewY), RGB(Red, Green, Blue)
Form1.DrawMode = 13

OldX = NewX
OldY = NewY

Theta = Theta + AngleStep
Radius = Radius - RadiusDecrement
```

Another tip for writing comments is to include some status information at the head of each routine that discusses who wrote the routine, when it was written, and a brief revision history. This information is especially useful when you have multiple people working on the same project. Listing 3.1 shows the complete DrawArc subroutine from the StarSX program.

Listing 3.1:   DrawArc Routine in StarSX

```
Private Sub DrawArc()

' Routine:        DrawArc
' Programmer:     Wayne S. Freeze
' History:
'    1Apr98:      Initial release - WSF.
'    5Apr98:      Modified to not draw the arc the first
'                 time this routine is called - WSF.
'
' Discussion:
'    Draw the arc of a circle from the coordinates (OldX, OldY)
'    to the point determined by Theta, Radius with center at
'    (CenterX, CenterY). The first time, Form1.DrawMode is set to
'    vbWhiteness, so the arc is not drawn. Set it to vbCopyPen so
'    subsequent arcs will be visible.

NewX = CenterX + Sin(Theta) * Radius
NewY = CenterY + Cos(Theta) * Radius

Form1.Line (OldX, OldY)-(NewX, NewY), RGB(Red, Green, Blue)
Form1.DrawMode = vbCopyPen

OldX = NewX
OldY = NewY

Theta = Theta + AngleStep
Radius = Radius - RadiusDecrement

End Sub
```

Following Coding Conventions

Coding conventions are another useful tool for preventing bugs. Coding conventions come in a couple of forms: they provide rules for naming variables and routines, and they identify which statements you want to avoid while programming. Both forms combine to create a style that must be comfortable for you to use.

Variable and Routine Names Microsoft recommends a rather complex way to prefix variables. While this convention conveys a lot of information about your variables, it makes them somewhat unreadable and definitely difficult to remember. Even though Microsoft makes this suggestion, you might notice that the properties for things like the TextBox and ListBox controls refer to the `Text` property rather than the `strText` property. The same goes for the rest of the properties and methods for the other controls and objects. I suggest that you use meaningful names but leave the type information off the variable name.

TIP

Find a variable quickly: If you right-click on a variable (or subroutine or function) and select the Definition option from the pop-up menu, you will be taken to the place in your program where the variable was defined. You can return to the same line you left by right-clicking again and selecting the Last Position option from the pop-up menu.

Subroutines and functions are two places where the more descriptive you make the name, the less likely you are to use the wrong one. Properties, methods, and events in your own user controls should also be descriptive. After all, when you compile your program into machine code, it doesn't matter in the least whether you used two characters or twenty characters!

Statements to Avoid Visual Basic includes a variety of different statements, many of which overlap other statements in terms of functionality. I strongly suggest that you choose a subset of these statements and use them, while ignoring the others. This means you'll need to remember the syntax for fewer statements, and you'll become more comfortable with the ways that you use those statements.

For instance, you can use `For/Next`, `Do Until/Loop`, `Do While/Loop`, and `While/Wend` to perform loops in your code. There is no reason to use all four. I suggest you pick one style and use it consistently. Personally, I prefer the `Do While/Loop` structure, but I find myself using the `For/Next` anytime I'm dealing with a collection of objects (`For Each`), or when I need to perform a process a fixed number of times (`For I= 1 to 10`). I never use the `Do Until/Loop` or the `While/Wend` statements.

NOTE   **There is an exception for every rule, and you'll see me use it fairly often:** Being a lazy programmer, I often use short variable names. The variable name I use most often is `i`. I typically use this whenever I write a `For/Next` loop as the index variable. (Can you tell I spent too much time writing FORTRAN programs over the years?)

I also recommend avoiding the `Gosub/Return` statement and the `GoTo` statement. Both are holdovers from BASIC's early days. `Gosub/Return` isn't really needed in Visual Basic, where you can declare real subroutines, and `GoTo` is against every structured programming rule ever written. I've debugged many programs written by professional programmers who used the `GoTo` statement, and I've frequently found it faster to rewrite the entire program rather than try to fix it.

WARNING   **More means less:** Visual Basic has the ability to include more than one statement in a single line of code. Don't do it! Breakpoints are set on the line of code, not the statement. This means that you can't stop your program on the third statement on a particular line of code.

Being a Lazy Programmer

After reading about the KISS and SMILE principles, object-oriented programming, and comments and coding conventions, you may be wondering, "What does this have to do with debugging my programs?" The answer is that following good, solid programming practices is key to creating programs that require less debugging and that can more easily be debugged. As long as I'm on my soapbox, I'm going to suggest a general philosophy that will help you to eliminate bugs before they become bugs. I call it the Lazy Programmer approach.

Here are the Ten Commandments of a Lazy Programmer:

1. Think about what you want to do before you write any code.

2. Make it work the first time—you prefer not to do it again.

3. Don't make a program more complicated than necessary, because this may introduce more problems into the program in the long run.

4. Write modular programs because they are easier to test and debug.

5. Use a wide variety of tools to reduce the amount of work required to create the program and to increase the reliability of the final product.

6. Reuse code where possible, since the code has already been written and is known to work properly.

7. Write the least amount of code to solve the problem.

8. Use a lot of comments for complex code, and make sure that you provide a good overview of how the program functions.

9. Use good coding conventions so that comments aren't necessary for simple tasks.

10. Use Visual Basic to write Windows programs.

In today's world, people are paid to work. The harder they work, the more money they make (well, at least in theory). While this should be true of most professions, it is the wrong way to pay programmers.

Programmers should be paid a flat fee for creating an acceptable program. That way, it is in the programmer's best interest to make it work right the first time, so he or she can move onto the next project. It also forces a programmer to think smart. After all, the correct measure of programming is not the number of lines of code written per year, but the number of acceptable programs written per year.

Isolating Bugs the Easy Way

Although you can use the techniques I've suggested so far to prevent some bugs, I don't need to tell you that you won't avoid all of them.

When you know you are getting the wrong result, or your program is not behaving properly, what do you do next? You can use the Visual Basic Debugger, but sometimes that's overkill for what may appear to be a simple problem. Here, I'll talk about some simple ways to help you find out what is going on in your program:

- The `MsgBox` statement can be used to display information about your program while it is running.

- By pressing Ctrl+Break, you can interrupt your program and use the Immediate window to find out what is happening with your program.

- The Debug object provides some facilities to your program while running in the Visual Basic development environment.

Displaying Information with MsgBox

As I mentioned earlier, I learned to program many years ago on a Hewlett Packard 2000F time-share system, and the only programming language was a version of BASIC. This version of BASIC was powerful at the time, but wasn't even close to the Visual Basic we know and love today. If your problem generated an error, it printed a cryptic error message and stopped running. There were no breakpoints and no watches. Hitting Break stopped your program without giving you an opportunity to check any of your variables.

In that situation, debugging became a matter of inserting Print statements at various places throughout the program to display critical variables. Sometimes, you would even put an Input statement after the Print statement, just to slow down the program to the point where you could see the results before they scrolled off the top of the terminal display.

Well, Visual Basic still remembers its roots. Probably the easiest way to debug a Visual Basic program is by placing statements in your program to display variable information and to interrupt execution. The MsgBox statement has the ability to both display information and interrupt your program while it is running.

Simply insert a statement like this in your program to see what value the variable x contains:

```
MsgBox Format(x)
```

Use the following type of statement to see what is in the variables x and y:

```
MsgBox Format(x) & ":" & Format(y)
```

Once you get the information you need, you can click the OK button to continue. As you can see in the example shown in Figure 3.1, the display isn't pretty, but then, you're the only one who is ever going to see it.

FIGURE 3.1:

Displaying a message box to see the contents of multiple variables

Using Ctrl+Break and the Immediate Window

While your program is running in the development environment, you can interrupt it at any time by pressing Ctrl+Break. You can also select Run ➢ Break from the Visual Basic IDE menu. Either method invokes the Visual Basic Debugger. This will even work while you are displaying a message box. But rather then use the full power of the Visual Basic Debugger, you can use the Immediate window to check on some values and perform some basic tasks.

The Immediate window allows you to enter a single Visual Basic statement and execute it immediately. Figure 3.2 shows an example.

FIGURE 3.2:

The Immediate window

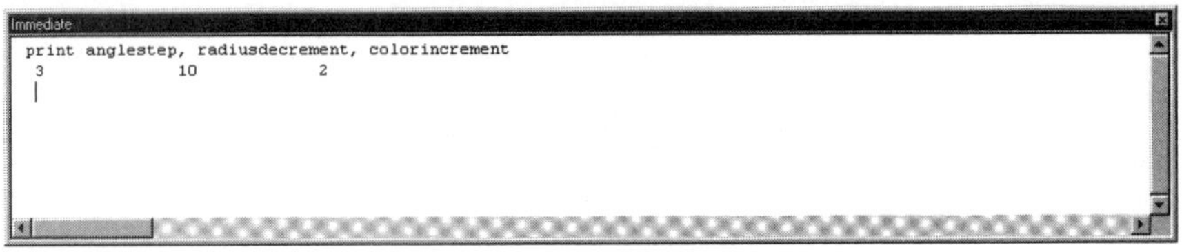

```
print anglestep, radiusdecrement, colorincrement
 3             10              2
```

Statements that declare variables or create subroutines can't be used in the Immediate window, but nearly any other statement can be used. For instance, you can display the contents of any of the variables that are in scope by using the Print statement. You can set the value of a variable by simply typing an assignment statement. You can even call functions, run subroutines, or invoke methods from the Immediate window.

The biggest limitation of using the Immediate window is that the variable or object must be available for you to reference. If you are waiting for input, your program may be able to access only global variables, because all of the other variables may be out of scope. To ensure that the variables you want to see are in scope, you need to insert a Stop statement where you want to check them, or set a breakpoint using the Visual Basic Debugger (discussed a bit later in this chapter).

WARNING   **Stop means End:** Use the Stop statement only when debugging your program. If you encounter a Stop statement while running a compiled program, it is treated as an End statement, and your program will be terminated.

Adding Debug.Assert

Okay, since your code is already perfect, how about making a small wager? Would you be willing to bet that everything is normal in several places throughout your program? The Debug.Assert statement let's you do just that.

For instance, you can add a statement like this one to your program:

```
Debug.Assert x > 0 and y = ""
```

This statement verifies that the variable x is greater than zero, and that y contains a null string. If x is really less than zero, the Assert method will fail and you will be transferred to the Visual Basic Debugger, with the Assert statement highlighted, as shown in Figure 3.3.

FIGURE 3.3:

The Visual Basic Debugger highlighting a failed Assert statement

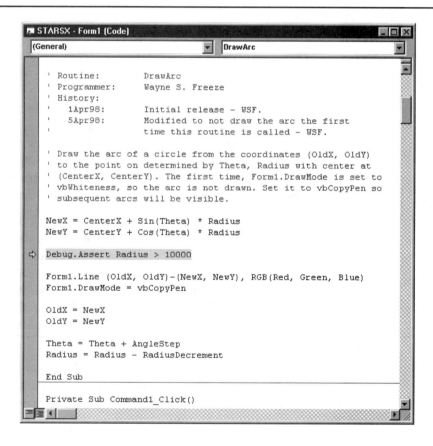

```
' Routine:        DrawArc
' Programmer:     Wayne S. Freeze
' History:
'    1Apr98:      Initial release - WSF.
'    5Apr98:      Modified to not draw the arc the first
'                 time this routine is called - WSF.

' Draw the arc of a circle from the coordinates (OldX, OldY)
' to the point on determined by Theta, Radius with center at
' (CenterX, CenterY). The first time, Form1.DrawMode is set to
' vbWhiteness, so the arc is not drawn. Set it to vbCopyPen so
' subsequent arcs will be visible.

NewX = CenterX + Sin(Theta) * Radius
NewY = CenterY + Cos(Theta) * Radius

Debug.Assert Radius > 10000

Form1.Line (OldX, OldY)-(NewX, NewY), RGB(Red, Green, Blue)
Form1.DrawMode = vbCopyPen

OldX = NewX
OldY = NewY

Theta = Theta + AngleStep
Radius = Radius - RadiusDecrement

End Sub

Private Sub Command1_Click()
```

Note that the `Assert` method works only in the development environment. When you compile your project, all references to the `Assert` method are dropped, so there is no need to use conditional compilation to remove these statements from your compiled program.

Adding Debug.Print

The `MsgBox` statement can be annoying, especially if it's inside a loop. Fortunately, the `Debug` object offers a viable alternative: the `Debug.Print` statement.

The `Debug.Print` statement works like a regular `Print` statement, except that it sends the output to the Immediate window. This can be useful when you want to check what is happening to a variable in a loop, as you can see in the example in Figure 3.4.

FIGURE 3.4:

Watching variables change in a loop

Using the Visual Basic Debugger

The biggest advantage of using an interpreted language is the ability to use a debugger that allows you to debug at the source-code level. The Visual Basic Debugger is a truly advanced tool that can help you identify problems with your program. Here, I'll go over the basic of setting breakpoints and watching expressions.

Debugging with Breakpoints

An alternative to using Ctrl+Break or the `MsgBox` statement to interrupt your program is to set a breakpoint. A *breakpoint* is a marker in your program that will temporarily interrupt your program and transfer control to the Immediate window. This works in the same way as the `Stop` statement described earlier. However, breakpoints are never included into a compiled program, so they can never be accidentally executed.

Setting a Breakpoint

To set a breakpoint, simply click on the gray area to the right of your statement. The statement will be highlighted in brown, and a brown dot will appear beside the statement in the gray area. Figure 3.5 shows a black-and-white rendition. The breakpoint can be set while your program is in break mode or while you are in design mode.

FIGURE 3.5:

Setting a break point

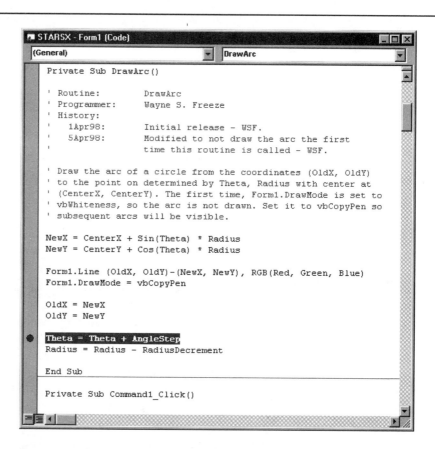

```
STARSX - Form1 (Code)
(General)                              DrawArc

   Private Sub DrawArc()

   ' Routine:        DrawArc
   ' Programmer:     Wayne S. Freeze
   ' History:
   '   1Apr98:       Initial release - WSF.
   '   5Apr98:       Modified to not draw the arc the first
   '                 time this routine is called - WSF.

   ' Draw the arc of a circle from the coordinates (OldX, OldY)
   ' to the point on determined by Theta, Radius with center at
   ' (CenterX, CenterY). The first time, Form1.DrawMode is set to
   ' vbWhiteness, so the arc is not drawn. Set it to vbCopyPen so
   ' subsequent arcs will be visible.

   NewX = CenterX + Sin(Theta) * Radius
   NewY = CenterY + Cos(Theta) * Radius

   Form1.Line (OldX, OldY)-(NewX, NewY), RGB(Red, Green, Blue)
   Form1.DrawMode = vbCopyPen

   OldX = NewX
   OldY = NewY

   Theta = Theta + AngleStep
   Radius = Radius - RadiusDecrement

   End Sub

   Private Sub Command1_Click()
```

Hitting a Breakpoint

When your program is running and encounters the breakpoint, the statement is highlighted in yellow, and the code window is displayed along with the Immediate window. You can then examine any variables local to the routine and look at any module-level variables or global variables. Figure 3.6 shows an example of what happens when you hit a breakpoint.

FIGURE 3.6:

Hitting a breakpoint

Breakpoints happen at the start: A breakpoint will be triggered before the break-pointed line of code is executed. If you have multiple statements on a single line, the program will be stopped before the first statement on the line is executed.

Leaving Break Mode

Once you have finished checking your program's state while in break mode, you have two ways to resume execution: continue with regular execution or go on in step mode.

Continuing with Normal Execution   You can select Run ➢ Continue to allow your program to continue normally. It will continue to the next breakpoint or until the end of the program if no more breakpoints are encountered.

Continuing in Step Mode Alternatively, you can resume in step mode after a breakpoint. In this mode, you can execute the current line of code and return to break mode. This is similar to setting a breakpoint on the next line of code. There are three options in step mode:

> **Step Into** This option lets you execute the current line of code and break at the next line of code executed, even if it is in a different subroutine.
>
> **Step Over** This option allows you to execute the current line of code and break at the line of code immediately following the current line, even it the current line is a call to a subroutine.
>
> **Step Out** This option lets you execute all of the statements starting with the current statement until the routine completes. Then the program will reenter break mode on the statement that immediately follows the statement that called the routine.

Step mode commands work only while you are in break mode.

Watching Expressions

Setting a breakpoint is not the only way to enter break mode. You can tell Visual Basic to watch an expression, and then enter break mode when the expression is true or when the value changes. If you don't specify either of these options, Visual Basic will just watch the expression and display it the next time you enter break mode. Note that unlike the Immediate window, which is updated continually as the program runs, the watch display is only updated when you enter break mode.

Setting a Watch

To set a watch, select Debug ➢ Add Watch to display the Add Watch dialog box, as shown in Figure 3.7. You fill in the Expression box with the expression you wish to watch. You can choose a simple variable as the expression, or you can choose a more complex expression involving variables, functions, properties, and methods that return a value.

FIGURE 3.7:

The Add Watch dialog box

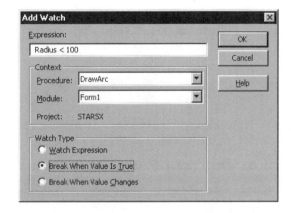

You can also specify the watch type, which describes the action to be taken when the expression is evaluated. When you choose the Watch Expression option, the expression is tracked, but no action is taken until you enter break mode. The Break When Value is True and the Break When Value Changes options are far more useful, because they enter break mode. You should think of these options as conditional breakpoints. While the expression can be as simple or as complicated as you make it, chances are you want to use something like `Radius < 100` or `ProcessingComplete = True` when you select either of the watch types that enter break mode.

NOTE

Watches are slow: Before you execute a statement, all of the watches will need to be recomputed, causing your program to slow down. In the interest of time, it is highly desirable to isolate the watch to a specific procedure or at least a specific module.

After you add a watch, the Watches window appears, listing all of the watches you set, as shown in Figure 3.8. You can highlight one of the watches and choose Debug ➤ Edit Watch or Debug ➤ Delete Watch (or right-click and select the appropriate option from the pop-up menu) to change or delete the selected watch.

FIGURE 3.8:

The Watches window before running your program

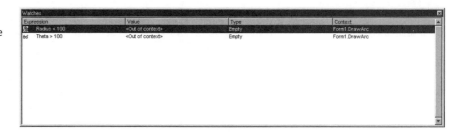

Running Your Program with a Watch

If you chose either the When Value is True or the Break When Value Changes option when you set your watch, when you run your program, the Watches window will appear when your program enters break mode. Figure 3.9 shows the Watches window and the Immediate window displayed when Radius < 100. Note that you can use the Immediate window to determine exact values for each watched variable.

FIGURE 3.9:

The Watches and Immediate windows in break mode

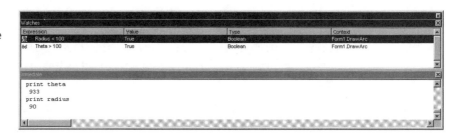

Tracking Down the Problem

As I said earlier in this chapter, I'm lazy. I know it. I admit it. This doesn't mean I don't work hard or that I'm not willing to devote the necessary time to a project. It's just that I want the most bang for the buck.

Under ideal circumstances, you should spend 50 (yes 50!) percent of your time in a project defining the requirements and designing the application. Another 25 percent should be spent in coding and unit testing, and the rest spent in system testing. However, in the real world, there's never enough time. Deadlines change, competitors release new products, and customers want new and different features.

In the real world, you never have enough time to define the requirements beyond "Do it now!" Project design is often done on the fly. This increases the time needed for coding and debugging the project. Because you did less design up front, you devote more time to debugging design flaws rather than simply debugging coding errors. Debugging design flaws is perhaps the most difficult debugging task of them all. Your code runs perfectly, but the program fails to perform its assigned task.

Correcting design flaws often involves making major changes to your application. You may need to add new database tables or restructure existing tables. You may need to make major changes to old forms, or even junk them and start over again from scratch. The beauty of writing Visual Basic programs is that much of the hard work is done for you automatically.

However, coding problems can still be a challenge to track down and fix. We've gone over the tools, now let's look at some problem errors. Visual Basic has a few traps of its own.

Finding Array Problems

Many controls use zero-based arrays. This means that the first element in an array has an index of zero. With Count items in the array, the last element will have an index of Count −1. However, just to keep you on your toes, some Visual Basic controls use a one-based array. Thus, valid indexes range from 1 to Count.

Remembering which type of array is used where is a challenge. When you get an error in this type of situation, you may want to pull up the documentation and review what the range of values should be.

Checking Parameter Ranges

Another area that often causes problems is ensuring that parameters are in the proper range before calling a function.

For instance, Left(mystring, len(mystring) − x) is a very useful expression. It will truncate the last x number of characters from the string mystring. This statement will work perfectly fine, until one time when x > len(mystring). Then you get that nasty runtime error saying "Invalid procedure call or argument."

Watching for Error Object Problems

The last area I want to mention involves the On Error statement and the Error object. Using an On Error statement without clearing the Error object creates a time bomb waiting to explode.

I spent an embarrassing amount of time (no, I'm not going to admit how much!) debugging a program when I first started using Visual Basic. I couldn't understand why a block of code was failing. I was doing everything right. I had an On Error Resume Next statement, followed by another statement, followed by an If statement that checked the Error object. Even though the statement succeeded, the If statement always found an error condition. It turns out that the Error object contained a minor error from another statement that I didn't care about. The statement that I thought was causing the error didn't change the Error object because no error had occurred. Therefore, the old value error condition that existed from before was caught in my If statement.

The moral of the story is that you should clear the Error object immediately before the statement you wish to check for errors. This prevents second-hand errors.

Final Thoughts

The best way to debug your program is to prevent bugs in the first place—hence, the KISS and SMILE principles and the Lazy Programmer philosophy. However, following this approach will not guarantee that your programs always will be 100 percent bug free.

When you suspect a bug, try to isolate where the problem is. The best way to do this is to look at your program and try to identify the code that could be causing the problem. Most likely, you can narrow your search considerably before you actually use any of the debugging techniques we discussed in this chapter.

Before you try to debug your program, consider making backup copies of all of your project's files. This will help you recover your original program after you've accidentally trashed it while trying to find the bug. I always try to put a project (or project group) into a single directory, so I just need to copy all the files in the directory to an empty directory to make a clean backup of the project.

One common problem in Visual Basic programs is determining when an event will occur. This is definitely a problem in a complex program where multiple events may be fired based on a single trigger. So if you are not sure of the order of the events or whether the event is even being called, simply put a message box in the event to display the name of the event.

Another common problem occurs when `If Then Else`, `Select Case`, `Do/Loop`, `While/Wend`, and `For/Next` are not coded properly. This usually happens when you have nested one of these statements inside another. The statement causing the problem is probably inside the wrong group of statements.

Use the `Debug.Assert` and `Debug.Print` methods liberally. Using `Debug.Print` inside a loop will generate a lot of output but is often helpful when debugging an infinite loop (and the output is easily recycled when you close the Immediate window).

Consider using the File System Objects described in Chapter 4 to create a log file where you can write debugging information. This concept is very useful when you are debugging a production application that fails only occasionally and you aren't getting enough information to isolate the error.

Use breakpoints and watches to trace your program's execution. When you have an extremely complex program, these tools are invaluable in helping you find your bug.

If breakpoints and watches aren't helping you, start stripping out code from your program one piece at a time. If the program starts working, look at the hunk of code you just deleted. The best way to delete code is not to use the Delete key, but to insert an apostrophe in front of the line and turn the line of code into a comment. Eventually, you will be able to isolate where the problem occurs.

When all else fails, try to duplicate the error in a small, stand-alone program. While Visual Basic is relatively protected against bugs, it's not totally bug free. If you think you've found a Visual Basic error, having a simple program that causes the error is very helpful when you contact Microsoft.

CHAPTER
FOUR

4

Using Disk Files

- Conventional file-access statements, functions, and controls

- The File System Objects approach

- The Drives collection and Drive object

- The Folders collection and Folder object

- The Files collection and File object

- The TextStream object

Every program uses disk files to some degree. The program itself is stored as a disk file. Any information that the program needs to remember between sessions also must be stored as a disk file. Databases are stored in a disk file. Even information in the Windows Registry is stored in a disk file. However, as you know, conventional disk files are also very useful.

Visual Basic provides two primary methods to access disk files. The older method uses conventional statements and functions to read and write data stored in sequential, random, and binary files. The newer method, which just became available in Visual Basic 6, uses a set of objects known as the File System Objects to access information stored on disk. Also associated with the File System Objects is the `Text-Stream` object, which can be used to read or write sequential text files. In this chapter, I'll talk about both approaches and how each works.

Using the Traditional File-Access Approach

The traditional way to access data on disk is through the use of file statements, functions, and controls. Some of these facilities have been around since BASIC was first written. It's no wonder that their capabilities overlap and their use can sometimes be confusing. Here, I'll try to clear up any confusion by reviewing the conventional statements, functions, and controls that allow you to access files in Visual Basic. Then I'll show you how they work in a few sample programs.

Making Statements

The statements for working with files are listed in Table 4.1. The `Open` statement allows you to gain access to a file. A file number in the range of 0 to 511 uniquely identifies an open file. (You can't use a file number that is already in use; the `Free-File` function gets a number that currently isn't being used.) The `Close` statement is used to clean up all file buffers and post any remaining data to the disk file.

TABLE 4.1:   Statements for Processing Files

Statement	Description
ChDir	Changes the current directory
Close	Closes access to a file
CurDir	Returns the current directory
FileCopy	Creates another copy of a file
Get	Retrieves data from random and binary files
Input #	Retrieves data from a sequential file
Kill	Deletes a file
Line Input #	Retrieves data from a sequential file
MkDir	Creates a directory
Open	Opens access to a file
Print #	Outputs data to a sequential file
Put	Outputs data to random and binary files
RmDir	Deletes a directory
Seek	Sets the current record pointer
SetAttr	Sets the attributes on a file
Write #	Outputs data to sequential files

A number of options are available to control file access. For sequential files, you can specify the mode of the file as Append, Input, and Output. You can specify access as Read, Write, or Read Write. Optionally, you can set file locking as Shared, Lock Read, Lock Write, or Lock Read Write. The record length of the file can be specified in the Len= clause. On a sequential file, this length is the size of the buffer; on a random file, this specifies the size of the record.

The Input # and Line Input # statements are used to read data written to the file with the Write # and Print # statements, respectively. The primary difference between the reading/writing pairs is that the Input # statement can read a series of variables while the `Line Input #` statement reads an entire line of the file into a string variable. The `Input #` and `Write #` statements work well with both binary and sequential files; the `Line Input #` and `Print #` statements work only with sequential files.

The `Get` and `Put` statements are used to read and write a single variable in a random file. You should use the `Type` statement to create a user-defined type so that you can read an entire record at one time. You also need to specify the length of each record in the `Open` statement's `Len=` clause. The first record in the file has a record number of 1.

The `Seek` statement moves the record pointer to the specified record number in a random file or the specified byte position in a sequential or binary file. You can use the `SetAttr` statement to set file attributes.

The remaining statements perform operations on unopened files. The `ChDir`, `CurDir`, `MkDir`, and `RmDir` statements work the same as the DOS commands with the same name. The `Kill` statement is the same as the Erase command. The `File-Copy` statement is basically the same as the Copy command.

Using Functions to Process Files

The file-processing functions are listed in Table 4.2. The most used file function is probably `EOF`, which determines when you've read all of the data from the file.

TABLE 4.2: Functions for Processing Files

Function	Description
Dir	Returns the complete path name to the specified file pattern; subsequent calls return the next file that matches the file pattern
EOF	Returns **True** if the file pointer is at the end of the file
FileDateTime	Retrieves date and time information about an unopened file
FileLen	Returns the length of an unopened file
FreeFile	Returns a free file number
GetAttr	Returns the file's attributes
Input	Returns data from a sequential or binary file

Continued on next page

TABLE 4.2 (CONTINUED):   Functions for Processing Files

Function	Description
Loc	Returns the relative location in the file
LOF	Returns the length of an opened file in bytes
Seek	Returns the current record pointer

The Loc function returns information about the position in the file:

- For a random file, it returns the relative record number.

- For a binary file, it returns the relative byte position within the file.

- For a sequential file, it returns a value that is roughly the byte position divided by 128.

Both the FileLen and LOF functions return the size of a file in bytes. The GetAttr function gets file attributes. The FileDateTime function returns the date the file was created or last modified.

The Input function works like the Input # statement, except that all of the data is returned rather than being parsed into multiple variables. The Seek function, similar to the Seek statement, returns the location of the record pointer.

The Dir function has two forms: one with a parameter and one without. If you specify a path to a file with wildcard characters, it will return the first name of a file in that directory that matches. If no match is found, then an empty string is returned. You can specify that you wish to include files with certain attributes, such as hidden and system. You also can retrieve directory files. Calling Dir a second time without any parameters will retrieve the next file in the directory that matches the original argument. You can repeat this process until you have retrieved all of the files in a particular directory.

TIP

Is the file really there? You can use the Dir function to determine if a file exists by specifying the exact filename. If the Dir function returns an empty string, then you know that the file doesn't exist.

Displaying File Information with Controls

In addition to the file-processing statements and functions, Visual Basic includes four intrinsic controls that can help you find information and perform useful functions with your files. These controls are listed in Table 4.3.

TABLE 4.3:   Controls for Displaying File Information

Control	Description
CommonDialog	Displays dialog boxes for opening and saving files
DirListBox	Displays a list of directories
DriveListBox	Displays a list of disk drives
FileListBox	Displays a list of files

The CommonDialog control displays standard dialog boxes for opening and saving files. Using this control helps your users by presenting familiar dialog boxes.

The DirListBox, DriveListBox, and FileListBox controls work together to display information about your directory structures. Information from the DriveListBox is passed onto the DirListBox, whose results are passed onto the FileListBox. This cascaded setup is fairly easy to implement and gives your application a professional look.

Selecting a File

Selecting a file is an easy task, as long as you use the proper tools. A long time ago, I built a quick-and-dirty program to help me match the pictures that appear in a book with the text and captions. I needed a tool that let me flip through a stack of images in both directions, since I often needed to back up a few slides as well as scroll forward.

The SlideShow program uses the DriveListBox, DirListBox, and FileListBox controls to display a list of files, as shown in Figure 4.1. The user selects the desired file or files to display and clicks the Show button. This action makes all of the file controls invisible and displays a picture box that contains the first selected image, as shown in Figure 4.2. Clicking the Next button displays the next selected file. After the last selected image is displayed, clicking the Next button has no effect.

FIGURE 4.1:

Selecting a file in the
SlideShow program

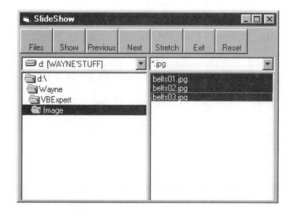

FIGURE 4.2:

Displaying a file in the
SlideShow program

In a similar fashion, clicking the Previous button displays each preceding image until the user reaches the first selected image. Clicking the Files button allows the user to select a different set of files. The file controls become visible again, and the picture control is invisible.

Cascading Changes

Key to using the DriveListBox, DirListBox, and FileListBox controls is the ability to cascade changes from one control to the next. In other words, changing the current drive implies that the current directory and list of files are now different. Likewise, changing the current directory changes the list of files that should be displayed.

I implement cascading changes through the Change events of the DriveListBox and DirListBox controls. As you can see in Listing 4.1, changing the current drive also changes the DirListBox's current path.

Listing 4.1: **DriveList_Change Event in SlideShow**

```
Private Sub DriveList_Change()

DirList.Path = DriveList.Drive

End Sub
```

Then I change the FileListBox's current path whenever the directory is changed. This code is shown in Listing 4.2.

Listing 4.2: **DirList_Change Event in SlideShow**

```
Private Sub DirList_Change()

FileList.Path = DirList.Path

End Sub
```

Not all changes that will affect these controls come from the user. I added a simple combo box called FileTypes that contains a list of file types I want to display. Each time the user selects a different value in FileTypes, I assign the value to the FileList.Pattern property and then Refresh the contents of the control, as shown in Listing 4.3.

Listing 4.3: **FileTypes_Click Event in SlideShow**

```
Private Sub FileTypes_Click()

FileList.Pattern = FileTypes.Text
FileList.Refresh

End Sub
```

I supply initial values for the FileTypes combo box in the Form_Load event, as shown in Listing 4.4.

Listing 4.4:   **Form_Load Event in SlideShow**

```
Private Sub Form_Load()

FileTypes.AddItem "*.jpg"
FileTypes.AddItem "*.gif"

End Sub
```

Processing Selected Files

After selecting the files to display, the user can click the Show button on the toolbar to display the first image file. As shown in Listing 4.5, I use the variable Current-Image to determine if a particular filename was selected by checking the FileList .Selected property. When this property is True, the user selected the file, and I call the ShowImage routine to display it.

Listing 4.5:   **Toolbar1_ButtonClick Event in SlideShow**

```
Private Sub Toolbar1_ButtonClick(ByVal Button As ComctlLib.Button)

Dim i As Integer

If Button.Key = "Files" Then
    SlideImage.Visible = False
    DirList.Visible = True
    FileList.Visible = True
    DriveList.Visible = True
    FileTypes.Visible = True

ElseIf Button.Key = "Show" Then
    CurrentImage = 0
    Do While CurrentImage < FileList.ListCount
        If FileList.Selected(CurrentImage) Then
            ShowImage CurrentImage
            Exit Do
        Else
```

```
            CurrentImage = CurrentImage + 1
         End If
      Loop

   ElseIf Button.Key = "Next" Then
      CurrentImage = CurrentImage + 1
      Do While CurrentImage < FileList.ListCount
         If FileList.Selected(CurrentImage) Then
            ShowImage CurrentImage
            Exit Do
         Else
            CurrentImage = CurrentImage + 1
         End If
      Loop

   ElseIf Button.Key = "Previous" Then
      CurrentImage = CurrentImage - 1
      Do While CurrentImage >= 0
         If FileList.Selected(CurrentImage) Then
            ShowImage CurrentImage
            Exit Do
         Else
            CurrentImage = CurrentImage - 1
         End If
      Loop

   ElseIf Button.Key = "Stretch" Then
      SlideImage.Stretch = Not SlideImage.Stretch
      ShowImage CurrentImage

   ElseIf Button.Key = "Exit" Then
      Unload SlideShow

   ElseIf Button.Key = "Reset" Then
      ResetSettings

   End If

   End Sub
```

The Next and Previous toolbar buttons use similar code. However, rather than setting `CurrentImage` to 0 before starting, they add or subtract one from the current value. Then they search in the appropriate direction looking for an image to display.

Accessing Files Sequentially

Sequential file access in Visual Basic implies that you are going to be using the `Line Input #` and `Print #` statements to read and write your data. The Sequential File Access program, shown in Figure 4.3, uses the `Line Input #` statement to fill a text box with the contents of a file. Using the `Print #` statement, you can save changes to the disk file.

FIGURE 4.3:

The Sequential
File Access program

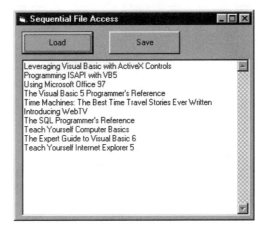

Reading a Sequential File

Clicking the Load button triggers the event shown in Listing 4.6. I use the Common-Dialog control's Open dialog box to get the name of the file, as shown in Figure 4.4.

Listing 4.6:   Command1_Click Event in Sequential File Access

```
Private Sub Command1_Click()

Dim s As String

On Error Resume Next
```

```
CommonDialog1.Flags = cdlOFNFileMustExist
CommonDialog1.ShowOpen
If Err = 0 Then
   Open CommonDialog1.FileName For Input As 1
   Line Input #1, s
   Text1.Text = s
   Do While Not EOF(1)
      Line Input #1, s
      Text1.Text = Text1.Text & vbCrLf & s
   Loop
   Close #1
End If

End Sub
```

FIGURE 4.4:

Opening a file in the Sequential File Access program

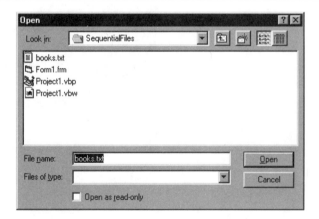

If the user clicks the Cancel button, a runtime error will be generated because I set the `CancelError` property to `True` at design time. This lets the user change his or her mind after looking for a file without overwriting the data in the text box.

I make sure that the file exists by setting the `CommonDialog1.Flags` property to `cdlOFNFileMustExist`. This prevents a runtime error from occurring when trying to open a nonexistent file.

Once I have a valid filename, I simply open the file for input and read the first line. I save the line in the `Text1` text box. Then I begin a loop that will continue reading lines of text from the file and appending it to the text box until I've reached the end of the file. When I reach the end of the file, I end the loop, close the file, and exit the routine.

Note that the `Line Input #` statement reads an entire line of text from the file, up to but not including the carriage return/line feed. As I append the text to the text box, I need to manually add the carriage return and line feed characters to properly display it.

Writing a Sequential File

The code for saving the contents of the text box to disk is shown in Listing 4.7. This code is similar to the code I used to read it. I display the CommonDialog box to perform the Save function to get a valid filename, as shown in Figure 4.5. I also set the `CommonDialog1.Flags` property so that it will automatically verify that the user wishes to overwrite an existing file before it returns the filename.

FIGURE 4.5:

Saving a file in the Sequential File Access program

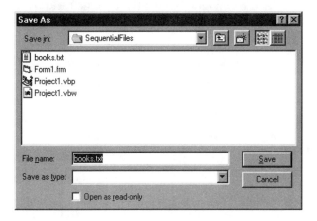

Listing 4.7:   **Command2_Click Event in Sequential File Access**

```
Private Sub Command2_Click()

Dim i As Integer
Dim s() As String

On Error Resume Next

CommonDialog1.Flags = cdlOFNOverwritePrompt
```

```
CommonDialog1.ShowSave
If Err = 0 Then
   s = Split(Text1.Text, vbCrLf)
   Open CommonDialog1.FileName For Output As 1
   For i = LBound(s) To UBound(s)
      Print #1, s(i)
   Next i
   Close #1
End If

End Sub
```

If I have a valid filename (`Err = 0`), then I will write the contents of the text box to disk. There are two ways I could do this. One way is to use a single `Print #` statement specifying `Text1.Text`. This would write the entire contents of the text box out in one fell swoop. The carriage return and line feed characters I explicitly added when I loaded the file into the text box would be included in the file when I wrote it. This means that the `Line Input #` statement would continue to work properly.

The other way is a bit more complicated, but it represents the traditional way that files are written. I take the contents of the text box and use the `Split` function to create a series of lines of text in the array `s`. This function also strips out the carriage return/line feed pairs from text. Having the data in this format is much more common when working with files.

I begin writing the data to disk by opening the file for output. Then I loop through each element of the `s` array and use the `Print #` statement to write it to the file. The `Print #` statement will append carriage return and line feed characters at the end of each line of text. When I'm finished, I simply close the file and exit.

The difference between the two approaches isn't much, but it might have an effect when you need to save your own data in a more specialized format. It's important to note that the `Print #` statement always appends a carriage return/line feed pair to the end of whatever it writes. If your data already includes these characters, you can prevent these characters from appearing by ending the `Print #` statement with a semicolon (`;`), as in the following statement:

```
Print #1, s(i);
```

Accessing Files Randomly

Random file access is a little more complicated than sequential file access. However, once you understand how it works, it really isn't all that hard to use.

Random files are constructed as a series of fixed objects called *records*. A record is usually implemented in Visual Basic as a Type structure. You can then address any particular record in the file by its record number. The first record in the file has a record number of 1, the second has a record number of 2, and so on. You can read or write any record in the file simply by specifying the proper record number. Unfortunately, you can't delete records in a random file, because there is no way to remove records once they are written.

TIP   **You can work magic:** Although you can't delete a record in a random file, you can include a field in your Type statement that indicates that the record has been deleted. Then you can include code in your program to detect deleted records and skip over them when scrolling through the records. You can also use a compress function that copies the current file into a new file without copying the records marked as deleted.

    The Random Access File program, shown in Figure 4.6, implements a simple address list tool. You can add new entries at the end and update any address in the list. It also includes the ability to scroll through the records from front to back or back to front.

FIGURE 4.6:

The Random Access File program

Random Access File Demo				
First	Next	Prev	Last	
John Doe				Open
123 Main Street				Append
Somewhere		SD	12345	
(123) 987-6543				Update

Issuing Global Declarations

Key to using random files is creating a data type with a fixed size that contains all of the information you need. In Listing 4.8, I create the Addr type containing Name, Addr, City, State, Zip, and Phone fields. I also define two other variables: File-Num to hold the file number and RecNum for the current record number. If FileNum equals 0, then the file hasn't been opened and any activities should be ignored except for opening the file.

Listing 4.8:   **Global Declarations in Random Access File**

```
Option Explicit

Private Type Addr
   Name As String * 40
   Addr As String * 40
   City As String * 30
   State As String * 2
   Zip As String * 5
   Phone As String * 16
End Type


Dim FileNum As Integer
Dim RecNum As Long
```

Opening a Random File

When the user clicks the Open button, the code in Listing 4.9 is triggered. I use the CommonDialog control to get the name of the file from the user. Then I make sure that the file has been closed (FileNum > 0 implies that it was opened as some point); if it hasn't, I close it. Then I open the file as a random file and specify the length of each record as Len(a). To do this, I needed to declare a local variable of type Addr to compute the length, but otherwise, I don't use this variable. If the file was opened successfully, I assign a value of 1 to FileNum; otherwise, I display an error message and set FileNum to 0 so that other routines will know that the file wasn't opened.

Listing 4.9:   **Command5_Click Event in Random Access File**

```
Private Sub Command5_Click()

Dim a As Addr

On Error Resume Next

CommonDialog1.ShowOpen
If Err = 0 Then
    If FileNum > 0 Then
        Close FileNum
    End If

    Open CommonDialog1.FileName For Random As 1 Len = Len(a)
    If Err <> 0 Then
        MsgBox Err.Description
        FileNum = 0

    Else
        FileNum = 1
    End If
End If

End Sub
```

Reading the First Record

Reading the first record in the file is merely a matter of verifying that the file has been open and using the Get statement to retrieve the first record into a local variable. I then copy the variable field by field into the text boxes on the form. Listing 4.10 shows this code.

Listing 4.10:   **Command1_Click Event in Random Access File**

```
Private Sub Command1_Click()

Dim a As Addr

If FileNum > 0 Then
```

```
    RecNum = 1

    Get FileNum, RecNum, a
    Text1.Text = a.Name
    Text2.Text = a.Addr
    Text3.Text = a.City
    Text4.Text = a.State
    Text5.Text = a.Zip
    Text6.Text = a.Phone
End If

End Sub
```

Reading the Next Record

Reading the next record is a little more difficult, since I need to make sure that I don't read a record past the end of file. I compute the last record in the file by dividing the number of bytes in the file by the length of each record. I save this result in the variable r. I then use the IIf function to make sure that the largest record number I can use is r. If RecNum +1 is greater than r, I use the value in r; otherwise, I use RecNum +1 for the next record number. Listing 4.11 shows the code for reading the next record.

Listing 4.11:   **Command2_Click Event in Random Access File**

```
Private Sub Command2_Click()

Dim a As Addr
Dim r As Long

If FileNum > 0 Then
    r = LOF(FileNum) / Len(a)
    RecNum = IIf(RecNum >= r, r, RecNum + 1)

    Get FileNum, RecNum, a
    Text1.Text = a.Name
    Text2.Text = a.Addr
    Text3.Text = a.City
    Text4.Text = a.State
    Text5.Text = a.Zip
```

```
        Text6.Text = a.Phone
End If

End Sub
```

Adding a New Record

Adding a new record to the file involves finding the last record number in the file and writing the new record into the next slot. I compute the last record by dividing the total file size in bytes (LOF(FileNum)) by the size of the record in bytes (Len(a)). Once I have this value, I just use the Put statement to write the record to the appropriate place in the file. Listing 4.12 shows the code for adding a new record.

Listing 4.12:   **Command6_Click Event in Random Access File**

```
Private Sub Command6_Click()

Dim a As Addr

If FileNum > 0 Then
    a.Name = Text1.Text
    a.Addr = Text2.Text
    a.City = Text3.Text
    a.State = Text4.Text
    a.Zip = Text5.Text
    a.Phone = Text6.Text

    RecNum = (LOF(FileNum) / Len(a)) + 1

    Put FileNum, RecNum, a
End If

End Sub
```

Updating an Existing Record

Updating a record is simply a matter of using the Put statement to write the record over an existing record, as shown in Listing 4.13.

Listing 4.13:   Command7_Click Event in Random Access File

```
Private Sub Command7_Click()

Dim a As Addr

If FileNum > 0 Then
    a.Name = Text1.Text
    a.Addr = Text2.Text
    a.City = Text3.Text
    a.State = Text4.Text
    a.Zip = Text5.Text
    a.Phone = Text6.Text

    Put FileNum, RecNum, a
End If

End Sub
```

In this case, I verify that the file is open and move the contents of the text boxes on the form to the local variable. Then I write that local variable to the file using the current record number.

Introducing File System Objects

The File System Objects are one of the more useful enhancements to Visual Basic 6. These objects make is very easy to navigate through the file system and perform basic file operations, such as creating, copying, moving, and deleting files and folders.

The examples I'll use to demonstrate the new system are taken from the File Viewer program. This program consists of two ActiveX controls: FileView and FileSelect. Both use the File System Objects to show a list of all of the files in the system and display the selected file using the specified format. Figure 4.7 shows the File Viewer program's file selection window.

FIGURE 4.7:

Selecting files in the File Viewer program

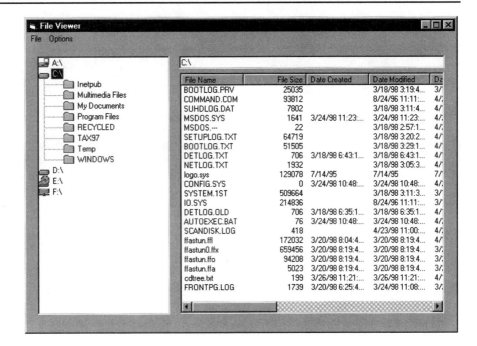

The `FileSystemObject` is the root object of the File System Objects. All of the other objects are created directly or indirectly from this object. This object also offers an assortment of methods that can be used to create, copy, move, and delete files and folders. Table 4.4 lists the `FileSystemObject` methods and properties.

TABLE 4.4:   FileSystemObject Properties and Methods

Property/Method	Description
`BuildPath` method	Assembles a path from the specified folder and filenames
`CopyFile` method	Copies one or more files to another location
`CopyFolder` method	Copies one or more folders and any files they contain to another location

Continued on next page

TABLE 4.4 (CONTINUED):   FileSystemObject Properties and Methods

Property/Method	Description
CreateFolder method	Creates a new, empty folder
CreateTextFile method	Creates a new, empty file
DeleteFile method	Removes one or more files from a folder
DeleteFolder method	Removes one or more folders from a folder
DriveExists method	Returns **True** if the specified drive is on the system
Drives property	Returns a **Drives** collection object containing all of the drives on the system
FileExists method	Returns **True** if the specified file exists
FolderExists method	Returns **True** if the specified folder exists
GetAbsolutePathName method	Returns the absolute path name of the specified folder
GetBaseName method	Returns the filename without extension of the specified file
GetDrive method	Returns a **Drive** object corresponding to the drive in the specified file or path name
GetDriveName method	Returns the drive name of the specified file or path name
GetExtensionName method	Returns the file extension of the specified filename
GetFile method	Returns a **File** object corresponding to the specified path and filename
GetFileName method	Returns the filename (including extension) of the specified filename
GetFolder method	Returns a **Folder** object corresponding to the specified folder name
GetFolderName method	Returns the folder name of the specified path name
GetParentFolderName method	Returns the name of the parent folder containing the specified file or folder name
GetSpecialFolder method	Returns a **Folder** object corresponding to the Windows folder, the System folder, or the folder used to hold temporary files
GetTempName method	Returns a name that can be used to create a temporary file or folder

Continued on next page

TABLE 4.4 (CONTINUED): FileSystemObject Properties and Methods

Property/Method	Description
MoveFile method	Moves one or more files to another location
MoveFolder method	Moves one or more folders and the files they contain to another location
OpenTextFile method	Opens the specified file and returns the corresponding TextStream object

You can use either of two methods to create a FileSystemObject. The following code shows the traditional way to create a new instance of an object in Visual Basic:

```
Dim fso as FileSystemObject
Set fso = New FileSystemObject
```

Note that the variable fso is defined to be of type FileSystemObject, which helps to promote better type checking.

As an alternative, you can use the CreateObject function to create a new FileSystemObject:

```
Dim fso as Object
Set fso = CreateObject("Scripting.FileSystemObject")
```

The main advantage of using the CreateObject function is that this code works properly in Visual Script; the traditional method will generate an error.

Working with Drives

The Drives property in the FileSystemObject returns a reference to the Drives collection. The Drives collection contains a series of Drive objects. Each Drive object corresponds to a floppy disk drive, a hard disk drive, a CD-ROM drive, or a network drive that is on your system. Table 4.5 lists the Drives collection properties.

TABLE 4.5: Drives Collection Properties

Property	Description
Count	Returns the number of Drive objects in the collection
Item	Returns a reference to a Drive object

Getting Information about Drives

The Drive object returns information about a single disk drive. Table 4.6 lists the Drive object properties. Most of the properties return basic information about the drive. However, the RootFolder property returns a Folder object, which contains the files and folders from the root directory of the drive. We'll examine the Folder object after we look at the Drive object and an example of its use.

> **NOTE**
>
> **AvailableSpace versus FreeSpace:** Although these properties appear similar, they are not. FreeSpace returns the actual free space on the drive. ActualSpace returns the space available to the user, which may be less due to Windows NT disk space quotas.

TABLE 4.6: Drive Object Properties

Property	Description
AvailableSpace	Returns the remaining space available for a user on a disk drive
DriveLetter	Returns the drive letter assigned to the drive
DriveType	Indicates the type of drive (floppy disk, hard disk, network, CD-ROM, or unknown)
FileSystem	Returns the type of file system installed on the drive (FAT, NTFS, or CDFS)
FreeSpace	Returns the total free space available on the drive
IsReady	Returns **False** when a floppy or CD-ROM is not present in the drive
Path	Returns the path to the disk drive
RootFolder	Returns a Folder object containing the folders and files in the root directory of the disk drive
SerialNumber	Returns the serial number of the disk drive
ShareName	Returns the share name of a network drive or an empty string for any other type of drive
TotalSize	Returns the total size of the disk drive
VolumeName	Returns the volume name of the disk drive

Are you ready? Before trying to access any of the files or folders on a particular drive, you should check the IsReady property. If you try to access information such as FreeSpace or look at any files or folders on a floppy or CD-ROM drive that is empty, an error will be generated. If the error is not handled properly, your program could abort.

Using the Drive Object in a Program

Listing 4.14 shows a code fragment from the File Viewer program. This code fragment begins by declaring a few local variables. The variable fso is assumed to exist as a module-level variable of type FileSystemObject. This routine will iterate through all of the Drive objects in the Drives collection, extracting the drive's path and adding to the collection of nodes used by the TreeView1 control (I'll cover the TreeView control in more detail in Chapter 7). Note that I look at the type of drive to assign the appropriate icon reference from the ImageList control. I also store the path information in the node's Key property and the name of the drive in the node's Text property.

Listing 4.14:   **Drive Information Retrieval in File Viewer**

```
Dim d As Drive    ' Current disk drive
Dim dl As String ' The Drive letter of the disk
Dim n As Node     ' Temporary TreeView node object


Set fso = New FileSystemObject
For Each d In fso.Drives
   dl = d.DriveLetter & ":\"
   If d.DriveType = Removable Then
      Set n = TreeView1.Nodes.Add(, , dl, dl, "floppy")
   ElseIf d.DriveType = CDRom Then
      Set n = TreeView1.Nodes.Add(, , dl, dl, "cdrom")
   ElseIf d.DriveType = Fixed Then
      Set n = TreeView1.Nodes.Add(, , dl, dl, "fixed")
   ElseIf d.DriveType = Remote Then
      Set n = TreeView1.Nodes.Add(, , dl, dl, "remote")
   Else
      Set n = TreeView1.Nodes.Add(, , dl, dl, "unknown")
   End If
Next d
```

Working with Folders

The `Folder` object corresponds to a folder on your disk drive. Since a folder can contain both files and subfolders, this object contains references to a `Folders` collection (the `SubFolders` property) and a `Files` collection (the `Files` property). Table 4.7 lists the properties and methods available in the `Folders` collection.

TABLE 4.7:   Folders Collection Properties and Methods

Property/Method	Description
Add method	Creates a new folder, adds it to the collection, and returns a reference to the new `Folder` object
Count property	Returns the number of `Folder` objects in the collection
Item property	Returns a reference to a `Folder` object

Since a folder is simply a place to hold other folders and files, a tree is often used to picture this arrangement. The leaves of the tree are files, and the branches are the folders. The folder that contains all of the other folders and files is known as the *root folder*. While all other folders have a parent, the root folder does not. This may require special programming when you move up the directory tree.

Getting Information about Folders

Physically, a folder is simply a special kind of file that contains a list of references for other files and folders. Thus, many of the properties associated with the `Folder` object are shared with the `File` object. Table 4.8 lists these properties and methods.

TABLE 4.8:   Folder Object Properties and Methods

Property/Method	Description
Attributes property	Returns an integer containing the file attributes set for this folder
Copy method	Copies this folder to the specified location
CreateTextFile method	Creates a new file in this folder, opens the file as a text stream, and returns a reference to the `TextStream` object
DateCreated property	Returns the date and time the folder was created

Continued on next page

TABLE 4.8 (CONTINUED):   Folder Object Properties and Methods

Property/Method	Description
DateLastAccessed property	Returns the date and time of the last access to the folder
DateLastModified property	Returns the date and time of the last time the folder was changed
Delete method	Deletes the folder associated with the Folder object
Drive property	Returns an object reference to the Drive object that contains this folder
Files property	Returns an object reference to the Files collection that contains the files found in this folder
IsRootFolder property	Returns True if the folder is the root folder of the disk drive
Move method	Moves this folder to the specified location
Name property	Returns the long name of this folder
ParentFolder property	Returns an object reference to the Folder object for the parent folder
Path property	Returns the complete path to this folder
ShortName property	Returns the short name of this folder
ShortPath property	Returns the complete path to this folder using short names for each intermediate folder
Size property	Returns the sum of the sizes of all files and subfolders
SubFolders property	Returns a reference to a Folder object containing the collection of subfolders in this directory
Type property	Returns the type of the object (for folders, this should always be File Folder)

Using the Folder Object in a Program

Listing 4.15 contains another code fragment from the File Viewer program. This fragment is taken from the TreeView1_NodeClick event. (Note that some of the code from the real TreeView1_NodeClick event has been deleted, since it wasn't relevant to this discussion of the Folder object.)

Listing 4.15: **TreeView1_NodeClick Event in File Viewer**

```
Private Sub TreeView1_NodeClick(ByVal Node As ComctlLib.Node)

Dim c As Node
Dim d As Drive
Dim fn As Folder
Dim fo As Folder

Set d = fso.GetDrive(fso.GetDriveName(Node.Key))
If d.IsReady Then
    Set fn = fso.GetFolder(Node.Key)
Else
    MsgBox "Drive " & d.DriveLetter & " is not ready."
    Exit Sub
End If

For Each fo In fn.SubFolders
    Set c = TreeView1.Nodes.Add(Node, tvwChild, _
        fo.Path & "\", fo.Name, "closedfolder")
Next fo

End Sub
```

I started building a TreeView structure containing the path to each of the disk drives on the system. The first thing I do in this routine is to get a reference to the Drive object that contains this folder and check to see if the physical drive is ready.

If the drive is ready, then I get the Folder object associated with the folder's path by using the GetDrive method. (Remember that I stored the path information in the node's Key property.) If the drive isn't ready, I display a message and exit the event.

Once I know that the drive is ready, I can process each of the subfolders in the Folder object stored in fn. I use the For Each construct to loop through all of the items in the collection. Then I add each folder I find to the TreeView's node collection as a child of the current folder. I construct a path using the folder's path and name. I also display the folder initially using the "closedfolder" icon in the TreeView, since the user hasn't had a chance to open the folder yet.

Working with Files

The `Files` collection refers to the set of files found in a single folder. Each `File` object corresponds to an individual file in the folder. Table 4.9 lists the `Files` collection properties.

TABLE 4.9:   Files Collection Properties

Property	Description
Count	Returns the number of `File` objects in the collection
Item	Returns a reference to a `File` object

Getting Information about Files

The `File` object contains information such as the file's short and long names, its size, and its attributes. This object also has date/time information showing when the file was created, last modified, and last accessed. Additionally, it contains an object reference to its parent folder.

By using the `File` object's `OpenTextStream` method, you can create a `TextStream` object for the file and manipulate the file using the `TextStream`'s methods (the `TextStream` object is discussed later in the chapter). Table 4.10 shows the `File` object properties and methods.

TABLE 4.10:   File Object Properties and Methods

Property/Method	Description
`Attributes` property	Returns an integer containing the file attributes set for this file
Copy method	Copies this file to the specified location
`DateCreated` property	Returns the date and time the file was created
`DateLastAccessed` property	Returns the date and time of the last access to the file
`DateLastModified` property	Returns the date and time of the last time the file was changed
`Delete` method	Deletes the file associated with the `File` object

Continued on next page

TABLE 4.10 (CONTINUED): File Object Properties and Methods

Property/Method	Description
Drive property	Returns an object reference to the Drive object that contains this file
Move method	Moves this file to the specified location
Name property	Returns the long name of this file
OpenAsTextStream property	Opens this file and return a TextStream object reference
ParentFolder property	Returns an object reference to the File object for the folder containing this file
Path property	Returns the complete path to this file
ShortName property	Returns the short name of this file
ShortPath property	Returns the complete path to this file using short names for each folder plus the short name for the file
Size property	Returns the size of the file
Type property	Returns the type of the file

NOTE

What type of type? The values of Type returned by the File object (and also the Folder object) are the same values defined in the Windows Registry under the key HKEY_CLASSES_ROOT. See Chapter 17 for more information about accessing the Windows Registry.

Using the File Object in a Program

The code fragment presented in Listing 4.15 demonstrated how to retrieve information for the folders. I used a TreeView control to display the folder hierarchy. Listing 4.16 shows how to get information about the files. I decided to use a ListView Report display to show the files. Using this control, it is easy to display the information associated with a file in a tabular format (I'll talk more about the ListView control and its Report view in Chapter 7).

Since I show only the files for the currently open directory in the ListView, I begin by clearing all of the items in ListView1. Then I use the For Each statement to process each file in fi. I use the file's path as the Key property for the ListItem and the file's long name as the text value. Then I add the file's size, creation date, last accessed and last modified dates, and file type to the list. Also, I decode the

Attributes property and add each attribute to a separate subitem before I finish the loop and start with the next File object.

Listing 4.16:	**TreeView1_NodeClick Event in File Viewer**

```
Private Sub TreeView1_NodeClick(ByVal Node As ComctlLib.Node)

Dim fi As File
Dim fn As Folder
Dim l As ListItem

ListView1.ListItems.Clear
For Each fi In fn.Files
    Set l = ListView1.ListItems.Add(, fi.Path, _
        fi.Name, "file")
    l.SubItems(1) = Format(fi.Size)
    l.SubItems(2) = Format(fi.DateCreated)
    l.SubItems(3) = Format(fi.DateLastModified)
    l.SubItems(4) = Format(fi.DateLastAccessed)
    l.SubItems(5) = Format(fi.Type)
    If fi.Attributes Mod 2 = 1 Then
        l.SubItems(6) = "Read only"
    End If
    If Int(fi.Attributes / 2) Mod 2 = 1 Then
        l.SubItems(7) = "Hidden"
    End If
    If Int(fi.Attributes / 4) Mod 2 = 1 Then
        l.SubItems(8) = "System"
    End If
    If Int(fi.Attributes / 32) Mod 2 = 1 Then
        l.SubItems(9) = "Archive"
    End If
    If Int(fi.Attributes / 64) Mod 2 = 1 Then
        l.SubItems(10) = "Alias"
    End If
    If Int(fi.Attributes / 128) Mod 2 = 1 Then
        l.SubItems(11) = "Compressed"
    End If
Next fi

End Sub
```

Reading and Writing a File Sequentially

The TextStream object is used to perform read and write operations on a single file. To create a TextStream object, use OpenTextStream method for the File object associated with the file you wish to access, or use the OpenTextFile method of the FileSystemObject.

Accessing TextStream Files

TextStream files can be accessed only sequentially; random access is not supported. They are also line-oriented. The TextStream object includes properties and methods that make it easy to process the file a single line at a time. Table 4.11 lists the properties and methods available for this object.

TIP

How should I store my information? TextStream files are good for holding temporary information or accessing data that needs to be read or written sequentially, such as a text document or image. TextStream files are also useful when you want to append information to the end of a log file. You may want to consider converting any file that is accessed randomly to a database file using the Jet engine. This will make it easier for you to write (and debug) your program (especially if you use the new ActiveX Data Objects) and probably will give you better performance in the long run.

TABLE 4.11:   TextStream Object Properties and Methods

Property/Method	Description
AtEndOfLine property	Returns **True** if the current position in the file is just before the end-of-line marker (carriage return)
AtEndOfStream property	Returns **True** if the current position in the file is at the end of the file
Close property	Closes a **TextStream** file
Column property	Returns the current column number of the current line of the **TextStream** file
Line property	Returns the current line number of the **TextStream** file
Read method	Returns the specified number of characters from the **TextStream** file

Continued on next page

TABLE 4.11 (CONTINUED): TextStream Object Properties and Methods

Property/Method	Description
AReadAll method	Returns the entire contents of the TextStream file
ReadLine method	Returns the next line from the TextStream file
Skip method	Reads and discards the specified number of characters from a TextStream file
SkipLine method	Reads and discards the next line of a TextStream file
Write method	Writes the specified string to a TextStream file
WriteBlankLines method	Writes the specified number of blank lines to a TextStream file
WriteLine method	Writes the specified string to a TextStream file, followed by an end-of-line marker

TIP

How much data am I going to read? If you plan to read large blocks of data into your program, you may find that a loop using the **Read** method may be more efficient than using the **ReadAll** method.

Using the TextStream Object in a Program

The ShowHex routine in the File Viewer program is shown in Listing 4.17. This routine is called when I need to display a file in hexadecimal/ASCII format, as shown in Figure 4.8. This display is useful when you need to understand the format of a file, especially if the file contains mixed ASCII and binary data. To simplify the code, I reference a routine called Hexify, which converts a single string of ASCII characters into the equivalent hex/ASCII display format.

Listing 4.17:   ShowHex Routine in File Viewer

```
Private Sub ShowHex()

Dim f As File
Dim s As String
Dim t As TextStream
Dim TempName As String
```

```
Dim x As TextStream
Dim b As Long
Dim CharsLoaded As Long
Dim TotalChars As Long

Set f = fso.GetFile(FName)
Set t = f.OpenAsTextStream(ForReading)
TempName = fso.GetTempName()
Set x = fso.CreateTextFile(TempName, True, False)

Do While Not t.AtEndOfStream
    s = t.Read(CharsLine)
    x.WriteLine Hexify(s)
    DoEvents
    Loop
t.Close
x.Close

RichTextBox1.Font.Name = "Courier New"
RichTextBox1.LoadFile TempName
fso.DeleteFile TempName

End Sub
```

FIGURE 4.8:

Displaying a file in hex/ASCII
format

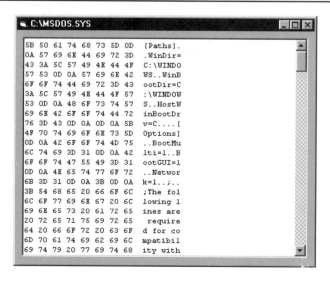

I begin this routine by creating a `File` object for the file I wish to display by using the `FileSystemObject`'s `GetFile` method and the module-level variable `FName`. Next, I actually open the file for reading by using the file's `OpenAsTextStream` method. Since I want to store the result of the conversion in a temporary file during the conversion process, I use the `GetTempName` of the `FileSystemObject` to create a temporary filename and open that file for writing using the `OpenAsTextStream` method.

Once I have both files open, I can begin processing the data. I use a `Do While/Loop` construct to read the input file until I reach the end of the input stream.

> **TIP**
>
> **When does a loop seem like an infinite loop, but is not?** A loop can appear infinite when you forget to put a call to `DoEvents` in the loop. A call to `DoEvents` allows Windows to check for other tasks that may need attention. Without this call, your system may appear to be locked up, and someone may decide to reboot before the loop finishes. If you don't believe me, comment out the call to `DoEvents` and display a large file in hex. You'll put that call back in rather quickly.

I read the desired number of characters and ignore the end-of-line information by using the `Read` method and specifying the number of characters I want to display in each line (`CharLine`). Then I write the data to the temporary file after converting it using the `Hexify` routine. Because this data is character-oriented, I use the `WriteLine` method, which will insert a carriage return/line feed (`vbCrLf`) pair at the end of each line. When I run out of data, I close both files.

With the data is ready for display, I load it into a RichTextBox control and delete the temporary file.

> **TIP**
>
> **RichTextBox versus TextBox:** The RichTextBox offers a lot of flexibility, and it also allows you to display more text than the TextBox's 32KB limit. If you think you might exceed the 32KB limit, use a RichTextBox to be safe.

Final Thoughts

The traditional file statements, functions, and controls show how Visual Basic has evolved over time. Today, they are a hodge-podge collection of conflicting capabilities and overlapping features. They still work, but I'm not sure that you should be developing applications using them.

In today's environment, however, most of the advanced file capabilities go unused, since it is far better to keep your data in a database than in a series of files. You still need sequential files to hold data to be imported or exported to and from your application. And you might want to store some types of information, such as application log files and some print files, outside the database. These requirements may be better served using the File System Objects.

With File System Objects, it is much easier to deal with the complex data structures that handle 10,000 or more files—a typical amount in a Windows 95, 98, or NT system. Also, I really like how the `FileSystemObject` handles `TextStream` files. The ability to load a file with just three statements is very useful to me, especially when combined with the new `Split` function, which allows me to parse files that were set up properly. (You'll see that I use this new approach in the examples throughout the rest of the book.) The `FileSystemObject` handles only `TextStream` files today, but I believe that support for more file structures will probably show up in Visual Basic 7. I can't wait.

CHAPTER

FIVE

5

Using Virtual Basic Functions

- Date functions

- Financial functions

- String functions

- Resource files

Oの of the strengths of Visual Basic is its range of useful functions. In this chapter, I'll talk about three main sets of functions: date, financial, and string functions. The demo programs I've written for this chapter are simple, but they serve to show you how many of the functions work.

Another useful feature of Visual Basic is that it allows you to store your resources in a file and then load them into memory as needed. Visual Basic 6 comes with a Resource Editor, which makes it easy to create resource files. In the final sections of this chapter, I'll explain how to use the Resource Editor and give you some tips on developing programs to run in multiple locales.

Using Date Functions

Worried about year 2000 problems? If you have been using the Visual Basic Date data type and date functions, you shouldn't have anything to worry about. The Date data type can represent any date and time value from 1 January 100 to 31 December 9999 and any time from 00:00:00 to 23:59:59.

NOTE   **Inside a date:** Visual Basic uses a standard IEEE 64-bit floating-point number to represent a date and time. Date information is stored as whole number of days before or after 30 December 1899. Thus, 1 January 1998 is 35,796 and 1 January 1899 is stored as –363. Time information is stored as a fractional number, where noon (12:00:00) is 0.5000 and midnight (0:00:00) is stored as 0.0000.

Table 5.1 lists the functions available in Visual Basic to handle dates. All of the functions use the Date data type to perform their processing.

TABLE 5.1:   Visual Basic Date Functions

Function	Description
CDate	Converts a string or numeric value to a Date value
Date	Returns or sets the system's current date
DateAdd	Adds a number to a date
DateDiff	Returns the difference between two Date values

Continued on next page

TABLE 5.1 (CONTINUED): Visual Basic Date Functions

Function	Description
DatePart	Returns the date part of a **Date** value
DateSerial	Returns a **Date** value for the specified year, month, and day
DateValue	Returns a **Date** value from the specified string containing date information
Day	Returns the day of month from a **Date** value
Format	Returns a **Date** value formatted as specified
FormatDateTime	Formats a **Date** value
Hour	Returns the hour of the day from a **Date** value
IsDate	Returns **True** if the specified value contains a valid date and/or time
Minute	Returns the minute of the hour from a **Date** value
Month	Returns the month of the year from a **Date** value
MonthName	Returns the name of a month for the specified month value
Now	Returns a **Date** value containing the current date and time
Second	Returns the second of the minute from a **Date** value
Time	Returns or sets the system's current time
Timer	Returns the number of seconds past midnight
TimeSerial	Returns a **Date** value for the specified string containing time information
TimeValue	Returns a **Date** value for the specified hour, minute, and second
Weekday	Returns a day of the week from a **Date** value
WeekdayName	Returns the name of a day for the specified weekday value
Year	Returns the year from a **Date** value

I've written a short program called Date/Time Demo that shows how to use many of the Visual Basic date functions. Figure 5.1 shows its window. Using the program is very simple. You enter the first parameter for the function you wish to try into the Input 1 box and the second parameter into the Input 2 box, then click the associated button. Note that most of the functions use only the first parameter and that some don't need any parameters at all.

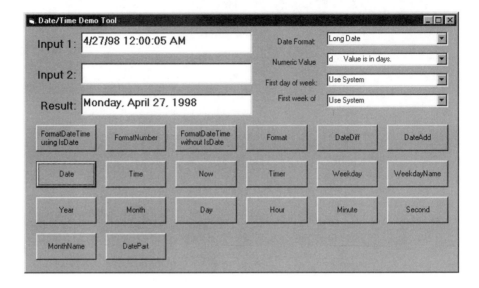

Dealing with Year 2000 Issues

Since Visual Basic can handle dates from 100 to 9999, what is the year 2000 problem all about? A long time ago, when disk prices were high, most data processing shops couldn't afford the extra disk space to store the century information. So years were always stored as a two-digit number.

Now that we are close to the end of the century, using two-digit years can be confusing. Does the date 1 Jan 02 represent 1 Jan 1902 or 1 Jan 2002? As a partial solution to the problem, many companies are saying that all two-digit years less than a certain value are assumed to be in the twenty-first century, and all other values are assumed to be in the twentieth century. Visual Basic assumes that two-digit years in the range of 00 to 29 have a prefix of 20, while years in the range of 30 to 99 have a prefix of 19.

NOTE   **Why do Visual Basic dates start with 1 Jan 100?** That's because Visual Basic assumes that any date with a two-digit year is in the range of 1930 to 2029.

Extended Date Fields

While it may appear that the solution is to simply add two more digits to any year values, this can cause other problems. For instance, consider an input form that accepts only two digits for the year. This form will need to be modified to accept four digits now. Also, any logic that may check for legal date values will need to be modified to accept the larger values.

You should also note that not all forms are as flexible as Visual Basic forms. On the big IBM mainframes, a form can contain only 80 characters in a single line. Adding two more digits to each date may mean that the form must be redesigned to accommodate the extra information. Likewise, reports that are column-oriented and printed on mainframe-type impact printers may have the same problem.

Leap Years

There may be other problems with the extended date field. With a four-digit year, you now need to be more careful about leap years. Leap years occur every four years, except when the year is evenly divisible by 100. Of course, years that are divisible by 400 are leap years. Now why is this important?

Consider what you need to do to compute the difference between two dates. First you must convert the two dates so that they represent some number of days past a certain year. Then you can compute the difference. However, how can you compute the days past a certain year if you don't know how to determine leap years accurately? (Now I know Visual Basic has functions to do this, but that's not necessarily true in the mainframe world.)

NOTE

Dates that don't causes any problems: Many dates exist only to be read by humans. Thus, if you store someone's birthday as a two-digit value and never use it as part of a calculation, this date format may not cause any problems. After all, even in the year 2050, you could probably assume that someone working for you with a birth year of 93 was born in 1993 and an employee who has a birth year of 10 was born in 2010, not 1910.

Some Solutions

The year 2000 problem can even affect Visual Basic programs. If you designed your program to store dates as strings and only stored two-digit years, you might have a problem. My suggestion is to try to use the Visual Basic Date data type whenever possible. Also, using functions such as DateDiff and FormatDateTime to perform the dirty work makes your life easier (remember the Lazy Programmer's Ten Commandments presented in Chapter 3).

If you can't use the Date data type for one reason or another, you should at least try to use character-based dates in the form of *yyyymmdd*, where *yyyy* holds a four-digit year, *mm* holds a two-digit month, and *dd* holds a two-digit day of month. One nice side effect of this format is that if you need to sort a file containing these values, the dates will always sort properly.

Converting Strings to Dates and Back Again

One of the most common tasks you encounter when dealing with dates is to convert date values to and from string values. Converting a date value to a string is a relatively simple process, limited only by the number of different date formats available. Converting string values is nearly as easy, but you may get an error unless you verify that the date is valid before you convert it.

Formatting Dates

FormatDateTime has a single parameter that specifies how the information should be formatted. You can specify that the default formatting (vbGeneralDate) should be used; this default is the short date if date information is present and short time if time information is present. Also, date information can be formatted as short or long (vbShortDate and vbLongDate), and time information can be formatted as short or long (vbShortTime and vbLongTime).

NOTE   **What is a short date?** Short dates (and for that matter, long dates) are defined as part of the Regional Settings specified in the Windows Control Panel. FormatDate-Time uses this information to format the date and time according to these settings. This means that the output should be appropriate for your locale. A short date or time is simply that—the shortest way of expressing the date and/or time possible. A long date or time is the longest way of expressing the date and/or time.

I use the `IsDate` function to verify that the string contains a valid `Date` value. Then I can use the `CDate` routine to convert the string value to a date. Finally, I use the `FormatDateTime` function to convert the date back to a string to be displayed in the text box. You can see how I did this in Listing 5.1.

Listing 5.1:   FormatDateTime with IsDate in Date/Time Demo

```
Private Sub Command1_Click()

If IsDate(Text1.Text) Then
   Text3.Text = FormatDateTime(CDate(Text1.Text), vbLongDate)
Else
   Text3.Text = "Invalid date or time."
End If

End Sub
```

Listing 5.2 shows another way to perform the same task, without using the `IsDate` function. I use the `On Error Resume Next` statement to permit the program to continue to run even if an error is encountered. Then I reset the `Err` object so that no prior error information exists. Next, I attempt to convert the contents of `Text1.Text` into a date value. If the value is properly formatted, then everything proceeds normally. Otherwise, an error will set the `Err.Number` to a value other than zero, which I can check with an `If` statement and then display an error message.

Listing 5.2:   FormatDateTime without IsDate in Date/Time Demo

```
Private Sub Command5_Click()

On Error Resume Next

Err.Clear
Text3.Text = FormatDateTime(CDate(Text1.Text), vbLongDate)
If Err.Number <> 0 then
   Text3.Text = "Invalid date or time."
End If

End Sub
```

Using Other Date-Conversion Functions

There are other functions that can help you convert values to and from `Date` variables:

- `DateSerial` takes values for days, months, and years and returns a `Date` value.

- `TimeSerial` does the same thing as `DateSerial` for hours, minutes, and seconds.

- `DateValue` and `TimeValue` perform the same thing as `CDate`, but return only date and time values, respectively. They also don't handle the range of input formats that the `CDate` routine can handle.

- `Day`, `Month`, `Year`, `Hour`, `Minute`, `Second`, `Week`, and `Weekday` all extract the named value from a `Date` value.

- `WeekdayName` and `MonthName` both return text information corresponding to a value for a weekday and month, respectively.

Creating Your Own Date Formats

The `Format` function is a general-purpose routine that allows you to convert information contained in most types of variables into a string. When dealing with date and time values, you can create your own format if one of the standard Visual Basic formats doesn't quite do the job.

The first parameter to format is the value to be displayed. The second parameter is the format to be used. The format can be either a named format, as listed in Table 5.2, or a string containing a sequence of individual character strings, as defined in Table 5.3.

TIP   **When is the first day of a week?** The `Format` function takes two additional parameters that allow you to specify the first day of the week and the first week of the year. The first parameter defaults to your system's default first day of the week. Otherwise, you specify the weekday (`vbSunday = 1`, `vbMonday = 2`, and so on) on which the week starts. The second parameter also defaults to the system's first week of the year value, but you can select the first week to be the week that 1 January falls on (`vbFirstJan1 = 1`), the first week of the year that has at least four full days (`vbFirstFourDays = 2`), or the first full week (`vbFirstFullWeek = 3`).

TABLE 5.2: Named Date and Time Formats

Named Format	Description
General Date	Displays the date as *mm/dd/yy* (e.g., 10/16/98), if date information is included and time as *hh:mm XM* if time information is included (e.g., 12:02:00 AM)
Long Date	Displays the date in your system's long date format (e.g., Tuesday, October 16, 1998)
Medium Date	Displays the date in your system's medium date format (e.g., 16-Oct-98)
Short Date	Displays the date in your system's short date format (e.g., 10/16/98)
Long Time	Displays the time in your system's long time format (e.g., 12:02:00 AM)
Medium Time	Displays the time in your system's medium time format (e.g., 12:02 AM)
Short Time	Displays the time in your system's short time format (00:02)

TABLE 5.3: Date Format Characters

Character String	Description
/	Displays the system default date separator
:	Displays the system default time separator
AM/PM	Displays an uppercase AM or PM as appropriate
am/pm	Displays a lowercase am or pm as appropriate
A/P	Displays an uppercase A or P as appropriate
a/p	Displays a lowercase a or p as appropriate
AMPM	Displays the system default AM/PM indicator as appropriate
c	Displays date information if present using the *ddddd* format and displays time information if present using the *ttttt* format
d	Displays the day of month without a leading zero (1–31)
dd	Displays the day of month with a leading zero if needed to make it two digits (01–31)
ddd	Displays the day as a three-character abbreviation (Sun, Mon, etc.)

Continued on next page

TABLE 5.3 (CONTINUED):   Date Format Characters

Character String	Description
dddd	Displays the day with its full name (Sunday, Monday, etc.)
ddddd	Displays the date using the short date format (same as the Short Date named format)
dddddd	Displays the date using the long date format (same as the Long Date named format)
h	Displays the hour without a leading zero (0–12)
hh	Displays the hour with a leading zero if needed to make it two digits (00–12)
m	Displays the month without a leading zero (1–12)
mm	Displays the month with a leading zero if needed to make it two digits (01–12)
mmm	Displays the month as a three-character abbreviation (Jan, Feb, etc.)
mmmm	Displays the month with its full name (January, February, etc.)
n	Displays the minutes without a leading zero (1–59)
nn	Displays the minutes with a leading zero if needed to make the display two digits (01–59)
q	Displays the quarter of the year (1–4)
s	Displays the seconds without a leading zero (0–59)
ss	Displays the seconds with a leading zero if needed to make the display two digits (00–59)
ttttt	Displays the time in the long time format (same as the Long Time named format)
w	Displays the day of the week as a number (1–7)
ww	Displays the day of the week of the year (1–54)
y	Displays the day of the year (1–366)
yy	Displays the year as a two-digit number (00–99)
yyyy	Displays the year as a four-digit number (0100–9999)

In Listing 5.3, you can see that all I do is grab the formatting information from the form as Input 2 and use it to format the date value from Input 1. Then I use the first day of the week value and the first week of year value from the combo boxes on the right side of the window to create the result, as shown in Figure 5.2.

Listing 5.3:   **The Format Function in Date/Time Demo**

```
Private Sub Command6_Click()

If IsDate(Text1.Text) Then
    Text3.Text = Format(CDate(Text1.Text), Text2.Text, _
        Combo3.ListIndex, Combo4.ListIndex)
Else
    Text3.Text = "Invalid date or time."
End If

End Sub
```

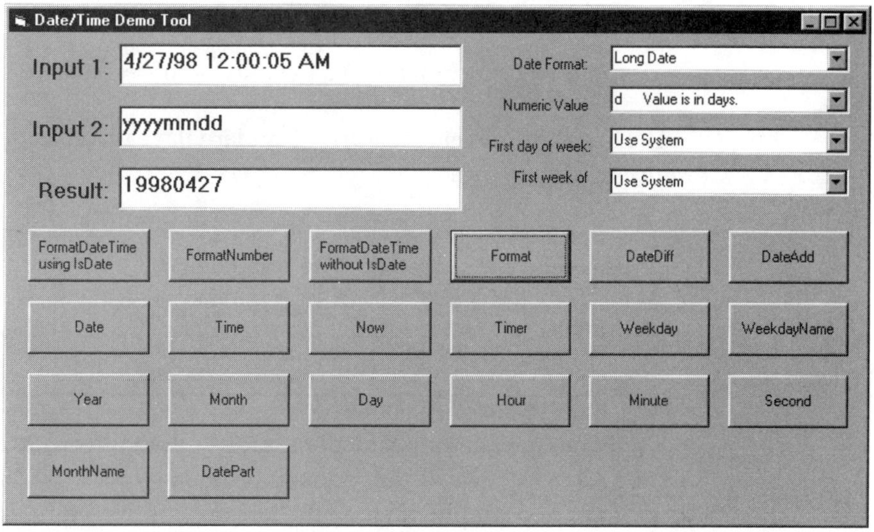

FIGURE 5.2:

Displaying a Date value using a special format string

TIP

Why use the Format function? The Format function is one of the older functions in Visual Basic and has been superceded in many ways. However, sometimes none of the more modern functions will return exactly what you need. For instance, suppose you want to create a log file to track certain events and you want to start a new log file each week. You could use the Format function to generate the filename by specifying lgyyyyww.log. During the seventh week of 1998, this would return a value of "lg199807.log," which would uniquely identify the log file for that week.

Getting Date and Time Information

Four different functions in Visual Basic return information about the current date and/or time:

- The Date function returns the current date from the computer's clock.

- The Time function returns the current time from the computer's clock.

- The Now function returns both the current time and date from the computer's clock.

- The Timer function returns the number of seconds past midnight.

The first three functions return a standard Date variable; the Timer function returns a Single value.

WARNING

Be careful with Date and Time statements: In addition to the Date and Time functions, there are also Date and Time statements in Visual Basic. They are used to set the date and time parts of your computer's clock. Use these statements with care, or you could wind up with the wrong date and/or time.

Using the date and time functions is fairly straightforward, as you can see in Listing 5.4, which shows the code for the Now function (the four functions work the same way). You simply call the function and use the return value as you desire. In this case, I format it and assign it to a text box for display.

Listing 5.4:	**The Now Function in Date/Time Demo**

```
Private Sub Command3_Click()

Text3.Text = FormatDateTime(Now, vbGeneralDate)

End Sub
```

Performing Date Arithmetic

One of the main causes of the year 2000 problem is that calculations involving dates with two-digit years will generate incorrect values. In most other languages, you need to write your own functions to perform date arithmetic. Visual Basic provides two tools that let you easily perform date arithmetic:

- DateAdd adds the specified number of days, weeks, hours, or whatever you want to a Date value.

- DateDiff returns the difference between any two dates using the units you specify.

In Listing 5.5, you can see how the DateAdd routine is a complex mess, but if you look at it closely, you can see that I verify that I have a legal Date value in Text1 .Text and a valid number in Text2.Text. Next, I add the number of days specified by Text2.Text to the date specified by Text1.Text. Note that I specified that Text2.Text contains days by using "d" as the first parameter. You can also specify other values for the units associated with the number in Text2.Text. These values are listed in Table 5.4.

TIP	**Schedule me in three weeks:** The DateAdd function is very useful if you need to compute a new date based on an existing date and some number of days or weeks later. For example, in a contact management system, you may want to schedule a follow-up call in three weeks from today. The DateAdd function makes this job trivial.

Listing 5.5: **The DateAdd Function in Date/Time Demo**

```
Private Sub Command9_Click()

If IsDate(Text1.Text) Then
    If IsNumeric(Text2.Text) Then
        Text3.Text = FormatDateTime(DateAdd("d", CLng(Text2.Text), _
            CDate(Text1.Text)))

    Else
        Text3.Text = "Invalid value to add to the date."
    End If

Else
    Text3.Text = "Invalid date or time."
End If

End Sub
```

TABLE 5.4: Units Used in DateAdd and DateDiff

Units	Description
d	Value is in days
h	Value is in hours
m	Value is in months
n	Value is in minutes
q	Value is in quarter years
s	Value is in seconds
w	Value is in weekdays
ww	Value is in weeks
yyyy	Value is in years

DateDiff works much the same as DateAdd, except that it computes the difference between two dates and returns the value in the unit specified. You can use this routine to compute how old something is by computing the difference between the two dates. So as I wrote this paragraph, I was able to use the DateDiff routine to compute that my son was born approximately 2,686,404 minutes ago. You can also use this routine to compute more mundane values, such as how many days until your retirement or how many weeks until the new Star Wars movie will be released.

Using Financial Functions

Financial functions are used primarily to compute information about interest rates, values of annuities, depreciation, and rates of return. These functions are useful for building accounting packages (but not for much else). Table 5.5 lists the financial functions available in Visual Basic.

NOTE   **Payments, receipts, and interest rates:** Payments and receipts are basically exchanges of cash. Payments are negative values; receipts are positive values. Thus, a payment of $100 is written as −100, and a receipt of $200 is written as 200 (or +200). Interest rates are expressed as percentage values between 0 and 1 (or 10% = 0.1). Note that interest rates are also based on the period. Assuming that you are dealing with a monthly annuity, you need to divide your annual interest rate by 12 to get the true interest rate. For example, 18% per year = 1.5% per month and would be entered into the computer as 0.015.

TABLE 5.5: Visual Basic Financial Functions

Function	Description
DDB	Uses the double-declining balance method to compute the depreciation of an asset
FV	Computes the future value of an annuity
Ipmt	Computes the amount of interest for a particular payment in an annuity

Continued on next page

TABLE 5.5 (CONTINUED):   Visual Basic Financial Functions

Function	Description
IRR	Computes the internal rate of return of an investment based on a series of payments and receipts
MIRR	Computes the modified internal rate of return of an investment based on a series of payments and receipts
Nper	Computes the number of periods in an annuity
NPV	Computes the net present value of an investment for a series of payments and receipts
Pmt	Computes the payment of an annuity
PPmt	Computes the principal for a particular payment in an annuity
PV	Computes the present value of an annuity
Rate	Computes the interest rate for an annuity
SLN	Uses the straight-line method to compute the depreciation of an asset
SYD	Uses the sum-of-years-digits method to compute the depreciation of an asset

Calculating Depreciation and Rate of Return

One group of functions is used to compute depreciation and rates of return according to several methods. The DDB, SLN, and SYN functions are fairly straightforward to use when you need to compute depreciation. The MIRR and IRR functions return values based on a stream of payments and receipts.

The MIRR and IRR functions receive an input stream contained in an array of Double values. You need to ensure that every cell in the array is used; otherwise, the MIRR and IRR functions may returned an invalid interest rate. To correct this problem, declare your array without a size (Dim Stream()), then use the ReDim statement to size your array to contain the exact number of elements you need: ReDim Stream(11). (Remember that, by default, Visual Basic assumes the lower bound of zero, so the redimensioned Stream array actually contains 12 elements.)

Computing Annuities

The other group of functions deals with annuities. Annuities are computed based on the following variables: present value, future value, number of periods, payment, and interest rate. To compute any one value, you need to know the rest.

To demonstrate the annuity functions, I created the Financial Function Demo Program, shown in Figure 5.3. The program provides fields for each of the variable values, plus Interest Payment and Principle Payment fields. You enter values into each of the fields and then click the button corresponding to the financial function you wish to try. Invalid entries will automatically turn the field's background red until an acceptable value is entered. Clicking one of the function buttons will set the background to blue for each field used as input in the calculation and turn the result field's background to green. A Reset button is also provided to give you some sample values to use while testing.

FIGURE 5.3:

The Financial Function Demo program

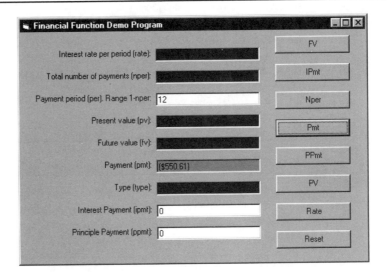

In Listing 5.6, you can see how simple these functions really are. First, I call Get-Data to get the data from each of the text fields and save it into a series of module-level variables. Then I set the BackColor property for each of the text fields in the display, except for the value I'm computing. Then I compute the payment based on the interest rate (r), number of periods (n), present value (p), future value (f), and payment type (t) and save the result in the appropriate text box. Finally, I set the text box color to green and return.

Listing 5.6:   **Annuity Payment Computing in Financial Function Demo**

```
Private Sub Command4_Click()

' compute Pmt

GetData

Text1.BackColor = &HFF0000        ' rate
Text2.BackColor = &HFF0000        ' nper
Text3.BackColor = &H80000005      ' per
Text4.BackColor = &HFF0000        ' pv
Text5.BackColor = &HFF0000        ' fv
Text7.BackColor = &HFF0000        ' type
Text8.BackColor = &H80000005      ' impt
Text9.BackColor = &H80000005      ' ppmt

Text6.Text = FormatCurrency(Pmt(r, n, p, f, t))
Text6.BackColor = &HFF00&         ' pmt

End Sub
```

WARNING   **Don't lose the name game:** Visual Basic isn't happy when you use duplicate names for items. Visual Basic has a function named **Pmt**, so if you name a variable **Pmt**, you won't be able to access the **Pmt** function. Avoid giving your variable, function, or subroutine a name already used by Visual Basic.

Using String Functions

Most modern applications spend more time moving information around internally and preparing it for display than on computing numbers. In Visual Basic, most of these manipulations involve strings. Hence, there are probably more functions involving strings than any other variable type. In general, string functions fall into one of two categories: those that format data for presentation and those that search and edit the contents of a string variable. Table 5.6 lists some of the more interesting string functions.

TABLE 5.6: Visual Basic String Functions

Function	Description
CStr	Converts nearly any variable into a string
Filter	Returns a string array extracted from another string array where each string meets the filter criteria
Format	Returns a string formatted according to the specified format criteria
FormatCurrency	Returns a string containing a number formatted according to the system's rules for currency
FormatDateTime	Returns a string containing a date/time value formatted according to the system's rules for dates and times
FormatNumber	Returns a string containing a number formatted according to the system's rules for numbers
FormatPercent	Returns a string containing a number formatted as a percentage
InStr	Returns the position of the first occurrence of the specified search string in another string
InStrRev	Returns the position of the last occurrence of the specified string in another string
IsDate	Returns **True** if the string contains a valid date or time value
IsNumeric	Returns **True** if the string contains a valid numeric value
Join	Concatenates an array of strings together
LCase	Converts a string to lowercase
Len	Returns the length of a string
Left	Returns the specified number of characters from the left side of the string
LTrim	Removes leading spaces from the left side of the string

Continued on next page

TABLE 5.6 (CONTINUED):   Visual Basic String Functions

Function	Description
Mid	Returns a substring extracted from the middle of the specified string
Replace	Changes one substring to another in the specified string
Right	Returns the specified number of characters from the right side of the string
RTrim	Removes trailing spaces from the right side of the string
Trim	Removes trailing spaces from the beginning and end of the string
Space	Returns a string containing the specified number of spaces
Split	Extracts a series of substrings from a string expression
Str	Converts a number into a string
StrComp	Compares two strings and returns the result
StrConv	Converts a string to uppercase, lowercase, propercase, to Unicode, or from Unicode
String	Returns a string containing the specified number of the specified characters
StrReverse	Reverses the order of characters in a string
Ucase	Converts a string into all uppercase characters

The String Demo Program shows how many of Visual Basic's string functions work. Its window is shown in Figure 5.4. Simply enter some data and click the button associated with the function you want to test. You can use the Test Data button in the lower-right corner of the window to build a multiple-line text string for use with the Split, Join, and Filter functions.

FIGURE 5.4:

The String Demo program

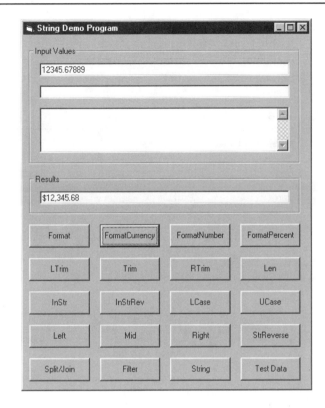

Formatting Data for Presentation

The FormatCurrency, FormatDate, FormatNumber, and FormatPercent functions can convert a number into the specified format. Similar to the FormatDateTime function discussed earlier in the chapter, these are intelligent functions that take into consideration your locale when formatting data.

The Format function is a very powerful routine designed to help you format data. This function handles nearly any type of data, including strings, numbers, and date/time values.

Usually, you will pass two parameters to Format: the value to be formatted and a format string. A format string can contain a sequence of formatting characters that tell the Format function how to display the value. A format string can also contain a named format that refers to a standard format string. Table 5.7 lists the named numeric formats.

TABLE 5.7:   Named Numeric Formats

Named Format	Description
General Number	Displays the number without the thousands separator
Currency	Displays the number with a leading dollar sign, thousands separator, and two decimal places
Fixed	Displays the number with at least one digit to the left of the decimal place and two to the right
Standard	Displays the same format as Fixed, but also includes the thousands separator
Percent	Multiplies the number by 100 and displays it with two digits to the right of the decimal point and a percent sign
Scientific	Displays the number as one digit, followed by multiple digits times an exponent raised to some power
Yes/No	If the number is zero, displays No; otherwise, displays Yes
True/False	If the number is zero, displays False; otherwise, displays True
On/Off	If the number is zero, displays Off; otherwise, displays On

---

WARNING   **Don't use Str:** The Str function is limited in its capabilities. You should use the FormatCurrency, FormatDateTime, FormatNumber, or FormatPercent function instead. If none of these functions meet your needs, use the **Format** function.

Searching and Editing Strings

Many of the functions for searching and editing strings are probably very familiar to you. You may have used Left, Right, Mid, LTrim, RTrim, and Trim. However, Visual Basic 6 also includes some powerful new functions: Split, Join, and Filter.

How many times have you found yourself needing to write a loop to split a string from a multiple-line text box into separate pieces, with each piece delimited by a carriage return/line feed? If you're like me, you've done this too many times.

The Split function searches through a single string looking for substrings separated by the specified delimiter string. Then each substring of characters is assigned to an element in a string array. When there are no more substrings to be processed, the function returns the string array.

The Join function is the opposite of the Split function. It creates a new string by taking a string array and concatenating each array element with the specified delimiter. Then it returns the new string.

In Listing 5.7, I use the Split function to convert the contents of a multiple-line text box into a string array. Then I use the Join function to put the string array back together with the delimiter specified in the Text1 text box.

Listing 5.7:   **The Split and Join Functions in String Demo Program**

```
Private Sub Command17_Click()

Dim x() As String

x = Split(Text3.Text, vbCrLf)

Text4.Text = Join(x, Text1.Text)

End Sub
```

The Filter function is another function that handles string arrays. It takes a string array and searches each element in it for the specified search element. If the element is found, then that element will be placed in another string array that will be returned when the process is complete. Listing 5.8 shows how to use the Join function.

Listing 5.8:   **The Join Function in String Demo Program**

```
Private Sub Command18_Click()

Dim x() As String

x = Split(Text3.Text, vbCrLf)

Text3.Text = Join(Filter(x, Text1.Text, True, vbTextCompare), vbCrLf)

End Sub
```

Using Resource Files

Resource files contain resources that are used by a Visual Basic program. They can contain five different types of data: strings, bitmaps, icons, cursors, and your own custom-designed resources. Each program is limited to only one resource file; however, multiple programs may share the same resource file. Your program may then call one of three different functions—LoadResData, LoadResPicture, or Load-ResString—to load the appropriate resource into memory.

A unique number called a resource ID references each resource in the file. In Visual Basic, this number may range from 1 to 32,767. It must be unique for the type of data being retrieved. Resource ID 1 is reserved for the program's icon. Unlike all other resources in a resource file, strings are not stored as individual items, but rather as a string table.

WARNING   **When is an integer not an integer?** Resource IDs are stored using an unsigned 16-bit value that can range from 0 to 65,535. However, since Visual Basic supports only signed 16-bit values, resource IDs must be less than or equal to 32,767. Although the Resource Editor may display values with resource IDs above 32,767, you can't edit them.

Working with Multiple Foreign Languages

When I said that a resource ID must be unique, I didn't tell the whole story. The true power of resource files comes into play when building international editions of your application. While each resource ID must be unique, there can be multiple flavors of each resource ID. Each flavor corresponds to a different locale. Thus, you could create a resource file in which every resource was duplicated in English and Spanish.

The routines that you use to access the resources are sensitive to the native language of your system. Thus, if you were using a Spanish-based version of Windows, your program would automatically load the resources tagged for Spanish. If you were using a German version of Windows, the program would load the first resource or string table found, since only English and Spanish were in the resource file. Thus, you can create a reasonable default for your locale.

TIP

Where am I? You can change your locale by clicking on Regional Settings in the Windows Control Panel and changing the language specified on the Regional Settings tab of the dialog box. But be aware that changing this value could have a significant impact on some of your applications (especially if they are using resource files).

Creating a Resource File

Unlike previous versions of Visual Basic, Visual Basic 6 now includes a resource file editor. This greatly simplifies the process that you use to create a resource file.

Enabling the Resource Editor

To use the Resource Editor, you must first enable it from the Add-In Manager dialog box, as shown in Figure 5.5. Select Add-Ins ➤ Add-In Manager from the Visual Basic menu to see this dialog box. Click on VB 6 Resource Editor and then put checkmarks in both the Loaded/Unloaded and Load on Startup checkboxes. This will load the Resource Editor immediately, and it also will be loaded the next time you start Visual Basic.

FIGURE 5.5:

The Add-In Manager
dialog box

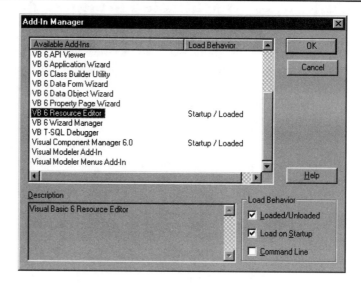

Opening a New Resource File

Next, you need to create the resource file. You can do this by selecting Project ➢ New Resource File from the Visual Basic menu. This will display the common file open dialog box. If you have an existing resource file you wish to use, simply select that name. Otherwise, choose a new name for the file and click the Open button to create the new resource file. You will see a message box asking you to verify that you want to create the new resource file. Click Yes to build the file.

WARNING   **Look before you open:** The Resource Editor will try to create the directory in a default directory where you probably don't want keep the file. So check the directory before you click the Open button.

Starting the Resource Editor

After you create the resource file, you will see the resource listed in the Project window under the Related Documents folder, as shown in Figure 5.6. To use the Resource Editor, click on the resource filename or select Tools ➢ Resource Editor.

FIGURE 5.6:

The Project window with a
resource file called stuff.res

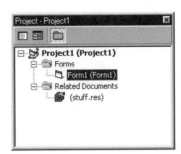

When the Resource Editor starts, you will see a display similar to the one shown in Figure 5.7. The window shows the contents of the resource file. Since I haven't loaded anything into the resource file, there are no contents yet.

FIGURE 5.7:

The Resource Editor window

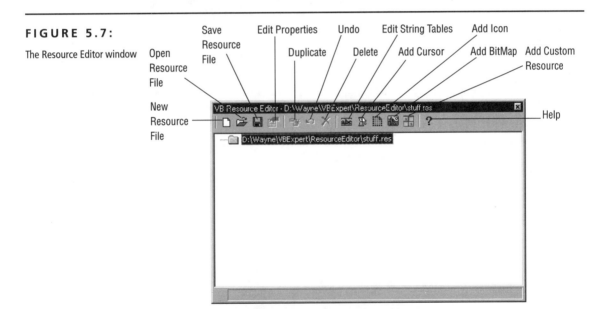

Adding Strings to the Resource File

Clicking on the Edit String Tables button brings up the String Table Editor. To create a new string table, click the Insert New String Table button (the buttons are labeled in Figure 5.8). The editor prompts you for the first string entry, as shown in Figure 5.8. English (United States) is created as the first string table. You can change the default value for this table by clicking on the table's name.

FIGURE 5.8:

The String Table Editor

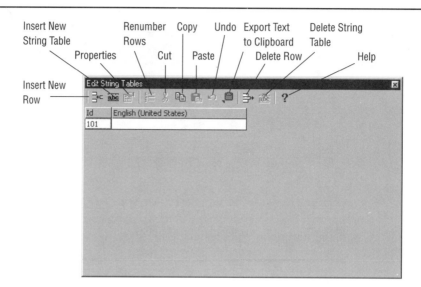

The default resource ID of the first string is 101. You can select this value and change it, or you can leave the default ID. Enter your first resource string in the field next to the ID. After you finish typing, press Enter, and you'll be prompted for the next value, as shown in Figure 5.9. Repeat this process until you are finished creating the table. If you need to make changes, you can go back to a field and edit any of the resource information you entered.

FIGURE 5.9:

Adding strings to the string table

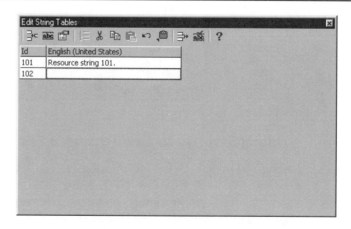

You can add another string table by clicking the Insert New String Table button again. This time, you will see a strange value for the string table name, as shown in Figure 5.10. This is the code page number (1056 in the example in the figure) associated with a different locale. You can click the drop-down arrow to see the complete list of locales available. When you are finished editing the string table, close the window to return to the main Resource Editor window.

FIGURE 5.10:

Adding a string table for a different locale

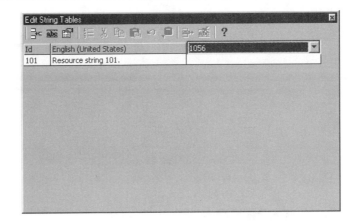

Adding Other Resources to the Resource File

Back at the main Resource Editor window, you can add any other resource using the same basic method as you use to add string tables. Click on the Add Cursor, Add Icon, Add Bitmap, or Add Custom Resource button to bring up an open file dialog box. When you select a file to be loaded into the resource file, you see a preview of the file. Figure 5.11 shows an example of loading an icon file.

FIGURE 5.11:

Adding an icon file to the resource file

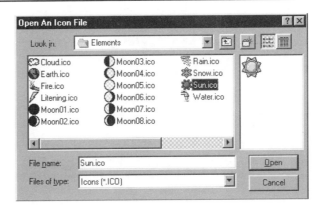

Clicking the Open button returns you to the Resource Editor window, where you can repeat the process to add more files to your resource file. Double-clicking on the resource icon opens another dialog box that allows you to modify the properties of the resource. Figure 5.12 shows the Edit Icon Properties dialog box. You can specify the locale of the resource and change the resource ID. For an icon file, you can also bring up an image viewer to see more details about the resource, such as its size and color depth.

FIGURE 5.12:

Modifying the icon resource's properties

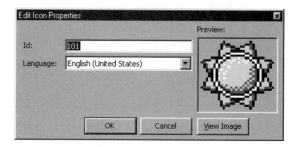

Closing the Resource File

Once you've added the resources you need, click the Save button or close the file. If you just close the file, you will see a "Modified" message in the status bar at the bottom of the window, as shown in Figure 5.13. If you haven't saved the resource file before you close it, you will be prompted to save it the next time you run your program.

FIGURE 5.13:

A modified resource file

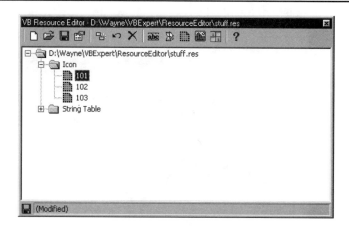

Accessing a Resource File

As mentioned earlier, there are three functions that you can use to access a resource file: LoadResData, LoadResPicture, and LoadResString. Each accepts a resource ID as a parameter. The LoadResData and LoadResPicture functions also have a format parameter indicating the type of data to be returned. Note that it is not necessary to specify a locale, because the routines determine that automatically.

The Resource File Demo Utility program is a rather simple program that demonstrates how to call the LoadResPicture and LoadResString functions to load information from a resource file. Figure 5.14 shows its window. You enter the resource ID in the text box next to the Show button in both the Strings section and the Bitmaps, Icons and Cursors section. For bitmaps, icons, and cursors, specify the format value in the box next to the resource ID.

FIGURE 5.143:

The Resource File
Demo Utility program

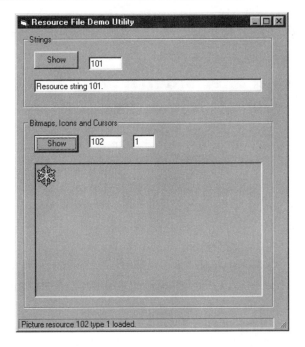

In Listing 5.9, you can see that all it really takes to load a resource is the single call to LoadResString. I added some error-checking code to prevent a runtime error from happening when an invalid resource ID was entered. In most cases, this code would be unnecessary, since you could be sure that all the resource IDs were properly coded (and a runtime error would be acceptable if they weren't).

Listing 5.9:   **LoadResString Function in Resource File Demo Utility**

```
Private Sub Command1_Click()

On Error Resume Next

Err.Clear
Text1.Text = LoadResString(Text2.Text)
If Err.Number <> 0 Then
    StatusBar1.Panels(1).Text = Err.Description
Else
    StatusBar1.Panels(1).Text = "String resource " & Text2.Text & "
loaded."
End If

End Sub
```

Making International Programs

Now that you understand how resource files work, there are a few things you may want to think about when you build your program. These apply when you want your program to work in different locales.

First of all, the text for all menu items, dialog box titles, command button captions, and any labels displayed in on a form should be kept in a resource file and loaded at runtime. This makes it easier to customize your program for different locales.

As a general rule, don't include text as part of an icon or image, unless you choose to replace all of your icons when the program is loaded. You should also take care to choose icons that are universal. Some icons, such as a mailbox, are perfectly fine in the United States but may confuse users in other countries.

Consider that the equivalent foreign phrase for your command button may be much larger than the English phrase, so you will need to allow extra space for the appropriate captions. You also may need to consider what happens if you need to concatenate phrases together to make a meaningful sentence. The order of the phrases may make sense in English, where verbs are in the middle of sentences, but not in German, where the verbs are at the end of the sentences.

Also, if you don't use `FormatCurrency`, `FormatNumber`, and `FormatDateTime` to display information, you may need to go back and revise your program. These routines are locale-sensitive and will display the information in the format that is appropriate to the locale.

If your programs use a language that is written from right to left, you'll be happy to know that Visual Basic comes equipped to handle this. Most controls in Visual Basic have the ability to accept input from right to left, as well as left to right. This makes it possible to build programs for the Arabic and Hebrew languages. Note that a special version of Windows is required to support these languages.

Final Thoughts

Visual Basic supports a wide range of functions, including those that can manipulate dates and times, financial values, strings, and resource files. Without them, your life would be a lot more difficult.

The `Date` data type and the date functions do more than just allow your programs to pass through the year 2000 without incident. They provide a level of isolation between your programs and the underlying data structure, much like objects provide that level of abstraction for more complex items.

Without the rich variety of financial functions, you would find yourself duplicating at least some of these functions in your own code. With them you win, not only because you spend less time developing these functions, but also because they are well tested and you should be able to trust their results. To put this another way, just watch the news and you'll see that every so often, some large firm has misstated profits or losses, made mistakes billing customers, or experienced some other financial problem that can be traced back to a glitch in a computer application. If this happens to the Fortune 500 firms, you know that it's a possibility for smaller organizations.

What do you do if you have a popular application, but someone wants it translated into another language? If you created your application using resource files, all you need to do is to create a new resource file with all of the messages, captions, and icons for the new language. Every element in a Visual Basic program that displays text can be updated on the fly with new values. The best way to get these values is from a resource file.

CHAPTER
SIX

6

Helping Your Users

- Form positioning and resizing

- Form loading speed

- Tab and access key handling

- Data checking techniques

- Long processing wait handling

- System information retrieval

In this chapter, I'm going to cover some tips and tricks that will make your programs even more interesting to your users. These tips and tricks cost very little in terms of programming effort, but they will make your users' lives easier.

Since nearly everything in Visual Basic revolves around forms, any improvements you can make to them can be helpful. You load forms, show forms, hide forms, unload forms, and resize forms. You move forms around on your screen, enter data into forms, and wait for forms to finish processing. It's easy to see how a few tweaks here and there could potentially go a long way toward improving a user's experience with your program.

Knowing how your user's system is configured also can be very useful. Information such as the screen's height and width is important when you want to center a form on the screen. You may want to have your program track the battery usage in a laptop to prevent a user from starting tasks when there are only about five minutes of battery life left.

Handling Forms

We'll begin with how and where the form appears on your user's screen. You can put it in the middle of the screen, put it back where it was the last time the user had it on the screen, control how it's resized (or not resized), and make it appear on the screen more quickly. All the techniques for handling forms discussed here are demonstrated in the Tips and Tricks Demo program.

Centering a Form

Centering a form on your screen is a relatively easy task. The `Screen` object contains a lot of valuable information, such as the active form, the active control, and the list of available fonts. The information we're interested in for this task is contained in the `Height` and `Width` properties.

Once you know the size of the screen, you can determine the size of your form using the form's `Height` and `Width` properties. Once you know the size of the screen and the size of the form, it is relatively simple to compute the left corner of the form.

The center of the screen is at location `Screen.Width/2` by `Screen.Height/2`. The center of your form is `Me.Width/2` by `Me.Height/2`. So the left corner of the form is at location Screen.Width/2 – Me.Width/2 by Screen.Width/2 – Me.Width/2 or, more simply, (Screen.Height - Me.Height)/2 by (Screen.Width - Me.Width)/2.

In Listing 6.1, I center the form when it is loaded using the above calculations, and then I display some information about your screen and the form's location on the screen. Note that while calculations don't care about the units of measure, all Visual Basic measurements are based in twips. If you want to convert to pixels, you need to divide by the TwipsPerPixel properties.

NOTE   **What is a twip?** Microsoft measures all units in Windows using twips. A twip is a typographic term that is short for twentieth of a printer's point. There are 1,440 twips to the inch (or 567 to the centimeter). This measurement unit is used to ensure that whatever you choose to print is always printed at the correct size. So even though your monitor may be larger than someone else's monitor, the objects drawn on both monitors will result in the same size images being sent to the printer.

Listing 6.1:   Form_Load Event in Form2 of Tips and Tricks Demo

```
Private Sub Form_Load()

Dim t As String

Me.Top = (Screen.Height - Me.Height) / 2
Me.Left = (Screen.Width - Me.Width) / 2

t = "This form is centered on your screen. Your screen size is "
t = t & FormatNumber(Screen.Width, 0) & " by "
t = t & FormatNumber(Screen.Height, 0)
t = t & " twips or " & FormatNumber(Screen.Width / Screen.TwipsPerPixelX, 0)
t = t & " by " & FormatNumber(Screen.Height / Screen.TwipsPerPixelY, 0)
t = t & " pixels. My upper left corner is at location "
t = t & FormatNumber(Me.Left, 0) & " by " & FormatNumber(Me.Top, 0)
t = t & "."

Label1.Caption = t

End Sub
```

TIP

Who Me? Often, you need to access the properties of a form, but you don't know the name of the form. Visual Basic provides an alternate name for the currently active form called **Me**. The name is very useful when you don't know the real name of the current form. For instance, you can put the code that centers the form (Listing 6.1) in any form, and it would work without any changes. This also makes it easier when you are creating form templates.

Remembering Where You Put a Form

Centering a form is somewhat specialized. While you may want to center an About form or a Splash form, you probably don't want to do it for every form. However, it might be nice to remember where you last placed the form from one time to the next.

The simplest way to remember the form's last position is to save it when the form is unloaded and get it again the next time the form is loaded. This means that you need to save the information about where the form was located in a place other than as variable in your program. If you make it a program variable, it will be lost, along with any other local storage, when the user exits the program.

In order to remember this information, you need to store it in a place that is external to the program. The most obvious place is the Windows Registry. After all, this is where Microsoft stores this type of information. There are two ways to access the Windows Registry from Visual Basic. The first is the GetSetting and SaveSetting functions that treat the Registry as simply an .INI file. The other way is to access the Registry using the Win32 API (we'll talk about this method a lot more in Part 4 of this book).

Moving the Form to Its Last Position

The GetSetting and SaveSetting functions store information in the Registry based on a three-part key composed of the application name, a section name, and a key name. The application name should be unique to your application. In the example in Listing 6.2, I use the value found in the App.Title object as the application name for the GetSetting function. I also use the name of the form (Me.Name) as the section name. I use the property I want to get as the key name. In this case, since I'm using the Top and Left properties, I use Top and Left as key names.

Listing 6.2: **Form_Load Event in Form3 of Tips and Tricks Demo**

```
Private Sub Form_Load()

Me.Top = GetSetting(App.Title, Me.Name, "Top", Me.Top)
Me.Left = GetSetting(App.Title, Me.Name, "Left", Me.Left)

Label1.Caption = App.Title
Label2.Caption = App.ProductName & " (" & App.EXEName & ")"
Label3.Caption = "Version: " & FormatNumber(App.Major, 0) & "."
Label3.Caption = Label3.Caption & FormatNumber(App.Minor, 0)
Label3.Caption = Label3.Caption & " (Build "
Label3.Caption = Label3.Caption & FormatNumber(App.Revision, 0) & ")"
Label4.Caption = "by " & App.CompanyName
Label5.Caption = App.LegalCopyright
Label6.Caption = App.LegalTrademarks
Label7.Caption = App.Comments

End Sub
```

One nice thing about the GetSetting function is that it allows you to specify default values for the setting. This means that while you are designing the application, you can put default values where you want the form placed on the screen. You can do this by specifying explicit values for the form's position, or you can do what I did in Listing 6.2—use the current values for the form's position. This means that the form will be loaded in the same position you left it in your development environment.

Saving the Form's Last Position

Logically, if you expect to retrieve information about the form's last location, you need to save it at some point. Thus, in the Form_Unload event shown in Listing 6.3, I save the current position of the form.

Listing 6.3: **Form_Unload Event in Form3 of Tips and Tricks Demo**

```
Private Sub Form_Unload(Cancel As Integer)

SaveSetting App.Title, Me.Name, "Top", Me.Top
```

```
SaveSetting App.Title, Me.Name, "Left", Me.Left

End Sub
```

> **NOTE**
>
> **Where are the settings really located?** The values from the `GetSetting` and `SaveSetting` routines are stored in the Windows Registry under the key `\HKEY_CURRENT_USER\Software\VB and VBA Program Settings\`. Within this folder will be a list of folders with application names corresponding to the `AppName` parameter used in the `GetSetting` and `SaveSetting` functions.

Deleting the Position Information from the Registry

Of course, since we are good programmers, we would never write a program that would leave around a bunch of junk that takes up space and may cause problems later. As a result, we need to create a routine that will delete this information from the Registry, as shown in Listing 6.4. Note that this routine can't reference the form as `Me.Name`, since you can't execute this routine from within the form. After all, when you exit the form, the information would be automatically saved, and that's the opposite of what you want to do.

Listing 6.4:   **Command3_Click Event in Form1 of Tips and Tricks Demo**

```
Private Sub Command3_Click()

DeleteSetting App.Title, "Form3", "Left"
DeleteSetting App.Title, "Form3", "Top"

End Sub
```

> **WARNING**
>
> **Duplicate names can cause problems:** Be careful when choosing a value for the application name. If you use the same name as an existing application, you will find yourself using the same entries in the Registry. If you use `App.Title` as I did in this example, make sure that you change the Application Title value in the Project Properties dialog box. The default value of `Project1` will certainly cause problems with the next program you write.

Resizing a Form

Resizing a form can be a complicated process. However, if you approach it the right way, it becomes very manageable. The first step is to understand how the resizing process works. The event `Form_Resize` will be called each time the size of the form is changed. The `Height` and `Width` properties then contain the new size for the form.

TIP

Resizing guidelines: You should add code that lets you resize a form when there is a benefit to having a larger form. A larger form is an asset when you can provide the user additional information. For example, a larger text box or picture box may show more information without scrolling. A larger form is also worthwhile if you can display additional controls that would also pass along more information to the user. If you can't provide additional value by making the form larger, then it probably isn't worth the effort.

Preventing Resizing

It's very easy to prevent someone from resizing a form. Simply create a couple of module-level variables to hold the form's `Height` and `Width` properties. Then save the `Height` and `Width` property values in those variables. In the `Form_Resize` event, you need to ensure that the window is not minimized or maximized. Then you can simply assign those values to the corresponding properties. This effectively prevents the height and width of the form from ever being changed. The code in Listing 6.5 shows how this is done.

Listing 6.5:   **Code from Form1 of Tips and Tricks Demo**

```
Dim FormHeight As Single
Dim FormWidth As Single

Private Sub Form_Load()

FormHeight = Me.Height
FormWidth = Me.Width

End Sub

Private Sub Form_Resize()

If Me.WindowState = vbNormal Then
    Me.Height = FormHeight
```

```
        Me.Width = FormWidth
    End If

    End Sub
```

Resizing Controls

While preventing a form from being resized is nice, it is more useful to allow the form to be resized and then take the appropriate action with the controls that are displayed on the form. The controls fall into two different categories:

• *Anchored* controls have two sides fixed in relation to the form itself. The other two sides stretch in proportion to the size of the forms.

• *Floating* controls stretch based on the control's relationship with other controls and the form itself.

Resizing Anchored Controls   Figure 6.1 shows a form consisting of four different anchored controls. The largest control is a PictureBox situated at the top-left corner of the form. Between the PictureBox control and the right side of the form is a vertical scroll bar. Below the PictureBox control is a horizontal scroll bar. In the bottom-right corner of the form between the two scroll bars is a Command-Button control. Listing 6.6 shows the code used to resize the form.

FIGURE 6.1:

A form with anchored controls

Listing 6.6:   **Code from Form4 of Tips and Tricks Demo**

```
Option Explicit

Dim CommandLeft As Single
Dim CommandTop As Single
Dim FormHeight As Single
Dim FormWidth As Single
Dim HScrollTop As Single
Dim HScrollWidth As Single
Dim PictureHeight As Single
Dim PictureWidth As Single
Dim VScrollLeft As Single
Dim VScrollHeight As Single

Private Sub Form_Load()

CommandLeft = Command1.Left
CommandTop = Command1.Top
FormWidth = Me.Width
FormHeight = Me.Height
HScrollTop = HScroll1.Top
HScrollWidth = HScroll1.Width
PictureHeight = Picture1.Height
PictureWidth = Picture1.Width
VScrollLeft = VScroll1.Left
VScrollHeight = VScroll1.Height

End Sub

Private Sub Form_Resize()

' Verify that the Window's state is not minimized or
' maximized and insure that the height and width is at
' least 1000 twips. Then reposition each control as
' needed.

If Me.WindowState <> 0 Then
    Exit Sub
End If
```

```
If Me.Height < 1000 Then
   Me.Height = 1000
End If

If Me.Width < 1000 Then
   Me.Height = 1000
End If

Command1.Top = Me.Height - FormHeight + CommandTop
Command1.Left = Me.Width - FormWidth + CommandLeft
HScroll1.Top = Me.Height - FormHeight + HScrollTop
HScroll1.Width = Me.Width - FormWidth + HScrollWidth
Picture1.Height = Me.Height - FormHeight + PictureHeight
Picture1.Width = Me.Width - FormWidth + PictureWidth
VScroll1.Left = Me.Width - FormWidth + VScrollLeft
VScroll1.Height = Me.Height - FormHeight + VScrollHeight

End Sub
```

This code works as follows:

- First I declare two variables for each control that needs to be moved, plus two more for the form's height and width.

- In the `Form_Load` event, I save the default values for each of the specified control's properties. Note that these values must be saved before the form is changed in any way; otherwise, the rest of the logic will fail.

- In the `Form_Resize` event, I verify that the form is not minimized or maximized. Changing the size while in either of these two states will cause a runtime error. So if the form is in one of those states, then I'll simply exit the event.

- I make sure that I don't resize the form so small that I end up setting one of the controls to a negative `height` or `width`. How did I pick 1000 for these values? I just tried values until I didn't get a runtime error when I tried to make the form as small as possible, and then made it a little larger so that it didn't look quite so funny.

- Finally, I resize each of the controls. Since I know something about the placement of each control (two out of the four sizing and positioning properties), all I need to do is to change the other properties.

For a control like the PictureBox that has fixed `Top` and `Left` values, I need to set the `Height` and `Width` properties. I do this by computing the size of the gap between the original height of the PictureBox and the original height of the form (`FormHeight - PictureHeight`). This gap should remain constant, since the horizontal scroll bar fits in this gap. Then I take this value away from the new height of the form and end up with the new height of the PictureBox (`Me.Height - FormHeight + PictureHeight`).

In the same way, I use the other seven constants to compute the varying dimensions and replace them in the `Form_Resize` event.

Resizing Floating Controls The approach you use to resize floating controls is very similar to the approach used for the anchored controls. However, the physical code can get quite complex, since now you must calculate the relative position of each control plus its size. If you have multiple columns of controls such as a ListView control beside a TreeView control, you may even want to put some sort of divider between the two controls to allow the user to determine the relative size of each control.

Loading Your Form Faster

Here's an interesting thought: If you do a `Me.Show` inside the `Form_Load` event, the form will show up quicker than if you let the form load normally. Normally means that the form will be entirely built and initialized before it is shown to the user. On a slow system, this could take a second or two—just long enough to be annoying. By using `Me.Show`, you show the form before it is completely loaded. The user may see a little flicker while the form is being initialized, but from the user's point of view, the computer is responding a bit faster.

WARNING   **Save resizing information first:** If you use my approach that saves resizing information from the form as designed in Visual Basic, you must save that information before you try to use the `Me.Show` method. If you don't, this information will be lost since the `Form_Resize` event will occur before the `Form_Load` event has been completed.

Another way to help speed up the process is to `Hide` your form when you are finished rather than unload it. This will make the display much faster, because the form doesn't need to go through the load process a second time.

Another simple little trick to help you speed up the initial form-loading process is to create a separate module file and add a subroutine called `Main`. Then you can change the Project Properties from a form name to calling `Sub Main`. In the `Sub Main` routine, you can initialize your global variables, then show your splash screen and wait for the user to click OK or for the splash screen to time out. Finally, you can show your main form. When you return from your main form, you simply exit the subroutine.

Using a `Sub Main` routine can be valuable when you have multiple forms that the user may want to see when the application starts. You can save the user's preference in the Windows Registry and retrieve it with the `GetSetting` function. Then it is a simple matter to display the desired form on startup.

TIP

Databases need speed, too: One of the biggest causes of delays in loading a form is the database. It takes time to load a database form and populate it with the first values. Anything you can do to improve the form-loading speed will be very noticeable to the user.

Processing the Tab and Access Keys

Anything that you can do to make it easier for your users to move around within the form will be appreciated. One way that you can do this is to make sure that pressing the Tab key takes them through the form in a logical manner. Another facility you can provide is access keys to controls and shortcut keys to menu options, so users have the option of using the keyboard to get around.

Handling Tabs

Every control that you place on the form is assigned a `TabOrder` property and will probably have a `TabStop` property, too. These properties are used to determine the form's ability to process the Tab key. Typically, the Tab key is used to move from one field or button to the next. This makes it easy for the user to fill in a form, such as the one shown in Figure 6.2.

FIGURE 6.2:

FIGURE 6.2:

A typical Visual Basic form

When you fill out the required information in one field, pressing the Tab key automatically takes you to the next field to be filled in. Also, after the last field has been filled out, pressing Tab takes you to the command button labeled Insert. The command buttons Delete and Update are followed in the tab sequence. Pressing Tab while on the Update button will position the cursor at the Name field.

Controlling the Tab Order

How tabs operate is based on a sequential number assigned by the IDE to the TabOrder property. The first field that will receive the focus when the form is displayed is the one with the lowest value in the TabOrder property. The last field to receive the focus in the form before starting at the beginning again has the highest value for TabOrder.

Thus, in any form, you should give strong consideration to the TabOrder of the fields. The ordering should naturally progress from one field to the next in order to make the user's work flow more naturally.

By default, Visual Basic assigns an ascending sequential value to the TabOrder property as the controls are added to the form. Most likely, this will be the wrong order. To correct this problem, you can start renumbering the controls at 0 and work you way through the entire set. However, the "lazy programmer" will remember that Visual Basic allows you to assign any value to the TabOrder property and will automatically renumber the control that currently has that value, plus all that follow.

So if you need to add a new control in between the second and third, simply set the `TabOrder` of the new control to 2, and the rest of the controls will still be in the proper order.

Skipping Fields

The `TabStop` property determines whether the control will receive the focus by tabbing. Thus, if you wish to let the user skip over a text field, simply set `TabStop` to `False`.

Note that some controls, such as the Label and the Frame controls, do not have the `TabStop` property. These controls can never receive the focus during tabbing, even through they have a valid value for `TabOrder`. Other controls, such as the Menu, Timer, Data, Image, ImageList, Line, and Shape controls, do not have either a `TabStop` or `TabOrder` property. They can never receive the focus.

Creating Access Keys

Access keys are merely a sequence of keys associated with a control, so that when a user presses the access key combination, the focus will be transferred to that control. Menu items also support access keys, but they are called *shortcuts*. Both types allow the user to press a key combination, such as Alt+A or Shift+Ctrl+F12, and switch the focus or execute a menu command. Access keys associated with controls always work with the Alt key; the shortcut keys associated with menu items use the Shift and Ctrl keys.

Defining Access Keys for Controls

To create an access key for a control, you simply edit the `Caption` property of the control you wish to transfer the focus to and insert an ampersand (&) before the character you wish to use as the access key. In Figure 6.3, you can see how I assigned the value `&Name` to the `Caption` property for `Label1` to create the access key for the Name field in the sample form shown earlier in Figure 6.2.

When the caption appears, the character will be underlined. Then when the user presses the Alt key plus the underlined character, the focus will be shifted to that control. If you define two or more controls with the same access key, the focus will shift to the next control in the `TabOrder` sequence.

FIGURE 6.3:

Defining an access key

If the control's `TabStop` property is `False` or the control doesn't have a `TabStop` property (like the Label control), the focus will be shifted to the first control in the `TabOrder` property where `TabStop` is `True`. If the control can perform an action— for example, it's a command button—then pressing the access key combination has the same effect as clicking the left button while the mouse pointer is over that control. For example, if you defined P as an access key for the Print button, pressing Alt+P is the same as clicking on the Print button.

> **TIP**   **Use labels with text boxes:** Label controls have a caption but can't receive the focus, and TextBox controls can receive the focus but can't have a caption. You can place a Label control immediately in front of the TextBox control and specify your access key. Then the focus will be transferred to the text box. Note this technique also works with frames and the individual tabs in a Tabstrip control.

Defining Shortcut Keys for Menus

To define a shortcut key for a menu item, enter it in the Menu Editor's Shortcut field. Figure 6.4 shows an example of defining the Ctrl+I shortcut for the Insert item on the Database menu. Note that the shortcut keys you define for menus will never conflict with the access keys you include in the `Caption` property of your controls (since neither will work).

FIGURE 6.4:

Using the Menu Editor
to define a shortcut to a
menu item

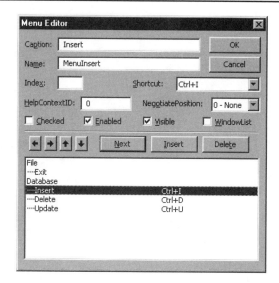

Checking User-Input Values

A typical application accepts and displays information from a database in a series
of text boxes, with each text box holding one field from your database. Ensuring
that only correct values are entered into each text box is the first step to guaranteeing that correct data is entered into the database.

There are several different things you can do to make sure that the data is correct:

- You can trap the individual characters as they are typed and allow only the
  proper ones to be accepted. This is done in the KeyPress event.

- You can use the Change event, LostFocus event, or Validate event to perform your edit checks after the user has filled out the field.

- You can use a combo box in place of a text box and let the user choose from
  a drop-down menu, or you can have the program automatically complete
  the field's value based on the characters typed.

I'll cover each of these techniques in the following sections. They are all demonstrated in the Control Tabs program.

Use Visual Basic controls to prevent errors: Visual Basic provides several controls that are particularly useful in data-entry applications. You can add Month-View and DateTimePicker controls to let your users choose dates from a calendar. For fields that require special formats, such as for phone numbers, you can use the MaskedEdit control. These and other useful controls are covered in Chapter 10.

Using the KeyPress Event to Check Data

The KeyPress event occurs each time that a user presses a key while a particular control has the focus. This keystroke can be captured and analyzed to determine what action should be taken. Thus, it is easy to make sure that the user can enter only the characters you want. You can let the user know that the entry is incorrect in a variety of ways.

In the example in Listing 6.7, I allow the user to enter only numbers. If the user enters an invalid character, I change the character to zero and sound a beep. Note that I only suppress printing characters. This means that the cursor keys and Backspace key will continue to work.

Listing 6.7: **Text6_KeyPress Event in Control Tabs**

```
Private Sub Text6_KeyPress(KeyAscii As Integer)

If Chr(KeyAscii) >= " " And Chr(KeyAscii) < "0" Then
    KeyAscii = 0
    Beep

ElseIf Chr(KeyAscii) > "9" And Chr(KeyAscii) <= "~" Then
    KeyAscii = 0
    Beep

End If

End Sub
```

WARNING **KeyPress only handles pressed keys:** While this statement seems kind of silly since it's obvious, remember that there are other ways to enter data into a text box. For example, using cut and paste allows the user to enter data into the text box and bypass the KeyPress event.

Using the Change Event to Check Data

Each time the contents of a text box are changed, the Change event is fired. This is true even if your program assigns a value to the Text property or the user cuts and pastes information into the control. However, the downside to using this event is that you don't know what was changed from the last time the event was called.

In Listing 6.8, I verify that the Text5 control contains a number less than ten characters long. If an improper value is entered, I turn the background to red; if the text box is empty, I turn the background to yellow.

Listing 6.8:   **Text5_Change Event in Control Tabs**

```
Private Sub Text5_Change()

If Len(Text5.Text) = 0 Then
    Text5.BackColor = &HFFFF&

ElseIf Not IsNumeric(Text5.Text) Or Len(Text5.Text) > 9 Then
    Text5.BackColor = &HFF&

Else
    Text5.BackColor = &H80000005
End If

End Sub
```

TIP   **Flag your errors:** No matter how you determine that the contents of a field are invalid, you should include a line like Text1.BackColor = &HFF& to indicate to the user that the value is incorrect. This tells the user in no uncertain terms that a field needs to be corrected. You can then reset it to normal with a line of code similar to Text1.BackColor = &H80000005.

Using the LostFocus Event to Check Data

You can also use the LostFocus event to perform edit checks. This event is triggered when the user or the program transfers the focus to another control. Since the LostFocus event of the current control is the last piece of processing that occurs before the next control gains focus, it is an ideal time to verify that the data entered in the current control is correct.

You can check the data and flag any information to be corrected later. You can also use this opportunity to display an error message to the user in a status bar (see Chapter 10 for details on adding StatusBar controls) or highlight the background of the control to indicate an error. This is the approach taken in Listing 6.9.

NOTE   **Resetting focus in the LostFocus event:** When your program handles the LostFocus event, the focus has already begun the process of shifting to the next control. If you try to use the **SetFocus** method inside the LostFocus event to bring the focus back to the current control, the next control will briefly receive the focus, and its **GotFocus** and **LostFocus** events will be fired.

Listing 6.9:   **Text1_KeyPress Event in Control Tabs**

```
Private Sub Text1_KeyPress(KeyAscii As Integer)

Text1.BackColor = &H80000005

End Sub

Private Sub Text1_LostFocus()

If Len(Text1.Text) = 0 Then
   Text1.BackColor = &HFFFF&
   StatusBar1.Panels(1).Text = "No value was entered for Name."

Else
   Text1.BackColor = &H80000005
End If

End Sub
```

Using the Validate Event to Check Data

One of the new features of Visual Basic 6 is the Validate event. This event is triggered just before the focus is switched to another control and the other control has the CauseValidation property set to True. If the other control does not have the CauseValidation property set to True, the Validate event will be triggered the next time you access a control with the CauseValidation property set to True.

This can greatly simplify your edit processing. Once in the Validate event, you can determine if the data is correct or incorrect. If the value is incorrect, all you need to do is set the Cancel parameter to False, and the focus will remain with the current control. Otherwise, the focus will shift to the next control normally. Listing 6.10 shows an example of using the Validate event.

Listing 6.10:   **Text3_Validate Event in Control Tabs**

```
Private Sub Text3_Validate(Cancel As Boolean)

If Len(Text3.Text) = 0 Then
    Text3.BackColor = &HFF&
    StatusBar1.Panels(1).Text = "No value was entered for City."
    Cancel = True
Else
    Text3.BackColor = &H80000005
End If

End Sub
```

TIP

To cause or not to CauseValidation: Set the CauseValidation on all controls to True, except for those situations where no processing is done against the data, such as a Help button or a Cancel button.

Using Combo Boxes to Enter Data

A few years ago, I started using a ComboBox control to help users fill in a particular field. This let users click the drop-down button to select from a list of items or enter their item directly into the field. Then I discovered that a number of people preferred to type their information into the field, because it was faster than clicking the drop-down button and scrolling through the list looking for the desired value.

This had the unfortunate side effect of letting users misspell some of the values in this field. I could have changed the `Style` property so that the control showed a drop-down list instead of a drop-down combo box. This would have corrected the problem with misspelled entries, but at a cost of not allowing the user to enter any new values. What I really wanted was a ComboBox control that let people enter any value they wanted, but also helped them spell some of the more common values.

Eventually, I solved the problem with the code you see in Listing 6.11. I preload the ComboBox control with the most common values that I think the user might enter. Then, based on their keystrokes, I attempt to guess what they are typing. This is similar to the AutoComplete feature you may have worked with in Microsoft Word (introduced in Word 97). Any characters users type will be preserved automatically, while the guess I provide is marked as selected text.

Listing 6.11:   SmartType Routine in Control Tabs

```
Sub SmartType(c As Object, n As Integer)

' c is the control
' n is the new character

Dim i As Integer
Dim l As Integer
Dim s As Integer
Dim t As String

' Stuff the new character into the Text property where the SelStart
' property is pointing. Then search the contents of the combobox for
' a matching prefix (left(combo1.text,combo1.selstart). If one is
' found, add the remaining characters to the Text property and set
' SelLength to go to the end of the string.

s = c.SelStart
l = c.SelLength
t = c.Text
```

```
t = Left(t, s) & Chr(n) & Right(t, Len(t) - s)
s = s + 1

i = 0
Do While (i < c.ListCount - 1) _
    And StrComp(Left(t, s), Left(c.List(i), s), vbTextCompare) <> 0
  i = i + 1
Loop

If UCase(Left(t, s)) = UCase(Left(c.List(i), s)) Then
   t = c.List(i)
   l = Len(t) - s
Else
   t = Left(t, s)
   l = 0
End If

c.Text = t
c.SelStart = s
c.SelLength = l

End Sub

Private Sub Combo1_KeyPress(KeyAscii As Integer)

If Chr(KeyAscii) >= " " And Chr(KeyAscii) <= "~" Then
   SmartType Combo1, KeyAscii
   KeyAscii = 0
End If

End Sub
```

For instance, assume that the ComboBox contained a State field. I would preload the control with the 50 states in alphabetical order. Thus, if the user typed **M**, I would respond with *Maine*, where the first *M* was not selected but the remaining *aine* was marked as selected text. If the user then typed **a**, then *ine* would be marked as selected. If the user typed an **r**, then I would guess *Maryland*. If this was the desired state, then the user need only tab to the next field. This method helps ensure correct, consistent spelling (and some of the states are harder to spell!).

Assuming the user started again by entering a **D**, I would guess *Delaware*, but if the user typed an **i** next, I would simply display those two letters, since there was not a state on my list that began with *Di*. This would permit the user to enter *District of Columbia* in its entirety, even though I didn't originally include it in the list of possible values.

In Listing 6.11, I intercept the user's character in the KeyPress event. If the character is a normal ASCII character somewhere between a space and a tilde, I pass it along to the SmartType subroutine to do all the dirty work. Note that I also cancel the KeyPress event, since the character will be added to the ComboBox as part of the SmartType subroutine.

The SmartType routine begins by creating temporary working copies of the control's text property and the information about the part of the text that is selected. Then I insert the new character at the insertion point (SelStart). Note that I take advantage of the Left and Right functions' ability to return an empty string if no characters were extracted.

Next, I search the list in the combo box, checking to see if there is a match between the characters already typed by the user (those before the insertion point) and the leading part of any of the items in the list. If a match is found, I save the value and determine the length of the text to be selected (the characters after the insertion point). If there isn't a match, I just display the characters the user has already typed, set the insertion point to the end, and don't mark any text as selected. In both cases, I update the control's properties with my working copies of the control's properties and wait for the user to enter the next character or go to another field.

TIP   **Don't keep your suggestions in your program:** Save your suggestions in a database table. This allows them to be easily modified by you or your user. You can also insert a few lines of code that could recognize when a new value is entered by the user and save it into the database table, thus automatically extending the list of suggestions.

Preventing Multiple Copies of Your Application from Running at the Same Time

Sometimes, you may take some shortcuts in building an application, assuming that your application will be run in single-user mode. This is not necessarily bad, but it can present problems in some cases.

Windows allows you to run the same application multiple times on the same machine. While technically you are still running in single-user mode (that is, only one person is sitting at the keyboard), different instances of the same application may be loaded at the same time. This means that you now need to be certain that one instance of the program doesn't interfere with other instances.

Another annoyance brought about by running multiple instances of the same application has to do with the "not-so-bright" user (and I know that every programmer has some prime candidates for the dumbest user contest). I have known individuals who would start the same application several times without ever leaving it. Then the duplicate windows with different data would seriously confuse them. Phone calls with someone whining, "I'm sure I was looking at <fill in the blank>, but now that data is gone and I'm looking at <something different>" were common. I'm sure that you would like to prevent a few phone calls like this to your office.

One way to avoid the problem is to simply not allow multiple instances of your application to run. You can do this by checking the `App.PrevInstance` property. This property is `True` when another copy of your application is running. By checking this property when your program starts, you can close your program before you get into a locking conflict or end up overwriting critical data.

Handling Long Processing Waits

How many times have you gotten annoyed when an application takes a long time to process something, and you can't do anything else with your system? Or worse, you think you system has become locked up and you don't know whether you should reboot. Here are a couple of tips to help with that situation:

- Anytime you are going to be processing something for a while (say, about a second or so) and your application will not be responding to any events, you should set the cursor to an hourglass, and then reset it when you are finished. This might happen when a user loads a large file or generates a large report.

- You should let the user know that the system is actually accomplishing something by displaying some indicator of how close you are to being done. The easiest way to do this is by using a ProgressBar control. This shows the user that you are indeed making progress, and it is relatively easy to use.

- You should make sure that Windows is free to respond to other requests. It's one thing if you lock up your application, but it's another if you lock up all of the other applications. The DoEvents routine is used to return control back to Windows. If there's nothing to be done, Windows will return to your application. You should try to ensure that the DoEvents function is called several times a second. This is frequent enough that Windows is still responsive, yet not so often that your program screeches to a halt.

TIP

How often should I update the progress bar? You should try to update the progress bar somewhere between 20 and 100 times during your processing loop. More frequently than that is just a waste of resources. Remember that the goal is to show the user that something is happening every few seconds. If you have a really long processing loop, consider breaking the processing into stages. Then you can display the name of the stage and reset the progress bar to zero for each one.

I've combined all three of these tips into a single package shown in Listing 6.12. This routine has two parameters: wait and times. If wait is True, then I initialize the progress bar and set the cursor to an hourglass before I start the loop and restore the cursor after the loop. Inside the loop, I call the DoEvents function and update the progress bar.

Listing 6.12:   **DoIt Routine in DoEvents**

```
Private Sub DoIt(wait As Boolean, times As Long)

' Routine:      DoIt
' Written by:   Wayne S. Freeze
' Description:
'     Do nothing the specified number of times. If
'     wait is True, then tell the user to wait for
'     a little while.

Dim i As Long
```

```
Dim m As Integer
Dim x As String

Form2.Show
Form2.Text1.Text = FormatDateTime(Now, vbLongTime)

' If we are going to show the users they need to wait,
' save the mousepointer so we can restore it later,
' then set it to an hourglass and initialize the
' progressbar control.

If wait Then
   m = Screen.MousePointer
   Screen.MousePointer = vbHourglass
   ProgressBar1.Min = 0
   ProgressBar1.Max = times
   ProgressBar1.Value = 0
End If

' Perform this killer loop the specified number
' of times. If we're showing waiting information
' to the users, take a break and update the progressbar.

For i = 1 To times
   x = x & " "
   If wait Then
      DoEvents
      ProgressBar1.Value = 1
   End If
Next i

' Restore the mousepointer if necessary and we're done.

If wait Then
   Screen.MousePointer = m
End If

End Sub
```

Getting Information about the User's System

Now we are going to cover three different ways to get information: the SysInfo control, the `Screen` object, and the `App` object. You can get most of the information from the properties of these controls and objects, but some information must be gathered through events as different actions occur in your user's system.

To demonstrate how to get and display system information, I wrote the System Information program. This program gathers information about the operating system, battery, screen, application, and system events and places that information on the corresponding tab.

Getting Operating System Information

The SysInfo control has three properties that will let you determine the type, version, and build level of the operating system. These are available through the `OSPlatform`, `OSVersion`, and `OSBuild` properties. Figure 6.5 shows this information gathered and saved in label captions.

FIGURE 6.5:

The Op Sys Info tab of the System Information program with operating system information

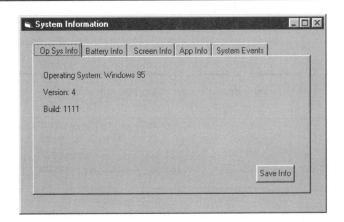

The code to capture this information is relatively simple, as shown in Listing 6.13. Note that I need to add one to the value of `OSPlatform`, because `OSPlatform`

returns values beginning with zero, while the first value in the **Choose** function has an index of one.

Listing 6.13:   **GetSysInfo Routine in System Information**

```
Private Sub GetSysInfo()

Label1.Caption = "Operating System: " & Choose(SysInfo1.OSPlatform + 1, _
    "Win32s", "Windows 95", "Windows NT")

Label2.Caption = "Version: " & SysInfo1.OSVersion

Label3.Caption = "Build: " & SysInfo1.OSBuild

End Sub
```

Getting Power and Battery Information

Information about batteries is gathered in the same way as the operating system information. Information from the battery-related SysInfo properties is collected, decoded, and displayed as the caption of a label. This information is useful only for laptops and servers with an integrated uninterruptible power supply (UPS). If you don't have a battery, then why worry about it, right?

NOTE   **Why doesn't it work on my computer?** Just because your computer has batteries doesn't mean that you can access information about them. Your hardware vendor needs to work with the battery manufacturer to properly design the computer and batteries, and supply the compatible drivers for Windows to determine this information. Not all machines can get battery information today, but I expect that more will be capable of doing this in the future.

There are five different pieces of battery information:

- The **ACStatus** property indicates whether the system is on battery power or AC power.

- The **BatteryFullTime** property returns the number of seconds that the battery should last with a full charge.

- The BatteryLifeTime property returns the number of seconds the battery should last.

- The BatteryLifePercent returns the relative percentage of a full charge remaining in the battery.

- The BatteryStatus returns a flag indicating whether the battery is charging or discharging, as well as the relative state of the battery's charge.

Figure 6.6 shows typical battery information for a laptop computer running on battery power.

TIP

Check your battery: It can be very useful for applications that run on a laptop using battery power to periodically check the battery status and notify the user to plug in the adapter or change the battery when it gets low. You can check Battery-Status or BatteryLifePercent periodically and prevent a user from starting a new operation if there isn't sufficient time or battery resources remaining to complete that operation.

FIGURE 6.6:

The Battery Info tab of the System Information program with battery information

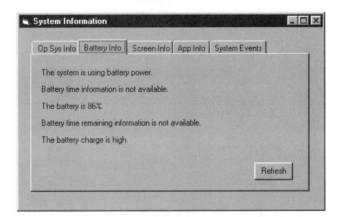

The routine in Listing 6.14 is a bit longer than the GetSysInfo routine, but it follows the same basic logic. You simply take the value of a property, decode it, and display it as a human-readable message in a label. For the most part, this is straightforward until you reach the BatteryStatus property. Unlike the other properties, this property includes two pieces of information: the relative level of battery charge remaining, and whether or not the battery is being charged. I just decode the battery's state and then if the battery is charging, I simply add a message to that effect to the end of the same label field.

Listing 6.14:   **GetBatteryInfo Routine in System Information**

```
Private Sub GetBatteryInfo()

If SysInfo1.ACStatus = 0 Then
    Label4.Caption = "The system is using battery power."
ElseIf SysInfo1.ACStatus = 1 Then
    Label4.Caption = "The system is using AC power."
ElseIf SysInfo1.ACStatus = 255 Then
    Label4.Caption = "The power status is unknown."
Else
    Label4.Caption = "Unknown ACStatus code: " & _
        FormatNumber(SysInfo1.ACStatus)
End If


If SysInfo1.BatteryFullTime = -1 Then
    Label5.Caption = "Battery time information is not available."
Else
    Label5.Caption = "The battery should last " & _
        FormatNumber(SysInfo1.BatteryFullTime) & " seconds."
End If


If SysInfo1.BatteryLifePercent = 255 Then
    Label6.Caption = "Battery life information is not available."
Else
    Label6.Caption = "The battery is " & _
        FormatNumber(SysInfo1.BatteryLifePercent, 0) & "%."
End If


If SysInfo1.BatteryLifeTime = -1 Then
    Label7.Caption = "Battery time remaining information is not available."
Else
    Label7.Caption = "The battery should last for another " & _
        FormatNumber(SysInfo1.BatteryLifeTime) & " seconds."
End If


If SysInfo1.BatteryLifePercent = 255 Then
```

```
      Label8.Caption = "Battery life remaining information is not available."
ElseIf SysInfo1.BatteryStatus = 128 Then
      Label8.Caption = "The system doesn't have a battery."
ElseIf SysInfo1.BatteryStatus Mod 8 = 4 Then
      Label8.Caption = "The battery charge is critical."
ElseIf SysInfo1.BatteryStatus Mod 8 = 2 Then
      Label8.Caption = "The battery charge is low."
ElseIf SysInfo1.BatteryStatus Mod 8 = 1 Then
      Label8.Caption = "The battery charge is high."
Else
      Label8.Caption = "BatteryStatus unknown: " & _
         FormatNumber(SysInfo1.BatteryStatus, 0) & "."
End If

If (SysInfo1.BatteryStatus / 8) Mod 16 = 1 Then
      Label8.Caption = Label8.Caption & "The battery is also charging."
End If

End Sub
```

Getting Screen Information

The SysInfo control contains information about the physical configuration of the screen. The Screen object contains additional information about the screen. Although there may appear to be some overlap between the two objects, there really isn't.

The Screen object supplies the absolute height and width of your display, while the SysInfo control's WorkAreaHeight and WorkAreaWidth return the height and width of the display after allowing for the space occupied by the Windows Taskbar. So you can place your form in the absolute center of the display (as described earlier in this chapter) or adjust your window size to fill only the available space left on the Desktop. You can see most of this information in Figure 6.7.

The routine shown in Listing 6.15 is basically the same as the previous information-gathering routines, except that now I'm using both the SysInfo control and the Screen object together to derive some information. Since Visual Basic performs most measurements in twips, I used the TwipsPerPixelX and TwipsPerPixelY conversion routines to get the measurements in pixels. The rest of the routine is relatively straightforward. Like the others, it retrieves the information from a property, decodes it if necessary, and displays it in a Label control.

FIGURE 6.7:

The Screen Info tab of the System Information program with display information

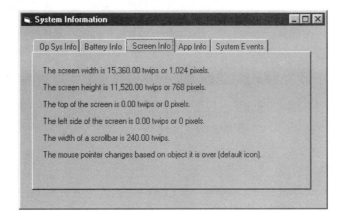

TIP

Can't add the Screen object to your project? You've been fooled. The Screen object is always available to a Visual Basic programmer. You don't need to explicitly add it to your project. On the other hand, the SysInfo control is not one of the standard default controls, so you must explicitly add it to your application.

Listing 6.15:   **GetScreenInfo Routine in System Information**

```
Private Sub GetScreenInfo()

Label9.Caption = "The screen width is " & _
    FormatNumber(SysInfo1.WorkAreaWidth) & " twips or " & _
    FormatNumber(SysInfo1.WorkAreaWidth / Screen.TwipsPerPixelX, 0) & " pixels."
Label10.Caption = "The screen height is " & _
    FormatNumber(SysInfo1.WorkAreaHeight) & " twips or " & _
    FormatNumber(SysInfo1.WorkAreaHeight / Screen.TwipsPerPixelY, 0) & " pixels."
Label11.Caption = "The top of the screen is " & _
    FormatNumber(SysInfo1.WorkAreaTop) & " twips or " & _
    FormatNumber(SysInfo1.WorkAreaTop / Screen.TwipsPerPixelX, 0) & " pixels."
Label12.Caption = "The left side of the screen is " & _
    FormatNumber(SysInfo1.WorkAreaLeft) & " twips or " & _
```

```
        FormatNumber(SysInfo1.WorkAreaLeft / Screen.TwipsPerPixelY, 0) & " pixels."
    Label13.Caption = "The width of a scrollbar is " & _
        FormatNumber(SysInfo1.ScrollBarSize) & " twips."

If Screen.MousePointer = vbDefault Then
    Label14.Caption = "The mouse pointer changes based on object " & _
        "it is over (default icon)."

ElseIf Screen.MousePointer = vbArrow Then
    Label14.Caption = "The mouse pointer is an arrow."

ElseIf Screen.MousePointer = vbCrosshair Then
    Label14.Caption = "The mouse pointer is a crosshair."

ElseIf Screen.MousePointer = vbIbeam Then
    Label14.Caption = "The mouse pointer is an I-beam."

ElseIf Screen.MousePointer = vbIconPointer Then
    Label14.Caption = "The mouse pointer is a square inside a square."

ElseIf Screen.MousePointer = vbSizePointer Then
    Label14.Caption = "The mouse pointer is a four sided arrow that " & _
        "points north, south, east and west."

ElseIf Screen.MousePointer = vbSizeNESW Then
    Label14.Caption = "The mouse pointer is a two sided arrow that " & _
        "points north east and south west."

ElseIf Screen.MousePointer = vbSizeNS Then
    Label14.Caption = "The mouse pointer is a two sided arrow that " & _
        "points north and south."

ElseIf Screen.MousePointer = vbSizeNWSE Then
    Label14.Caption = "The mouse pointer is a two sided arrow that " & _
        "points north west and south east."

ElseIf Screen.MousePointer = vbSizeWE Then
    Label14.Caption = "The mouse pointer is a two sided arrow that " & _
        "points west and east."

ElseIf Screen.MousePointer = vbUpArrow Then
```

```
        Label14.Caption = "The mouse pointer is a single sided arrow that " & _
            "points north."

    ElseIf Screen.MousePointer = vbHourglass Then
        Label14.Caption = "The mouse pointer is an hourglass."

    ElseIf Screen.MousePointer = vbNoDrop Then
        Label14.Caption = "The mouse pointer contains a no drop icon."

    ElseIf Screen.MousePointer = vbArrowHourglass Then
        Label14.Caption = "The mouse pointer contains an arrow and an " & _
            "hourglass."

    ElseIf Screen.MousePointer = vbArrowQuestion Then
        Label14.Caption = "The mouse pointer contains an arrow with a " & _
            "question mark."

    ElseIf Screen.MousePointer = vbSizeAll Then
        Label14.Caption = "The mouse pointer is a size all icon."

    ElseIf Screen.MousePointer = vbCustom Then
        Label14.Caption = "The mouse pointer is a custom icon."

    End If

    End Sub
```

Getting Application Information

Remember the Program Properties dialog box we discussed in Chapter 2? Most of that information ends up in the App object. Like the Screen object, the App object is always available to your program. It can be used to generate information such as the version and copyright, as shown in Figure 6.8.

FIGURE 6.8:

The App Info tab of the
System Information program
with application information

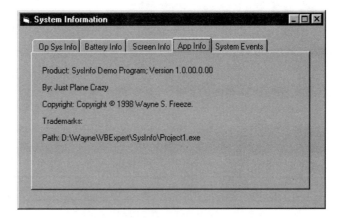

As with the SysInfo control and the Screen object, using the App object is
mostly a matter of moving and perhaps formatting information directly from its
properties. Whether you fill in this information and include a display in your
program is really up to you. But if it is this easy, you ought to take credit for your
intellectual property. Listing 6.16 shows how this is done.

Listing 6.16:   GetAppInfo Routine in System Information

```
Private Sub GetAppInfo()

Label15.Caption = "Product: " & App.ProductName & "; Version " & _
   FormatNumber(App.Major, 0) & "." & FormatNumber(App.Minor) & _
   "." & FormatNumber(App.Revision)
Label16.Caption = "By: " & App.CompanyName
Label17.Caption = "Copyright: " & App.LegalCopyright
Label18.Caption = "Trademarks: " & App.LegalTrademarks
Label19.Caption = "Path: " & App.Path & "\" & App.EXEName & ".exe"
Label20.Caption = App.Comments

End Sub
```

Tracking System Events

Thought all this stuff was easy? Up till now, it has been. But it's time to get a little more complicated and tricky.

There is a lot of stuff going on inside your computer all the time that you never really think about. However, you may consider watching some of these events a little more closely. For instance, with the Plug-and-Pray (I meant Play) architecture, users can change their system configuration on the fly. If you have Windows 98 and some new Universal Serial Bus (USB) devices, it may be useful to know when one of those devices is added or removed. If you have a laptop, you also have this problem, since PCMCIA devices can be added and removed on the fly. Also, if you have a long-running server-based application, do you need to be notified when the clock changes from Daylight Savings Time and back again?

Picking Events of Interest

Along with the ability to provide you basic information about your system, the SysInfo control also can allow your program to handle events for these and other conditions. Table 6.1 lists the events that can be trapped with the SysInfo control.

TABLE 6.1: SysInfo Control Events

Event	Description
ConfigChangeCanceled	A proposed configuration change was canceled.
ConfigChanged	The configuration was changed.
DeviceArrival	A device was added to the system.
DeviceOtherEvent	A nonstandard event was raised by a device.
DeviceQueryRemove	A request was made to remove a device from the system. You can cancel the request.
DeviceQueryRemoveFailed	Someone canceled a request to remove a device.
DeviceRemoveComplete	A device has been removed from the system.
DeviceRemovePending	Everyone responded yes to a request to remove a device from the system, but the device hasn't been removed yet.
DevModeChange	A user has changed a device mode setting.

Continued on next page

TABLE 6.1 (CONTINUED): SysInfo Control Events

Event	Description
DisplayChanged	A user has changed the display characteristics.
PowerQuerySuspend	A user requested to suspend the system.
PowerResumeEvent	The system has been resumed after being suspended.
PowerStatusChanged	The PowerStatus property was changed.
PowerSuspend	The system is about to enter the suspend state.
QueryChangeConfig	A user requested to change the configuration.
SettingChanged	A system-wide parameter such as the Windows Taskbar was changed (e.g., moved or resized).
SysColorsChanged	The system colors were changed.
TimeChanged	The system clock was changed.

For the most part, these events fall into four categories:

Hardware and system configuration These occur when changes are made to the hardware configuration. For the most part, your application can ignore these events unless you need access to a specific device and need to know if the user attempted to remove it.

Power issues These events are not much use on most desktop machines, but it can be important to know when a laptop's battery is getting low or has finished recharging. You can also intercept a request to suspend and either cancel it or write the user's work to a temporary file so that the user is protected in case the user's laptop doesn't resume properly. Also, you should try to minimize activities that consume power, like performing disk I/O and accessing the CD-ROM, when running on batteries to help extend their life.

> **TIP**
>
> **It only fails when you need it the most:** Experience with laptops has taught me to save my work completely before I suspend it. Nine times out of ten, my machine recovers without a blink. But—just often enough to be frustrating—a problem occurs and I need to reboot the machine.

Display changes Two events relate to the display: One event will occur when the display has been changed, and another will occur when the color depth has changed.

Time changes The last category of events contains just a single event, the `TimeChanged` event. Most likely, this event will occur only twice a year, when you convert to and from Daylight Savings Time. Of course, any change to the system clock also will trigger this event.

Handling Display Changes Sometimes, looking at other applications may give you ideas that you can use in your own. For instance, when you change your display size, Microsoft Word will resize its window automatically so that all parts of it remain visible. (Word only handles this change as the display size shrinks; when it is expanded, you need to manually restore the window size.)

You could easily modify your application to remember the initial display size, so if the display size changed, you could change its height to keep the same size gap between the bottom of the screen and the bottom of your window. Then you could shift the window horizontally to maintain the same size gap.

Handling Time Changes Having been responsible for computers that ran 24 hours a day, 7 days a week for many years, I ran into some issues related to converting to Daylight Savings Time and back again. One popular issue concerned what happens to a program when it sees 2:12am twice. In most cases, the programs didn't really care about the time for any calculations. At most, the time was treated as just another block of text and was moved around and then printed so that the user could read it. But some programs needed to know how much time elapsed between two events. I was always able to fix the programs so that they were stopped before the time change and restarted after the time change.

Nowadays, it is much harder to make adjustments for time changes because of all the interactive requirements of the web and client/server programming. I recommend that most people should track events in terms of GMT and convert to and from local time as necessary. However, sometimes this just isn't practical. Using the `TimeChange` event is a way to recognize that the system clock has been changed and your processing may need to be adjusted accordingly.

TIP

How long has it been? If you have a complex Internet application and you are worried about time changes, you should try to keep all time values based on GMT or Universal time and never change your clock to accommodate Daylight Savings Time. This is especially true if your application spans multiple time zones and receives inputs based on the clock of the client computer.

Logging System Events

Figure 6.9 shows a relatively simple log facility that records system events while your program is running.

FIGURE 6.9:

The System Events tab of the System Information program with a system event log

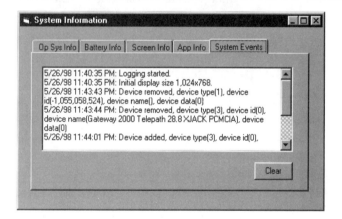

In Listing 6.17, you see a SysInfo event that occurs each time that the display resolution is changed. In this case, I merely record the information in a text box for later analysis, but you may wish to take some action based on this information.

Listing 6.17:   **SysInfo1_DisplayChanged Event in System Information**

```
Private Sub SysInfo1_DisplayChanged()

Text1.Text = Text1.Text & FormatDateTime(Now, vbGeneralDate) & _
    ": Display changed, new size " & _
    FormatNumber(SysInfo1.WorkAreaWidth / Screen.TwipsPerPixelX, 0) & "x" _
    & FormatNumber(SysInfo1.WorkAreaHeight / Screen.TwipsPerPixelY, 0) & _
```

```
"." & vbCrLf

End Sub
```

Saving the System Information

After we've gone to all this trouble of gathering system information, it might be nice to save this information to a file. If you have a user who is experiencing a problem and you're not sure what is causing it, you might want to see some of this information. The need to see this information is directly proportional to the distance between your location and the user's location. It's no big deal if you can walk next door and check someone's PC. If the user is across the country, being able to see information about his or her system becomes much more important.

I decided that it would be very useful to add a button that copied all of the information displayed into a single text file. That way, the file could be sent as an e-mail attachment, and it could provide a clue as to what the user's problem might be.

This routine is very straightforward, as you can see in Listing 6.18. I simply ask the user for a filename that I can use to save the information using the Common-Dialog box control. Then I create a text stream object to which I will write all of the Caption and Text properties.

Listing 6.18: **Command1_Click event in System Information**

```
Private Sub Command1_Click()

Dim fso As FileSystemObject
Dim i As Integer
Dim j As Integer
Dim t As TextStream

On Error Resume Next

Set fso = New FileSystemObject

CommonDialog1.CancelError = True
CommonDialog1.Filter = "All Files (*.*)" & _
    "|*.*|Environmental Log Files (*.elf)|*.elf"
CommonDialog1.FilterIndex = 2
```

```
CommonDialog1.Flags = cdlOFNExplorer + cdlOFNOverwritePrompt

CommonDialog1.ShowSave
If Err.Number > 0 Then
    Exit Sub
End If

Err.Clear
Set t = fso.CreateTextFile(CommonDialog1.FileName, True)
If Err.Number > 0 Then
    MsgBox "Unable to create the file."
    Exit Sub
End If

t.WriteLine "Envirnmental Log File"
t.WriteLine vbCrLf & "Operating System Information"
t.WriteLine Label1.Caption
t.WriteLine Label2.Caption
t.WriteLine Label3.Caption
t.WriteLine vbCrLf & "Battery Information"
t.WriteLine Label4.Caption
t.WriteLine Label5.Caption
t.WriteLine Label6.Caption
t.WriteLine Label7.Caption
t.WriteLine Label8.Caption
t.WriteLine vbCrLf & "Screen Information"
t.WriteLine Label9.Caption
t.WriteLine Label10.Caption
t.WriteLine Label11.Caption
t.WriteLine Label12.Caption
t.WriteLine Label13.Caption
t.WriteLine vbCrLf & "System Events"
t.WriteLine Text1.Text
t.WriteLine vbCrLf & "End of data"

t.Close

End Sub
```

Final Thoughts

There are many things you can do in Visual Basic to make it easier for the user to use your application. Simple things like remembering the size and position of a window may seem almost trivial to you, but to some users those are the features that make or break an application.

Unfortunately, some of the most interesting facilities in Windows aren't normally available to Visual Basic programmers. While Visual Basic has come a long way in terms of its ability to dig inside Windows, it still lags behind C++ in this area. The SysInfo control and Screen object are big steps in this direction, but there are more goodies buried in the Windows API, which I'll talk about in Chapter 16.

PART II

Useful Visual Basic Objects and ActiveX Controls

CHAPTER

SEVEN

7

Displaying Information with the Big Controls

- The TreeView control

- The ListView control

- The FileSelect ActiveX control

- The MSFlexGrid control

- The MSChart control

Four of the most powerful controls in Visual Basic are the TreeView, ListView, MSFlexGrid, and MSChart controls. I call them the "Big Controls." They form two natural groupings: those that are used to view collections of hierarchical objects (TreeView and ListView) and those that provide spreadsheet capabilities (MSFlex-Grid and MSChart).

In this chapter, I'm going to describe how I used the TreeView and ListView controls to build an application that lets you see the contents of a file, in either hexadecimal or ASCII format, or as an image. Then, I'll explain how I used the MSFlexGrid and MSChart controls together in a program that builds a very primitive spreadsheet program, called Charter. The Charter program will reappear in various chapters as I add capabilities to it that will bring it a little closer to a real spreadsheet program.

Using TreeView and ListView

Two of the most interesting controls that display information to the user are the TreeView and ListView controls. The TreeView control displays information hierarchically. The ListView control displays information as a series of icons, as item names, or as a multi-column report.

In this chapter, I'll continue working with the File Viewer program that you first saw in Chapter 4. As you remember, this program displayed the computer's directory structure in a TreeView control, because of its naturally hierarchical organization. The files found inside a directory were stored in a ListView control as a series of rows and columns, where each row contained information about a single file, and each column contained a particular type of information about a file.

The project I'm going to use to demonstrate the TreeView and ListView controls is an ActiveX control called FileSelect. The purpose of this control is to display a tree view of directories and a list view of the files in a selected directory. When the user clicks on one of the filenames in the list view, the filename will be returned to the host application. A sample of how this control looks is shown in Figure 7.1.

FIGURE 7.1:

FIGURE 7.1:

The FileSelect control at work

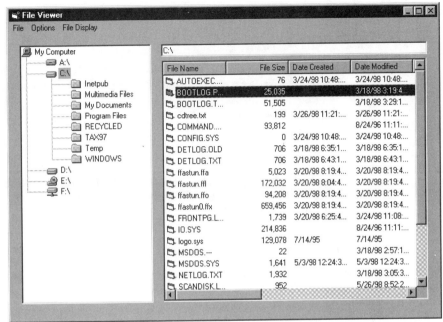

Managing Hierarchies with the TreeView Control

The TreeView control is most useful when you need to manage a hierarchical set of items. These items are stored in a collection of Node objects. Each Node object contains information about the object being displayed in the tree view, plus information about the node's placement in the tree view's hierarchy. The TreeView control automatically expands and contracts the tree depending on the node that the user clicked. It also traps clicks and double-clicks on individual nodes.

The Node object stores information about a single object contained in the TreeView control. Each Node object contains a Text value, which is displayed on the screen, and a Key value, which is used to uniquely identify the object. Aside from a few other properties containing information specific to the node, such as the Expanded-Image and Image properties, which hold ImageList references for an opened image and a closed image, respectively, the rest of the properties are devoted to maintaining information about the tree's structure.

TIP

The Key to the FullPath: The Key property in each node item must be unique. The FullPath property returns a string containing each of the Text values separated by the value in the PathSeparator property. However, when working with files, I find it easier to use just the Key property to hold the complete file path. This also allows me to take the file's path and quickly find the actual Node object by using the path as a value for Key.

For any given node, you can locate its parent node, its first child, its last child, its sibling, and the root node from which it is descended. You can also change most of these values by simply setting a new node reference to them. This makes it easy to traverse the tree structure associated with the TreeView control and to move information around.

Adding New Nodes to the TreeView Control

Like all collections in Visual Basic, you create new items by using the collection's Add method. Unlike some of the collections, however, the Nodes collection Add method is rather complex. In addition to supplying values for the Text, Key, and Image properties, you also need to describe its relationship to another node.

WARNING

Use caution when changing node's relationships at runtime: It is possible (and easy) to change the nodes so that a node's child could also be its parent. This destroys the hierarchical structure of the TreeView control and will result in run-time errors, infinite loops, or both.

In Listing 7.1, you can see a short example of how to add a new generation of nodes to a single node. In this case, I have a reference to a Node object and its corresponding Folder object. I'm going to create new nodes for each of the subfolders in the Folder object. Each of these new nodes will be a child of the specified node, since the subfolders are contained in the specified folder.

Listing 7.1:   **AddNodes Routine in File Viewer**

```
Private Sub AddNodes(n As Node, fn As Folder)

Dim c As Node
Dim fo As Folder
```

```
n.Sorted = False
For Each fo In fn.SubFolders
    Set c = TreeView1.Nodes.Add(n, tvwChild,
        fo.Path & "\", fo.Name, "closedfolder")
    c.ExpandedImage = "openfolder"
Next fo

n.Sorted = True

End Sub
```

I begin by turning off sorting until I finish adding the new nodes. Then I turn sorting back on. Next, I loop through the subfolders in the collection and use the `TreeView1.Nodes.Add` method to create a new node. Since these nodes are all children of the specified node, I specify the parent node and tell the Add method that the new node is its child. I use the full path name as the Key value (note that I added the final backslash), use the folder's name as the Text property, and specify that the default icon is a `"closedfolder"`. Since I can't specify the image that is displayed when the node is expanded on the Add method, I explicitly specify that an `"openfolder"` should be displayed each time the node is expanded. Finally, I restore the Sorted property to reorder the newly added nodes.

TIP

Don't sort while you're loading: If you're going to load a number of new nodes to a TreeView control, turn off the automatic sorting property while you're loading the records, then turn it back on afterwards. As with any rule of thumb, your actual performance will vary, but in general, it is faster to resort the nodes after the new nodes have been added than to insert them in sorted order. Note that this tip also applies when you use the ListView control, as well as in many other situations where you have a choice about sorting before or after you insert information.

Deleting Nodes from the TreeView Control

While it's not common to delete nodes from a TreeView control, sometimes it's necessary. This can happen if you need to refresh the contents of a node because an external source has changed or because the data has been deleted and is now invalid.

The subroutine in Listing 7.2 shows how to delete all of the child nodes from a specified node.

Listing 7.2:   **DeleteNodes Routine in the File Viewer Program**

```
Private Sub DeleteNodes(n As Node)

Do While n.Children > 0
   DeleteNodes n.Child
   TreeView1.Nodes.Remove n.Child.Key
Loop

End Sub
```

When deleting a node from a Nodes collection, you must remember that there may be many levels of nodes beneath the node you're trying to delete. This means that you can't simply delete the node, because any child nodes would remain in the collection and their relationship information would be invalid, since they would point back to a parent node that no longer exists.

To prevent this problem, I wrote the DeleteNodes subroutine to be recursive; that is, it can call itself. I begin by checking this specified node to see if it has any children. If it has children, I call the DeleteNodes subroutine again with the first child's node to delete its children. This process will repeat until it reaches a node with no children. In that case, the routine will return and the Remove method will be used to delete the childless node. Then I go back and check to see if there are any children left and repeat the process until all the children have been deleted. Eventually, I will reach a point where I have deleted all of the children of the original node, and I can return to where the subroutine was originally called.

Responding to TreeView Events

Once the TreeView control has been loaded with some nodes, you can show the contents to the user and wait for responses. The TreeView control will respond to three events: Click, DblClick, and NodeClick. The NodeClick event returns the node the user clicked on; the other events do not return information. You can get the currently selected node by looking at the SelectedItem property.

Listing 7.3 contains the code I wrote to handle the Db1Click event. This routine will determine if the tree needs to be expanded or contracted, and it will load new data or delete existing data as necessary.

Listing 7.3:   **TreeView1_DblClick Event in File Viewer**

```
Private Sub TreeView1_DblClick()

Dim Node As Node
Dim d As Drive
Dim fn As Folder

Set Node = TreeView1.SelectedItem

If Node.Key = "My Computer" Then
   Exit Sub
End If

If Not Node.Expanded And Node.Children = 0 Then
   Set d = fso.GetDrive(fso.GetDriveName(Node.Key))
   If d.IsReady Then
      Set fn = fso.GetFolder(Node.Key)
   Else
      MsgBox "Drive " & d.DriveLetter & " is not ready."
      Exit Sub
   End If
   AddNodes Node, fn
   AddFiles fn
   Node.Expanded = True
   Node.EnsureVisible

ElseIf Node.Expanded Then
   DeleteNodes Node

End If

End Sub
```

The first step is to determine the selected node. Then if the node is the "My Computer" node, I exit the routine because I don't want to expand or contract the list of drives displayed.

Next, I determine if I need to add more nodes to expand the tree. I check the `Node.Expanded` and `Node.Children` properties to make sure that the node is not expanded and that the node doesn't have any children.

Before I add any new nodes, I need to verify that the drive containing the files is ready. If it is, then I simply call the `AddNodes` routine (shown in Listing 7.1), followed by the `AddFiles` routine that will add the individual files to the ListView control (in Listing 7.4, coming up soon).

The last two steps I perform are to expand the tree to show the children of this node, using the `Node.Expanded` method, and to make sure that the first of the newly displayed nodes is visible in the tree view's display area, using the `Node.Ensure-Visible` method.

Collapsing the tree is very simple. I merely delete all of the child nodes of the currently selected node using the `DeleteNodes` subroutine. This ensures that the next time I need the data, the program will load only the most current data available.

Of course, all of this work is not strictly necessary. I could have loaded the contents of the entire file system all at once. However, you need to consider what problems that will cause. A typical C: drive on your system may contain as many as 20,000 files, depending on what products you have installed. My C: drive, for instance, contains more than 13,000 files related to Windows, Office 97, and Visual Studio, plus a few other smaller utilities. All of my data files reside on my D: drive, which contains another 3,000 files. It would take a long time to load all 16,000 files into the TreeView control at initialization.

TIP

Loading later leads to less labor: I prefer to load information into a TreeView control only when I need to. This not only ensures that the most recent copy of the data is loaded, but also results in a much shorter delay when initially loading the data (of course, users will experience some delays when the additional information is loaded as it's needed). For example, I once used a TreeView control in a Visual Basic newsreader program to display all of the available newsgroups. I got acceptable performance when I tried to load a few hundred groups, but when I tried to load all 10,000 plus newsgroups, my system screeched to a halt. It was only when I loaded the newsgroups as I needed them that I got an acceptable level of performance.

Listing Items with the ListView Control

The ListView control allows you to display information in four different ways: Icon, Small Icon, List, and Report. These four different views are the same four ways you can display information in My Computer (although the Report view is known as the Details view). Of the four views, the Report view is my favorite. It provides an easy way to display tabular data, which is difficult to do with any other controls (except the Grid controls).

Key to using the ListView control is building a collection of ListItem objects. Each object represents the information displayed as a single entry in the control. For the most part, ListItem objects are similar to Node objects. Both contain a Key value, which uniquely identifies the object in the collection, and a Text value, which is shown on the control's display area. However, there are two primary differences between a ListItem object and a Node object:

- Unlike the Node object, the ListItem object is flat, so there is no need to store any information about a particular item's relationship to the other items in the collection.

- A ListItem object can contain additional information related to the main object. For example, a ListItem object might contain a person's name, as well as additional information about that person such as birth date, address, education, and so on.

Using Column Headers

When you use the Report view, you need to define the columns that you want to appear. While you can define them in your program, you may find it easier to define them at design time. To do this, right-click on the control and select properties or choose custom properties from the Properties dialog box.

In the Column Headers tab of the Property Pages dialog box, shown in Figure 7.2, you can insert a column for each item you plan to display in the control. Note that you need to define a Text column, plus one column header for each subitem you wish to use.

FIGURE 7.2:

The Column Headers tab
of the ListView Property
Pages dialog box

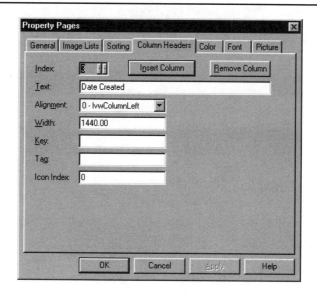

Adding New Items to the ListView Control

Listing 7.4 shows the subroutine that I call to load information about the files contained in a particular folder into the ListView control.

Listing 7.4:   **AddFiles Routine in File Viewer**

```
Private Sub AddFiles(fn As Folder)

Dim fi As File
Dim l As ListItem
Dim t As String
Dim i As Long

On Error Resume Next

Text1.Text = n.Key

i = 0
ListView1.ListItems.Clear
For Each fi In fn.Files
   Set l = ListView1.ListItems.Add(, fi.Path, fi.Name, "file", "file")
```

```
t = FormatNumber(fi.Size, 0)
l.SubItems(1) = Space(14 - Len(t)) & t
l.SubItems(2) = Format(fi.DateCreated)
l.SubItems(3) = Format(fi.DateLastModified)
l.SubItems(4) = Format(fi.DateLastAccessed)
l.SubItems(5) = Format(fi.Type)
If fi.Attributes Mod 2 = 1 Then
    l.SubItems(6) = "Read only"
End If
If Int(fi.Attributes / 2) Mod 2 = 1 Then
    l.SubItems(7) = "Hidden"
End If
If Int(fi.Attributes / 4) Mod 2 = 1 Then
    l.SubItems(8) = "System"
End If
If Int(fi.Attributes / 32) Mod 2 = 1 Then
    l.SubItems(9) = "Archive"
End If
If Int(fi.Attributes / 64) Mod 2 = 1 Then
    l.SubItems(10) = "Alias"
End If
If Int(fi.Attributes / 128) Mod 2 = 1 Then
    l.SubItems(11) = "Compressed"
End If
i = i + 1
If i Mod 25 = 0 Then
    DoEvents
End If

Next fi

End Sub
```

I begin by saving the name of the folder into the Text1 textbox. Then I clear the current collection of ListItems using the ListItems collection Clear method. Next, I loop through each file in the folder by using the For Each statement.

For a particular file, I begin by creating a new ListItem object by using the ListItems.Add method. Since I don't care about the order of these objects (at least for now), I can omit the Index parameter. The Key value must be unique, so I use the complete path name of the file. Then I use the filename for the Text parameter. Finally, I list the names used for normal-sized icons and small icons. Because I don't have ready access to the icons that correspond to the file's type, I'm going to cheat by using just one type of icon for all files.

TIP

When big is the same as small: When using the ListView control, you need to specify two ImageList references containing the icons to be displayed (remember that an ImageList can contain only one size of icons), one for large icons and one for small icons. Since each `ListItem` entry needs an icon reference in both Image-List controls, using the same name for the icon in each ImageList simplifies your programming.

Once I have created the new `ListItem`, I can now put information in the rest of the `SubItems`. This is a relatively straightforward process for text information—all I need to do is to assign a string value to the specific `SubItem`. However, adding numeric information presents a significantly different problem.

Numeric information is stored as a string value in the `ListItem`. While this might be okay under most circumstances, it does cause a problem when you need to sort data. A string containing the value 2 will sort after a string containing 1,234,567,890, and unless you're in Congress, you'll recognize that 2 is smaller than 1,234,567,890.

To compensate for this problem, I decided to right-justify the number inside the string. The easiest way to do this is to format the number into a temporary string and then pad it with enough spaces to the front of the string to make it a constant length. In this case, I wanted to create a string in which the length of the spaces and the formatted number total 14 characters, so I used the `Space` function to create a string of 14 minus the length of the formatted string.

The rest of this routine is devoted to filling out the rest of the `SubItems`. The only trick (if you can call it that) is that I put each file attribute in a separate field. This allows me to sort the data on a particular attribute, and all files with that attribute will be grouped together. Note that I stop to execute the `DoEvents` function every 25 files. This value is a compromise between performance, screen flicker, and Windows responsiveness. You may want to try a few different values and see how it impacts your system.

Sorting the Collection

In the previous section, I described how I prepared the subitems so that they could be easily sorted. I'm going to use the SortKey, SortOrder, and Sorted properties to do the real work.

To sort a column, all you need to do is to set Sorted to False, assign the column number you want to sort to the SortKey property, and then set Sorted to True. You can also specify the sort order by setting the SortOrder property to 0 for ascending and 1 for descending.

The easiest way to indicate which column to sort is by using the ColumnClick event. This event occurs whenever a user clicks on a column header. It passes the ColumnHeader object corresponding to the button the user pressed as a parameter. From the ColumnHeader object, you can determine the SortKey for the column you wish to sort by subtracting one from ColumnHeader.Index.

The routine shown in Listing 7.5 not only sorts the contents of the ListView control based on the column clicked by the user, but sorts in the opposite direction if the contents of the control were already sorted on that column.

Listing 7.5:   **ListView1_ColumnClick Event in File Viewer**

```
Private Sub ListView1_ColumnClick(ByVal ColumnHeader As _
    ComctlLib.ColumnHeader)

If ListView1.SortKey = ColumnHeader.Index - 1 Then
   ListView1.Sorted = False
   ListView1.SortOrder = (ListView1.SortOrder + 1) Mod 2
   ListView1.Sorted = True

Else
   ListView1.Sorted = False
   ListView1.SortKey = ColumnHeader.Index - 1
   ListView1.SortOrder = lvwAscending
   ListView1.Sorted = True
End If

End Sub
```

I start the routine by seeing if the current value of SortKey is the same as the column the user clicked. If it is, then I choose the opposite sort order by adding one to the current SortOrder value and then returning the Mod 2 value. Otherwise, I set SortKey to the column the user clicked and then set the default Sort-Order to ascending. In both cases, I disable sorting before I make any changes, and then enable it again after the changes are complete.

Responding to ListView Events

After you've added the ListView control to your form and written the code to initialize it, you need to handle the event when the user selects an item. You have a number of choices for events for this purpose: the Click event, the DblClick event, and the ItemClick event. The Click and DblClick events are the standard events associated with most Visual Basic controls. However, the ItemClick event is unique to the ListView control.

The ItemClick event returns a single value: a ListItem object containing a reference to the item that the user clicked. From there, you can process the item as you desire. The ItemClick event occurs before either the Click or DblClick events. Note that Click and DblClick events will still occur if the user clicks on a part of the ListView control where no items are displayed.

Listing 7.6 shows how I return the name of a file that the user clicked to the program using the FileSelect control.

Listing 7.6:   **ListView1_ItemClick Event in File Viewer**

```
Private Sub ListView1_ItemClick(ByVal Item As ComctlLib.ListItem)

Raise FileSelect(Item.Key)

End Sub
```

TIP

Selecting full rows in ListView: One problem with the version of the ListView control included with Visual Basic 5 was that the user had to click on the text or the icon to select a row in Report view. Often users (myself included) would click somewhere to the right of the text and consequently not select the desired item. Now you can set the FullSelect property to True, which will allow the user to click anywhere on the row to select the item.

Using MSFlexGrid and MSChart

Two of most complex controls in Visual Basic are the MSFlexGrid and MSChart controls. The MSFlexGrid control gives you the raw capabilities to build a spreadsheet. The MSChart control allows you to build your own two- and three-dimensional charts. Using these controls together to build a general-purpose spreadsheet tool like Microsoft Excel is an obvious choice, so that's the program I wrote. I call this program Charter, since its primary purpose is to draw charts. Figure 7.3 shows the MSFlexGrid view, and Figure 7.4 shows the MSChart view.

FIGURE 7.3:

Using the MSFlexGrid control to manipulate spreadsheet data

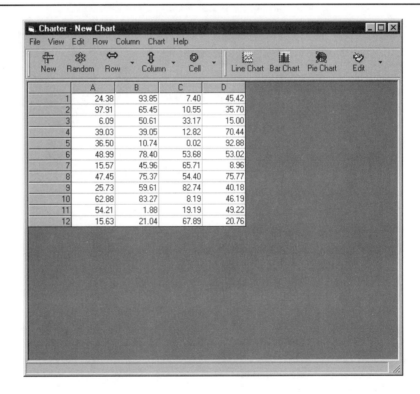

FIGURE 7.4:

Using the MSChart control to
display graphical information

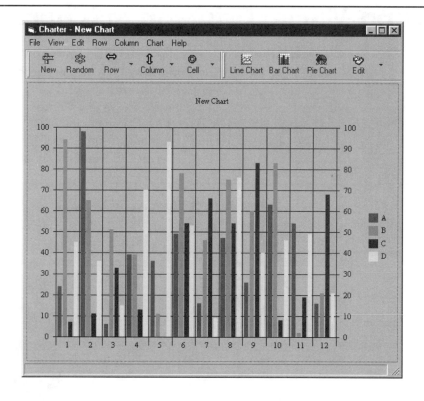

MSFlexGrid + MSChart < Excel: Neither of these tools is a replacement for
Excel. The best way to think of these controls is as a lightweight version of Excel,
much like Access is a lightweight database when compared to SQL Server. One big
difference is that Excel can perform calculations while MSFlexGrid can't. (Of
course with a little work, anything can be changed, and we'll take a look at over-
coming this limitation in Chapter 17.) If you really need to build complex charts or
perform data analysis, you can always embed an Excel spreadsheet or chart into
your program.

Displaying Data with the MSFlexGrid Control

The MSFlexGrid control displays a set of rows and columns on your form.
Data can be loaded into individual cells by using the TextMatrix property and

supplying the appropriate row and column coordinates. You can also store a picture in a cell by assigning a picture to the CellPicture property.

Microsoft ships two other grid controls with Visual Basic 6: MSHFlexGrid and DataGrid. The primary difference between the MSHFlexGrid control and the MSFlexGrid control is that the MSHFlexGrid control has the ability to display hierarchical information using merged cells and multiple views. The DataGrid control is tightly coupled to a database and can update data directly in the database, but the MSFlexGrid and MSHFlexGrid controls cannot.

TIP

Developing database applications: One of the most useful tools to have while debugging a database program is the DataGrid control. With a minimal amount of programming (just put DataGrid, TextBox, and CommandButton controls on a blank form), you can enter a query, refresh the data, scroll through the results, and even update them if necessary. I've found it useful to even leave it in production applications (though I usually prevent users from updating the database), because it provides a quick way to view tabular data.

Creating a Basic MSFlexGrid

Adding the MSFlexGrid control to your application is almost as simple as putting the control on your form, setting a few properties, and starting to use it. That's exactly what I do in Listing 7.7.

Listing 7.7:   **NewChart Routine in Charter**

```
Private Sub NewChart()

Dim i As Integer
Dim j As Integer

MSFlexGrid1.Cols = 5
MSFlexGrid1.Rows = 13
MSFlexGrid1.FixedCols = 1
MSFlexGrid1.FixedRows = 1
MSFlexGrid1.AllowUserResizing = flexResizeBoth

For i = 1 To MSFlexGrid1.Cols - 1
   MSFlexGrid1.Col = i
   For j = 1 To MSFlexGrid1.Rows - 1
```

```
        MSFlexGrid1.Row = j
        MSFlexGrid1.CellAlignment = flexAlignGeneral
        MSFlexGrid1.Text = ""
    Next j
Next i

MSFlexGrid1.Row = 0
For i = 1 To MSFlexGrid1.Cols - 1
    MSFlexGrid1.Col = i
    MSFlexGrid1.CellAlignment = flexAlignCenterCenter
    MSFlexGrid1.Text = Chr(Asc("@") + i)
Next i

MSFlexGrid1.Col = 0
For i = 1 To MSFlexGrid1.Rows - 1
    MSFlexGrid1.Row = i
    MSFlexGrid1.CellAlignment = flexAlignRightCenter
    MSFlexGrid1.Text = FormatNumber(i, 0)
Next i

ChartStartCol = 1
ChartStartRow = 1
ChartStopCol = MSFlexGrid1.Cols - 1
ChartStopRow = MSFlexGrid1.Rows - 1

SetChartType VtChChartType2dLine

CommonDialog1.FileName = ""

Form1.Caption = "Charter - New Chart"
MSChart1.TitleText = "New Chart"

End Sub
```

I set the number of columns and rows to 5 and 13, respectively, with the first column and row fixed. In this case, *fixed* implies that the first row and column will always be displayed after the user has scrolled rows and/or columns that follow them off the display. This makes the fixed column and row an ideal location for column headers and row headers.

Next, I initialize the non-fixed part of the grid to empty strings. This merely ensures that any previous data in the grid has been erased. I also set the alignment to the flexGeneralAlign. Then I initialize the column headers to the letters *A* through whatever. Note that after 26 columns, I'll have some pretty strange letters. This could be easily fixed by adding a second character starting with the twenty-seventh column à la Excel, but since I doubt that anyone would want that many columns in this program, I'm willing to live with the limitation.

I use a similar loop to set the header values for each row. Since I'm using an Integer for the loop counter (the Cols property is a Long), my program lets you have up to 32,767 rows before it crashes, but somehow I doubt that you would want that many. The MSFlexGrid control is really only limited by available memory.

To wrap up this routine, I set the coordinates of the data that will be used for charting to cover the entire table. (I'll talk about these values and what they mean a little later in this chapter.) Next, I call a subroutine called SetChartType, which I use to set the default chart type for this grid. Then I set the default filename associated with this grid to an empty string. Finally, I set the chart's title to "New Chart" and I also use the chart's title in the form's caption.

Loading Data into MSFlexGrid

The MSFlexGrid control has a couple of different properties that can be used to access the data stored in the grid. My favorite way is to use the TextMatrix property, which takes two parameters: row and column. Thus, to me, the grid's storage area looks just like a normal two-dimensional array. The code to do this is shown in Listing 7.8.

Listing 7.8:   **StuffGrid Routine in Charter**

```
Private Sub StuffGrid()

Dim i As Integer
Dim j As Integer

For i = 1 To MSFlexGrid1.Cols - 1
   For j = 1 To MSFlexGrid1.Rows - 1
      MSFlexGrid1.TextMatrix(j, i) = FormatNumber(Rnd * 100, 2)
   Next j
Next i

End Sub
```

There is an alternate method you should be aware of. By specifying values for the Col and Row properties, you can assign a value to the Text property that will be saved in the cell. This method also works for the Picture property, which you would use if you want to display an image in a particular cell. This technique is shown in Listing 7.9.

Listing 7.9:   **StuffGridA Routine in Charter**

```
Private Sub StuffGridA()

Dim i As Integer
Dim j As Integer

For i = 1 To MSFlexGrid1.Cols - 1
   MSFlexGrid1.Col = i
   For j = 1 To MSFlexGrid1.Rows - 1
      MSFlexGrid1.Row = j
      MSFlexGrid1.Text = FormatNumber(Rnd * 100, 2)
   Next j
Next i

End Sub
```

Which method is better? Without detailed measurements, it would be difficult to tell. My guess is that the approach in Listing 7.9 would be slightly slower. This is because it accesses the control's properties more frequently in order to set the current row and column, plus it needs to perform the arithmetic to compute the next location at the end of each loop. However, for all practical purposes, unless you have a very large grid, the two methods are interchangeable. If you have a very large grid and you are having performance problems through this part of the code, I suggest trying both methods to see how each affects your application.

Using the Keyboard to Move Around the Grid

One of the MSFlexGrid control's weak spots is its support of the keyboard. Essentially, there isn't any. So, I added some event handling to provide some of the basic functions necessary to move around the grid and enter data into a cell.

While I guess I could have handled all of this code in only one event, I chose to separate the code that actually stuffs characters into a cell from the code that manages the nonprinting ASCII characters. This is because it was easier to convert keystrokes into ASCII characters in the KeyPress event, and it was easier to deal with the individual keys for movement in the KeyUp event.

Handling the KeyPress Event

In Listing 7.10, all I really do is verify that I have a printing ASCII character and append it to the contents of the Text property. The movement process will ensure that the Text property points to the current cell. This is done automatically when the user selects a different cell by moving the mouse pointer or by the KeyUp event when the user moves to a different cell using the cursor keys.

> **NOTE**   **Two main groups of ASCII characters:** There are ASCII characters that can be printed or displayed and those that can't. I often refer to the first group as *printing* or *printable* characters (an old term I learned back when I wrote BASIC programs on a Teletype). The second group is made up of nonprinting, or control, characters that are used to perform specific functions, such as tab or backspace, but in themselves do not result in another character being displayed on the screen. The second group has values ranging from 0 to 31 decimal (1F hex). The first group has values ranging from 32 decimal (20 hex) to 127 decimal (7F hex).

Listing 7.10:   **MSFlexGrid1_KeyPress Event in Charter**

```
Private Sub MSFlexGrid1_KeyPress(KeyAscii As Integer)

If KeyAscii >= 32 And KeyAscii <= 127 Then
   MSFlexGrid1.Text = MSFlexGrid1.Text & Chr(KeyAscii)
End If

End Sub
```

Handling the KeyUp Event

The KeyUp event is a little more complex, as you can see in Listing 7.11. Essentially, I select each key I want to handle and process it separately. In the case of the cursor keys, I move the current cell indicated by Row and Col in the direction indicated by the key. In order to prevent the cursor from moving beyond the edge of the grid, I use the IIf function to select either the next cell or the appropriate edge. This allows me to handle this situation in a single line (okay two lines, since I had to format the program listing to fit on the page) rather than taking several lines for a regular If statement.

Listing 7.11:   MSFlexGrid1_KeyUp Event in Charter

```
Private Sub MSFlexGrid1_KeyUp(KeyCode As Integer, Shift As Integer)

If KeyCode = vbKeyDown Then
   MSFlexGrid1.Row = IIf(MSFlexGrid1.Row + 1 > MSFlexGrid1.Rows, _
      MSFlexGrid1.Rows, MSFlexGrid1.Row + 1)

ElseIf KeyCode = vbKeyUp Then
   MSFlexGrid1.Row = IIf(MSFlexGrid1.Row - 1 > 1, _
      1, MSFlexGrid1.Row - 1)

ElseIf KeyCode = vbKeyLeft Then
   MSFlexGrid1.Col = IIf(MSFlexGrid1.Col - 1 > 1, _
      1, MSFlexGrid1.Cols + 1)

ElseIf KeyCode = vbKeyRight Then
   MSFlexGrid1.Col = IIf(MSFlexGrid1.Col + 1 > MSFlexGrid1.Cols, _
      MSFlexGrid1.Cols, MSFlexGrid1.Cols + 1)

ElseIf KeyCode = vbKeyDelete Then
   MSFlexGrid1.Text = ""

ElseIf KeyCode = vbKeyBack Then
   If Len(MSFlexGrid1.Text) > 0 Then
      MSFlexGrid1.Text = Left(MSFlexGrid1.Text, _
         Len(MSFlexGrid1.Text) - 1)
   End If
End If

End Sub
```

Besides the cursor keys, I handle the Delete key and the Backspace key. If the user hits the Delete key, I set the value of the Text property to an empty string. If the user presses the Backspace key, I remove the last character (if there is one) from the Text property.

This is one routine that could be expanded to handle more keyboard input. It would be nice to include keys like Ctrl+Home to move to the beginning of a line and PageUp and PageDown to scroll through the grid more quickly. It would also be nice to support the F2 key to allow using the cursor keys to move around inside the cell while editing its contents.

Selecting Data

Selecting data in the MSFlexGrid control is done by pressing the left mouse button and holding it while moving the cursor over the desired range of cells. This range can be described by the location of two cells: the first cell that was selected and the cell at the diagonal corner of the highlighted rectangle. The location of the first cell is found by using the Col and Row properties of the MSFlexGrid control. The second cell is found by using the ColSel and RowSel properties.

Listing 7.12 shows a code fragment that sets the boundaries for the data that will be sent to the MSChart control. I assume that the user selected an area on the screen, clicked the Cell button on the toolbar, and chose Select Chart Area. If the user has not made this selection, the ColSel and RowSel properties will have the same value as the Col and Row properties. While not desirable, it will make a rather interesting pie chart.

Listing 7.12:   **Toolbar1_ButtonMenuClick Event in Charter**

```
ElseIf ButtonMenu.Parent.Key = "Cell" Then
    If ButtonMenu.Key = "Select Chart Area" Then
        ChartStartCol = IIf(MSFlexGrid1.Col <= MSFlexGrid1.ColSel, _
            MSFlexGrid1.Col, MSFlexGrid1.ColSel)
        ChartStopCol = IIf(MSFlexGrid1.Col > MSFlexGrid1.ColSel, _
            MSFlexGrid1.Col, MSFlexGrid1.ColSel)
        ChartStartRow = IIf(MSFlexGrid1.Row <= MSFlexGrid1.ColSel, _
            MSFlexGrid1.Row, MSFlexGrid1.RowSel)
        ChartStopRow = IIf(MSFlexGrid1.Row > MSFlexGrid1.Col, _
            MSFlexGrid1.Row, MSFlexGrid1.RowSel)

    End If
End If
```

In order to ensure that ChartStopCol is never less than ChartStartCol, I use the IIf function to determine the smaller value, assign that to the ChartStartCol, and repeat the process to determine the larger value for ChartStopCol. Then I repeat both calculations to find the appropriate values for the ChartStartRow and ChartStopRow variables.

Changing the Alignment of Data in the Grid

Building on the same logic I used for selecting data, I added a feature that will allow the user to set the alignment of a particular cell or range of cells. This code is shown in Listing 7.13.

Listing 7.13: **AlignCell Routine in Charter**

```
Private Sub AlignCell(a As Integer)

Dim c As Integer
Dim i As Integer
Dim j As Integer
Dim lc As Integer
Dim lr As Integer
Dim r As Integer
Dim uc As Integer
Dim ur As Integer

lc = IIf(MSFlexGrid1.Col <= MSFlexGrid1.ColSel, _
   MSFlexGrid1.Col, MSFlexGrid1.ColSel)
uc = IIf(MSFlexGrid1.Col > MSFlexGrid1.ColSel, _
   MSFlexGrid1.Col, MSFlexGrid1.ColSel)
lr = IIf(MSFlexGrid1.Row <= MSFlexGrid1.RowSel, _
   MSFlexGrid1.Row, MSFlexGrid1.RowSel)
ur = IIf(MSFlexGrid1.Row > MSFlexGrid1.RowSel, _
   MSFlexGrid1.Row, MSFlexGrid1.RowSel)
c = MSFlexGrid1.Col
r = MSFlexGrid1.Row

For i = lc To uc
   MSFlexGrid1.Col = i
   For j = lr To ur
      MSFlexGrid1.Row = j
      MSFlexGrid1.CellAlignment = a
   Next j
Next i
```

```
MSFlexGrid1.Col = c
MSFlexGrid1.Row = r

End Sub
```

Looking at Listing 7.13, you can see that I start this routine by declaring a lot of local variables. These variables will be used to hold things like the current row and column (r and c), the bounds of the selected area (lc, lr, uc, and ur), and a couple of loop counters (i and j).

Then I initialize these variables holding the selected area using the IIf function as I did in Listing 7.12. I also save the current values of Row and Col, since these values will need to change to point to the cell where I will set the CellAlignment property.

Next, I set up a nested loop to go through all of the cells in the selected area. Inside the loop, I set the Row and Col properties to point to the desired cell, and then set the CellAlignment property to the desired value. After the loop is finished, I reset the original values for Row and Col and exit the subroutine.

You can follow this same procedure to change other properties, such as the cell's font information, the cell's text style, or the picture alignment.

TIP

Storing other useful information for your grid: Since the MSFlexGrid control really only stores and displays string information, you may want to consider creating a table of cells containing your own information. This information could be things like the type of information stored in the cell (Number, Date, String, and so on), formatting information (Short Date, General Number, and so on), or any other information you may find useful. You can use the column and row header cells to store default values for a particular column or row, and you can use the cell at location 0,0 to store global table information.

Saving MSFlexGrid Data to a Disk File

Saving data from the MSFlexGrid control is a relatively straightforward task, depending on which format you wish to use. In this case, I choose to build my own file format called the Junk file format, or .JNK. It consists of some header information, followed by the contents of each individual cell. A character whose

ASCII value is 255 separates each major piece of information I write to the file. Inside that piece of information, I separate individual fields by using a character with the ASCII value 254.

I could have used a more common file format, such as the Comma Separated Value (CSV) format, but my .JNK format lets me put additional information into the file that I couldn't save with a standard format. It also has the side effect of being easier to parse when loading the file back into memory.

The subroutine in Listing 7.14 shows how I save the information from the grid to disk. This subroutine takes a single parameter called dialog. If dialog is True, then I force the user to go through a Save As dialog box to specify a filename. If dialog is False, then I simply save the file using the current filename, unless the current filename is an empty string. In that case, I force the user to go through the Save As dialog box again.

Listing 7.14:   **SaveChart Routine in Charter**

```
Private Sub SaveChart(dialog As Boolean)

Dim i As Integer
Dim j As Integer
Dim t As TextStream

On Error Resume Next

If dialog Or Len(CommonDialog1.FileName) = 0 Then
   CommonDialog1.CancelError = True
   CommonDialog1.Filter = "All Files (*.*)" & _
      "|*.*|Charter Documents (*.jnk)|*.jnk"
   CommonDialog1.FilterIndex = 2
   CommonDialog1.Flags = cdlOFNExplorer + cdlOFNOverwritePrompt

   CommonDialog1.ShowSave
   If Err.Number > 0 Then
      Exit Sub
   End If

End If

Err.Clear
Set t = fso.CreateTextFile(CommonDialog1.FileName, True)
```

```
If Err.Number > 0 Then
   MsgBox "Unable to create the file."
   Exit Sub
End If

t.Write "Charter Junk File" & Chr(254)
t.Write MSChart1.TitleText & Chr(254)
t.Write FormatNumber(MSFlexGrid1.Cols, 0) & Chr(254)
t.Write FormatNumber(MSFlexGrid1.Rows, 0) & Chr(254)
t.Write FormatNumber(ChartStartCol, 0) & Chr(254)
t.Write FormatNumber(ChartStopCol, 0) & Chr(254)
t.Write FormatNumber(ChartStartRow, 0) & Chr(254)
t.Write FormatNumber(ChartStopRow, 0) & Chr(255)

For i = 0 To MSFlexGrid1.Cols - 1
   MSFlexGrid1.Col = i
   For j = 0 To MSFlexGrid1.Rows - 1
      MSFlexGrid1.Row = j
      t.Write FormatNumber(MSFlexGrid1.CellAlignment, 0) & Chr(254)
      t.Write MSFlexGrid1.Text & Chr(255)
   Next j
   DoEvents
Next i

t.Close

Form1.Caption = "Charter - " & CommonDialog1.FileTitle

End Sub
```

Working my way through the code, I begin by deciding whether I need to display the Save As dialog box. If I do, then I prepare the CommonDialog control to display a list of all files and .JNK files. I set the CancelError property to True so that I can tell if the user clicks the Cancel button while the dialog box is displayed. I also ask the user if it is okay to overwrite an existing file by setting the Flag property to cdlOFNOverwritePrompt before invoking the ShowSave method.

After the ShowSave method completes, I check the Err object to see if the user hit the Cancel button. If so, I simply abort the process and exit the subroutine. If the user didn't click the Cancel button, I assume that I have a valid filename in `CommonDialog1.FileName` that I can use to create a text stream object.

Once I have the text stream object, I use it to write out the information associated with the chart. First, I write a header line indicating that this is a genuine Charter Junk file. Then I write out the chart title, the number of columns, the number of rows in the grid, plus the charting coordinates.

Then I write out the information for each cell. In this case, I have only two pieces of information: the cell's alignment and the cell's contents. An enhanced version of this program could have additional information, such as a format string for each cell or an equation, as output.

Comma Separated Value File Format Rules

The CSV format is probably the most widely accepted format to import and export data to and from a spreadsheet program. The rules for building a CSV file are relatively simple:

- Each row of the spreadsheet is a single line of text followed by a carriage return/line feed pair (`vbCrLF`).

- Each line of text contains a list of cell values separated by commas.

- If the cell value is numeric, then the value is listed with the decimal point in the appropriate place.

- If the cell value contains text, then the text value must be enclosed in double quotation marks ("). Any double quotations marks contained inside the text value must be prefixed by a second double quotation mark. Thus, the string Clark "Superman" Kent would be appear in a CSV file as "Clark ""Superman"" Kent".

Loading MSFlexGrid Data from a Disk File

Writing the data to a disk file is usually much easier than reading it back in. However, the new `Split` function will prove to be very useful in this situation. Listing 7.15 shows how I handled loading data from a file.

Listing 7.15:   OpenChart Routine in Charter

```
Private Sub OpenChart()

Dim i As Integer
Dim j As Integer
Dim k As Integer
Dim t As TextStream
Dim x() As String
Dim y() As String
Dim z As String

On Error Resume Next

CommonDialog1.CancelError = True
CommonDialog1.Filter = "All Files (*.*)" & _
    "|*.*|Charter Documents (*.jnk)|*.jnk"
CommonDialog1.FilterIndex = 2
CommonDialog1.Flags = cdlOFNExplorer
CommonDialog1.ShowOpen
If Err.Number > 0 Then
    Exit Sub
End If

Err.Clear
Set t = fso.OpenTextFile(CommonDialog1.FileName)
If Err.Number > 0 Then
    MsgBox "Unable to open the file."
    Exit Sub
End If

z = t.ReadAll
y = Split(z, Chr(255))
x = Split(y(0), Chr(254))

If x(0) <> "Charter Junk File" Then
    MsgBox "Invalid file type"
    Exit Sub
End If

MSChart1.TitleText = x(1)
```

```
MSFlexGrid1.Cols = CInt(x(2))
MSFlexGrid1.Rows = CInt(x(3))
ChartStartCol = CInt(x(4))
ChartStopCol = CInt(x(5))
ChartStartRow = CInt(x(6))
ChartStopRow = CInt(x(7))

k = 1
For i = 0 To MSFlexGrid1.Cols - 1
   MSFlexGrid1.Col = i
   For j = 0 To MSFlexGrid1.Rows - 1
      MSFlexGrid1.Row = j
      x = Split(y(k), Chr(254))
      MSFlexGrid1.CellAlignment = CInt(x(0))
      MSFlexGrid1.Text = x(1)
      k = k + 1
   Next j
Next i

t.Close

Form1.Caption = "Charter - " & CommonDialog1.FileTitle

End Sub
```

You can see that I used the CommonDialog control to find the file the user wants to open. With a valid filename, I create a text stream object and read it into the variable z in one big chunk.

Next, I parse the file into the array y using the Split function with Chr(255) as the separator value. The first chunk of data, y(0), holds the header information. The next chunk of data, y(1) holds the data for the first cell, up to the last element of y, which holds the data for the last cell in the spreadsheet. Then I parse each element of y using the Split function again, but this time I use Chr(254) as the separator value. From here, it is very easy to load the data into the various elements of this program in the same order that they were originally written.

One test that I make after I parse the first record of the file is to verify that this is a valid Charter Junk file. Once I see this field, I assume that the file format is compatible with the program. Therefore, I can safely bypass some checks that I would normally perform, such as making sure that the values for the number of rows and column are numeric before I convert them.

Now I know this is not the most efficient way to load a file, but for this project, it's appropriate. After all, we are dealing with data files that might get as large as two or three kilobytes, not files that can approach a megabyte or more. Of course, the same techniques I used here would also work for bigger files, as explained next.

Loading Bigger Files   To handle loading large files, I would create a function that would return the next chunk of data that ends in a Chr(255). This function would read 4KB chunks of data from the file and hold it in a static variable—let's call it buffer. I would also have a static variable that would point to the last location processed in the static variable—let's call this variable pointer.

Initially, buffer would be empty and pointer would point to the end of buffer. On the first call, the function would recognize that it needs more data, so it would read the first chunk of data from the file into buffer and reset pointer to the beginning of buffer. I would probably read 4096 bytes of data, though I might be tempted to read a full cluster if I were dealing with relatively large file sizes.

Once I had data in the buffer, I would scan through it, starting at the position indicated by pointer, looking for the first Chr(255) value I could find, using the InStr function. If I found it, then I would extract the information from the start of the buffer to the location of the Chr(255) and save it to be returned as the value of the function. Then I would adjust pointer to point to the location just past the Chr(255) and return. If I didn't find the Chr(255) in the current value of buffer, I would append it to a temporary variable and repeat the process until I found a Chr(255) or an end-of-file condition.

Of course, if I had to deal with even larger files, I would create my own ActiveX control so I could manage multiple buffers and perform asynchronous reads. That way, I could be scanning one buffer at the same time I'm loading data into another buffer. But debugging that kind of program will drive anyone nuts, so that's why I decided to stick with the relatively simple routine I used here.

Displaying Charts with the MSChart Control

The MSChart control gives you the ability to include a dozen different types of charts into your application. This is most useful when you are dealing with complex data that varies over time, such as financial or other quantifiable data.

Like its cousin, the MSFlexGrid control, the MSChart control is very powerful, but it is missing a number of features—most notably, those needed to deal with the user interface. With a lot of work and patience, you can handle the missing features yourself and take advantage of the control's many functions. (Discussing all of these functions would take up most of this book, but the default values are more than acceptable for most applications.)

Charting the Course of Your Data

When choosing data for your chart, it is important to think about the values that you wish to plot. You should look for values that are close in size, but not too close. If you have data points that are too close, you won't be able to see any difference in the values. However, if they are too far apart, any information they may contain relative to each other will be lost. I suggest that you try to scale the data so that it occupies at least one half of the chart.

I also suggest that you use no more than four series of data points with no more than a dozen data points in each series. Pie charts should have only one series of data with no more than five or six slices. Smaller charts should have fewer data points; larger charts can have more. Putting too much information in a single chart makes a chart difficult to read; even worse, it can lead users to making bad decisions because they misunderstood the information.

Getting Information from MSFlexGrid

While it would be nice if both the MSChart and MSFlexGrid controls used a common storage object, it's not really necessary. A true spreadsheet will usually have a lot of additional information that doesn't need to be passed to the charting tool. In this case, I'm just going to copy the selected cells to the chart tool.

In Listing 7.16, I begin copying by disabling the Repaint property on the chart. Then I set the number of columns and rows of data in the chart based on the ChartStartCol, ChartStartRow, ChartStopCol, and ChartStopRow values.

WARNING   **Don't refresh on every change:** Repainting a chart is an expensive operation. Unless you disable repainting, the user will see a lot of screen flicker as each change is displayed. Also, the process will take a lot longer to complete, since repainting a graphic image can take a fair amount of system resources.

Listing 7.16: **ShowChart Routine in Charter**

```
Private Sub ShowChart()

Dim i As Integer
Dim j As Integer

MSChart1.Repaint = False

MSChart1.ColumnCount = ChartStopCol - ChartStartCol + 1
MSChart1.RowCount = ChartStopRow - ChartStartRow + 1

For i = ChartStartCol + 1 To ChartStopCol
   For j = ChartStartRow + 1 To ChartStopRow
      MSChart1.Column = i - ChartStartCol + 1
      MSChart1.Row = j - ChartStartRow + 1
      MSFlexGrid1.Col = i
      MSFlexGrid1.Row = j
      If IsNumeric(MSFlexGrid1.Text) Then
         MSChart1.Data = CInt(MSFlexGrid1.Text)
      Else
         MSChart1.Data = 0
      End If
   Next j
Next i

For i = ChartStartCol To ChartStopCol
   MSChart1.Column = i - ChartStartCol + 1
   MSChart1.ColumnLabel = MSFlexGrid1.TextMatrix(0, i)
Next i

For i = ChartStartRow To ChartStopRow
   MSChart1.Row = i - ChartStartRow + 1
   MSChart1.RowLabel = MSFlexGrid1.TextMatrix(i, 0)
Next i

MSChart1.Repaint = True

End Sub
```

In the heart of the routine, I set up a nested loop to copy the data values one cell at a time. Note that the first row and column of the data grid are used for the row and column headers. I select the current cell in the chart control by setting values for the Column and Row properties before setting the Col and Row properties for the MSFlexGrid control. Note that I adjust the values for the MSChart control to ensure that they start with 1.

For each value in the chart, I check to see if the spreadsheet's cell contains a numeric value. If I find one, then I convert it to an integer and save it into the chart's Data property. Otherwise, I stuff a zero into the chart's Data property. You might wonder why the chart's Data property is an integer. What about the loss of accuracy when the data is converted to an integer? When you generate a chart, the images you see can only be so accurate. You will probably not be able to tell the difference between values with two digits of accuracy or those with three or more.

After I load the data, I copy the row and column headers from the grid to the appropriate label properties on the MSChart control, then I set the Repaint property to True, which will force the new chart to be drawn on the screen.

Note that actual data is stored in the DataGrid object, which is referenced by using the MSChart control's DataGrid property.

> **NOTE**
>
> **The DataGrid control versus the DataGrid object:** You will notice a reference to a DataGrid object in the MSChart control. This object is not the same as the DataGrid control. The DataGrid object holds information about the data displayed in the MSChart control; the DataGrid control is an updated version of the DBGrid control from Visual Basic 5, which contains the results of a database query.

Choosing the Chart Type

Setting the chart type is a very easy task. You simply choose which chart type you want to use and assign it to the ChartType property. However, doing this from a menu, as shown in Figure 7.5, is a slightly more complex task. Each menu item typically has its own event, so you end up with a bunch of little events that are used to select a chart type.

Handing a MenuChart Event To address this problem, I chose to create a control array of menu items. I did this in the Menu Editor by creating a menu item for each possible chart type. Then I assigned each menu item a sequential index value starting with zero, as shown in Figure 7.6. This means that I can handle the menu event with a single subroutine like the one shown in Listing 7.17.

FIGURE 7.5:

The menu for choosing a chart type in the Charter program

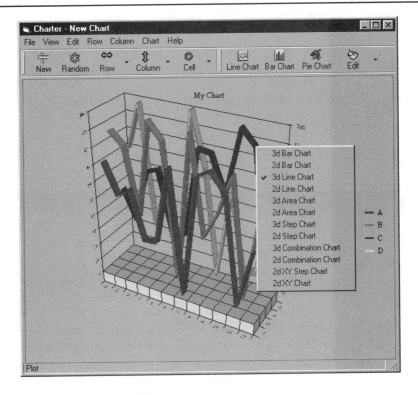

FIGURE 7.6:

Creating a menu array with the Menu Editor

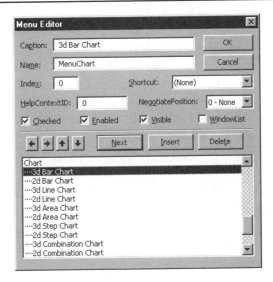

Listing 7.17:   **MenuChart_Click Event in Charter**

```
Private Sub MenuChart_Click(Index As Integer)

If Index <= 9 Then
    SetChartType Index

ElseIf Index = 10 Then
    SetChartType 14

ElseIf Index = 11 Then
    SetChartType 16

End If

End Sub
```

In this event, all I do is translate the Index parameter so that it corresponds to the ChartType property. When I created the menu item using the Menu Editor, I had to use sequential index values, even though the ChartType property doesn't use sequential chart types. So I used the values for ChartType that were sequential and assigned an Index value of 10 for ChartType 14 and a value of 11 for ChartType 16. I then translated the menu choices and called the SetChartType subroutine to actually set the ChartType property.

Setting the Chart Type   In Listing 7.18, you can see the three lines of code that actually set the ChartType property. Note that I took the time to disable Repaint before I set ChartType and reset it again afterwards. Then I set the Checked property for each of the menu items to False with a simple For/Next loop. I then used a series of If statements to set the appropriate menu item's Checked property.

Listing 7.18:   **SetChartType Routine in Charter**

```
Private Sub SetChartType(t As Integer)

Dim i As Integer

MSChart1.Repaint = False
MSChart1.chartType = t
MSChart1.Repaint = True
```

```
For i = 0 To 11
    MenuChart(i).Checked = False
Next i

If t <= 9 Then
    MenuChart(t).Checked = True

ElseIf t = 14 Then
    MenuChart(10).Checked = True

ElseIf t = 16 Then
    MenuChart(11).Checked = True

End If

End Sub
```

Why did I go to all the trouble of using two subroutines? Since I want to set the ChartType property from several different locations in the program, like in the NewChart routine (Listing 7.7) and the MenuChart_Click event (Listing 7.17), I prefer to have this code in just one place. This allows me to add new features—like putting some buttons on a toolbar—to perform the same function and know that the menu items are always in sync.

Adding a Chart Title

Assigning a title to the MSChart control can be a very simple operation; however, it isn't terribly user friendly. It is far better to put a sample chart title on the screen and allow the user to double-click on the title on the chart and edit it directly on the screen. Figure 7.7 shows how this works in the Charter program.

Setting the MSChart control's AllowSelections property to True allows the user to click on an object and have your program respond to the event. While some functions—such as dragging a chart object from one place on the screen to another—are automatic, keyboard handling is not. To allow the user to edit the chart's title (or any other chart object), you need to write some code for the Key-Press and KeyUp events.

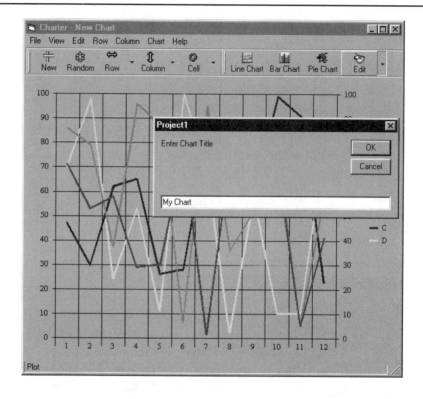

First, I'll show you how to assign a title, and then I'll go over the code for letting the user change that title.

Assigning a Title

Listing 7.19 shows the code for assigning a title to a chart.

Listing 7.19: **Toolbar1_ButtonMenuClick Event in Charter**

```
If ButtonMenu.Parent.Key = "Edit" Then
    If ButtonMenu.Key = "Title" Then
        MSChart1.TitleText = InputBox("Enter Chart Title", , _
            MSChart1.TitleText)

    End If

End If
```

Handling the KeyPress Event   Listing 7.20 shows the code needed to append a character to the end of the chart's `TitleText` property. Notice how similar it is to the `KeyPress` event I used for the MSFlexGrid control (Listing 7.10). The only difference is that I need to determine which part of the chart the user selected. To do this, I used the `GetSelectedPart` method to return the part type in the variable p. The other parameters are not used (at least not for the chart's title), but are required, so I used some dummy variables. Once I have the selected part, I append the character to the `TitleText` property if the character is a printing character.

Listing 7.20:	**MSChart1_KeyPress Event in Charter**

```
Private Sub MSChart1_KeyPress(KeyAscii As Integer)

Dim i1 As Integer
Dim i2 As Integer
Dim i3 As Integer
Dim i4 As Integer
Dim p As Integer

MSChart1.GetSelectedPart p, i1, i2, i3, i4

If p = VtChPartTypeTitle Then
   If KeyAscii >= 32 And KeyAscii <= 127 Then
      MSChart1.TitleText = MSChart1.TitleText & Chr(KeyAscii)
   End If
End If

End Sub
```

Handling the KeyUp Event   In the KeyUp event, I added code to handle the Delete key, the Backspace key, and the Enter key:

- When the Delete key is pressed, I erase the contents of the title, but leave a single blank character in the `TitleText` property. This ensures that the title can still be selected on the chart. If I set the `TitleText` property to an empty string, then the title would disappear and the chart itself might be redrawn to use the now empty space.

- The Backspace key deletes the last character in the TitleText property. Note that I still leave a single blank character if the user attempts to delete the last character.

- When I see the Enter key (vbCr), I assume that the user has finished making changes and select the chart itself, which deselects the title. As with the Get-SelectPart method, the SelectPart method requires four parameters that aren't used when selecting the chart itself.

Listing 7.21:   MSChart1_KeyUp Event in Charter

```
Private Sub MSChart1_KeyUp(KeyCode As Integer, Shift As Integer)

Dim i1 As Integer
Dim i2 As Integer
Dim i3 As Integer
Dim i4 As Integer
Dim p As Integer

MSChart1.GetSelectedPart p, i1, i2, i3, i4

If p = VtChPartTypeTitle Then
   If KeyCode = vbKeyDelete Then
      MSChart1.TitleText = " "

   ElseIf KeyCode = vbKeyBack Then
      If Len(MSChart1.TitleText) > 1 Then
         MSChart1.TitleText = Left(MSChart1.TitleText, _
            Len(MSChart1.TitleText) - 1)
      Else
         MSChart1.TitleText = " "
      End If

   ElseIf KeyCode = Asc(vbCr) Then
      TitleEdit = False
      MSChart1.SelectPart VtChPartTypeChart, 0, 0, 0, 0
   End If

End If

End Sub
```

Final Thoughts

All the controls discussed in this chapter are very powerful, but remember that they have their limitations. TreeView and ListView work best with relatively small amounts of data since the process to add entries into the control takes longer with each entry added. Also, they both work best with read-only data, again because the update process is very slow. Because of this, I prefer to load data when you need it as opposed to when you load the form. This is because most users prefer to see a few smaller delays than one big delay.

The ListView control is one of my favorites because it allows me to easily display tabular information. In the File Viewer program, I used this control to display a list of filenames plus related file information. But it easily could be used to display a list of e-mail messages, a list of items in a database table, or any other type of list.

The MSChart and MSFlexGrid controls both are designed to provide lightweight versions of Excel charting and spreadsheets capabilities. If used in the right circumstances, they can add significant value to your application. For instance, consider an application that is used to balance a number of factors to achieve a desired a result. This could be choosing a series of stocks and bonds to maximize your profit, or choosing a mix of materials to make dog food to minimizes your cost (in other words, any of the classic linear programming problems). You could display each the factors as a series of numbers and let the user change them directly, or you could display the information as a bar chart and let the user click on a bar and drag it to make it larger or smaller to increase or decrease the impact of that factor.

The MSFlexGrid control and its cousins are a natural way to display the information from a database table. I include the DataGrid control (first cousin to MSFlexGrid) in nearly every database application I build, because it is easy to use and offers an unedited and untranslated view of the data in the table. This helps me to quickly identify problems and inconsistencies in the data. While a stand-alone query tool offers just as many advantages (if not more), sometimes you don't have access to the tool when you need it (like when you're visiting a user on site).

The MSChart control is a very flexible tool. In addition to chart titles, you can also include legends, axis labels, footnotes, and many other objects. You can change the font type, size, and style for any text-based objects. You also can change the color and brush style for any non–text-based objects on the screen.

Just remember that the MSFlexGrid and MSChart controls are not designed to replace Excel. Excel offers more chart formats as well as the ability to do complex data analysis. You can always embed an Excel chart into your application and take advantage of its power. However, if you don't need all of that power, the MSChart control makes is easy to convert raw data in your program into information for your user.

CHAPTER

EIGHT

8

Reading and Sending E-Mail Messages

- E-mail transfer with the Simple MAPI controls

- An overview of the Collaboration Data Objects (CDO)

- The CDO objects and their relationships

- CDO programming

Messaging Application Program Interface (MAPI) is a facility that lets your programs use e-mail services under Windows. Visual Basic includes two tools that let you access the MAPI services: Simple MAPI and the Collaboration Data Objects (CDO). Simple MAPI consists of two controls that provide you with an easy way to read messages from your inbox and send messages via your outbox.

CDO is a newer interface that allows you to access the full set of MAPI services, rather than the limited subset offered in the Simple MAPI controls. Similar to the File System Objects or Data Access Objects (used to access a Microsoft Jet database), CDO is object-oriented.

Neither method actually supplies the e-mail services you are using. Rather, they simply refer your request to your preferred e-mail system. In my case, this is Outlook Express. However, you can use any MAPI-compliant mail system. Just click on the Mail icon in the Windows Control Panel to configure MAPI to work with your e-mail program.

Using Simple MAPI

Simple MAPI consists of two controls:

- The MAPISession control is used to establish a MAPI session. Once the session is established, the `SessionId` property is used to connect the MAPIMessages control to the MAPISession control.

- The MAPIMessages control is then used to retrieve messages from your inbox and send messages to other users.

Figure 8.1 shows an example of using the Simple MAPI controls to read e-mail.

Using Simple MAPI
controls to read e-mail

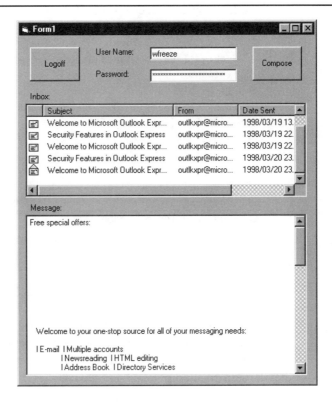

Establishing a MAPI Session

Establishing a MAPI session requires supplying a user name and a password, and then invoking the MAPISession control's SignOn method. Listing 8.1 shows a routine in which I use the same command button to sign on and to sign off MAPI, changing the label to indicate the next command.

Listing 8.1:   Command1_Click Event in MAPI Demo

```
Private Sub Command1_Click()

On Error Resume Next

If Command1.Caption = "Logon" Then
    MAPISession1.UserName = Text1.Text
```

```
        MAPISession1.Password = Text2.Text
        MAPISession1.SignOn
        If Err.Number <> 0 Then
            MsgBox "Invalid signon attempt, please try again"
            Exit Sub
        End If
        MAPIMessages1.SessionID = MAPISession1.SessionID
        Command1.Caption = "Logoff"
        FetchMessages

    Else
        ListView1.ListItems.Clear
        MAPISession1.SignOff
        Command1.Caption = "Logon"

    End If

    End Sub
```

When the user signs on, I capture the `UserName` and `Password` properties from the appropriate text boxes and invoke the `SignOn` method. If the sign-on fails because of a bad user name or password, I detect the error and display a message indicating that the sign-on attempt failed and the user needs to try again.

TIP

Security should not be user friendly: When users can't log on to your system, tell them as little as possible about why their logon attempt failed. You never know when someone may be trying to gain unauthorized access. If you tell someone that he or she entered a bad password, then you've cut an intruder's work in half—that person now knows that the user name is correct and only needs to guess the password.

Once the sign-on is complete, I link the MAPIMessages control to the MAPISession control by setting the `MAPIMessages.SessionId` property to the value of the `MAPISession.SessionId` property. Next, I switch the command button's caption to Logoff so that the next time it is clicked, the log-off process will be executed. Then I call the subroutine `FetchMessages` to get the messages from the inbox.

The sign-off process is a lot simpler. I merely clear the list of e-mail messages that I retrieved with the `FetchMessages` routine (shown in the next section). Then I call the `SignOff` method and reset the command button's caption to read Logon.

Fetching MAPI Messages

Once you have a MAPI session, fetching the messages is a relatively easy process, as shown in Listing 8.2. It consists of two parts: calling the Fetch method to retrieve the messages from the server and retrieving the information about each individual message.

Listing 8.2:   **FetchMessages Routine in MAPI Demo**

```
Private Sub FetchMessages()

Dim c As String
Dim i As Integer
Dim k As String
Dim l As ListItem

MAPIMessages1.Fetch

For i = 0 To MAPIMessages1.MsgCount - 1
   MAPIMessages1.MsgIndex = i
   k = "x" & Format(MAPIMessages1.MsgIndex)
   c = IIf(MAPIMessages1.MsgRead, "opened", "closed")
   Set l = ListView1.ListItems.Add(, k, "", , c)
   l.SubItems(1) = MAPIMessages1.MsgSubject
   l.SubItems(2) = MAPIMessages1.MsgOrigAddress
   l.SubItems(3) = MAPIMessages1.MsgDateReceived
   l.SubItems(4) = FormatNumber(MAPIMessages1.AttachmentCount, 0)
Next i

End Sub
```

The Fetch method is rather self-explanatory, but the process for loading the message header information into the ListView control can use some explaining.

Since the messages are stored as a series of properties with subscripts, I need to build a loop to get the header information for each message. Each message is selected by setting the MsgIndex property to a valid message number. Then I create a temporary variable k, which consists of an x followed by the MsgIndex. This will generate a unique key, which can be used in the ListItem object. I also create another temporary variable c that contains the name of the icon to be displayed. If the message has already been read (MsgRead = True), then I use an open envelope. Otherwise, I display a closed envelope.

Next, I create the ListItem object using k and c. Then I assign the MsgSubject, MsgOrigAddress, MsgDateReceived, and AttachmentCount properties to the first four subitems in the ListItem and continue the loop until I have processed all of the messages.

NOTE   **Plenty of properties:** In this example, I showed only a few of the many properties that describe a single e-mail note. You can add a list of people who received the note, including their e-mail addresses, and a list of the attachments by name. Plus, you can find out the type of message, whether a receipt was requested, and the message's conversation ID.

Reading a MAPI Message

If getting the list of MAPI messages was easy, then the process to read one of those messages is down right trivial. The ItemClick event of the ListView control will occur when the user clicks on the desired message. Then all you need to do is to extract the MsgIndex from the item's key by discarding the first character and converting it back to a number. Next, assign this value to the MsgIndex property. Then you can get the text of the message from the MsgNoteText property. Listing 8.3 shows how this is done.

Listing 8.3:   **ListView1_ItemClick Event in MAPI Demo**

```
Private Sub ListView1_ItemClick(ByVal Item As ComctlLib.ListItem)

MAPIMessages1.MsgIndex = CInt(Right(Item.Key, Len(Item.Key) - 1))
RichTextBox1.Text = MAPIMessages1.MsgNoteText & vbCrLf

End Sub
```

Sending a MAPI Message

If reading a message was trivial, then the block of code in Listing 8.4 is embarrassing. To send a message, simply use the Compose method to create a new blank message. Then use the Send method and specify a dialog parameter of True. This starts the underlying mail system (in my case, Outlook Express) and has it display its message composition screen, as shown in Figure 8.2. You then fill out the information and click the Send button when you're done.

Listing 8.4:   Command2_Click Event in MAPI Demo

```
Private Sub Command2_Click()

MAPIMessages1.Compose
MAPIMessages1.Send True

End Sub
```

FIGURE 8.2:

The message composition window from Outlook Express

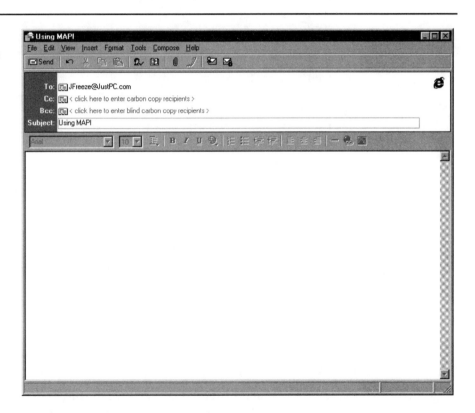

Sending a MAPI Message Revisited

Okay, I admit it—I cheated. In the previous section, I showed you the minimum code you need to send a message. Now let's look at a little more complex example. I'm going to add the ability to send a .JNK document from the Charter program (which I introduced back in Chapter 7) via e-mail, similar to the e-mail capabilities in Microsoft Word and Excel. Listing 8.5 shows the SendChart routine, which provides this feature.

Listing 8.5:   **SendChart Routine in Charter**

```
Private Sub SendChart()

SaveChart False

If Len(CommonDialog1.FileName) > 0 Then
   MAPISession1.LogonUI = True
   MAPISession1.SignOn

   MAPIMessages1.SessionID = MAPISession1.SessionID
   MAPIMessages1.Compose
   MAPIMessages1.MsgSubject = "A Charter document (" & _
      CommonDialog1.FileTitle & ")"
   MAPIMessages1.AttachmentName = CommonDialog1.FileTitle
   MAPIMessages1.AttachmentPathName = CommonDialog1.FileName

   MAPIMessages1.Send True
   MAPISession1.SignOff

End If

End Sub
```

Saving the Chart

The first step in this process is to save the chart as a disk file. I call the SaveChart subroutine with a parameter of False so that I perform a Save operation rather than a Save As operation.

Next, I verify that the user did, in fact, save the file. Therefore, if there is a filename in the CommonDialog control's FileName property, then I assume that the file has been saved successfully under that filename.

Prompting for Sign-On Information

I already showed you how to sign on to MAPI using your own user name and password fields. This time, I'm going to be lazy and allow MAPI to prompt you for that information. I do this by setting `LogonUI` to `True` and executing the `SignOn` method. Once I have access to MAPI, I need to copy the MAPI `SessionId` property from the MAPISession control to the MAPIMessages control.

Creating and Sending the Message

To create a new message, I use the `Compose` method. Then I can assign a subject (`MsgSubject`) and specify the name of an attachment (`CommonDialog1.FileName`) and the type of attachment (Charter document). If you wish, you can assign default values for any or all of the other MAPIMessages control's properties.

To send the message, I simply use the `Send` method. If you specify `True` for the dialog parameter, your mail program's message composition window will appear with all of the default values you supplied in your program. The user can modify any of these parameters and send (or cancel) the message. If you specify `False` for the dialog parameter, the message will be put together and automatically sent to the list of recipients that you specified. Note that if you didn't specify any recipients, the mail won't be sent and you'll receive a runtime error. Once you've sent your message, it's time to sign off from MAPI.

Introducing Collaboration Data Objects

CDO consists of a comprehensive group of objects that allow you to access MAPI services. These objects provide you with access to the same facilities and tools that Outlook 98 uses.

You can use CDO to send and receive e-mail, including e-mail messages with attachments. You can maintain a series of message folders where you can save messages. You can create collaboration documents, build schedules, and maintain your address book. In short, CDO offers the full capabilities of MAPI; the Simple MAPI controls that we just discussed do not.

NOTE **The technology name game:** CDO is based on technology that has been around for a while under a couple of different names. Version 1.0 was known as OLE Messaging. Version 1.1 brought the name Active Messaging. Version 1.2 is now known as Collaboration Data Objects.

Adding CDO to Your Program

CDO includes a complex set of interrelated objects that allow you easy access to most of the MAPI functions. I'm going to cover many of the objects and methods that are useful for writing CDO programs, focusing on what it takes to send and receive e-mail, access your address book, and manage your message folders.

To add the CDO objects to your program, select Microsoft CDO 1.21 Library in the Project ➢ References dialog box. You should also have installed Windows messaging and a MAPI client such as Outlook 98 or Outlook Express. The programs in this chapter were written with Outlook Express as my default e-mail program and my default Simple MAPI client, as shown in Figure 8.3. Outlook 98 was also installed, though largely unused.

FIGURE 8.3:

The Outlook Express Options dialog box

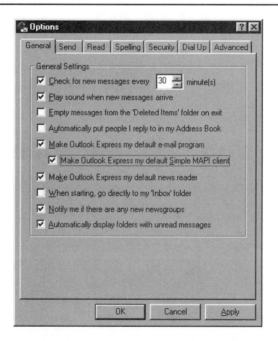

TIP   **It ain't here:** The CDO objects are not included with Visual Basic 6. Whether this is deliberate or not, I'm not sure. However, you can find the necessary CDO files on your system when you install Outlook 98. Look for the file called CDO.DLL.

The relationship between the various objects in the CDO is rather complicated, as you can see in Figure 8.4.

FIGURE 8.4:

The Collaboration Data Objects

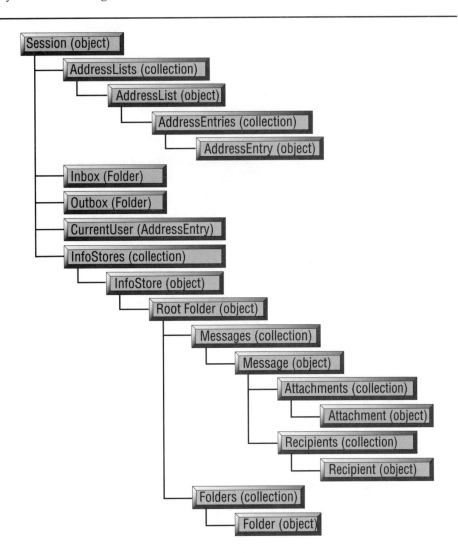

Table 8.1 lists properties that are common to all of the objects in CDO. Each object always contains a reference to the Session object. The Session object is the object from which all of the other objects will be derived. The Parent object contains an object reference to the object's parent, except for the Session object, which has no parent.

TABLE 8.1: Properties Common to CDO Objects

Property	Description
Application	Returns the name of the object library, Collaboration Data Objects
Class	Returns a unique number that identifies the object
Count	Specifies the number of items in a collection
Field	Returns information from the MAPI subsystem based on the appropriate index, property tag, or name value
Fields	Contains a collection of Field objects
ID	Returns a unique string that identifies the specific instance of the object
Index	Returns an Item's position within a collection
Item	Returns an object from inside a collection
Name	Returns the text name of the object
Parent	Returns the parent of the object (for the Session object, Nothing is returned)
Session	Returns a reference to the Session object

The Fields object returns information directly from the MAPI interface. The Application object always returns the value Collaboration Data Objects. (I guess this property is useful in a product that changes it name with every new version.)

Getting the Class

Class is a particularly useful property. No matter which object you reference, it is present. It returns a numeric value that corresponds to the name of the object that contains it. The values it returns are listed in Table 8.2. In some cases, where only a single object exists in a collection, the object itself will be returned rather than the collection. Since the Class property is common to both the collection and the object, you can easily determine which object you are dealing with.

TABLE 8.2:   Values Returned by the Class Property

Library Object	Class Value	Constant Name
AddressEntries collection	21	CdoAddressEntries
AddressEntry	8	CdoAddressEntry
AddressEntryFilter	9	CdoAddressEntryFilter
AddressList	7	CdoAddressList
AddressLists collection	20	CdoAddressLists
AppointmentItem	26	CdoAppointment
Attachment	5	CdoAttachment
Attachments collection	18	CdoAttachments
Field	6	CdoField
Fields collection	19	CdoFields
Folder	2	CdoFolder
Folders collection	15	CdoFolders
GroupHeader	25	CdoGroupHeader
InfoStore	1	CdoInfoStore
InfoStores collection	14	CdoInfoStores
MeetingItem	27	CdoMeetingItem
Message	3	CdoMessage
MessageFilter	10	CdoMessageFilter
Messages collection	16	CdoMesssages
Recipient	4	CdoRecipient
Recipients collection	17	CdoRecipients
RecurrencePattern	28	CdoRecurrencePattern
Session	0	CdoSession

Checking for the Same Object

The IsSameAs method is used in many places in CDO to determine if two object pointers are referring to the same instance of an object. This is useful when you arrive at the same object by two different paths. The IsSameAs method returns True if both objects are the same instance of the object.

Using the Session Object

The Session object is the root object of the CDO system. All other CDO objects are derived from this object. Until you execute the Session object's Logon method to establish a link to the MAPI system, none of its properties are available for use.

Assigning Session Object Properties

Table 8.3 lists some of the Session object properties. The AddressLists property returns a reference to one or more address books. The CurrentUser property returns an AddressEntry object containing information about the currently logged on user. OperatingSystem and Version contain the name of the operating system and the version number of the CDO library respectively.

TABLE 8.3: Selected MAPI.Session Object Properties

Property	Description
AddressLists	Returns either a single AddressList object or an AddressLists collection
CurrentUser	Returns information about the current user as an AddressList object
Inbox	Returns a Folder object containing the current user's inbox
InfoStores	Returns either a single InfoStore object or an InfoStores collection
OperatingSystem	Returns the name of the operating system
Outbox	Returns a Folder object containing the current user's outbox
OutOfOffice	When set to True, means that the OutOfOfficeText will be used to reply to any e-mail
OutOfOfficeText	Contains the message included with the automatic reply to an e-mail message when OutOfOffice is True
Version	Returns the version of the object library as a string

The Inbox and Outbox properties return a Folder object containing the information in the user's inbox and outbox. The InfoStores property returns either a reference to an InfoStore object or an InfoStores collection. The key property in the InfoStore object is RootFolder, which is just another Folder object.

Using Session Object Methods

Table 8.4 lists the `Session` object methods. The first method you should use when you begin writing a CDO program is the `Logon` method. This method establishes a link to the MAPI system and grants you access to the data stored there. When you're finished, you should use the `Logoff` method to cleanly close the link to the MAPI system.

TABLE 8.4: Session Object Methods

Method	Description
AddressBook	Displays the address book in a dialog box and allows the user to select one or more entries
CompareIds	Returns **True** if the specified objects are the same
CreateConversationIndex	Either creates a new index or returns an existing index to be used to create a new message as part of a conversation thread
DeliverNow	Requests that all undelivered messages are sent immediately
GetAddressEntry	Returns an **AddressEntry** object for the specified entry ID
GetAddressList	Returns an **AddressList** object from a directory service
GetArticle	Returns a **Message** object for the specified article number
GetDefaultFolder	Returns a **Folder** object for the specified type of folder (see Table 8.5)
GetFolder	Returns a **Folder** object for the specified folder ID
GetInfoStore	Returns an **InfoStore** object that can access both public folders and the user's personal folders
GetMessage	Returns an **Appointment**, **MeetingItem**, or **Message** object from a message source
GetOption	Returns the calendar-rendering option for this session
Logoff	Terminates the MAPI access
Logon	Starts a MAPI session
SetLocaleIDs	Defines a user locale
SetOption	Sets a calendar-rendering option for this session

Configuring a Session

The GetOption and SetOption methods configure how calendars are displayed. The SetLocaleIDs method is used to set the locale for the session. The AddressBook method displays the address book and lets the user select one or more addresses that can be used when creating a message. The DeliverNow method sends all of the queued messages immediately. The CreateConversationIndex returns a new conversation index that can be used to identify the proper order for a series of messages with the same ConversationTopic.

Getting Information

The GetInfoStore method returns an InfoStore object, which contains a set of Folder objects. The GetFolder method returns the requested Folder object. The GetArticle method returns a Message object corresponding to the specified ArticleID and FolderID. The GetMessage returns the message based on the supplied MessageID. The GetAddressList method returns an Address-List object from a directory service. This can be either your local address book or a global address list. The GetDefaultFolder method returns one of the Folder objects, based on the value listed in Table 8.5.

TABLE 8.5:   Folder Types Used with GetDefaultFolder

Folder Type	Value	Constant Name
Calendar	0	CdoDefaultFolderCalendar
Contacts	5	CdoDefaultFolderContacts
Deleted Items	4	CdoDefaultFolderDeletedItems
Inbox	1	CdoDefaultFolderInbox
Journal	6	CdoDefaultFolderJournal
Notes	7	CdoDefaultFolderNotes
Outbox	2	CdoDefaultFolderOutbox
Sent Items	3	CdoDefaultFolderSentItems
Tasks	8	CdoDefaultFolderTasks

Working with InfoStores

The InfoStores collection contains a collection of InfoStore objects. Each InfoStore object contains a RootFolder, which contains a Folder object that contains a collection of Folder objects and Message objects. Table 8.6 lists some of the InfoStore object properties.

TABLE 8.6: Selected InfoStore Object Properties

Property	Description
ProviderName	Contains the name of the message store provider
RootFolder	Contains the root Folder of the message store

Working with Folders

The Folders collection contains a series of Folder objects, where each Folder object contains a Folders collection and a Messages collection. Table 8.7 lists some methods of the Folders collection.

TABLE 8.7: Selected Folders Collection Methods

Method	Description
Add	Adds a new folder to the Folders collection
Delete	Deletes all Folder objects in the Folders collection
GetFirst	Returns an object reference to the first Folder object in the collection
GetLast	Returns an object reference to the last Folder object in the collection
GetNext	Returns an object reference to the next Folder object in the collection
GetPrevious	Returns an object reference to the previous Folder object in the collection
Sort	Sorts the Folder objects in the Folders collection

The Folder object contains a few interesting properties, which are listed in Table 8.8. Each folder can contain other folders as well as a list of messages, and they are stored in the Folders property and the Messages property, respectively. The HiddenMessages property contains folder-related information used by MAPI.

The `FolderID` is a unique value within an `InfoStore`. You can use the `Session` `.GetFolder` method to retrieve a folder with this value.

TABLE 8.8: Selected Folder Object Properties

Property	Description
FolderID	Specifies the unique identifier of this `Folder` object
Folders	Contains a collection of subfolders
HiddenMessages	Contains a collection of hidden messages
Messages	Contains a collection of messages

Working with Messages

There are three basic kinds of messages:

- A *sent* message is created in a private folder and sent to a public folder or a recipient.

- A *posted* message is created in a public folder.

- A *saved* message is created and saved in a private folder.

The `Messages` collection contains a series of `Message` objects. The properties are the usual set available with any collection object. Some of the `Messages` collection methods are listed in Table 8.9 (you'll notice that they are the same as the ones available in the `Folders` collection).

TABLE 8.9: Selected Messages Collection Methods

Method	Description
Add	Adds a new message to the `Messages` collection
Delete	Deletes all of `Message` objects in the `Messages` collection
GetFirst	Returns an object reference to the first `Message` object in the collection
GetLast	Returns an object reference to the last `Message` object in the collection
GetNext	Returns an object reference to the next `Message` object in the collection
GetPrevious	Returns an object reference to the previous `Message` object in the collection
Sort	Sorts the `Message` objects in the `Messages` collection

The Add method adds a new message to the Messages collection. Note that until the Message.Update method is used, the message will not be saved. Also, you should create the message in the Outbox folder if you wish to send it to another user. Appointment messages should be created in the Calendar folder.

The Delete method erases a message from the collection. The GetFirst, GetNext, GetPrevious, and GetLast methods help you move through the collection, though I prefer to use the For Each statement. The Sort method allows you to sort the messages before you retrieve them.

Assigning Message Object Properties

The Message object is at the heart of the CDO system. Its properties and methods reflect the information in a single message. Table 8.10 lists some of the Message object properties.

TIP   **Everything might not be in stock:** When looking at this impressive list of properties, you should remember that there might not be information in every single property. Selecting a property without information will result in a runtime error. So use caution and lots of error handling when accessing these properties.

T A B L E 8 . 1 0 :   Selected Message Object Properties

Property	Description
Attachments	Contains a reference to an Attachments collection
Categories	Returns a string array containing a set of keyword items associated with this message
ConversationIndex	Specifies a value that allows you to determine where this message falls in the set of messages having the same ConversationTopic
ConversationTopic	Contains the subject of the conversation thread
DeliveryReceipt	When set to True, requests a delivery receipt when the message is delivered
Encrypted	When set to True, requests that the message be encrypted if possible.
FolderID	Specifies the unique identifier associated with the folder that contains the message
Importance	Specifies the relative importance of the message
ReadReceipt	When set to True, requests a read receipt when the message is read

Continued on next page

TABLE 8.10 (CONTINUED): Selected Message Object Properties

Property	Description
Recipients	Returns a `Recipient` object or a `Recipients` collection containing the information about who received the mail
Sender	Returns an `AddressEntry` object containing information about the person who created the message
Sensitivity	Describes the sensitivity of the message
Sent	When set to `True`, means that the message was sent through the MAPI subsystem
Signed	When set to `True`, means that the message includes a digital signature
Size	Contains the approximate size of the message, including all attachments plus all other associated properties
StoreID	Specifies the unique identifier associated with the `InfoStore` that contains the message
Subject	Contains the subject of the message
Submitted	When set to `True`, means that the message has been submitted to the MAPI subsystem
Text	Contains the body of the message
TimeCreated	Contains the local date and time the message was created
TimeExpired	Contains the local date and time the message becomes invalid
TimeLastModified	Contains the local date and time the message was last modified
TimeReceived	Contains the local date and time the message was received
TimeSent	Contains the local date and time the message was sent
Type	Contains the type of message
Unread	When set to `True`, means that the user hasn't read the message

Message Essentials The message itself is stored in the Text property. The subject is stored in the Subject property. The Sender property is an AddressEntry object. The Recipients property is either a Recipient object or a Recipients collection containing information about who received the mail. Any attachments are stored in the Attachments collection.

Message Status Also included with the Message object is a series of flags containing status information. Categories returns a string array containing the keywords associated with the message. `DeliveryReceipt` requests a return message indicating when the message was received by the recipient's mail system. `ReadReceipt` requests a return message indicating when the recipient first read the message.

WARNING   **Property arrays and property arguments equal confusion:** Use of methods and properties that have optional arguments may conflict with the use of arrays. The first parenthesis is associated with the optional parameters. Thus, you would have to write `Msg.Categories()(1)` to reference element one in the string array.

When `Encrypted` is `True`, the message must be decrypted before it can be read. CDO does not manage any encryption processes, so you'll need to handle this yourself.

`Importance` and `Sensitivity` both communicate information about the priority and security of the message. `Size` gives you some idea of the relative size of the message, but don't try to match this with the number of bytes in the `Text` property; the value in `Size` includes all of the attachments, plus any other information contained in the properties.

The `ConversationIndex` and `ConversationTopic` properties both convey information about a series of messages with a common thread. The `FolderID` property returns the unique identifier for the folder that contains this message. `StoreID` is similar to `FolderID`, but refers to the `InfoStore` object that contains the message store, which contains the folder. `Type` holds information about the message type. The `Sent` and `Submitted` flags contain information about the status of the mail transmission of message.

Date and Time Values   A number of date and time values are included with each message. You can determine when the message was created (`TimeCreated`), last modified (`TimeLastModified`), received (`TimeReceived`), and sent (`TimeSent`). It also includes a `TimeExpired` property to indicate when a message is no longer valid.

Using Message Object Methods

Table 8.11 lists the methods available for the `Message` object. You can use the `CopyTo` method to create a copy of a message in another folder or the `MoveTo` method to move the message into another folder. The `Delete` method removes the message from the folder.

TABLE 8.11: Selected Message Object Methods

Method	Description
CopyTo	Creates a copy of the **Message** object
Delete	Deletes a **Message** object and all of subfolders and messages
Forward	Returns a new **Message** object
MoveTo	Moves the **Message** object and all of its subfolders and messages to the specified location
Options	Displays a modal dialog box to set the options for the message
Reply	Returns a new **Message** object that has been prepared as a reply to the current recipient
ReplyAll	Returns a new **Message** object that has been prepared as a reply to all recipients
Send	Saves the changes made to the **Message** object and moves it to the outbox in preparation to being sent to the recipients
Update	Saves the changes made to the **Message** object

The Reply, ReplyAll, and Forward methods all create a new message based on the current message that has been prepared so that the user may edit and send the new message. The Options method displays a dialog box to modify any of the options set for this message.

The Update method saves the message into the folder. The Send method performs an Update and then moves the message to the outbox so that it will be sent when the user triggers the Session.DeliverNow method.

Working with Attachments

The Attachments collection contains the standard collection properties of Count and Item, plus the methods listed in Table 8.12. The Add method adds a new Attachment to the collection. The Delete method is used to remove an Attachment from the collection.

TABLE 8.12: Selected Attachments Collection Methods

Method	Description
Add	Adds a new **Attachment** object to the collection
Delete	Removes all of the **Attachment** objects from the collection

Assigning Attachment Object Properties

Table 8.13 lists some `Attachment` object properties. The `Position` property specifies the character position in the `Text` property that will be replaced by the attachment. A value of 0 means that the attachment is not visible in the document. A value of −1 means that the attachment is handled some other way.

TABLE 8.13:   Selected Attachment Object Properties

Property	Description
Position	Specifies the position in the `Text` document where the attachment should be inserted
Source	Specifies the source of the attachment
Type	Specifies the type of the attachment

The `Type` property specifies the type of the attachment. This can be the contents of a file, a link to a file, an OLE reference, or a reference to an existing message. The `Source` specifies the source of the attachment.

Using Attachment Object Methods

Table 8.14 lists some of the `Attachment` object methods. The `Delete` method removes that attachment from the collection. The `ReadFromFile` method is used to copy a file or OLE document into the MAPI subsystem. This method can't be used with an attachment type of file link or a reference to an existing message. The `WriteToFile` is the inverse operation of the `ReadFromFile` method. It saves the contents of the attachment as specified in the `Type` property.

TABLE 8.14:   Selected Attachment Object Methods

Method	Description
Delete	Removes the attachment from the `Attachments` collection
ReadFromFile	Loads an attachment from the specified location
WriteToFile	Saves an attachment to the specified location

Working with Recipients

The `Recipients` collection contains the list of people who have received (or will receive) the message. The `Resolved` property indicates if all of the addresses for the recipients have been resolved. If they haven't, you should use the `Recipients.Resolve` method to resolve all of the objects in the collection or use the `Recipient.Resolve` method to resolve them one at a time.

Some of the `Recipients` collection methods are listed in Table 8.15. The `Add` method adds a new recipient to the collection. The `AddMultiple` method adds a list of recipients, separated by semicolons, to the collection. The `Delete` method clears the collection. The `GetFirstUnresolved` and `GetNextUnresolved` methods are used to step through the list of unresolved addresses. The `Resolve` method is used to convert each `Recipient` object into a valid messaging address. This method can optionally display a dialog box to prompt the user for information needed to resolve the address.

TABLE 8.15:   Selected Recipients Collection Methods

Method	Description
Add	Adds a new recipient to the collection
AddMultiple	Adds multiple recipients to the collection
Delete	Deletes all of the `Recipient` objects in the collection
GetFirstUnresolved	Returns the first unresolved address in the collection
GetFreeBusy	Returns the availability of each recipient to attend a meeting at the specified date and time
GetNextUnresolved	Returns the next unresolved address in the collection
Resolve	Attempts to convert a `Recipient` object into a full messaging address

Assigning Recipient Object Properties

Table 8.16 lists some of the properties of the `Recipient` object. The `Address` property contains the full address for the recipient. It corresponds to the `Type` and `Address` properties of the `AddressEntry` object. The `AddressEntry` property contains an object reference to the complete `AddressEntry` object for the recipient. The `AmbiguousNames` property returns an `AddressEntries` collection containing possible matches for the recipient.

TABLE 8.16:   Selected Recipient Object Properties

Property	Description
Address	Specifies the full address of the recipient
AddressEntry	Contains a reference to an **AddressEntry** object containing the information about the recipient
AmbiguousNames	Returns an **AddressEntries** collection containing a list of suggestions for an unresolved **Recipient** object
DisplayType	Describes how to display the recipient information
MeetingResponseStatus	Contains the response to a meeting request
Type	Specifies how the message is directed to the user

The DisplayType property contains information about how the recipient should be displayed as part of the message. The MeetingResponseStatus contains information about how a recipient responded to the meeting request. The Type property specifies how the message is directed to the user—To, Cc, or Bcc.

Using Recipient Object Methods

Table 8.17 lists some of the Recipient object methods. The Delete method is used to remove a recipient from the collection. The Resolve method works the same as the Recipients.Resolve method, but acts on only the single Recipient object. The GetFreeBusy method returns the ability of the recipient to attend a meeting at the specified time.

TABLE 8.17:   Selected Recipient Object Methods

Method	Description
Delete	Removes this **Recipient** object from the collection
GetFreeBusy	Returns the availability of the recipient to attend a meeting at the specified date and time
Resolve	Attempts to convert the recipient into a full messaging address

Working with Address Lists

The AddressLists collection contains a group of AddressList objects and is a standard collection that can be traversed with a For/Next statement. Each AddressList object in the collection corresponds to a MAPI address book.

Table 8.18 lists two properties of the AddressList object. The AddressEntries property contains a reference to an AddressEntries collection. The IsReadOnly property indicates if entries may be added or removed from the AddressEntries collection. Note that this property does not affect any statements about the ability to modify any of the individual entries in the AddressEntries collection.

TABLE 8.18:   Selected AddressList Object Properties

Property	Description
AddressEntries	Contains an object reference to the AddressEntries collection
IsReadOnly	When set to True, means that the AddressList object can't be changed

Working with Address Entries

The AddressEntries collection contains a series of AddressEntry objects. The properties are the usual set available with any collection object. The methods listed in Table 8.19 are the same as the ones available in the Folders collection.

TABLE 8.19:   Selected AddressEntries Collection Methods

Method	Description
Add	Adds a new address to the AddressEntries collection
Delete	Deletes all of AddressEntry objects in the AddressEntries collection
GetFirst	Returns an object reference to the first AddressEntry object in the collection
GetLast	Returns an object reference to the last AddressEntry object in the collection
GetNext	Returns an object reference to the next AddressEntry object in the collection
GetPrevious	Returns an object reference to the previous AddressEntry object in the collection
Sort	Sorts the AddressEntry objects in the AddressEntries collection

The Add method adds a new message to the AddressEntries collection. The Delete method removes all of the entries in the collection. The GetFirst, GetNext, GetPrevious, and GetLast methods provide ways to retrieve items in order from the collection. The Sort method allows you to reorder the members of the collection.

Assigning AddressEntry Object Properties

Table 8.20 lists the key properties of the AddressEntry object. The Address property contains a messaging address. The exact format of the address depends on the Type. The Type property specifies the routing method used to send a message. Some valid types are SMTP, FAX, and X400.

TABLE 8.20: Selected AddressEntry Object Properties

Property	Description
Address	Contains a messaging address
DisplayType	Describes the contents of the AddressEntry object, plus how it should be displayed
Manager	Returns an AddressEntry object containing the manager of this individual, if available
Members	Returns an AddressEntries collection with the members of the distribution list
Type	Specifies the messaging router that will be used to reach the recipient

DisplayType contains information about the contents of the AddressEntry object and how it should be formatted on the screen. If DisplayType is a distribution list, then this property will contain an object reference to an AddressEntries collection containing the AddressEntry objects in the distribution list. The Manager property, if present, contains an AddressEntry for the manager of the person described in the AddressEntry object.

Using AddressEntry Object Methods

Table 8.21 lists some of the AddressEntry object methods. The Delete method deletes an AddressEntry object. The Details method displays a dialog box containing information about this AddressEntry object. The GetFreeBusy method returns a string containing one character per time period indicating the person's availability during the specified range of time. The Update method is used to commit any changes made to the AddressEntry object to permanent storage.

TABLE 8.21:   Selected AddressEntry Object Methods

Method	Description.
Delete	Deletes an AddressEntry object from the AddressEntries collection
Details	Displays a modal dialog box containing the information about this AddressEntry object
GetFreeBusy	Returns a string indicating if the person is free or not available for a meeting at the specified times
Update	Commits the changes to an AddressEntry object

Programming with CDO

Using the Collaboration Data Objects is very similar to using the File System Objects, but just a little more complicated. The concept of organizing a file system into Drives, Folders, and Files collections corresponds to organizing an e-mail system into InfoStores, Folders, and Messages collections. The main structural difference between the two is that CDO has a richer set of properties and methods to perform tasks at the folder and file level.

I wrote the CDO Demo program to demonstrate some of the key capabilities of CDO. Figure 8.5 shows an example of reading a message with this program. Selecting a folder from the left side of the form will display its contents in the ListView box on the right side of the form. Below that ListView box is a message block containing the selected e-mail message. Across the top is a series of buttons that allow you to compose a new message, reply to an existing message, display a message's properties, send the messages in the outbox, delete a message in a folder and save a message into a folder.

FIGURE 8.5:

Reading a message with the
CDO Demo program

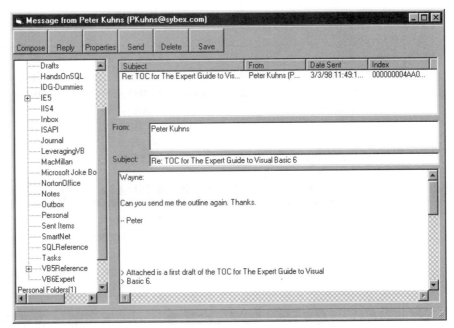

Initializing the MAPI Session

The first step in using CDO to access MAPI is to create the MAPI.Session object
and use the Logon method to establish a connection, as shown in Listing 8.6. After
I log on to MAPI, I load all of the InfoStores and their folders into the TreeView
control, as explained in the next section. Since this process takes a relatively long
period of time, I use the Me.Show method to show the form quickly, even before
all of the information has finished loading.

Listing 8.6:   **Form_Load Event in CDO Demo**

```
Private Sub Form_Load()

Me.Show

Set ms = New MAPI.Session
ms.Logon
```

```
LoadInfoStore

End Sub
```

Note that I didn't define ms in this routine. It is a module-level variable that will be used by the program to access any MAPI.Session facilities. I've also defined msg as a MAPI.Message object and msf as a MAPI.Folder object for the same reason.

Loading InfoStore Information

Loading the InfoStores collections into the TreeView control is simply a matter of iterating through the InfoStores collections in the MAPI.Session object and adding them to the TreeView control, as shown in Listing 8.7. Since the InfoStore objects are at the base of the MAPI storage hierarchy, I add them as root-level nodes in the TreeView. I use the InfoStore.ID object as the key to the node, since it is guaranteed to be unique. Figure 8.6 shows the results.

FIGURE 8.6:

Loading InfoStores collections

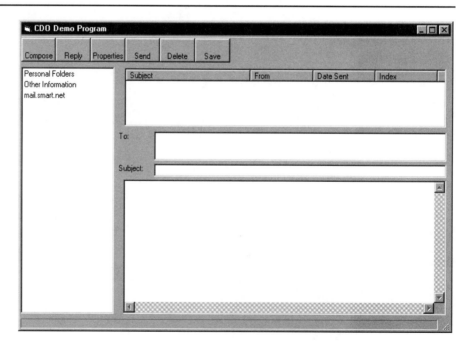

Listing 8.7:   **LoadInfoStore Routine in CDO Demo**

```
Private Sub LoadInfoStore()

Dim mi As MAPI.InfoStore
Dim mp As Integer
Dim n As Node

mp = Screen.MousePointer
Screen.MousePointer = vbHourglass

For Each mi In ms.InfoStores
    Set n = TreeView1.Nodes.Add(, , mi.id, mi.Name)
    n.Tag = ""
    LoadFolders mi.RootFolder.Folders, n, mi.id
    DoEvents
Next mi

Screen.MousePointer = mp

End Sub
```

After I load the InfoStore information into a root node, I then pass the RootFolder .Folders collection, the current TreeView node, and the ID property for the InfoStore object to the LoadFolders subroutine that will load the contents of the folders into the TreeView (discussed in the next section).

Note that I turn the cursor to an hourglass while loading this information. It lets the user know that this step is going to take a little while to finish. I also put in a call to DoEvents at the end of each loop to allow Windows to do some higher-priority work while this program is running.

Loading the MAPI Folders

Loading folders into a TreeView control can be rather tricky, unless you decide to write a recursive subroutine. If you studied computer science at some point, you probably had to write a routine that called itself. Usually, you would calculate the factorial of a number or some other equally simple function. However, this is not so straightforward when dealing with situations where folders are nested inside of folders, which are nested...well, you get the idea. The routine I wrote to handle this is shown in Listing 8.8. The results can be seen in Figure 8.7.

FIGURE 8.7:

Loading folder information

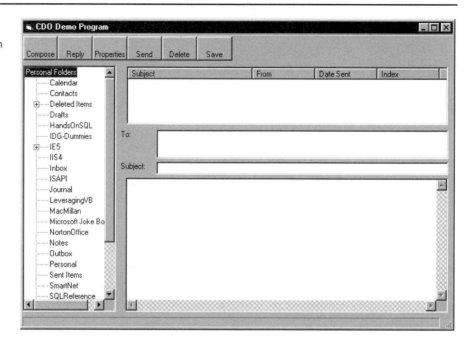

> **NOTE**
>
> **Just the factorial please:** A factorial of a number is computed by taking the product of every number less than or equal to that number. For instance 5! = 1 x 2 x 3 x 4 x 5 or 120. Another way to compute it is 5! = 5 x 4!; 4! = 4 x 3!; 3! = 3x 2!; 2! = 2 x 1! 1! = 1.

Listing 8.8:   **LoadFolders Routine in CDO Demo**

```
Private Sub LoadFolders(ms As MAPI.Folders, p As Node, i As Variant)

Dim f As MAPI.Folder
Dim n As Node

For Each f In ms
    Set n = TreeView1.Nodes.Add(p, tvwChild, f.id, f.Name)
```

```
        n.Tag = i
        LoadFolders f.Folders, n, i
        DoEvents
    Next f

End Sub
```

In this case, I want to load a folder and call the same routine again to load any subfolders that the folder may contain. If there are no folders to load, the For Each statement will not execute any of the looped statements and the routine will return. If there is at least one folder, then the For Each statement will process each folder and call itself again to process any folders that may be contained in that folder.

Confused? Let's examine the code. I pass ms as a collection of Folder objects, p as the current TreeView node, and i as the ID of the InfoStore object. As I loop through the Folders collection (ms), I create a new Node object for each folder. This node will be the child of the node that represents the parent folder (p). This duplicates the folder hierarchy. I use the folder's ID value as the key and the folder's name for the Text property. I save the InfoStore value into the Tag property. I'll use this information later to let me go directly to this particular folder.

After I've added this folder, I call the LoadFolders routine again. However, this time, I use the Folders collection that is contained in this folder (f.Folders), the node I just created (n), and the same i value I used earlier, since this is still part of the same InfoStore.

TIP

I know it works: When writing recursive subroutines, it is often best to write it assuming that it will work. More often than not, it will work. If it doesn't, you can add a Debug.Print statement to print out the parameters to the routine. Looking at the pattern in this output will help you understand why your routine isn't working.

Displaying the Contents of a Folder

Once you loaded all of the folders into the TreeView control, you want to display the messages that are in a particular folder. To do this, you need to handle the NodeClick event, as shown in Listing 8.9. In this event, I grab the folder ID property from the Node.Key property and get the InfoStore ID property from the Node.Tag property. Then I can use the GetFolder method to get the Folder object associated with these values and load the messages into the ListView control by using the LoadMessages routine (discussed next).

Listing 8.9:   **TreeView1_NodeClick Event in CDO Demo**

```
Private Sub TreeView1_NodeClick(ByVal Node As ComctlLib.Node)

If Len(Node.Tag) > 0 Then
    Set msf = ms.GetFolder(Node.Key, Node.Tag)
    msi = Node.Tag
    LoadMessages msf, Node.Tag

End If

End Sub
```

The LoadMessages routine, shown in Listing 8.10, loops through the Messages object and copies selected properties for each message into the ListView control. Figure 8.8 shows the results.

FIGURE 8.8:

Loading messages from a folder

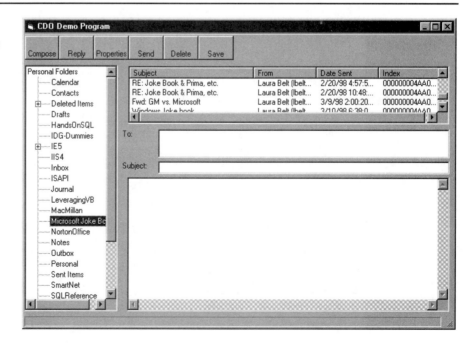

Listing 8.10:   LoadMessages Routine in CDO Demo

```vb
Private Sub LoadMessages(f As MAPI.Folder, id As Variant)

Dim l As ListItem
Dim m As MAPI.Message
Dim mp As Integer

mp = Screen.MousePointer
Screen.MousePointer = vbHourglass

On Error Resume Next

ListView1.ListItems.Clear
Text1.Text = ""
Text2.Text = ""
Text3.Text = ""
For Each m In f.Messages
    Set l = ListView1.ListItems.Add(, m.id, m.Subject)
    l.SubItems(1) = m.Sender.Name & " (" & m.Sender.Address & ")"
    l.SubItems(2) = FormatDateTime(m.TimeSent)
    l.SubItems(3) = m.id
    l.Tag = id
    DoEvents
Next m

Screen.MousePointer = mp

End Sub
```

You can see that I clear the ListView before I load it. This lets me refresh the contents of the folder by simply calling this routine again. Besides the subject and sender's e-mail address, I also keep track of the message's ID property and the ID of the InfoStore. Note that I clear the text boxes used to display a message, since they no longer contain a valid message from the list of messages stored in the ListView.

Displaying a Message

Clicking on a message in the ListView control triggers the `ItemClick` event, as shown in Listing 8.11. This routine retrieves the `Message` object and saves the reference in the module-level variable `msg` for later processing. Then it displays the message in the appropriate text boxes on the main form, as shown in Figure 8.9.

Listing 8.11:   ListView1_ItemClick Event in CDO Demo

```
Private Sub ListView1_ItemClick(ByVal Item As ComctlLib.ListItem)

On Error Resume Next

Set msg = ms.GetMessage(Item.Key)
Text1.Text = msg.Text
Text2.Text = msg.Sender
Text3.Text = msg.Subject
Label1.Caption = "From: "
Me.Caption = "Message from " & msg.Sender.Name & " (" & _
    msg.Sender.Address & ")"

End Sub
```

FIGURE 8.9:

Displaying a message

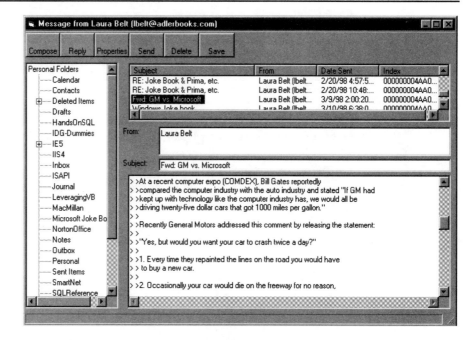

Processing a Message

The toolbar on top of the form contains a series of buttons that perform various e-mail tasks:

- To write a message, click the Compose button.

- To send a message after entering the information, click the Send button.

- To reply to a message, click the Reply button, type the response, and then click the Send button.

- To change message properties, click the Properties button to see a separate form with a list of the key properties and their values for the message.

- To save the contents of the message in the folder in which it was created, click the Save button (instead of the Send button to send it).

- To remove the message from the system permanently, click the Delete button.

These buttons are processed in the ButtonClick event, as shown in Listing 8.12.

Listing 8.12:   Toolbar1_ButtonClick Event in CDO Demo

```
Private Sub Toolbar1_ButtonClick(ByVal Button As ComctlLib.Button)

Dim f As Form
Dim r As MAPI.Recipient
Dim x() As String

On Error Resume Next

If Button.Key = "Compose" Then
   Me.Caption = "Composing new message."
   Label1.Caption = "To:"
   Text1.Text = ""
   Text2.Text = ""
   Text3.Text = ""
   Set msg = ms.Outbox.Messages.Add

ElseIf Button.Key = "Reply" Then
   Me.Caption = "Replying to " & msg.Sender.Name & _
      " (" & msg.Sender.Address & ")"
   Set msg = msg.Reply
```

```
      Text3.Text = "Re: " & msg.Subject
      Text2.Text = ""
      For Each r In msg.Recipients
          Text2.Text = Text2.Text & r.Address & ";"
      Next r
      x() = Split(msg.Text, vbCrLf)
      Text1.Text = ">" & Join(x(), vbCrLf & ">")
      Label1.Caption = "To:"

   ElseIf Button.Key = "Properties" Then
      ShowProperties ms.GetMessage(ListView1.SelectedItem.SubItems(3), _
          ListView1.SelectedItem.Tag)

   ElseIf Button.Key = "Send" Then
      msg.Text = Text1.Text
      msg.Recipients.AddMultiple Text2.Text
      msg.Subject = Text3.Text
      msg.Sender = ms.CurrentUser
      msg.Update
      msg.Recipients.Resolve
      msg.Send
      Text1.Text = ""
      Text2.Text = ""
      Text3.Text = ""
      Me.Caption = StdHeader
      LoadMessages msf, msi

   ElseIf Button.Key = "Save" Then
      msg.Text = Text1.Text
      msg.Recipients.AddMultiple Text2.Text
      msg.Subject = Text3.Text
      msg.Sender = ms.CurrentUser
      msg.Update
      Text1.Text = ""
      Text2.Text = ""
      Text3.Text = ""
      Me.Caption = StdHeader
      LoadMessages msf, msi
```

```
ElseIf Button.Key = "Delete" Then
    msg.Delete
    Set msg = Nothing
    Text1.Text = ""
    Text2.Text = ""
    Text3.Text = ""
    Me.Caption = StdHeader
    LoadMessages msf, msi

End If

End Sub
```

Composing a Message

To compose a new message, you use the Messages.Add method. This method adds a new message to the folder where the Messages collection exists.

When programming using CDO, you should create new messages in either the inbox or the outbox. In this case, I created the message in the outbox folder and saved the reference in the module-level variable msg.

Sending a Message

Clicking the Send button copies the message body to the Text property, adds the users to the Recipients collection using the AddMultiple method, and collects information about the sender from the CurrentUser object. It then performs an Update against the Message object to save this information to permanent storage.

I use the Recipients.Resolve method to examine each of the addresses and determine the closest match. If the Resolve method was unable to determine the proper addresses, an address selection dialog box appears, as shown in Figure 8.10. After the addresses have been resolved, I use the Send method to Update the message again, and then move it to the outbox with the rest of the messages that are ready to be transmitted.

FIGURE 8.10:

Resolving addresses with the
Check Names dialog box

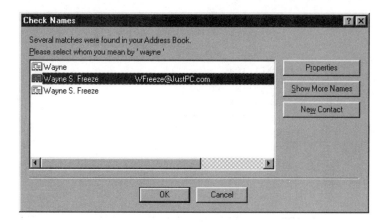

Replying to a Message

Replying to a message is not much more difficult than creating a new message. You use the Reply method against the current message to create a new message. All of the properties of the old message have been changed to reflect the reply status. For instance, the old sender is now the recipient, and the old recipient is now the sender.

What remains to be done is to insert the > character in front of each line of text and insert a *Re:* in front of the old subject line. The first is easy with the new Split and Join functions. Simply split the text into separate lines using vbCrlf and then join them back together using vbCrLF & ">". This will insert the > character in front of every line except for the first, which is easily handled outside this function.

TIP

Split and Join versus Replace: You could also use the Replace function to search through the message and replace every carriage return/line feed pair with a carriage return/line feed pair and a > character. This should be even more efficient than the Split/Join approach.

Viewing a Message's Properties

Clicking the Properties button displays the CDO information associated with a message, as shown in Figure 8.11. The Properties dialog box shows information such as the number of attachments, various status flags, the subject line, and the list of recipients. This helps you understand the state of the various pieces of information associated with a message.

FIGURE 8.11:

Message properties

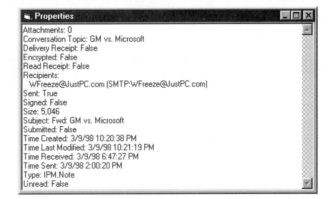

```
Properties                                                    _ □ ×
Attachments: 0
Conversation Topic: GM vs. Microsoft
Delivery Receipt: False
Encrypted: False
Read Receipt: False
Recipients:
  WFreeze@JustPC.com (SMTP:WFreeze@JustPC.com)
Sent: True
Signed: False
Size: 5,046
Subject: Fwd: GM vs. Microsoft
Submitted: False
Time Created: 3/9/98 10:20:38 PM
Time Last Modified: 3/9/98 10:21:19 PM
Time Received: 3/9/98 6:47:27 PM
Time Sent: 3/9/98 2:00:20 PM
Type: IPM.Note
Unread: False
```

Saving a Message

Saving a message is very similar to sending a message, except I don't bother to resolve any addresses and I don't perform the Send method. Note that I do refresh the current folder after saving or sending a message. This lets you see your new message if your current folder happens to be the outbox or the same folder where the original message was before you replied to it.

Deleting a Message

Deleting a message is also easy. Simply perform the Delete method against the message you want to delete. You don't need to worry about performing an Update first. Just remember to refresh the current folder and erase the currently displayed message.

Final Thoughts

The Simple MAPI controls are sufficiently powerful for many applications. Consider this: You can write a relatively simple program that can scan your inbox for mail, delete unwanted messages, and automatically reply to routine messages. For example, if you maintained a Frequently Asked Questions (FAQ) list, your program could scan through your inbox looking for "send" and the name of your FAQ. When a match is found, your program could send the requester a copy of the FAQ and delete the message from you inbox. You would never have to see it or worry about it.

Also, remember in Chapter 6 when I created a flat file containing environmental data about a user's system? It would be a simple matter to include a small bug-reporting form in the application. The form could collect a description of the bug and contact information, then compose an e-mail message using that information, and even include environmental data as an attachment. The note would then be sent to an address for bug reports (where another Simple MAPI program could automatically delete it).

I've barely touched on what the Collaboration Data Objects can do. It is very easy to use them to maintain your address book and contact list. You can also use them to schedule meetings and to filter your messages so you only see what you want to see. You could build an archive program that searched through all of your active folders in an `InfoStore` and created folders in another `InfoStore` that could contain all messages related to a particular person or subject. You could even duplicate messages between folders if the message spans more than one topic. This might simplify searching for information after the files have been removed from your current folders.

After studying these objects, you will have a much better understanding of how Outlook 98 works. However, CDO is not for everyone. It is more difficult to use than the Simple MAPI controls. Yet once you get used to it, the extra functions are worth the extra complexity.

CHAPTER

NINE

9

Printing with Visual Basic

- The `Printer` object

- Printer selection

- Printouts with multiple character fonts

- Printouts with shapes and images

- Your own print preview window

Many people have speculated that someday there would be no need for printed output. My belief is that this will never happen—at least not in my lifetime. Too many people rely on paper for various purposes. The classic example of the senior executive who has a secretary print out e-mail and then writes replies on paper for the secretary to retype and send is all too true.

Of course, there are some valid reasons for generating paper output. Invoices, bills, packing lists, and other such documents really need to be on paper, since most computer systems still don't talk to each other directly. Also, it is much easier to stuff a piece of paper in your pocket than haul around a computer. Printing a list of grocery items your spouse e-mailed you earlier in the day makes much more sense than carrying your computer through the store (especially if you don't own a laptop!).

In this chapter, we will focus on printing using the `Printer` object and other tools that make it easy to generate output for your printer. I'll start with an overview of the `Printer` object and then talk about the different ways you can select a printer. Then I'll discuss how to generate output, followed by how to build your own print preview window.

Introducing the Printer Object

The `Printer` object is the primary method used to access the printer. It has many properties and methods in common with the Picture control, plus a few that are unique to the `Printer` object. Table 9.1 lists the properties and methods common to both objects, and Table 9.2 lists the properties and methods specific to the `Printer` object.

NOTE   **The Printer object versus the Picture control:** These are very similar in nature and function. Both offer a canvas for you to create your own artwork. The only significant differences between them relate to the physical differences between a video display and a printer—you can clear a screen but not a printer page, and you can start another page in the printer but you can't do that with a video display.

TABLE 9.1:   Printer Object and Picture Control Properties and Methods

Property/Method	Description
Circle method	Draws a circle or an ellipse
CurrentX property	Specifies the horizontal coordinate of the cursor
CurrentY property	Specifies the vertical coordinate of the cursor
DrawStyle property	Specifies the pattern used to draw the line
DrawWidth property	Specifies the width of the line in pixels
FillColor property	Specifies the interior color for shapes
FillStyle property	Specifies the pattern used to fill shapes
Font property	Specifies the font characteristics for text output
ForeColor property	Sets the color used to draw the shapes and characters on the object
hDC property	Specifies the device context used to access the device
Height property	Specifies the height of the work area in twips
Line method	Draws a line between the specified coordinates
PaintPicture method	Draws the picture at the specified location
Print method	Outputs the specified text to the object
Pset method	Draws a point at the specified location
Scale method	Defines the coordinate system used to describe the work area
ScaleHeight property	Contains the Height in the units specified by ScaleMode
ScaleLeft property	Contains the Left position in the units specified by ScaleMode
ScaleMode property	Specifies the unit of measure for the Scale properties
ScaleTop property	Contains the Top in the units specified by ScaleMode
ScaleWidth property	Contains the Width in units specified by ScaleMode
ScaleX method	Computes a value for the specified width value in a different scale
ScaleY method	Computes a value for the specified height value in a different scale
TextHeight method	Computes the height of the specified string using ScaleMode and the specified font information

Continued on next page

TABLE 9.1 (CONTINUED): Printer Object and Picture Control Properties and Methods

Property/Method	Description
TextWidth method	Computes the width of the specified string using ScaleMode and the specified font information
Width property	Contains the width of the work area in twips

TABLE 9.2: Printer Object-Specific Properties and Methods

Property/Method	Description
EndDoc method	Finishes the current print operation and releases the output to the print spooler or printer
Fonts property	Contains an object reference with the list of fonts that can be used with the printer
KillDoc method	Finishes the current print operation and discards the output
NewPage method	Ejects the current page and begins a new page
Orientation property	Specifies if the printer's paper is placed in portrait mode or landscape mode
Page property	Specifies the current page number
PaperSize property	Specifies the size of the paper in the printer
PrintQuality property	Specifies the relative quality of the output
TrackDefault property	Specifies whether to change the default Printer object whenever the Windows default Printer object is changed
Zoom property	Specifies the scaling factor of the output

Printing in Windows

Printing in Windows is relatively simple. You can begin using the Print method to write some text to the printer, use the PaintPicture method to insert a graphical image below the text, and then use the EndDoc method to send the page to the printer.

It's important to understand that Windows treats a printer as a graphical device, like a video display or plotter. You can easily write one line of text after another, starting from the bottom of the page and going to the top, or you can write every other line on one pass and then fill in the blank lines on the next pass—it really doesn't matter. The important point is that you must finish putting everything on the page before you call the NewPage or the EndDoc method.

Printing from Applications

As far as your application is concerned, a printer is a printer is a printer. For the most part, the exact details of each printer don't matter. All output is arranged and printed a page at one time. Your program generates a page of output, and it is sent to the Print Manager to hold in a temporary file. This file is also known as a *spool file*.

The Print Manager continues to hold your output until you use either the End-Doc method or the KillDoc method. The EndDoc method tells the Print Manager to release the spool file and begin printing it. The KillDoc method tells the Print Manager to delete the spool file immediately, before it is sent to the printer.

Selecting a Printer

Windows supports multiple printers on each system. One printer is defined to be the system default. The others are defined and available for use.

There are two basic ways to select a printer:

- Load all of the DeviceNames into a ComboBox control and let the user select a printer from there.

- Use the CommonDialog control and the ShowPrinter method to let the user choose printing options as well as another printer.

Loading Device Names into a Combo Box

The Printers collection consists of a set of Printer objects. Changing the printer associated with the Printer object is as simple as using the Set statement to make the Printer object refer to a specific member of the Printers collection. You can do this by loading all of the DeviceNames into a ComboBox control, as shown in

Listing 9.1. Then you can switch printers whenever the user clicks on a new printer DeviceName, as shown in Listing 9.2.

Listing 9.1: **LoadPrinters Routine in Printer**

```
Private Sub LoadPrinters()

Dim pr As Printer

For Each pr In Printers
    Combo1.AddItem pr.DeviceName
Next pr

Combo1.Text = Printer.DeviceName

End Sub
```

Listing 9.2: **Combo1_Click Event in Printer**

```
Private Sub Combo1_Click()

Set Printer = Printers(Combo1.ListIndex)

End Sub
```

Using this approach, you are temporarily defining a printer to be the default printer for this application; you aren't changing the system default printer. You usually don't want to reset the default printer for Windows, because whoever selected it probably did so because most of that user's output is going to be sent there.

Showing the Printer Dialog Box

While selecting a printer from the Printers collection is a relatively effortless task, sometimes your users need to do more than simply selecting the printer. They may need to choose a different paper size or input tray, or change any of the properties available with the Printer object. In this situation, you should use the CommonDialog control and the ShowPrinter method. This provides the standard printer selection dialog box that you see in Figure 9.1.

FIGURE 9.1:

FIGURE 9.1:

The Printer dialog box

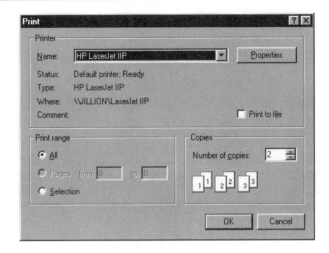

The Printer dialog box offers a number of options. Users can select the range of pages to be printed and the number of copies to be created. They also can access the Printer Properties dialog box, shown in Figure 9.2, and change any of the printer's properties, such as paper size, orientation, paper source, and graphics resolution.

FIGURE 9.2:

The Printer Properties dialog box

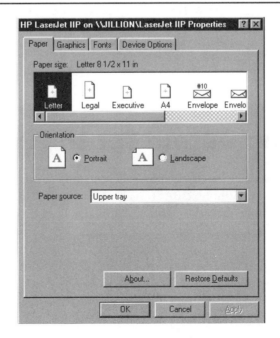

It is important to realize that the CommonDialog control doesn't talk to the printer at all. It merely collects information that your application may or may not send to the printer. Note that you also can set default values or disable some of these fields, such as the range of pages to be printed, by using the Flags property.

The block of code in Listing 9.3 shows how to use the CommonDialog control to change the system default printer to whatever the user selects. Also, two copies of the document will be printed by default, unless the user explicitly changes the number of copies.

Listing 9.3:   **MenuConfigure_Click Event in Printer**

```
Private Sub MenuConfigure_Click()

CommonDialog1.Copies = 2
CommonDialog1.PrinterDefault = True
CommonDialog1.ShowPrinter

End Sub
```

WARNING   **Setting PrinterDefault may cause problems:** Any changes the user makes to the default printer in the CommonDialog control with PrinterDefault set to True will be reflected in the default Windows system printer. Since you may not want the user to be able to make changes to the default system printer, use caution when setting this property to True.

Creating Output for the Printer

Unlike the original BASIC, Visual Basic presents a lot of issues to deal with when you print text. BASIC is line-oriented; Visual Basic generates output a page at a time. Each character in BASIC takes up the same amount of space, so aligning text into columns isn't a big deal. With Visual Basic, characters can vary in height and width. Also, you can now include graphics ranging from a simple line to a bitmapped image—an option that didn't exist in the original BASIC.

In the following examples, I'm going to perform a number of operations on a PictureBox control to illustrate how to perform these functions. The beauty of Visual Basic is that the same operations can be performed on a `Printer` object or a PictureBox control without any changes.

Printing Text

Printing text in BASIC is done with the `Print` statement. Similarly, in Visual Basic, you use the `Print` method. This method works on the object you wish to print. This object can be an entire form, the `Debug` object, the `Printer` object, or a Picture control. We've already talked about how the `Debug.Print` method directs output to the Immediate window (in Chapter 3). The other methods display their output on their respective objects:

- `Form1.Print` sends output to `Form1`'s background.

- `Picture1.Print` sends the output to the `Picture1` control.

- `Printer.Print` sends the output to the printer.

> **WARNING**   **Recycled paper versus recycled electrons:** When testing your printing programs, remember that most of the methods and properties you will use on the `Printer` object also can be used with the Picture control. So for most of the examples in this chapter, I use the Picture control to show you how the various methods and properties work. Feel free to try any of these programs out using the `Printer` object by substituting `Printer` for `Picture1`, sending your results directly to your printer. Only your recycler knows the difference.

Printing to and beyond the Edges

The `Print` method works much as you would expect. Each time you call the `Print` method, the output will begin at the start of the next line, except if the previous `Print` method ended with a comma or semicolon. In that case, the print would be continued on the same line. Listing 9.4 contains an example of code that allows printing beyond the right edge, and Figure 9.3 shows the results.

Listing 9.4: **Command1_Click Event in Print**

```
Private Sub Command1_Click()

Dim i As Integer

Picture1.Cls
For i = 1 To 100
    Picture1.Print "abcdefg";
Next i

End Sub
```

FIGURE 9.3:

Any printed output beyond
the right edge of the control
is lost.

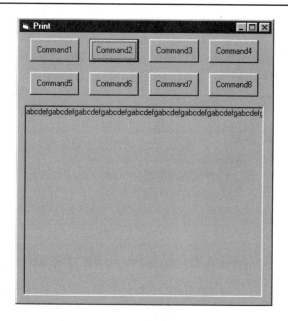

One limitation of this approach is that, eventually, you will reach the end of the object. If you continue to print to the object, the text will fall off the end of the paper or screen and not be visible. Likewise, if you continue to print on the same line, it will also fall off the edge and be lost. Neither of these conditions will generate an error or a warning. Listing 9.5 contains an example of code that allows printing beyond the bottom edge, and Figure 9.4 shows the results.

Listing 9.5:   **Command2_Click Event in Print**

```
Private Sub Command2_Click()

Dim i As Integer

Picture1.Cls
For i = 1 To 100
    Picture1.Print "abcdefg"
Next i

End Sub
```

FIGURE 9.4:

Any printed output beyond
the bottom edge of the
page is lost

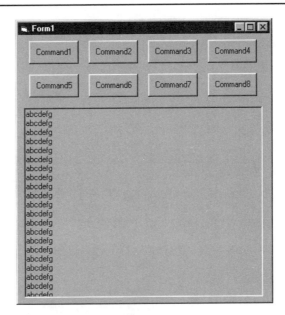

NOTE   **Clearing the object:** The Cls method is used to clear the contents of a form or of
a Picture control and to reposition the cursor to the beginning.

Printing in Columns

Just like in the original BASIC, if you separate values by commas, each value will start at the beginning of the next print zone. Print zones are aligned based on absolute measurements, not characters. This makes it easier to create columns, as long as your data is not wider than a print zone. If it's wider, you need to be careful to ensure that you are starting the data in the proper print zone. The code shown in Listing 9.6 creates columns with commas. Figure 9.5 shows its output.

Listing 9.6:   **Command3_Click Event in Print**

```
Private Sub Command3_Click()

Picture1.Cls
Picture1.Print "abc", "def", "ghi", "jkl", "mno", "pqr", _
    "stu", "vwx"
Picture1.Print "abcdef", "ghijkl", "mnopqr", "stuvwx"
Picture1.Print "abcdefghijkl", "mnopqrstuvwx"
Picture1.Print "abcdefghijklmnopqrstuvwxyz", _
    "abcdefghijklmnopqrstuvwxyz"

End Sub
```

FIGURE 9.5:

When you use commas, columns will line up as long as they are close to the same size.

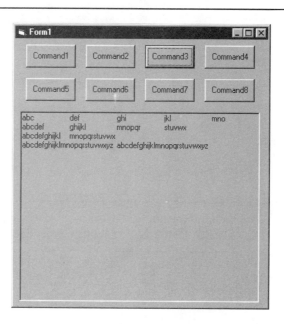

Things go better with Tab: One of the functions available for the `Print` method is the Tab function. The Tab function will position the output cursor at a particular column in the output field. The width of a column is determined by the average width of all of the characters in the current font. This is not the most accurate way to align columns of information, but it is better than relying on the effect of commas and semicolons.

Positioning the Cursor

Another way to control printing alignment is by positioning the cursor. Each object (Form, `Picture`, and `Printer`) maintains a cursor that describes the current position on the object. Two properties describe the location of the cursor: `CurrentX` is the horizontal component, and `CurrentY` is the vertical component. These properties can be read to find the current location or assigned a value to reset the cursor to a new position. As usual with these objects, all measurements are made in twips. (Recall that one twip is exactly one-twentieth of a printer's point, and there are 1440 twips to the inch or 567 to the centimeter.)

The code in Listing 9.7 shows how to move around a PictureBox control using the CurrentX and CurrentY properties. I save the values of CurrentX and CurrentY into the string t before I execute the `Print` method so that these values remain unaffected by the printing process. Figure 9.6 shows the output.

Listing 9.7:   Command4_Click Event in Print

```
Private Sub Command4_Click()

Dim t As String

Picture1.Cls
t = FormatNumber(Picture1.CurrentX, 0) & "," & _
    FormatNumber(Picture1.CurrentY, 0)
Picture1.Print t

Picture1.CurrentX = 0
Picture1.CurrentY = 2880
t = FormatNumber(Picture1.CurrentX, 0) & "," & _
    FormatNumber(Picture1.CurrentY, 0)
Picture1.Print t
```

```
Picture1.CurrentX = 2880
Picture1.CurrentY = 0
t = FormatNumber(Picture1.CurrentX, 0) & "," & _
    FormatNumber(Picture1.CurrentY, 0)
Picture1.Print t

Picture1.CurrentX = 2880
Picture1.CurrentY = 2880
t = FormatNumber(Picture1.CurrentX, 0) & "," & _
    FormatNumber(Picture1.CurrentY, 0)
Picture1.Print t

End Sub
```

FIGURE 9.6:

You can use the CurrentX and CurrentY properties to control the position of a PictureBox control.

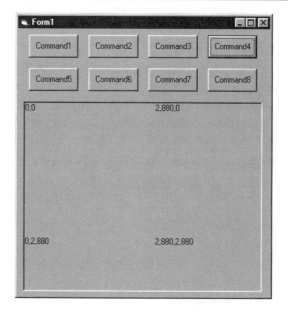

Positioning Text

So far, I haven't talked about where the cursor is oriented with respect to the text you're going to print. Maybe it's obvious, but the cursor is always at the upper-left corner of an imaginary box that surrounds the text. The actual size of the box is determined by the size of the tallest character in the text string, the sum of the widths of each individual character in the text string, and the font used to display the text string.

Because this is a rather complicated process, Visual Basic includes two methods that return the size of the string: TextWidth and TextHeight. Also, if you have embedded carriage returns, these methods will compute the total size of the box based on the size of the longest line and the total number of lines.

The code in Listing 9.8 shows how to display the same string of text in four different quadrants surrounding the center point of the cursor. Figure 9.7 shows the results.

NOTE **Why is there a small space below the text string and behind the text string?** This is because the TextWidth method allows for space after the last character in the string, and the TextHeight method includes space above and below the string. This way, you don't need to worry about where to place the next string.

Listing 9.8: **Command5_Click Event in Print**

```
Private Sub Command5_Click()

Dim t As String

t = "Hello"

Picture1.Cls
Picture1.CurrentX = 1440
Picture1.CurrentY = 1440
Picture1.Print t

Picture1.CurrentX = 1440 - Picture1.TextWidth(t)
Picture1.CurrentY = 1440
Picture1.Print t

Picture1.CurrentX = 1440
Picture1.CurrentY = 1440 - Picture1.TextHeight(t)
Picture1.Print t

Picture1.CurrentX = 1440 - Picture1.TextWidth(t)
Picture1.CurrentY = 1440 - Picture1.TextHeight(t)
Picture1.Print t

End Sub
```

FIGURE 9.7:

You can use the TextHeight and TextWidth methods to control the position of text.

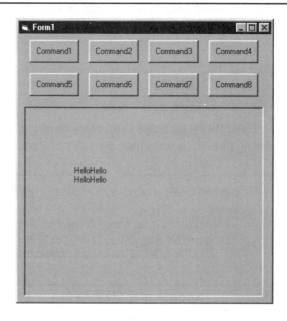

In this example, I begin by printing the first string starting at 1 inch from the top and 1 inch from the left margin (remember, 1440 twips equal 1 inch). Next, I print the second string immediately to the right of the first string. I compute its new X coordinate by subtracting the width of the string.

The third string is printed above the second. Its X coordinate is computed by subtracting the width of the string from the 1440-twips X coordinate. Its Y coordinate is computed by subtracting the height of the string from the 1440-twips Y coordinate. Finally, the last string is printed above the first by subtracting the height of the string from the 1-inch Y coordinate.

Changing Font Characteristics

One of the nice features of Visual Basic is that it has the ability to use multiple fonts in a single object. This means that you can make a block of text bold, italic, or underlined. You can also change the size or even the name of the font you wish to use. This allows you to present information more dramatically by emphasizing certain items.

Doing this in Visual Basic is fairly easy. All you need to do is change the Font object associated with the object you are using. In Listing 9.9, you can see that I copied the same code from the code shown in the previous section and inserted some changes to Picture1's Font property.

Listing 9.9:   Command6_Click Event in Print

```
Private Sub Command6_Click()

Dim t As String

t = "Hello"

Picture1.Cls
Picture1.CurrentX = 1440
Picture1.CurrentY = 1440
Picture1.Print t

Picture1.Font.Bold = True
Picture1.CurrentX = 1440 - Picture1.TextWidth(t)
Picture1.CurrentY = 1440
Picture1.Print t

Picture1.Font.Italic = True
Picture1.CurrentX = 1440
Picture1.CurrentY = 1440 - Picture1.TextHeight(t)
Picture1.Print t

Picture1.Font.Size = 18
Picture1.CurrentX = 1440 - Picture1.TextWidth(t)
Picture1.CurrentY = 1440 - Picture1.TextHeight(t)
Picture1.Print t

Picture1.Font.Size = 8
Picture1.Font.Bold = False
Picture1.Font.Italic = False

End Sub
```

As you can see in Figure 9.8, most of these changes did not materially change how the information is aligned. However, in the upper-left corner, where I changed the font size to 18, you can see that the text is pulled slightly away from the other three text blocks. This is because the padding areas above, below, and to the right of the text are greater in an 18-point font than in the standard 8-point font.

You can change font characteristics to emphasize text.

Generating Simple Graphics

Generating simple graphics is a relatively easy task. Visual Basic includes the Circle, Line, and PSet methods for drawing circles, lines, and points, respectively.

The code in Listing 9.10 shows how to create a circle with a radius of 0.5 inch (720 twips) centered at a location 1 inch down and 1 inch over (1440 by 1440 twips). Then a square is drawn, with each side 1 inch long (hint: 2160 twips equal 1.5 inches). Finally, I make a point in the exact center of the circle and the square. Figure 9.9 shows the results.

Listing 9.10:   Command7_Click Event in Print

```
Private Sub Command7_Click()

Picture1.Circle (1440, 1440), 720

Picture1.Line (720, 720)-(2160, 720)
Picture1.Line (2160, 720)-(2160, 2160)
Picture1.Line (2160, 2160)-(720, 2160)
Picture1.Line (720, 2160)-(720, 720)

Picture1.PSet (1440, 1440)


End Sub
```

FIGURE 9.9:

You can use Visual Basic's drawing methods to create a square, a circle, and a point.

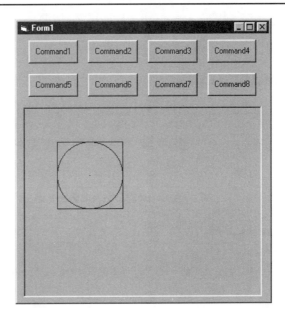

Inches, Centimeters, Pixels, or Twips

You can use any of the four measuring systems when you specify coordinates for these graphic methods, as follows:

- Set the `ScaleMode` property to 5 to specify coordinates in inches.

- Set the `ScaleMode` property to 7 to specify coordinates in centimeters.

- Set the `ScaleMode` property to 3 to specify coordinates in pixels.

- Set the `ScaleMode` property to 1 to specify coordinates in twips.

At one time or another, I've tried each of these scales and had problems. I forgot to set `ScaleMode` when I created a new control, or somehow `ScaleMode` would get reset back to twips. Or worse, the scales were user-defined—so who knew what values were legal coordinates? Finally, I gave up and decided to memorize 1,440 twips = 1 inch. Now I write code like `1440*2` instead of `2.0` inches. Performance-wise, there shouldn't be a difference, since the compiler should optimize that `1440*2` to `2880`.

Including Images

Printing images is merely a matter of using the PaintPicture method to place the image on the page at the specified location. The code in Listing 9.11 shows how to include two different images on the same object at the same time. Figure 9.10 shows the results.

Listing 9.11:   Command8_Click Event in Print

```
Private Sub Command8_Click()

Picture1.Cls
Picture1.PaintPicture LoadPicture(App.Path & "\p944ts.bmp"), 144, 720
Picture1.PaintPicture LoadPicture(App.Path & "\cj&sam.bmp"), 2880, 1440

End Sub
```

FIGURE 9.10:

I used the PaintPicture method to print these pictures of my three children.

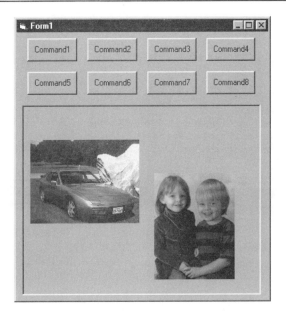

Pulling It Together

Listing 9.12 contains a subroutine that demonstrates how to format a single page from a spreadsheet, including the gridlines and random values for the data.

Listing 9.12:   **Sample01 Routine in Print**

```
Private Sub Sample01()

Dim g As Single
Dim i As Single
Dim j As Single
Dim t As String

For i = 1440 To 1440 * 10 Step 720
    Printer.Line (1440, i)-(1440 * 7, i)
Next i

For i = 1440 To 1440 * 7 Step 1440
    Printer.Line (i, 1440)-(i, 1440 * 10)
Next i
```

```
g = (720 - TextHeight("Cell: G20")) / 2

Printer.Font.Bold = True
For i = 1 To 5
   t = Chr(Asc("@") + i)
   Printer.CurrentY = 1440 + g
   Printer.CurrentX = 1440 + 1440 * i + (1440 - Printer.TextWidth(t)) / 2
   Printer.Print t
Next i

For i = 1 To 17
   t = FormatNumber(i, 0)
   Printer.CurrentY = 1440 + 720 * i + g
   Printer.CurrentX = 2880 - Printer.TextWidth(t) - g
   Printer.Print t
Next i

Printer.Font.Bold = False
For i = 1 To 5
   For j = 1 To 17
      t = FormatNumber(Rnd * 10000, 2)
      Printer.CurrentY = 1440 + 720 * j + g
      Printer.CurrentX = 2880 + 1440 * i - Printer.TextWidth(t) - g
      Printer.Print t
   Next j
Next I

Printer.EndDoc

End Sub
```

The routine begins by declaring some local variables: g is used to hold a gap value, i and j are general-purpose loop counters, and t is a temporary string variable used to hold data prior to printing.

The first real work is to draw 20 horizontal lines starting at 1 inch (1440 twips) and stopping at 10 inches (1440 * 10 twips) with a $\frac{1}{2}$-inch (720-twips) gap between each line. Each line is 7 inches long (1440 * 7 twips). Next, I draw vertical lines starting at 1 inch (1440 twips) and stopping at 7 inches, with a 1-inch gap between lines. Each line is 10 inches long. This draws the grid where I can fill in information. Next, I compute a gap value for g that is used to center the text vertically within a cell. This value is based on one half of the difference between the height of one cell (720 twips) and the height of some sample text (`"Cell: G20"`). I divide it in half to get the distance between the top of the cell and the top of the text.

Next, I print the column headers and row headers in bold. I compute the actual header value and save it into t. This means that I can compute the `TextWidth` and print the value while only computing it once. The column headers are positioned down g twips from the top of the cell and centered in the cell.

The row headers are right-justified and also positioned down g twips from the top of the cell, but I leave a gap of g between the right edge of the cell and the left edge of the text. I did this simply because it looked a little better with the same distance between the top, left, and bottom edges of the text and the cell. I could have just as easily put the text right up against the right edge of the cell. Or I could have appended a couple of spaces between the edge of the text and the cell wall. You can use whatever method you feel comfortable with.

Then I generate some random numbers to print and print them using the same technique I used to position the row headers. Note that I turned bold off before I print the main text, since I want to emphasize the headers, not the text itself. Finally, I send the spool file to the printer with the `EndDoc` method. Figure 9.11 shows the results.

TIP

Go slowly and think about the entire page at one time: When building code to format a printed page, the trick is to go slowly and build the individual pieces, testing them one step at a time. Start with your header and footer. Make sure that they are showing up where you expect them. Next, add in the code to produce the first few lines of your output. Are the columns aligned properly? Are they justified correctly? (Sometimes, it is easier to do this with fake data rather than real data.) Once you are satisfied that everything looks good, add the rest of the lines and enjoy the finished product.

FIGURE 9.11:

An example of a printed spreadsheet page

	A	B	C	D	E
1	7,055.48	562.37	9,109.64	3,820.11	807.15
2	5,334.24	9,495.57	2,268.66	3,009.71	4,579.71
3	5,795.19	3,640.19	6,951.16	9,485.71	9,057.30
4	2,895.63	5,248.68	9,800.03	9,798.29	2,613.68
5	3,019.48	7,671.12	2,439.31	4,013.74	7,852.12
6	7,747.40	535.05	5,338.73	2,782.80	3,789.03

Building a Print Preview Window

Now that you know how to prepare output for the printer, what about creating a print preview window to see what the output looks like before you actually send it to the printer? Since you know that most of the same methods and properties apply to both the Picture control and the `Printer` object, you can base your preview window on the Picture control. However, before we begin this project, let's consider a few basic issues.

Creating Output for a Particular Page

For a print preview window, we need to be able to build the print output one page at a time. This means that for any given value of `Page`, we need to be able to create the printer document for that particular page. This can be more difficult than it looks.

Consider a word processor. To print any random page from the document means that you must clearly know where each page starts. For example, if someone inserted a line at the beginning of a 100-page document, you must go through and repaginate the entire document before you can print it. (Well this isn't strictly true, all you really need to repaginate is the pages prior to the page you want to print, but you get the point.) This can be a very time-consuming process. Spreadsheets are a little easier when all of their rows are fixed in height, but you can't always assume that is the case. Database reports can be tougher still, since they can get very large and complicated. How do you handle this? Generating output is a relatively straightforward task in BASIC. You simply use the `Print` statement.

The trick to building a print preview window with Visual Basic is to recognize that you should have only a method to generate the output for a specific page and then apply that method for each page as needed to complete the output. When sending the output to the printer, you simply generate all of the desired pages. When sending the output to the preview window, you generate one page and wait until the user requests the next page.

Using Common Routines

The first step in this process is to build some common routines that can be used to handle the differences between the `Printer` object and the Picture control.

Beginning a New Page

The `WriteNewPage` routine is called before I start writing anything to the preview window or the printer, as you can see in Listing 9.13. It accepts two parameters: the `PrintObject` and the `PageNumber`. The `PrintObject` contains an object reference to either a `Printer` object or the Picture control where the output will be sent. If the object is a `Printer`, then I need to execute the `NewPage` method on every page after the first. If this object is a Picture control, then all I need to do is clear the screen.

Listing 9.13:   **WritePage Routine in Charter**

```
Private Sub WriteNewPage(PrintObject As Object, PageNumber As Integer)

If TypeOf PrintObject Is Printer Then
   If PageNumber > 1 Then
      PrintObject.NewPage
   End If
Else
   PrintObject.Cls

End If

End Sub
```

Ending a Print Session

After beginning a new page, I need to handle how I end the print session. This is even easier. I only need to execute the EndDoc method for the `Printer` object, since I don't really want to clear the Picture control until after the user has finished viewing it. That will be handled automatically when I start the next print preview. The WriteEndDoc routine is shown in Listing 9.14.

Listing 9.14:   **WriteEndDoc Routine in Charter**

```
Private Sub WriteEndDoc(PrintObject As Object)

If TypeOf PrintObject Is Printer Then
    PrintObject.EndDoc
End If

End Sub
```

Painting the Image

Listing 9.15 contains the simplest of the preview routines. It merely paints the specified image at the specified location. It really doesn't need to be a separate routine; however, I included it here to show how the rest of the routines function. Basically, I supply all of the arguments necessary, followed by the `PrinterObject`, as parameters for this routine. Then I translate them into the single statement to paint a picture. Note that since both the `Printer` object and the Picture control both support the `Line` method, there isn't any difference between how they are handled in this routine.

Listing 9.15:   **WritePicture Routine in Charter**

```
Private Sub WritePicture(pic As Object, x1 As Single, y1 As Single, _
    PrintObject As Object)

PrintObject.PaintPicture pic, x1, y1

End Sub
```

Centering Text in a Rectangle

Remember how I described myself as lazy? The next routine, shown in Listing 9.16, is definitely one that looks nasty at first, but when you've had a chance to use it a bit, you will see how it can save a lot of work in the long run. This routine is called `WriteCenter` and has two siblings, `WriteLeft` and `WriteRight`, which you can read for yourself when you load this program.

Listing 9.16:   WriteCenter Routine in Charter

```
Private Sub WriteCenter(OutputText As String, PrintObject As Object, _
    Optional x1 As Variant, Optional y1 As Variant, _
    Optional x2 As Variant, Optional y2 As Variant, _
    Optional NewBold As Variant, Optional NewItalic As Variant, _
    Optional NewUnderline As Variant, Optional NewSize As Variant, _
    Optional NewFontName As Variant)

Dim OldBold As Boolean
Dim OldItalic As Boolean
Dim OldUnderline As Boolean
Dim OldSize As Integer
Dim OldFontName As String

If Not IsMissing(NewBold) Then
    OldBold = PrintObject.Font.Bold
    PrintObject.Font.Bold = NewBold
End If

If Not IsMissing(NewItalic) Then
    OldItalic = PrintObject.Font.Italic
    PrintObject.Font.Italic = NewItalic
End If

If Not IsMissing(NewUnderline) Then
    OldUnderline = PrintObject.Font.Underline
    PrintObject.Font.Underline = NewUnderline
End If

If Not IsMissing(NewSize) Then
    OldSize = PrintObject.Font.Size
    PrintObject.Font.Size = NewSize
End If

If Not IsMissing(NewFontName) Then
```

```
        OldFontName = PrintObject.Font.Name
        PrintObject.Font.Name = NewFontName
    End If

    If Not (IsMissing(x1) Or IsMissing(x2)) Then
        PrintObject.CurrentX = x1 + (x2 - x1) / 2
    ElseIf Not IsMissing(x1) Then
        PrintObject.CurrentX = x1
    End If

    If Not (IsMissing(y1) Or IsMissing(y2)) Then
        PrintObject.CurrentY = y1 + (y2 - y1) / 2
    ElseIf Not IsMissing(y1) Then
        PrintObject.CurrentY = y1
    End If

    PrintObject.CurrentX = PrintObject.CurrentX - _
        PrintObject.TextWidth(OutputText) / 2
    PrintObject.CurrentY = PrintObject.CurrentY - _
        PrintObject.TextHeight(OutputText) / 2
    PrintObject.Print OutputText

    If Not IsMissing(NewFontName) Then
        PrintObject.Font.Name = OldFontName
    End If

    If Not IsMissing(NewSize) Then
        PrintObject.Font.Size = OldSize
    End If

    If Not IsMissing(NewUnderline) Then
      PrintObject.Font.Underline = OldUnderline
    End If

    If Not IsMissing(NewItalic) Then
        PrintObject.Font.Italic = OldItalic
    End If

    If Not IsMissing(NewBold) Then
        PrintObject.Font.Bold = OldBold
    End If

    End Sub
```

All this routine does is to center the specified text string inside the rectangle defined the by x1, y1 and x2, y2 parameters, or centered at the location specified by x1, y1, or centered over the current cursor position. However, to make your life easier, I included most of the common font changes that you might make during the course of your program. Thus, you can easily specify any changes in the default font for a particular print item. This routine will ensure that only the specified changes are made and that the defaults are properly restored at the end of the routine.

This routine can be broken down into three parts. The first part checks to see if a parameter was supplied. If one is supplied, then the current property value is saved and the property is then set to the new value.

The second part is the actual positioning of the cursor and printing of the text. In this case, I compute the center point of where I want to print the text. If both x, y coordinates are supplied, I choose the center of the rectangle defined by them. If only one x, y coordinate is supplied, then I assume that the coordinate is the physical point where the text should be centered. If no x, y coordinates are supplied, then I assume that the current cursor position is where the text should be centered. Once I have the center point, all I do is subtract one half of the TextHeight method to determine the starting y coordinate, and subtract one half of the Text-Width method to determine the starting x coordinate. Then I can simply use the Print method to display the text.

The third part of the routine is to clean up any definitions I may have changed. Once that is done, I'm finished with this routine.

WARNING   **Be careful of variable types when using Optional:** The only acceptable variable type for an optional parameter is Variant. This means that it is easy to pass a String when you really need to pass an Integer. You should choose very meaningful variable names here to help the users determine the appropriate data type when Visual Basic prompts them with the list of parameters for the function.

A Simple Print Preview Example

You may have noticed that the listings for the print preview window code are from the Charter application, which I first discussed in Chapter 6. I thought it would be nice if I added the ability to send both the chart and the grid to the printer. Listing 9.17 shows how easy it is to print a report using the common routines. First, I select the entire chart and copy it to the clipboard. Then I simply use the `WritePicture` routine to either display the picture in the preview window or print it on the physical printer, depending on the parameter passed to this routine.

Listing 9.17:   **PrintChart Routine in Charter**

```
Private Sub PrintChart(o As Object)

MSChart1.SelectPart VtChPartTypeChart, 0, 0, 0, 0
MSChart1.EditCopy
WritePicture Clipboard.GetData, 1440, 1440, o
WriteEndDoc o

End Sub
```

A More Complex Print Preview Example

Listing 9.18 contains a more complex example of how the print preview functions work. This is essentially the same function as in Listing 9.12 earlier in the chapter, but it is much shorter due to the processing done in the `Write` routines.

Listing 9.18:   **PrintGrid Routine in Charter**

```
Private Sub PrintGrid(o As Object)

Dim i As Single
Dim j As Single
Dim t As String

WriteNewPage o, 1

WriteCenter MSChart1.TitleText, o, 0, 720, 1440 * 8.5, 720, True, , , 24

For i = 0 To MSFlexGrid1.Rows
   WriteLine 1440, 1440 + i * 720, 1440 + 1440 * MSFlexGrid1.Cols, _
      1440 + i * 720, o
Next i

For i = 0 To MSFlexGrid1.Cols
```

```
    WriteLine 1440 + i * 1440, 1440, 1440 + i * 1440, _
        1440 + MSFlexGrid1.Rows * 720, o
Next i

For i = 1 To MSFlexGrid1.Cols - 1
    WriteCenter Chr(Asc("@") + i), o, 1440 + 1440 * i, 1440, _
        2880 + 1440 * i, 1440 + 720, True
Next i

For i = 1 To MSFlexGrid1.Rows - 1
    WriteRight FormatNumber(i, 0) & "  ", o, 2880, 720 * (i + 1), 2880, _
        2160 + 720 * (i + 1), True
Next i

For i = 1 To MSFlexGrid1.Cols - 1
    For j = 1 To MSFlexGrid1.Rows - 1
        WriteRight MSFlexGrid1.TextMatrix(j, i) & "  ", o, 2880 + 1440 * i, _
            1440 + 720 * j, 2880 + 1440 * i, 2160 + 720 * j
    Next j
Next i

WriteEndDoc o

End Sub
```

I begin this routine by calling the WriteNewPage to make sure that I'm on the first page. I continue by displaying the chart title at the top of the page. Since I can override the default values for this statement, I choose to output the title in 24-point bold. Then I draw the lines to form the grid.

Next, I display the column headers and row headers. Again, because it's easy to override the default font characteristics, I can easily specify that these values are written in bold without doing a lot of work to get this result. Also, I know that the defaults are restored, so I don't need to worry about them during the next call. Note that I output a couple of spaces after each right-justified field to make sure that the field doesn't touch the right end of the cell.

Then I output the actual contents of the cells in much the same fashion as I output the row headers. Finally, I call the WriteEndDoc routine to close the spool file and send it to the printer.

Final Thoughts

I've written enough code over time using the `Printer` object to decide that there has to be a better way. Fortunately, there are a couple. First, you can use the RichTextBox control to help format your text. This may not be a lot easier, but you may be able to build a series of small RichText documents that contain the proper formatting for your data, and then merge them together into one large RichText document to send to the printer. You can even save the report as a disk file by using the `Save-File` method, so it could be included as an attachment in an e-mail message.

Another option is to create your own Word or Excel documents and use the native power of those applications to perform your formatting and printing. This is even more powerful than the RichText approach, since you can easily combine text and graphics into a single report.

Consider the case of a systems integrator who recommends a series of hardware and software services. It might be desirable to format a summary letter based on some key information from the recommendations, plus include charts and graphs that discuss the recommendations even further. The report would end with a list of recommended hardware and software with detailed pricing information. While you could do this yourself in Visual Basic, it screams Word and Excel. The only problem is that the data is in your database, and Word and Excel can't read a database.

Of course, the option that most programmers will take, especially the lazy programmers working with databases, will be to use Crystal Reports or the new Microsoft Data Reporter. Both make it easy to create your own custom reports from the database with far less effort than any of the options discussed in this chapter. While the results may not be as nice as the custom reports you can write by hand or create using Word and Excel, the report writers provide a fast, easy way to build reports. They offer the ability to add more reports down the road, without requiring you to release a new version of the software.

No matter which way you look at it, you have a rich selection of tools to help you create your own custom documents and reports.

Providing Useful Controls for Your Users

- Menus and status bars

- Toolbars and CoolBars

- The MonthView and DateTimePicker controls

- The MaskedEdit control

Buried deep within Visual Basic are a large number of controls that you can easily add to your program. Many of these controls are hidden in three big controls that are called the Microsoft Windows Common Controls. The others are stand-alone, but provide you with simple tools that can make your programs more powerful and easier for your users to use.

Nearly all applications developed for Windows include a series of menu commands, status bars, and toolbars. Along with providing a well-designed drop-down menu structure, with a very simple set of code, you can display a pop-up menu whenever a user right-clicks on an item. Communicating status information to the user is also important, which is why you may want to take a closer look at including status bars in your applications. In the space on the form that a single command button may occupy, you can include a small toolbar that allows your users to quickly perform multiple tasks.

In addition to the Menu, StatusBar, Toolbar, and CoolBar controls, I'll also talk about some controls that are especially useful for data-entry programs. The Month-View and DateTimePicker controls make it easy for your users to work with dates. The ImageCombo control lets you add images to your combo box lists. Finally, the MaskedEdit control helps your users enter values in special formats.

Adding Menus

The most fundamental tool to allow the user to perform functions in Windows programs is the Menu control. While you might not normally think of the menu bar as a control since it doesn't appear in the Visual Basic IDE toolbox, it is in fact a control. It has properties and events just like a normal control, and you can even create a control array with a number of menu items that can be accessed by a single index value.

NOTE   **The menu is the root of all functions:** When creating a menu hierarchy, I try to ensure that every function that is available in my application has a menu entry. This means that the user can always expect to find a particular function somewhere on a menu. I may choose to include a toolbar, which duplicates some of the functions already on the menus. I may also choose to put shortcut buttons on the form or use shortcut keys. But no matter whatever other means there are for selecting functions, I make sure that every one of those functions is already available somewhere on the menu bar.

All menu items are created with the Menu Editor. Each entry in the Menu Editor is a single control and contains a series of properties and a single event. Table 10.1 lists the Menu control properties and events.

TABLE 10.1:   Menu Properties and Events

Property/Event	Description
Caption property	Displays as the text of the menu item
Checked property	When set to True, displays a checkmark in front of the caption
Click event	Occurs when the user selects the menu item
Enabled property	When set to True, displays the menu item in black and allows it to be selected; when set to False, displays the menu item in gray and doesn't allows it to be selected
HelpContextId property	References a help item in a help file
Index property	Uniquely identifies a menu item in a Menu control array
Name property	Provides the name of the menu item
Parent property	Identifies the menu item's parent object, which is usually the form itself
Tag property	Stores data in the menu control
Visible property	When set to True, displays the menu item; when set to False, hides the menu item (and all subordinate items)
WindowList property	When set to True, displays all the child windows in an MDI application

---

TIP

Put your menu items on groups: You should use a menu separator to group common items together. This is done by setting the Caption property to a single dash (-). The dash draws a single line across the drop-down menu, providing the user with a visual clue to common elements.

Designing Your Menu Structure

When creating your menu structure, you should consider the impact of the Windows interface guidelines. These guidelines call for five different top-level menu items: File, Edit, View, Window, and Help. While none of these menu items are required, using them helps your users by putting common functions where they expect to find them. Look at some other applications to see what types of menu items those developers choose to include.

You should not feel limited to just these menu items, nor should you believe that all of these menu items absolutely must be included in your application. What you include is up to you. However, if you choose to include a menu item to exit your program, your users would be best served by an Exit subitem under the File menu item rather than somewhere else. Figure 10.1 shows a typical menu item arrangement for an application (the Charter program, which was discussed in Chapter 7).

FIGURE 10.1:

A typical application with a menu bar

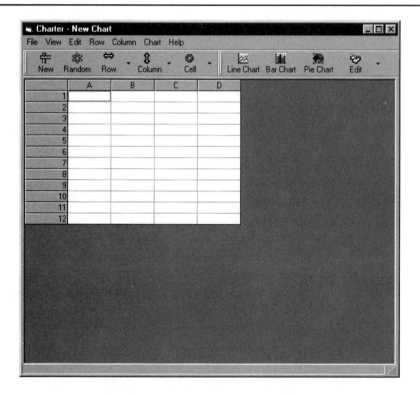

Two other Windows interface guidelines for menus provide a bit more information about the subitems for the user. Whenever you define a shortcut key that performs the same function as a menu item, you should try to display that as part of the subitem entry. Also, you should use an ellipsis (…) after any menu subitems that display a dialog box when they are selected.

The File Menu

The File menu should be the first item on your menu bar. The drop-down menu should include any file-related or document-oriented items. The following are typical File menu subitems:

New This item creates an empty document.

Open This item opens an existing document.

Close This item closes the current document. If the current document is not saved, the program should give the user a chance to save the document before closing it.

Separator A separator line divides the first three choices from the ones below.

Save This item saves the current document.

Save As This item saves the current document and prompts the user for a new name and/or location.

Separator A separator line divides the Save subitems from the ones below.

Print Setup This item shows the Printer Setup dialog box using the CommonDialog control's `ShowPrinter` method.

Print Preview This item shows a preview of how the current document would look after being printed.

Print This item prints the current document.

Separator A separator line divides the Print subitems from the one below.

Exit This item closes all open documents and exits the current program.

TIP

Exit before starting: When I start building a Visual Basic application, I always include two menu items: `File` and `Exit`. In the `Click` event for `Exit`, I add a single statement: `Unload Me`. This gives me the framework to add more menu items and provides a nice way to exit my application while I'm building it.

The Edit Menu

The second top-level menu item is Edit. This menu item holds normal editing controls, such as those listed below:

Undo This item undoes the effects of the previous change to the current document.

Repeat This item repeats the last action.

Separator A separator line divides the top two items from the ones below.

Cut This item copies the selected items from the current document to the clipboard and deletes them from the document.

Copy This item copies the selected items from the current document to the clipboard but leaves them in the document.

Paste This item pastes the items from the clipboard to the current document at the cursor position.

Separator A separator line divides the clipboard-related items from the ones below.

Find This item searches the current item for the specified information.

Replace This item performs the same function as Find but replaces the information with a new value once it has been found.

Separator A separator line divides the search functions from the ones below.

Delete This item removes the selected items from the document.

Duplicate This item performs the same function as Copy and Paste.

As I said before, don't feel that you must include any or all of these items. Also, you should feel free to include additional items that are appropriate to your application.

> **TIP**
>
> **Protect your users from themselves:** Often users will select menu items that they probably shouldn't. If your program doesn't offer an undo capability, you should give users a chance to change their minds. Have your program ask users to verify that they really want to delete a selected item (such as a large block of text or a database entry) or that they want to close a file or exit the program without saving their changes.

The View and Window Menus

Next to the Edit menu item should be the View menu item. You should place any menu items that affect how the user sees the information presented on the form under this menu item. For example, you might include a function for switching from outline form to raw format to normal view of a document. Zoom In, Zoom Out, and Show Ruler are other common menu subitems displayed on the View menu.

After the first three menu items, you're on your own until you reach the last two. The next to last top-level menu item is Window. This menu item exists only in MDI (Multiple Document Interface) applications and serves primarily to allow the user to see, select, and arrange the currently active document windows.

The Help Menu

The last top-level menu item on your menu bar should be the Help menu. This should contain the following subitems:

Help Topics This item displays the standard Help window.

Contents and Index This item displays the contents and index dialog boxes for the help file.

Separator A separator line divides the top two items from the one below.

About This item displays an About dialog box with information about the application.

Creating Menu Arrays

Just like regular control arrays, menu arrays can be very useful when you want to have a single event to handle a number of similar controls. For example, you can select the Chart top-level menu item on the Charter application and see a list of available charts:

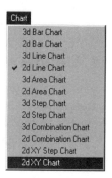

Since only one of these charts may be selected at a time, I thought it would be nice to allow the user to click on the name of a chart and have a checkmark appear next to it. This would mean that I would have to set the Checked property to False for all other controls. In this case, there are a dozen different charts to choose from. If I used independent menu controls for each chart, I would have a dozen different routines to code, and I would need to explicitly set Checked to False for each individual control.

Instead, I use a menu array. Then I need to handle only one event, as shown in Listing 10.1. This event calls a simple subroutine that will update the menu controls and set the actual chart type, as shown in Listing 10.2. The only complication is that the valid chart types don't form a contiguous range of values, but a control array must have a contiguous range of Index values. I handle this with a simple If statement, as you can see in Listing 10.1.

Listing 10.1:   **MenuChart_Click Routine in Charter**

```
Private Sub MenuChart_Click(Index As Integer)

If Index <= 9 Then
    SetChartType Index

ElseIf Index = 10 Then
```

```
         SetChartType 14

     ElseIf Index = 11 Then
         SetChartType 16

     End If

     End Sub
```

In the subroutine shown in Listing 10.2, after selecting the chart type, I loop through each of the menu controls and set the Checked property to False. Then I use an If statement to set the Checked property to True for the selected chart type.

Listing 10.2:   SetChartType Routine in Charter

```
     Private Sub SetChartType(t As Integer)

     Dim i As Integer

     MSChart1.Repaint = False
     MSChart1.chartType = t
     MSChart1.Repaint = True

     For i = 0 To 11
         MenuChart(i).Checked = False
     Next i

     If t <= 9 Then
         MenuChart(t).Checked = True

     ElseIf t = 14 Then
         MenuChart(10).Checked = True

     ElseIf t = 16 Then
         MenuChart(11).Checked = True

     End If

     End Sub
```

Looking at these two routines, you might wonder why I didn't set the Checked property in the menu's Click event, which would have saved me from having to use the second set of If statements in the SetChartType subroutine. While that is true, the situation is a bit more complex.

When dealing with a user interface that includes toolbars and pop-up menus, it is often useful to have one common point where you set and reset various attributes of your program. In this case, I also have a toolbar that can choose the chart type. Putting the set of If statements in the SetChartType subroutine allows me to have a common point for performing all of the updates to the user interface.

Building Pop-Up Menus

One of the latest trends in Windows programming is to provide pop-up menus in your application. Pop-up menus are easy to build. You simply use the Menu Editor to create a menu with one or more submenus, and then you use the PopUp statement to show the menu.

NOTE   **Hiding your pop-up menus:** By default, any pop-up menu you create will be displayed as part of the regular menu bar. Setting the Visible property to False will prevent the menu from being displayed in the menu bar but still allow it to be displayed using the PopUp statement.

In Listing 10.3, you can see how easy it is to create a pop-up menu. I display this menu anytime the user right-clicks anywhere on the chart, while the entire chart is selected. When the MouseDown event occurs, I check to see if the right mouse button was clicked. I then determine the part of the chart that was selected, since I only want to display the pop-up menu when the entire chart is selected. After I get the chart part, I check to see which mouse button triggered this event. If the right button was clicked, I check to see if the entire chart was selected. If so, I display the pop-up menu for selecting a chart type, as shown in Figure 10.2.

FIGURE 10.2:

The Charter program's
pop-up menu

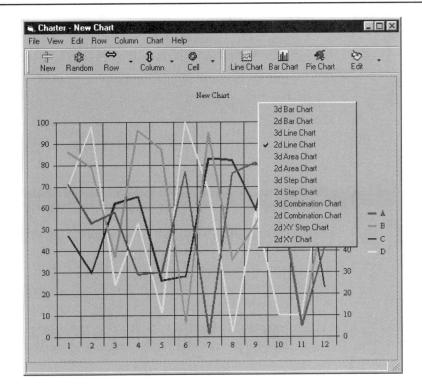

Listing 10.3:   MSChart1 Routine in Charter

```
Private Sub MSChart1_MouseDown(Button As Integer, Shift As Integer,_
    X As Single, Y As Single)

Dim i1 As Integer
Dim i2 As Integer
Dim i3 As Integer
Dim i4 As Integer
Dim p As Integer

MSChart1.GetSelectedPart p, i1, i2, i3, i4
```

```
If Button = vbRightButton Then
    If p = VtChPartTypeChart Then
        PopupMenu MenuChartList
    End If
End If

End Sub
```

Adding Status Bars

The status bar provides one of the most useful ways to present noncritical information to the user. In the case of Microsoft Word's status bar, for example, you can see the current page number, the total number of pages in the document, the relative position of the cursor in the document, plus some additional information such as the status of the CapsLock and Insert keys.

A StatusBar control consists of two basic components: a series of one or more panels up to a maximum of sixteen, plus a resize grip at the right side of the control.

Adding a StatusBar control is relatively easy. Simply draw the control anywhere on the form and watch it automatically go to the bottom of the form and stretch itself from one side to the other. The only piece of information retained from what you drew on the form is the height of the StatusBar. Can life be any easier?

Table 10.2 lists the key properties available in the StatusBar control. You should use the Property Pages dialog box rather than the regular Properties dialog box to define the properties for this control. With the Property Pages dialog box, you can define not only the properties available for this control, but also specify properties for each of the Panel objects that are contained in the control.

TABLE 10.2: Selected StatusBar Properties

Property	Description
Align	Describes how the status bar is placed on the form
Panels	Provides an object reference to the Panels collection, which contains the information about each panel

Continued on next page

TABLE 10.2 (CONTINUED):   Selected StatusBar Properties

Property	Description
SimpleText	When the Style property is set to sbrSimple (1), holds the text to be displayed in a panel
Style	When set to sbrSimple (1), displays a single panel containing the string in the SimpleText property; when set to sbrNormal (0), displays up to 16 panels as defined by the Panels collection

The StatusBar control has two modes of operation. The simplest mode is when the status bar displays only a single panel with text. You can choose this mode by setting the Style property to sbrSimple. Then anytime you want to display information to the user, simply assign a text value to the SimpleText property, and it will be displayed in the panel. You enter the text you want to appear in the General tab of the Property Pages dialog box, which is shown in Figure 10.3.

FIGURE 10.3:

The General tab of the StatusBar Property Pages dialog box

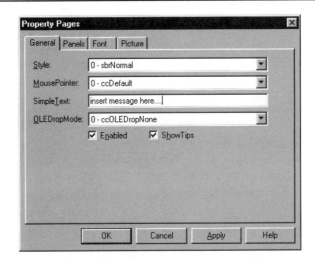

The other mode of operation is when you define one or more panels, which allows you to take full advantage of the all the features of the StatusBar control. Setting the Style property to sbrNormal is all it takes. This is also the default mode. Then you can set the properties for each panel on the Panels tab of the StatusBar Property Pages dialog box, as shown in Figure 10.4.

FIGURE 10.4:

The Panels tab of the StatusBar Property Pages dialog box

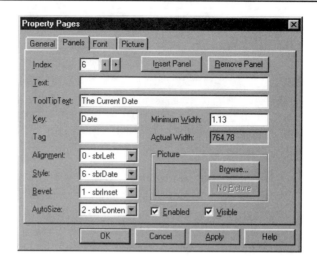

Defining Panels in the Status Bar

By default, the StatusBar control comes with only one panel. You can define additional panels through the Panels tab of the StatusBar Property Pages dialog box (see Figure 10.4).

To add other panels, simply click the Insert Panel button. To remove the current panel, click the Remove Panel button. To scroll through the panels, either type the index value of the panel you wish to see or click on the left/right arrows to scroll through the existing panels. Then all you need to do is to fill in the blanks for the properties of that particular panel. Table 10.3 lists the panel properties. When you run your program, the panels will be displayed in the status bar in the order of their Index values.

TABLE 10.3: Panel Properties

Property	Description
Alignment	Describes how the text appears in the panel
AutoSize	Adjusts the panel's size when the width of the form is adjusted or to fit the size of the contents

Continued on next page

TABLE 10.3 (CONTINUED):   Panel Properties

Property	Description
Bevel	Describes how the panel is displayed in the status bar
Index	Specifies a number that uniquely identifies the panel
Key	Provides a text reference to the panel
MinWidth	Specifies the minimum size of a panel
Picture	Identifies a Picture object to be displayed in the panel
Style	Contains the style of information in a panel
Text	Contains the text to be displayed in the panel
ToolTipText	Contains the text that will be displayed as a ToolTip when the mouse cursor passes over the panel
Width	Specifies the width of the panel

Panel Styles

There are eight different styles of panels. The default type is text, which can display both an image and a string of characters (examples are coming up soon). If you include an image, its height will automatically be resized to fit into the panel. The placement of the image depends on the alignment you choose for the panel:

- If you specify left alignment, any image will be displayed starting at the left edge of the panel, followed immediately by the text.

- If you specify right alignment, the image will be displayed against the right edge of the panel and the text will be immediately to the image's left edge.

- If you specify center alignment, the image will return to the left edge of the panel and any text will be placed in the center.

The other seven styles do not let you display an image. They exist to display system information such as the status of the CapsLock key, the NumLock key, the Ins key, and the Scroll Lock key. You can also display the current date and time, plus whether the KANA character mode (KANA is a simplified Japanese character set) is enabled.

Panel Sizing

The AutoSize property works with the MinWidth and the Width properties to determine the size of panel. Panel sizing works as follows:

- You can set AutoSize to sbrNoAutoSize, in which case the width of the panel is determined by the Width property.

- You can set AutoSize to sbrContents, which will automatically resize the panel based on the size of the text value.

- You can set AutoSize to sbrSpring, which will expand the panel to fill the available space after the widths for all the panels with fixed and content sizing have been calculated. If more than one panel has an AutoSize of sbr-Spring, then the space will be evenly distributed among the panels.

Panel ToolTips

You should also include ToolTipText for each status bar Panel object. This way, you can make sure that the user is fully aware of what the status bar contents really mean. A ToolTip also provides a useful way to communicate what will happen if the user clicks or double-clicks on the panel.

Panel Names

The Key property is similar to the Key property in many other controls. It is used to uniquely identify the Panel object by name. This allows you to rearrange the order of the status bar panels from time to time (perhaps you inserted a new panel for a new feature) without rewriting your existing code.

Status, Please

When using a StatusBar control in my applications, I like to make the first panel a general-purpose text panel whose AutoSize property is set to sbrSpring. This lets me better communicate information to the user.

For instance, this is a useful way to tell a user that he or she has made a mistake when editing a field. I can flag the field in error by setting the field's background to red and then display a specific error message in the status bar.

Unlike when you use a message box to communicate this type of information, the user isn't required to take any action to clear the error message display in order to correct the error. It also helps the user to associate the error message with the appropriate field in case multiple errors were found.

Displaying Information in a Status Bar

Displaying information in a status bar is very easy. Simply assign a string value to the Text property or a picture to the Picture property of the desired panel. Note that you can do this only when the Style property is set to sbrText. This is because the other panels automatically generate their own information and don't use these properties. Figure 10.5 shows an example of a status bar with text.

FIGURE 10.5:

A status bar with the text "Illegal value in interest rate per period"

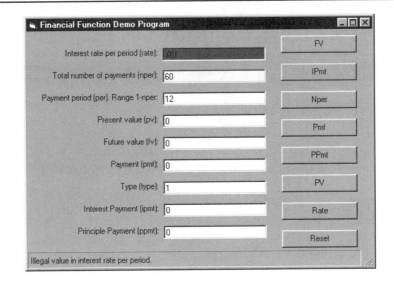

Listing 10.4 shows the code that produced the status bar message in Figure 10.5. This is from the Financial Function Demo program described in Chapter 5. I used the CheckData subroutine to verify that the specified object has a numeric value in the Text property. If not, then the error message passed to this routine will be displayed in the Errors panel of the StatusBar control, and the background of the object will be changed to red.

Listing 10.4:   CheckData Routine in Financial Function

```
Private Sub CheckData(d As Object, m As String)

If Not IsNumeric(d.Text) And Len(d.Text) <> 0 Then
    StatusBar1.Panels("Errors") = m
    d.BackColor = &HFF&
```

```
Else
    StatusBar1.Panels("Errors") = ""
    d.BackColor = &H80000005
End If

End Sub
```

Responding to Click Events in a Status Bar

The StatusBar control can also respond to click and double-click events. Table 10.4 lists the four types of events you can work with in your status bars.

TABLE 10.4: StatusBar Events

Event	Description
Click	Occurs whenever the user clicks anywhere on the panel
DblClick	Occurs whenever the user double-clicks anywhere on the panel
PanelClick	Occurs when the user clicks on a panel; occurs before the Click event
PanelDblClick	Occurs when the user double-clicks on a panel; occurs before the DblClick event

Panel Clicks versus Regular Clicks

It is important to note that if a user clicks over a panel, both the PanelClick event and the Click event will occur in that order. This also applies to the PanelDblClick and DblClick events.

The main difference between the PanelClick and the regular Click events is that the PanelClick event will contain a copy of the Panel object. From this object, you can determine which panel the mouse pointer was over when the user clicked.

Animation in a Status Bar

Listing 10.5 contains some code from an utterly useless program that I wrote to have a little fun with a few controls. The object of this code is to animate a moon in the first panel of the status bar. To do this, I added a StatusBar control to the bottom of the form. I also included an ImageList control to hold the series of images to be displayed and a Timer control that will be used to determine when to switch the images. The status bar looks like this:

Listing 10.5:   **StatusBar Events for Animating a Moon in Weather Maker**

```
Dim NextPicture As Integer

Private Sub Form_Load()

NextPicture = 1
Timer1.Enabled = False
Timer1.Interval = 200
StatusBar1.Panels("Moon").Picture = ImageList1.ListImages.Item(1).Picture

End Sub

Private Sub StatusBar1_PanelClick(ByVal Panel As ComctlLib.Panel)

If Panel.Key = "Moon" Then
    Timer1.Enabled = Not Timer1.Enabled

End If

End Sub

Private Sub Timer1_Timer()

NextPicture = (NextPicture Mod 8) + 1
StatusBar1.Panels("Moon").Picture = _
    ImageList1.ListImages.Item(NextPicture).Picture

End Sub
```

In the `Form_Load` event, I set the variable `NextPicture`, which holds the Image-List index of the next picture, to 1. Next, I disable the Timer and set the Timer's `Interval` to 200 milliseconds. Finally, I load the initial picture into the StatusBar.

I use the `PanelClick` event to start and stop the animation. To do this, I make sure that the user clicked in the Moon panel, and then I merely toggle the `Timer .Enabled` property. In the Timer event, I compute the index of the next picture, and then I copy the picture from the ImageList to the StatusBar.

Adding Toolbars

Everyone loves those neat little buttons most Windows programs put under the menu bar. Toolbars make programs easier to use, because they make the most popular functions readily available with a single mouse-click. Users aren't forced to search through the menus to find the functions they need.

Creating a Toolbar

You can add your own toolbars to your Visual Basic programs by using the Toolbar control. In the space on the form that a single command button might occupy, you can include a small toolbar that can perform multiple tasks.

TIP

Once is enough: When designing an application, you should isolate all of the functions that can be performed by a user using a toolbar, menu, or some other method into a single subroutine or function—even if it is just a single line of code. Then you can call it from each toolbar or menu event. This means that when you need to update this logic, you only need to change it one place, not in each individual event.

A Toolbar control consists of a set of independent buttons that, when clicked, will trigger an event in which you can perform the desired function. Each button can contain an icon, a text caption, or both. Toolbar buttons can also have a drop-down menu, similar to the drop-down toolbar buttons in Internet Explorer 4. Figure 10.6 shows a program with a typical toolbar (although you probably won't find buttons for making weather in a typical program).

FIGURE 10.6:

A program with a sample
toolbar

Creating a toolbar is a very simple process. Just click on the Toolbar icon in the
toolbox and draw a Toolbar control on the form. Then you can set Toolbar properties on the General tab of the Toolbar Property Pages dialog box, as shown in Figure 10.7. Some of the more interesting Toolbar control properties are listed in
Table 10.5.

FIGURE 10.7:

The General tab of the
Toolbar Property Pages
dialog box

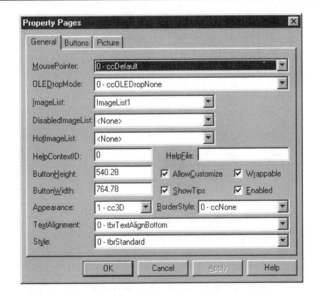

TABLE 10.5: Selected Toolbar Properties

Property	Description
Align	Specifies how the toolbar is placed on the form
AllowCustomize	Allow users to customize the toolbar using the standard Customize Toolbar dialog box
Appearance	Specifies whether the toolbar is displayed with 3D effects or as flat
BorderStyle	Specifies the type of border displayed around the entire toolbar
DisabledImageList	References an ImageList control containing a list of icons that will be displayed if the button is disabled
HotImageList	References an ImageList control containing a list of icons that will be displayed when the cursor hovers over a button
ImageList	References an ImageList control containing a list of icons that will be displayed in a button
ShowTips	When set to **True**, shows ToolTips
Style	Specifies how the buttons will appear on the toolbar
TextAlignment	Specifies if text is displayed below or to the right of the button
ToolTipText	Specifies the text to be displayed when the mouse pointer is held over the control for about a second
Wrappable	When set to **True**, specifies that if the form is resized, the buttons will be displayed on a second line if necessary

NOTE   **Overlapping ToolTips:** You can specify ToolTips for the entire control or for each individual button. Don't do both, or they will overlap each other.

Toolbar Alignment and Wrapping

You can specify how the toolbar will be positioned on the form by setting the Align property. You can automatically place the toolbar along any edge of the form or leave it at the default of tbrAlignNone.

Be lazy: Set the `Align` property to `vbAlignTop` to automatically resize the Toolbar control when the form is resized.

You can also set the `Wrappable` property to `True` to display all of the buttons on the toolbar in case the user resizes the form, making it too small for all of the buttons to fit. If this happens with `Wrappable` set to `True`, the buttons will be wrapped to the next line, and the height of the toolbar will be increased.

The ImageList Control for the Toolbar

After you've put your Toolbar control on the form, create an ImageList control and add any images that you want to display on the toolbar. Then display the Properties dialog box and select the ImageList you just created.

If you want to display a different icon when the button is disabled or when the mouse pointer passes over it, create an additional ImageList control for each function and load it with the desired icons. Make sure that each icon has the same value for Key in each of the ImageLists; each button can specify only one image value. Depending on the situation, the icon to be displayed will be taken from the appropriate ImageList.

Be sure that your small icons are really small: Set the icon size before you add any images to the ImageList control.

Transparent Toolbar Buttons

If you like the new toolbars used in Office 97 and Internet Explorer 4, you can set the `Style` property to `tbrFlat`. This makes the toolbar flat without distinct buttons, as shown in Figure 10.8. When the mouse pointer passes over the button, a border will be drawn around it, thus highlighting the button.

FIGURE 10.8:

A toolbar with transparent buttons

Adding Buttons to a Toolbar

Once you've added a Toolbar control and defined the ImageList controls, you can select the Buttons tab of the Toolbar's Property Pages dialog box to create the buttons that will be displayed on the toolbar. Figure 10.9 shows an example of this dialog box with the properties for the Snow button that appears in the sample toolbars shown in Figures 10.7 and 10.8.

FIGURE 10.9:

The Buttons tab of the Toolbar's Property Pages dialog box, with properties for the Snow button

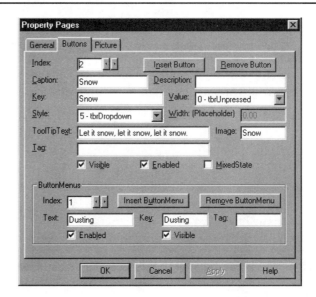

Each button is automatically assigned a unique index value, starting with 1. To add buttons, click the Insert Button button. To remove a button, click the Remove Button button. Table 10.6 lists some of the more useful properties for a toolbar button.

TABLE 10.6: Selected Toolbar Button Properties

Property	Description
Caption	Specifies the text displayed below or beside the button
Description	Specifies the text displayed next to the button in the Customize Toolbar dialog box
Image	References an image in an ImageList

Continued on next page

TABLE 10.6 (CONTINUED):   Selected Toolbar Button Properties

Property	Description
Key	Specifies a string that uniquely identifies the button
MixedState	When **True**, sets the button in an indeterminate state
Style	Describes how the button is displayed
ToolTipText	Specifies the text displayed when the mouse pointer is held over the button for about a second
Value	Holds the state of the button; can be either **trbUnpressed** (0) or **tbrPressed** (1)
Visible	When set to **True**, displays the button on the toolbar

The Button's Icon

Probably the most important of the button properties is the Image property. This is either an index or key value to an image in the ImageList controls we just discussed. Remember that the same reference must exist in all ImageList controls that you specified on the General tab of the Toolbar Property Pages dialog box.

Button Styles

The Style property is also important, although you probably won't need to change its default value. The default value (tbrDefault) will create a normal button that is activated when you click on it. The following are your other choices for the button Style property:

- The tbrCheck style creates a button that works like a checkbox. When you press the button, it remains pressed until you press it again, then it returns to its normal state.

- If you specify tbrSeparator, the button becomes a separator on the toolbar. In normal mode, this will leave a gap between buttons. In transparent mode, this will appear as a vertical line.

- You can create a group of buttons where only one button at a time can be pressed by creating a series of buttons with a style of tbrButtonGroup. Two buttons with a Style of tbrSeparator must separate the button group.

- A button with the `tbrPlaceholder` style is used to create a location for other objects, such as a ComboBox or ImageCombo control, on the toolbar. Although the Toolbar control is not truly a container for these controls, you can easily move and resize the combo box to the location of the placeholder button after the toolbar has been moved or resized.

- A button with the `tbrDropDown` style works like a normal button, with a drop-down arrow next to it. When the user clicks the drop-down arrow, a menu of items will appear below the button, and the user can select one any of these items.

TIP

Stating the obvious: This may be obvious to some readers, but it is possible to set the value of these buttons on the fly. This is especially useful for the button group and check style buttons, where you may want their states to mimic the state of processing in your application.

Mixed State Buttons

The `MixedState` property is useful when you are not sure if a button should be displayed as pushed or not. The classic case for this situation is when the user has selected a block of text, and some of the text contains bold characters and some does not. In this instance, you would want to display the Bold button in a mixed state until the selection is changed or until the user clicks the button and changes the selected text to all bold or not bold.

Button Menus

Adding a button menu to a button is even easier than adding a button. Simply fill in the information at the bottom of the Buttons tab of the Property Pages dialog box. The `Text` property contains the entry that will appear in the drop-down menu, and the `Key` property is used to uniquely identify the menu item.

Handling a Toolbar's Events

Using a Toolbar control in your program is relatively simple (but what isn't in Visual Basic, right?). You merely write a few lines of code to handle a few events and you're finished. Table 10.7 lists some interesting Toolbar events.

TABLE 10.7:   Selected Toolbar Events

Event	Description
ButtonClick	Occurs when a users clicks one of the buttons on the toolbar
ButtonDropDown	Occurs when a user clicks the drop-down arrow next to a button
ButtonMenuClick	Occurs when a user selects an item from the button's drop-down menu
Change	Occurs after a user has changed the toolbar using the Customize Toolbar dialog box

Listing 10.6 contains the code I've written to respond to a Toolbar control Button-Click event. This routine receives a Button object as a single parameter. From this parameter, you will most likely want to look at the Key property, to determine the button that was pushed, and the Value property, to determine its state.

With that understanding, I merely need to determine which button was clicked, and then perform the appropriate routine to handle the button's function. Note that the Snow button also has a button menu, so I take advantage of that by keeping a variable called DefaultSnow to hold the most recently selected value from the button menu. I then verify that it has valid data (Len(DefaultSnow) > 0) before using the default value.

> **TIP**
>
> **History repeats itself:** Sometimes, you want to dynamically assign the series of values to a button menu. This would work well for a Redo button, where clicking the Redo button itself would repeat the most recent change, and the drop-down menu could list the ten most recent changes.

Listing 10.6:   **Toolbar1_ButtonClick Routine in Weather Maker**

```
Private Sub Toolbar1_ButtonClick(ByVal Button As ComctlLib.Button)

If Button.Key = "Sunshine" Then
    SetWeather "The sun is shining. It's a beautiful day."

ElseIf Button.Key = "Snow" Then
    If Len(DefaultSnow) > 0 Then
        SetWeather DefaultSnow
```

```
      Else
          SetWeather "The snow is falling."
      End If

  ElseIf Button.Key = "Rain" Then
      SetWeather "The rain is expected to stop later today."

  ElseIf Button.Key = "Lightning" Then
      SetWeather "Scattered thunderstorms are expected this evening."

  ElseIf Button.Key = "Clouds" Then
      SetWeather "It's partly cloudy today with patches of sunshine."

  End If

  End Sub
```

Handling a ButtonMenuClick event is also very easy. Much like I did with the ButtonClick event, in Listing 10.7, I use the Key property to discover which button was pushed and determine which action should be taken.

Listing 10.7:   Toolbar1_ButtonMenuClick Routine in Weather Maker

```
Private Sub Toolbar1_ButtonMenuClick(ByVal ButtonMenu As _
    ComctlLib.ButtonMenu)

If ButtonMenu.Key = "Dusting" Then
    DefaultSnow = "The snow storm will end shortly leaving only a dusting."
    SetWeather DefaultSnow

ElseIf ButtonMenu.Key = "Close" Then
    DefaultSnow = "Schools will be closed today, due to snow."
    SetWeather DefaultSnow

ElseIf ButtonMenu.Key = "Blizzard" Then
    DefaultSnow = "The blizzard will continue for the next 72 hours."
    SetWeather DefaultSnow

End If

End Sub
```

Customizing Your Toolbar

Before we leave the subject of toolbars, let's take a look at how users can customize them. Assuming that you set the `AllowCustomize` property to `True`, all a user needs to do to make changes to a toolbar is double-click on the toolbar (but not on one of the buttons), and the Customize Toolbar dialog box will appear, as shown in Figure 10.10.

FIGURE 10.10:

The Customize Toolbar
dialog box

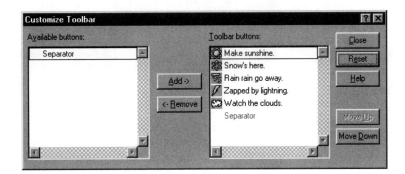

This dialog box allows users to add and remove buttons from the toolbar. Also, they can change the order of the buttons. When the user makes a change to the toolbar, the `Change` event will be triggered. You can then use the `SaveToolbar` method to save the new Toolbar control configuration to the Windows Registry, as I did in Listing 10.8, and use the `RestoreToolbar` method to restore it the next time your program runs.

Listing 10.8:   Toolbar1_Change Routine in Weather Maker

```
Private Sub Toolbar1_Change()

Toolbar1.SaveToolbar "Weather Maker", "Form1", "Toolbar1"

End Sub
```

TIP
Stitching new buttons on your toolbar: Another way to build customizable toolbars is to simply define all possible buttons on the toolbar. This takes advantage of the fact that a button that is not visible will not occupy any space on the toolbar. Then all you need to do is to include the code to handle the buttons in the appropriate events and create a Toolbar customization form with one checkbox for each button. You can then place a checkmark next to the desired item, which means that the button is displayed (`Visible = True`), or uncheck it to indicate that it's not displayed (`Visible = False`).

Adding CoolBars

One of the new features that became available in Office 97 is a new style of toolbar. An improved version of this toolbar is used in the Internet Explorer 4 web browser. These toolbars replace conventional three-dimensional buttons with flat buttons that become highlighted when you pass the cursor over them (the `tbr-Flat` setting for the Toolbar `Style` property, discussed earlier). Also, for the first time, you can include a drop-down menu of items from a toolbar button (the `tbrDropDown` setting for the Button `Style` property, also discussed earlier).

An integral part of these enhancements is a new toolbar container called a CoolBar. A CoolBar container consists of one or more bands, and each band can contain a toolbar, combo box, textbox, or other control. These controls are accessed via the Band control's `Child` property.

Figure 10.11 shows you an example of a CoolBar control with five bands:

- The first band is empty.
- The second band contains a combo box control.
- The third band contains a conventional toolbar with raised buttons.
- The fourth band contains a caption.
- The fifth band contains a toolbar with flat buttons.

FIGURE 10.11:

A sample CoolBar with five bands

The bands can be rearranged and resized based on the user's preference. You can force each band to be the same height or allow the CoolBar to vary the heights as needed. The CoolBar control lets you move bands from one row onto another, and it will even create a new row if necessary. Rows will be deleted if there are no bands in them. Also, although the CoolBar is usually displayed horizontally at the top of the form, you can reorient the control so that it can be displayed vertically along the side or in the middle of the form.

TIP   **Where is the CoolBar control?** The Toolbar and CoolBar controls are found in the Microsoft Windows Common Control Library and Library 3, respectively. If you need them, simply add them using the Project ➤ Components dialog box.

Creating a CoolBar

Adding a CoolBar to your program is a snap. Simply select the CoolBar icon in the toolbox and draw it on your form. Then you can set properties in the CoolBar Property Pages dialog box, as shown in Figure 10.12. Table 10.8 shows some of the CoolBar properties.

FIGURE 10.12:

The General tab of the CoolBar Property Pages dialog box

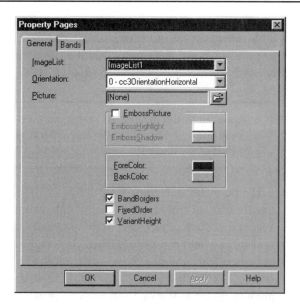

TABLE 10.8: Selected CoolBar Properties

Property	Description
Align	Sets the location of the CoolBar relative to the form
Bands	Specifies a collection of **Band** objects to be displayed on the CoolBar
Orientation	Sets whether the band is displayed horizontally or vertically
RowCount	Specifies the number of rows in the CoolBar
VariantHeight	If set to **False**, specifies that each band must be the same height

CoolBar Alignment

Unlike the Toolbar control, the CoolBar control doesn't automatically position itself. Go to the Property Pages dialog box and set the Align property to vbAlignTop. Then the control will reposition itself to the top of the form and stretch itself so that it extends from one side of the form to the other.

CoolBar Controls

The CoolBar acts as a control container, just like a Frame or PictureBox control. To add controls to your CoolBar, simply draw them on top of the CoolBar. If you want to paste a control, make sure that the CoolBar has the focus before you paste the control.

NOTE   **Children of the hWnd:** The CoolBar control supports only controls containing the hWnd property. Since the Label control lacks the **hWnd** property, it can't be used as a child of the CoolBar.

The most natural control to put on your CoolBar is the Toolbar control. In fact, the Toolbar control has had several enhancements over the version released in Visual Basic 5. As discussed in the previous section, the Style property now lets you choose between the old three-dimensional buttons and the new transparent buttons. (Transparent buttons are used in Office 97 and Internet Explorer 4.) If you set the Toolbar's Style to transparent, you should also change the Appearance property to flat to duplicate Office 97's look.

Adding Controls to a Band

In order to use the CoolBar controls, you need to create a band and then set Band.Child to the control. You can do this at design time by using the Bands tab of the Coolbar Property Pages dialog box, as shown in Figure 10.13, or at runtime by using the Bands collection's Add method. Table 10.9 lists some of the Band control's properties.

FIGURE 10.13:

The Bands tab of the CoolBar Property Pages dialog box

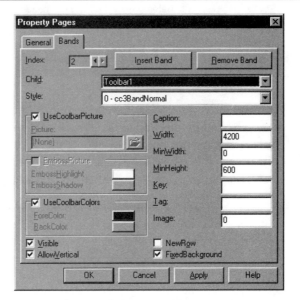

TABLE 10.9: Selected Band Properties

Property	Description
Caption	Specifies the caption displayed on a band
Child	Specifies the control that is attached with the band
Height	Sets the height of the band
Index	Specifies a number that is used to uniquely identify a particular band
Key	Specifies a text value that uniquely identifies a particular band
MinHeight	Specifies the minimum height of the band

Continued on next page

TABLE 10.9 (CONTINUED): Selected Band Properties

Property	Description
MinWidth	Specifies the minimum width of the band
NewRow	If set to True, specifies that the band begins a new row
Position	Sets the relative position of the band within the CoolBar
Style	Determines if the band can be resized
Visible	If set to True, displays the band at runtime
Width	Sets the width of the band

You specify a value for the Band control's Caption property for information to be displayed in the band. Since the user can expand and compress a band at runtime, you can specify minimum heights and widths for each band to ensure that the user doesn't shrink the band beyond usefulness. You can also set the Band control's Style property to prevent the band from being resized.

> **NOTE**
>
> **No Labels needed:** You can use the Band control's Caption property to achieve the same effect as using a Label control as the Band' control's Child.

Programming Your CoolBar

After deciding to use a CoolBar control in your program, you have a big choice to make: Do you want to restore the CoolBar to its original configuration each time, or do you want to save the configuration between sessions? If you don't care to save the CoolBar's configuration, then you can define a band at design time and link it to its child control.

However, if you are going to use the CoolBar, you might as well do it right. Unfortunately, this means a little more work on your part. Unlike the Toolbar control, the CoolBar control doesn't have convenient methods to save and restore the control's settings. You need to build this functionality yourself. Also, because the Position property is read-only, you can't merely save the information about a band and restore it later.

The approach I used in the Weather Maker program (see Figure 10.8, shown earlier) was to create a CoolBar without any bands but with the controls that I could use later as the children of the bands at design time. Then at runtime, I dynamically add the bands in the proper order using the position information from the last time, and then I save the position information when the program ends.

Saving Position Information

Listing 10.9 contains the routine I use to save the position information. I simply loop through each band in the CoolBar's Bands collection. Then I save the name of the child control, the width of the band, and the NewRow property. I use the application's EXEName and "CoolBar" as a high-level part of the key. I append a C, W, or N after the band's position to create the last part of the key. This gives me values like 1C and 2C for control names for the first two bands in the CoolBar.

Listing 10.9:   SaveBandInfo Routine in Weather Maker

```
Private Sub SaveBandInfo()

Dim b As Band

For Each b In CoolBar1.Bands
    SaveSetting App.EXEName, "CoolBar", FormatNumber(b.Position, 0) & "C", _
        b.Child.Name

    SaveSetting App.EXEName, "CoolBar", FormatNumber(b.Position, 0) & "W", _
        b.Width

    SaveSetting App.EXEName, "CoolBar", FormatNumber(b.Position, 0) & "N", _
        Format(b.NewRow, "True/False")

Next b

End Sub
```

Adding a Band

Adding a band to a CoolBar can be rather complicated, as shown in Listing 10.10. This routine takes three parameters:

- The first is b, which holds the band's position in the CoolBar.

- The next parameter is d, which contains the default name of the child control.

- The last parameter is w, which contains the default width of the band.

The last two parameters supply default values that will be used only if these are not set in the Registry.

To make the code a little simpler, I compute the three values I need when creating a new band. Since the Add method needs an object reference for the control, I use the form's Controls collection to get the object reference based on the name of the control. Next, I get the proper values for the NewRow and Width properties from the Registry. Then I create the band by using the Coolbar1.Bands.Add method, the NewRow value, and the child control reference. Finally, I set the band's width by setting the Width property directly.

Listing 10.10:   GetBandInfo Routine in Weather Maker

```
Private Sub GetBandInfo(b As Integer, d As String, w As String)

' b = band position
' d = default control
' w = default width

Dim c As Object    ' object pointer to the child control
Dim n As Boolean   ' NewRow
Dim x As Single    ' width

c = Me.Controls(GetSetting(App.EXEName, "CoolBar", _
   FormatNumber(b, 0) & "C", d))
n = IIf(GetSetting(App.EXEName, "CoolBar", FormatNumber(b, 0) & "N", _
   "False") = "True", True, False)
x = CSng(GetSetting(App.EXEName, "CoolBar", FormatNumber(b, 0) & "W", w))

CoolBar1.Bands.Add , , , , n, c

CoolBar1.Bands.Item(b).Width = x

End Sub
```

Loading the CoolBar

Using the GetBandInfo routine from Listing 10.10, I wrote the GetCoolBarInfo routine shown in Listing 10.11. This routine merely loads each individual band and supplies default values for the control name and the band width, which will be used if there aren't corresponding values in the Registry.

Listing 10.11:   GetCoolBarInfo Routine in Weather Maker

```
Public Sub GetCoolBarInfo()

GetBandInfo 1, "Toolbar1", "4500"
GetBandInfo 2, "ImageCombo1", "3200"

End Sub
```

Resizing the CoolBar Control

After all this, there's still one more routine that we need to talk about. Whenever the CoolBar needs to add a new row of bands, you need to move the controls around on the form; otherwise, the taller CoolBar control could overlap other information on your form. The HeightChanged event occurs after the Resize event and should be use to handle the changes to the control and the form.

When the form is loaded for the Weather Maker program, I save the current height of the CoolBar control into the variable OldHeight. Then, when a row is added or removed from the CoolBar control, the code in Listing 10.12 is called.

Listing 10.12:   CoolBar1_HeightChanged Routine in Weather Maker

```
Private Sub CoolBar1_HeightChanged(ByVal NewHeight As Single)

If Me.WindowState = vbNormal Then
    Me.Height = Me.Height + NewHeight - OldHeight
End If

Text1.Top = Text1.Top + NewHeight - OldHeight
OldHeight = NewHeight

End Sub
```

This code simply adjusts the height of the form based on the NewHeight parameter and the OldHeight variable. Note that I do this only when the form is shown as a normal window. If the form is maximized, I don't need to make the form any larger; when it's minimized, I don't worry about it.

After adjusting the form, I merely adjust the top of the text box by the same amount. If I had other controls on the form, I would need to adjust them individually as well. Note that I don't need to adjust the StatusBar control, because it was adjusted automatically when the form was resized.

Finally, I save the value of NewHeight as OldHeight, which I'll need the next time a row is added or removed from the CoolBar.

Using Controls to Aid Data Entry

If you've built any database applications, you know that the best way to prevent problems is to ensure that the cleanest possible data gets into the database in the first place. In many cases, the data is entered into your database by an end user running one of your application programs. It may be called an Inquiry/Update program, a Data Entry program, or by some fancy application name, but its purpose is to allow an end user to enter, edit, and view the data in your database.

Writing one of these kinds of programs can be as challenging as you want. The more you can do to make the user's life easier, the better the data that will go into your database. Some checks can be very easy. Is the value of the field numeric? Were too many characters entered into the field? Was the field empty? Is the date valid? However, in many cases, these questions are too simple.

If you only check whether the date is valid, you might have someone scheduling an appointment for March 8, when the current date is May 7. Or what happens when someone enters a birthday of 7/27/15? Visual Basic will interpret the date as 7/27/2015, not 7/27/1915.

How about if someone entered a telephone number as 13015556? Your application may assume it is a valid phone number since it contains seven digits, but in this case, the first four digits are actually a 1 followed by an area code.

To help avoid these and other problems associated with data entry, you can use several handy Visual Basic controls: MonthView, DateTimePicker, ImageCombo, and MaskedEdit.

Using the MonthView Control

The MonthView control displays a calendar showing one or more months on your form. Here's an example showing one month:

This control is extremely helpful when users are trying to schedule an activity. Because of the control's visual nature, the date entered by someone using Month-View probably will be accurate.

Users can choose a date in several ways:

- Click on a date in the currently displayed month.
- Scroll through the months until they find the month they want.
- Click on the month or year and directly choose a new value for either.

The MonthView control also allows your users to select a range of dates by clicking on one date and then clicking on a second date while holding down the Shift key. You then can verify that the selected range is legal before accepting the date.

Your program can mark any date of your choice in bold to indicate special dates, like weekends or holidays. It can also specify the number of months you wish to view at a single time with the MonthView control. This makes it easier when users want to schedule activities over a period of several months.

Adding MonthView to Your Program

The MonthView control is very easy to add to your application. Simply click on the MonthView icon in the toolbox and put it on your form. However, unlike many controls, this control has a fixed size. No matter how big or small an area you indicate, the control will position itself in the upper-left corner and will occupy whatever space it needs. This is due to the fact that the control paints itself a full month at a time.

How to change the unchangeable: While you can't directly change the size of MonthView's calendar, you can indirectly change it. By selecting a different size for the font, you can increase or decrease the amount of space occupied by the control.

Table 10.10 lists some of the more common properties and methods for the MonthView control. (Most of the ones not included in the table are the typical properties common to all ActiveX controls.)

TABLE 10.10:   Selected MonthView Properties and Methods

Property/Method	Description
`ComputeControlSize` method	Returns the size of the control for a specified number of rows and columns
`Day` property	Specifies the currently selected day of month
`DayBold` property	Specifies an array of **Boolean** values, indexed by a **Date** value; when **True**, means that the date should be displayed in bold in the calendar
`DayOfWeek` property	Specifies the currently selected day of week
`MaxSelCount` property	Specifies the maximum number of days that can be selected
`Month` property	Specifies the currently selected month
`MonthBackColor` property	Sets the background color of the calendar
`MonthColumns` property	Specifies the number of columns of months displayed on the form
`MonthRows` property	Specifies the number of rows of months displayed on the form
`MultiSelect` property	When set to **True**, permits the user to select multiple dates
`SelEnd` property	Specifies the last date selected
`SelStart` property	Specifies the first date selected
`ShowToday` property	Highlights today's date on the calendar
`ShowWeekNumber` property	When set to **True**, specifies that each week is preceded by the week of the year value
`StartOfWeek` property	Determines the first day of the week
`TitleBackColor` property	Sets the background color of the calendar's title bar

Continued on next page

TABLE 10.10 (CONTINUED):   Selected MonthView Properties and Methods

Property/Method	Description
TitleForeColor property	Sets the foreground color of the calendar's title bar
TrailingForeColor property	Sets the foreground color for the dates before and after the current month
Value property	Returns the currently selected date
VisibleDays property	Specifies an array of **Dates**; an index of 1 returns the first date on the form, 2 returns the second, and so on, up to the number of the last date on the form
Week property	Specifies the currently selected week
Year property	Specifies the currently selected year

The Months Display   Before using the MonthView control, you need to determine how many months of information you wish to display. Showing 12 months may be nice, but it would take up most of your display, leaving little room for anything else. However, if you are constantly scheduling activities over several months, then displaying more than one month at a time may be desirable.

MonthView Size   Changing the size of the MonthView control isn't difficult at all—simply specify values for the MonthRows and MonthColumns properties. You can even change these values at runtime. To help you determine how much space the control will take when you change it at runtime, you can use the Compute-ControlSize method. For any given number of rows and columns, this method will return the new values for height and width in twips.

Date Information   Of course, all of the typical information about a date is available, including the day of month, day of week, month, week, and year. The MonthView control also can handle a range of dates beginning with a specified start date (SelStart) and continuing to a specified end date (SelEnd). These values may not be further apart than the MaxSelCount property. Note that you must enable this feature by setting the MultiSelect property to True.

Calendar Colors   If you need to change the default Windows colors, the Month-View control allows you to specify a number of colors for the different parts of the calendar. You can specify the calendar's background (MonthBackColor), the title's background (TitleBackColor), the title's foreground (TitleForeColor), and color of the days not in the current month (TrailingForeColor).

Programming the MonthView Control

MonthView is one of the easiest controls to use. By default, the current date is displayed on the calendar. However, simply by changing the contents of Value, you can display any initial date. This control can also be used as a data-bound control with a database, so simply scrolling through the database will show the current date value as a calendar. For the most part, this is all you should probably need. If you need to do little more checking on these values, you can use the events listed in Table 10.11. In the next set of listings, you can see how I handled these events in the Date Control program

TABLE 10.11: Selected MonthView Events

Event	Description
DateClick	Occurs when the user clicks on a date
DateDblClick	Occurs when the user double-clicks on a date
GetDayBold	Occurs when the user scrolls the calendar
SelChange	Occurs each time the user selects a date range

DateClick Event Handling Listing 10.13 shows an example of code that handles a DateClick event. The date that was clicked is passed as a parameter to the event. You can examine the date to ensure it is valid and change the Value if it isn't.

Listing 10.13:   **MonthView1_DateClick Event in Date Control**

```
Private Sub MonthView1_DateClick(ByVal DateClicked As Date)

Text1.Text = "MonthView: DateClick event" & vbCrLf
Text1.Text = Text1.Text & "Date clicked: "
Text1.Text = Text1.Text & FormatDateTime(DateClicked, vbLongDate)

End Sub
```

SelChange Event Handling Whenever you select a new date value or range, the SelChange event is fired, as you can see in the code fragment in Listing 10.14. You can examine the range of values to determine if it is valid. For instance, does the range begin on the proper day of the week, or does the range include a weekend? If for any reason you don't want the range of dates to be selected, all you need to do is to set Cancel to True, and the previous selection will be restored.

Listing 10.14:   **MonthView1_SelChange Event in Date Control**

```
Private Sub MonthView1_SelChange(ByVal StartDate As Date, _
   ByVal EndDate As Date, Cancel As Boolean)

Text1.Text = "MonthView: SelChange event" & vbCrLf & "Date range: "
Text1.Text = Text1.Text & FormatDateTime(StartDate, vbLongDate)
Text1.Text = Text1.Text & " to " & FormatDateTime(EndDate, vbLongDate)

End Sub
```

GetDayBold Event Handling The GetDayBold event is triggered just before the calendar is drawn. It allows you to specify the dates that should be displayed in bold by setting the corresponding entry in the State array to True. The code in Listing 10.15 shows how to display the weekend in bold. Since each calendar begins with Sunday, I simply start with the first value in the State array, and turn every seventh one after that to True. Then I do the same thing for the Saturdays.

Listing 10.15:   **MonthView1_GetDayBold Event in Date Control**

```
Private Sub MonthView1_GetDayBold(ByVal StartDate As Date, _
   ByVal Count As Integer, State() As Boolean)

Dim i As Integer

For i = 0 To Count Step 7
   State(i) = True
Next i

For i = 6 To Count Step 7
   State(i) = True
Next i

End Sub
```

Using the DateTimePicker Control

If you read the previous section, you know that the MonthView control is really cool. However, most of us do not have room on our forms for a calendar, especially if there is more than one date on the form. This is where the DateTimePicker control comes in handy. On the form, it looks just like a normal combo box:

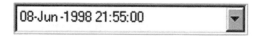

But instead of displaying a drop-down list of choices, DateTimePicker shows a calendar, just like MonthView's display:

In place of the drop-down button, you can substitute a set of up/down arrows. This allows the user to place the cursor over the value to be changed, and then scroll through a list of valid values by clicking the arrows (the arrows are required if you want to allow the user to change time values):

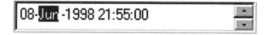

Adding DateTimePicker to Your Program

Table 10.12 lists some of the most interesting properties for the DateTimePicker control. The five properties that begin with Calendar modify the drop-down calendar part of the display. These properties all correspond to the MonthView control properties that control the display of the calendar.

TABLE 10.12: Selected DateTimePicker Properties

Property	Description
CalendarBackColor	Sets the background color of the calendar
CalendarForeColor	Sets the foreground color of the calendar
CalendarTitleBackColor	Sets the background color of the calendar's title bar
CalendarTitleForeColor	Sets the foreground color of the calendar's title bar
CalendarTrailingForeColor	Sets the foreground color for the dates before and after the current month
CheckBox	Displays a checkbox next to the value; if not checked, **null** will be returned as **Value**
CustomFormat	Holds an alternate format to display date and/or time values
Day	Specifies the currently selected day of month
DayOfWeek	Specifies the currently selected day of week
Format	Specifies standard or custom format to display the value
Hour	Specifies the currently selected hour
MaxDate	Specifies the maximum date the user can enter
MinDate	Specifies the minimum date the user can enter
Minute	Specifies the currently selected minute
Month	Specifies the currently selected month
Second	Specifies the currently selected second
UpDown	Modifies dates with up/down buttons instead of a drop-down calendar
Value	Returns the currently selected date
Year	Specifies the currently selected year

Up/Down Counter and Time Values The UpDown property causes the control to display an up/down counter at the end of the text area instead of a drop-down arrow. This is required when you want to input time values, since Microsoft didn't implement a drop-down clock.

A Checkbox for Enabling/Disabling When the CheckBox property is True, the DateTimePicker control displays a checkbox to the left of the date/time information. This checkbox functions like an enable switch. Without a check in the checkbox, the data is grayed out and the user can't modify it. It also sets the Value property to null. With a check in the checkbox, the control functions normally.

Minimum and Maximum Dates The MinDate and MaxDate properties are useful when you want to exclude a range of dates as being invalid. You can use Now as a MinDate value for any events that have yet to occur. Likewise, you can use Now as a MaxDate value for events that should have already occurred.

TIP

Hiring any babies? Depending on the circumstances, you may want to exclude more dates. For instance, consider the situation when you need to enter applicants' birth dates when they apply for a job. Now it is obvious that you can exclude any date starting with today since that would mean they haven't been born yet. However, you might want to exclude any birth dates less than 14 years ago since most companies won't hire someone younger than 14 (except maybe for that 8-year-old hacker who got into the Pentagon's computer network). Likewise, if you have a mandatory retirement age of 65, any birth date prior to 65 years ago also should be invalid.

Date and Time Formats The Format and CustomFormat properties are a very useful pair of properties. These properties control the way that the date and time information is displayed in the DateTimePicker control. You can set the Format property to one of several standard formats, such as short date or long date and time. Alternatively, you can select a custom format, and the string in the Custom-Format property will be used. Table 10.13 lists the custom format characters.

T A B L E   1 0 . 1 3 :   Custom Format Characters for the DateTimePicker Control

Character String	Description
d	Displays the day of month without a leading zero (1–31)
dd	Displays the day of month with a leading zero if needed to make it two digits long (01–31)
ddd	Displays the day as a three-character abbreviation (Sun, Mon, etc.)
dddd	Displays the day with its full name (Sunday, Monday, etc.)

Continued on next page

TABLE 10.13 (CONTINUED): Custom Format Characters for the DateTimePicker Control

Character String	Description
h	Displays the hour without a leading zero (0–12)
hh	Displays the hour with a leading zero if needed to make it two digits long (00–12)
H	Displays the hour in 24-hour time format without a leading zero (0–23)
HH	Displays the hour in 24-hour time format with a leading zero if needed to make it two digits long (00–23)
M	Displays the month without a leading zero (1–12)
MM	Displays the month with a leading zero if needed to make it two digits long (01–12)
MMM	Displays the month as a three-character abbreviation (Jan, Feb, etc.)
MMMM	Displays the month with its full name (January, February, etc.)
m	Displays the minutes without a leading zero (0–59)
mm	Displays the minutes with a leading zero if needed to make the display two digits long (01–59)
s	Displays the seconds without a leading zero (0–59)
ss	Displays the seconds with a leading zero if needed to make the display two digits long (00–59)
t	Displays AM or PM as a single character (A or P)
tt	Displays AM or PM as two characters (AM or PM)
X	Uses the `Callback` events (`CallbackKeyDown`, `Format`, and `FormatSize`) to get information needed to format the custom date/time value
y	Displays the day of the year (1–365)
yy	Displays the year as a two-digit number (00–99)
yyyy	Displays the year as a four-digit number (0100–9999)

NOTE **All date/time format characters are not alike:** The characters used to build the `CustomFormat` are slightly different than those used to build format strings for the `Format` function.

Programming the DateTimePicker Control

The DateTimePicker control has all of the standard events that you would find in any ActiveX control; however, it also has some rather unique events that make this control interesting to program. Table 10.14 lists these events and the following listings show examples of their use.

TABLE 10.14: Selected DateTimePicker Events

Event	Description
CallbackKeyDown	Occurs when the user presses a key while over an X format character
CloseUp	Occurs when the drop-down month is closed
Format	Occurs when formatting an X format character
FormatSize	Occurs to provide an estimate of the space required for formatting

FormatSize Event Handling   The X format allows you to define your own date or time format. You can use any number of X formats in the CustomFormat property. However, you need to make sure that each X format is unique, since your code will need to determine what to do with that particular format.

The DateTimePicker routine calls the FormatSize event for each X format before the date/time value is formatted. This is done to reserve space in the output string. So for each X format you use, you need to return the maximum size of the string you will return in the Format event. In the example in Listing 10.16, I return a maximum length of 5 for the XX format.

Listing 10.16:   DTPicker1_FormatSize Event in Date Control

```
Private Sub DTPicker1_FormatSize(ByVal CallbackField As String, _
   Size As Integer)

If CallbackField = "XX" Then
   Size = 5
End If

End Sub
```

Format Event Handling   The Format event is called each time an X format is found in the custom format string. The routine should look at the Date value and the X format passed in the CallbackField parameter, and then it should return the formatted value as FormattedString, as shown in Listing 10.17:

Listing 10.17:   DTPicker1_Format Event in Date Control

```
Private Sub DTPicker1_Format(ByVal CallbackField As String, _
   FormattedString As String)

If CallbackField = "XX" Then
   Select Case Format(DTPicker1.Value, "q")
   Case "1"
      FormattedString = "1st Q"
   Case "2"
      FormattedString = "2nd Q"
   Case "3"
      FormattedString = "3rd Q"
   Case "4"
      FormattedString = "4th Q"
   End Select

End If

End Sub
```

Using the ImageCombo Control

The ImageCombo control is similar to the ComboBox control. The difference is that you have the option of displaying an image next to each of each of the entries. Figure 10.14 shows an example that uses weather icons next to the choices.

The ImageCombo control also uses a standard Collection object to hold the entries, so you can use the For Each statement to access the individual members. If you don't specify an ImageList or don't specify an image for any of the drop-down items, the control will appear just like a regular ComboBox control to the user.

The ImageCombo control

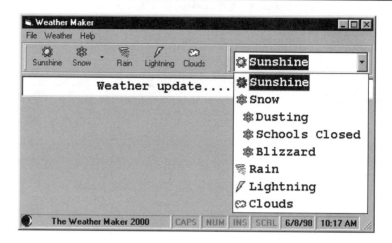

TIP

A picture is worth a thousand words (or at least a thousand bytes): Sometimes, you want a user to enter visual information into the program, but you want to store it as a text field. This could range from the color of a new car (what color does sandalwood look like?), a fabric pattern, or a type of jewelry. Using a small (or not so small) image gives the user a visual clue to what the text field should contain.

Adding ImageCombo to Your Program

Since the ImageCombo box has more capabilities than a regular ComboBox, there are some additional properties you may want to review and set, as listed in Table 10.15. For example, you can make searches of the ComboItems collection case-insensitive by setting the CaseSensitive property to False. You can specify the default indentation for any item in the list (and the text window) by setting the Indentation property (this value is overridden by the value in a particular ComboItem's Indentation property).

TABLE 10.15: Selected ImageCombo Properties and Methods

Property/Method	Description
CaseSensitive property	When set to False, searches the list in a case-insensitive fashion
ComboItems property	Specifies an object reference to the ComboItems collection
GetFirstVisible method	Returns the first ComboItem that is displayed when the drop-down arrow is pressed
Indentation property	Specifies the number of spaces that the image and text will be indented; each space is equivalent to 10 pixels
SelectedItem property	Returns an object reference to the currently selected ListItem
SetFirstVisible method	Sets the first ComboItem that will be displayed when the drop-down arrow is pressed
Text property	Specifies the text value of the currently selected ComboItem

Table 10.16 contains some of the key properties associated with a particular ComboItem. The Image property contains either a Key or Index reference to an image in an ImageList control. The SelImage also contains a Key or Index reference to an image in an ImageList control. This image will be displayed next to the currently selected item, both in the ImageCombo's window and in the drop-down box. As I mentioned before, the value of the Indentation property overrides the control's default value. A value of 1 in this field will move the image and text to the right by 10 pixels; a value of 2 will move them 20 pixels.

TABLE 10.16: Selected ComboItem Object Properties

Property	Description
Image	References an ImageList image that will be displayed next to the text
Indentation	Specifies the number of spaces the entry will be indented; each space is 10 pixels
Index	Specifies a unique number that identifies the object in the collection
Key	Specifies a unique text string that identifies the object in the collection
Selected	When set to True, means that this object is the currently selected object in the collection

Continued on next page

TABLE 10.16 (CONTINUED): Selected ComboItem Object Properties

Property	Description
SelImage	References an ImageList image that will be displayed in place of Image when the item is selected
Text	Specifies the text that will be displayed in the drop-down list and in the ImageCombo text area itself

TIP

Make it obvious: You can set the SelImage property to a different image to highlight the default value (or currently selected value) in the ImageCombo's drop-down box. You can also use the Indentation property to show a hierarchical relationship between the items in the drop-down box.

Programming the ImageCombo Control

Programming the ImageCombo control is very similar to programming a regular ComboBox. You add items to the list of items to be displayed in the drop-down box, and you handle the interaction with the user in the Click and Change events. However, since the ImageCombo uses a regular Visual Basic collection to hold the list of items, you must use the ListItem.Add method rather than the ComboBox's AddItem method.

The ComboItems.Add method creates a new ComboItem object and assigns values for the following properties: Index, Key, Text, Image, SelImage, and Indentation. For the Weather Maker program, to simplify matters, I used the same value for the Key and Text properties. I indented the three types of Snow options that I used in the drop-down toolbar button and used the same icon as the default value. This code is shown in Listing 10.18.

Listing 10.18:   LoadImageCombo Routine in Weather Maker

```
Private Sub LoadImageCombo()

ImageCombo1.ComboItems.Add , "Sunshine", "Sunshine", "Sunshine"
ImageCombo1.ComboItems.Add , "Snow", "Snow", "Snow"
ImageCombo1.ComboItems.Add , "Dusting", "Dusting", "Snow", , 1
ImageCombo1.ComboItems.Add , "Schools Closed", "Schools Closed", "Snow", , 1
```

```
ImageCombo1.ComboItems.Add , "Blizzard", "Blizzard", "Snow", , 1
ImageCombo1.ComboItems.Add , "Rain", "Rain", "Rain"
ImageCombo1.ComboItems.Add , "Lightning", "Lightning", "Lightning"
ImageCombo1.ComboItems.Add , "Clouds", "Clouds", "Clouds"

End Sub
```

The following is a code fragment that sets the `SelectedItem` property to a particular item in the `ComboItems` collection. Note that I'm using a `Set` statement rather than a regular assignment statement. This is because I'm creating an object reference.

```
Set ImageCombo1.SelectedItem = ImageCombo1.ComboItems.Item(s)
```

Using the MaskedEdit Control

The MaskedEdit control is a special kind of text box that permits the user to enter characters that match the specified input mask. This control is useful when your users need to enter numbers in special formats, such as social security numbers, telephone numbers, and credit card numbers.

NOTE **Invalid social security numbers:** The middle two digits of a social security number (AAA-*BB*-CCCC) are never 00. The programmers at the Social Security Administration use social security numbers with 00 for testing their programs.

Adding MaskedEdit to Your Program

Using the MaskedEdit properties, listed in Table 10.17, you can build an input mask for a field. You can also specify the format for the entry and control how text is entered.

TABLE 10.17: Selected MaskedEdit Properties

Property	Description
AllowPrompt	When set to `True`, means that the `PromptChar` is a valid input character
AutoTab	When set to `True`, means that the control will automatically tab to the next field when this field is full

Continued on next page

TABLE 10.17 (CONTINUED):   Selected MaskedEdit Properties

Property	Description
ClipMode	Includes/excludes literal characters when the user performs a cut or copy operation
ClipText	Holds the selected text, excluding any mask characters
Format	Specifies up to four format strings that are used to display the information in the control
FormattedText	Specifies the text after formatting; this value will be displayed in the control when it doesn't have the focus
Mask	Specifies a series of mask characters describing the input format
MaxLength	Specifies the maximum length of the data
PromptChar	Specifies a single character that is used to prompt the user for input
PromptInclude	When set to **True**, means that the prompt character is included in the **Text** property; for bound controls, **True** means that the **Text** property will be saved in the database and **False** means that the **ClipText** property will be saved
SelLength	Specifies the length of the selected text
SelStart	Specifies the starting position of the selected text
SelText	Holds the selected text
Text	Holds the value displayed in the control while editing

The Input Format   Of all the properties of the MaskedEdit control, the `Mask` property is at the heart. It specifies the input format that the user must match in order for the input to be accepted. The input format consists of a series of characters, as listed in Table 10.18. If the user enters a character that doesn't match the input format, it will not be displayed. If you wish, you can trap the invalid character in the `ValidationError` event.

TABLE 10.18:   Valid Mask Characters

Mask Character	Description
#	A required numeric character
.	A decimal point indicator as defined in Windows; treated as a literal

Continued on next page

TABLE 10.18 (CONTINUED): Valid Mask Characters

Mask Character	Description
,	A thousands separator as defined in Windows; treated as a literal
/	A date separator as defined in Windows; treated as a literal
:	A timer separator as defined in Windows; treated as a literal
\	Treat the next character as a literal
&	A character placeholder
>	Convert the following characters to uppercase
<	Convert the following characters to lowercase
A	A required alphanumeric character
a	An optional alphanumeric character
9	An optional numeric character
C	Same as & (ensures compatibility with Microsoft Access)
?	A required alphabetic character
Other	Any other character is treated as a literal

Building an input mask is not a difficult task. Simply choose the format that best reflects how your users enter their data, and insert the edit characters and literals as needed. The following are some common input masks:

(###) ###-####	Telephone number
####-####-####-####	Credit card number
>A<AAAAAAAAAA	A name field with the first character always in uppercase and the following characters always in lowercase
>AAAAAAAAAAA	A name field with all characters converted to uppercase
?#:##	A time value
##/##/##	A date value

The Prompt Character When the user is prompted to enter information into a MaskedEdit box, the PromptChar is used to fill in the spaces in the Mask before it is displayed to the user. Generally, you will use the underscore character (_) as the prompt character, but you may want to supply a value like a zero or a space, depending on the input mask. For instance, if you set PromptChar to 0 and Mask to ###-##-####, the user will see 000-00-0000 in the field. The user would then overtype the zeros with the appropriate values. Note that if you use a value for PromptChar that is also legal in the input mask, then you need to set the AllowPrompt property to True.

The Unformatted Value The ClipText property contains the unformatted value of the contents of the Text property. This means if the Text property contains a formatted number with commas and dollar signs, the ClipText property merely contains the number. This value then can be easily used in other places. Specifying True for the ClipMode property means that cut and copy operations will also use the ClipText value rather than the contents of the Text property.

Prompt Inclusion Setting the PromptInclude property to True has two effects:

- The prompt character actually becomes part of the Text property. If the user doesn't enter any information in this field, the input mask with the prompt characters will be used as the default value for the control.

- When this control is used as a database-bound control, the data from the Text property will be saved in the database. When PromptInclude is set to False, the data from the ClipText property will be saved in the database.

Programming the MaskedEdit Control

As I noted earlier, you can trap invalid characters entered into a MaskedEdit control with the ValidationError event. Listing 10.19 shows the code I execute each time the user enters an invalid character in the MaskedEdit box. In this case, I exploit the full multimedia potential of the original IBM PC/XT computer and generate an audible signal to communicate to the user that he or she goofed.

Listing 10.19:   MaskEdBox1_ValidationError Event in Weather Maker

```
Private Sub MaskEdBox1_ValidationError(InvalidText As String, _
    StartPosition As Integer)

Beep

End Sub
```

Final Thoughts

Menus are an important part of the look and feel of any Windows program. Properly designed menus make your users' lives easier since they already know how to use many of the basic functions your application will perform.

Let's assume for a minute that you don't want to be lazy. You could write your own routines that would allow users to drag the individual buttons around the toolbar to change the order of the buttons. You could also allow users to drag a button off the toolbar to delete it. Finally, you could show the users a window with every possible button and let them drag new buttons from that window to the toolbar. Then you could play music while the buttons are being moved; perhaps play an animated video or two. Maybe you could even change the weather. But who would really want to spend all that time and effort (unless they were working for Microsoft)? The lazy programmer would just use the Customize Toolbar dialog box.

One thing that is relatively easy to do with toolbars is to use specify an ImageList for the HotImageList. Merely moving your mouse pointer over a button is all that it takes for the toolbar to change a button's image from the one in the standard ImageList to one that is in the HotImageList. This makes that particular button stand out and grab the user's attention.

The CoolBar is a pretty control, but I'm not sure that it's needed in most applications. Unless you have a bunch of different toolbars, the CoolBar is probably not necessary. However, transparent buttons on a toolbar are cool, even without the CoolBar.

The GetDayBold method in the MonthView control is a powerful tool that allows you to provide visual information to the user about what dates should be selected or not selected. Assume that you are writing an application for a business that books performances for bands and other entertainers. You could display a calendar for a particular entertainer and show the dates that have already been booked in bold. The remaining dates would be free to be booked.

The ImageCombo control is essentially a replacement for the regular ComboBox control. There is nothing you can do with a ComboBox control that you can't do with an ImageCombo control. The only price you pay is that you need to distribute the Microsoft Windows Common Controls file with your application. Since this file also contains the Toolbar, StatusBar, ProgressBar, TreeView, ListView, plus a few other controls, you'll probably end up distributing this file anyway.

Verifying input data is much easier when you use the MaskedEdit control. This is especially true for formatted fields such as social security numbers and telephone numbers. However, for all of its usefulness, it can be a cumbersome control to use. The new DateTimePicker and MonthView controls offer better ways to enter date and time values.

PART III

Internet Applications

CHAPTER
ELEVEN

11

Transferring Files over the Internet

- Internet requirements

- The FTP and HTTP protocols

- The Internet Transfer control

- A file update utility

Nearly all client/server applications built today are supported across the Internet. Most of these applications are built around web servers, such as Internet Information Server, and web browsers, such as Internet Explorer. However, some functions require special-purpose applications that use the Internet to transfer data between applications. For example, custom programs can perform functions like synchronizing clocks and exchanging real-time information.

I'll begin this chapter with a brief review of the requirements for communicating over the Internet, including IP addresses, domain names, port numbers, protocols, and URLs. Then I'll quickly go over the workings of the two protocols that Visual Basic's Internet Transfer control supports: FTP and HTTP. The remainder of the chapter is devoted to using the Internet Transfer control.

Reviewing Internet Requirements

The Internet is something evil that keeps growing larger and larger like the blob did in the 1950's movie. At least this appears true if you've watched any TV news programs lately. Since the job of the TV newscaster is to encourage viewers to watch the rather long commercials between the small spots of news, the full story about the Internet is never shown.

The Internet exists primarily to allow one computer network to connect to another. It has a hardware component that provides a physical connection from one network to another, and it has a software component that ensures that what one computer sends to another is understood by both. While a discussion of the hardware involved in networking can be very interesting, the software component is much more important to the Visual Basic programmer.

Some Internet History

The origins of the Internet date back to the late 1960s, when the Department of Defense's Advanced Research Projects Agency (known as ARPA) began funding research projects into computer networks. For the most part, the work was done in a university setting, with some research being done by private research corporations.

continued on next page

In December 1969, four computers were connected together in what was known as the ARPANET. Throughout the 1970s and '80s, ARPA (then known as DARPA) encouraged universities and other organizations working on its project to connect to the ARPANET. In 1985, the National Science Foundation (NSF) created its own independent network known as NSFNET. The term Internet came to be when these two networks were connected.

It's important to understand that because most of the work was done by universities, many of their personal philosophies became incorporated into the design of the Internet. One of the most important things is that nothing is fixed in place. Anything and everything is open to discussion and change, which means that no one person or organization is really in charge of the Internet.

Assigning IP Addresses and Domain Names

Every computer on the Internet is assigned a unique address, known as an *Internet Protocol* (IP) *address*. An IP address is 32 bits long and is written in the form *aaa.bbb.ccc.ddd*, where each value represents a number in the range of 0 to 255. When one computer sends a piece of information to another, it sends the message to the other computer's IP address.

Since IP addresses are difficult to remember, people started assigning names to their computers. However, since the Internet was formed in a university environment where people don't like giving up control of their domain, a hierarchical naming convention was eventually developed. This gave people the ability to name their computers whatever they wanted, yet provided a method to guarantee that the name would be unique across the Internet.

This technique is known as *domain names*. Domain names are mapped to an IP address, which in turn is used in the actual communications with the computer. Domain names are built from groups of characters separated by periods. For instance, www.JustPC.com is a valid domain name. The .com is the top-level domain. It is used to indicate that the computer is commercial. Some other top-level domains are .edu for education, .gov for government, .net for network, and .org for nonprofit organizations.

Other top-level domains may reflect geographic locations, such as .us for the United States, .ca for Canada, and .uk for United Kingdom. Within a country, mid-level domains may be used to further refine the address. For example, mail.bcpl.lib.md.us is a valid domain name for the Baltimore County Public Library in the state of Maryland in the United States.

The remainder of the address for both domains is up for grabs. An organization called InterNIC is currently responsible for managing the .com and .net top-level domains. Organizations may request any mid-level name and will be granted permission to use that name if it is not in use by someone else (and as long as they pay the appropriate registration fees).

Once you have a mid- and top-level name, you can choose your own machine names. In my case, I use www.JustPC.com as my web server, ftp.JustPC.com as my FTP server, and JustPC.com as my mail server.

Since all information sent via the Internet must use a valid IP address, a process must exist that will translate a domain name into an IP address. This process is called a *Domain Name Server* (*DNS*). The DNS takes a domain name and returns a valid IP address. If your computer is attached to the Internet, it either has a hardcoded IP address of a DNS or it receives this information dynamically when a connection is established, via a modem or when the computer is first turned on.

Using Port Numbers and Protocols

Simply knowing how to send a message to a computer is not sufficient. Most computers need to access various services across the Internet, and some computers provide those services. There needs to be a way to separate the incoming traffic and direct the information to the appropriate program. This is done through the use of ports.

A *port* is simply another address that is local to the computer. Various functions access various ports. For instance, a web server will listen on port 80 for requests and will respond with the requested information. An FTP server listens on port 21. Port numbers can range from 0 to 65,535 (or $2^{16}-1$).

Over the years, Internet users have agreed on a list of well-known port addresses. These addresses reflect the port numbers that people should try to use when they want to access a particular type of server. Some well-known port numbers for some of the most common Internet services are listed in Table 11.1.

NOTE

Many port numbers are well known: A lot of port numbers belong on this list (for instance, Doom uses port 666 for multi-user game play). I omitted some numbers from the table because they aren't very common. For a more complete list, look at the file C:\Windows\Services.

TABLE 11.1:   Some Well-Known Port Numbers

Name	Port Number	Description
Daytime	13	Daytime protocol—returns date and time information
ftp-data	20	FTP (File Transfer Protocol), default data port—transfers files between systems
ftp	21	FTP, control port
Telnet	23	Telnet—provides terminal access to a remote computer
Smtp	25	SMTP (Simple Mail Transport Protocol)—transfers mail between systems
Time	37	Time protocol—returns date and time information
Domain	53	DNS (Domain Name Server)—converts a domain name into an IP address
Finger	79	Finger protocol—returns information about a remote computer or user
www-http	80	WWW (World Wide Web), HTTP (HyperText Transport Protocol)—retrieves HTML-formatted documents
Pop3	110	POP3 (Post Office Protocol) version 3 protocol—retrieves e-mail messages
nntp	119	NNTP (Network News Transport Protocol)—retrieves news articles

When looking at Table 11.1, you may notice that many of the port numbers are also associated with a protocol. *Protocols* are a way for one computer to request information from another and understand its response. For the most part, protocols are well-documented command strings and ranges of valid responses. The Internet Transfer control supports two protocols: the File Transfer Protocol and the HyperText Transfer Protocol, which I'll cover soon. But first I want to finish up here with one last item you need for Internet applications: a Universal Resource Locator.

Using Universal Resource Locators

Universal Resource Locators, or URLs, are very familiar to anyone who has spent a little time surfin' the 'net. Most people assume that URLs are useful only when dealing with web pages; however, a URL is truly a universal tool because it allows you to specify the location of nearly any resource on the Internet. It encompasses most Internet protocols and even allows you to include user names and passwords when that information is required.

The format of a URL is:

```
<protocol>://[<user-info>]<host>[<port-info>]/[<url-path>]
```

where:

- `<protocol>` specifies the protocol and can be any of the following: FTP, HTTP, GOPHER, MAILTO, NEWS, NNTP, TELNET, WAIS, or FILE.

- `<user-info>` is optional and is used to specify a user name or user name and password. A user name is specified by `username@`, and a user name and password are specified by `username:password@`. If this parameter is not specified, then the user name and password will default to a server-supplied value.

- `<host>` is the domain name or IP address of the machine you wish to access.

- `<port-info>` is optional and takes the form of `:<port-number>`. If this parameter is not specified, it will default to the well-known port value for the specified `<protocol>`.

- `<url-path>` is also optional and usually consists of a fully qualified path name for a file. Note that other information may be included as part of the `<url-path>` such as parameters for a CGI-BIN script or additional information such as `;type=typecode` for an FTP transfer.

NOTE   **Web browsers and more:** In addition to the HTTP protocol, most web browsers can access FTP sites and Gopher sites. More complex packages such as Internet Explorer also support the News, NNTP, and MailTo protocols through the use of integrated tools like Outlook. Usually, if you don't specify a protocol, the browser will assume that you want to use HTTP.

Reviewing the Protocols Supported by the Internet Transfer Control

Microsoft has provided Visual Basic programmers with the Internet Transfer control to access remote servers on the Internet. The Internet Transfer control bundles two common Internet protocols: the File Transfer Protocol (FTP) and the HyperText Transfer Protocol (HTTP). This control handles all of the grunge work and makes transferring files relatively easy.

Before I go into the details about how the Internet Transfer control works, I would like to take a moment to review the FTP and HTTP protocols. Of course, if you already know how these protocols work and don't need a refresher, feel free to skip to the next section.

Using the File Transfer Protocol

One of the oldest protocols still in use today is the File Transfer Protocol, known as FTP, which was first developed in 1971. It was designed to move files from one computer to another and to handle the translation problems that invariably occur when different types of computers try to communicate.

In order to access an FTP server, you must provide a user name and a password. This information is used to determine what level of access you will be granted.

Many FTP servers allow people to access the server by using "anonymous" as a user name and an e-mail address as the password. This permits people to access public information without having a predefined user name and password. (This was a popular technique for distributing information in the days prior to the World Wide Web.)

NOTE   **Anonymous FTP:** Most FTP servers that allow you to log on as anonymous ask you to send your e-mail address as your password. This allows the person responsible for the server to track usage at an individual level. While it may be tempting to use bclinton@whitehouse.gov as a password, you should be a responsible netizen (citizen of the Internet) and use your real e-mail address.

FTP Commands and Responses

To understand a protocol, I find it best to think of a series of commands and responses like you might see during a DOS session. For instance, in DOS, if you type a CD command followed by a path name, the computer processes your request and either returns an error or returns a command prompt. FTP works along these lines.

If you send a command to an FTP server, you will receive a three-digit response code describing how the server processed your command:

- Codes that begin with 1 mean the command was successful, but you need to wait for another response code before issuing your next command.

- Codes that begin with 2 describe the successful completion of a command.

- Codes that begin with 3 mean that the server needs more information before it can complete the request.

- Codes that begin with 4 mean that the system was too busy to process the command and that you should try again later.

- Codes that begin with 5 represent some kind of error; you should resolve the error before trying the command again.

FTP commands are grouped together as a session. You first must log on to the server. Then you can execute multiple commands to upload and download files, create and delete directories, and perform other tasks. When you are finished, you close the connection to the server. This will log you off the server. Note that you log on to the server only once, and the server remembers things like the current directory you are accessing.

FTP and URLs

A typical FTP URL might look like this:

```
ftp://wfreeze:mypass@ftp.justpc.com/vb/inet/project1.exe
```

This would download the file project1.exe in the /vb/inet directory on the ftp.justpc.com server. It would use *wfreeze* as the user name with a corresponding password of *mypass*.

Typically, when you use a URL with an FTP server, you will log on, execute a command, and log off again. This process will be repeated for each URL you execute. In some cases, such as when you want the user to download a single file, it's okay to log off after executing the command. However, if you want a user to be able to create a directory and then upload multiple files, it is more efficient to use a regular FTP program rather than go through the logon and logoff process for each command executed.

Using the HyperText Transport Protocol

When most people think of the World Wide Web, they think of web pages that are coded in HTML, but that's only part of the web. In order to simplify transfer of documents and files, another file transport protocol was developed. This is known as the HyperText Transport Protocol, or HTTP.

NOTE   **HTTP is not HTML:** Although this may appear to be obvious, many people get confused. HTTP is one way to transfer a document from a server to a client. HTML is a language used to encode a specific type of document. A web browser combines the ability to retrieve an HTML document and display it. A browser could also use FTP to retrieve an HTML document and display it, and you can also use HTTP to retrieve and save an .EXE file.

HTTP Commands

Like FTP, HTTP also uses commands to access information. Unlike FTP, HTTP commands are not used as part of a session. Each command is issued as a stand-alone command, and the server doesn't have any previous memory of any other commands. This means that security information, if required, as well as any identity information the client wishes to send, must be sent each time.

While not as rich as the set of commands in FTP, the HTTP commands allow you to retrieve an entire document and send documents to the web server. The exact set of commands varies from web server to web server, but all allow you to retrieve an entire document or only the document's header information. Also, most web servers can receive information and process it using a program on the web server.

The server will respond to each command sent with a multiple-line message. The first line contains the version of HTTP the server understands followed by a space and a three-digit reply code. The reply code is similar to the reply code used by FTP, with the same meanings for the leading digit. It differs only in the actual meaning of each individual code.

Header Information

Accompanying the request sent to the server and the server's response to the client is usually one or more lines of header information. Headers are composed of a keyword ending in a colon (:), followed by a space and then the value.

Headers are used to convey information such as the e-mail address of the person making the request, the authorization information, the name of the client software, or the date the document was last modified. Headers are also used to describe the type of document being sent, by sending information such as the length of the document, the type of the document, and how the document was compressed.

Using the Internet Transfer Control

The Internet Transfer control, also known as the Inet control, allows you to build programs that transfer files using FTP or HTTP. This control encapsulates the HTTP and FTP protocols and makes it easy for you to add file-transfer capabilities.

You may want to use this control to upload data to the corporate mainframe from a remote site that doesn't have a full-time network connection. Another use might be to extract data from a web page for later analysis. This would be great for tracking the status of various stocks and bonds.

One application I like is one that contacts a remote system to get the list of current files for your application and compares that list to the files on your system. Then the program downloads and installs the update files. I'm going to describe how to build this kind of application later in this chapter.

Adding an Internet Transfer Control

Unlike most Visual Basic controls, the Internet Transfer control does not display a graphic image at runtime. At design time, you see it as a small box with an icon on it. This is similar in function to the MAPI controls I talked about in Chapter 8.

Like the other types of Visual Basic controls, the Internet Transfer control includes a number of properties that determine how it operates. Table 11.2 lists the most important Internet Transfer control properties.

TABLE 11.2:   Selected Internet Transfer Control Properties

Property	Description
AccessType	Specifies whether directly connected to the Internet or though a proxy server
Document	Specifies the name of the document to be used with the **Execute** method
hInternet	Specifies a handle to an Internet object created by the Wininet.DLL API
Password	Specifies the password associated with a particular user name
Protocol	Specifies the protocol used to talk to the remote server—usually FTP, HTTP, or HTTPS
Proxy	Specifies the name of a proxy server and port number to be used
RequestTimeout	Sets the number of seconds without activity before an error is returned
RemoteHost	Specifies the name of the remote server
RemotePort	Specifies the port number on the remote server—usually 21 for FTP and 80 for HTTP
ResponseCode	Specifies the response code returned by the server
ResponseInfo	Specifies text information associated with the response code
StillExecuting	When set to **True**, means that the previous method is still executing
URL	Specifies the name of a document on a remote server and the protocol needed to access it
UserName	Specifies a valid user name on the remote system

Specifying the Protocol and URL

The most important property is the Protocol property. This determines if the control will use FTP or HTTP to transfer a file.

The next most important property is the URL property. This property holds a lot of information such as the Protocol to be used, the name of the RemoteServer, the RemotePort number, the UserName and Password, plus the name of the Document to be retrieved.

Set the URL first: Setting the URL property will in turn set the `Protocol`, the `RemoteHost`, the `RemotePort`, the `Password` and the `UserName`, and the `Document` properties. Note that the reverse is also true. Setting any or all of these properties will update the URL property with the new information.

Setting the Transfer Time

It is important to remember that transferring files across the Internet can take a lot of time. This means that your program will issue a request to the server through the Internet Transfer control, and then will need to wait until the request is completed. You can use the `StillExecuting` property to determine when the request has been completed. (You can also wait for `State = 12` in the `StateChanged` event, as described shortly.)

Handling Response Codes and Proxy Servers

Sometimes, it is important to see the response code that the server returned. This information is available in the `ResponseCode` property. Any text information that the server returned with the response code is available in the `ResponseInfo` property.

Finally, if you access the Internet through a proxy server, you can include that information in the `AccessType` and `Proxy` properties.

Using Internet Transfer Control Methods

The Internet Transfer control has five methods and one event, as listed in Table 11.3.

TABLE 11.3:   Internet Transfer Control Methods and Event

Method/Event	Description
`Cancel` method	Terminates a currently outstanding request and closes the connection to the remote server
`Execute` method	Executes the specified command
`GetChunk` method	Retrieves a buffer full of data from the remote server
`GetHeader` method	Retrieves header information from a file on the remote server
`OpenURL` method	Retrieves information from the remote server
`StateChanged` event	Occurs each time the control's state changes

Interacting with the Server

There are two main ways to interact with the server. The first is to use the OpenURL method, and the second is to use the Execute method with the GetChunk and GetHeader methods as needed.

The OpenURL method retrieves the document specified by the URL as either a String or Byte Array. If you are transferring binary information, you should use a Byte Array to hold the results; otherwise, the information may be changed during its conversion to a string.

The Execute method is more flexible than the OpenURL method, but it may require a bit of programming to complete the task. The Execute method is used to submit a command to the server for execution, and you will wait for the appropriate response from the server. In some cases, you will need to use the GetChunk or GetHeader method to retrieve the server's response. Sometimes, the result will be a new file on your system, which you will need to open to see its contents. In other cases, the command won't return any results, so you don't need to worry about any special processing.

Canceling a Request

If you wish to stop your request, simply use the Cancel method. Note that you may need to clean up any files that may have been partially transferred if you use this method.

Tracking the Progress

The StateChanged event is used to track the progress of your request. See Table 11.4 for a list of the states that will be reported in this event. Many of the states will pass quickly while the connection is being established or while the command is being sent to the server. However, you can expect your program to remain in state 5 and state 7 for some time while waiting for the server to respond or send information.

TIP   **When is it going to be done?** You can wait for a request to be completed either by watching the StillExecuting property or by setting a trap in the State-Changed event. Using the StateChanged event is desirable when you want to display a message to the user indicating that all processing is complete (the process ended with a state of 12—everything worked okay) or that there was some sort of a problem (state of 11).

TABLE 11.4: State Information Returned by the StateChanged Event

State	Description
0	No state information is available
1	Looking up the IP address for the remote server
2	Found the IP address for the remote server
3	Connecting to the remote server
4	Connected to the remote server
5	Requesting information from the remote server
6	The request was sent successfully to the remote server
7	Receiving a response from the remote server
8	The response was received successfully from the remote server
9	Disconnecting from the remote server
10	Disconnected from the remote server
11	An error was detected when communicating with the remote computer
12	The request was completed; all data has been received

Issuing FTP Commands

The Internet Transfer control will automatically establish an FTP session the first time you execute an FTP command. Table 11.5 lists the FTP commands for the control.

TABLE 11.5: FTP Commands for the Internet Transfer Control

FTP Command	Description
CD *dir*	Changes the current directory to the specified directory on the remote computer
CDUP	Changes the current directory to the parent directory on the remote computer

Continued on next page

TABLE 11.5 (CONTINUED): FTP Commands for the Internet Transfer Control

FTP Command	Description
CLOSE	Closes the connection to the remote computer
DELETE *file*	Deletes the specified file on the remote computer
DIR [*dir*]	Returns the list of files from the specified directory (use **GetChunk** to get the information)
GET *file1 file2*	Retrieves the specified file (*file1*) from the remote computer and saves it as the specified file (*file2*) on the local computer
LS [*dir*]	Same as **DIR**
MKDIR *dir*	Creates the specified directory on the remote computer
PUT *file1 file2*	Sends the specified file (*file1*) from the local computer and saves it as the specified file (*file2*) on the remote computer
PWD	Returns the current directory from the remote computer (use **GetChunk** to get the information)
QUIT	Terminates the current user's session on the remote computer
RECV *file1 file2*	Same as **GET**
RENAME *file1 file2*	Changes the name of the specified file (*file1*) to the specified name (*file2*) on the remote computer
RMDIR *dir*	Deletes the specified directory
SEND *file1 file2*	Same as **PUT**
SIZE *dir*	Returns the size of the specified directory (use **GetChunk** to get the information)

WARNING   **Security, security, security:** Just because a command is listed here does not mean it can be used. Your user name and password will determine your level of access to the files on the server, as well as which commands you will be able to execute.

Closing a Session

The session will remain active until you explicitly close it with the Quit or Close commands. If you used the Quit command to log on as a different user, then you need to update the values in UserName and Password properties before you issue the next command.

Sending and Receiving Files

You can send a file to the remote computer by using the PUT command. The PUT command has two parameters: the name of the file on the local computer and the name of the file on the remote computer. Both are required to successfully transfer a file. The SEND command is another name for the PUT command.

The GET command works the same as the PUT command, but it retrieves a file from the remote machine. Two parameters are required for this command also. The first parameter is the name of the remote file, and the second is the name of the local file. Like the PUT command, both parameters are required to successfully transfer the file. The RECV command is a synonym for the GET command.

Working with Directories

One of the side effects of a session-oriented protocol like FTP is that the server can remember certain information from one command to the next. So commands like CD, CDUP, and PWD allow you to traverse the directory structure on the remote computer and let you specify filenames relative to the current working directory.

You can also create and delete directories using the MKDIR and RMDIR commands. You can retrieve a list of files using the DIR command. (Note that the LS command is a synonym for the DIR command.) When using the DIR command, you need to use the GetChunk method to retrieve the contents of the directory. The chunk of information returned is merely a list of files in the current directory on the remote system. Each file is listed on a single line with a carriage return/line feed pair between them. No size or other information is returned in this value. (Note that you can also specify the name of a file or directory, and that information will be returned in place of the list of files in the current working directory.)

Issuing HTTP Commands

There are very few commands for HTTP transfers when compared to the list of commands for FTP. However, HTTP was designed to be a lightweight tool that would let people easily download documents from the server, so fewer commands are necessary. Table 11.6 lists the HTTP commands for the Internet Transfer control

TABLE 11.6:   HTTP Commands for the Internet Transfer Control

HTTP Command	Description
GET	Retrieves the document specified in the URL property (use GetHeader to retrieve header information and GetChunk to get the rest of the information)
HEAD	Gets the header information (use GetHeader to retrieve header information)
POST	Sends data to the server
PUT	Replaces the page specified in the URL property with the specified data

Of the four commands available in the Internet Transfer control for HTTP transfers, the GET command will be the most used. This command is used to retrieve a document based on the supplied URL. The HEAD command is used to retrieve only the document's header information. Both commands need to use the Get-Header method to retrieve header information, and the GET command uses the GetChunk method to retrieve the body of the document.

The POST command is used to send data back to the server. This is most often used with HTML forms that need to transmit data to the server for processing. The PUT method is used to add a new document or file to the web server or update an existing document. This command may not work with all web servers, and it will most likely require information in the headers for authorization information.

Programming with the Internet Transfer Control

I wrote a program I call the Internet Updater, which demonstrates the use of the Internet Transfer control. The Internet Updater is used to update an application by examining each file in the application and choosing those files that have newer versions. Files with newer versions than those residing on the user's system are then downloaded.

The program begins by loading into memory a local file that contains the status of the local files. Then it will download a similar file that contains the information about the current version of the application. Then it will recommend which files should be updated, as shown in the example in Figure 11.1. The users can choose to accept the recommendation or adjust it as they see fit. Finally, they can download the files onto their system. When the download is complete, the local list will be updated and saved.

FIGURE 11.1:

The Internet Updater program

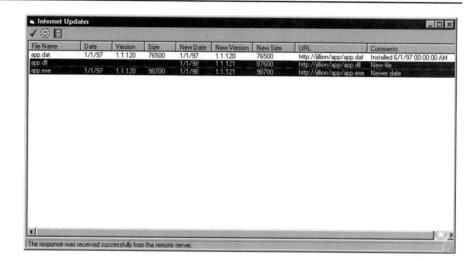

Creating the Local and Remote Information Files

In order to determine which files should be updated, you need a list of files available for download and a list of files on your system. In addition to the file lists, you also need two more pieces of information—the current version of the file and where to locate the file. All of this information is contained in two files, one on the local machine and one on the remote machine.

Remote File Information   As you can see in the example below, the format of the remote file is very simple. Each file in the list occupies a single line of text, with the individual fields separated by commas. The fields are File Name, Creation Date, Version, File Size, and URL to retrieve the file.

```
app.exe, 1/1/98, 1.1.121, 98700, http://jillion/app/app.exe
app.dll, 1/1/98, 1.1.121, 87600, http://jillion/app/app.dll
app.dat, 1/1/97, 1.1.120, 76500, http://jillion/app/app.dat
```

Local File Information The format of the local file is similar to the remote file, but it contains a little more information in the beginning. The local file has the following information:

- The first line of the file contains the URL to retrieve the remote file.

- The user name and password to access the system are on the second and third lines.

- The fourth line contains the root directory where the application files are stored.

- Starting with the fifth line is a list of files similar to the files found on the remote system, except that the last field tracks when the file was installed rather than a URL.

Here is an example of a local information file, before updates:

```
http://jillion/app/app.ver
anonymous
wfreeze
d:\app
app.exe, 1/1/97, 1.1.120, 98700, Installed 6/1/97 00:00:00 AM
app.dat, 1/1/97, 1.1.120, 76500, Installed 6/1/97 00:00:00 AM
```

When you compare the remote and local information files, notice that the remote file includes a new file that is not currently on the local system (app.dll). You should also notice that the app.exe file has been updated; it now has a date of 1/1/98 and a version level of 1.1.121. The local file after it has been updated will look like this:

```
http://jillion/app/app.ver
anonymous
wfreeze
d:\app
app.dat, 1/1/97, 1.1.120, 76500, Installed 6/1/97 00:00:00 AM
app.dll, 1/1/98, 1.1.121, 87600, Installed 6/7/98 10:54:42 PM
app.exe, 1/1/98, 1.1.121, 98700, Installed 6/7/98 10:54:42 PM
```

Retrieving the Remote File

As you saw in Figure 11.1, I track all of the information from the files in a ListView control (I talked about the ListView control in Chapter 7). Loading the local information into the ListView is very straightforward, especially when using the Split function, so I won't cover it here. Loading the remote file is a bit more interesting, however.

In Figure 11.2, you see the Properties window for the Internet Updater program. It contains the same four pieces of information found at the beginning of the local file: the URL of the remote file, the user name and password to access the remote file, and the directory where you can find the application on the local system.

FIGURE 11.2:

The Internet Updater Properties window

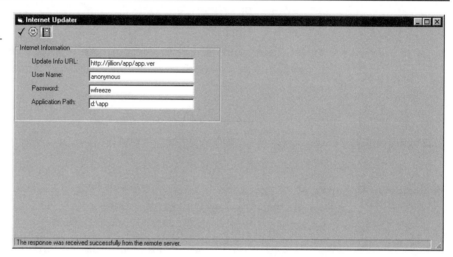

Loading Information from the Remote System The LoadRemoteInfo subroutine in Listing 11.1 uses three of these four fields to establish a connection to the remote system. It works as follows:

- Begin by initializing the Internet Transfer control (Inet1).

- Assign the URL of the remote file to the URL property of Inet1.

- Assign values for the UserName and Password properties.

- Use the OpenURL method to retrieve a string containing the remote file.

- Use the Split function to break the string apart into its separate lines.

- Call the AnalyzeInfo function to take the information I just retrieved and update the ListView control.

You may have noticed something interesting here. Nowhere did I mention any code that was specific for the HTTP or FTP protocol. I used the Internet Transfer control's ability to load information from either type of server and left the ultimate decision on what protocol to use up to the implementers.

Listing 11.1:   **LoadRemoteInfo Routine in Internet Updater**

```
Private Sub LoadRemoteInfo()

Dim d As String
Dim x() As String

Inet1.URL = Text1.Text
Inet1.UserName = Text2.Text
Inet1.Password = Text3.Text

d = Inet1.OpenURL(, icString)

x = Split(d, vbCrLf)

AnalyzeInfo x

End Sub
```

Analyzing the Information   The AnalyzeInfo routine, shown in Listing 11.2, looks like one big mess. It probably is, too. This routine grew out of a much smaller routine, but I wanted to add a few extra functions.

Listing 11.2:   **AnalyzeInfo Routine in Internet Updater**

```
Private Sub AnalyzeInfo(x() As String)

Dim b As Boolean
Dim c As Integer
Dim i As Integer
Dim j As Integer
Dim l As ListItem
Dim y() As String
```

```
On Error Resume Next

' Make sure that nothing is marked as selected

For Each l In ListView1.ListItems
    l.Selected = False
Next l

' Process the remote file one line at a time

For i = 0 To UBound(x)
    y = Split(x(i), ",")
    For j = 0 To 4
        y(j) = Trim(y(j))
    Next j

    b = False
    b = Len(ListView1.ListItems(y(0)).Text) > 0
    If b Then
        ListView1.ListItems(y(0)).SubItems(4) = y(1)
        ListView1.ListItems(y(0)).SubItems(5) = y(2)
        ListView1.ListItems(y(0)).SubItems(6) = y(3)
        ListView1.ListItems(y(0)).SubItems(7) = y(4)

        If ListView1.ListItems(y(0)).SubItems(1) < y(1) Then
            ListView1.ListItems(y(0)).Selected = True
            ListView1.ListItems(y(0)).SubItems(8) = "Newer date"

        ElseIf ListView1.ListItems(y(0)).SubItems(2) < y(2) Then
            ListView1.ListItems(y(0)).Selected = True
            ListView1.ListItems(y(0)).SubItems(8) = "Newer version"

        End If

    Else
        Set l = ListView1.ListItems.Add(, y(0), y(0))
        l.Selected = True
        l.SubItems(1) = ""
        l.SubItems(2) = ""
        l.SubItems(3) = ""
        l.SubItems(4) = y(1)
        l.SubItems(5) = y(2)
        l.SubItems(6) = y(3)
```

```
            1.SubItems(7) = y(4)
            1.SubItems(8) = "New file"

        End If

    Next i

    c = 0
    For Each 1 In ListView1.ListItems
        If 1.Selected Then
            c = c + 1
        End If
    Next 1

    If c = 0 Then
        MsgBox "No updates are needed."

    ElseIf c = 1 Then
        MsgBox "One file should be updated."

    Else
        MsgBox FormatNumber(c, 0) & " files should be updated."

    End If

    End Sub
```

I start by going through each item in the ListView control and making sure it is not selected. This is important, since I've set MultiSelect to True and I want the user to be able to override any of the recommendations I make in this routine.

After I clear any selections, I begin to process each line of the remote file. The first thing I do is to separate the line into a string array using the Split function with a comma as a delimiter. Then I remove any leading and trailing spaces from each member of the array by using the Trim function.

Next, I get a little tricky. I need to know if the filename stored in y(0) is in the ListView. To do this, I rely on the On Error Resume Next statement to prevent my program from dying if I use an invalid key value. First, I set a temporary variable (b) to False. Then I check to see if the Text property of the ListItem with a key value of y(0) is greater than zero and assign b a value of True. In other words, if there is an entry in the ListView with that filename, b will be set to True. If there isn't, the statement will fail and not change the previous value of b. I think this approach is much better than building a loop to search the entire ListView for a particular value.

Once I know that the value is in the ListView, I merely fill in the values for the New Date, New Version, New Size, and URL. Then I can compare the dates. If the new date is newer than the current date, I indicate this in the Comment column and select the row for processing later. If the dates are compatible, I then check the version information.

If the filename didn't exist in the ListView, I create a new row using the filename as the Key and Text values. Then I assign empty strings to the current values (since there aren't any current values), and I assign the new values to the new columns. Finally, I set the Comments field to indicate that this is a new file.

At the end of this routine, I decide to get cute and count the number of files I need to download by counting the number of selected rows in the ListView control. Then I display the appropriate message box letting the users know that the update analysis has been finished and tell them how many files need to be downloaded.

Updating Files In Listing 11.3, I perform the actual update process. I scan through the ListView looking for selected rows. If a row is selected, I call the GetFile routine to download the file using the URL stored in the URL column (SubItems(7)), and the application directory (Text4.Text) and the filename (ListItems(i).Text). Then I copy the value from the new columns to the current columns since this is now the current data, and I set the Comments column to reflect the date and time the new files were installed.

Listing 11.3:   **UpdateInfo Routine in Internet Updater**

```
Private Sub UpdateInfo()

Dim i As Integer

For i = 1 To ListView1.ListItems.Count
    If ListView1.ListItems(i).Selected Then

        GetFile ListView1.ListItems(i).SubItems(7), _
            Text4.Text & "\" & ListView1.ListItems(i).Text

        ListView1.ListItems(i).SubItems(1) = _
```

```
        ListView1.ListItems(i).SubItems(4)
    ListView1.ListItems(i).SubItems(2) = _
        ListView1.ListItems(i).SubItems(5)
    ListView1.ListItems(i).SubItems(3) = _
        ListView1.ListItems(i).SubItems(6)

    ListView1.ListItems(i).SubItems(8) = _
        "Installed " & FormatDateTime(Now, vbGeneralDate)

    ListView1.ListItems(i).Selected = False
  End If
Next i

SaveInfo

MsgBox "Update completed."

End Sub
```

Retrieving Files from the Remote Server   I use the GetFile routine, shown in Listing 11.4, to retrieve a file from the remote server. The parameters s and d contain the URL and local path name for the file, respectively. I use the OpenURL method to retrieve the file on the remote system, similar to how I used it with the LoadRemoteInfo subroutine. The only difference is that this time I return the contents as a byte array. This ensures that no binary information is lost, which is particularly important when you are dealing with .EXE and .DLL files. After I receive the data, I open the local file for binary access, write the contents of the byte array, and then close it.

Listing 11.4:   **GetFile Routine in Internet Updater**

```
Private Sub GetFile(s As String, d As String)

Debug.Print s, d

Dim x() As Byte

Inet1.URL = s
Inet1.UserName = Text2.Text
```

```
Inet1.Password = Text3.Text

x = Inet1.OpenURL(, icByteArray)

Open d For Binary Access Write As #1
Put #1, , x()
Close #1

End Sub
```

Watching State Information

I find it interesting to watch the state of the Internet Transfer control. It provides some insight into what is happening when. This is especially true when you are trying out different features of the control. In Listing 11.5, I handle the StateChanged event. I simply convert State into a descriptive string and display it in the status bar.

Listing 11.5:   Inet1_ StateChanged Routine in Internet Updater

```
Private Sub Inet1_StateChanged(ByVal State As Integer)

StatusBar1.Panels(1).Text = GetState(State)

End Sub
```

Translating the State value into a string is just a matter of using one big Select Case statement, as you can see in Listing 11.6.

Listing 11.6:   GetState Function in Internet Updater

```
Private Function GetState(s As Integer) As String

Select Case s
  Case 0
    GetState = "No state information is available."

  Case 1
    GetState = "Looking up the IP address for the remote server."
```

```
Case 2
   GetState = "Found the IP address for the remote server."

Case 3
   GetState = "Connecting to the remote server."

Case 4
   GetState = "Connected to the remote server."

Case 5
   GetState = "Requesting information from the remote server."

Case 6
   GetState = "The request was sent successfully to the remote server."

Case 7
   GetState = "Receiving a response from the remote server."

Case 8
   GetState = "The response was received successfully from the " & _
      "remote server."

Case 9
   GetState = "Disconnecting from the remote server."

Case 10
   GetState = "Disconnected from the remote server."

Case 11
   GetState = "An error has occurred while communicating with the " & _
      "remote server."

Case 12
   GetState = "The request was completed, all data has been received."

Case Else
   GetState = "Unknown state: " & FormatNumber(State, 0)

End Select

End Function
```

Final Thoughts

A program like Internet Updater can be a powerful tool. Because I wanted to keep this program general, I used the `OpenURL` method rather than the `Execute` method. The `Execute` method would have required me to determine the protocol being used, and issuing different commands based on the protocol would have been a lot more work. I originally designed this program just to retrieve the list of remote files from a web server and to use FTP to retrieve the files themselves. However, I felt that everyone might not have access to both an FTP server and a web server in real life, hence the changes that leave the final decisions up to you.

You can also use the Internet Transfer control for many other things than updating your application. It is a good solution for uploading information to a mainframe for batch processing. (I know this is old-fashioned, but many places still use batch processing on mainframes for a lot of their work.) It also can be useful if you want to download web pages and perform an analysis on their data. This could be information such as stock quotes, price information, or top-ten lists. You could even program it to download the latest Dilbert cartoon each morning so it is ready for your viewing when you arrive at work.

I should also point out that the Internet Transfer control also supports the HTTPS secure protocol for transferring files. This may be important if you need to transport secure information. Also the "reserved" protocol (`Protocol = 3`) that's in the documentation actually refers to the Gopher protocol. Gopher was a short-lived solution to making the Internet easier to surf. It began to get popular about a year before the World Wide Web sprang up. It made it easy to traverse a tree structure of files on different servers. It was a big improvement on using anonymous FTP to surf for information, but it lacked the web's graphical appeal. Its use declined after the World Wide Web began its phenomenal rise in popularity. While there may be a few Gopher servers still in existence, most of the Gopher servers I was involved with were converted to web servers a long time ago.

CHAPTER
TWELVE

12

Building Client/Server Programs with Winsock

- The Winsock control

- Internet client programs

- Internet server applications

- Client/server applications

In Chapter 11, you saw how to access two common Internet servers, FTP and HTTP, by using the Internet Transfer control. That control is designed to hide the grungy details of the real Internet protocols from application programmers. However, what do you do if you really need to deal with those grungy details? The Visual Basic Winsock control provides the answer.

The Winsock control gives you access to a lower level of entry to the Internet. This is the level at which the real Internet client/server applications are built. Your programs interact with other Internet programs at the protocol level, using a standard protocol or defining one of your own.

Winsock is a short name for Windows Sockets. Sockets were first developed at the University California at Berkeley for the Unix system to facilitate communications between two processes. This concept was extended to allow the processes to run on different machines that were connected via a TCP/IP-based network. The Berkeley modifications became very popular among the early pioneers of the Internet and eventually became the standard by which most applications communicate with each other. Today, the term *socket* is used a lot when building Internet applications, and nearly all systems support a socket-level interface to the Internet.

Reviewing the Network Service Protocols

As you study how the Internet works, you'll find that there's always a *protocol* for something you want to do. This is just the Internet's way to describe the interaction between computers. Network service protocols describe how two computers talk to each other. Network service protocols differ from application protocols (like FTP and HTTP) in that these protocols operate at a much lower level. The Winsock control supports two network service protocols: TCP and UDP.

The TCP, or Transmission Control Protocol (yes, this is the TCP in TCP/IP), creates a virtual-circuit connection between two computers. Both computers can talk to each other as if they were directly connected to each other. While this type of connection is very reliable, it is expensive to set up in terms of time and network resources. However, in most cases, the more reliable transport mechanism is worth the cost.

The UDP, or User Datagram Protocol, is a connectionless protocol that sends a message from one computer to another without any guarantees that the message will be delivered. Its main advantage is that it has less overhead than TCP. However, with the exception of a few lightweight application protocols, it is not often used on the Internet.

One way to understand the difference between TCP and UDP is that TCP requires a connection to another computer before you can send and receive data, while UDP doesn't. Messages merely show up at a UDP server. You can then determine their address and send a message back to the sender if you choose to. If you don't reply, the sender has no way of knowing if you successfully received the message.

With TCP, one machine must be configured as a *listener*. It must wait for another machine to connect before any messages can be sent or received. However, once the connection is established, messages can be freely sent between the two machines. If one machine were to encounter problems, the other machine would know about the difficulty—it would receive an explicit message closing the connection or a timeout would occur, triggering an error condition. Either way, the machine would know that the other machine was not available.

Using the Winsock Control

Believe it or not, using the Winsock control is very easy once you understand a few basic concepts. Nearly everything works in an asynchronous fashion; that is, you make a request and wait for an event to occur indicating that the processing is complete. This approach makes sense when you consider that those requests must be passed through a network connection to another machine, and then the machine making the request needs to wait for a response from the other machine. The network connection can vary in speed from an FDDI token ring transmitting 100 million bits per second to a network that can barely transmit 28.8 thousand bits per second. Rather than tie up your application, as well as Windows resources waiting for data, using the request/wait-for-event approach makes the most sense.

Adding a Winsock Control

When building your application, you can either connect to another system or listen for another system to connect to yours, but not both. If you wish to do both, you need to use more than one Winsock control. You can also build servers that communicate with multiple computers by using multiple copies of Winsock.

The properties listed in Table 12.1 provide configuration information for the socket connection. The `Protocol` property specifies which protocol you want to use. Since nearly all Internet servers use TCP, including those that also accept UDP, you will probably want to use TCP. This is especially true if you are building your own application protocol.

TABLE 12.1: Selected Winsock Control Properties

Property	Description
BytesReceived	Contains the number of bytes in the receive buffer
LocalHostName	Contains the name of the local machine
LocalIP	Contains the IP address of the local machine
LocalPort	Contains the port number used on the local machine (0 means assign a random port number)
Protocol	Specifies either TCP or UDP
RemoteHostIP	Contains the IP address of the remote machine
RemoteHostName	Contains the name of the remote machine
RemotePort	Contains the port number used on the remote machine
SocketHandle	Contains a reference to the underlying Winsock API handle
State	Contains the state of the control

Specifying Names, Addresses, and Ports

The `LocalHostName` and `LocalIP` address are read-only properties that describe your local system. The `RemoteHostName` and `RemoteIP` properties contain information about the other computer. You need only specify the `RemoteHostName` property, and the Winsock control will convert the name into an IP address.

The `LocalPort` property specifies which port you want to use to receive information from the remote host. Specifying a value of 0 means that the control will use an unassigned port. The `RemotePort` property specifies which port you want to use on the remote computer. Zero is not a legal value for this property.

> **WARNING**   **Servers shouldn't hide:** In order to access your server application, people need to know which port they should use. Thus, you should never use a port value of **0** for your server application, since the Winsock control will automatically assign your application to a random port number each time you start the server.

Getting the State of the Control

The State property indicates the current state of the control at the point in time you reference the State property. Table 12.2 lists the various values of the State property.

TABLE 12.2: Values for the State Property

State	Value	Description
sckClosed	0	The socket is closed
sckOpen	1	The socket is open
sckListening	2	The socket is listening
sckConnectionPending	3	The connection is pending
sckResolvingHost	4	The remote host name is being translated to an IP address
sckHostResolve	5	The remote host name has been resolved to an IP address
sckConnecting	6	The socket is connecting to the remote computer
sckConnected	7	The socket is connected to the remote computer
sckClosing	8	The remote computer has closed the connection
sckError	9	An error has occurred

Most of these values are relatively unimportant, but knowing if the socket is closed, open, or listening for a connection can be important in your program. You can verify that the socket is closed before using the Connect or Listen methods. Likewise, you know that you can safely close the connection if the connection is already open, and you have finished processing or are merely listening for a new connection.

Using Winsock Control Methods

Table 12.3 lists the methods that you can use with the Winsock control. As you would expect, they involve listening, connecting, and transferring data.

TABLE 12.3: Winsock Control Methods

Method	Description
Accept	Accepts a connection request in the ConnectionRequest event
Bind	Selects the local network adapter and local port number
Close	Closes the listening socket for TCP connection and resets the control so you can change protocols
Connect	Establishes a TCP connection to the remote host
GetData	Retrieves data from the receive buffer and clears the buffer
Listen	Waits for another computer to connect to your computer (TCP protocol only)
PeekData	Retrieves data from the receive buffer but does not clear the buffer
SendData	Sends data to the remote computer

Listening and Connecting

The Listen method works with TCP connections. This method waits until someone attempts to connect to your machine, then it fires the ConnectionRequest event. Inside this event, you can use the Accept method to accept the connection and begin communicating. You can also switch the Winsock controls at this point and free your listener control to handle another incoming request.

The Connect method also works with TCP connections. This method is used to create a connection to someone else's machine. Once the connection has been made, the Connect event will be fired.

You can reserve a port on your machine by using the Bind method. This will prevent any other applications from listening to this port. You can also use the Bind method to specify which network adapter in your computer you wish to use. Since each adapter has a unique IP address, all you need to do is specify the IP address of the adapter you wish to use.

Sending and Retrieving Data

Data is sent from your computer to a remote computer by using the SendData method. When data arrives at your computer, it is stored in a receive buffer, and then the DataArrival event will be triggered.

You can retrieve the data by using the GetData method. This method will automatically convert the contents of the receive buffer into whatever data type you specify. You can also look at the data before you retrieve it by using the PeekData method (this requires a TCP connection).

TIP

Which type of data should I use? You can receive the data in nearly any format Visual Basic supports, but only two make sense: Strings and Byte Arrays. Use Strings for character-oriented data where there is no need to preserve every bit of data. Use Byte Arrays when you are dealing with binary data, because a Byte Array will hold every bit from the receive buffer without change. Also, both Strings and Byte Arrays can easily hold variable amounts of data, so you won't lose data if the amount of data in the receive buffer is larger than you expected.

Using Winsock Control Events

The events available for the Winsock control are listed in Table 12.4. I've already mentioned how some of these can be used with the Winsock control methods.

TABLE 12.4: Winsock Control Events

Event	Description
Close	Occurs when the remote computer closes a TCP connection
Connect	Occurs when a connection has been made
ConnectionRequest	Occurs when a connection request is received
DataArrival	Occurs when data is received from the remote computer
Error	Occurs when an error condition arises
SendComplete	Occurs when the data transfer to the remote computer is complete
SendProgress	Occurs periodically during a data transfer

Connecting and Closing

The Connect event happens when your Connect method has established a connection with a remote computer. The ConnectionRequest event occurs when someone wants to connect to your machine.

The Close event occurs when the other party has closed the connection between the machines. You should use the Close method at that point to ensure that this part of the connection is properly closed. Note that the Close event will not occur if you initiate closing the connection.

All of these events apply to TCP connections only.

Tracking the Data

Both TCP and UDP connections make use of the DataArrival, SendComplete, and SendProgress events. The DataArrival event is triggered whenever data has arrived at your computer. Note that the DataArrival event may occur more than once, depending on the amount of data being sent.

The SendComplete event occurs when all of the data you sent with the SendData method has been delivered. The SendProgress event will be triggered periodically while data is being sent. This event is useful to track the progress of the data transfer.

Encountering Errors

The last event is the Error event. If a socket error is encountered while the program is running, this event will be triggered with the error number (Number), error description (Description), and related help file information (HelpFile and HelpContext). Setting the CancelDisplay parameter to True prevents the error information from being automatically displayed.

Building an Internet Client Program

One somewhat forgotten feature of the Internet is the Quote of the Day server. A program can connect with the server using either TCP or UDP on port 17. The server is available on many computers, including Windows NT.

Looking for a good quote? Try installing Windows NT Server's Simple TCP/IP Services. Among other things, you'll find the Quote of the Day server.

Getting a quote is very easy. When using a TCP connection, simply connect to the server and wait for the quote. When using a UDP connection, simply send a message to the server. The message will be discarded, and the server will return your quote.

Figure 12.1 shows Quote, a program I wrote to retrieve a quote from a Quote of the Day server. The user can choose to use TCP and specify the remote server and port.

FIGURE 12.1:

Configuring the
Quote program

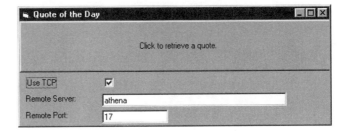

Once the client program has been configured, the user can simply click the command button to display the quote:

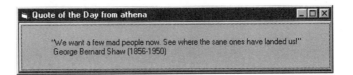

The form is automatically resized so that only the command button is showing, and the configuration information is saved in the Registry. If desired, the user can click the button again and retrieve the next message.

If the user right-clicks on the command button, a pop-up menu appears with three choices:

- The Configure option restores the configuration screen.

- The Reset option deletes the configuration from the Windows Registry and resets the configuration information to the default.

- The Exit option stops the program.

Requesting the Quote

Most of the work in the Quote program is done in the command button's click event, as shown in Listing 12.1.

Listing 12.1: **Comand1_Click Event in Quote**

```
Private Sub Command1_Click()

If Len(Text1.Text) > 0 Then
   Me.Caption = "Quote of the Day from " & Text1.Text
   Command1.Left = 0
   Command1.Top = 0
   Me.Width = Command1.Width + 60
   Me.Height = Command1.Height + 380

   Winsock1.RemoteHost = Text1.Text
   If IsNumeric(Text2.Text) Then
      Winsock1.RemotePort = CInt(Text2.Text)
   End If

   If Check1.Value = vbChecked Then
      Winsock1.Protocol = sckTCPProtocol
      Winsock1.Connect

   Else
      Winsock1.Protocol = sckUDPProtocol
      Winsock1.SendData "Hello"
   End If

Else
   Me.Height = Text2.Top + Text2.Height + 410
End If

End Sub
```

This routine begins by verifying that the user has entered a value for the remote host. If so, it resizes the form so that only the command button is shown. If not, it resizes the form so that the configuration information is visible.

Next, I set the necessary properties for communication with the server. I assume that the server name is valid and save it in RemoteHost. Then I verify that the port number is numeric and assign it to RemotePort. Finally, I determine which protocol I want to use by examining Check1. If Check1 is checked, then I set Procotol to TCP and issue the Connect method to send a connection request to the remote server. If Check1 is not checked, I set Protocol to UDP and just send a junk message to the server. Once either message has been sent, the routine ends and I wait for the DataArrival event to occur.

Receiving the Quote

If requesting the quote seems easy, receiving the quote is even easier. Listing 12.2 shows how I handle the DataArrival event.

Listing 12.2:   Winsock1_DataArrival Event in Quote

```
Private Sub Winsock1_DataArrival(ByVal bytesTotal As Long)

Dim x As String

Winsock1.GetData x, vbString
Command1.Caption = x

Winsock1.Close

End Sub
```

In the DataArrival event, I simply use the GetData method to retrieve the data from the receive buffer. In this case, I saved the data into a string and then assigned the string to the command button's caption.

After I've processed the data, I close the connection. I did this for two reasons:

- With a TCP connection, I want to end the session.
- If I'm using a UDP connection, I want to close the control so that I can reset the Protocol property the next time the user clicks the command button.

Note that I don't allow more than one packet of data to be retrieved. The amount of data I'm receiving is very small (at most, a few hundred characters), so it's very likely to be sent in a single packet. Also, if there is a problem and the data doesn't arrive, more data is only a click away.

WARNING   **The lost data of Winsock:** It's very easy to lose data in the `DataArrival` event, if you assume that the `DataArrival` event will be called only once. The more data you send across the Internet, the more likely the data will be sent in multiple packets. Each time a packet arrives at your computer, it will be placed in the receive buffer, and the `DataArrival` event will be triggered. The `GetData` method allows you to retrieve some or all of the data in the `DataArrival` event. If you make the mistake of grabbing only part of the data from the receive buffer, the rest will be discarded, and an error code of 10040 will be generated.

Building an Internet Server Program

Now that we have built a client program using Winsock, let's focus on the server side. I could have built a server program for the Quote program, but I wanted to demonstrate how easy it was to manage multiple connections with a single program. So I decided that my Windows 95 machine needed a Telnet server.

I decided to limit the commands in my Telnet Server program to just four: Date, Time, Who, and Exit. However, you are free to add any other commands you want. I've also included a primitive security system to the server. It accepts a user name and a password and then verifies that the pair is legal.

TIP   **Where oh where is my Telnet client?** Start a DOS session on either Windows 95 (or 98) or NT and type **telnet *hostname***, where *hostname* is the name of the computer on which you are running the Telnet Server program.

The Telnet Server program takes advantage of two features of Visual Basic and the Winsock control:

- You can create additional copies of elements in a control array.

- You can accept an incoming TCP connection request on a different Winsock control than it was received.

I created a form with two different socket controls. One is named `PublicSocket`, which is used to receive connection requests. The other, called `PrivateSocket`, is used to maintain a particular Telnet session. Each session will have its own copy of `PrivateSocket` to prevent confusion between the sessions.

Starting the Server

In Listing 12.3, you can see that all I need to do is set the value for the `LocalPort` to 23 (the well-known port for Telnet) and listen for a connection.

Listing 12.3: **TForm_Load Routine in Telnet Server**

```
Private Sub Form_Load()

Dim i As Integer

For i = LBound(SessionState) To UBound(SessionState)
    SessionState(i) = 0
Next i

PublicSocket.LocalPort = 23
PublicSocket.Listen

LogIt "Server started on " & PublicSocket.LocalHostName & " (" & _
    PublicSocket.LocalIP & ")"

End Sub
```

Note that I initialize the `SessionState` array to 0. I'll use this array to track the progress of a user's logon.

I also use a routine called `LogIt` saying that the server has been started. Since I'm building a traditional Visual Basic program with a form, I decided to include a text box to display a running log of the various activities that are going on inside the server. `LogIt` merely writes the string to the text box, preceded by the current date and time, as shown in Figure 12.2.

The Telnet Server's
console log

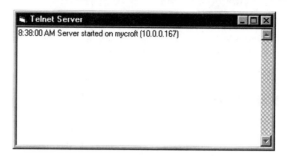

Handing Multiple Connection Requests

Of all the routines in this program, the one in Listing 12.4 is the most important—
it shows how to transfer a session from one socket to another. I use the Public-
Socket's ConnectionRequest event to receive a connection request from a client
program and pass it along to a PrivateSocket.

Listing 12.4:   PublicSocket_ConnectionRequest Event in Telnet Server

```
Private Sub PublicSocket_ConnectionRequest(ByVal requestID As Long)

Dim Found As Boolean
Dim i As Integer
Dim s As String

Found = False
i = PrivateSocket.LBound
Do While Not Found
   If PrivateSocket(i).State = sckClosed Then
      Found = True
   ElseIf i < PrivateSocket.UBound Then
      i = i + 1
   Else
      i = i + 1
      Load PrivateSocket(i)
      Found = True
   End If

Loop
```

```
PrivateSocket(i).LocalPort = 0
PrivateSocket(i).Accept requestID
PrivateSocket(i).SendData "User name: "

LogIt "Connection Request from " & PublicSocket.RemoteHost & _
    " (" & PublicSocket.RemoteHostIP & ") Session - " & _
    FormatNumber(i, 0)

End Sub
```

The first step in this process is to find a free PrivateSocket in the Private-Socket control array. I set up a loop that will scan through each element of the array looking for a closed socket. If I reach the end of the array and haven't found one, I create a new element using the Load statement.

TIP　　**A control array knows no bounds:** If you need more elements in a control array, use the Load statement to create a new instance of the control. The new element inherits all of the default properties from the base element.

Once I've found an available PrivateSocket control, I set the LocalPort property to 0 so that it will use any available port value. Then I execute the Accept method to accept the connection request. At this point, the connection is bound to the element of the PrivateSocket control array and not the PublicSocket control. This leaves the PublicSocket control free to continue listening for additional connection requests and lets the PrivateSocket control manage the Telnet session.

Once the Telnet connection request has been accepted, I send a message to the user asking for his or her user name. I handle the rest of the logon process in the Data-Arrival event. I also use the LogIt subroutine to add an entry to the server's log.

Running the Telnet Session

The DataArrival event occurs as responses are received from the client program. In a Telnet session, each incoming packet of data usually contains a single character. Since a single character by itself isn't really useful, I append it to the Tag property in the PrivateSocket until I receive a carriage return character. Then I send the entire input line onto another routine for processing. Listing 12.5 shows the code for responding to Telnet messages.

Listing 12.5: **PrivateSocket_DataArrival Event in Telnet Server**

```
Private Sub PrivateSocket_DataArrival(Index As Integer, ByVal bytes _
    Total As Long)

Dim s As String

PrivateSocket(Index).GetData s, vbString

If Asc(s) = 8 Then
    If Len(PrivateSocket(Index).Tag) > 0 Then
        PrivateSocket(Index).Tag = Left(PrivateSocket(Index).Tag, _
            Len(PrivateSocket(Index).Tag) - 1)

        PrivateSocket(Index).SendData s
    End If

ElseIf s = vbCrLf Then
    PrivateSocket(Index).SendData vbCrLf
    ProcessInput Index
    PrivateSocket(Index).Tag = ""

    If SessionState(Index) = 2 Then
        PrivateSocket(Index).SendData vbCrLf & "C:>"
    End If

Else
    PrivateSocket(Index).Tag = PrivateSocket(Index).Tag & s
    PrivateSocket(Index).SendData s

End If

End Sub
```

I begin the routine by retrieving the data into the string s. Then I check to see if the user entered a backspace character (Ctrl+H), which has an ASCII value of 8. If so, I delete the last character in the Tag property, assuming that there is at least one character to delete. After I delete the character, I send the backspace character to the user so that their cursor is also moved back one space.

Next, I check to see if the user entered a carriage return/line feed pair. If so, I echo the carriage return/line feed to the client and call the ProcessInput routine to handle the entire line of text. When the ProcessInput routine has finished, I clear the Tag field and send a new prompt character if the session is still active (SessionState(Index) = 2).

If I don't see a backspace or a carriage return, I simply append the input character to the end of the input buffer and wait for the next packet of information from the user.

Processing a Line of Input

The next routine, ProcessInput, needs to handle three types of input depending on the SessionState. Listing 12.6 shows this routine.

Listing 12.6: **ProcessInput Routine in Telnet Server**

```
Private Sub ProcessInput(Index As Integer)

If SessionState(Index) = 0 Then
    SessionUser(Index) = UCase(Trim(PrivateSocket(Index).Tag))
    PrivateSocket(Index).SendData "Enter password: "
    SessionState(Index) = 1

ElseIf SessionState(Index) = 1 Then
    If ValidLogon(SessionUser(Index), _
        UCase(Trim(PrivateSocket(Index).Tag))) Then

        PrivateSocket(Index).SendData "Welcome to " & _
            PublicSocket.RemoteHost & " Telnet Server." & _
            vbCrLf & "Session " & FormatNumber(Index, 0) & "   " & _
            FormatDateTime(Now, vbLongDate)

        LogIt "Logon (" & FormatNumber(Index, 0) & ") " & SessionUser(Index)
        SessionState(Index) = 2

    Else
        PrivateSocket(Index).SendData "Illegal user name and password." & _
            vbCrLf

        DoEvents
```

```
        PrivateSocket(Index).Close

        LogIt "Illegal logon attempt (" & FormatNumber(Index, 0) & ") " & _
            SessionUser(Index)
        SessionState(Index) = 0

      End If

  Else
      RunIt Index

  End If

  End Sub
```

When `SessionState` is 0, I'm expecting a user name as input. I save the user name in the `SessionUser` array and change the `SessionState` to 1.

When the `SessionState` is 1, I've seen a user name and I'm waiting for a password to be entered. Once I receive the password, I verify that the combination is valid by using the `ValidLogon` function. You can change the function to do whatever you want, but all I did was to verify that the password was "EXPERT" and ignored the user name.

If I determine that the password is acceptable, I send a logon message to the user and another to the server's log display, and set the `SessionState` to 2. Figure 12.3 shows the results of a successful logon. A `SessionState` of 2 means that the user was able to sign on properly, and the input buffer contains a command to be executed. My solution is to pass the command onto yet another routine, shown in the next section, which will process the commands.

If the password isn't valid, I send a message to the user letting that user know that he or she can't log on, and I disconnect that user from the system. Figure 12.4 shows the results of an unsuccessful logon. Then I set the `SessionState` to 0, meaning that the next line of text I expect to see is someone's user name.

FIGURE 12.3:

A successful logon
to the Telnet server

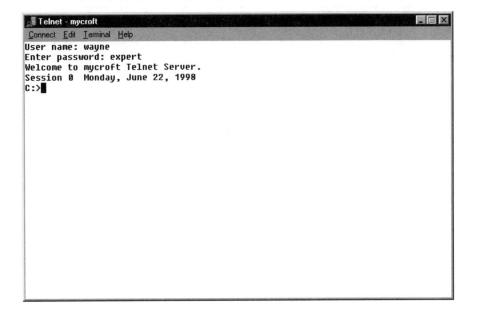

FIGURE 12.4:

An unsuccessful logon

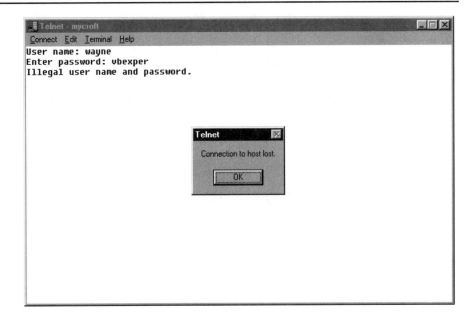

> **TIP**
> **Who says Visual Basic is slow?** In order to allow a message to be sent before the session is disconnected, you need to insert a call to **DoEvents** between sending the message and disconnecting the session. This allows Windows to send the message before the disconnect message is sent.

Processing a Command

In Listing 12.7, you see my version of `command.com`. This routine executes commands submitted by the user and returns the results. It takes one parameter: the index of `PrivateSocket`.

Listing 12.7:   **RunIt Routine in Telnet Server**

```
Private Sub RunIt(Index As Integer)

Dim i As Integer

Dim w As Winsock

LogIt "Executing (" & FormatNumber(Index, 0) & ") - " & _
   PrivateSocket(Index).Tag

If UCase(PrivateSocket(Index).Tag) = "EXIT" Then
   PrivateSocket(Index).SendData "Logoff"
   DoEvents
   PrivateSocket(Index).Close
   LogIt "Logoff (" & FormatNumber(Index, 0) & ")"
   SessionState(Index) = 0

ElseIf UCase(PrivateSocket(Index).Tag) = "TIME" Then
   PrivateSocket(Index).SendData FormatDateTime(Now, vbLongTime)

ElseIf UCase(PrivateSocket(Index).Tag) = "DATE" Then
   PrivateSocket(Index).SendData FormatDateTime(Now, vbLongDate)

ElseIf UCase(PrivateSocket(Index).Tag) = "WHO" Then
   PrivateSocket(Index).SendData "Current users" & vbCrLf
   For Each w In PrivateSocket
      If w.State <> sckClosed Then
         PrivateSocket(Index).SendData SessionUser(w.Index) & vbCrLf
      End If
   Next w
```

```
ElseIf UCase(PrivateSocket(Index).Tag) = "HELP" Then
    PrivateSocket(Index).SendData "List of valid commands" & vbCrLf & _
                    "------------" & vbCrLf & _
                    "Date - Display the current date." & vbCrLf & _
                    "Exit - End the telnet session." & vbCrLf & _
                    "Time - Display the current time." & vbCrLf & _
                    "Who  - List the users on the server." &vbCrLf

ElseIf UCase(PrivateSocket(Index).Tag) <> "" Then
    PrivateSocket(Index).SendData "Illegal command."

End If

End Sub
```

The first thing this routine does is to log the command to the server's console. Then I use a big If statement to process the command.

The Exit command sends a logoff message to the user and then closes the socket. Note that I call DoEvents between sending the logoff message and closing the session. Then I set SessionState back to 0, meaning that I'm waiting for a user name to be entered. Figure 12.5 shows the results of executing the Exit command.

FIGURE 12.5:

Logging off the Telnet server

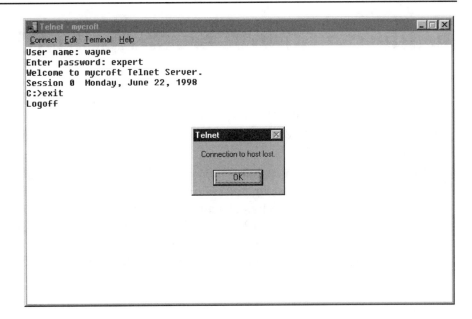

The Date and Time commands merely return the current date and time values. The Who command works its way through the collection of `PrivateSockets` and displays the user names associated with each active socket. The Help command lists the commands supported on this server, as shown in Figure 12.6.

FIGURE 12.6:

Using the Help command

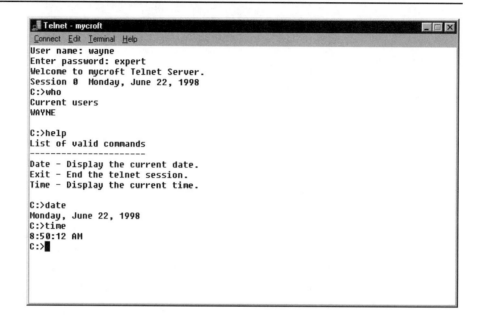

```
Telnet - mycroft                                                    _ □ X
Connect  Edit  Terminal  Help
User name: wayne
Enter password: expert
Welcome to mycroft Telnet Server.
Session 0  Monday, June 22, 1998
C:>who
Current users
WAYNE

C:>help
List of valid commands
----------------------
Date - Display the current date.
Exit - End the telnet session.
Time - Display the current time.

C:>date
Monday, June 22, 1998
C:>time
8:50:12 AM
C:>█
```

Building a Client/Server Application

So far, I've talked about how to write a client for standard Internet server and how to write a server for a standard Internet client. Now we're ready for Sea Wars, a combination client and server program built into one. It is loosely modeled after the game Battleship (I played Battleship when I was a kid, and perhaps you did, too).

This implementation is somewhat different than the original game, as you can see by looking at Figures 12.7 and 12.8. The most obvious difference is that the playing area is rectangular and not square. However, that difference is really irrelevant since the game board can be any size you choose. The second difference is that there are only four ships, one of each size. This is a limitation I imposed to simplify the program because we're primarily interested in how the program communicates with another copy of itself, not so much in building a real game. Finally, the high-quality artwork for each ship speaks for itself.

FIGURE 12.7:

A view of your own ships

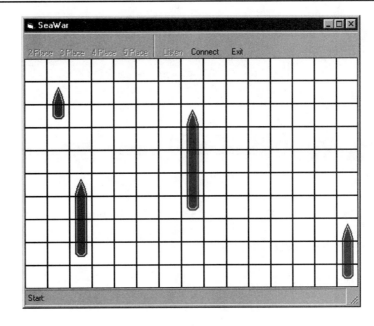

FIGURE 12.8:

A map of your ships and your opponent's ships

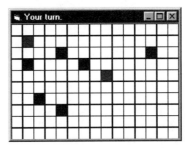

Playing the Game

Because this is a two-player game, you need to run two copies of the program, one copy for each player. The two machines need to be connected via a TCP/IP connection. While there is no reason why you can't run more than one copy of the program on the same system, it is somewhat resource-intensive and you may run out of system resources on Windows 95. However, you will be limited to only one listening program using port 777, because a TCP/IP port can't be shared.

> **NOTE**
>
> **TCP/IP does not mean Internet:** Even though the Internet is based on TCP/IP, you do not need to be connected to the Internet to use TCP/IP. Many intranets are based on TCP/IP. They can leverage TCP/IP-based software such as web browsers and e-mail servers to provide good solutions for local area networks. Many larger organizations do this, but it is also becoming common for families with two or three PCs to hook them together using a small TCP/IP network to share resources such as printers and disk space.

In order to establish a connection between the two machines, one machine must listen for a connection request from the other machine. Technically, the machine that is listening is the server and the machine that initiates the connection is the client. However, this is more of a peer-to-peer relationship once the connection has been established.

You need to enter some information before you can play the game, as shown in Figure 12.9. You need to supply the name of the remote computer only if you plan to connect to it. Both the connector and the listener need to know the port number to establish the connection. The connector sends the number of rows and columns. Both systems will automatically configure their windows to these values once the connection is fully established. Finally, the player's name is exchanged between machines.

Once the connection is fully established, each user must put ships on the grid. They do this by clicking one of the ship buttons at the top of the screen and then clicking on the cell where the front of the ship should be placed. Unfortunately, one of the limitations of the current game is that ships can be placed only in the vertical position. After a ship has been placed, its button becomes disabled. After all four ships have been placed, the players are ready to start the game.

The game play then shifts to the opponent's window, where the person who made the connection moves first. By clicking on one of the squares, the first player will attack the corresponding square on the opponent's local window. Then that computer will respond with either a hit or miss, and the opponent's window will be updated to reflect a hit (red) or a miss (blue). Then the other player may attack the first player in a similar way. When all of the squares occupied by a ship have been hit, the ship is sunk. When all of a player's ships are sunk, the game is over.

FIGURE 12.9:

Sea Wars configuration
information

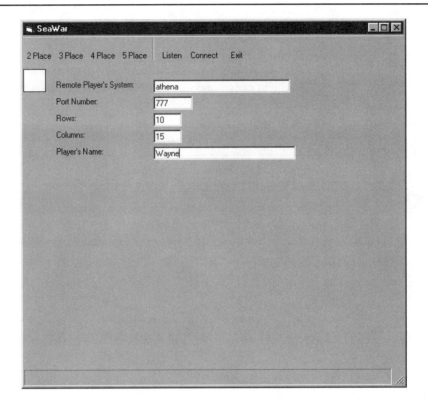

Developing the Protocol

The examples earlier in this chapter demonstrate the mechanics of how to create a
program that can issue a connection request and another program that listens for
connection requests. Now I want to move up a level and deal with how two programs can interact with each other. In this case, one program is going to send a
message to the other program, which in turn may respond with yet a different
message. The messages and how they are exchanged are called a *protocol*. For Sea
Wars, I developed a simple protocol.

Each message in Sea Wars consists of a statement name followed immediately
by a colon, an argument, and a carriage return/line feed. The statements are case-
insensitive, so that Hit, HIT, hit, and hiT all mean the same thing. Arguments are
either a numeric value without a decimal point or a string of characters beginning
immediately after the colon and continuing until the carriage return character. A
maximum of one argument is permitted per statement. Also, even though some

statements do not have an argument, the colon and the carriage return/line feed are still required.

In general, a single message will arrive in a single packet. However, it is possible that multiple messages may arrive in a single packet as long as the proper command and response rules are followed. Table 12.5 lists the statements available in this protocol.

TABLE 12.5: Protocol Statements Used in Sea Wars

Statement	Argument	Description
attack	cell index	Attack a particular cell on the grid
hit	cell index	Response to attack indicating that a ship was at that location.
miss	cell index	Response to attack indicating that nothing was damaged during the attack
name	string	Response to seawars containing the opponent's name
numcols	integer	Response to seawars containing the number of columns in the grid
numrows	integer	Response to seawars containing the number of rows in the grid
seawars	string	Acknowledge the connection request and return the opponent's name
start	n/a	Indicate that you have placed your ships and are ready to play
sunk	size	Inform you that you sunk a ship of size size
youwon	n/a	Inform you that your opponent has lost

Waging a Battle

The seawars statement does two things: It acknowledges the connection request, and it returns the name of the listening player. The name statement is used to supply the connecting player's name to the listening player. The start and youwon statements merely pass along state information, so no parameters are required.

The attack, hit, and miss statements all use a cell index as an argument. Since the number of rows and columns is known, all I need to do is to pass the index to the cell. The sunk statement informs the opponent that the last attack statement sunk the specified type of ship.

Setting the Scene

The numrows and numcols statements are straightforward. They supply the number of rows and columns of the game area.

The current implementation assumes that the number of columns will be received before the number of rows. This is okay for this situation, but if you are implementing the game on multiple platforms, you might want to revise the design to allow the rows and columns to be received in any order.

Exchanging Protocol Statements

The following script describes the protocol exchange between two copies of Sea Wars. The script assumes that the players have supplied the necessary information prior to trying to connect. The players are Samantha (running the listener program) and Christopher (running the connecting program).

Samantha	Listens on port 777
Christopher	Connects to listener on port 777
Samantha	`Seawars: Samantha`
Christopher	`Name: Christopher`
	`NumCols: 15`
	`NulRows: 10`

Both programs draw the playing areas for placing their ships and for targeting their opponent's ships. Then the users will place their ships on their local playing area. After all the ships are placed, both computers will continue the game by sending the start command.

Samantha	`Start:`
Christopher	`Start:`
	`Attack: 5`
Samantha	`Miss: 5`
	`Attack: 1`
Christopher	`Hit: 1`
	`Attack: 10`

Samantha	Miss: 10
	Attack: 16
Christopher	Hit: 1
	Sunk: 2
	Attack: 15

The game will continue like this, with each player responding to the previous set of messages with the results of their opponent's last attack and the player's new attack. This process will continue until the end of the game, when the following commands might be exchanged.

Samantha	Miss: 44
	Attack: 84
Christopher	Hit: 84
	Sunk: 5
	YouWon:

Requesting a Connection

To start the game after filling in the necessary information in the text boxes, the user can click either the Listen button to wait for another computer to connect or the Connect button to connect to the other computer. This is controlled by the `Toolbar1_ButtonClick` event, as shown in Listing 12.8.

Listing 12.8:   Toolbar1_ButtonClick Event in Sea Wars

```
Private Sub Toolbar1_ButtonClick(ByVal Button As ComctlLib.Button)

If Button.Key = "Listen" Then
   Toolbar1.Buttons("Connect").Enabled = False
   Winsock1.LocalPort = CInt(Text2.Text)
   Winsock1.Listen

ElseIf Button.Key = "Connect" Then
   Toolbar1.Buttons("Listen").Enabled = False
   If Len(Text1.Text) > 0 Then
```

```
        Winsock1.RemoteHost = Text1.Text
        Winsock1.RemotePort = CInt(Text2.Text)
        Winsock1.Connect
      End If

  ElseIf Button.Key = "Exit" Then
     Unload Opponent
     Unload Me

  End If

  End Sub
```

If the user clicked the Listen button, I disable the Connect button so that users can't change their minds about how they are going to connect. Then I assign the value in Text2.Text to the Winsock1.LocalPort property. Finally, I issue the Listen method to wait for another user to connect to this system. When the other system connects with this one, the ConnectionRequest event will occur.

Clicking the Connect button will disable the Listen button. Then I use the Winsock control to request a connection to the system specified in the Text1 text box. I use the same port value for the RemotePort property as I used when I processed the Listen method. This is because both machines must agree on the same port when making a connection.

Making a Connection

In the listening system, the ConnectionRequest event will occur when the connection request is received, as shown in Listing 12.9. In this event, I need to close the socket if it is not already closed, and then accept the request number. Once the request is accepted, the listening system will respond to the connecting system with the SeaWars statement, including the name of the user from the Text5 text box.

Listing 12.9:   **Winsock1_ConnectionRequest Event in Sea Wars**

```
Private Sub Winsock1_ConnectionRequest(ByVal requestID As Long)

If Winsock1.State <> sckClosed Then
   Winsock1.Close
End If
```

```
Winsock1.Accept requestID

Winsock1.SendData "SeaWars: " & Text5.Text & vbCrLf

End Sub
```

Receiving Data

All requests received from the other machine arrive through the `DataArrival` event, as shown in Listing 12.10. This includes requests generated by the connecting system and the listening system. This routine is designed to receive a stream of input and break it into separate statements for processing.

> **NOTE**
>
> **A difference that makes no difference:** Once a TCP connection is established, the distinction between the connecting system and the listening system goes away. Both systems may freely use the **SendData** method to send data and the **DataArrival** event to receive data without any restrictions. So while it's common for one system to send data and then wait to receive data from the other system, it's not necessary.

Listing 12.10:   **Winsock1_DataArrival Event in Sea Wars**

```
Private Sub Winsock1_DataArrival(ByVal bytesTotal As Long)

Dim i As Integer
Dim x As String
Dim y() As String

Winsock1.GetData x, vbString
y = Split(x, vbCrLf)

For i = 0 To UBound(y)
    If Len(y(i)) > 0 Then
        ProcessInput (y(i))
    End If
Next i

End Sub
```

The routine begins by using the GetData method to retrieve data from the receive buffer. I then use the Split function to separate the input data into single lines of text. Finally I loop through the array to process each line of text, while skipping any blank lines.

Processing Protocol Statements

The ProcessInput routine receives all of the protocol statements from the other computer and generates most of the protocol statements for this computer. The only other routines that issue protocol statements are the ConnectionRequest event that I've already discussed and the Water_Click event on the opponent form, which I'll discuss a little later in this chapter.

Listing 12.11 contains the ProcessInput subroutine I referenced in Listing 12.10. This routine takes a single protocol statement, decodes it, and takes the appropriate action.

Listing 12.11:   ProcessInput Routine in Sea Wars

```
Private Sub ProcessInput(x As String)

Dim i As Integer
Dim j As Integer
Dim k As Integer
Dim l As Integer

StatusBar1.Panels(1).Text = x

i = InStr(1, x, ":")

Select Case LCase(Left(x, i - 1))

Case "attack"
    j = CInt(Mid(x, i + 1))
    If Len(Water(j).Tag) = 0 Then
        Winsock1.SendData "Miss: " & FormatNumber(j) & vbCrLf
        Water(j).BackColor = RGB(0, 0, 255)

    Else
        Winsock1.SendData "Hit: " & FormatNumber(j) & vbCrLf
        Water(j).BackColor = RGB(255, 0, 0)
```

```
            Water(j).Picture = Nothing
            k = CInt(Water(j).Tag)
            Water(j).Tag = ""
            Ships(k) = Ships(k) - 1
            If Ships(k) = 0 Then
                Winsock1.SendData "Sunk: " & FormatNumber(k) & vbCrLf
            End If

            If Ships(2) + Ships(3) + Ships(4) + Ships(5) = 0 Then
                Winsock1.SendData "YouWon: " & vbCrLf
                DoEvents
                MsgBox "You lost."
            End If
        End If
        GameState = 4
        Opponent.Caption = "Your turn."
        Beep

    Case "hit"
        j = CInt(Mid(x, i + 1))
        Opponent.Water(j).BackColor = RGB(255, 0, 0)

    Case "miss"
        j = CInt(Mid(x, i + 1))
        Opponent.Water(j).BackColor = RGB(0, 0, 255)

    Case "name"
        OpponentName = Mid(x, i + 1)

    Case "numcols"
        NumCols = CInt(Mid(x, i + 1))

    Case "numrows"
        NumRows = CInt(Mid(x, i + 1))
        DrawMyGrid
        Opponent.Show 0
        DrawOpponentGrid

    Case "seawars"
        OpponentName = Mid(x, i + 1)
        NumRows = CInt(Text3.Text)
        NumCols = CInt(Text4.Text)
```

```
        Winsock1.SendData "Name: " & Text5.Text & vbCrLf
        Winsock1.SendData "NumCols: " & FormatNumber(NumCols, 0) & vbCrLf
        Winsock1.SendData "NumRows: " & FormatNumber(NumRows, 0) & vbCrLf

        DrawMyGrid
        Opponent.Show 0
        DrawOpponentGrid
        GameState = 1

    Case "start"
        GameState = GameState + 1

    Case "sunk"
        j = CInt(Mid(x, i + 1))
        MsgBox "Sunk " & FormatNumber(j, 0) & " place ship."

    Case "youwon"
        MsgBox "Winner!"

    End Select

    End Sub
```

The first step in this routine is to display the incoming statement in the status bar. This allows me to watch the protocol exchange while the program is running. Next, I find the character position of the colon. Then I create a Select Case statement using the characters in the statement up to but not including the colon as the Select argument.

The first case I handle is the Attack statement. I extract the cell location from the remaining characters in the input statement. I use the Tag property of the Water control array element pointed to by the specified cell location to determine if there is a ship in that cell.

If the Tag property contains an empty string, then no ship is present. A Miss message will be returned to the other computer, and the BackColor of the square will be set to blue (RGB (0, 0, 255)).

If a ship is there, then the Tag property contains the size of the ship. Obviously, a Hit message must be returned. I set the BackColor of the square to red (RGB(255, 0, 0)) and disable the picture. Next, I decrement the Ships array element corresponding to the ship size by 1. This array element begins with the number of pieces in the ship. As pieces of the ship are killed off, the value is decremented until it reaches 0, meaning that the ship is destroyed.

If the ship is destroyed, then I send a Sunk statement to the other computer, letting the player know that the ship has been sunk. If all the ships are sunk (the sum of all ship elements), then the game is over and the remote system is the winner.

At the end of this section, I set GameState to 4, meaning that the local player's turn is over and it is time for the other player to make an attack. (I'll explain GameState in a bit, in the "Attacking an Opponent" section.) I also remind the local user that it is the other player's turn by setting the caption on the opponent window accordingly. Finally, I use the Beep statement to remind the user that it's the other player's turn.

The Hit statement is very easy to process, since I set the BackColor of the specified cell to red. Likewise, the Miss statement is easy to process, but this time I set BackColor to blue.

In the name statement, I simply set the variable OpponentName to the value of the rest of the protocol statement. This value is used when setting the Caption on the Opponent form to indicate when it is the other player's turn.

The NumRows and NumCols statements convey the size of the playing grid before the playing grid is built. I assume that NumCols will be received before NumRows, so I defer building grids (the local grid and the opponent's grid) until after I receive the NumRows value. Note that the statements will never be received by the connecting system, and the listening system will never generate these statements, so I need to create the playing grids somewhere else on the connecting system.

I use the SeaWars statement to begin the game. It comes from the listener to the connector as an acknowledgment of the connection and also to pass the name of the listener's user to the other machine. Once I send this information, I create and draw my own grids. When I receive the Start statement, I increment the GameState by one.

Since the Sunk statement means that my last attack killed a ship, I pass the information along to the player using a message box. Likewise, the YouWon statement means that the player sunk all of the opponent's ships. I just issue a message box letting the player know that he or she won. The game is over.

Building the Game Board

The Sea Wars program takes advantage of Visual Basic's ability to add new elements to a control array using the Load statement. Each form contains one Picture control called Water that is the zeroth element of a control array. To create this Picture control, simply put a Picture control on the form and change its Index property from blank to 0. The routine for creating the playing grid is shown in Listing 12.12.

Listing 12.12:   DrawMyGrid Routine in Sea Wars

```
Private Sub DrawMyGrid()

Dim i As Integer
Dim j As Integer

Text1.Visible = False
Text2.Visible = False
Text3.Visible = False
Text4.Visible = False
Text5.Visible = False

For i = 1 To NumRows * NumCols - 1
   Load Water(i)
   Water(i).Visible = True
Next i

For i = 0 To NumRows - 1
   For j = 0 To NumCols - 1
      Water(i * NumCols + j).Left = Water(0).Width * j
      Water(i * NumCols + j).Top = Water(0).Height * i + _
         Toolbar1.Height
      Water(i * NumCols + j).Tag = ""
   Next j
Next i

Me.Height = Toolbar1.Height + NumRows * Water(0).Height + _
   StatusBar1.Height + 400
Me.Width = NumCols * Water(0).Width + 120

End Sub
```

This routine begins by making the text boxes invisible (Visible = False); otherwise, they would show through the playing grid. Then I use a For/Next loop to create new copies of Water to fill the required number of rows and columns. Note that the controls initially have the Visible property set to False, so I need to set that property to True as I create them.

After creating the number of controls I need, I place them on the form. I do this by creating a nested For/Next loop that iterates through each column and row. Inside the loop, I multiply the Width of the control by the column number to get a new value for Left, thus the Water control in column 0 will have its Left property set to 0. The Water control in column 1 will have its Left property set to the width of the Water control.

I do the same thing for the Height property, except I need to allow space for the toolbar. I also set the Tag property to an empty string, because I'll use it later to hold information about what type of ship (if any) is present in that cell. At the end of the routine, I resize the form so that it displays only the grid, the status bar, and the toolbar.

I use a very similar routine to create the Opponent form. There are only two real differences. First, I don't need to worry about the text box controls, the toolbar, and the status bar, because the only controls on this form will be the array of Water controls. Second, since I don't use the Tag property, I don't need to initialize it.

Attacking an Opponent

The last routine I want to discuss it the Water_Click event in the Opponent form, which is shown in Listing 12.13. This routine will send the Attack statement to the remote computer based on the control array index value.

Listing 12.13:   Water_Click Event in Sea Wars

```
Private Sub Water_Click(Index As Integer)

If Form1.GameState = 4 Then
   Form1.Winsock1.SendData "Attack: " & FormatNumber(Index, 0)
   Me.Caption = Form1.OpponentName & "'s turn."
   Form1.GameState = 5
End If

End Sub
```

What is probably most interesting about this routine is that I use the public variable `GameState` to determine when the user is allowed to send the `Attack` message. This variable keeps track of the game's state throughout the program. Table 12.6 lists the `GameState` values.

TABLE 12.6:   GameState Values

GameState	Description
0	Before connection
1	After connection, but before all ships have been placed
2	Either the listener program has finished placing all the ships and is waiting for the connector program or the connector program has finished and is waiting for the listener
3	In the listener program, both programs have finished placing all of the ships; in the connector program, the connector has finished placing all the ships and is waiting for the listener
4	Ready to play, my turn
5	Ready to play, your turn

`GameState` begins at 0 before a connection. After the two systems are connected, `GameState` contains a value of 1. `GameState` values 2, 3, and 4 are entered as the two players place their ships. `GameState` is incremented by one when it receives a message from the other machine that the player has placed all of his or her ships and is ready to start. `GameState` is incremented by one on the listening machine and by two on the connecting machine when the player has placed all of his or her ships. This leaves the listening machine with a `GameState` of 3 and the connecting machine with a `GameState` of 4 when both are ready to begin playing.

A `GameState` of 4 also means that the player may make an attack upon the opponent. The connecting machine makes the first move and sets `GameState` to 5. After the listening machine receives the attack statement and responds with the results, `GameState` will be set to 4, allowing the player to issue his or her own attack. At this point, `GameState` will alternate between the two values, depending on whose turn it is, until the game is finished.

Final Thoughts

The example of a client program I presented first, the Quote program, is very simple. It has no security, and it has no error checking. It merely serves to demonstrate how easy it is to write an Internet client program using the Winsock control. For an application like Quote, it doesn't matter whether I use the UDP or TCP protocol. The messages are very short—just one each way—and even if one gets lost, it really doesn't matter.

However, losing messages does matter for most applications, including the Telnet Server program described in this chapter. Using a reliable transport is important, so Telnet Server uses TCP only. Also, remember that a reliable transport is not necessarily a secure transport. Telnet server and client programs are not secure in that any information sent between the client and server could be intercepted.

You can easily extend the Telnet Server program by adding more commands to the existing program. You might want a `Dir` command to list the files on your machine. You could also add a simple editor so that you could view and change files on your machine.

Sea Wars is a relatively simple program that communicates with itself. While it uses a Winsock and TCP communications link, it uses its own application protocol. This is necessary since it needs to exchange information unique to itself. The best way to write this kind of program is to focus on the protocol exchange itself.

The term *protocol* can sound intimidating, but once you understand how a protocol works, you will realize using and developing a protocol is not that difficult. Although the protocol I developed for Sea Wars is not very robust, it does serve to introduce some of the basic concepts you should know when developing your own protocols.

The most important thing to understand is how the two computers will talk to each other. The first step is to create a dialog script showing the messages that are being passed between the two systems. Next, take that script and formalize the statements. While formalizing the statements, you'll probably want to make some changes that simplify the processing. In Sea Wars, the `NumCols` and `NumRows` statements were originally one statement with the two arguments. However, since all of the other statements had only one argument, it was easier to break this statement into two and use the same mechanism to decode the parameter.

One change that could be made to Sea Wars is adding the ability to put the ships in any direction rather than just vertically. Also it would be nice to have better graphics, including water for the background, nice-looking ships, and animated explosions. This is also a program that would lend itself to some sounds, such as the launching of a missile when an attack is made or an explosion when a ship is hit.

One other change I would consider is to replace the Picture control array with a single large Picture control. It would be more difficult to place the graphics and to detect where the cursor was when the user clicked to attack, but the larger Picture control would perform better on slower systems.

The real power of the Winsock control is that it lets you program directly at the protocol level. You can write your own client programs to read POP3 and IMAP4 mail, or you can write your own NNTP newsreader program. You can build nearly any type of client/server program using the Winsock control if you develop your own communications protocols. The low level of network access provided by the control makes this relatively easy.

PART IV

Advanced Programming Techniques

Adding Scripting Support to Your Application

- The MSScript control

- VBScript programming

- A programmable calculator

- Equation calculations in a spreadsheet

Do you want to allow your users to customize their copies of your application? Would you like to let your users automate repetitive tasks? Is there a need for a scripting language in your application? Are you interested in putting a really cool feature in your application? If you answered yes to any of these questions, then your application really needs MSScript.

MSScript began life as VBScript—a lightweight version of Visual Basic designed to compete with JavaScript in web browsers. Today, the MSScript ActiveX control is used to provide general-purpose scripting services within an application. The MSScript control supports both VBScript and JavaScript scripting languages. Since I'm somewhat biased, I'm going to focus on how to use VBScript and not bother with JavaScript. The same techniques I discuss here apply to JavaScript as well. Only the actual scripting code used will differ.

In this chapter, I will build two new programs: a simple program that allows you to test functions in VBScript and a really programmable calculator. I'm also going to revisit the Charter program and add the ability to perform simple calculations using the MSScript control (also known as the ScriptControl).

NOTE   **VBScript is not Visual Basic for Applications.** It is important not to confuse VBScript and Visual Basic for Applications (VBA). VBA is included with products like Microsoft Word and Microsoft Excel, and it is a much richer language than VBScript. VBA has a more sophisticated development environment than VBScript. It is possible to develop complete applications using VBA. VBScript, on the other hand, is designed primarily as a macro language and is not very suitable for developing applications.

Using the ScriptControl

Using the ScriptControl is merely a matter of adding the control to your program, defining the objects the script programs can access, and then running the scripts as needed.

Before we go any further, I should warn you that using the ScriptControl is not for everyone. The ScriptControl is one of the least-documented controls available in Visual Basic. Most of the documentation for MSScript and VBScript was developed for people building web applications. You can incorporate the ScriptControl into your own programs, but expect to spend some time getting the feel of this control and its quirks. Also, be sure to save your programs (both Visual Basic and VBScript) often.

Adding a ScriptControl

If you have tried the ScriptControl already, you may have had trouble finding information about it because Microsoft's documentation is really hidden. To find the documentation for this control, type **WinHelp MSScript** from a DOS session, or choose Start ➢ Run from the Taskbar.

Table 13.1 lists the key properties associated with the ScriptControl.

TABLE 13.1: Selected ScriptControl Properties

Properties	Description
AllowUI	When set to **True**, means that the script program can display user interface (UI) elements such as a **MsgBox**
CodeObject	Returns the set of objects that were created with the **AddObject** method using the script name for the object
Error	Returns an **Error** object containing information about the script error
Language	Contains either VBScript or JScript
Modules	Contains a collection of **Module** objects
Procedures	Contains a collection of **Procedure** objects
SitehWnd	Contains a reference to a **hWnd** that will be used to display GUIs
State	Describes how events of objects added with the **AddObject** method will be handled
Timeout	Specifies the maximum number of milliseconds the script will run before an error will be generated
UseSafeSubset	Prevents access to selected objects and procedures that can compromise an application's security

The Language property determines whether you use VBScript or JavaScript. The default value is VBScript, and if you are a Visual Basic advocate like me, no other option really exists. The AllowUI property determines if your script program can display visual elements like InputBox and MsgBox.

The Modules and Procedures properties return object references to the Modules and Procedures collections. The Modules collection contains the name and object reference for each module available in the ScriptControl. There is always at least one module in every ScriptControl called the Global module. Within each module is a collection of Procedures and a collection of object references (CodeObject) available to the procedures in that module. The Procedures collection contains the name, number of arguments, and whether the procedure returns a value or not for each procedure in the module.

The CodeObject property contains all of the routines defined with the AddCode method. The objects are referenced using the name of the subroutine or function; however, you must know the name of the routine at design time.

TIP   **Don't hard-code:** Although you can hard-code references to your script programs using the CodeObject property, you probably shouldn't bother. One of the reasons for using the ScriptControl is to allow the user to change the application without recompiling the application. Given the dynamic nature of script programs, you will be better served using the Run and Execute methods.

The Timeout property offers a safety shield to prevent a script program from going into an infinite loop and locking up the system. You can specify the maximum amount of time that a script can run before a warning message is displayed (if the AllowUI property is True). If the user chooses the End option, the Timeout event will occur. If you specify a value of −1, no timeouts will occur. A value of 0 means that the ScriptControl will monitor the execution of the script and will trigger the Timeout event if it determines that the script is hung.

Using ScriptControl Methods

The ScriptControl contains methods to execute code, add code and objects to the scripting engine, and reset the scripting engine to its initial state. Table 13.2 lists the ScriptControl methods. These methods apply to either the global module or any of the local modules that may be defined.

TABLE 13.2: ScriptControl Methods

Methods	Description
AddCode	Adds a subroutine to the ScriptControl
AddObject	Makes an object available for the script programs
Eval	Evaluates an expression
ExecuteStatement	Executes a single statement
Reset	Reinitializes the scripting engine
Run	Executes a subroutine

There are four different ways to execute a program using the ScriptControl. The simplest way is with the Eval method. This method returns the value of the specified expression. For instance x = ScriptControl1.Eval "1+2" will assign a value of 3 to the variable x. The Eval method can also reference functions and variables that are defined in either the global module or the local module, if the method was invoked from a local module. It also can access any resource declared as public in any module.

NOTE

Wait for me to finish: When you run a script using the ScriptControl, you can't change most of the properties or use any of the methods until the script has finished. Trying to do so will result in the error "Can't execute; script is running."

You can also execute a single statement by using the ExecuteStatement method, as in:

```
ScriptControl1.ExecuteStatement "MsgBox ""VBScript is fun"""
```

This method works just like the Eval method and can access resources in the module it was declared, in public variables declared in any module, and in the global module.

Another way to execute script code is to use the Run method. This method allows you to execute any subroutine declared in the ScriptControl. The subroutine may call any other subroutine or access any objects according to the rules that are used to create modules. You also can specify an array containing the parameters to be passed to the subroutine.

The AddCode method adds a block of code of code to the ScriptControl. During this process, the syntax of the code is checked, and the first error found will trigger the Error event.

WARNING **One-way street:** Be sure to keep a separate copy of the code to which you added the ScriptControl. There is no way to retrieve code from the control once it has been added.

Using ScriptControl Events

Table 13.3 lists the only two events that are available with the ScriptControl. The Timeout event occurs after the user chooses End from the dialog box, after the script program has timed out. The Error event occurs whenever an error is encountered in the script program. You should use the Error object, described next, to determine the cause of the error and take the appropriate action.

TABLE 13.3: ScriptControl Events

Event	Description
Error	Occurs when the scripting engine encounters an error condition
Timeout	Occurs in timeout conditions when the user selected End from the dialog box

---

WARNING **No runs, no hits, no Error event:** If you don't have an Error event in your application, any errors found by MSScript will trigger a runtime error in your application. Even a little syntax error while trying to add a script to a module can cause your application to end with a runtime error.

Getting Error Information

The Error object contains information about error conditions that arise while using the ScriptControl. Table 13.4 lists the properties and methods for the Error object.

TABLE 13.4:   Error Object Properties and Methods

Property/Method	Description
Clear method	Clears the script error
Column property	Contains the source code column number where the error occurred
Description property	Describes the error
HelpContext property	Contains a help context reference describing the error
HelpFile property	Contains a help filename containing the help file context
Line property	Contains the source code line number where the error occurred
Number property	Contains the error number
Source property	Describes the general type of error
Text property	Contains the line of source code where the error occurred

The Source property describes the error as a runtime or compile-time error and the language as VBScript or JScript. The Text property contains the line of source code where the error condition was found. The Line and Column properties contain the exact location of the error in the script. The actual error number is available in the Number property, and the standard description of the error is in the Description property.

If you want to provide your users with a more detailed explanation, you can use the CommonDialog control with the HelpContext and HelpFile properties to display the Visual Basic help page for that error. (Note that you will need to install the associated help file on your system for this to work.)

The Clear method is used to reset the Error object. Using the AddCode, Eval, ExecuteStatement, or Reset methods will also clear the Error object before these methods begin processing. For more information about error handling, see Chapter 20.

Programming with VBScript

Writing VBScript programs is as easy as writing Visual Basic programs. The same basic (yes, the pun was intended) language is at the heart of both. However, just because VBScript looks like Visual Basic doesn't mean that anything you can do in Visual Basic you can do in VBScript.

Following Data Type Rules

First of all, VBScript supports only the Variant data type. Thus, the only reason you would use a Dim statement is to declare an array. VBScript doesn't support all of the features of the Dim, Public, and Private statements used to declare variables.

You can continue to use variables with different data types. You can still create Date values, String values, and Double values, but they must be created according to the rules of the Variant data type.

Using VBScript Statements

Data types aren't the only things missing. VBScript also lacks several statements. It's missing all of the statements related to file I/O, such as Open, Close, Read, and Input. Other statements that are not available are Write. GoSub, On GoSub, On GoTo, On Error, and DoEvents. Table 13.5 contains a complete list of all of the available VBScript statements.

TABLE 13.5:   Statements Supported in VBScript

Statement	Description
Call	Invokes a subroutine
Const	Declares a constant value
Dim	Declares variables
Do/Loop	Executes a loop until a condition or while a condition is True
Erase	Reinitializes the contents of a fixed-size array and frees all of the memory allocated to a variable-sized array
For/Next	Executes a loop while iterating a variable
For Each/Next	Executes a loop while iterating through a collection of objects
Function/End Function	Declares a routine that will return a value
If/Then/Else/End If	Conditionally executes one set of statements or another
On Error	Takes the specified action if an error condition arises
Option Explicit	Requires that all variables must be declared before their use
Private	Declares private variables
Public	Declares public variables
Randomize	Initializes the random-number generator

Continued on next page

TABLE 13.5 (CONTINUED): Statements Supported in VBScript

Statement	Description
ReDim	Changes the size of an array
Select Case/End Select	Chooses a single condition from a list of possible conditions
Set	Assigns a reference to an object or creates a new object
Sub	Declares a subroutine
While/Wend	Executes a loop while a condition is True

Using VBScript Functions

Not all functions are carried over to VBScript, just like not all of the statements are carried over. A complete list of functions available in VBScript is shown in Table 13.6.

TABLE 13.6: Functions Available in VBScript

Function	Description
Abs	Returns the absolute value of a number
Array	Returns a variant containing an array with the specified values
Asc/AscB/AscW	Returns the ASCII value of a character
Atn	Returns the arctangent of the argument
Chr/ChrB/ChrW	Returns a character for a specific ASCII value
Cbool	Converts a value to Boolean
Cbyte	Converts a value to Byte
Ccur	Converts a value to Currency
Cdate	Converts a value to Date
CDbl	Converts a value to Double
Cint	Converts a value to Integer
CLng	Converts a value to Long
Cos	Returns the cosine of the argument
CreateObject	Creates a new instance of the specified object

Continued on next page

TABLE 13.6 (CONTINUED): Functions Available in VBScript

Function	Description
CSng	Converts a value to `Single`
Date	Returns the current date
DateSerial	Converts month, day, and year values to a `Date` value
DateValue	Returns a date part of a `Date` value
Exp	Returns the exponential of the argument
Filter	Returns a string array that meets the specified filter criteria
Fix	Returns the integer part of a number (`Fix (1.2) = 1` and `Fix(-1.2) = -1`)
FormatCurrency	Formats a value as currency
FormatDateTime	Formats a value as a date or time
FormatNumber	Formats a number
FormatPercent	Formats a number as a percentage
GetObject	Returns a reference to an automation object
Hex	Returns a string containing the hexadecimal value of a number
InputBox	Displays a dialog box with a prompt for an input value
InStr/InStrB	Returns the starting position of the specified substring
InStrRev	Similar to `InStr` but starts at the end of the string.
Int	Returns an integer part of a number. (`Fix (1.2) = 1` and `Fix (-1.2) = -2`)
IsArray	Returns `True` if the argument is an array
IsDate	Returns `True` if the argument contains a valid `Date` value
IsEmpty	Returns `True` if the argument has been initialized
IsNull	Returns `True` if the argument contains valid data
IsNumeric	Returns `True` if the argument contains a valid number
IsObject	Returns `True` if the argument contains an object
Join	Joins together a series of strings (opposite of `Split`)
Lcase	Converts a string to lowercase characters
Left/LeftB	Returns the leftmost part of a string or byte array
Len/LenB	Returns the length of a string or byte array

Continued on next page

TABLE 13.6 (CONTINUED): Functions Available in VBScript

Function	Description
LoadPicture	Loads a picture object
Log	Returns the log of the argument
LTrim	Removes leading spaces from a string
Mid/MidB	Returns a substring from the middle of a string or byte array
MsgBox	Displays a dialog box with a message
Oct	Returns a string containing the octal value of a number
Replace	Replaces one substring with another substring the specified number of times
RGB	Returns a color based on values for red, green, and blue
Right/RightB	Returns the rightmost part of a string or byte array
Rnd	Returns the next random number from the random-number generator
Round	Rounds a value to the specified number of decimal places
Rtrim	Removes trailing spaces from a string
Sgn	Returns −1 if the argument is negative, 0 if it's zero, +1 if it's positive
Sin	Returns the sine of the argument
Space	Fills a string with the specified number of spaces
Split	Breaks apart a string into multiple strings based on a substring (opposite of **Join**)
Sqr	Returns the square root of the argument
StrComp	Compares strings
String	Fills a string with a specified character the specified number of times
StrReverse	Reverses the order of the characters in the string
Tan	Returns the tangent of the argument
Time	Returns the current time
TimeSerial	Converts hour, minute, and second values to a **Date** value
TimeValue	Returns the time part of a **Date** value
Trim	Removes leading and trailing spaces from a string
TypeName	Returns a string containing the name of the type of variable
VarType	Returns an integer containing the type of variable

Using VBScript Objects

Unless you use the `AddObject` method to add more objects, VBScript knows about only a handful of objects, as listed in Table 13.7. If you set `UseSafeSubset` to True, then only the `Err` and `Dictionary` objects will be available. `FileSystemObject` and the other objects derived from it (`Drive`, `Drives`, `File`, `Files`, `Folder`, `Folders`, and `TextStream`) are considered unsafe, since they allow a script program direct access to disk files.

TABLE 13.7: Objects Available in VBScript

Object	Description
Dictionary	Stores a collection of key and data values
Drive	Accesses information about a disk drive; part of FileSystemObject
Drives	Stores a collection of Drive objects; part of FileSystemObject
Err	Holds information about runtime errors
File	Accesses information about the files in a directory; part of FileSystemObject
Files	Stores a collection of File objects; part of FileSystemObject
FileSystemObject	Provides object-oriented access files and directories
Folder	Accesses folders; part of FileSystemObject
Folders	Stores a collection of Folder objects; part of FileSystemObject
TextStream	Accesses the contents of a file; part of FileSystemObject

Building a Simple MSScript Program

By now, you've probably noticed that the first thing I do when I want to try out a new feature in Visual Basic is to create a minimal program that can be easily modified to try out the new feature. That's exactly how the program shown in Figure 13.1 was built.

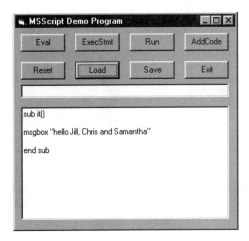

FIGURE 13.1:

The MSScript Demo program

This program isn't pretty, but it allows you to test most of the major features of the ScriptControl. You can enter an expression, statement, or program into the large text window, and click on the Eval, ExecStmt, AddCode, or Run button to process your code. The Run button requires that you enter the name of the subroutine that you want to run in the small text box below the buttons.

The other buttons work as follows:

- The Reset button reinitializes the ScriptControl.

- The Load button copies a disk file into the text box.

- The Save button saves the text box into a disk file.

- The Exit button ends the program.

Adding Code to the Scripting Engine

There are two types of code you can add to the scripting engine: subroutines and module-level variable declarations. Figure 13.2 shows how you would add a global variable, and Figure 13.3 shows how to add a function. Note that you don't need to declare types for the variables or functions, because the only type available is Variant.

FIGURE 13.2:

Adding a global variable

FIGURE 13.3:

Adding a function

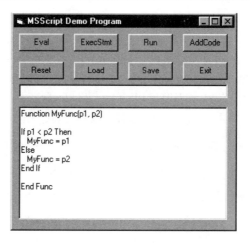

When you click the AddCode button, the event shown in Listing 13.1 is triggered. The AddCode method of the ScriptControl is used to add the contents of the large text box. This method will perform any necessary syntax checking, and it will make the code available for use with the Eval, ExecuteStatement, and Run methods. I use the On Error Resume Next statement to prevent compile-time errors in the script code from creating runtime errors in the main program.

Listing 13.1:   **Command7_Click Event in MSScript Demo**

```
Private Sub Command7_Click()

On Error Resume Next

ScriptControl1.AddCode Text1.Text

End Sub
```

All at once or a little at a time—the choice is yours: You can add all of your code in a single shot or load each declaration or routine separately. Which approach you choose should be based on how you plan to let your users edit the code. If they are supposed to edit each subroutine independently of the others, then you should probably load each routine separately. If you're planning to let users modify a series of declarations and routines, adding them all at one time is better.

Evaluating an Expression

In Figure 13.4, you see the results of evaluating a simple mathematical expression. Figure 13.5 shows that strings and functions can be included in the expression.

FIGURE 13.4:

Evaluating a simple expression

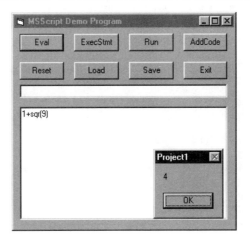

FIGURE 13.5:

Strings can be evaluated also.

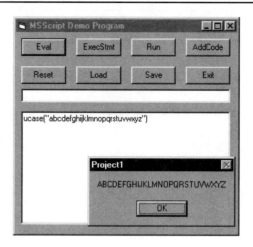

<table>
<tr><td>**NOTE**</td><td>**Expressions need formatting, too:** Expressions passed to the Eval method for processing must conform to the standard syntax rules for Visual Basic. The expression must fit on a single line, or each line but the last line must end with a blank followed by the underscore character.</td></tr>
</table>

The code in Listing 13.2 runs when the user clicks the Eval button. I use the On Error Resume Next statement to prevent runtime errors from occurring when I evaluate an expression. Then I simply call the Eval method and format the results. I used the Format function rather than one of the newer functions because it will format nearly any value; FormatNumber, FormatDateTime, and the rest require specific data types.

Listing 13.2:   **Command5_Click Event in MSScript Demo**

```
Private Sub Command5_Click()

On Error Resume Next

MsgBox Format(ScriptControl1.Eval(Text1.Text))

End Sub
```

Executing a Statement

The ExecuteStatement method is similar to the Eval method, except that a complete Visual Basic statement is allowed. Multiple statements are permitted, provided that they are separated by colons (:) and placed on a single line (although you can use the space/underscore technique to split the text across several physical lines). Figures 13.6 and 13.7 show how to use the ExecuteStatement statement to perform functions that require more than one statement.

FIGURE 13.6:

Assigning values to a module-level variable

FIGURE 13.7:

Displaying a value from a module-level variable

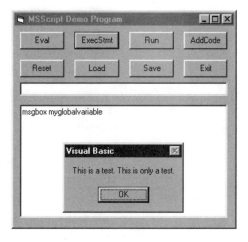

Are you beginning to see a pattern here? After setting the On Error statement, I simply use the ExecuteStatement method of the ScriptControl to execute the statement in the Text1 text box. Listing 13.3 shows the routine that runs when the user clicks the ExecStmt button.

Listing 13.3:   Command4_Click Event in MSScript Demo

```
Private Sub Command4_Click()

On Error Resume Next

ScriptControl1.ExecuteStatement Text1.Text

End Sub
```

Running a Program

The Run method differs from the Eval and ExecuteStatement methods in that the code must be added using the AddCode method before you can use the Run method. The code you add must be a complete subroutine or function, and it can even accept parameters. Figure 13.8 illustrates adding a subroutine, and Figure 13.9 shows the results of running that subroutine.

FIGURE 13.8:

Adding a subroutine

FIGURE 13.9:

Running the subroutine

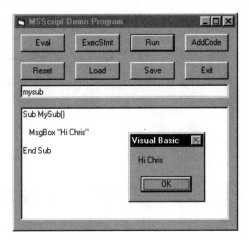

Listing 13.4 shows how to run your subroutine. This time, rather than passing the actual code itself to the Run method, I merely pass the name of the subroutine I want to run.

Listing 13.4:   **Command1_Click Event in MSScript Demo**

```
Private Sub Command1_Click()

On Error Resume Next

ScriptControl1.Run Text2.Text

End Sub
```

Handling Errors

Handling compile-time and runtime errors in the MSScript Demo program is really a two-step process. I've already pointed out the first step, which is to use an On Error statement with the AddCode, Eval, ExecuteStatement, and Run methods. This prevents a runtime error from stopping your application. The other step is to use the Error event to trap runtime and compile-time errors in your script program. Figure 13.10 shows a typical compile-time error that is trapped and reported to the user.

FIGURE 13.10:

Trapping a compile-time error

The Error event is triggered when an error occurs in your script, either at compile-time or at runtime. The complete information about the error is contained in the Error object. As you can see in Listing 13.5, in this event, I choose to display the line that contains the error (ScriptControl1.Error.Text) and the description of the error (ScriptControl1.Error.Description). After I display the error message, I clear the error using the Clear method.

Listing 13.5:	**ScriptControl1_Error Event in MSScript Demo**

```
Private Sub ScriptControl1_Error()

MsgBox ScriptControl1.Error.Text & vbCrLf & "Error: " & _
    ScriptControl1.Error.Description
ScriptControl1.Error.Clear

End Sub
```

Designing a Calculator

As another example of using the ScriptControl, I developed a really programmable calculator—and that's what I called the program, as you can see in Figure 13.11. Every button triggers a VBScript routine. You can edit these routines and change the button captions to make the calculator do whatever you want. You can also save your code into a disk file and load it back again. The only problem is that you will need to do all of the work one keystroke at a time.

FIGURE 13.11:

The Really Programmable
Calculator program

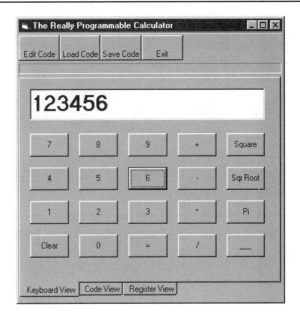

The basic design of this program is relatively simple. The form contains a large display for the digits and a control array of command buttons that the user can click. Each of the command buttons calls a VBScript subroutine to perform the appropriate function.

The program's views are contained in an SSTab control with three tabs:

- The first tab holds the Keyboard View, which contains the display window and the calculator's keypad (see Figure 13.11).

- The second tab holds the Code View, which is used to display and edit the VBScript routines, as shown in Figure 13.12.

- The third tab shows the Register View, which holds some text boxes that can be used in intermediate calculations, as shown in Figure 13.13.

FIGURE 13.12:

The Code View tab

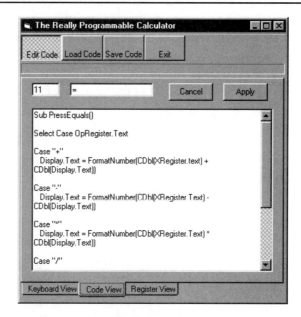

FIGURE 13.13:

The Register View tab

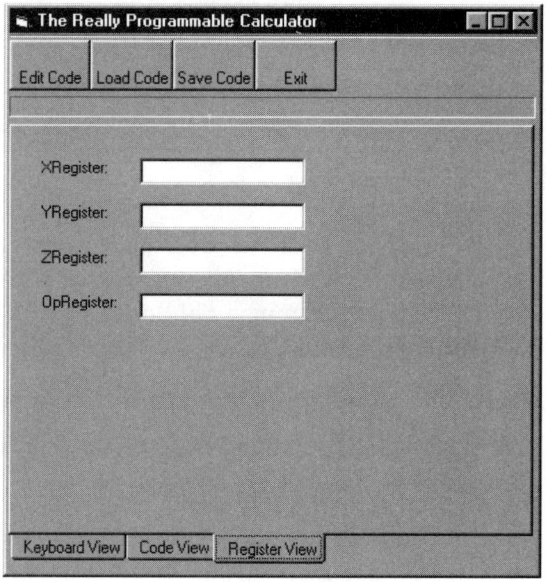

Besides the three views, the calculator also includes a toolbar with a status bar beneath it. The toolbar is used to control some of the higher-level functions, such as editing the code assigned to a key, saving and loading the entire VBScript program, and shutting down the program. The status bar displays various error messages that may occur while the calculator is running.

The calculator has two modes: the normal mode and the edit mode. When the Edit Code button is not pressed, the calculator works as you would expect. However, when the Edit Code button is pressed, clicking on any of the keypad buttons will immediately switch to the Code View tab and show the code associated with that key. The user can then edit the code and click the Apply button to accept the changed code. Normally, clicking the Apply button will switch back to the Keyboard View. However, if there is a syntax error, the Code View display will remain, the error message will be displayed in the status bar, and the cursor will be positioned at the error. Clicking the Cancel button will discard any changes and return the user to the Keyboard View.

Handling KeyButton Events

Whenever the user clicks on one of the keys on the calculator's keypad, the Key-Button_Click event will occur. Listing 13.6 shows how I handle this event.

Listing 13.6:   **KeyButton_Click Event in Programmable Calculator**

```
Private Sub KeyButton_Click(Index As Integer)

On Error Resume Next

CurrentButton = Index
StatusBar1.Panels(1).Text = ""

If Toolbar1.Buttons.Item("EditCode").Value = tbrPressed Then
   CodeBlock.Text = Code(Index)
   CodeNam.Text = KeyButton(Index).Caption
   KeyPos.Text = CStr(Index)
   SSTab1.Tab = 1

Else
   If KeyButton(Index).Caption <> "___" Then
      ScriptControl1.Error.Clear
```

```
            ScriptControl1.Run CodeName(Index)
         End If
      End If

      End Sub
```

I start this routine by using the On Error Resume Next to prevent runtime errors from ending the program. Next, I save the Index of the currently pressed button and clear any messages that may be in the status bar.

Then I determine which mode the program is in by looking at the Edit Code button on the toolbar. If it's pressed, then I get the code for the key button and display it in the CodeBlock text box on the Code View tab. I save the name of the subroutine in the CodeNam text box, and save the index of the button in the Key-Pos text box. Then I display the Code View tab (SSTab1.Tab = 1).

Updating the VBScript Routine

After making changes to the VBScript code in the Code View tab, the user can click the Apply button to save the changes. This will trigger the code shown in Listing 13.7.

Listing 13.7: **Set_Click Subroutine in Programmable Calculator**

```
Private Sub Set_Click()

Dim i As Integer
Dim k As Integer

On Error Resume Next

If Toolbar1.Buttons("EditCode").Value <> tbrPressed Then
   Exit Sub
End If

k = CInt(KeyPos.Text)
If Err.Number = 0 Then
   If k >= 0 And k <= MaxButtons - 1 Then
      ScriptControl1.AddCode CodeBlock.Text & vbCrLf
      If ScriptControl1.Error.Number = 0 Then
```

```
            Code(k) = CodeBlock.Text
            i = InStr(4, CodeBlock.Text, "()", vbTextCompare)
            CodeName(k) = Mid(CodeBlock.Text, 5, i - 5)
            KeyButton(k).Caption = CodeNam.Text
            SSTab1.Tab = 0
          End If
        End If
     End If

     End Sub
```

I begin this routine by using the On Error Resume Next statement to prevent runtime errors from crashing my program. Next, I put in a safety check that ensures that I'm in edit mode when I attempt to save the changes, since it is possible to switch to this display without being in edit mode.

The real meat of this routine begins by converting the value in the button number field (KeyPos.Text) to the variable k. Then I verify that the data is valid by checking the Number property of the Err object and checking to see if it contains a valid KeyButton index.

If everything is correct so far, I use the Add method to add the code to the Script-Control. If there are no syntax errors, I save the code into the Code array and extract the name of the subroutine, then save it in the CodeName array. Next, I update the caption displayed on the button from the CodeNam.Text field. Finally, I switch back to the Keyboard View by setting the SSTab1.Tab property to 0.

Note that I don't have any code to handle the error condition. That's because the code in the ScriptControl's Error event will take care of displaying the error message and positioning the cursor at the place where the error was detected. This handling is described next.

Trapping Script Errors

All script errors, whether they are compile-time or runtime errors, will cause the Error event to be triggered. In Listing 13.8, I handle both types of errors. Unlike the error handling in the MSScript Demo program (Listing 13.5), here I help the user identify and correct the error in a more user-friendly fashion.

Listing 13.8:   **ScriptControl1_Error Event in Programmable Calculator**

```
Private Sub ScriptControl1_Error()

Dim i As Integer
Dim k As Integer

If SSTab1.Tab <> 1 Then
    SSTab1.Tab = 1
    CodeBlock.Text = Code(CurrentButton)
End If

k = 1
For i = 1 To ScriptControl1.Error.Line - 1
    k = InStr(k, CodeBlock.Text, vbCrLf)
Next i

CodeBlock.SetFocus
CodeBlock.SelStart = k + 2 + ScriptControl1.Error.Column
k = InStr(CodeBlock.SelStart, CodeBlock.Text, vbCrLf)
CodeBlock.SelLength = k - CodeBlock.SelStart

StatusBar1.Panels(1).Text = ScriptControl1.Error.Description
ScriptControl1.Reset
Beep

End Sub
```

I begin the routine by seeing if the Code View tab is already visible. If it is not, then I make it visible and load the code related to the current button. Next, I use a For/Next loop to find the line containing the error. I scan the text box looking for carriage return/line feed pairs (vbCrLf). Since each line ends with a carriage return/line feed pair, I look for the line before the error, knowing that two characters after that is the start of the line I want.

Once I have the character offset to the start of the line with the error, I can find the starting position of the error by simply adding the Error object's Column property. By setting the text box's SelStart property, the cursor will be placed in front of that character. Then I can highlight the rest of the line of code by setting the SelLength property to the number of characters left in the line. I do this by searching for the position of the next carriage return/line feed pair and subtracting the current value of the SelStart property.

I finish this routine by copying the error's description into the status bar. Then I clear the error condition by using the Reset method. Finally, I provide a multimedia beep to let the user know something isn't right.

Defining Objects for the VBScript Program

My Really Programmable Calculator program defines several objects that can be used in the VBScript program. I do this when I load the calculator form, as you can see in Listing 13.9. I also set the SSTab control to the Keyboard View, initialize the FileSystemObject, and call the LoadCode routine to load the default script program.

Listing 13.9:   Form_Load Event in Programmable Calculator

```
Private Sub Form_Load()

ScriptControl1.AddObject "Display", Display
ScriptControl1.AddObject "XRegister", XRegister
ScriptControl1.AddObject "YRegister", YRegister
ScriptControl1.AddObject "ZRegister", ZRegister
ScriptControl1.AddObject "OpRegister", OpRegister

SSTab1.Tab = 0

Set fso = New FileSystemObject

LoadCode

End Sub
```

Defining the objects is a very simple process. All you need to do is call the AddObject method and specify the object's script name and real name. Inside your script program, you will refer to the object by its script name, while you will continue to refer to the object by its real name in your Visual Basic 6 application.

Loading the VBScript Program

Here's a quick hack job that lets me load the calculator's VBScript code from a disk file. As you can see in Listing 13.10, it isn't very pretty, but it works.

Listing 13.10:   LoadCode Script Routine in Programmable Calculator

```
Private Sub LoadCode()

Dim i As Integer
Dim j As Integer
Dim k As Integer
Dim s As String
Dim t As TextStream
Dim x() As String

On Error Resume Next

Set t = fso.OpenTextFile(App.Path & "\calc.mod")
s = t.ReadAll
t.Close

x = Split(s, "'~")

For i = 0 To MaxButtons - 1
   KeyButton(i).Caption = Trim(Mid(x(i + 1), 9, 10))
   j = InStr(1, x(i + 1), "Sub ", vbTextCompare)
   Code(i) = Mid(x(i + 1), j, Len(x(i + 1)) - j + 1)
   k = InStr(j + 4, x(i + 1), "()", vbTextCompare)
   CodeName(i) = Trim(Mid(x(i + 1), j + 4, k - j - 4))
   ScriptControl1.AddCode Code(i)
Next i

End Sub
```

I start this routine by declaring a bunch of local variables and inserting my usual On Error Resume Next statement. As I did with the VBScript updating routine, I'm going to let the Error event perform the work if an error arises.

I open the "calc.mod" file (the beginning of this file is shown in Listing 13.11) using the OpenTextFile method of the FileSystemObject and load the file into a memory with a `ReadAll` method. This is followed by a call to the `Split` function to split the contents of the file into individual subroutines using the array `x`. Each subroutine is separated by a marker consisting of an apostrophe followed by a tilde (`'~`). This is a valid comment in Visual Basic, so it doesn't hurt if it is included as part of the program.

Listing 13.11:   **Start of the Calc.mod File**

```
' Revised: 6/14/98 3:01:11 PM
'~
'Key:          7
Sub Press7()

Display.Text = Display.Text & "7"

End Sub
'~
'Key:          4
Sub Press4()

Display.Text = Display.Text & "4"

End Sub
'~
```

The section before the first marker I call the file's header. Basically, I throw this information away when I load the file; however, it is useful to have when looking at the raw file. This information will be loaded into `x(0)`. Immediately following the marker is the information for the first button, `KeyButton(0)`. Then the next marker will appear, followed by the next block of code. This will continue in the same order as the buttons until all 20 buttons have been defined.

The information associated with a single button has some strict formatting requirements. The marker is on a line by itself. A line containing the text to be displayed as button's caption immediately follows the marker. The characters in positions nine through eighteen will be used at the key's caption.

The next line of the file contains the subroutine definition. The format is the typical definition Visual Basic subroutine definition like `sub xxx()`. To parse this line, I look for the keyword `sub` then I look for the empty parentheses (). The characters in between (xxx) are the name of the subroutine.

Once I have collected all of this information, I simply use the AddCode method to install the entire block of code into the scripting engine. The scripting engine ignores the lines of comments, which is why I formatted the additional information as comments.

NOTE

One little, two little, three little subroutines: After a little experimenting, I found that the AddCode and the ExecuteStatement methods are relatively insensitive to the amount of code processed. Each line of code must end in a carriage return/line feed pair, including the last. Beyond that, the number of subroutines or statements doesn't appear to matter when using the ScriptControl.

Writing the Calculator Script Program

The calculator script program is relatively straightforward. As buttons on the calculator's keypad are clicked, data is entered into the display register or a task is processed. When one of the keys from 0 to 9 is clicked, the digit is appended to the Display text box. Listing 13.12 shows the code run when the numeral 1 key is clicked.

Listing 13.12: **Press1 Script Routine in Programmable Calculator**

```
'Key:            1
Sub Press1()

Display.Text = Display.Text & "1"

End Sub
```

Clicking the plus (+) key causes the code in Listing 13.13 to be run. The code executes the PressEquals routine if a mathematical operator was saved in OpRegister. Then it saves the current mathematical operator in OpRegister. It also saves the Display register in the XRegister before clearing the Display register. The code for the other mathematical operators (−, *, and /) works in the same way.

Listing 13.13: **PressAdd Script Routine in Programmable Calculator**

```
'Key:             +
Sub PressAdd()
```

```
    If Len(OpRegister.Text) > 0 then
       PressEquals
    End If

    OpRegister.Text = "+"
    XRegister.Text = Display.Text
    Display.Text = ""

    End Sub
```

Pressing the equal sign (=) completes the calculation process and displays the results. As shown in Listing 13.14, the code selects the appropriate mathematical operation and performs it based on the current value of OpRegister. The result is saved in the Display register, and the XRegister and the OpRegister are both cleared at the end of this routine.

Listing 13.14:   PressEquals Script Routine in Programmable Calculator

```
'Key:         =
Sub PressEquals()

Select Case OpRegister.Text

Case "+"
   Display.Text = FormatNumber(CDbl(XRegister.text) + CDbl(Display.Text))

Case "-"
   Display.Text = FormatNumber(CDbl(XRegister.Text) - CDbl(Display.Text))

Case "*"
   Display.Text = FormatNumber(CDbl(XRegister.Text) * CDbl(Display.Text))

Case "/"
   Display.Text = FormatNumber(CDbl(XRegister.Text) / CDbl(Display.Text))

End Select

XRegister.Text = ""
OpRegister.Text = ""

End Sub
```

Calculating Equations in a Spreadsheet

Of all of the programs I've written for this book, I felt that the Charter program could benefit the most from using the ScriptControl. The ability to evaluate expressions in the grid part of the program could add significant value to this simple spreadsheet program. Figure 13.14 shows how I can enter an equation into a cell.

Adding this capability requires modifying many of the existing functions because of a new global variable called `Equations`. The `Equations` variable is a string array, where each element in the string array corresponds to a cell on the grid. Rather than go through every routine that was changed, I'm just going to cover those that are related to using the ScriptControl.

FIGURE 13.14:

Entering an equation into Charter

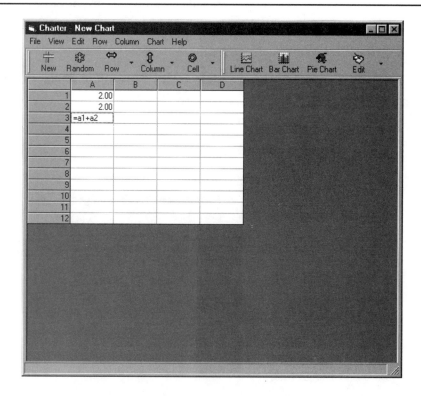

Initializing the ScriptControl

As you've seen elsewhere in this chapter, you need to initialize some aspects of the ScriptControl before you can use them. In this case, since I want to be able to access the grid from the ScriptControl, I need to create a reference to the MSFlex-Grid control using the AddObject method. Since this needs to be done only once, I do it in the Form_Load event, as shown in Listing 13.15. Note that there is no requirement for the name inside the scripting engine to be the same as the name of the real object, so this time I called the internal name Grid rather than typing all of those characters.

Listing 13.15:   Form_Load Event in Charter

```
Private Sub Form_Load()

NewChart

Set fso = New FileSystemObject

Picture1.Width = Printer.Width
Picture1.Height = Printer.Height

ScriptControl1.AddObject "Grid", MSFlexGrid1
ScriptControl1.AddCode _
    "Function Eval(r, c)" & vbCrLf & _
    "If IsNumeric(Grid.TextMatrix(r,c)) Then" & vbCrLf & _
    "   Eval = CDbl(Grid.TextMatrix(r,c))" & vbCrLf & _
    "Else" & vbCrLf & _
    "   Eval = CDbl(0)" & vbCrLf & _
    "End If " & vbCrLf & _
    "End Function" & vbCrLf

MSFlexGrid1.Visible = True
MSChart1.Visible = False
Picture1.Visible = False
HScroll1.Visible = False
VScroll1.Visible = False
Command1.Visible = False
MSFlexGrid1.ZOrder 0

End Sub
```

The other thing I want to do when the program first starts is to create a short function that will allow me to access the contents of a cell as a Double. This function will also return a value of 0 if the cell is empty or contains a non-numeric value.

Entering an Equation into a Cell

Entering an equation into a single cell is as simple as typing an equal sign and then typing the equation. The equation will continue to be displayed in the cell until the user moves the cursor to another cell; then the LeaveCell event will occur. Listing 13.16 shows the code to achieve this.

Listing 13.16:   MSFlexGrid1_LeaveCell Event in Charter

```
Private Sub MSFlexGrid1_LeaveCell()

If Left(MSFlexGrid1.Text, 1) = "=" Then
    Equations(MSFlexGrid1.Row, MSFlexGrid1.Col) = Mid(MSFlexGrid1.Text, 2)
    MSFlexGrid1.Text = Compute(Equations(MSFlexGrid1.Row, MSFlexGrid1.Col))
End If

Recalculate

End Sub
```

The LeaveCell event contains the code that will save contents of the cell into Equations array if the first character of the cell is an equal sign. If so, then it computes a new value for the cell using the Compute function and saves the result in the cell.

Finally, I recalculate the contents of the entire grid using the Recalculate routine. This is done even if there wasn't an equation in the cell. It's possible that someone simply typed a new number into the cell, and the cell might be used in an equation somewhere else in the grid. Without recalculating the entire spreadsheet, any cells that use this value in their calculations would display an incorrect value.

Computing the Value of a Cell

The function shown in Listing 13.17 translates the equation that the user typed in into one that the scripting engine can evaluate. The basic problem this function has to handle is to translate cell references of the form <letter><number> into Eval(<row>, <column>). For example, a reference to A1 must be converted to Eval(1,1), and a reference to B7 must be converted to Eval(7,2).

Listing 13.17:   Compute Function in Charter

```
Private Function Compute(e As String) As String

Dim i As Integer
Dim j As Integer
Dim s As String
Dim t As String

On Error Resume Next

t = UCase(e)

For i = 1 To MSFlexGrid1.Cols - 1
   For j = 1 To MSFlexGrid1.Rows - 1
      s = Chr(j + 64)
      s = s & FormatNumber(i, 0)
      t = Replace(t, s, "Eval(" & FormatNumber(i, 0) & "," & _
         FormatNumber(j, 0) & ")")
   Next j
Next i

Compute = FormatNumber(ScriptControl1.Eval(t), 2)

End Function
```

There are basically two ways to handle this process. The first way is to parse the equation and determine which values are cell references and which values are not. This is the way that Microsoft Excel works. It's also the way I probably would have done it, except that it would have taken a lot more code to accomplish, and it really wouldn't make much of a difference given the size of the grids I'm using in this program.

So I chose to use the second way—a brute force approach. I search the equation for every possible cell reference and replace that cell reference with the corresponding reference to the Eval function. I compute the letter part of the cell reference by adding 64 to the column number and converting the sum to a character. (Note that a value of 65 corresponds to an *A*, 66 corresponds to a *B*, and so forth.) Then I append the row number to create the cell reference. Finally, I use the Replace function to replace every occurrence of the cell reference with the corresponding call to the Eval function.

After I've processed all possible call references, I use the scripting engine's Eval method to compute a new value for the cell. Then I format the result and return it as the value of the function.

Recalculating the Grid

The last major step of this process is to loop through each cell in the grid and update the cell's displayed value. That's exactly what happens in Listing 13.18. I set up a loop to check every cell, and if the cell has an equation, then I update the value in the cell by using the Compute function.

Listing 13.18:   **Recalculate Routine in Charter**

```
Private Sub Recalculate()

Dim i As Integer
Dim j As Integer

For i = 1 To MSFlexGrid1.Rows - 1
   For j = 1 To MSFlexGrid1.Cols - 1
      If Len(Equations(i, j)) > 0 Then
         MSFlexGrid1.TextMatrix(i, j) = Compute(Equations(i, j))
      End If
   Next j
Next i

End Sub
```

Using the ScriptControl in Your Own Programs

The hardest part about using the ScriptControl is finding the right situation in which to add it. Here, I'll offer some suggestions of when you might want to use it.

Many business applications have rules that are unique to a particular business. Using the ScriptControl allows you to customize your application without recompiling for each business. All you need to do is to code the business-specific rules in VBScript for each organization. Then they could be loaded at runtime. A good example of this is computing sales tax for a particular state. Some items are taxable, and some are not. Even the tax rate may vary depending on the item. Using VBScript allows you to easily write a specific program for a state and quickly change it whenever the state changes its laws related to computing sales tax.

Another place where you might consider using the ScriptControl is in game playing. Many games such as SimCity and Civilization are rather complex and often involve tedious tasks that can follow a specific strategy. For instance, an advanced Civilization game player could benefit from a VBScript program that would automatically choose the next advance based on the advance just completed and the advances achieved by the other players.

Yet another place where VBScript might prove valuable is to create a batch-processing facility. Suppose you have a tool like Photoshop, where you can perform various tasks based on keyboard and/or mouse movements. Then suppose that you need to apply that same transformation ten or fifty times. Rather than doing it by hand, it might be useful to write a little VBScript program that would allow you to repeat the transformation as many times as needed. This would not only save time, but it also could reduce mistakes.

Final Thoughts

I really consider the MSScript Demo program I talked about at the beginning of this chapter as a throwaway program because it isn't intended to perform a useful function other than testing. Including a new feature like a ScriptControl into an existing application can be confusing when problems arise. The most powerful feature of Visual Basic is its ability to add small amounts of code to your program and see how it works immediately.

When I wrote the MSScript Demo program, I didn't just type in all of the code and press F5. If you take a close look at the names of the command buttons, you can see how this program evolved as I experimented with the features. Originally, the Command1 command button performed both the AddCode and the Run functions in the same routine. I added the Command2 and Command3 buttons to allow me to load and save my scripts (I didn't show this in the text, so check the CD-ROM for the full program) because I got tired of retyping my scripts each time the program died.

The Command4 and Command5 buttons showed up because I wanted to try the ExecuteStatement and Eval methods. About this time, I added the Error event to provide a little diagnostic information about why the script failed. The Command6 and Command7 buttons were added when I wanted to test the AddCode method separately from the Run method. Specifically, I wanted to create global variables to see how they worked with the Eval and ExecuteStatement methods. Finally, I added the Exit button (Command8) because I had an empty space on the form and couldn't think of anything better to add. I highly recommend using the technique of adding a section of code at a time whenever you need to try something new and don't have a good feel for how it works.

The Calculator program would need a lot of work before I would let non-programmer types use it. Little things like being able to specify a filename to load or save and simplifying the file format that I use to save the VBScript code need to be revisited and changed. I might even change the routine so that it worked more like a Visual Basic event, where I passed the caption of the button that was pressed rather than associating a different subroutine with each key. I could also use a Load event to initialize the calculator, add methods that could be used to change the layout of the existing buttons, and even create new buttons on the fly.

The Charter program has been enhanced many times in this book. It shows the kind of program that is easy to build if you use the right tools. The three major controls I use in this program—MSScript, MSChart, and MSFlexGrid—represent over 2.5MB of code that I didn't have to write. With these controls, it's no wonder why it is easy and fast to develop complex projects in Visual Basic!

CHAPTER

FOURTEEN

14

Incorporating Animated Agents into Your Programs

- An overview of Microsoft Agent

- Microsoft Agent software installation

- The MSAgent control

- Speech recognition programming

- Animated game development

One of the features introduced with Microsoft Office 97 was the Office Assistant, a cute little animation designed to help users get the most out of the application. Some users think that this is entertaining; others find it infuriating. But no matter how you feel about animated paper clips and scratch paper cats, tools like the Office Assistant are here to stay.

Creating your own Office Assistant-like characters can be a difficult task; however, Microsoft has made it easier with a new technology called Microsoft Agent. This technology allows you to incorporate Office Assistant-like characters into your own programs.

An Agent is a character that, when active, will always overlay everything on the screen. It can speak through the use of the text-to-speech engine, by displaying text in a little balloon like a cartoon character, or both. It can also respond to spoken commands under your program's control. A menu with the commands can be used if a microphone is not available.

Microsoft Agent is not a standard part of Visual Basic, but it is included on your Visual Basic CD-ROM. Look on your CD-ROM for the directory \Common\ Tools\VB\MSAgent for the files.

Introducing Microsoft Agent

The Microsoft Agent technology is primarily directed at web developers, although there is good support for conventional application developers. From a Visual Basic point of view, you add the Microsoft Agent ActiveX control to your program and begin reaping the benefits of the technology.

Microsoft Agent represents a new generation past the original Office Assistants. Instead of living inside a small square with a frame, only the character, or *Agent*, itself is displayed. You can choose from three different characters—Merlin the Magician, Robby the Robot, and Genie the Genie—or you can create your own characters. Figure 14.1 shows Merlin, Genie, and Robby.

Introducing Merlin, Genie, and Robby

Like the Office Assistants in Office 97, Agents are animated figures capable of expressing emotions such as boredom, confusion, happiness, and sadness. They can gesture at various locations on the screen and move around. They can also pop in from nowhere, or just roll up and disappear. Here's an example of Genie's entrance:

The Microsoft Agent software also includes speech engines that allow the Agent to speak and to listen. The Lernout & Hauspie TruVoice text-to-speech engine allows your Agent to speak. The Microsoft Command and Control speech engine is included to perform speech recognition. Two other tools provided with the software are the Microsoft Agent Character Editor, which allows you to build your own characters, and the Microsoft Agent Linguistic Information Sound Editing Tool, which you can use to improve the quality of the Agent's speech.

The Microsoft Agent software runs from the Agent server. The Agent server controls all of the Agents that are used on the computer at any point in time. No matter how many applications may be using characters, only one server will exist on your system. The Agent server starts automatically the first time a character is requested, and it is stopped when the last character is unloaded.

TIP

The Agent on the net: The MSAgent control and the related objects can be used in web browsers and other Internet tools that support HTML documents. Many of the methods allow you to automatically download the needed components on the fly from Microsoft's web site. Of course, downloading this information takes time, so the Agent software is sufficiently intelligent to download only what it needs over time. And if the information is available locally, that's even better.

Installing and Configuring Microsoft Agent

Installing Microsoft Agent is very straightforward. You just need to load the software and then copy the character files to your hard disk. Once you've installed Microsoft Agent, you can configure some settings for the characters through the Agent server properties. I'll go through the installation and configuration steps here. But before you begin the installation, check that your system meets the requirements for the software:

- To get the maximum benefit from Microsoft Agent, you should have at least a Pentium 166 with at least 32MB of memory, running either Windows 95 or newer, or Windows NT 4.0 or newer.

- A Windows-compatible sound card is necessary if you want the characters to speak or listen to you. And, of course, some kind of microphone is required if you want to perform speech recognition.

- Disk space requirements range from a low of about 670KB for just the base Agent software to about 20MB if you plan to install everything.

If you're running Visual Basic 6, you probably won't have any problems running Microsoft Agent (assuming all of the necessary peripherals are in place, of course).

Installing the Software

Installing the software is merely a matter of running each of the file-installation programs. Each of the software packages is saved in a self-installing .EXE file. You should install the services in the order they are presented here.

TIP   **Close before installing:** None of the Microsoft Agent installation programs require you to reboot your system. However, you should exit any programs just as a precaution before installing any software.

Installing the Microsoft Agent

Run the MSAGENT.EXE program to install the basic Microsoft Agent services. The program will begin by asking you if you want to install Microsoft Agent 1.5. Click on the Yes button. Then the End User License Agreement will be displayed. Click Yes to accept the license. Finally, the installation program will run, extracting and installing the files necessary to use Microsoft Agent.

Installing the Text-to-Speech Engine

Run the CGRAM.EXE program to install the Lernout & Hauspie TruVoice text-to-speech engine. The program will ask you if you want to install this software. Click the Yes button. Then the End User License Agreement will be displayed. Click the Yes button, and the installation program will install the file for the text-to-speech engine.

Installing the Command and Control Speech Engine

Run the ACTCNC.EXE program to install the Microsoft Command and Control speech engine. The program will show you the End User License Agreement. As with the other installation programs, after you accept the terms of the license, the installation will proceed to install the command and control files.

After the files have been installed, the Microphone Wizard will help you configure the microphone. First, you choose the type of microphone, as shown in Figure 14.2. Click Next a few times, and you will be asked to read a sentence into the microphone, as shown in Figure 14.3. The system will attempt to adjust the microphone levels for optimal speech recognition. The wizard may prompt you to read the sentence several times while optimizing the settings. Just follow the instructions until the wizard completes.

FIGURE 14.2:

Selecting the type of microphone

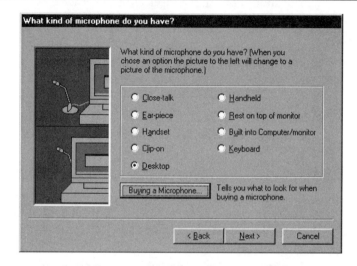

FIGURE 14.3:

Making sure that the microphone is working

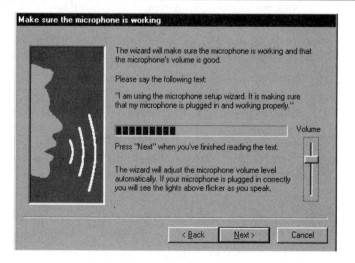

> **TIP**
>
> **Step up to the mike:** The closer the microphone is to your mouth, the more accurately the speech recognition engine will work. The close proximity to your mouth means that the microphone will pick up less background noise. The best type of microphone to use is a close-talk microphone, where the microphone is placed just in front of your mouth. If you don't have a close-talk microphone, then try to keep the room as quiet as possible.

If you want to change the microphone settings later, you can run the wizard again. Double-click on the Microsoft Agent icon in the Taskbar's system tray and select the Speech Input tab on the Microsoft Agent Properties dialog box. Click the Adjust Microphone button to begin working with the wizard again. I'll talk more about the Microsoft Agent server properties you can adjust after finishing up with the installation steps.

Installing the Microsoft Agent Character Editor

The Microsoft Agent Character Editor is an optional component that you only need if you plan to create your own characters. To install it, run the ACE.EXE program. It will ask you if you wish to install the software. If you click Yes, it will then ask if you agree with the End User License Agreement. Clicking Yes again will install the software.

Installing the Sound Editing Tool

You only need the Microsoft Agent Linguistic Information Sound Editing Tool (LISET) if you want to optimize the Agent's speech. To install LISET, simply run LISET .EXE and reply Yes when it asks if you want to install the software. Click Yes again if you agree to the licensing terms. Then the software will be expanded and installed onto your system.

Installing the Characters

After the software has been installed, you need to install the files that contain each of the characters. Microsoft currently has the three characters you saw earlier: Genie the Genie, Merlin the Magician, and Robby the Robot. There is also an enhanced version of Merlin called MerlinSfx, which has special sound effects that accompany his actions.

> **WARNING**   **One Merlin is fine, but two are trouble:** While both Merlin characters can be loaded onto the same hard disk, an application can only load one at a time. If you attempt to load a second Merlin, your program will stop with a runtime error.

The installation notes about where to place the characters aren't clear. However, most developers are placing their characters in the \Program Files\Microsoft Agent\Characters\ directory. The location isn't critical, but every program that uses an Agent needs to know where the characters are stored.

Configuring the Agent Server

Whenever the Agent server is active, you will see the Agent icon on the Taskbar's icon tray:

Double-clicking on the Agent icon in the icon tray displays the Microsoft Agent Properties dialog box, as shown in Figure 14.4. By setting properties in this dialog box, you can specify how the character will act:

- You can select whether the character displays the words he says in a balloon, along with the font to be used for the text.

- You can enable or disable whether the character's speech is played through the speakers, and whether or not the character's sound effects (if present) are also played through the speakers.

- You can adjust the speaking speed.

Note that these adjustments are global and will affect all characters.

The Speech Input tab, shown in Figure 14.5, contains all the properties related to speech input. If you didn't install the Microsoft Command and Control speech engine, these properties will be disabled.

FIGURE 14.4:

The Output tab of the
Microsoft Agent Properties
dialog box

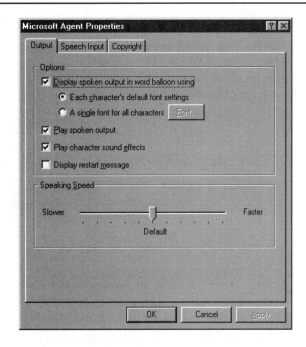

FIGURE 14.5:

The Speech Input tab of the
Microsoft Agent Properties
dialog box

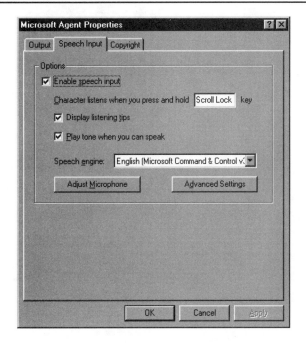

By default, the character will only hear commands when the user presses and holds the Scroll Lock key. You can change this value to another key or set it to None, which means that the character is continually listening for commands. Other properties let you display a listening tip, play a tone when the character is waiting for speech input, and select the speech engine you wish to use. A *listening tip* visually cues the user to when the character is listening to speech input, like this:

You can start the Microphone Wizard from the Speech Input tab by clicking the Adjust Microphone button. You can also click the Advanced Settings button to reach the Microsoft Speech Recognizer Properties dialog box, as shown in Figure 14.6.

FIGURE 14.6:

The Microsoft Speech Recognizer Properties dialog box

From here, you can click the Training button to help train your computer to better understand your speech. The Training Wizard, shown in Figure 14.7, will ask you to read from a variety of documents that will allow the speech recognition engine to analyze your speech and try to improve the performance of the speech engine.

FIGURE 14.7:

The Microsoft Speech Recognizer Training Wizard

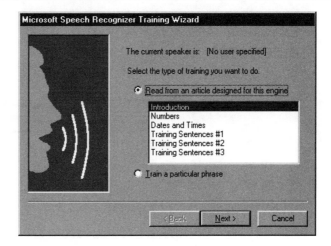

Using the MSAgent Control

Understanding the MSAgent control can be a rather formidable task because there are so many objects and properties available. However, using the defaults for most of them is not only acceptable, but also recommended. Figure 14.8 shows a hierarchy of the objects used in the MSAgent control.

Objects used in the
MSAgent control

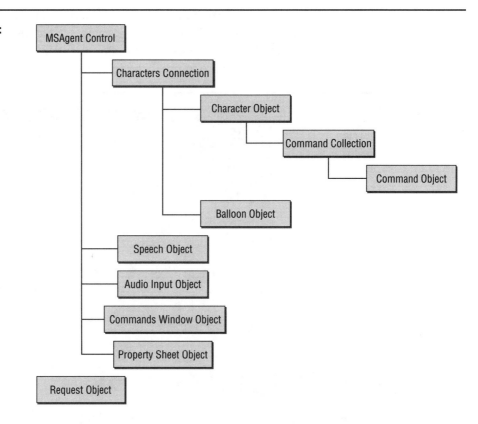

Adding the MSAgent Control to Your Program

Most of the properties of the MSAgent control are references to other objects that
exist within the scope of the control. The most important of these objects is the
Characters collection, which contains references for all of the currently loaded
characters. Other objects contained in the control are AudioOutput, Commands-
Window, PropertySheet, and SpeechInput. Table 14.1 lists some important
properties of the MSAgent control.

TABLE 14.1: Selected MSAgent Control Properties

Property	Description
AudioOutput	Contains an object reference to the AudioOutput object
Characters	Contains an object reference to the Characters collection
CommandsWindow	Contains an object reference to the CommandsWindow object
Connected	Contains True if the control is connected to the Agent server
PropertySheet	Contains an object reference to the PropertySheet object
SpeechInput	Contains an object reference to the SpeechInput object
Suspended	Contains True if the Agent server is suspended

The Connected property is True if the control is connected to the Agent server. Normally, the Connected property is set to True when your program starts or when the control is loaded in your web page, but if you create a new instance of the control at runtime, you may need to set the Connected property to True to force a connection. The Suspended property indicates the state of the Agent server. You can't change this value directly, but you can ask the user to restart the server by choosing Restart from the Taskbar pop-up menu.

Using MSAgent Control Events

The MSAgent control also includes an assortment of events that you can use to track the execution of your characters or respond to user requests. Unlike the normal Click and DblClick events, these contain the following information:

- The character's name
- The mouse button that triggered the event
- The state of the Ctrl, Alt, and Shift keys
- The x, y location of the mouse measured in pixels

Table 14.2 lists the MSAgent control events.

TABLE 14.2: MSAgent Control Events

Event	Description
ActivateInput	Occurs when a character becomes input-active
BalloonHide	Occurs when a character's balloon is hidden
BalloonShow	Occurs when a character's balloon is shown
Bookmark	Occurs when a bookmark is encountered while using the **Speak** method
Click	Occurs when the user clicks on the character; includes button clicked, Shift key status, and x, y location of the cursor
Command	Occurs when the user issues a command
DblClick	Occurs when the user double-clicks on the character; includes button double-clicked, Shift key status, and x, y location of the cursor
DeactivateInput	Occurs when the character becomes non–input-active.
DragComplete	Occurs when the user has finished dragging the character
DragStart	Occurs when the user starts dragging a character
Hide	Occurs when a character is hidden
IdleComplete	Occurs when the server ends the idle state of a character
IdleStart	Occurs when the server places a character into the idle state
Move	Occurs after a character has been moved
RequestComplete	Returns the **Request** object after the server has finished a queued request
RequestStart	Returns the **Request** object before the server starts processing a request
Restart	Occurs when the server goes from a suspended to an active state
Show	Occurs when a character is displayed with the **Show** method
Shutdown	Occurs when the user shuts down the Agent server
Size	Occurs when the size of the character changes

Issuing Character Commands

The Command event occurs when the user sends a command to the character, either by speaking or by choosing a command from the command menu. The UserInput object will be returned as a value to the event. This object contains information for up to three commands (the best match and up to two alternatives) that the speech recognition engine believes are possible matches, as listed in Table 14.3.

TABLE 14.3:   The UserInput Object Used in the Command Event

Property	Description
CharacterID	The name of the character that received the command
Name	The name of the command
Confidence	A value in the range of −100 to +100 indicating how close the spoken input was to the Voice property
Voice	The string of characters that was matched against the spoken input
Alt1Name	The name of the first alternate command
Alt1Confidence	Same as Confidence but for Alt1Name
Alt1Voice	Same as Voice but for Alt1Name
Alt2Name	The name of the second alternate command
Alt2Confidence	Same as Confidence but for Alt2Name
Alt2Voice	Same as Voice but for Alt2Name
Count	The number of alternatives returned

Each returned command includes the name of the command, the string containing the voice text, and a confidence number in the range of −100 to +100 that indicates how well the spoken words match the command. The event also includes the number of commands returned. If the command was selected via a menu, Count will be set to 1 and the Confidence value will be set to +100. If the server was unable to match the spoken words with a command, Count will be set to 0.

Shutting Down and Restarting

The Shutdown and Restart events occur when the user stops the server and restarts it again directly from outside the program's control. These events will occur in all programs that have an active connection to the server.

Hiding, Showing, Moving, and Resizing

The Hide event is triggered whenever a character is hidden. Why this character is hidden is also included as an argument to this event. Similarly, the Show event occurs when the character is shown.

The Move event is triggered after the character is moved to a new location on the screen, with the coordinates specified in pixels. Similar to the Move event are the DragStart and DragComplete events; however, these events are sent only to the input-active character. When the size of a character is changed via its Height and Width properties, the Size event will be triggered.

WARNING   **It's not my fault:** Many of the events in the MSAgent control are triggered system-wide for all applications using Agents. You should verify the character name passed to check that the event applies to your program.

Activating and Deactivating

The ActivateInput and DeactivateInput events occur at the beginning and the end of the period of time that a particular character can receive input. More specifically, the ActivateInput is triggered when the character becomes input-active, and the DeactiveInput event occurs when the character becomes non–input-active.

Working with Characters

The Characters collection contains a series of Microsoft Agent characters. The Character object is the primary object that you will manipulate. It contains the properties and methods that are necessary to make your character come alive.

Table 14.4 lists the properties and methods available for the Characters collection.

TABLE 14.4:   Characters Collection Properties and Methods

Property/Method	Description
Character method	Returns the specified Character object from the collection
Item property	Returns the specified Character object from the collection (same as the Character method)
Load method	Loads a character into the collection
Unload method	Removes a character from the collection

Loading and Unloading Characters

Before you use a particular character, you must first load it. When using the Load method, you must specify where the character information may be found. This location may be a path and filename or an HTTP URL to Microsoft's web site.

When you're finished with a character, you can use the Unload method to unload it, thus saving memory and other resources. However, you will need to Load the character again the next time you want to use it.

Referencing a Character

You can reference a particular character by using the Item property or the Character method. In fact, you can omit both keywords and simply specify the name of the character that you wish to use. The first three statements in the following code all perform the same function. In the last three statements, I declare a variable as type Object and create an object reference to it. This provides the quickest way of all to reference the character.

```
Agent1.Characters.Character("Genie").Speak "Hello Chris."
Agent1.Characters.Item("Genie").Speak "Hello Chris."
Agent1.Characters("Genie").Speak "Hello Chris."

Dim MyAgent as Object
Set MyAgent = Agent1.Characters.Character("Genie")
MyAgent.Speak "Hello Chris."
```

Using Character Files

There are three types of character files:

- The .AAF file contains the character animation information.

- The .ACF file contains the character data.

- The .ACS file contains both the character animations and the character data.

The three types of files are optimized for different situations. The .AAF and .ACF files are designed to let users download just enough data over the Internet to perform their immediate task. You use the Character object's Get method to retrieve the pieces of information you need. The .ACS file is designed for use on your local hard disk, when the amount of information you want to access is not a problem.

Assigning Properties to the Character Object

Table 14.5 lists the Character object's properties. By changing the values of Height and Width, you can change the size of the character. By changing the Top and Left properties, you can change the character's location on the screen. All four of these properties use measurements in pixels, not twips.

TABLE 14.5: Selected Character Object Properties

Property	Description
Balloon	Returns an object reference to a **Balloon** object
Commands	Returns an object reference to a **Commands** collection
Description	Contains a description of the character (may not be present with all characters)
ExtraData	Contains extra data about the character (may not be present with all characters)
HasOtherClients	When set to **True**, other applications are using this character
Height	Contains the height of the character in pixels
IdleOn	When set to **True**, the server plays the **Idle** animation after the character has been idle for a while.
Left	Contains the distance between the left edge of the character and the left edge of the screen, measured in pixels

Continued on next page

TABLE 14.5 (CONTINUED): Selected Character Object Properties

Property	Description
MoveCause	Contains an Integer that describes who last moved the character
Name	Contains the name of the character
Pitch	Contains a **Long** value with the character's speech output pitch setting (TTS)
SoundEffectsOn	When set to **True**, sound effects are automatically played for your character if included in the character information
Speed	Contains a **Long** value containing the user's current setting for the speed of the character's speech
Top	Contains the distance between the top edge of the character and the top edge of the screen, measured in pixels
VisibilityCause	Contains an Integer that describes who last changed the character's Visible property
Visible	When set to **True**, the character is currently displayed on the screen
Width	Contains the width of the character in pixels

Some of these properties, such as the character's Name, Description, and ExtraData, are set when the character is created using the Agent Character Editor. Both the Description and the ExtraData properties contain optional information that may not be available in all characters.

Setting the IdleOn property to True will let the Agent server automatically provide animations when the character hasn't been referenced in a while. The SoundEffectsOn property controls whether or not the character's sound effects will be played. Of the characters shipped with Microsoft Agent 1.5, only the MerlinSfx character contains sound effects, so this property won't make much of a difference with any of the other characters. The Pitch and Speed properties reflect the options set by the user in the Microsoft Agent Properties dialog box.

Since a particular character may be controlled by multiple applications, several of the properties are available to coordinate multiple access. You can see if you have exclusive use of the character by checking the HasOtherClients. You can find out who or what last moved the character with the MoveCause property, and you can check who last changed the Visible property with the Visibility-Cause property.

Using Character Object Methods

When working with Agents, most of the functions involve requests that you will pass to an individual character to perform. These functions include speaking, gesturing, playing animations, and moving around on the screen. To perform these functions, you use the methods listed in Table 14.6.

TABLE 14.6:   Character Object Methods

Method	Description
Activate	Changes which character is active
GestureAt	Plays the animation where the character will gesture at the specified location on the screen
Get	Retrieves information about a character
Hide	Removes the character from the screen
Interrupt	Interrupts the current animation of another character and continues with the next animation in the queue
MoveTo	Moves the character to the specified location on the screen
Play	Plays the specified animation
Show	Displays the character on the screen
Speak	Uses the text-to-speech engine to say the specified text and displays the text in the balloon
Stop	Cancels the current animation and the rest of the animations in the queue
StopAll	Stops the specified list of requests
Wait	Waits for the specified request to be completed

Because many of the actions that a character will perform take a relatively long period of time, most of the methods issue a command to the Agent server and then return control to your program. The Agent server maintains a queue with these commands and will execute them in the order that they were submitted to the server, unless you take explicit action to change what is happening.

Displaying and Hiding Characters Once you have used the Load method to load a character into the Characters object, you can use the Show method to display the character on the screen. Normally, the character will play a short animation rather than simply appearing on the screen. For instance, the Robby the Robot animation will begin by showing a door opening on your screen and then walking through the door, as you can see in Figure 14.9. You have the option to skip this animation and have the character appear immediately on the screen.

FIGURE 14.9:

Robby the Robot's Show animation

The opposite of the Show method is the Hide method. Normally, the Hide method will play a short animation rather than having the character simply vanish. However, you can specify that the character should skip this animation, which will cause the character to disappear immediately.

Moving Characters You can move your character around the screen by using the MoveTo method. This method requires an x, y location (in pixels) to specify where you want to move the character and a value to indicate the speed at which the character should be moved. An animation will be played while the character is moving. If you specify a value of 0 for speed, the character will immediately jump to the new location without any animation.

TIP

Jump before you show: You can use the MoveTo method before you use the Show method to display the character if you set the MoveTo speed to 0. Otherwise, using the MoveTo method before the Show method will cause an error.

The animation consists of two parts: the normal animation and the return animation. The normal animation takes the character from the neutral position to the desired position. The return animation takes the character back to the neutral state.

Making Characters Point   The GestureAt method also plays an animation. This animation is used to point at a location specified by an x, y coordinate on the screen. Figure 14.10 shows an example. The routine is smart enough to pick the appropriate animation to point in the correct direction relative to the character's current location.

FIGURE 14.10:

Merlin's gesture

Playing with Your Characters   All of the other animations are handled by the Play method. This method adds the animation to the end of the queue at the Agent server. Each animation will be played in turn, unless a Stop, StopAll, or Interrupt method is used. Table 14.7 lists some of the animations handled by the Play method.

TABLE 14.7:   Selected Play Method Animations for Genie, Merlin, and Robby

Animation	Description
Acknowledge	Nods head
Alert	Straightens and raises eyebrows
AlertReturn	Returns to neutral state
Blink	Blinks eyes
Confused	Scratches head
ConfusedReturn	Returns to neutral state
DontRecognize	Holds hand to ear
DontRecognizeReturn	Returns to neutral state

Continued on next page

TABLE 14.7 (CONTINUED): Selected Play Method Animations for Genie, Merlin, and Robby

Animation	Description
Explain	Extends arms to the side
ExplainReturn	Returns to neutral state
Greet	Bows (Genie and Merlin) or waves (Robby)
GreetReturn	Returns to neutral state
Pleased	Claps hands and smiles (Genie), smiles and holds hands together (Merlin), or straightens body and smiles (Robby)
PleasedReturn	Returns to neutral state
Read	Gets scroll and reads it (Genie), opens book and looks up (Merlin), or tears off printout and reads it (Robby)
ReadReturn	Returns to neutral state
Sad	Looks sad
SadReturn	Returns to neutral state
Suggest	Displays light bulb
SuggestReturn	Returns to neutral state
Surprised	Looks surprised
SurprisedReturn	Returns to neutral state
Think	Looks up with hand on chin (Genie and Merlin) or tilts head and scratches (Robby)
ThinkReturn	Returns to neutral state
Wave	Waves
WaveReturn	Returns to neutral state
Write	Writes and looks up
WriteReturn	Returns to neutral state

If an animation doesn't leave the character in a neutral state, and the next animation starts with the character in the neutral state, then the return animation associated with the last animation will be played automatically. For example, when you tell Merlin to play the Wave animation, Merlin finishes with his hand up. Then when you play the Surprised animation, the WaveReturn animation will be played automatically before the Surprised animation is started.

Making Animations Speak The Speak method uses the text-to-speech engine to convert the string of words into audible speech. The words will also be displayed in the character's balloon as they are spoken. In addition, this method includes a number of speech tags that can be used to modify how the speech sounds Table 14.8 lists the available speech tags and what they do.

TABLE 14.8: Speech Tags Used with the Speak Method

Tag	Description
Chr	Specifies the character of the voice; valid values are Normal, Monotone, and Whisper
Ctx	Sets the context of the output text; valid values are Address, Email, and Unknown
Emp	Emphasizes the next word
Lst	Repeats the character's last spoken statement; this tag must be alone in the parameter for the Speak method
Map	Sends one block of text to the speech-to-text engine and displays the other in the balloon
Mrk	Triggers the Bookmark event with the specified number
Pau	Pauses the speech for the specified number of milliseconds
Pit	Sets the baseline pitch; this value can range from 50 to 400 hertz
Rst	Resets all tags to their default settings
Spd	Sets the baseline speaking speed
Vol	Sets the baseline speaking volume

Synchronizing Characters If you have a program with more than one Agent, you will need a way to synchronize the various characters. Synchronization can be accomplished by using the Wait and Activate methods. Each of the methods we've discussed here (GestureAt, Hide, MoveTo, Play, Show, and Speak) can return a Request object. The Wait method uses the Request object and will delay one character's action until the action of another character has been completed.

WARNING   **Wait not, want not:** You can't use the Wait method on the same character that created the Request object. Doing so will cause an error.

The Activate method is also important because it allows you to make a different character input-active. Without this method, you would need to play an animation or speak some words to switch the input-active state from one character to another.

Stopping Animations   To cancel the current animation and the rest of the animations in the queue, use the Stop method. You can also use the Stop method to cancel the animation associated with a particular Request object. The StopAll method can cancel all animations or other requests by request type. The Interrupt method is used to cancel the current animation and begin processing the next animation in sequence. All of these methods are not queued and take effect immediately.

Handling Characters over the Internet   The Get method is used primarily in Internet applications where character information and animations are loaded from a web server. This method allows you to retrieve three types of information: an animation, a state date, or a wave file. The requests are sent to the Agent server, which will get the information from the specified location if needed. By using the Get method, you will only download those animations you need, thus minimizing download time.

WARNING   **You can't play what you don't have:** You must use the Get method to retrieve character information and animation information before you use it. For example, before you use the Show method, you must download the Show animation. Of course, if you are using character data from your local hard disk, this warning doesn't apply.

Working with Commands

In order to do voice recognition, you need to define the words and phrases you want to handle to put in the Commands collection. While this collection has a few different properties and methods than the typical collection, the Visual Basic For Each statement will work the same as in any other collection.

When running your program, a user can see a list of the commands understood by the Agent character by right-clicking on the Agent icon in the system tray and selecting Open Commands Window. This displays a Command window with the list of commands, as shown in Figure 14.11. The user also can see the same list of commands as a pop-up menu by right-clicking on the Agent character, as shown in Figure 14.12. Since this is a standard pop-up menu, the user can select any of the menu items, and it will be handled just as if he or she spoke the corresponding phrase.

FIGURE 14.11:

A typical Commands window

FIGURE 14.12:

A pop-up menu showing the same commands

The properties of the Commands collection are listed in Table 14.9. The Caption property contains the text that will be displayed as a heading in the Commands window in the Agent server (if the Visible property is True). The Voice property contains the text that will be passed to the voice recognition software if the user chooses this entry from the Commands window.

TABLE 14.9: Commands Collection Properties

Property	Description
Caption	Displays the specified text in the Commands window and the pop-up menu
Count	Contains the number of objects in the Commands collection
Item	Returns the specified Command object
Visible	When set to True, means that the command's caption will appear in the character's pop-up menu
Voice	Specifies the text that will be passed to the voice recognition engine for processing

The methods of the Commands collection are listed in Table 14.10. The Add method adds a new Command object to the Commands collection. The Insert method is also used to add new Command objects to the Commands collection; however, with the Insert method, you also can specify the relative location where the new object will be placed. This method is useful because it affects the order of the items in the pop-up menu and the Commands window.

TABLE 14.10: Commands Collection Methods

Method	Description
Add	Adds a new command to the collection
Command	Returns the specified Command object
Insert	Adds a new command to the collection at the specified location
Remove	Removes the specified command from the collection
RemoveAll	Removes all of the commands in the collection

The name of the game: The first parameter of the Add and the Insert methods is Name. This value is used to retrieve a specific Command object using either Item or Command, but it is not stored in the Command object. You will not be able to retrieve this value after you use it.

The Remove and RemoveAll methods are used to remove the specified member or all the members from the collection, respectively. The Command method is similar to the Item property; it returns the Command object with the specified name.

Assigning Command Object Properties

Table 14.11 lists the properties available for the Command object. The speech recognition engine attempts to find a match between the words you spoke and the words in the Voice property. The ConfidenceText property will be displayed in the Listen Tip window if the confidence level of the match is less than the value in the Confidence property. Confidence levels must be in the range of −100 to +100.

T A B L E 14.11:   Command Object Properties

Property	Description
Caption	Displays the specified text in the Commands window and the pop-up menu
Confidence	Contains the confidence level for this command
ConfidenceText	Contains the text displayed when the confidence level of the input is less than Confidence
Enabled	When set to True, the command is enabled in the pop-up menu
Visible	When set to True, means that the command's caption will appear in the character's pop-up window
Voice	Contains the text that will be matched by the speech recognition engine

The Caption property contains the text that will be displayed on the pop-up menu and the Command window if the Visible property is True. If the Enabled property is False, the Caption will be grayed out; otherwise, the Caption will be displayed normally.

Working with Balloons

The `Balloon` object contains a series of properties that control how the balloon will be displayed on the screen. Table 14.12 lists these properties. All but a few of these properties should be very familiar to you. The `BorderColor` property allows you to change the color of the border. The `FontCharSet` allows you to specify which character set should be used to display the text inside the balloon.

TABLE 14.12:   Balloon Object Properties

Property	Description
BackColor	Specifies the background color of the balloon
BorderColor	Specifies the color of the balloon's border
CharsPerLine	Specifies the average number of characters that can be displayed in a single line of the balloon
Enabled	When set to **True,** means that the balloon will be enabled
FontBold	When set to **True,** means that the balloon's text will be displayed in bold
FontCharSet	Specifies the type of character set used by the font
FontItalic	When set to **True,** means that the balloon's text will be displayed in italics
FontName	Specifies the name of the font used to display the characters
FontSize	Specifies the size of the characters to be displayed
FontStrikethru	When set to **True,** means that a single line will be drawn through the center of the characters displayed in the balloon
FontUnderline	When set to **True,** means that the characters displayed in the balloon will be underlined
ForeColor	Specifies the color of the characters
NumberOfLines	Specifies the number of lines of text that the balloon will hold
Visible	When set to **True,** means that the balloon will be displayed

Probably the most important properties of the `Balloon` object are `NumberOfLines` and `CharsPerLine`. The `NumberOfLines` property is fairly straightforward—it simply specifies the number of lines that will be displayed inside the balloon. The

CharsPerLine property specifies the number of average characters you will be able to display in a single line. It doesn't mean that you will always be able to display that many characters in a line, unless you are using a nonproportional font such as Courier.

TIP   **It's hard to scroll when there are no scroll bars:** Since the balloon doesn't come equipped with scroll bars, you need to plan the size of the balloon carefully. Using too small a balloon or too much text will make the text difficult to read, and using too large a balloon will waste screen space. Also, you should remember that the words appear as they are spoken. Since most people (and computers) speak slower than they read, you might not need as much space as you think you do.

Working with Requests

The Request object is the only object that is not directly part of the MSAgent control. This object is returned by many methods that operate asynchronously, such as Character.Play and Character.Speak. Since these methods will operate while your application continues to run, you can periodically check to see the progress of the method. You can also pass this object to the Character.Wait method to ensure that your requested action has finished before continuing onto the next one. Table 14.13 lists the properties available for the Request object.

TABLE 14.13: Request Object Properties

Property	Description
Description	Contains a text description of the error
Number	Contains an error code; if this value is 0, no error occurred
Status	Contains the status of the request

The Number property will contain 0 if the request was completed successfully; otherwise, it will contain an error number. The Description property will contain a text message that describes the error. The Status property describes the request's current state. Table 14.14 lists the status codes and their meanings.

TABLE 14.14: Request Object Status Codes

Status	Description
0	The request was successful.
1	The request failed.
2	The request is pending.
3	The request has been interrupted.
4	The request is in progress.

Two events are also available when using the `Request` object: `RequestStart` and `RequestComplete`. These events will be fired if you create a global `Request` object to track the status of a specific method. These events will be triggered only in the client object making the request.

WARNING **Upgrade now:** In VBScript 1.0, the `RequestStart` and `RequestComplete` events will be triggered even if you don't issue the request using a global reference object. This problem was fixed in VBScript 2.0 (which is included with Visual Studio 98).

Using Other Agent Objects

Microsoft Agent provides a few other objects. The `SpeechInput` object contains information about the speech engine that is extracted from the Speech Input tab of the Microsoft Agent Properties dialog box (see Figure 14.5). The `AudioOutput` object contains some of the items from the Output tab (see Figure 14.4). The properties in both objects are read-only except for the `SpeechInput.Enabled` property, which you can set programmatically.

The `CommandsWindow` object and the `PropertySheet` object contain information about the placement of those windows on the screen.

Building a Simple MSAgent Program

The first computer program I ever wrote was the standard Hello World program. It's such a classic program that sometimes I just can't resist using it again. However, I've enhanced the program just a bit since that very first one. I now call it the Hello Jill program, named after my wife, Jill, who means the world to me.

I rewrote the program using the MSAgent control. It was very interesting to see the Genie pop up and say, "Hello Jill!"

I also was curious about the rest of the Agents. With a few quick patches, I had the program I'm going to talk about here.

Figure 14.13 shows the Hello Jill window. To run it, simply select the character you wish to use, type what you would like the character to say into the text box, click the Speak button, and then sit back and wait for your speech.

FIGURE 14.13:

Running the Hello Jill program

Making Global Declarations for Hello Jill

Unlike most of the programs I've discussed in this book, I'm going to include the entire Hello Jill program in the text. (Don't worry, I counted only 22 lines of code, including the blank lines.) Listing 14.1 shows the global declarations.

Listing 14.1: **Global Declarations for Hello Jill**

```
Option Explicit

Const AgentPath = "c:\Program Files\Microsoft Agent\Characters\"
```

I start this program by specifying Option Explicit. If you don't understand why I did this, go back and reread Chapter 2. I specify a constant I call AgentPath, which holds the path name where I store the characters. For some reason, Microsoft chose not to store this information in the Registry where all programs could find it. (Maybe this will be fixed in the next release.)

Initializing the MSAgent Control

Initializing the MSAgent control is fairly straightforward, as shown in Listing 14.2. All I need to do is use the Characters.Load method to load the Agent information into the Characters collection. This will let me choose any of these characters later in the program.

Listing 14.2: **Form_Load Event in Hello Jill**

```
Private Sub Form_Load()

Agent1.Characters.Load "Genie", AgentPath & "Genie.acs"
Agent1.Characters.Load "Merlin", AgentPath & "MerlinSfx.acs"
Agent1.Characters.Load "Robby", AgentPath & "Robby.acs"

Combo1.AddItem "Genie"
Combo1.AddItem "Merlin"
Combo1.AddItem "Robby"
Combo1.Text = "Genie"

End Sub
```

To load a character, I need to specify the name of the Agent and the name of file where the Agent's information is saved. Note that I used `MerlinSfx` rather than `Merlin` because I'm curious about the sound effects. I then initialized the `Combo1` control with a list of the Agents available in the program so I can let the users choose which Agent they would like to see and hear.

Speaking the Message

Now that I have my collection of Agent characters and a combo box filled with Agent names, I let the user choose any one of these and then click the command button. This triggers the `Click` event you see in Listing 14.3.

Listing 14.3:   **Command1_Click Event in Hello Jill**

```
Private Sub Command1_Click()

Agent1.Characters.Character(Combo1.Text).Show
Agent1.Characters.Character(Combo1.Text).Speak Text1.Text
Agent1.Characters.Character(Combo1.Text).Hide

End Sub
```

I start the routine by showing the character specified by the user. Then I use the Speak method to have the character speak the words in the text box. Finally, I Hide the character until the next time I want to use him.

Using the Speech Recognition Engine

The next program I developed to test the MSAgent control is called (unimaginatively) the Agent Demo Program. It demonstrates how to play animations and use the speech recognition engine. It is designed to listen for spoken commands and execute them. It will also accept commands selected from the pop-up menu. Here's an example of what you might get if your command was Say Hello Merlin:

Making Global Declarations for Agent Demo

Listing 14.4 contains the global declarations I need in this program. The Option Explicit clause should be familiar by now, and the AgentPath was used in the Hello Jill program. I declare object variables for my Agent character and a Request object that I use to track the execution of an animation.

Listing 14.4:	Global Declarations for Agent Demo

```
Option Explicit

Const AgentPath = "c:\Program Files\Microsoft Agent\Characters\"

Dim MyAgent As IAgentCtlCharacter
Dim MyRequest As IagentCtlRequest
```

Initializing the Commands Collection

In order to accept input from the microphone, I must define a set of commands that the speech recognition engine can use when analyzing speech. But before I do that, I need to Load an Agent character. I create an object reference to the character so I only need to type MyAgent rather than Agent1.Characters("Merlin"). Listing 14.5 shows the routine for initializing the Commands collection.

Listing 14.5: **Form_Load Event in Agent Demo**

```
Private Sub Form_Load()

Agent1.Characters.Load "Merlin", AgentPath & "MerlinSfx.acs"
Set MyAgent = Agent1.Characters("Merlin")
MyAgent.Show

MyAgent.Commands.Caption = "MyAgent Commands"
MyAgent.Commands.Visible = True
MyAgent.Commands.Voice = "MyAgent Commands"
MyAgent.Commands.Add "Bye bye", "Bye bye", "... bye bye ...", True, True
MyAgent.Commands.Add "Down", "Down", "... down ...", True, True
MyAgent.Commands.Add "Happy", "Happy", "... happy ...", True, True
MyAgent.Commands.Add "Hello", "Hello", "Hello Merlin", True, True
MyAgent.Commands.Add "Left", "Left", "... left ...", True, True
MyAgent.Commands.Add "Move", "Move", "... move ...", True, True
MyAgent.Commands.Add "Right", "Right", "... right ...", True, True
MyAgent.Commands.Add "Sad", "Sad", "... sad ...", True, True
MyAgent.Commands.Add "Up", "Up", "... up ...", True, True

End Sub
```

Unlike most other ActiveX controls, the MSAgent control doesn't allow you to define many properties at design time. You are forced to do this at runtime. So after I've created and shown the Agent, I set Commands.Caption and Commands.Voice to "MyAgent Commands", and then I set the Commands.Visible property to True. This information will be displayed in the Commands window of the Agent server.

Then I initialize each command that the speech recognition engine will support. The parameters, in order, are as follows:

- The Name property must be a unique key value to retrieve a member from the collection.

- The Caption property will be displayed in pop-up menus and the Agent server's Command window.

- The Voice property contains the text that the speech recognition engine should try to match.

- The Enabled and Visible properties control how the Caption is displayed in the pop-up menu and the Command window.

It's all in a name: Since you can't retrieve the Name property from the Command object, I usually assign the same value to the Name and Caption properties. That way, I know what the missing Name property should be.

In the code in Listing 14.5, notice that rather than focusing on complex phrases that the speech recognition engine should try to match, I focus on a keyword that best describes the command. Then I use an ellipsis before and after the word that indicates that zero or more other words (also known as garbage words) may proceed or follow the keyword, as in this line:

```
MyAgent.Commands.Add "Move", "Move", "... move ...", True, True
```

I find this often makes the recognition process more reliable. However, you should use this feature carefully, because it may also cause some problems with false matches. In this example, if the user said "move up," both "move" and "up" would be potential matches.

Processing Spoken Commands

The real guts of this program are contained in the Command event, as shown in Listing 14.6. The UserInput object contains the name of the command that the speech recognition engine determines is the best match, so in this routine, I process each of the individual commands.

Listing 14.6:   **Agent1_Command Event in Agent Demo**

```
Private Sub Agent1_Command(ByVal UserInput As Object)

Select Case LCase(UserInput.Name)

Case "bye bye"
   MyAgent.Speak "Bye bye"
   MyAgent.Play "Wave"
   Set MyRequest = MyAgent.Hide

Case "down"
   MyAgent.GestureAt MyAgent.Left, Screen.Height / Screen.TwipsPerPixelY
```

```
       MyAgent.Speak "All fall down."

   Case "happy"
      MyAgent.Play "Pleased"
      MyAgent.Speak "I'm happy."

   Case "hello"
      MyAgent.Speak "Hello Merlin."
      MyAgent.Play "DoMagic1"
      MyAgent.Speak "Abracadabra, hocus pocus."
      MyAgent.Play "DoMagic2"
      MyAgent.Speak "Visual Basic now can" & \Map=""spoke ith""=""spoketh""\."

   Case "left"
      MyAgent.GestureAt 0, MyAgent.Height
      MyAgent.Speak "Left is that away."

   Case "move"
      MyAgent.MoveTo Screen.Width / Screen.TwipsPerPixelX * Rnd, _
                     Screen.Height / Screen.TwipsPerPixelY * Rnd
      MyAgent.Speak "I like flying."

   Case "right"
      MyAgent.GestureAt Screen.Width / Screen.TwipsPerPixelX, MyAgent.Height
      MyAgent.Speak "Keep to the right."

   Case "sad"
      MyAgent.Play "Sad"
      MyAgent.Speak "I'm sad."

   Case "up"
      MyAgent.GestureAt MyAgent.Left, 0
      MyAgent.Speak "The sky is falling."

   Case Else
      MyAgent.Speak "I didn't understand you."
      MyAgent.Play "Confused"

End Select

End Sub
```

The processing for the `"happy"` command is typical of most of the commands I handle in this routine. The `"happy"` command tells the Agent server to play the `"Pleased"` animation and then speak the words "I'm happy."

My favorite is the `"hello"` command. In this command, Merlin speaks three different times with an animation played in between each bit of speech. This activity takes a fair amount of time and can be entertaining. Note that in the second speech, the text includes a speech output tag. The `\Map=` tag allows the character to speak one thing and show something else in the character's balloon.

The `"move"` command simply invokes the animation that moves the character from one place on the screen to another random location. Note that I had to convert the twips value to pixels for this method to work properly.

The `"up"` command (and the `"down"`, `"left"`, and `"right"` commands for that matter) directs the character to point at a location on the screen and speak a phrase.

If I can't find a match of any of these commands, I will play the `"Confused"` animation and let the user know that the character didn't understand what was said.

TIP   **Play Misty for me:** There are a large number of animations available for each character (for example, the Merlin character includes more than 100 different animations). See the documentation included with the Microsoft Agent software for more details about the animations available for each character.

Waiting for a Request to Complete

When I originally wrote the code to handle the `"bye bye"` command, I wanted Merlin to say "bye bye," wave, then disappear before the program stopped. After I performed the `Hide` method, I inserted an `Unload Me` statement. Doing this caused the program to stop before Merlin had a chance to even begin speaking.

What was happening was that when the program finished, it dropped the connection to the Agent server, which immediately canceled all of the queued requests. So to handle this situation, I added the `MyRequest` object to the global declarations (see Listing 14.4, earlier in the chapter) and used it with the `Hide` request. I also needed to code the `RequestComplete` event, as shown in Listing 14.7. Then when the `Hide` method is finished, the `RequestComplete` event is fired, and the program ends properly.

Listing 14.7:   **Agent1_RequestComplete Event in Agent Demo**

```
Private Sub Agent1_RequestComplete(ByVal Request As Object)

Unload Me

End Sub
```

Stopping the Character

What do you do if you're playing a long animation and don't want to wait for it to finish? How about if you queue up a couple of individual animations, plus some text for the character to speak (as I did when I processed the `"hello"` command in Listing 14.6), and want to stop all of them? Using the `StopAll` method will cancel the current animation, plus all of the other animations that are in the queue. I used this method with the `Click` event of the Cancel button, as you can see in Listing 14.8.

Listing 14.8:   **Command1_Click Event in Agent Demo**

```
Private Sub Command1_Click()

MyAgent.StopAll

End Sub
```

Developing an Animated Game

When I started working with Microsoft Agent, my kids loved watching the little blue guy named Genie, who appears in a puff of smoke and talks to them. When they could talk back to that little blue guy and see him understand what they were saying, they went absolutely nuts! So one night after they went to bed, I started writing what would eventually become the I'm Thinking of a Color program.

NOTE

I'm thinking of a color? In case you don't know, playing I'm thinking of a color is very similar to playing I'm thinking of a number. The host secretly picks a color, and then the players take turns trying to guess the color. The first person to correctly guess the color is the winner.

The first generation of this program supported only the host (which was the computer) and one player (a human). While that was interesting, I thought about the three different Agent characters from Microsoft and decided to try to use all of them. There are a lot of applications that can benefit from using one Agent, but here's one that can use three. You can see the three Agents in the program's window, as shown in Figure 14.14.

FIGURE 14.14:

The I'm Thinking of a Color program

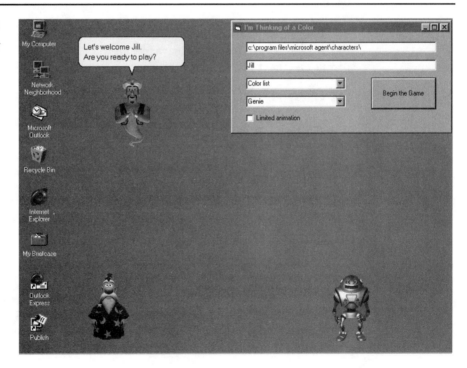

Making Global Declarations for I'm Thinking of a Color

This program begins by declaring variables for the host (TheHost) and the players (Player). I also create a global Request object for use in synchronizing the various characters. TheColor holds the color chosen by the host. AColor is used to hold the guess from either one of the computer players or the human player. AllColors holds a memory of the colors guessed during the game. The YesFlag is True when the user responds Yes to a question. Listing 14.9 shows the global declarations.

Listing 14.9:   **Global Declarations for I'm Thinking of a Color**

```
Option Explicit

Dim TheHost As IAgentCtlCharacter
Dim Player(2) As IAgentCtlCharacter
Dim RequestWait As IAgentCtlRequest

Dim PlayerInitialized As Boolean

Dim AColor As Integer
Dim TheColor As Integer
Dim AllColors(99) As Integer
Dim YesFlag As Boolean
```

Getting Started

This program uses a combo box to hold the list of available colors. It allows the users to view the colors to see exactly which ones were included in the program, but in this version of the program, they can't change the colors. The other combo box is used to hold a list of the Agents. Users can select anyone to be the host, and the remaining characters will become the players. Listing 14.10 shows how this is set up.

Listing 14.10:   Form_Load Event in I'm Thinking of a Color

```
Private Sub Form_Load()

Combo1.AddItem "black"
Combo1.AddItem "blue"
Combo1.AddItem "brown"
Combo1.AddItem "green"
Combo1.AddItem "orange"
Combo1.AddItem "pink"
Combo1.AddItem "purple"
Combo1.AddItem "red"
Combo1.AddItem "silver"
Combo1.AddItem "tan"
Combo1.AddItem "violet"
Combo1.AddItem "white"
Combo1.AddItem "yellow"

Combo1.Text = "Color list"

Combo2.AddItem "Genie"
Combo2.AddItem "Merlin"
Combo2.AddItem "Robby"

Combo2.Text = "Genie"

PlayerInitialized = False

End Sub
```

Running the Game

When the user clicks the command button to start the game, the `Command1_Click` event will be triggered, as shown in Listing 14.11.

Listing 14.11: **Command1_Click Event in I'm Thinking of a Color**

```
Private Sub Command1_Click()

Dim i As Integer

Randomize

If Not PlayerInitialized Then
    PlayerInit
End If

If Check1.Value = 0 Then
    PlayerWelcome
Else
    PlayerWelcomeQuick
End If

For i = 1 To 3
    PlayGame (i)
Next i

If Check1.Value = 0 Then
    PlayerByeBye
Else
    PlayerByeByeQuick
End If

End Sub
```

This routine is in overall control of the game. It begins by initializing the Agent characters if necessary. Then it plays either the long welcome message or the short message, depending on the state of the Check1 check box. This feature helps me test the game while preserving all of the fun interactions.

After the welcome message is displayed, three individual games are played (though in hindsight, rounds would have been a better term). Then I play the appropriate "bye bye" message when the games are finished. To play again, the user clicks the command button.

Initializing the Characters

Initializing the characters is relatively straightforward. The only tricky part is that I save two of the characters in the character object array, Player. Listing 14.12 shows the routine.

Listing 14.12:   PlayerInit Routine in I'm Thinking of a Color

```
Private Sub PlayerInit()

Dim p As Integer

Agent1.Characters.Load Combo2.Text, Text1.Text & Combo2.Text & ".acs"
Set TheHost = Agent1.Characters(Combo2.Text)

p = 1
If Combo2.Text <> "Genie" Then
   Agent1.Characters.Load "Genie", Text1.Text & "genie.acs"
   Set Player(p) = Agent1.Characters("Genie")
   p = p + 1
End If

If Combo2.Text <> "Merlin" Then
   Agent1.Characters.Load "Merlin", Text1.Text & "merlin.acs"
   Set Player(p) = Agent1.Characters("Merlin")
   p = p + 1
End If

If Combo2.Text <> "Robby" Then
   Agent1.Characters.Load "robby", Text1.Text & "robby.acs"
   Set Player(p) = Agent1.Characters("Robby")
End If

AddCommands

PlayerInitialized = True

End Sub
```

Note that only Player(1) and Player(2) are valid. Player(0) is a placeholder for the human player. This way, if I find another character I wish to include, I can add another player without disturbing the logic.

Adding the Commands

The AddCommands routine, shown in Listing 14.13, uses code similar to the code I used in the Agent Demo program to initialize the Commands collection (shown earlier, in Listing 14.5).

Listing 14.13: **AddCommands Routine in I'm Thinking of a Color**

```
Sub AddCommands()

Dim i As Integer
Dim l As String

TheHost.Commands.Caption = "I'm Thinking of a Color"
TheHost.Commands.Voice = "I'm Thinking of a Color"
TheHost.Commands.Visible = True
TheHost.Commands.Add "cheat", "cheat", "what is the color", True, True
TheHost.Commands.Add "yes", "yes", "... yes ...", True, True
TheHost.Commands.Add "stop", "stop", "stop", True, True
TheHost.Commands.Add Text2.Text, Text2.Text, Text2.Text, True, True

For i = 0 To Combo1.ListCount - 1
    l = Combo1.List(i)
    TheHost.Commands.Add l, l, "... " & l & " ...", True, True
Next i

End Sub
```

Note that all of these commands belong to TheHost character. Since the user only interacts with the host and none of the other players, the other players don't need any commands defined.

I added a cheat command, "what is the color", to help me debug the program, and a stop command that allows me to quickly exit the program. Then I add all of the colors that are contained in the combo box.

Receiving Commands

As in the Agent Demo program, the Command event is very important in the I'm Thinking of a Color program. All input from the user is received and processed in this routine, as shown in Listing 14.14.

Listing 14.14:   Agent1_Command Event in I'm Thinking of a Color

```
Private Sub Agent1_Command(ByVal UserInput As Object)

Dim i As Integer

If UserInput.Name = "yes" Then
   YesFlag = True

ElseIf UserInput.Name = "stop" Then
   YesFlag = True
   TheHost.StopAll
   Player(1).StopAll
   Player(2).StopAll
   Unload Me

ElseIf UserInput.Name = "cheat" Then
   TheHost.Speak "The color is " & Combo1.List(TheColor) & "."

ElseIf UserInput.Name = Text2.Text Then
   TheHost.Speak "Hi " & UserInput.Name & "."

ElseIf UserInput.Name = "" Then
   TheHost.Play "Confused"
   TheHost.Speak "I'm not sure what you said, " & Text2.Text & _
      ". Please try again."

Else
   AColor = 0
   Do While UserInput.Name <> Combo1.List(AColor)
      AColor = AColor + 1
   Loop

End If

End Sub
```

If the user's command is easy to process, like the `"stop"` command, I process it immediately. Otherwise, I set a global variable indicating that the input was received. Then I can look for this value elsewhere in the program.

If I receive a `"stop"` command, I set the YesFlag to True and then issue a StopAll command for each of the characters. This ensures that all of the queued requests are purged from the Agent server. Then I can stop the program using an Unload Me statement.

Passing along a color is just a matter of scanning through the list of colors in the combo box for the same value, and then setting the global variable AColor with the relative position in the list. When I'm ready to process this input, I just look for the value in the global variable.

Beginning the Game

The PlayerWelcome routine, shown in Listing 14.15, is typical of what is required when you have interaction among multiple characters. The routine begins by introducing the game. I use the RequestWait variable to hold the result from the Speak method the host uses to introduce the first computer player. Then I play the `"Pleased"` action for the host.

Listing 14.15:   PlayerWelcome Routine in I'm Thinking of a Color

```
Private Sub PlayerWelcome()

TheHost.Show
TheHost.MoveTo 325, 50, 1500
TheHost.Speak "Welcome to the I'm thinking of a color game."
TheHost.Speak "I think of a color and three contestants try to guess it."
TheHost.Speak "Player number one is a computer annimation from Microsoft."
Set RequestWait = TheHost.Speak("Let's welcome " & Player(1).Name & ".")
TheHost.Play "Pleased"

Player(1).Wait RequestWait
Player(1).MoveTo 100, 100, 0
Player(1).Show
TheHost.GestureAt 100, 100
Player(1).MoveTo 100, 450, 1500
Player(1).Play "Greet"
TheHost.Play "Pleased"
```

```
TheHost.Play "PleasedReturn"
Set RequestWait = Player(1).Speak("Hello " & TheHost.Name & ".")
Player(1).Play "GreetReturn"

TheHost.Wait RequestWait
TheHost.Speak "Player number two is also a computer annimation from " & _
    "Microsoft."
Set RequestWait = TheHost.Speak("Let's give a big hand for " & _
    Player(1).Name & ".")
TheHost.Play "Pleased"

Player(2).Wait RequestWait
Player(2).MoveTo 100, 100, 0
Player(2).Show
TheHost.GestureAt 100, 100
Player(2).MoveTo 550, 450, 1500
Player(2).Play "Greet"
TheHost.Play "Pleased"
TheHost.Play "PleasedReturn"
Set RequestWait = Player(1).Speak("Hi " & TheHost.Name & ".")
Player(2).Play "GreetReturn"

TheHost.Wait RequestWait
TheHost.Speak "Player number three is a human from outside this computer."
TheHost.Speak "Let's welcome " & Text2.Text & "."
TheHost.Play "Pleased"

Set RequestWait = TheHost.Speak("Are you ready to play?")

Player(1).Wait RequestWait
Player(1).Play "Pleased"
Set RequestWait = Player(1).Speak("Yes. Let's go!")

Player(2).Wait RequestWait
Player(2).Play "Pleased"
Set RequestWait = Player(2).Speak("I'm ready!")

Player(1).Play "PleasedReturn"
Player(2).Play "PleasedReturn"

YesFlag = False
Do While Not YesFlag
```

```
    DoEvents
Loop

TheHost.Wait RequestWait

End Sub
```

The first thing I do for player one is make that player wait until the host has finished his introduction. I do this by using the `Wait` method with the `RequestWait` object. Then I perform a series of animations and speeches, ending in player one setting the `RequestWait` object. The host then uses the `Wait` method with the `RequestWait` object.

When studying the code, remember that most of the character's methods merely place a request in the Agent server's queue for that character. The requests in the queue will be executed one at a time until the queue is empty. Without the first `Wait` by player one, that player's first action will be placed in the queue and executed immediately. Thus, while the host was still introducing the game, player one would arrive on the screen and start moving around.

With the `Wait` method, player one's `MoveTo` and `Show` methods will not begin until the host has finished introducing player one. Likewise, the host will wait until player one has finished saying hello before introducing player two.

Interacting with the human is a little more difficult since there isn't a `Wait` method available. Also, all of the user commands are received in the `Command` event, not through a regular function like `InputBox`. This means that processing user input is a bit more complicated.

However, there's always the `DoEvents` routine. Remember that in the `Command` event, I set the variable `YesFlag` to `True` whenever the user said yes. I'm going to sit in a tight spin loop while the `YesFlag` is `False`. I stick in a call to `DoEvents` inside the loop, so that the system is free to receive and process the user command.

TIP   **Waiting with spin loops:** There are many times when you need to wait for a different process to complete before continuing with the current process. One way of waiting is to perform a loop on a global variable that another part of the program will change. This loop is called a *spin loop*. However, since Windows 95 is not a true multitasking system, this loop will lock up your system. To correct this limitation, just put a call to `DoEvents` inside the loop. This will return control back to Windows, so it can continue processing other work, including the part you're waiting on.

Final Thoughts

The Microsoft Agent software offers a unique way for you to differentiate your application from the competition. While adding the code to display an Agent and letting him speak isn't difficult, planning how to effectively use the Agent is. Agents shouldn't detract from the main purpose of your application; they should somehow augment what the application is trying to do. For example, Agents would be useful as helpers in showing people how to accomplish something. You could have the Agent move to various locations, push buttons, or make text appear. You could also use the Agent characters to help challenged users by reading the contents of various fields and captions and accepting spoken commands.

You should consider this chapter as only an introduction to the Microsoft Agent software. There's a lot more that you can do with this technology. For instance, it is very easy to incorporate Agents into VBScript code, so web developers can easily add Agents to their web pages. In fact, if you are using an HTML-capable e-mail program such as Microsoft Outlook or Outlook Express, you can even add Agents to your e-mail messages so that they could read the message to the recipient.

With the proper programming, one Agent could be shared among several applications. After all, people generally have only one application active at a time. You may have noticed that Microsoft Office 97, Excel, Word, and Access all share the same little animated paper clip. This saves memory since each animation takes between 2.5MB and 3.5MB of disk space. It also saves other system resources.

The I'm Thinking of a Color game I presented here could use a little work. I didn't go through the entire program in this chapter, but I did cover how everything works. The rest of the program is similar to the `PlayerWelcome` routine, where I control how the players interact with each other and the host. The hardest part was trying to coordinate the interaction between the human and the various Agent characters, and I showed you how to do that. You can review the complete program on the CD-ROM.

You could improve the game by incorporating the ability to add and delete colors and putting in an ImageCombo control to display a graphic of the color next to the word. It would also be nice to keep score. I had originally envisioned a nice scoreboard similar to the classic baseball scoreboard with the player names, the score, and maybe a series of scores for each individual game with the number of guesses that it took to get the answer. You might even be able to configure the number of rounds that would make up a single game.

Another improvement would be to add more animations and different actions for each of the characters, especially those that aren't input-active at the moment. This might be something like blinking eyes or looking toward the character who is speaking. Also, you could add some background music similar to what Jeopardy uses. And thinking of backgrounds, since the characters float on top of whatever else is on the screen, it might be nice to put up some sort of background so the user doesn't see just the normal Desktop.

CHAPTER

FIFTEEN

15

Communicating with Other Programs

■ The Shell function and SendKeys and AppActivate methods for running other programs

■ The CreateObject and GetObject functions for references to other program's objects

■ OLE automation for accessing Visual Basic class objects

■ A custom ActiveX EXE program

In today's programming environment, it's easy to write programs that talk to each other. You may want to communicate with standard applications, such as Microsoft Word or Excel, or you may want to communicate with other programs you wrote.

Consider the WinZip program as an example of a program that communicates with other programs. When you open a .ZIP file, you see the list of files inside. Double-clicking on one of these files will extract it to a temporary location and then run the appropriate program to read the file. In the case of Word documents, WinZip doesn't just start a new copy of the Word to process the file but first tries to use an existing Word session; if it can't, then it starts a new session.

TIP

Get WinZip: If you have to deal with .ZIP files or other compressed files, you should have the WinZip utility program. WinZip is fast, works well, and is very stable. It's probably the best piece of shareware money can buy.

Moving business rules that span many programs to a common location is fast becoming a standard industry practice. Visual Basic allows you to do this by using Class objects, similar to how Excel and Word allow you to access their object structure. In fact, you can even store your Class objects on a different machine from the one running your program and allow multiple machines (including web servers) to access your Class objects.

In this chapter, I'm going to cover two main approaches to communicating with other programs. The first approach uses the SendKeys statement to send keystrokes to another program, which thinks your program is really a user sitting behind a keyboard and reacts accordingly. The second approach is to use OLE automation to interact with other programs like Microsoft Excel and Word, as well as with your own ActiveX EXE programs.

Running Another Program

The traditional way to run another program from your Visual Basic program is to use the Shell function. After the program is started, you can give it the focus by using the AppActivate statement. Then you can use the SendKeys statement to send keystrokes to the program.

TIP   **Do it with DOS:** Any program you can run from a DOS prompt can be run in the Shell function. DOS commands included in command.com can't be executed using the Shell function. However, you can execute command.com, as well as any batch file that includes any of the command.com commands.

Starting a Program with the Shell Function

The Shell function takes two parameters:

- The fully qualified path name of the program you wish to run

- The WindowStyle parameter, which specifies how the program will initially be started (see Table 15.1)

The Shell function returns a Double value containing the new program's task ID. This value can be used with the AppActivate statement, which is discussed in the next section.

TABLE 15.1:   WindowStyle Values for Programs Started with the Shell Function

WindowStyle Constant	Value	Description
vbHide	0	The program's window is initially hidden and given the focus.
vbNormalFocus	1	The program's window starts normally and is given the focus.
vbMinimizedFocus	2	The program's window starts minimized and is given the focus (default).
vbMaximizedFocus	3	The program's window starts maximized and is given the focus.
vbNormalNoFocus	4	The program's window starts normally and is not given the focus.
vbMinimizedNoFocus	6	The program's window starts minimized and is not given the focus.

Transferring Focus with the AppActivate Statement

By using the task ID value returned by the Shell function, you can transfer the focus to that application any time you want. You can have your Visual Basic application wait until it has the focus before it transfers the focus to the specified program, or your application can transfer the focus immediately.

You can also switch the focus to any other application by specifying the title of the application. This value is the same value as the text found in the title bar of the main window. If the value you specified doesn't match any of the currently running applications, then the application whose title matches the most leading characters will be activated. For example, if you specify Charter but that application isn't running, the application with Chamber in the title bar might receive the focus.

> **NOTE**
>
> **What's in a name?** The value in the title bar is not the same as the filename of the program. In Visual Basic, you can set this value dynamically by using the startup form's Caption property.

Sending Keystrokes with the SendKeys Statement

The SendKeys statement takes advantage of the fact that each keystroke is sent to a Windows program as a separate message. These messages result in calls to the Visual Basic KeyDown, KeyPress, and KeyUp events; other languages handle the messages according to their own rules. Since DOS programs don't process keystrokes this way, the SendKeys statement can communicate only with Windows applications.

Because you can't represent some keys in a single character (for example, the function keys require two to three characters—*F1* through *F12*), SendKeys allows you to form these characters using multi-character sequences. Table 15.2 shows the characters that can be used in SendKeys statements.

TABLE 15.2: Characters Used in SendKeys Statements

Key	Code
%	{%}
^	{^}

Continued on next page

TABLE 15.2 (CONTINUED):   Characters Used in SendKeys Statements

Key	Code
+	{+}
~	{~}
(	{(}
)	{)}
[	{[}
]	{]}
{	{{}
}	{}}
Backspace	{BACKSPACE} or {BKSP} or {BS}
Break	{BREAK}
CapsLock	{CAPSLOCK}
Delete (Del)	{DELETE} or {DEL}
Down arrow	{DOWN}
End	{END}
Enter	{ENTER} or ~
Esc	{ESC}
F1	{F1}
F2	{F2}
F3	{F3}
F4	{F4}
F5	{F5}
F6	{F6}
F7	{F7}
F8	{F8}
F9	{F9}
F10	{F10}
F11	{F11}

Continued on next page

TABLE 15.2 (CONTINUED):   Characters Used in SendKeys Statements

Key	Code
F12	{F12}
Help	{HELP}
Home	{HOME}
Insert (Ins)	{INSERT} or {INS}
Left arrow	{LEFT}
NumLock	{NUMLOCK}
PageDown	{PGDN}
PageUp	{PGUP}
Right arrow	{RIGHT}
ScrollLock	{SCROLLLOCK}
Tab	{TAB}
Up arrow	{UP}

The plus (+), caret (^), and percent (%) keys represent the Shift, Ctrl, and Alt keys, respectively, and are used to modify the next character in the sequence. For example, Alt-F is represented by the string %F. You can combine the characters used for Alt, Ctrl, and Shift by using them together. For example, Ctrl-Shift-Z is represented by the string ^+Z.

Parentheses represent multiple keys being pressed at the same time. For example, pressing the *a* and *b* keys at the same time is represented by the string (ab).

Braces contain special characters that can't be specified by a single character. For example, the F1 key is represented by {F1}. You can also specify the number of times a character is repeated inside the braces—the string {z 28} will send the *z* character 28 times. The brackets ([and]) don't have any particular meaning to SendKeys, but they must be enclosed in braces anyway.

WARNING   **Windows accepts, but DOS rejects:** You can only use the **SendKeys** statement with Windows programs. DOS-based programs can't receive these keystrokes.

Programming with Shell, AppActivate, and SendKeys

To demonstrate how to use Shell, AppActivate, and SendKeys, I wrote the Notepad Writer program, shown in Figure 15.1. This program starts Notepad (or any program you specify in the Program textbox) when you click the Start button. Tabbing to the Character Input textbox and typing a character will send it to Notepad and then return for another character. In the Block Input textbox, you can type a long string of characters and enter them in a single batch. This is necessary if you want to enter a multi-character string, such as {f1} or %f.

FIGURE 15.1:

The Notepad Writer program

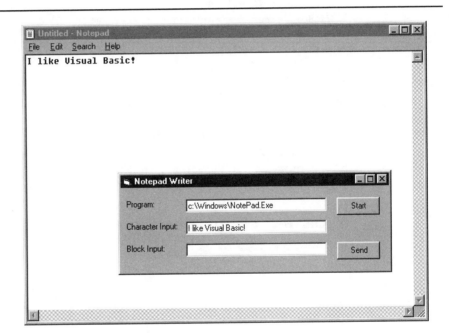

Starting the Program

Clicking the Start button (Command2) triggers the event shown in Listing 15.1, which starts the program specified in the Text1 textbox.

Listing 15.1:   **Command2_Click Event in Notepad Writer**

```
Private Sub Command2_Click()

On Error Resume Next

Err.Clear
np = Shell(Text1.Text, vbNormalNoFocus)

If Err.Number <> 0 Then
    MsgBox "Error " & FormatNumber(Err.Number, 0) & ": " & Err.Description
    np = 0
End If

End Sub
```

The routine begins by clearing the Err object. Then I use the Shell function to start the program, while keeping the focus. The function will return the task ID of the new program into the variable np. Then I check the Err object for errors. If I find an error, I display error information in a MsgBox and set np to 0.

Processing a Single Character

When a user types a character in the Text2 textbox, the KeyPress event is triggered, as shown in Listing 15.2.

Listing 15.2:   **Text2_KeyPress Event in Notepad Writer**

```
Private Sub Text2_KeyPress(KeyAscii As Integer)

If np <> 0 Then
    AppActivate np
    SendKeys Chr(KeyAscii), True
    Text2.SetFocus
End If

End Sub
```

I check to see if I have a running program to talk to by looking at the variable np. If it contains a nonzero value, I switch the focus to the program by using the

AppActivate statement and the task ID value in np. Then I convert the KeyAscii value to a character and send it to the program using the SendKeys statement.

The SendKeys statement will wait for the character to be processed by the other program before returning control back to this program. I then use the Text2 SetFocus method to reset the focus back to the Text2 textbox so that I'm ready to process the next character.

Processing a String of Characters

Processing a string of characters is nearly identical to processing single characters. Instead of converting the character value to ASCII, I simply send the string of characters in the Text3 textbox to the program, as you can see in Listing 15.3.

Listing 15.3:   Command1_Click Event in Notepad Writer

```
Private Sub Command1_Click()

If np <> 0 Then
    AppActivate np
    SendKeys Text3.Text, True
    Text3.SetFocus
End If

End Sub
```

Using an Application's Objects

Back in Chapter 7, I showed you how to use the MSFlexGrid and MSChart controls to build a simple utility (called the Charter program) that creates a chart from the data you enter. However, there is a much better way to perform the same function—use Microsoft Excel.

Excel comes with its own set of objects that you can use from your Visual Basic program to perform functions in Excel. Simply add the Excel object reference by choosing Project ➤ References and then checking Microsoft Excel 8.0 Object Library, as shown in Figure 15.2. Then with a little work, you too can build a program like the one shown in Figure 15.3.

FIGURE 15.2

Adding the Excel 8.0 Object Library

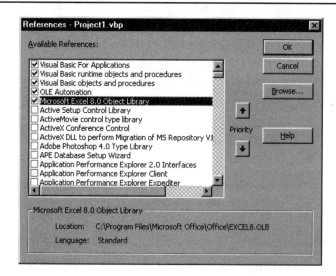

FIGURE 15.3:

The Excel Demo program

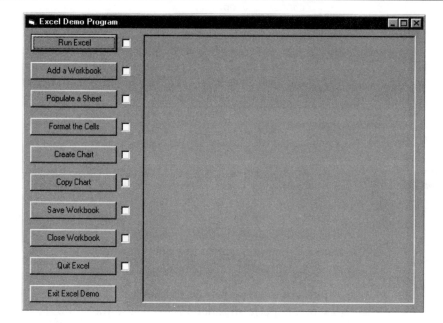

Not only can you use Excel in this fashion, you also can use many popular programs including Word, Internet Explorer, PowerPoint, Photoshop, Access, and more. Check the References dialog box to see a list of objects available on your system.

Cutting Out the Middleman

For a number of years, I was actively involved with data analysis. I used a number of different programming tools to reduce millions of transactions into a report that could be easily understood by a nontechnical manager.

The end result of this analysis was an Excel workbook with a number of charts showing key indicators and trend information. A few spreadsheets were also included to show the details that could not be shown in a chart. To produce this workbook, I went through a number of steps, with the last few generating files that I could import into Excel. I then had to update all of the charts by hand with the proper date and verify that the charts were displayed properly.

If the Excel objects were available, I would have built a Visual Basic program that produced the charts and spreadsheets from the raw data, cutting out the middle steps. Without the manual efforts, I believe that I could have reduced the time to prepare the reports from a day or two to less than an hour.

Creating and Getting Objects

Key to using another application's object is the ability to create a reference to an object on the fly. Here's where the `CreateObject` and `GetObject` routines come into play. These routines allow you to create an object on the fly and then use the object's methods and properties to perform various tasks.

The `CreateObject` function returns an object reference for the specified type of object. The top-level object for Excel is `Excel.Application`. From this object, you can create object references for all of the other objects in Excel.

> **I object Your Honor:** Finding information about the Excel objects is very easy—just look in the Excel documentation files for information about Visual Basic for Applications (VBA) programming. The objects you use to write your VBA macros are the same objects you will use from Visual Basic 6. The only difference is that you need to start with the top-level object, `Excel.Application` in Visual Basic 6. Excel's VBA already assumes that information.

The `GetObject` function also returns an object reference, but this routine works a little differently. You may specify the name of a file, and the system will automatically determine the best way to try to view it. Thus, if you type in the following line of code, you will receive an object reference for Excel, and Excel will load that workbook automatically:

```
MyObj = GetObject("C:\My Documents\Book1.XLS")
```

You also can specify the object type as the second parameter:

```
MyObj = GetObject( , "Excel.Application")
```

This form will also start Excel, but it will not load any documents. The difference between just specifying the object type with the `GetObject` function and using this specification with the `CreateObject` function is that the `GetObject` function will attempt to use an existing Excel program, while the `CreateObject` function always uses a separate copy of Excel.

The first step in using Excel to perform your processing is to create a copy of Excel to use. In the Excel Demo program, I start by using the `GetObject` function to find an existing copy of Excel, as shown in Listing 15.4. If that fails, then I know there isn't an existing copy of Excel and I need to create my own copy. I do this with the `CreateObject` function. `MyExcel` reflects whether I'm using an already running copy of Excel (`False`) or my own private copy (`True`).

Listing 15.4:   **Command1_Click Event in Excel Demo**

```
Private Sub Command1_Click()

On Error Resume Next
```

```
Err.Clear

Set ExcelApp = GetObject(, "Excel.Application")
If Err.Number <> 0 Then
    Err.Clear
    Set ExcelApp = CreateObject("Excel.Application")
    If Err.Number <> 0 Then
        MsgBox "Error: " & Err.Description
    Else
        MyExcel = True

    End If

Else
    MyExcel = False

End If

ExcelApp.Visible = True

Check1.Value = vbChecked
Command2.SetFocus

End Sub
```

Once I have a valid object for Excel, I make the spreadsheet program visible. Then I end this routine by putting a little check beside the button and setting the focus on the next command button. Figure 15.4 shows this stage.

TIP   **Caution—objects at work:** By default, Excel will be hidden from view when created this way. It will not even be visible on the Windows Taskbar. However, by making it visible, I can watch what is happening during each step of the process.

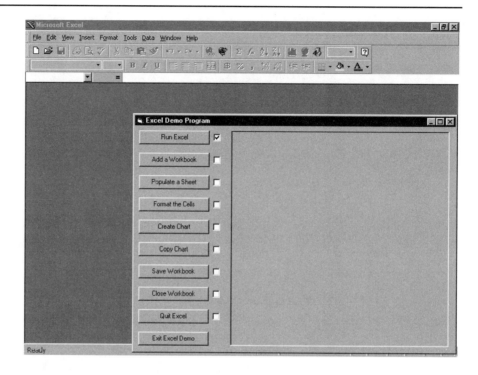

Creating a Workbook and Worksheet

After creating the basic Excel object, the next step is to create a spreadsheet to work with. As shown in Listing 15.5, this is really a two-step process. First, I create a new workbook by using the `ExcelApp.Workbooks.Add` method. (A workbook is a container for worksheets and charts.) Then using the workbook object, I create a reference to the first worksheet in the workbook. Figure 15.5 shows the results.

Listing 15.5:   Command2_Click Event in Excel Demo

```
Private Sub Command2_Click()

Set ExcelWkb = ExcelApp.Workbooks.Add
Set ExcelSht = ExcelWkb.Worksheets(1)

Check2.Value = vbChecked
Command3.SetFocus

End Sub
```

FIGURE 15.5:

Creating a workbook
and a worksheet

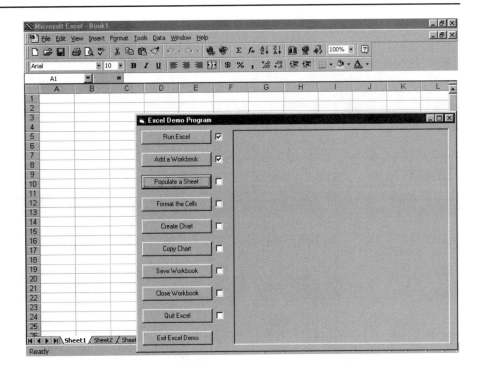

Adding Data to the Worksheet

Now that I have a worksheet, I can insert data into it by using the ExcelSht.Cells property, as shown in Listing 15.6. The format of the parameters is *row, column*. In this case, I merely assign each cell a random value between 0 and 100. Figure 15.6 shows the results of adding the data. Note that I can easily change this assignment to put any data in any cell that I wish. I could also include formulas.

Listing 15.6:   Command3_Click Event in Excel Demo

```
Private Sub Command3_Click()

Dim i As Integer
Dim j As Integer

For i = 1 To 4
   For j = 1 To 10
      ExcelSht.Cells(j, i) = Rnd() * 100
```

```
    Next j
Next i

Check3.Value = vbChecked
Command4.SetFocus

End Sub
```

FIGURE 15.6:

Inserting data into the worksheet

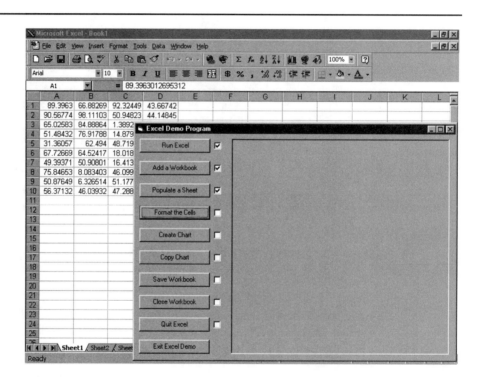

Formatting Cells

After looking at the unevenly aligned columns, I decided to use a standard numeric format with two decimal places to display my data. To do this, I determine which range of cells I want to change by using the Range property. I use the Excel notation of A1:D10 to change the four columns and ten rows of data. Then I set the NumberFormat property to 0.00, meaning that the values should be displayed with two decimal places. Listing 15.7 shows the code, and Figure 15.7 shows the formatted cells.

Listing 15.7:	**Command4_Click Event in Excel Demo**

```
Private Sub Command4_Click()

ExcelSht.Range("A1:D10").NumberFormat = "0.00"

Check4.Value = vbChecked
Command5.SetFocus

End Sub
```

FIGURE 15.7:

Formatted cells in the worksheet

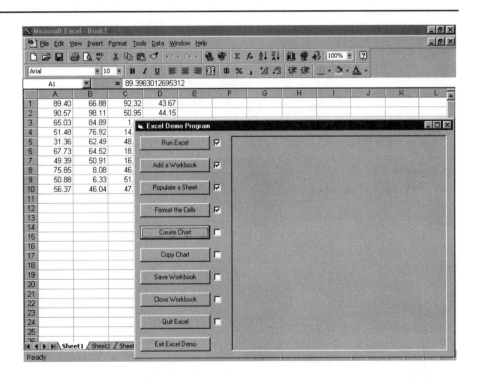

Charting the Results

The next step of this process, shown in Listing 15.8, creates a chart in Excel. I begin by adding a new chart to the workbook. Then I set the type of chart that will be displayed. Next, I select the range of cells and how they will be oriented in the chart. Finally, I assign titles to the top of the chart and each axis, and mark this section as complete. Figure 15.8 shows the chart.

Listing 15.8:   Command5_Click Event in Excel Demo

```
Private Sub Command5_Click()

Set ExcelCht = ExcelWkb.Charts.Add
ExcelCht.ChartType = xlLineMarkers
ExcelCht.SetSourceData ExcelSht.Range("A1:D10"), xlColumns
ExcelCht.HasTitle = True
ExcelCht.ChartTitle.Characters.Text = "My Data"
ExcelCht.Axes(xlCategory, xlPrimary).HasTitle = True
ExcelCht.Axes(xlCategory, xlPrimary).AxisTitle.Characters.Text = "X-Axis"
ExcelCht.Axes(xlValue, xlPrimary).HasTitle = True
ExcelCht.Axes(xlValue, xlPrimary).AxisTitle.Characters.Text = "Data Series"

Check5.Value = vbChecked
Command6.SetFocus

End Sub
```

TIP

Micro macros: By now you are probably saying to yourself, "This is nice but learning how to use the Excel objects is much harder than using MSChart." There's a little trick that makes this nearly trivial (well at least to anyone who is familiar with Excel). Use the Record New Macro facility to record the steps you want to include in your code. Then use the Edit Macro facility to look at the code. You will see a bunch of Visual Basic statements that can be included in your own code. Just remember to use the proper base object in your program.

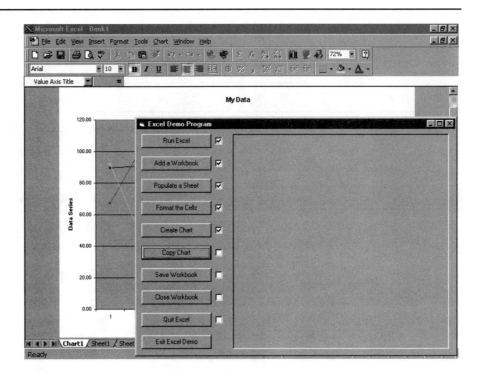

Copying the Chart

Now that Excel has a copy of the chart, I can select and copy the chart to the Windows clipboard by using the ChartArea.Select and ChartArea.Copy methods, as shown in Listing 15.9. Then it becomes a simple matter to get it from the clipboard and save it into the Image control on the form. Figure 15.9 shows the chart copied into my program.

Listing 15.9:   **Command6_Click Event in Excel Demo**

```
Private Sub Command6_Click()

ExcelCht.ChartArea.Select
ExcelCht.ChartArea.Copy

Image1.Picture = Clipboard.GetData(vbCFBitmap)
```

```
Check6.Value = vbChecked
Command7.SetFocus

End Sub
```

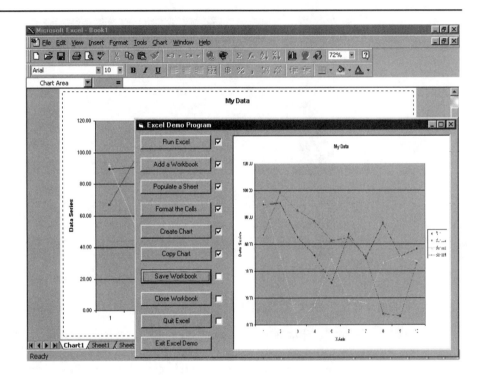

Saving the Workbook

Once I've copied the chart from Excel to my program, I want to save the work-book to a disk file just in case I decide to make any changes later. Before I save the file, I check to see if the file exists and purge it if necessary. Then I use the SaveAs method to save the file. Listing 15.10 shows the routine.

Listing 15.10: **Command7_Click Event in Excel Demo**

```
Private Sub Command7_Click()

If Len(Dir(App.Path & "\test.xls")) <> 0 Then
```

```
Kill App.Path & "\test.xls"
End If

ExcelWkb.SaveAs App.Path & "\test.xls"

Check7.Value = vbChecked
Command8.SetFocus

End Sub
```

Closing the Workbook

The `Close` method is used to close the workbook, as shown in Listing 15.11. The first parameter specifies whether or not to save the workbook. Since I had previously saved it, this option should be `False`.

Listing 15.11:	Command8_Click Event in Excel Demo

```
Private Sub Command8_Click()

ExcelWkb.Close False

Check8.Value = vbChecked
Command9.SetFocus

End Sub
```

Exiting Excel

With everything else complete, it's time to close the Excel session. The code for exiting is shown in Listing 15.12. If I created the `ExcelApp` with the `GetObject` function, I don't need to stop the Excel program since I didn't start it. Someone else was using it previously, and I don't want to disrupt anyone's work. However, if I started this particular instance of Excel, then I need to close it with the `Quit` method.

Listing 15.12:   Command9_Click Event in Excel Demo

```
Private Sub Command9_Click()

If MyExcel Then
    ExcelApp.Quit
End If

Check9.Value = vbChecked
Command10.SetFocus

End Sub
```

Writing ActiveX Programs

Another way to communicate with other programs is to write an ActiveX EXE program. This approach is similar to using an application's objects (as I did in the Excel Demo program), but you create your own object model and put it in an ActiveX EXE program.

Using ActiveX

Visual Basic allows you to create three different types of ActiveX programs: the ActiveX control, the ActiveX DLL, and the ActiveX EXE. Each of these has its own characteristics and uses.

Using ActiveX Controls

As a Visual Basic programmer, you've already come to know and love the ActiveX control. The control has a visual component that must be placed in a container. (Even though some controls aren't visible on your screen at runtime, they are visible at design time.) A container may be a Visual Basic form, a Visual Basic Picture control, or an Internet Explorer web page. An ActiveX control is always run as part of its parent's process (known as *running in process*).

Using ActiveX DLLs

The ActiveX DLL is also an in-process component and shares its parent's address space. This type of ActiveX program is designed for unattended operation. It is used to store objects created through the Visual Basic Class facility.

Using ActiveX EXEs

The ActiveX EXE is an out-of-process component. It runs in a totally separate address space and may even run on a different computer. This is the way that programs like Microsoft Word and Excel are created. Like Word and Excel, the ActiveX EXE may have a visual interface, but that is not required. You can run the program in the background and never know it is being used. Running in a different address space (out of process) is a little slower than being in process, but it does protect your program, in that crashing a user program will not affect the ActiveX EXE.

NOTE   **I started Excel and I can't find it:** In the Excel Demo program I made Excel visible when I set the `ExcelApp.Visible` property to `True` in the `Command1_Click` event. But if you modify that program and remove that statement, you will never see Excel on your screen or on your Taskbar. Yet Excel is still available to perform its functions as usual. When writing your own ActiveX EXE program, remember if there is no need for the program to be visible, you should keep it hidden from the user to prevent confusion.

Introducing Honest Wayne's Used Airplane Lot

As an example of developing an ActiveX program, I packaged the business rules for a fictitious business known as Honest Wayne's Used Airplane Lot. This business sells surplus World War II airplanes to customers around the world. To simplify the work to implement its business rules, the rules have been consolidated into a single ActiveX EXE file. This allows these rules to be shared between the web developers group and the Visual Basic developers group.

Creating the Airplane and Airplanes Objects

The program is based on a Visual Basic class called Fleet and contains two sets of objects: Airplane and Airplanes. The Airplane object contains properties that relate to a single model of airplane. The Airplanes object contains a set of Airplane objects. Don't confuse this with a collection of Airplane objects—this is not a traditional Visual Basic collection that you can process using a For Each statement. I've also written a small client program to interact with the ActiveX EXE server program.

NOTE   **Business second, fun first:** I should note that these programs are not very realistic in either their content or their specific actions. I attribute this to writing them rather late at night. However, the same techniques apply to more serious business problems. By isolating the code that accesses your data from the code that interacts with the user, you can improve overall program stability.

The Airplane object itself is rather simple, containing only five properties that describe a single model of airplanc. It contains the Name associated with the Model, the Role where the airplane is used, the Quantity on hand, and the Cost (the minimum sales price). Listing 15.13 shows the definition of the Airplane object.

Listing 15.13:   **Airplane Object Definition**

```
Public Name As String       ' Mustang
Public Role As String       ' Fighter
Public Model As String      ' P-51D
Public Quantity As Integer  ' 7
Public Cost As Single       ' 550000.00
```

The Airplanes object contains a series of properties and methods that can be used to access the information, as listed in Table 15.3.

TABLE 15.3:   The Airplanes Object Properties and Methods

Property/Method	Description
ErrorDescription method	Describes the results of the SellOne method
FleetSize property	Contains the number of airplanes in the fleet or for a specific model
FleetValue property	Contains the total value of all of the airplanes in the inventory
IsModel method	Returns True if the Model is valid

Continued on next page

TABLE 15.3 (CONTINUED):   The Airplanes Object Properties and Methods

Property/Method	Description
IsRole method	Returns True if the Role is valid
Name method	Returns the Name of an airplane given the Model
Role method	Returns the Role of an airplane given the Model
SellOne method	Evaluates an offer for an airplane

The IsModel and IsRole methods are used to determine if the Model or Role is valid. The Name and Role methods return information based on the specified Model. The FleetSize property returns either the size of the total fleet or the number of available airplanes for a particular Model. The FleetValue property returns the total dollar value of all the planes on the lot. The SellOne method evaluates an offer for a specific Model and returns a status value that can be interpreted by the ErrorDescription method.

Starting the Server

Every Class object has two optional events: Class_Initialize and Class_ Terminate. I use the Class_Initialize event to build a small collection with information about nine different airplanes. I'll use this collection in place of a set of database files.

TIP   **Database rules, too.** If you are planning on incorporating your business rules into an ActiveX EXE program, then you really should be using a database to hold your data. Some of the rules will be best coded as relationships in your database, while others are better coded directly as objects in the ActiveX EXE program.

The server is started when the client program calls the CreateObject function, as shown in Listing 15.14. Then Windows searches for the object on the specified system.

Listing 15.14:   **Client's Form_Load Event in Wayne's Used Airplane Lot**

```
Private Sub Form_Load()

Set MyPlanes = CreateObject("Fleet.Airplanes", "Mycroft")
```

```
Text5.Text = "Current size of the fleet is " & _
    FormatNumber(MyPlanes.FleetSize(""), 0) & " and its value is " & _
    FormatCurrency(MyPlanes.FleetValue) & "."

End Sub
```

When the object is found and a new copy is created, the Class_Initialize event is triggered, as shown in Listing 15.15. Then the client accesses some statistics about the fleet of aircraft by using the FleetSize and FleetValue properties. Figure 15.10 shows the result.

Listing 15.15:   **Server's Class_Initialize Event in Wayne's Used Airplane Lot**

```
Private Sub Class_Initialize()

AddOne "T-6", "Texan", "trainer", 12, 100000
AddOne "P-38", "Lightning", "Fighter", 0, 1000000
AddOne "P-40", "Warhawk", "Fighter", 4, 350000
AddOne "P-47", "Thunderbolt", "Fighter", 2, 450000
AddOne "P-51", "Mustang", "Fighter", 4, 500000
AddOne "B-17", "Flying Fortress", "Bomber", 2, 1200000
AddOne "B-25", "Mitchell", "Bomber", 5, 500000
AddOne "B-29", "Super Fortress", "Bomber", 1, 2000000
AddOne "C-47", "Skytrain", "Cargo", 9, 200000

End Sub
```

FIGURE 15.10:

Starting the client program

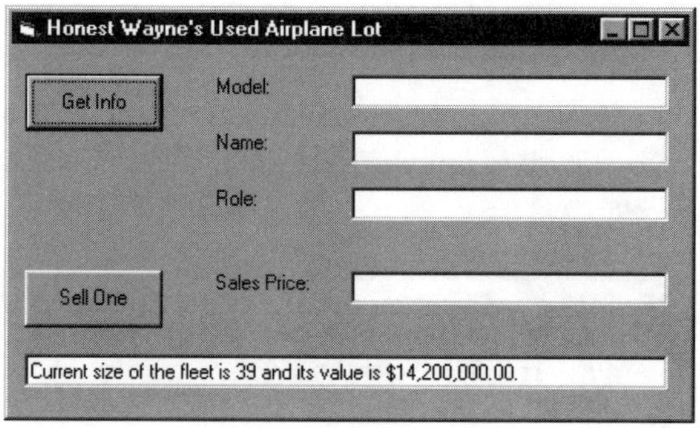

The Class_Initialize event calls the AddOne subroutine, shown in Listing 15.16, to add some airplanes to the collection. Normally, this event would be used to ensure that all variables are initialized properly and perform tasks like opening the database.

Listing 15.16:   **Server's AddOne Routine in Wayne's Used Airplane Lot**

```
Private Sub AddOne(ym As String, yn As String, yr As String, _
    yq As Integer, yc As Single)

Dim y As Airplane

Set y = New Airplane

y.Model = ym
y.Name = yn
y.Role = yr
y.Quantity = yq
y.Cost = yc

xAirplanes.Add y, ym

End Sub
```

The AddOne routine is straightforward. It creates a new Airplane object using the Set New statement. It then assigns the list of supplied values to the new object. Next, it uses the collection's Add method to put the newly created object into the xAirplanes collection.

Getting Information about an Airplane

Clicking the Get Info button triggers the Command1_Click event, shown in Listing 15.17. This routine begins by checking to see if the model entered in the Text1 text box is valid. If the model is valid, then it retrieves information about the model, such as its name, role, and the number airplanes available. Figure 15.11 shows an example.

Listing 15.17:   Client's Command1_Click Event in Wayne's Used Airplane Lot

```
Private Sub Command1_Click()

If MyPlanes.IsModel(Text1.Text) Then
   Text2.Text = MyPlanes.Name(Text1.Text)
   Text3.Text = MyPlanes.Role(Text1.Text)
   Text5.Text = "There are " & _
      FormatNumber(MyPlanes.FleetSize(Text1.Text), 0) & _
      " " & Text1.Text & " " & Text2.Text & "s available."
Else
   Text5.Text = "Invalid model."

End If

End Sub
```

FIGURE 15.11:

Getting information about
an airplane

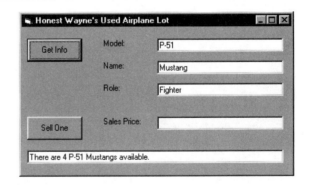

The IsModel function in the Airplanes object appears to the programmer using this object as the IsModel method Airplanes object. As shown in Listing 15.18, this routine scans through the items in the xAirplanes collection to see if there is a match between the specified model and one of the models in the collection. If a match is found, then the function returns True; otherwise, False is returned.

Listing 15.18:   Server's IsModel Function in Wayne's Used Airplane Lot

```
Public Function IsModel(ym As String) As Boolean

Dim a As Airplane

IsModel = False

For Each a In xAirplanes
   If LCase(ym) = LCase(a.Model) Then
      IsModel = True
   End If
Next a

End Function
```

The FleetSize routine, shown in Listing 15.19, returns either the total number of airplanes on the lot or the total number of airplanes for a particular model. Calculating the number of airplanes on the lot means looping through the xAirplanes collection and adding up the quantities. For a single model, all I need to do is to return the Quantity property.

Listing 15.19:   Server's FleetSize Routine in Wayne's Used Airplane Lot

```
Public Property Get FleetSize(ym As String) As Integer

Dim a As Airplane
Dim s As Integer

s = 0

If Len(ym) = 0 Then
   For Each a In xAirplanes
      s = s + a.Quantity
   Next a

Else
   s = xAirplanes.Item(ym).Quantity

End If
```

```
FleetSize = s

End Property
```

Placing an Order

Clicking the Sell One button fires the Command2_Click event, shown in Listing 15.20. This event verifies that the value entered in the Text4 text box is numeric and then calls the SellOne method.

Listing 15.20:   Client's Command2_Click Event in Wayne's Used Airplane Lot

```
Private Sub Command2_Click()

Dim r As Integer

If IsNumeric(Text4.Text) Then
    r = MyPlanes.SellOne(Text1.Text, CSng(Text4.Text))
    If r = 0 Then
        Text5.Text = "Sold."
    Else
        Text5.Text = MyPlanes.ErrorDescription(r)
    End If
End If

End Sub
```

The SellOne method evaluates a bid for an airplane, as shown in Listing 15.21. It first checks to see if there are any airplanes available. If there aren't any, an error code is returned. Then the cost is evaluated to see if the asking price is at least ten percent over the airplane's cost. If not, a different error code is returned to indicate that the price was too low. If everything is proper, the bid will be accepted and the quantity of that model of airplane will be decremented by one. The program displays the "Sold" message, as shown in Figure 15.12.

Listing 15.21:   **Server's SellOne Function in Wayne's Used Airplane Lot**

```
Public Function SellOne(ym As String, yc As Single) As Integer

If xAirplanes.Item(ym).Quantity > 0 Then
    If (xAirplanes.Item(ym).Cost) * 1.1 < yc Then
        SellOne = 0
        xAirplanes.Item(ym).Quantity = xAirplanes.Item(ym).Quantity - 1
    Else
        SellOne = 2 ' price too low
    End If

Else
    SellOne = 1 ' no planes available

End If

End Function
```

FIGURE 15.12:

Buying a P-51 Mustang
for $575,000

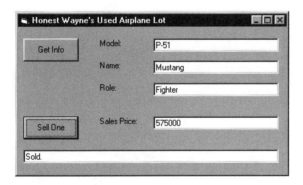

Any other value indicates an error condition, and the message associated with the error is returned, as shown in Figure 15.13. The ErrorDescription method, shown in Listing 15.22, merely translates a return code from the SellOne method into a text description.

Listing 15.22:   **Server's ErrorDescription Function in Wayne's Used Airplane Lot**

```
Public Function ErrorDescription(e As Integer) As String

Select Case e

Case 1
   ErrorDescription = "No airplanes available."

Case 2
   ErrorDescription = "Sales price too low."

Case Else
   ErrorDescription = "Unknown error: " & FormatNumber(e, 0)

End Select

End Function
```

FIGURE 15.13:

Bidding too low for
a Mustang

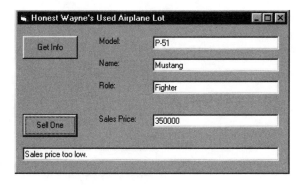

Final Thoughts

The Notepad Writer program I wrote to demonstrate how to use `Shell`,
`AppActivate`, and `SendKeys` is an interesting tool that lets you send characters
from one program to another. While this is a neat trick, you might wonder if it
is really useful. The answer is yes. Imagine a toolbar full of buttons that could

send to another program a series of keystrokes to perform a task. You could program the keystrokes just like some people program macros.

Another idea would be to use this program to test another program. Imagine that you have an application that you would like to put through a standard test. Rather than typing every single keystroke, you could use the SendKeys statement to send the keystrokes to the program. This accomplishes two things. First, each test is the same as the previous test, so you don't have to worry about someone entering the wrong set of keystrokes. Second, because the same keystrokes are entered each time, it is possible to reproduce problems, thus making it easier to isolate bugs in your code.

As you saw in my Excel Demo program, I like using an application's objects to build programs. This lets me take advantage of the work that others have done. Why build your own spreadsheet when you can use Excel? Why build a word processor when you can use Word? As more and more programs adopt Visual Basic for Applications as a macro language, I expect to see more applications adopting this object-oriented approach.

Another idea that may prove useful would be to generate PowerPoint slides from live data. Consider the case of someone preparing a presentation using production schedules or stock values. The user could acquire that information automatically and update the slides by running a single program.

You also could combine Word, Excel, and PowerPoint with a Visual Basic program that helps people generate business proposals. Consider the case of a company that sells office furniture. The salesperson would collect information from the prospective buyers about the quantity and style of the furniture they want and key that information into a series of Visual Basic forms. This information would be processed using a database, which contains furniture information, costs, and estimated availability. Then the information would be used to create an Excel spreadsheet showing the detailed pricing, a Word document containing an executive summary of the proposal, and a PowerPoint slide show for the salesperson's proposal presentation.

Although the other approaches I covered in this chapter have value, building your own objects may net you the biggest bang for the buck. In my Honest Wayne's Used Airplane Lot program, I showed you how to build an ActiveX EXE program that used an object model similar to Excel and Word. (Well, maybe not as complex, but the idea is the same.)

Your own objects could provide standard functions to access information in your database and perform database updates. They could also provide utility functions such as validation checks to ensure that a value is valid, comparisons of two objects to determine if they are the same, and encoding and decoding database values.

In general, application programmers will be more productive because they don't need to worry as much about the actual data manipulation and can focus on issues related to user interface design. It also prevents the problem where two application programmers write slightly different algorithms to perform the same function, which could lead to the programs providing slightly different answers.

ActiveX programs also have the advantage that they can run on a different computer than the one running your application program. Thus, you could dedicate a server to running your program and let all of the other machines reference its objects across the network. This would include web servers as well as traditional Visual Basic programs. This approach may lead to better performance, since you are offloading work from your web server and your users' PCs.

CHAPTER

SIXTEEN

16

Writing Win32 API Programs

- An overview of Win32 API programming

- Win32 API calls from Visual Basic programs

- The time zone information function

- Windows, environment, and process information functions

- Program and file execution functions

- System color functions

- The icon retrieval function

- The Windows shutdown function

Visual Basic is a rich programming language, but some things are just not available in Visual Basic. For instance, you can't determine what time zone the computer is in. You can't set a value in an environment string. You can't run a program and wait for it to finish before continuing in your application. You can't determine the appropriate program to view a particular type of file.

Using the Win32 API, you can do all of these things and more. The Win32 API is the complete interface to Windows. Any function you can perform in Windows can be performed using the Win32 API. In this chapter, I'm going to cover some Win32 API routines that I find particularly interesting.

WARNING

Warning—hazardous material: The material in this chapter may be hazardous to your system's health and your sanity. Although using Win32 API calls in your program is generally safe, problems may arise that can crash your program, Visual Basic, and possibly even your system. While every attempt was made to make sure that the information and programs included in this book are correct, use them at your own risk!

Introducing the Win32 API

Microsoft Windows is written in C. That simple statement means that C programmers has a distinct advantage when accessing Windows facilities. For the most part, Microsoft has done a good job of adding new facilities to Visual Basic with each new release, but the C folks have done an equally good job of introducing new features.

Also, for some reason, the Visual Basic group has ignored some of the more useful Windows facilities. Fortunately, Visual Basic does have the ability to call external routines located in a dynamic link library (DLL). Since the Win32 API is implemented as a bunch of subroutines in a set of DLL files, it's easy to use this capability to make Win32 API calls.

TIP **Look before you call:** Many Win32 API calls are already available in Visual Basic. Each revision of Visual Basic adds new objects and controls, like the `Screen` object and the SysInfo control. It also adds new options and parameters to existing functions, controls, and objects. So if you haven't reviewed the syntax of a routine like `MsgBox` for a while, take a look at it before you decide that you need to make a direct call to the `MessageBox` API function.

Win32 API Character Sets

The Win32 API supports three different character sets:

- The ANSI character set (often referred to as ASCII), where each character occupies one byte

- The Double Byte Character Set (DBCS), which designates certain characters as an indicator that the next byte should be included when forming a character

- The Unicode character set, in which all characters are two bytes wide

The DBCS and Unicode character sets are important when writing international programs. Languages like Japanese include hundreds of characters.

The impact of the multiple character sets is that the routines handling string values must know which character set is being used. It's possible to recognize the difference between ANSI and DBCS by examining the contents of the data. The real issue is how to tell the difference between the ANSI character set and the Unicode character set.

To handle this problem, Microsoft has created two sets of routines, one to handle ANSI parameters and one to handle Unicode parameters. Both routines have a common API name (for example, `MessageBox`). The Unicode version of the routine appends a `W` to the end of the name (as in `MessageBoxW`); the ANSI version appends an `A` (as in `MessageBoxA`).

However, this is not the end of the problem. Windows 95 and 98 are based on the ANSI character set, but Windows NT is based on Unicode. To complicate matters even more, both Visual Basic and OLE 2.0 use Unicode. In order to make your Visual Basic program compatible with both ANSI and Unicode, Microsoft converts all string values to ANSI when making an API call.

Win32 API Data Types

Since Windows is a C world, all of the Win32 API calls use C data types. For the most part, Visual Basic data types are compatible with C data types. However, there are a few data types that may cause you some extra work. Table 16.1 lists the C data types and their corresponding Visual Basic data types. The following sections explain some of the issues related to data types.

TABLE 16.1: Win32 API Data Types

C Data Type	Visual Basic Data Type	Size	Comments
char	Byte	8 bits	
BYTE	Byte	8 bits	
uchar	Byte	8 bits	Unsigned value
short	Integer	16 bits	
WORD	Integer	16 bits	
int	Long	32 bits	
UINT	Long	32 bits	Unsigned value
BOOL	Long	32 bits	Boolean value
DWORD	Long	32 bits	
LONG	Long	32 bits	
float	Single	32 bits	
double	Double	64 bits	
VARIANT	Variant	n/a	
VARIANTARG	Variant	n/a	
LPSTR	String	n/a	Null-terminated string
not used	Boolean	16 bits	Not used in the Win32 API
not used	Currency	64 bits	Not used in the Win32 API

Boolean Values

Generally, C and Visual Basic assume that any nonzero value is True and a value of zero means False. However, the convention in C is to use a value of 1 for True. This is different from Visual Basic's use of −1 as True. This means that you should always test BOOL values for either = 0 or <> 0 rather than testing for = 1 or = -1.

Unsigned Values

C allows a programmer to specify a variable as unsigned. This means that a 16-bit value can range from 0 to 65,384 rather than from −32,768 to 32,767. Visual Basic doesn't support unsigned data types. However, this generally doesn't cause a problem with the API call itself. It just means that instead of seeing a 32768, you're going to see −32768, the value 32769 will be displayed as −32769, and so forth.

Unused Visual Basic Data Types

The Win32 API does not use the Currency data type or Visual Basic's Boolean data type.

Both the Single and Double floating-point data types are not used in the core Win32 API. They can be used in your own DLLs if you desire. Just make sure that you use the correct type in both places, since Single and Double values are passed to external routines using different techniques.

Variants are also not used by the core Win32 API. However, Variants are compatible with the OLE 2.0 variant data type. So there shouldn't be a problem with using Visual Basic Variants when using OLE 2.0.

Strings

Besides the issues of Unicode versus ANSI, there is another issue about using Strings in Win32 API calls. C strings consist of a series of characters terminated by a Null character. Visual Basic Strings are formatted as a length field followed by the characters. Figure 16.1 illustrates the differences. Obviously, this will cause a problem when you call a Win32 API routine where a string is needed.

FIGURE 16.1:

C Strings versus Visual Basic Strings

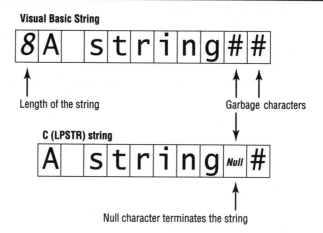

Visual Basic handles this condition in two ways. For parameters that are passed by value (ByVal), Visual Basic will transparently create a temporary copy of the string using the C format. Then it passes a pointer to this string to the DLL routine. If the routine makes any changes to the string, it will make them to the copy, not to the original string.

For strings that are not passed by value (ByRef), Visual Basic creates a BSTR pointer to the string in your program. (A BSTR pointer simply points to a series of characters, which may or may not be null-terminated.) This allows the DLL routine to modify the contents of the string without worrying about the length. This poses a problem for the Visual Basic programmer. Because the length of the string is not passed to the calling program, you need to fill the string with null characters (or spaces or whatever, depending on the call) so that the routine will never go beyond the end of the string. If the routine returns a string that is less than the length of the string, all you need to do is throw away the fill characters.

If more data is written into the string than the space you have allowed, at a minimum, you won't be able to access any data beyond the end of the string. Since the length of the string hasn't been changed from Visual Basic's perspective, there can't be valid data beyond the end of the string. It is very likely that the variables stored beyond the memory space of the string will be overwritten. This will lead to one of three possible results:

- Nothing will happen because the variables aren't used or are reinitialized before they are used again.

- Your program will generate incorrect data, which will probably go unnoticed until you show the data to your client.

- Your program will die a horrible death, and you won't be able to find out why.

WARNING   **Crash, Bang, Boom!** Probably the leading cause of failures in Visual Basic programs using the Win32 API is improperly handling strings that have been passed by reference. To prevent problems, it is important that you make sure that you have more characters in the string than can be returned. Otherwise, your data could be overwritten and your program could crash.

Calling a Win32 API Routine

To call a Win32 API routine from your Visual Basic program, you need to create the reference to that routine and interpret the data returned. Visual Basic 6 provides some help in the form of a utility called the API Text Viewer, which lets you copy and paste Win32 API statements. Then you can use the routine just as if it were a regular Visual Basic subroutine or function.

Declaring a Win32 API Call

You use the `Declare` statement to create a reference to a subroutine or function residing in a DLL file, using one of the syntax forms below:

```
[ Public | Private ] Declare Function name Lib lib [ Alias alias ] _
    [ ( args ) ] As type
[ Public | Private ] Declare Sub name Lib lib [ Alias alias ] _
    [ ( args ) ]
```

where:

- *name* is the name of the routine that you will use in your program.

- *lib* is the name of the library that contains the routine. You need to specify the full path name for the library unless the library is in your \Windows\ System directory. The .DLL extension is also required, except for the three main Windows libraries, user32, kernel32, and gdi32.

- *alias* contains the real name of the routine. If specified, this is a string value containing the real name of the routine found in the DLL. If not specified, *name* is assumed.

- *args* is the list of arguments for the routine, including type information.

- *type* is the data type of the value returned by the function.

WARNING **Case is Important:** In the Win32 API, the name of a routine is case-sensitive. Make sure that you've used the correct case when specifying values for *name* and *alias*.

The list of arguments consists of individual *arg* clauses separated by commas. Each *arg* is formed by the syntax below:

```
[ Optional ] [ ByVal ] [ ByRef ] [ ParamArray ] argname [ () ] _
    [ As type ]
```

where:

- Optional means that the argument need not be specified when the routine is called.

- ByVal means that the argument is passed by value.

- ByRef means that the argument is passed by reference.

- ParamArray means that the routine can receive an unspecified number of arguments of type Variant, starting at this position. This must be the last argument in the Declare statement and can't be used with the Optional, ByVal, or ByRef clauses.

- *argname* contains the name of the argument.

- () indicates that the argument is an array.

- *type* is the data type of the argument.

A typical Declare statement looks like this:

```
Public Declare Function GetTimeZoneInformation Lib "kernel32" _
    (lpTimeZoneInformation As TIME_ZONE_INFORMATION) As Long
```

Defining Win32 API Structures and Constants

Many Win32 API calls return data in a C structure. A C structure is equivalent to a Visual Basic Type statement. Also, many calls make reference to various constants that can are used to interpret results or select options. Constants can be defined in Visual Basic using the Const statement. The following are some examples of structures and constants:

```
Public Const TIME_ZONE_ID_UNKNOWN = 0
Public Const TIME_ZONE_ID_STANDARD = 1
Public Const TIME_ZONE_ID_DAYLIGHT = 2

Public Type SYSTEMTIME
        wYear As Integer
        wMonth As Integer
        wDayOfWeek As Integer
        wDay As Integer
        wHour As Integer
        wMinute As Integer
        wSecond As Integer
        wMilliseconds As Integer
End Type

Public Type TIME_ZONE_INFORMATION
        Bias As Long
        StandardName(31) As Integer
        StandardDate As SYSTEMTIME
        StandardBias As Long
        DaylightName(31) As Integer
        DaylightDate As SYSTEMTIME
        DaylightBias As Long
End Type
```

Using the API Text Viewer

Visual Basic 6 comes with a useful utility, called the API Text Viewer, that helps you write the declarations you need to call a Win32 API routine. The API Viewer is easy to use. Simply specify the type of information you desire (declares, constants, or types) and then enter the first few letters of the value. The API Viewer will find the reference in its database. Figure 16.2 shows an example of finding `GetTimeZoneInformation`.

FIGURE 16.2:

The API Text Viewer

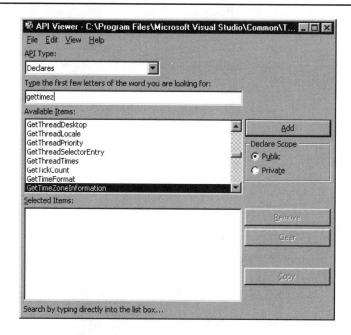

Clicking the Add button adds the item to the list of selected items, which you can copy to the Windows clipboard by clicking the Copy button. From the clipboard, you can easily paste the information into your Visual Basic program.

Pulling It All Together

To add Win32 API routines to a program, start Visual Basic and create a new standard EXE program. Add a module. Then start the API Viewer application. Choose the necessary statements from the API Viewer and copy them to the clipboard. Paste them into the module.

Listing 16.1 contains the Win32 API definitions for the `GetTimeZoneInformation` function, after the constants and type definitions have been corrected. This

GetTimeZoneInformation function provides some information that Visual Basic is sorely lacking, namely which time zone your computer is in. This becomes important when you want to coordinate times between people in multiple time zones. After all, if you only know something happened at 11:00 a.m. in your time zone, how do you know whether this event happened before or after an event that occurred at 11:30 a.m. in what may be a different time zone? If you have the time zone information, you can take the appropriate action.

Listing 16.1:   **Get Time Zone Header Information in Win32API**

```
Public Const TIME_ZONE_ID_UNKNOWN = 0
Public Const TIME_ZONE_ID_STANDARD = 1
Public Const TIME_ZONE_ID_DAYLIGHT = 2

Public Declare Function GetTimeZoneInformation Lib "kernel32" _
    (lpTimeZoneInformation As TIME_ZONE_INFORMATION) As Long

Public Type SYSTEMTIME
        wYear As Integer
        wMonth As Integer
        wDayOfWeek As Integer
        wDay As Integer
        wHour As Integer
        wMinute As Integer
        wSecond As Integer
        wMilliseconds As Integer
End Type

Public Type TIME_ZONE_INFORMATION
        Bias As Long
        StandardName(31) As Integer
        StandardDate As SYSTEMTIME
        StandardBias As Long
        DaylightName(31) As Integer
        DaylightDate As SYSTEMTIME
        DaylightBias As Long
End Type
```

Note that the GetTimeZoneInformation routine is found in the kernel32 library and that it returns a Long value. If you read the documentation, you will see that the three constants TIME_ZONE_ID_UNKNOWN, ZONE_ID_STANDARD, and TIME_ZONE_ID_DAYLIGHT represent return values from the GetTimeZoneInformation function.

Also note that the StandardName and DaylightName members return Integer arrays rather than Strings. Each number in the Integer array corresponds to a single Unicode character. The first element of the array that contains a binary zero marks the end of the string. You can use the Chr function to convert each number to a character.

Listing 16.2 shows the code that uses this function. For the most part, this looks much like any other Visual Basic program (well, except for the identifiers in all uppercase).

Listing 16.2:   Command1_Click Event in Win32API

```
Private Sub Command1_Click()

Dim i As Integer
Dim r As Long
Dim tz As TIME_ZONE_INFORMATION

r = GetTimeZoneInformation(tz)

Text1.Text = FormatNumber(r, 0)
If r = TIME_ZONE_ID_STANDARD Then
    Text1.Text = Text1.Text & " ("
    Do While tz.StandardName(i) <> 0
        Text1.Text = Text1.Text & Chr(tz.StandardName(i))
        i = i + 1
    Loop
    Text1.Text = Text1.Text & ")"

ElseIf r = TIME_ZONE_ID_DAYLIGHT Then
    Text1.Text = Text1.Text & " ("
    Do While tz.DaylightName(i) <> 0
        Text1.Text = Text1.Text & Chr(tz.DaylightName(i))
        i = i + 1
    Loop
    Text1.Text = Text1.Text & ")"

Else
    Text1.Text = Text1.Text & "(Unknown)"
```

```
End If

Text2.Text = FormatNumber(tz.Bias / 60, 0)
Text3.Text = FormatNumber(tz.StandardBias / 60, 0)
Text4.Text = FormatNumber(tz.DaylightBias / 60, 0)

End Sub
```

I display the return value in the Text1 text box. This value contains a flag, which indicates if the computer is on Standard Time or Daylight Savings Time. The Text2 text box contains the number of hours that you would need to add to get UTC time. This value is referred to as Bias. The Text3 and Text4 text boxes describe how many hours need to be added to Bias to get Standard Time and Daylight Saving Time. Figure 16.3 shows the results.

FIGURE 16.3:

Output from the GetTime-ZoneInformation function

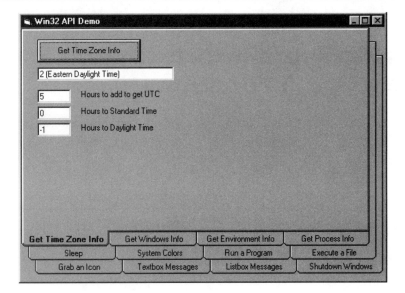

It's a C World After All

If you want to use the Win32 API calls in your program, spend a few dollars and a few hours (well maybe quite a few) learning Visual C++.

In the first example presented here, I was unable to find the three constants without resorting to the Visual C++ header files. The routine worked (well, it least it didn't crash my program), but most of the results were wrong. I also got wrong results in the **Type** definition of `TIME_ZONE_INFORMATION`. Originally, the `StandardName` and `DaylightName` members of the **Type** were declared to have an upper bound of 32. After looking at the code in the VC++ header file, I found that the values were supposed to have 32 elements, so an upper bound of 31 was correct, not 32.

The moral of the story is that if you really want to do Win32 API programming, you better know C.

Using Some Interesting Win32 API Functions

Now that I've given you some background and explained how to build a program that makes Win32 API calls, let's see what the Win32 API has to offer. Table 16.2 lists some of the routines available in the Win32 API.

TABLE 16.2: Some Interesting Win32 API Functions

Routine	Description
CloseHandle	Closes access to a handle
CreateProcess	Starts a new program
DestroyIcon	Destroys an icon
DrawIcon	Draws an icon on a device context
ExitWindowsEx	Shuts down Windows

Continued on next page

TABLE 16.2 (CONTINUED): Some Interesting Win32 API Functions

Routine	Description
ExtractIcon	Gets one or more icons from an EXE or a DLL file
FindExecutable	Finds the program associated with the specified file
GetComputerName	Retrieves the name of the computer
GetCurrentProcess	Returns a handle to the current process
GetCurrentProcessId	Returns the current process number
GetEnvironmentVariable	Retrieves the contents of an environment variable
FileTimeToSystemTime	Converts a FileTime value to a SystemTime value (Visual Basic supports neither data type, but it's easy to convert from SystemTime to a Date value)
GetPriorityClass	Retrieves information about the priority of a process
GetProcessTimes	Retrieves information about the specified process
GetProcessWorkingSetSize	Retrieves information about the specified process
GetSysColor	Retrieves the color of the specified object
GetSystemDirectory	Returns the directory path where the Windows system directory is located
GetTimeZoneInformation	Retrieves information about the time zone where the computer is located
GetUserName	Retrieves the name of the current user
GetWindowsDirectory	Retrieves the directory path where Windows is installed
OpenProcess	Returns a handle to an existing process
SendMessage	Sends a message to a handle
SetEnvironmentVariable	Set the contents of an environment variable
SetSysColors	Sets the list of objects to the list of a specified colors
ShellExecute	Runs the program associated with a file
Sleep	Waits the specified amount of time

Continued on next page

TABLE 16.2 (CONTINUED): Some Interesting Win32 API Functions

Routine	Description
WaitForInputIdle	Waits until the specified program has been initialized and is waiting for input
WaitForSingleObject	Waits until the specified program has finished or until the specified time-out interval occurs

To demonstrate how each of these Win32 API routines work, I built the Win32 API Demo program. I already showed you how the GetTimeZoneInformation routine works (in Listings 16.1 and 16.2). In the rest of this chapter, I'll explain how this program works in the following areas:

- Getting Windows, environment, and process information

- Having a program wait for a specified amount of time

- Changing system colors

- Running a program

- Loading and displaying a file

- Retrieving an icon

- Accessing text box capabilities

- Shutting down Windows

Getting Windows Information

One of the benefits of using the Win32 API is that you can access a lot of information about your computer that you can't normally access in Visual Basic. You can get information such as the name of your computer, your user name, your hardware configuration, plus a lot more. Some of this information is easy to access, and some is not. I'm going to begin by discussing some of the easier routines.

To see the results of using these functions in the Win32API Demo program, select the Get Windows Info tab and click the Get Windows Info button. You'll see something like the display shown in Figure 16.4.

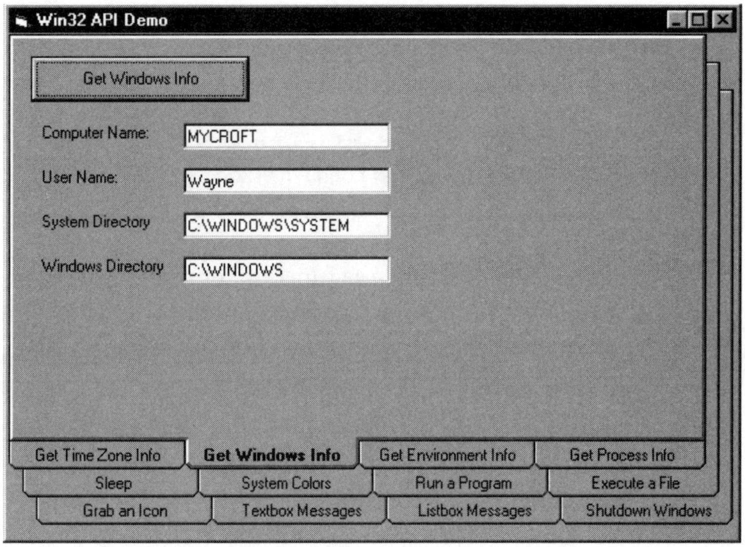

FIGURE 16.4:

Getting your user name and
your computer's name

FIGURE 16.4:

Getting your user name and
your computer's name

Listing 16.3 shows the header information for calling the Windows information
functions.

Listing 16.3:   Get Windows Information Header in Win32API

```
' =============================================================
' = Get Windows Information                                   =
' =============================================================

Public Const MAX_COMPUTERNAME_LENGTH = 31
Public Const MAX_PATH = 260
Public Const UNLEN = 256

Public Declare Function GetComputerName Lib "kernel32" _
    Alias "GetComputerNameA" (ByVal lpBuffer As String, _
    nSize As Long) As Long

Public Declare Function GetSystemDirectory Lib "kernel32" _
    Alias "GetSystemDirectoryA" (ByVal lpBuffer As String, _
    ByVal nSize As Long) As Long
```

```
Public Declare Function GetUserName Lib "advapi32.dll" _
    Alias "GetUserNameA" (ByVal lpBuffer As String, _
    nSize As Long) As Long

Public Declare Function GetWindowsDirectory Lib "kernel32" _
    Alias "GetWindowsDirectoryA" (ByVal lpBuffer As String, _
    ByVal nSize As Long) As Long
```

The GetComputerName function returns the name of your computer that is used for Windows networking. This value was set when your computer was started. The maximum size of this field is MAX_COMPUTERNAME_LENGTH.

The GetUserName function returns the name of the user who is currently logged on to your computer. The maximum length of this field is UNLEN. This value may be useful for determining capabilities of someone using your program since the user had to supply a valid password.

The GetSystemDirectory function returns the name of the Windows system directory. The maximum length of this field is MAX_PATH. On a Windows 95 or 98 system, this function will usually return C:\Windows\System. On a Windows NT system, this will usually return C:\WinNT\System32.

The GetWindowsDirectory function returns the name of the Windows directory. The maximum length of this field is MAX_PATH. On a Windows 95 or 98 system, this function will usually return C:\Windows. On a Windows NT system, this will usually return C:\WinNT.

In Listing 16.4, you can see the code that I wrote to call each of these four functions.

Listing 16.4: **Command2_Click Event in Win32API**

```
Private Sub Command2_Click()

Dim r As Long
Dim s As Long
Dim t As String

t = String(CInt(MAX_COMPUTERNAME_LENGTH + 1), Chr(0))
s = MAX_COMPUTERNAME_LENGTH
r = GetComputerName(t, s)
Text5.Text = Left(t, s)
```

```
t = String(UNLEN + 1, Chr(0))
s = UNLEN
r = GetUserName(t, s)
Text6.Text = Left(t, s)

t = String(MAX_PATH + 1, Chr(0))
s = MAX_PATH
r = GetSystemDirectory(t, s)
Text22.Text = Left(t, InStr(1, t, Chr(0)))

t = String(MAX_PATH + 1, Chr(0))
s = MAX_PATH
r = GetWindowsDirectory(t, s)
Text23.Text = Left(t, InStr(1, t, Chr(0)))

End Sub
```

I start by filling the string that the function will return with Null characters (Chr(0)). This ensures that Visual Basic has reserved sufficient space to hold the return value and that the Win32 API function won't accidentally overwrite something and cause a problem.

The easiest way to do this is to use the String function and pass it the maximum length of the field plus one and the Null character. This ensures that if the function returns a value whose length is the maximum permitted, there will be still be a Null character at the end of the field. This also makes it easy to find the end of the string, since the first Null character marks the true length of the string.

Then I assign the maximum length value to a temporary variable for the call. With the GetWindowsDirectory and the GetSystemDirectory routines, it isn't necessary to make this assignment. I could simply pass this value directly to the routine. But in the GetUserName and GetComputerName routines, this value is passed by reference, and the variable will hold the length of the returned string.

Since the GetWindowsDirectory and GetSystemDirectory routines don't return the length of the returned string, it is necessary to scan the returned string for the first Null character to find the true length. The InStr function makes this job a snap. This function should always find a Null character because the function itself should return a string of characters followed by a Null, and because I made sure that there is at least one Null beyond the maximum length of the return value.

Each of these routines returns a status value indicating if the routine was successful. If `r = 0`, then the call failed. If `r <> 0`, then the call succeeded. However, since I don't really care about the status code, I can safely ignore it and use the result of the function call.

Getting and Setting Environment Information

Using environment variables was common in DOS programs. You could define the root directory for an application in an environment variable and then detect it in your application to locate any necessary files. This practice has largely been replaced through the use of the Windows Registry, but sometimes you might still run into situations where environment variables may be useful. A typical example is when you want to return a value from your Visual Basic program that would affect how your batch file runs.

Visual Basic allows you to read environment strings through the Environ function, but it doesn't permit you to set them. However, the Win32 API includes functions to do both.

In the Win32API Demo program, select the Get Environment Info tab to bring up the controls to get and set environment variables. Simply fill in the name of an environment variable (for example, TEMP) and click the Get Environment Info button to retrieve its value, as shown in Figure 16.5. Then you can update the value and click the Set Environment Info button to make the change.

FIGURE 16.5:

Getting and setting environment information

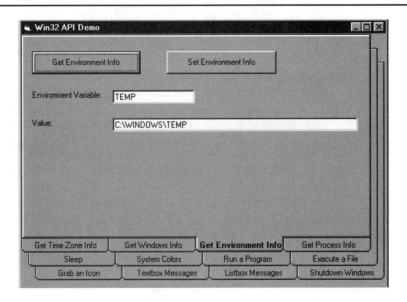

Listing 16.5 shows the header information for calling the environment information routines.

Listing 16.5:   Get Environment Information Header in Win32API

```
' ===========================================================
' = Get Environment Information                             =
' ===========================================================

Public Declare Function GetEnvironmentVariable Lib "kernel32" _
    Alias "GetEnvironmentVariableA" (ByVal lpName As String, _
    ByVal lpBuffer As String, ByVal nSize As Long) As Long

Public Declare Function SetEnvironmentVariable Lib "kernel32" _
    Alias "SetEnvironmentVariableA" (ByVal lpName As String, _
    ByVal lpValue As String) As Long
```

Retrieving Environment Information

To retrieve information from the function, simply pad a string buffer with Null characters and then pass the name of the environment variable, the buffer, and the size of the buffer to the GetEnvironmentVariable function. The function will either return 0, meaning that the function failed (probably the variable doesn't exist), or the number of characters returned in the string buffer. Listing 16.6 shows the routine for getting environment information.

Listing 16.6:   Command3_Click Event in Win32API

```
Private Sub Command3_Click()

Dim r As Long
Dim s As Long
Dim t As String

t = String(2049, Chr(0))
s = 2084

r = GetEnvironmentVariable(Text7.Text, t, s)
If r = 0 Then
```

```
       Text8.Text = "Variable not found."
   Else
       Text8.Text = Left(t, r)
   End If

   End Sub
```

Setting an Environment Variable

Setting an environment variable is even easier than getting one. Simply pass the name of the variable and its new value to the function and check for a 0 value to see if the routine failed. Listing 16.7 shows how this is done.

Listing 16.7:   **Command4_Click Event in Win32API**

```
   Private Sub Command4_Click()

   Dim r As Long

   r = SetEnvironmentVariable(Text7.Text, Text8.Text)

   If r = 0 Then
       Text8.Text = "Update unsuccessful"
   End If

   End Sub
```

Getting Process Information

One aspect that has always fascinated me about computers is performance analysis. I like watching how much processor time and memory my programs occupy. Unfortunately, Window 95 and 98 don't track this information, but Windows NT does.

However, you can still get information about a process in Windows 95 and 98, as shown in Figure 16.6. On a Windows NT system, you can watch the time values increase each time you click the Get Process Info button, as shown in Figure 16.7.

FIGURE 16.6:

Getting process information from Windows 95

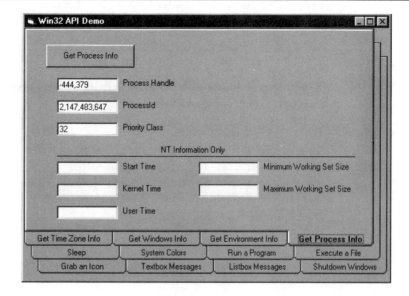

FIGURE 16.7:

Getting processing information from Windows NT

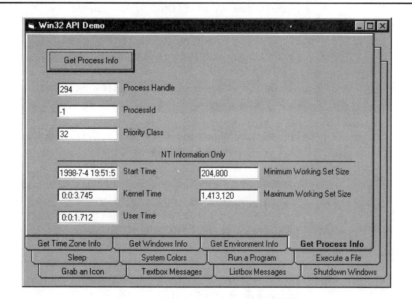

Listing 16.8 shows the header information for using the Win31 API functions to get information about a running program.

Listing 16.8:   **Get Process Information Header in Win32API**

```
' ============================================================
' = Get Process Information                                  =
' ============================================================

Public Const HIGH_PRIORITY_CLASS = &H80
Public Const IDLE_PRIORITY_CLASS = &H40
Public Const NORMAL_PRIORITY_CLASS = &H20
Public Const REALTIME_PRIORITY_CLASS = &H100

Public Type FILETIME
        dwLowDateTime As Long
        dwHighDateTime As Long
End Type

Public Declare Function FileTimeToSystemTime Lib "kernel32" _
    (lpFileTime As FILETIME, lpSystemTime As SYSTEMTIME) As Long

Public Declare Function GetCurrentProcess Lib "kernel32" _
    () As Long

Public Declare Function GetCurrentProcessId Lib "kernel32" _
    () As Long

Public Declare Function GetPriorityClass Lib "kernel32" _
    (ByVal hProcess As Long) As Long

Public Declare Function GetProcessTimes Lib "kernel32" _
    (ByVal hProcess As Long, lpCreationTime As FILETIME, _
    lpExitTime As FILETIME, lpKernelTime As FILETIME, _
    lpUserTime As FILETIME) As Long

Public Declare Function GetProcessWorkingSetSize Lib "kernel32" _
    (ByVal hProcess As Long, lpMinimumWorkingSetSize As Long, _
    lpMaximumWorkingSetSize As Long) As Long
```

The GetCurrentProcess function returns a pseudo handle to the current process. This value will be used for most of the other routines in this section. Unlike a real handle, the pseudo handle doesn't need to be closed when you are finished using it. However, if you do call the CloseHandle function, the call will have no effect.

The GetCurrentProcessId function returns the process ID for the current process. This value is guaranteed to be unique throughout the system while your program is running.

The GetPriorityClass function returns the general priority class for the process. This value is combined with each thread's priority to set the base priority for each thread. The priority class is broken into four basic groups:

• Real-time runs code at a priority higher than the operating system itself.

• High priority runs programs, which must respond quickly no matter what the computer's workload is like.

• Normal priority is where most applications should be run.

• Idle runs a program only when no other programs need the computer's resources.

WARNING   **Real-time out:** Running in real-time priority, or even high priority, for more than a few moments can cause serious problems with functions such as disk I/O transfers. Don't use it unless you know exactly what you're doing.

The GetProcessTimes function returns the time the application started, the time it finished, the amount of user processor time accumulated, and the amount of kernel processor time accumulated. These measurements are made using the FILETIME data structure, which is essentially a 64-bit integer. The start and stop time values are actual calendar entries, while the user and kernel processor time values are accumulated time values. This routine applies only to a Windows NT system. On a Windows 95 or 98 system, it will return an error.

To read the contents of a FILETIME structure, it is easiest to convert it to a SYSTEMTIME structure using the FileTimeToSystemTime routine. This routine converts the FILETIME values to a set of year, months, days, hours, minutes, seconds, and thousandths of a second. Each of these values is a normal 16-bit integer, which can be easily processed by Visual Basic programs. You can use a FILETIME structure to hold a date and time value by specifying the number of 100-nanosecond increments from 1 January 1601. You also can use it as a general counter that tracks the number of 100-nanosecond intervals that have accumulated during processing. The Get-ProcessTimes routine uses this structure for both.

The GetProcessWorkingSetSize routine returns the minimum working set size that will be allocated to the program. It also returns the maximum working set size that the memory manager will try to keep when the system becomes short on memory. This routine is also a Windows NT-only function. Windows 95 and 98 will return an error condition when it is called.

Retrieving Process Information

Listing 16.9 shows how easy it is to get information about your process. I don't bother checking for a zero value from the GetCurrentProcessId and GetCurrent-Process routines, because I assume that since my program is running, they should work. I do make sure that I have a valid process handle before I try to use it to extract any information based on the handle.

Listing 16.9: **Command5_Click Event in Win32API**

```
Private Sub Command5_Click()

Dim Pid As Long
Dim hProcess As Long
Dim pc As Long
Dim r As Long
Dim STime As FILETIME
Dim ETime As FILETIME
Dim KTime As FILETIME
Dim UTime As FILETIME
Dim minws As Long
Dim maxws As Long

Pid = GetCurrentProcessId
Text9.Text = FormatNumber(Pid, 0)

hProcess = GetCurrentProcess
Text10.Text = FormatNumber(hProcess, 0)

pc = GetPriorityClass(hProcess)
Text11.Text = FormatNumber(pc, 0)
```

```
If hProcess <> 0 Then
   pc = GetPriorityClass(hProcess)
   Text11.Text = FormatNumber(pc, 0)

   r = GetProcessTimes(hProcess, STime, ETime, KTime, UTime)
   If r <> 0 Then
      Text12.Text = FileTimeToString(STime)
      Text13.Text = FileTimeToString(KTime)
      Text14.Text = FileTimeToString(UTime)
   End If

   r = GetProcessWorkingSetSize(hProcess, minws, maxws)
   If r <> 0 Then
      Text15.Text = FormatNumber(minws, 0)
      Text16.Text = FormatNumber(maxws, 0)
   End If

End If

End Sub
```

Next, I grab the priority information using the GetPriorityClass function and display it to the user. Then I call GetProcessTimes to get information about when the program started and how much of the computer's resources were used to this point. Since the program is still running, the data in the lpExitTime parameter is undefined, so I don't bother displaying it. The GetWorkingSetSize routine returns information about memory allocation. If I get a valid return code, I simply format the information and display it.

Handling FILETIME Structures

To handle the results of the FILETIME structures I receive from the GetProcess-Times function, I created the FileTimeToString function, as shown in Listing 16.10.

Listing 16.10:   FileTimeToString Routine in Win32API

```
Public Function FileTimeToString(f As FILETIME) As String

Dim r As Long
Dim s As SYSTEMTIME
Dim t As String
```

```
    r = FileTimeToSystemTime(f, s)
    If r <> 0 Then
        t = FormatNumber(s.wYear, 0, , , vbFalse)
        t = t & "-" & FormatNumber(s.wMonth, 0)
        t = t & "-" & FormatNumber(s.wDay, 0)
        If t = "1601-1-1" Then
            t = ""
        End If
        t = t & " " & FormatNumber(s.wHour, 0)
        t = t & ":" & FormatNumber(s.wMinute, 0)
        t = t & ":" & FormatNumber(s.wSecond, 0)
        t = t & ":" & FormatNumber(s.wMilliseconds, 0)

    Else
        t = "Error in converting value"

    End If

    FileTimeToString = t

    End Function
```

Since Visual Basic doesn't handle 64-bit integers (at least in version 6), I use the FileTimeToSystemTime Win32 API. This converts the very big integer into a series of integers for each different unit of time. Then I simply convert each of the SYSTEMTIME fields into the appropriate value. Note that I don't bother to convert the milliseconds to a fraction of a second; instead, I simply display it as its own unit of measure.

I also suppress the year, month, and day values when they equal "1601-1-1". When I see this value, it's because the data was used to accumulate the number of 100-nanosecond intervals, so it doesn't hold a real date value.

Sleeping for a While

From time to time, your program may need to wait for a while. You can always use a DoEvents spin loop, but that can be sometimes wasteful. The Sleep function may be a viable alternative.

You can see how this works by displaying the Sleep tab of the Win32API Demo program and clicking the Sleep button. This disables the program for five seconds by calling the Sleep routine. To create Figure 16.8, I took a DOS session (please don't make fun of me, I still like to use DOS for copying files and looking at directories), moved it around the window for a few seconds, and captured the result. It's pretty ugly.

FIGURE 16.8:

Sleeping for a while

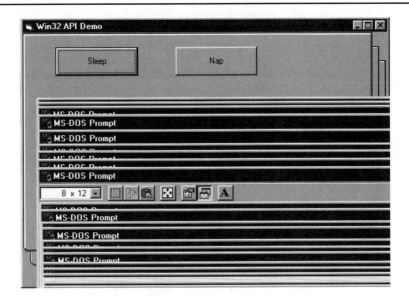

Clicking on the Nap button allows the form to be repainted normally while the program is waiting for the naps (one-tenth second pauses) to finish. It doesn't suffer from the problems that are encountered when the program sleeps for the entire five seconds.

As shown in Listing 16.11, the Sleep function takes a single parameter: A Long value that contains the number of milliseconds the program should wait before it begins execution. During this time, your program is completely idle. It can't respond to any messages, including system messages. Use this routine with care! If you specify a value of 0, the current time slice is ended and the program will resume the next time it's dispatched.

FIGURE 16.9:

Taking a series of short naps

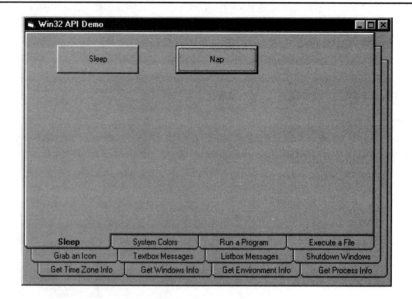

Sleeping at the wrong time can be dangerous: The Sleep routine stops your program from all activities including functions that Visual Basic usually performs on your behalf, such as repainting the form and handling user interactions. If you use the Sleep routine while a window is being created, it can't respond to messages, which could eventually hang your entire system until the sleep period is over.

Listing 16.11:   Get Sleep Header Information in Win32API

```
' =============================================================
' = Get Sleep Information                                      =
' =============================================================

Public Declare Sub Sleep Lib "kernel32" _
    (ByVal dwMilliseconds As Long)
```

Going to Sleep

Using the Sleep subroutine is very easy. I simply call it with the number of milliseconds I wish to wait until the program resumes execution, as shown in Listing 16.12. This routine displays a message box, then waits five seconds and displays another message box.

Listing 16.12:   Command6_Click Event in Win32API

```
Private Sub Command6_Click()

MsgBox "Ready for bed."

Sleep (5000)

MsgBox "Waking up."

End Sub
```

Taking a Nap

The problem with using the Sleep routine as in Listing 16.12 is that it prevents your program from responding to normal messages such as those that request your program to repaint itself. Listing 16.13 is a hybrid of the traditional DoEvents spin loop and the Sleep routine. I call this "taking a nap." Rather than sleeping for the entire five seconds, this routine only pauses for a tenth of a second before making a call to DoEvents to allow it to catch up with any necessary processing.

Listing 16.13:   Command7_Click Event in Win32API

```
Private Sub Command7_Click()

Dim i As Integer

MsgBox "Ready for bed."

For i = 1 To 50
   Sleep (100)
   DoEvents
Next i
```

```
MsgBox "Waking up."

End Sub
```

Playing with System Colors

The next two routines—GetSysColor and SetSysColor—allow you to change the system's color configuration, much like the Display applet in the Control Panel. They affect the entire system, not just your local program. The changes last until the next time the system is rebooted or until you change them again in the current session.

> **WARNING**
>
> **Think twice before you change it:** These routines are capable of changing the system color scheme for your computer. With very little work, it is possible to get the color information so messed up that you can't use your computer (for example, setting all of the colors on your system, including fonts, to Windows Desktop Green). You might need to reboot you system in order to resolve the problem.

To see for yourself, simply click on the System Colors tab, then click the three buttons in sequence:

- The Get System Color button changes the background color of the text box to the right of the button.

- The Set System Colors button changes all of the button face objects on the screen to red. This includes all windows for all programs and the background of such objects as menu bars, toolbars, scroll bars, and so on.

- The Reset System Colors button restores the system colors from the text box's background color (saved when you clicked the Get System Color button), as shown in Figure 16.10.

Unlike the other routines I've discussed in this chapter, this pair of routines actually allows you to make a major change in the Windows environment. You can change the value of any of the standard Windows colors. As typical of many Win32 API calls, there are many constants associated with the functions, as you can see in Listing 16.14. Each constant represents a different aspect of the Windows color scheme you can change.

FIGURE 16.10:

Restoring the button
face color

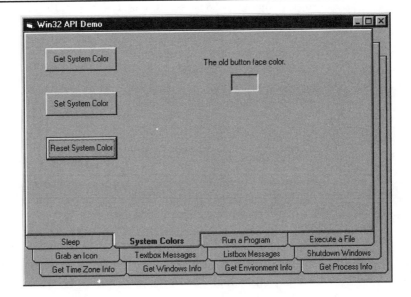

Listing 16.14:   Get System Color Information Header in Win32API

```
' ============================================================
' = Get System Color Information                             =
' ============================================================

        Public Const COLOR_ACTIVEBORDER = 10
        Public Const COLOR_ACTIVECAPTION = 2
        Public Const COLOR_APPWORKSPACE = 12
        Public Const COLOR_BACKGROUND = 1
        Public Const COLOR_BTNFACE = 15
        Public Const COLOR_BTNHIGHLIGHT = 20
        Public Const COLOR_BTNSHADOW = 16
        Public Const COLOR_BTNTEXT = 18
        Public Const COLOR_CAPTIONTEXT = 9
        Public Const COLOR_GRAYTEXT = 17
        Public Const COLOR_HIGHLIGHT = 13
        Public Const COLOR_HIGHLIGHTTEXT = 14
        Public Const COLOR_INACTIVEBORDER = 11
        Public Const COLOR_INACTIVECAPTION = 3
```

```
Public Const COLOR_INACTIVECAPTIONTEXT = 19
Public Const COLOR_MENU = 4
Public Const COLOR_MENUTEXT = 7
Public Const COLOR_SCROLLBAR = 0
Public Const COLOR_WINDOW = 5
Public Const COLOR_WINDOWFRAME = 6
Public Const COLOR_WINDOWTEXT = 8

Public Declare Function GetSysColor Lib "user32" _
    (ByVal nIndex As Long) As Long

Public Declare Function SetSysColors Lib "user32" _
    (ByVal nChanges As Long, lpSysColor As Long, _
    lpColorValues As Long) As Long
```

The GetSysColor routine returns a Long value containing the color of a specific system object, such as a button face or button text.

The SetSysColors routine takes an array of system objects and a second array of color values, where each element of the color value array corresponds to the same element in the system objects array. You specify the number of system objects in the array (and the number of elements in the color array for that matter) as the first value to the function. Note that both the system objects and their colors are stored as normal variables. When you call the routine, you must specify the first element of the array rather than the array itself.

Retrieving and Saving the Color

The routine in Listing 16.15 is fairly simple. It just retrieves the color of the button face object and saves it as the background color of the Text17 text box.

Listing 16.15: **Command8_Click Event in Win32API**

```
Private Sub Command8_Click()

Dim c As Long

c = GetSysColor(COLOR_BTNFACE)
Text17.BackColor = c

End Sub
```

Setting the Color

The next routine, shown in Listing 16.16, sets the button face object to red. Note that even though I am passing an array to the routine, I need to pass the first element of the array. The routine will find the subsequent elements without any problems.

Listing 16.16:   Command9_Click Event in Win32API

```
Private Sub Command9_Click()

Dim c As Long
Dim elements(2) As Long
Dim colors(2) As Long

elements(0) = COLOR_BTNFACE
colors(0) = RGB(255, 0, 0)

c = SetSysColors(1, elements(0), colors(0))
End Sub
```

Restoring the Color

Finally, I restore the button face color from the Text17 text box using the same technique that I used to set it.

Listing 16.17:   Command10_Click Event in Win32API

```
Private Sub Command10_Click()

Dim elements(2) As Long
Dim c As Long
Dim colors(2) As Long

elements(0) = COLOR_BTNFACE
colors(0) = Text17.BackColor

c = SetSysColors(1, elements(0), colors(0))

End Sub
```

Running a Program

Using the Win32 API to run a program may make more sense then you think. The Shell function in Visual Basic already provides a way to start a program, but you can use the Win32 API calls to start your own program and control its initial environment. You can also track the program's execution and wait for it to complete.

For example, to play Solitaire, click the Run a Program tab and click the Play Solitaire button. After Solitaire has started, a message box will appear letting you know that the game has been started, as shown in Figure 16.11. Before you click OK in the message box, notice that the program is still responding to messages. You can move another window over the demo program's window, and it will be repainted properly. After you click the OK button, notice that the program is frozen and won't even repaint itself. After you close Solitaire, the demo program runs normally.

FIGURE 16.11:

Playing Solitaire from the Win32 API Demo program

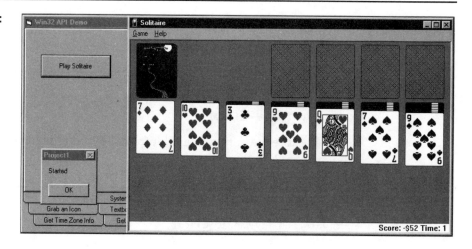

Running your own program under the Win32 API looks complicated from the number of data structures involved, as shown in Listing 16.18, but it really isn't that bad.

Listing 16.18:   Process Header Information in Win32API

```
' ===============================================================
' = Process                                                     =
' ===============================================================

Public Const CREATE_NEW_CONSOLE = &H10
Public Const CREATE_NEW_PROCESS_GROUP = &H200
Public Const CREATE_SUSPENDED = &H4
Public Const DEBUG_PROCESS = &H1
Public Const DEBUG_ONLY_THIS_PROCESS = &H2
Public Const DETACHED_PROCESS = &H8
Public Const INFINITE = &HFFFF

Public Const SYNCHRONIZE = &H100000

Public Type PROCESS_INFORMATION
        hProcess As Long
        hThread As Long
        dwProcessId As Long
        dwThreadId As Long
End Type

Public Type STARTUPINFO
        cb As Long
        lpReserved As String
        lpDesktop As String
        lpTitle As String
        dwX As Long
        dwY As Long
        dwXSize As Long
        dwYSize As Long
        dwXCountChars As Long
        dwYCountChars As Long
        dwFillAttribute As Long
        dwFlags As Long
        wShowWindow As Integer
        cbReserved2 As Integer
        lpReserved2 As Long
        hStdInput As Long
        hStdOutput As Long
```

```
        hStdError As Long
End Type

Public Declare Function CloseHandle Lib "kernel32" _
    (ByVal hObject As Long) As Long

Public Declare Function CreateProcess Lib "kernel32" _
    Alias "CreateProcessA" _
    (ByVal lpApplicationName As String, _
    ByVal lpCommandLine As String, _
    ByVal lpProcessAttributes As Long, _
    ByVal lpThreadAttributes As Long, _
    ByVal bInheritHandles As Long, _
    ByVal dwCreationFlags As Long, _
    ByVal lpEnvironment As Long, _
    ByVal lpCurrentDriectory As String, _
    lpStartupInfo As STARTUPINFO, _
    lpProcessInformation As PROCESS_INFORMATION) As Long

Public Declare Function OpenProcess Lib "kernel32" _
    (ByVal dwDesiredAccess As Long, _
    ByVal bInheritHandle As Long, _
    ByVal dwProcessId As Long) As Long

Public Declare Function WaitForInputIdle Lib "user32" _
    (ByVal hProcess As Long, _
    ByVal dwMilliseconds As Long) As Long

Public Declare Function WaitForSingleObject Lib "kernel32" _
    (ByVal hHandle As Long, _
    ByVal dwMilliseconds As Long) As Long
```

The PROCESS_INFORMATION structure contains information returned by the Create-Process function after the process was started. The hProcess and hThread items contain handles for the process and its primary thread. The dwProcessId and dw-ThreadId functions return unique ID values for the process and its primary thread.

When starting a process with the CreateProcess function, you need to fill out some information that determines how the process will be started. This information is stored in the STARTUPINFO control block. For the most part, these parameters aren't important. They just need to be properly initialized to the zero or null state before the CreateProcess function is called.

The `CreateProcess` function is at the heart of running a program. It takes a command, the name of a program, or both and attempts to start the program based on this information, plus the name of the default directory. For the most part, these parameters should be set to a default value when launching a standard Windows program.

The `CloseHandle` routine simply closes a handle. Unless you have a good reason to keep a process handle open, you should close it. This will prevent problems later on when the program tries to close itself, since Windows keeps track of all open handles. Besides, you can always convert a process ID into a handle using the `OpenProcess` routine.

The `OpenProcess` routine converts a process ID value into a valid process handle. Note that on Windows NT systems, you may need to worry about access rights to the program.

The `WaitForInputIdle` function waits for a process to enter into a state where the program is waiting for input from the user. When starting a program, this is one way to verify that the program's initialization phase has been completed.

The `WaitForSingleObject` function waits for a process to complete or for it to time out. In either case, the program that called `WaitForSingleObject` will resume processing. The return value indicates whether the process completed, the timeout value was reached, or an error occurred somewhere while processing this command.

Most of the work to run a program has been encapsulated into two routines: The `RunProg` function runs a program, and the `WaitProg` function waits for a program to finish.

Starting a Program

The `RunProg` function, shown in Listing 16.19, begins by initializing the STARTUP-INFO with zeros or null strings except for the length of the control block. I set the cb element to the length of the structure.

Listing 16.19:   RunProg Function in Win32API

```
Public Function RunProg(prog As String) As Long

Dim p As PROCESS_INFORMATION
Dim s As STARTUPINFO
```

```
Dim r As Long

s.cb = Len(s)
s.dwFlags = 0
s.lpDesktop = vbNullString
s.lpReserved = vbNullString
s.lpTitle = vbNullString

r = CreateProcess(prog, vbNullString, 0, 0, True, _
    NORMAL_PRIORITY_CLASS, 0, vbNullString, s, p)
If r <> 0 Then
    r = CloseHandle(p.hThread)
    If r <> 0 Then
        r = WaitForInputIdle(p.hProcess, INFINITE)
        r = CloseHandle(p.hProcess)
    End If
End If

RunProg = p.dwProcessId

End Function
```

Then I use the control block, plus the name of the program and a few other null parameters to call the CreateProcess function. If this function returns a successful return code, I close the thread handle (hThread) with the CloseHandle function.

Next, I use the WaitForInputIdle function to suspend the calling program until the newly created program is waiting for user input and there is nothing in the input queue to be processed. I do this to ensure that the program has been completely initialized. Once I've finished with the process handle, I close the handle. Then I can return the process ID as the value of the function and return.

Waiting for a Program to Finish

Waiting for the program to finish is easy. I call the OpenProcess function to get a handle to the specified process ID. Then I call the WaitForSingleObject using that handle and tell it I'm willing to wait an infinite amount of time for the program to finish. When the function returns, I close the handle and return. Listing 16.20 shows the WaitProg subroutine.

WaitProg Routine in Win32API

```
Public Sub WaitProg(Pid As Long)

Dim r As Long
Dim pHandle As Long

pHandle = OpenProcess(SYNCHRONIZE, 0, Pid)

r = WaitForSingleObject(pHandle, INFINITE)

r = CloseHandle(pHandle)

End Sub
```

The WaitForSingleObject function works much like the Sleep routine. Both prevent your program from handling any messages or responding to user input until
the routine is finished. So, rather than specifying INFINITE as a timeout value, you
might want to use a small value, such as 50 or 100 milliseconds, inside a DoEvents
spin loop. Another option would be to specify a timeout value of 0 and periodically
call the WaitForSingleObject function. If the function returns a value of WAIT_
TIMEOUT, then the program is still running. If the function returns a value of
WAIT_FAILED, then the program is no longer running.

Launching the Program

Listing 16.21 shows how I used both the RunProg and the WaitProg routines to
launch the Solitaire program. I call MsgBox after the program is started and again
after the program has finished.

Command11_Click Event in Win32API

```
Private Sub Command11_Click()

Dim p As Long

p = RunProg("c:\windows\sol.exe")

MsgBox "Started"
```

```
If p <> 0 Then
    WaitProg p
End If

MsgBox "Finished"

End Sub
```

Running a File

One of the nice features of Windows is that it lets the user double-click on a file and have the operating system determine which program should be used to view the file. Visual Basic doesn't offer this feature, but it is available with a simple Win32 API call named ShellExecute.

To see how this works, click on the Execute a File tab and enter the name of the file you wish to open in the text box. Clicking the Execute File button starts the program to display the file. Figure 16.12 shows an example.

FIGURE 16.12:

Viewing a file with the Win32 API Demo program

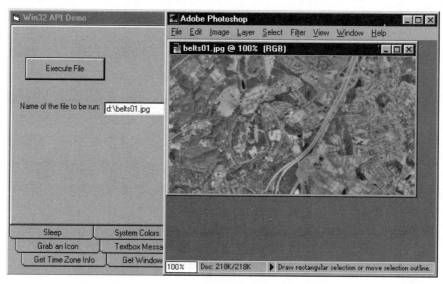

As shown in Listing 16.22, the ShellExecute function takes the name of a file and will load the program associated with the file type, then load and display the file. If the file is a program, it will automatically load and execute the program.

Listing 16.22:   Run a File Header Information in Win32API

```
' ==========================================================
' = Run the program associated with a file                 =
' ==========================================================

' Error conditions
Public Const ERROR_BAD_FORMAT = 11&
Public Const ERROR_FILE_NOT_FOUND = 2&
Public Const ERROR_PATH_NOT_FOUND = 3&
Public Const SE_ERR_ACCESSDENIED = 5
Public Const SE_ERR_ASSOCINCOMPLETE = 27
Public Const SE_ERR_DDEBUSY = 30
Public Const SE_ERR_DDEFAIL = 29
Public Const SE_ERR_DDETIMEOUT = 28
Public Const SE_ERR_DLLNOTFOUND = 32
Public Const SE_ERR_FNF = 2
Public Const SE_ERR_NOASSOC = 31
Public Const SE_ERR_OOM = 8
Public Const SE_ERR_PNF = 3
Public Const SE_ERR_SHARE = 26

' ShowCmd values
Public Const SW_HIDE = 0
Public Const SW_MINIMIZE = 6
Public Const SW_RESTORE = 9
Public Const SW_SHOW = 5
Public Const SW_SHOWMAXIMIZED = 3
Public Const SW_SHOWMINIMIZED = 2
Public Const SW_SHOWMINNOACTIVE = 7
Public Const SW_SHOWNA = 8
Public Const SW_SHOWNOACTIVATE = 4
Public Const SW_SHOWNORMAL = 1

Public Declare Function ShellExecute Lib "shell32.dll" _
    Alias "ShellExecuteA" _
    (ByVal hWnd As Long, ByVal lpOperation As String, _
    ByVal lpFile As String, ByVal lpParameters As String, _
    ByVal lpDirectory As String, ByVal nShowCmd As Long) As Long
```

ShellExecute needs a handle to a window (hWnd) in case a message box needs to be displayed.

The lpOperation argument can be one of the following:

- open opens the file with the program associated with its file type.
- print prints the file with the program associated with the file type.
- explore opens the directory in a window.

A null string will default to open.

The lpFile argument contains the name of the file to be executed, and lp-Parameters contains a list of parameters to be passed to a program if lpFile specifies an executable program. The default directory is specified in lpDirectory, and the nShowCmd parameter contains one of the SW constants listed in Listing 16.22. These constants describe how the program is displayed when it's started.

Getting the Filename

To make the ShellExecute function a little easier to use, I built the routine shown in Listing 16.23. The StartMeUp routine takes the name of the file as a parameter and extracts the current directory from it by looking for the last backslash and grabbing all of the characters that precede it. If I don't find the backslash, I use the current value of App.Path as the default directory. Then I call the ShellExecute routine to start the program that will open the file.

Listing 16.23:   **StartMeUp Routine in Win32API**

```
Public Function StartMeUp(f As String)

Dim i As Integer
Dim d As String

i = InStrRev(f, "\")
If i > 0 Then
    d = Left(f, i - 1)

Else
    d = App.Path

End If
```

```
StartMeUp = ShellExecute(Form1.hWnd, "open", f, vbNullString, d, _
    SW_SHOWNORMAL)

End Function
```

Displaying the File

The program to display the file is shown in Listing 16.24. It simply takes the contents of the text box beside the command button and uses it to call the StartMeUp function.

Listing 16.24:   Command12_Click Event in Win32API

```
Private Sub Command12_Click()

If StartMeUp(Text18.Text) <= 32 Then
    MsgBox "Unable to start the application associated with the file"

End If

End Sub
```

If the function returns a value less than 33, some sort of error occurred while trying to start the application—either the file doesn't exist or there isn't a program associated with the file.

Grabbing an Icon

Have you ever wanted to get the icon associated with a file? It's a little harder than I originally thought, but not really all that bad. The biggest drawback is that it is a relatively expensive operation. You can see this for yourself when you choose View ➤ Options and select the File Types tab in Windows Explorer. This tab displays the icons along with the file type information, as shown in Figure 16.13, and Windows takes a fair amount of time to load this information the first time it needs it.

The File Types tab of the
Windows Explorer Options
dialog box

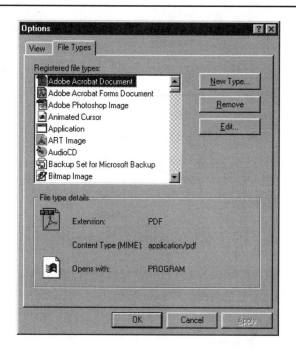

TIP

Get it the first time only: Save any icons you get in an ImageList control so that you can use them in a TreeView, ListView, or ImageCombo control. Specify the file type as the key so you can easily determine if you have already retrieved the icon.

To grab an icon with the Win32 API Demo program, simply click on the Grab an Icon tab and fill in the filename you wish to use. When you click the Grab an Icon button, the program attempts to determine the filename of the program that is associated with the file's type and then grabs the first icon in the program file. It will save the name of the program in the Program Name field and display the icon in the Icon Image square, as shown in Figure 16.14.

FIGURE 16.14:

Grabbing an Icon based on file type

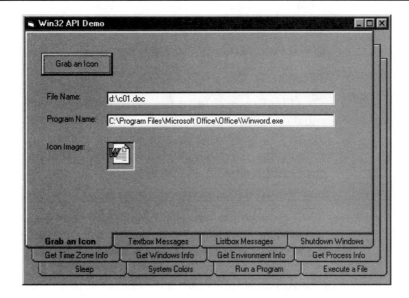

There are only four routines needed to retrieve an icon, as you can see in Listing 16.25.

Listing 16.25:   Get Icon Header Information in Win32API

```
' ===========================================================
' = Get the icon associated with a program                  =
' ===========================================================

Public Declare Function DestroyIcon Lib "user32" _
    (ByVal hIcon As Long) As Long

Public Declare Function DrawIcon Lib "user32" _
    (ByVal hdc As Long, ByVal x As Long, ByVal y As Long, _
    ByVal hIcon As Long) As Long

Public Declare Function ExtractIcon Lib "shell32.dll" _
    Alias "ExtractIconA" _
    (ByVal hInst As Long, ByVal lpszExeFileName As String, _
    ByVal nIconIndex As Long) As Long
```

```
Public Declare Function FindExecutable Lib "shell32.dll" _
   Alias "FindExecutableA" _
   (ByVal lpFile As String, ByVal lpDirectory As String, _
   ByVal lpResult As String) As Long
```

The FindExecutable routine returns the filename of the program associated with the file. Note that the filename is supplied in two parts to this routine: The filename itself is passed as the lpFile parameter, and the current directory is passed in the lpDirectory parameter. The filename of the executable program is returned in lpResult.

The ExtractIcon routine takes the name of an executable file and extracts an icon from it. It needs a handle to an instance, which you can get from the App .hInstance object. Since a program can have more than one icon, you can get the number of icons by specifying −1 for the nIconIndex parameter. Otherwise, you would specify 1 for the first icon, 2 for the second, and so forth. The function returns a Long containing either the number of icons in the file or a handle to the icon.

The DrawIcon function takes a device context (hdc), a set of coordinates (x and y), and a handle to an icon, and draws the icon on the device context. Since the ExtractIcon function returns a handle to the icon, you need to close the handle using the DestroyIcon function.

The routine for getting an icon is shown in Listing 16.26. I start this routine by padding a string (t) with Null characters that will hold the name of the program associated with the file type. Then I clear the Picture1 control, where I will display the icon and call the FindExecutable routine to get the name of the program containing the icon. If the FindExecutable routine worked, it will return a value greater than 32. If it doesn't, I issue an error message and return.

Listing 16.26:   Command13_Click Event in Win32API

```
Private Sub Command13_Click()

Dim r As Long
Dim t As String
Dim hIcon As Long

t = String(MAX_PATH + 1, Chr(0))
```

```
Picture1.Cls
r = FindExecutable(Text19.Text, d, t)
If r > 32 Then
    Text20.Text = Left(t, InStr(1, t, Chr(0)))

    r = ExtractIcon(App.hInstance, Text20.Text, -1)
    If r > 0 Then
        hIcon = ExtractIcon(App.hInstance, Text20.Text, 1)
        r = DrawIcon(Picture1.hdc, 0, 0, hIcon)
        r = DestroyIcon(hIcon)
    End If

Else
    Text20.Text = "No associated application."

End If

End Sub
```

If the program was found, I compute the true length of the string by looking for the first Null (Chr(0)) character and save the result it in the Text20 text box. Next, I determine the number of icons available by calling the ExtractIcon routine with an icon number of −1. If the number of available icons is greater than zero, I get a handle to the first icon in the file. Then I draw the icon on the Picture control and destroy the handle to the icon.

Using New Functions for Text Boxes

The text box is just another specialized window in the Windows operating system. It has a lot of capabilities that are simply not available in Visual Basic. These capabilities can be accessed using the Win32 API.

Windows is based on the concept of messages and lots of big and little rectangles on the display that send and receive messages. A window can be a form, a command button, or even a text box. Any object in your Visual Basic program that has an hWnd property is a true window that can send and receive messages.

A message corresponds to a request or accompanies a piece of data. For example, a window might receive the WM_CLEAR message, which instructs the window to clear the contents of the window. A WM_CHAR message might accompany a character that is to be processed by a window. A text box may simply display the character in its own space, while a form may pass the message onto a command button for processing if the mouse pointer is over the button's window area.

The SendMessage function is one way to send requests to another window for processing. In the Win32 API Demo program, I used the SendMessage function to make a text box read-only. To see how this works, click on the Textbox Messages tab. Then type some text into the text box, as shown in Figure 16.15. Clicking the Make Read Only button prevents you from making any changes in the text box. Clicking the Restore Read/Write button allows you to make changes again. Also, you can restore the contents of the text box to its previous value by pressing the Escape key. (The Listbox Messages tab in the demo program works in a similar manner.)

FIGURE 16.15:

Making a text box read-only or read/write

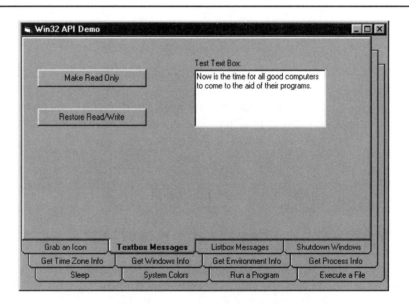

The SendMessage function takes four parameters, as shown in Listing 16.27.

Listing 16.27:   Send Message Header Information in Win32API

```
' ==============================================================
' = Send Message                                               =
' ==============================================================

Public Const CB_FINDSTRING = &H14C
Public Const CB_FINDSTRINGEXACT = &H158
Public Const CB_LIMITTEXT = &H141
Public Const CB_SETITEMHEIGHT = &H153
Public Const CB_SETLOCALE = &H159
Public Const CB_SHOWDROPDOWN = &H14F

Public Const EM_CANUNDO = &HC6
Public Const EM_EMPTYUNDOBUFFER = &HCD
Public Const EM_GETFIRSTVISIBLELINE = &HCE
Public Const EM_GETLINE = &HC4
Public Const EM_GETLINECOUNT = &HBA
Public Const EM_GETWORDBREAKPROC = &HD1
Public Const EM_LIMITTEXT = &HC5
Public Const EM_LINEFROMCHAR = &HC9
Public Const EM_LINEINDEX = &HBB
Public Const EM_LINELENGTH = &HC1
Public Const EM_LINESCROLL = &HB6
Public Const EM_SETREADONLY = &HCF
Public Const EM_SETSEL = &HB1
Public Const EM_SETTABSTOPS = &HCB
Public Const EM_SETWORDBREAKPROC = &HD0
Public Const EM_UNDO = &HC7

Public Const LB_FINDSTRING = &H18F
Public Const LB_GETTEXTLEN = &H18A
Public Const LB_GETTOPINDEX = &H18E
Public Const LB_SETTABSTOPS = &H192
Public Const LB_SETTOPINDEX = &H197

Public Const WM_CLEAR = &H303
Public Const WM_CLOSE = &H10
Public Const WM_COMMAND = &H111
Public Const WM_COMMNOTIFY = &H44
Public Const WM_COPY = &H301
```

```
Public Const WM_CUT = &H300
Public Const WM_GETFONT = &H31
Public Const WM_GETHOTKEY = &H33
Public Const WM_GETMINMAXINFO = &H24
Public Const WM_GETTEXT = &HD
Public Const WM_GETTEXTLENGTH = &HE
Public Const WM_PAINT = &HF
Public Const WM_PASTE = &H302
Public Const WM_SIZE = &H5
Public Const WM_SYSCOMMAND = &H112
Public Const WM_UNDO = &H304


Public Declare Function SendMessage Lib "user32" Alias "SendMessageA" _
    (ByVal hWnd As Long, ByVal wMsg As Long, ByVal wParam As Long, _
    lParam As Any) As Long
```

The hWnd parameter is the handle to the window that will receive the message. The wMsg parameter contains the message number to be sent. The wParam and lParam parameters contain additional information that is related to the message, such as the character being received, or return information, such as a string of characters from the current line of the text in the window.

Using the SendMessage function is both easy and difficult at the same time. Calling the function is very easy—simply specify the handle of the window that will receive the message, include the message number itself and any other required information, and make the call. Choosing the appropriate message is hard. Not all messages available in Windows can be used safely. Also, many messages duplicate functions already available in Visual Basic. The trick is to find the messages that work and to avoid the messages that don't work.

Marking a Window as Read-Only

The EM_SETREADONLY message is one example of a message that works properly with Visual Basic and doesn't duplicate a function already available. The EM_SET-READONLY message marks a window as read-only. If the user tries to enter any text into this field, it will be ignored. This includes paste operations as well as when the user enters characters from the keyboard. In order to mark the window as read-only, I need to specify a value of 1 for the wParam parameter, as shown in Listing 16.28.

Listing 16.28:   **Command14_Click Event in Win32API**

```
Private Sub Command14_Click()

Dim r As Long

r = SendMessage(Text21.hWnd, EM_SETREADONLY, 1, 0)

End Sub
```

Restoring a Window to Read/Write

To restore the window to read/write, I call SendMessage with EM_SETREADONLY and a wParam of 0, as shown in Listing 16.29.

Listing 16.29:   **Command15_Click Event in Win32API**

```
Private Sub Command15_Click()

Dim r As Long

r = SendMessage(Text21.hWnd, EM_SETREADONLY, 0, 0)

End Sub
```

Adding an Undo Buffer

Adding an undo buffer is a useful addition to a text box. Listing 16.30 shows how to use the EM_CANUNDO and the EM_UNDO messages to allow the user to undo the latest change by pressing the Escape key.

Listing 16.30:   **Text21_KeyPress Event in Win32API**

```
Private Sub Text21_KeyPress(KeyAscii As Integer)

Dim r As Long
If KeyAscii = 27 Then
    r = SendMessage(Text21.hWnd, EM_CANUNDO, 0, 0)
```

```
          If r <> 0 Then
          r = SendMessage(Text21.hWnd, EM_UNDO, 0, 0)

      End If

      KeyAscii = 0

   End If

   End Sub
```

In the `KeyPress` event of the text box, I check to see if the user pressed the Escape key (`KeyAscii = 27`). If so, I check to see if the text box can undo the latest change. This means I send the `EM_CANUNDO` message to the text box. A nonzero response means that the change can be undone. In that case, I pass the `EM_UNDO` message to instruct the window to undo the last change. Finally, I set the `KeyAscii` value to 0 to prevent the character from being added to the text box.

Shutting Down Windows

Probably the most dangerous Win32 API routine I'm going to talk about in this chapter is `ExitWindowEx`. This routine will literally shut down Windows. You have the usual shutdown options available— Logoff, Reboot, and Shutdown— plus one new one. The Force option allows you to shut down the computer immediately without checking to see if it is okay to shut down.

WARNING **You can't turn back, unless you get lucky:** Once you execute the `Exit-WindowsEx` function, you can't stop the shutdown process, unless you have a program that can respond to the `WM_QUERYENDSESSION` message that is issued as part of the normal shutdown process. See the discussion of the SysInfo control in Chapter 6 for more details about how to trap and respond to shutdown requests in Visual Basic.

To shut down Windows from the Win32 API Demo program, select the Shut down Windows tab, click the Shutdown button, and respond OK to the message box display, as shown in Figure 16.16. Windows will shut itself down and wait for you to restart the system.

Shutting down Windows from
the Win32 API Demo program

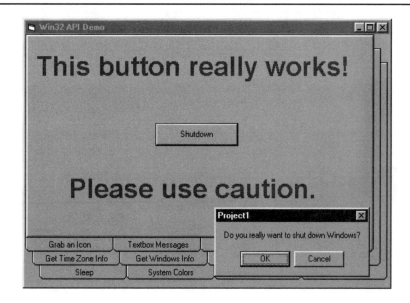

The ExitWindowsEx function takes two parameters, one of which you can only
pass a value of 0. The other parameter takes any of the EWX constants listed in
Listing 16.31.

Listing 16.31:   Shutdown Windows Header Information in Win32API

```
' ===============================================================
' = Shutdown Windows                                            =
' ===============================================================

Public Const EWX_FORCE = 4
Public Const EWX_LOGOFF = 0
Public Const EWX_REBOOT = 2
Public Const EWX_SHUTDOWN = 1

Public Declare Function ExitWindowsEx Lib "user32" _
    (ByVal uFlags As Long, ByVal dwReserved As Long) As Long
```

For a normal shutdown, you would use EWX_SHUTDOWN. The EWX_FORCE option
does not bother querying other applications if they are prepared to shut down; it

kills the system as quickly as possible. This means that there is a possibility of corrupt data on the disk because an application did not have the opportunity to post its data to disk before the shutdown was performed.

The program to shut down Windows is shown in Listing 16.32. When the command button is pressed, I verify that the user really wants to shut down Windows. If so, then I call the ExitWindowEx routine to perform a normal shutdown. There are statements that follow this function, but they won't be executed if the shutdown request was successful.

Listing 16.32:   Command18_Click in Win32API

```
Private Sub Command18_Click()

Dim r As Long

r = MsgBox("Do you really want to shut down Windows?", vbOKCancel)

If r = vbOK Then
    r = ExitWindowsEx(EWX_SHUTDOWN, 0)
    If r <> 0 Then
        MsgBox "Shutdown in progress."
    Else
        MsgBox "Shutdown unsuccessful."
    End If
End If

End Sub
```

Final Thoughts

Using the Win32 API can add value to your programs. You can get access to information that you need but Visual Basic doesn't provide. As you also saw, using the Win32 API is not an exact science. You need a good working knowledge of Windows and C in order to understand what is going on. You should expect problems the first time you try a function, but once you've solved them, you shouldn't expect problems until the next version of Visual Basic or Windows.

There are three reasons that anyone would use the Win32 API from Visual Basic:

- You need information from Windows that Visual Basic doesn't provide. A good example of this is getting time zone information.

- You want or need to perform a function you can't do in Visual Basic. A good example of this is the `Sleep` function.

- You want to improve performance.

I usually don't buy the improved performance argument. Although using Win32 API calls to improve performance may speed up some aspects of your program, it costs a lot to maintain the more complex code. With the speed of the current release of Visual Basic, I don't think that the performance enhancements justify the additional costs. If you feel otherwise, perhaps you should consider the impact of replacing Visual Basic with Visual C++, since you might squeeze a little more performance out of the application.

I never realized the Visual Basic was missing time zone information until I tried to write my own e-mail program. I wanted to include a qualifier that described that I was using Eastern Daylight Saving Time (EDT) on one of the headers I was building. Nowhere in Visual Basic could I find that information. I eventually decided that it wasn't worth the effort, and I just marked the messages as local time.

The `Sleep` routine is an interesting tool that I wish Visual Basic provided. In several programs, I've come across places where I would like to wait for a few moments, but I didn't want to create a `DoEvents` spin loop or build a timer routine to count the seconds. The `Sleep` routine allows me to build a `Sleep` spin loop that is much closer to what I really wanted—a low-overhead delay function.

Getting an icon for a file type and launching a program to process a particular type of file are some worthwhile functions that should be in Visual Basic. As time goes on, you may see more and more general-purpose applets that perform small, specialized tasks. Without a mechanism to determine what program processes which types of file, it will be impossible to take advantage of these applets.

CHAPTER

SEVENTEEN

Making Visual Basic Do What You Want

- Your own screen saver

- Your own icons on the Windows Taskbar system tray

- A job scheduler program

- Windows Registry access

- A Registry tool

Visual Basic is my tool of choice when programming in Windows. With version 6.0, there are very few things you can't do in Visual Basic, especially if you use the Win32 API functions, which I covered in the previous chapter.

In this chapter, I'm going to build a few programs that take Visual Basic into areas that you may not have thought possible. I'll go through the ten steps necessary to build your own screen saver. Then I'm going to show you a goodie that Microsoft put on your CD-ROM and didn't bother to tell you about—the Systray control, which lets you add your own icon in the system tray. You should take a few minutes to look at the source code for this ActiveX control. Finally, I'll show you how easy it is to access information in the Windows Registry.

Building Screen Savers

Have you ever wanted to write your own screen saver program? Maybe you had something simple in mind, like a slide show program where you slowly scroll through a set of pictures. It turns out that building a screen saver program is a lot easier than you might think. Windows takes care of all the hard stuff, such as determining when to run the screen saver. All you need to do is to display the pretty graphics whenever Windows tells you to.

A screen saver is simply a normal program that has a file type of .SCR and responds to two different command-line arguments:

- /c is used to configure the screen saver.
- /s is used to start the screen saver.

Determining when to start the screen saver is Windows responsibility; you just need to indicate when to end it. To help you build your own screen saver, I've put together a ten-step process, complete with source code and commentary:

1. Start a new Visual Basic project.
2. Create the display part of the screen saver.
3. Display the form in full-screen mode without a title bar.
4. Unload the form on any user-initiated mouse or keyboard events.
5. Add a second form to configure the screen saver.

6. Add a module to your project.

7. Add a Sub Main routine to control the screen saver.

8. Adjust the program's properties.

9. Install your program into the \Windows directory.

10. Configure your screen saver.

Step 1 is simple. In fact, you don't really have to start with a blank Visual Basic project, but you do need to create a copy of the program you can edit and change. The other steps require a bit more explanation.

Creating the Display Portion

The display portion of the screen saver is an intentional infinite loop. It should display a set of pictures or draw a set of graphics and then loop around and start all over again. It should be designed to be self-scaling; in other words, it should adapt itself to any display size. In the case of a slide show, you might center the pictures if they are too small to fill the whole screen. A graphics program would be scaled so that the whole screen is used.

Since the display part of the screen saver is separate from the configuration part, you should retrieve any configuration information from the Windows Registry using the GetSetting routine.

Declaring Module-Level Variables

For my screen saver program, I decided to use a modified version of the StarSX program, which I talked about in Chapter 3. Listing 17.1 shows the module-level variables I use.

Listing 17.1:   **Module-Level Variables for ScreenSaver's Pic Form**

```
Option Explicit

Dim AngleStep As Single
Dim Color As Long
Dim ColorIncrement As Long
Dim Delta As Single
Dim RadiusDecrement As Single
```

```
Dim TimeDelay As Long

Dim CenterX As Long
Dim CenterY As Long
Dim Radius As Single
Dim Theta As Single
```

I will retrieve the first group of values (`AngleStep`, `ColorIncrement`, `Delta`, `RadiusDecrement`, and `TimeDelay`) from the Registry. The rest I will initialize when I begin drawing the figure.

Drawing the Star

The `DrawArc` routine, shown in Listing 17.2, is the same as the one in Chapter 3, except for some minor details. Rather than use a Timer control, I now use the `Sleep` Win32 API function to slow down the drawing process. I also rewrote the method that I used to increment color and created a separate subroutine that can be used by both the `Pic` form and the `Config` form. The revised logic lets me keep just one variable for color, and I break out the RGB (Red, Green, and Blue) components to create the color I display. Because of the way the logic works, the value for `Color` now ranges from 0 to 1535 (256 color levels times six different color bands minus one, since I'm starting at zero).

Listing 17.2:   DrawArc Routine for ScreenSaver's Pic Form

```
Private Sub DrawArc()

Static OldX As Single
Static oldY As Single

Dim NewX As Single
Dim NewY As Single

Dim r As Integer
Dim g As Integer
Dim b As Integer

NewX = CenterX + Sin(Theta) * Radius
NewY = CenterY + Cos(Theta) * Radius
```

```
        ColorToRGB r, g, b, Color

        Pic.Line (OldX, oldY)-(NewX, NewY), RGB(r, g, b)
        Pic.DrawMode = vbCopyPen

        OldX = NewX
        oldY = NewY

        Theta = Theta + AngleStep
        Radius = Radius - RadiusDecrement
        Color = (Color + ColorIncrement) Mod 1535
        DoEvents
        Sleep TimeDelay

        End Sub
```

The DrawStarSx routine, shown in Listing 17.3, is called to display a single StarSX image. It acquires the parameters from the Windows Registry using the GetSetting function. I then initialize the rest of the module-level variables and call the DrawArc routine until the Radius value is less than the specified value for Delta. Note that I use the form's Height and Width properties to determine the values that depend on the screen size, such as the center of the form (CenterX and CenterY) and the initial radius of the circle (Radius).

Listing 17.3:   DrawStarSx Routine for ScreenSaver's Pic Form

```
Public Sub DrawStarSx()

Color = CInt(GetSetting("StarSX", "Pic", "Color", "1"))
TimeDelay = CLng(GetSetting("StarSX", "Pic", "TimeDelay", "50"))
AngleStep = CSng(GetSetting("StarSX", "Pic", "AngleStep", "3.00"))
ColorIncrement = CLng(GetSetting("StarSX", "Pic", "ColorIncrement", "2"))
Delta = CSng(GetSetting("StarSX", "Pic", "Delta", "10"))
RadiusDecrement = CSng(GetSetting("StarSX", "Pic", "RadiusDecrement", "10"))

Pic.DrawMode = vbNop
CenterX = Me.Width / 2
CenterY = Me.Height / 2
Radius = 0.95 * IIf(CenterX < CenterY, CenterX, CenterY)
Theta = 0
```

```
Do While Radius > Delta
  DrawArc
Loop

End Sub
```

Don't limit yourself: You can make your program a true multimedia experience by playing background music or other sounds to accompany your screen saver's display. Use the Visual Basic Multimedia control (MCI) to play background MIDI tunes or various .WAV files to coincide with the graphic presentation.

Loading the Form

The first step the Form_Load event, shown in Listing 17.4, performs is to show itself when it first loads. Then it performs an infinite loop that clears the form and displays a StarSX picture. This is one of the few cases where you really want to use a Do While True statement, since the resulting infinite loop ensures that the screen saver will not end until it is interrupted by another process.

Listing 17.4:   Form_Load Event for ScreenSaver's Pic Form

```
Private Sub Form_Load()

Me.Show

Do While True
  Me.Cls
  DrawStarSX

Loop

End Sub
```

I didn't discuss the Form_Unload event, since it contains only a single statement, End. This ensures that whenever I unload this form for whatever reason, the program will stop completely.

Displaying the Form in Full-Screen Mode

It's very easy to maximize a form in Visual Basic. You just set the form's Window-State property to 2 (vbMaximized). However, this leaves the title bar in place, which would look rather dumb on a screen saver. You also might want to set the screen's background to black to make the graphics stand out better.

To prepare the form for the screen saver, you need to set the following properties:

Property	Setting
Caption	" "
ControlBox	False
MaxButton	False
MinButton	False
WindowState	vbMaximized

The first four values disable the title bar, and the last property runs the form in full-screen mode. You can set these values dynamically in your program, or you can set them as part of the form's design-time properties. I choose to do it at design time, since I can set WindowState to vbNormal while testing the program and then change it to vbMaximized when I'm ready to compile a real test version of the program.

NOTE   **Should a screen saver save screens?** The original concept behind a screen saver was to minimize the burn-in effect on computer monitors. If the same screen is shown for a long period of time, the images begin to burn into the phosphor. A screen saver prevents this by displaying a moving image on the screen. Technological advances in modern computer monitors have minimized the burn-in effect, so a screen saver is no longer necessary. Today, screen savers are used primarily because of their entertainment value.

Unloading the Form on User-Initiated Events

A typical screen saver will stop the program if the user presses any key, moves the mouse, or clicks either mouse button. The way to stop the screen saver program is to simply unload the form. The Form_Unload event will execute the End statement, ensuring that the program is stopped properly.

Simply putting the Unload Me statement in the MouseDown and KeyDown events will take care of stopping the screen saver. You also need the Unload Me statement in the MouseMove event. Visual Basic sometimes moves the mouse as part of loading and displaying a form. To ensure that Visual Basic doesn't stop your screen saver before it starts, use the code in Listing 17.5 to ignore the first two mouse movements and end the program on the third.

Listing 17.5: **Form_MouseMove Event for ScreenSaver's Pic Form**

```
Private Sub Form_MouseMove(Button As Integer, Shift As Integer, _
    X As Single, Y As Single)

Static c As Integer

If c > 2 Then
    Unload Me

Else
    c = c + 1

End If

End Sub
```

TIP

Screen saver hot spots: A traditional screen saver ends whenever someone moves the mouse, clicks a mouse button, or presses a key. This doesn't mean that you have to be traditional. You could ignore mouse movements and instead create a hot spot on your screen where the user could click a mouse button. A mouse click on the hot spot could either display a pop-up menu or launch the configuration form without stopping the screen saver.

Adding a Configuration Form

The first form takes its startup parameters from the Windows Registry, so you need a method to put those values in the Registry in the first place. It doesn't really matter how this form looks, although you do need to make it easy to use.

Since StarSX the screen saver was built from StarSX the toy, I simply reused the same controls I used in the original StarSX program. Of course, I took a little time to make them look a little nicer, because I'm not sharing the form with the graphics anymore. Figure 17.1 shows the StarSX configuration settings.

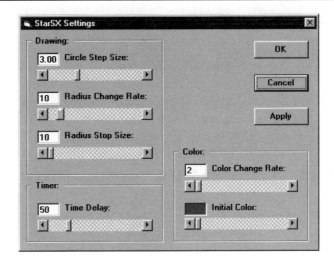

I added three buttons to the form:

- The OK button saves the current settings to the Registry and closes the window.

- The Apply button merely saves the current settings to the Registry.

- The Cancel button closes the window without making any changes.

TIP

If you don't know, cheat: Sometimes the best way to design an application is to look at other applications that perform similar functions. In this case, I looked at some other screen saver dialog boxes to see how best to lay out my own screen saver.

Adding a Module and a Sub Main Routine

Visual Basic can launch a program by loading a form or by calling the `Main` subroutine. While you can use either in this program, I choose the `Main` subroutine because it offers a cleaner interface to start either the `Config` form or the `Pic` form. However, to use a `Sub Main`, you need to add a module to your program.

TIP

Use Sub Main to start your program: A `Main` subroutine will run before any forms are shown. This way, it is easy to decide which form you want to show at the start of the program. You might want to show the last form used in a database application or select the appropriate form based on someone's user name. This is also useful if you want to display a splash screen before you load the main form.

I start the `Main` subroutine by checking to see if there was a previous copy of this program already running. If so, I end the program since there is no reason to run two screen saver programs at the same time. I then start the `Config` form or the `Pic` form, depending on what command-line value is supplied by Windows. Listing 17.6 shows this subroutine

---

Listing 17.6: **Main Subroutine in ScreenSaver**

```
Public Sub Main()

If App.PrevInstance Then
    End

ElseIf Left(LCase(Command()), 2) = "/c" Then
    Config.Show

ElseIf Left(LCase(Command()), 2) = "/s" Then
    Pic.Show

End If

End Sub
```

Adjusting the Program's Properties

You need to set a few program properties before you can compile your program. Figure 17.2 shows the Project Properties dialog box for StarSX.

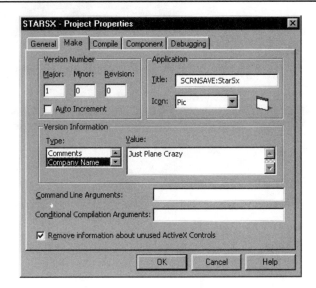

The Application Title property must be set to SCRNSAVE: followed immediately by the title of your program. It is important that SCRNSAVE be in all uppercase letters; otherwise, Windows will not recognize your program as a screen saver.

You also need to set the startup object to Sub Main to start that subroutine. Assuming that you are ready to try out your screen saver, you can compile the program into an .EXE file.

Installing and Configuring Your Screen Saver

Once you've compiled your program, you're ready to install it. The .EXE file must be renamed to .SCR and moved to the Windows directory (typically \Windows on Windows 95 and \WnNT on NT workstation).

To use your new screen saver, open the Control Panel and select the Display applet. Then select the Screen Saver tab. Click on the combo box's drop-down arrow and select the name of your screen saver, as shown in Figure 17.3.

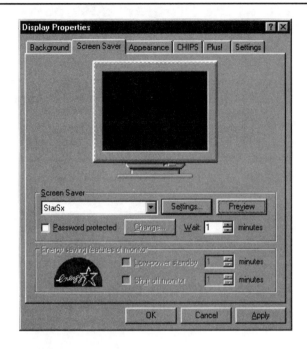

The screen saver has six different parameters. Each of these parameters controls the image displayed on the screen. There are two parameters that control the basic image generated: Circle Step Size and Radius Change Rate. These parameters correspond to the variables `AngleStep` and `RadiusDecrement`. Changing these values only slightly will often result in radically different pictures. Some interesting values for these two parameters are listed in Table 17.1.

TABLE 17.1:   Selected Values for Circle Step Size and Radius Change Rate

Circle Step Size	Radius Change Rate
4.00	10
4.00	1
3.25	2
3.14	1

Continued on next page

TABLE 17.1 (CONTINUED): Selected Values for Circle Step Size and Radius Change Rate

Circle Step Size	Radius Change Rate
2.90	8
2.70	7
2.00	6
1.58	3
1.57	1
0.80	10
0.70	2
0.50	2
0.04	1

The remaining parameters have a more minor effect on the image:

- Radius Stop Size stops the picture when the size center goes below this value. The larger the value, the quicker the picture will stop.

- Color Change Rate controls how quickly the colors change. A value of zero means that the color will never change.

- Initial Color is self-explanatory. However, note that even in a 24-bit color environment, only 1536 colors will be used (see the ColorToRGB routine in this program on the CD-ROM for more details).

- Time Delay is also self-explanatory—the smaller the value, the quicker the drawing will be completed. Note that the accuracy of this value is limited to about 55, due the accuracy of the Windows clock. A value of zero disables the timer and will draw most pictures in less than a second.

The program will automatically configure itself for the default values you saw earlier in Figure 17.1. These values will generate a screen much like the one shown in Figure 17.4.

Displaying an Icon in the System Tray

Have you ever looked at the system tray over in the right corner of the Windows Taskbar and wondered what it would take to use it in your own programs? I have. When I started writing this book, I planned to go through how to use the Win32 API to display my own icon in the system tray. However, when I looked through the Visual Basic CD-ROMs, I found the source code for an ActiveX control, called Systray, that did everything I wanted. So I changed my mind and decided to use it rather than write my own program (remember, the lazy programmer doesn't mind reusing code whenever possible).

Adding the Systray Control

Table 17.2 lists the properties of the Systray control. The Index, Name, Object, Parent, and Tag properties have the same meanings as in other ActiveX controls. The TrayIcon property holds the icon that will be displayed in the system tray.

The TrayTip property holds a string of text that will be displayed above the icon in the toolbar when the mouse pointer hovers over the icon for about a second or so.

TABLE 17.2: Systray Control Properties

Property	Description
Index	Contains a number that uniquely identifies the control in a control array
InTray	When set to **True**, means that **TrayIcon** is shown in the system tray; when set to **False**, means that the icon is not displayed
Name	Specifies the name of the control
Object	Returns an object reference to the control
Parent	Returns an object reference to the control's container
Tag	Contains user-supplied information
TrayIcon	Specifies the icon to be displayed
TrayTip	Specifies the ToolTip text that will be displayed when the mouse pointer is held over the icon in the system tray

The InTray property is used to enable and disable the Systray icon. When InTray is False, the control is inactive. Setting InTray to True displays the icon in the system tray, and the control will trap the mouse events listed in Table 17.3.

WARNING **Don't stop too quickly:** Ending a program while the InTray property is still True may leave the icon in the system tray while in the Visual Basic IDE. This can cause Visual Basic to crash or other nasty things. Be sure to set InTray to False before stopping your program.

TABLE 17.3: Systray Control Events

Event	Description
MouseDblClick	Occurs when the mouse is double-clicked on the icon in the system tray
MouseDown	Occurs when one or more mouse buttons are pressed while the mouse cursor is over the icon in the system tray

Continued on next page

TABLE 17.3 (CONTINUED): Systray Control Events

Event	Description
MouseMove	Occurs when the mouse cursor is moved over the icon in the system tray
MouseUp	Occurs when one or more mouse buttons are released while the mouse cursor is over the icon in the system tray

Programming the Systray Control

Only a few programs can benefit from the Systray control. These tend to be long-running programs that need very little interaction with the user. For example, the Telnet Server program I built in Chapter 12 is a good example of a program that would benefit from the Systray control. This program runs by itself and services Telnet requests. Since you don't need to interact with it very often, you'll probably keep it minimized. However, a minimized program takes space on the Taskbar, which is often at a premium on a busy system. Using a system tray icon to anchor the Telnet Server allows you easy access to the program when necessary, without taking up a valuable amount of real estate elsewhere on the Taskbar.

Another program that would benefit from the Systray control is a job scheduler, and that's the program I wrote. Basically, this program starts tasks at a specified time and automatically reschedules them for their next execution. Since this is a long-running program, like the Telnet Server, there is no need for it to occupy space on the Taskbar. When you want to check the status of existing tasks, you can click on the program's icon in the system tray to see a window like the one shown in Figure 17.5. You also can easily add new tasks or change existing tasks by right-clicking on the scheduled tasks box. Figure 17.6 shows the dialog box that appears.

FIGURE 17.5:

The Scheduler program's schedule display

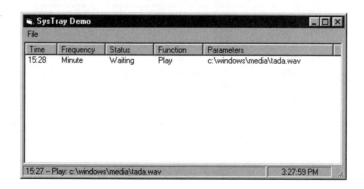

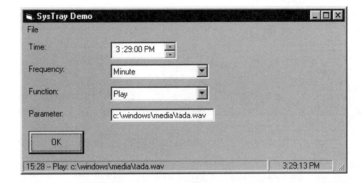

Special note to Jill: After losing almost a whole chapter due to a system crash,
my wife asked me why I couldn't write a little program that would copy my working files to our LAN server every hour or so. This is that program. Thanks Jill.

Starting the Scheduler

The Scheduler program begins by initializing both combo boxes on the main form,
as shown in Listing 17.7. I load the information about the currently active schedules. I get the number of entries from the `Scheduler\Main\Count` key and then
use a `For/Next` loop to load each individual entry.

Listing 17.7:   **Form_Load Event in Scheduler**

```
Private Sub Form_Load()

Dim c As Integer
Dim l As ListItem

Combo1.AddItem "Minute"
Combo1.AddItem "Hour"
Combo1.AddItem "Day"
Combo1.AddItem "Once"

Combo2.AddItem "Beep"
Combo2.AddItem "Play"
```

```
Combo2.AddItem "Run"

c = GetSetting("Scheduler", "Main", "Count", "0")

For CurrentEvent = 1 To c
   Set l = ListView1.ListItems.Add(, "x" & FormatNumber(CurrentEvent, 0), _
      GetSetting("Scheduler", FormatNumber(CurrentEvent, 0), "Time", ""))
   l.SubItems(1) = GetSetting("Scheduler", FormatNumber(CurrentEvent, 0), _
      "Frequency", "")
   l.SubItems(2) = GetSetting("Scheduler", FormatNumber(CurrentEvent, 0), _
      "Status", "")
   l.SubItems(3) = GetSetting("Scheduler", FormatNumber(CurrentEvent, 0), _
      "Function", "")
   l.SubItems(4) = GetSetting("Scheduler", FormatNumber(CurrentEvent, 0), _
      "Parameter", "")
Next CurrentEvent

ListView1.ZOrder 0

CurrentIcon = 1
Set cSysTray1.TrayIcon = ImageList1.ListImages(1).ExtractIcon
cSysTray1.InTray = True
Timer1.Interval = 1000
Timer1.Enabled = True
Me.Hide

End Sub
```

After I load the scheduling information, I grab the icon to be displayed in the system tray from ImageList1. Then I set cSysTray1.InTray to True, which displays the icon in the tray and enables the mouse movements. Note that I could have assigned the TrayIcon value at design time; however, I decided to be cute, as you'll see in a moment.

I end this routine by setting a Timer control to interrupt every second. For a serious scheduling program, this time interval may be too small. Setting it to five or even thirty seconds may be more acceptable. However, setting the interval to one second lets me more accurately track what is happening in the program. It also simplifies the programming, since I don't need to worry about the clock drifting or restarting the program exactly on the minute boundary.

Controlling Program Flow

The Timer routine, shown in Listing 17.8, controls the flow of this program. Every time the clock ticks, I check the ListView control to see if there are any tasks to be run. If there is one, I call the RunMe subroutine with the appropriate information.

Listing 17.8:   **Timer1_Event in Scheduler**

```
Private Sub Timer1_Timer()

Dim l As ListItem

Set cSysTray1.TrayIcon = ImageList1.ListImages(CurrentIcon).ExtractIcon
CurrentIcon = CurrentIcon Mod 8 + 1
StatusBar1.Panels(2) = FormatDateTime(Now, vbLongTime)

For Each l In ListView1.ListItems
   If l.Text = FormatDateTime(Now, vbShortTime) And _
         l.SubItems(2) = "Waiting" Then
      RunMe l.SubItems(3), l.SubItems(4)
      UpdateStatus l
   End If
Next l

End Sub
```

Note that the first thing I do in this routine is to switch the icon displayed in the Taskbar to the next one in the ImageList control. Since I have eight icons I can loop through, I compute the current icon by taking the remainder after dividing the value by eight (using the Mod operator) and adding one. This will always give me a value between one and eight.

Running the Program

Listing 17.9 shows the RunMe subroutine for the Scheduler program. I decided to use the StartMeUp routine that I talked about in Chapter 16 (Listing 16.23) to run a program. This let me create a batch file to copy the files from my working directory to my server.

Listing 17.9:   **RunMe Routine in Scheduler**

```
Private Sub RunMe(c As String, p As String)

StatusBar1.Panels(1).Text = FormatDateTime(Now, vbShortTime) & " - " _
    & c & ": " & p

cSysTray1.TrayTip = StatusBar1.Panels(1).Text

If c = "Beep" Then
    Beep

ElseIf c = "Play" Then
    MMControl1.FileName = p
    MMControl1.Command = "Open"
    MMControl1.Wait = True
    MMControl1.Command = "Play"
    MMControl1.Command = "Close"

ElseIf c = "Run" Then
    StartMeUp p

End If

End Sub
```

NOTE **Beeps versus tadas:** When I originally wrote this program, the **RunMe** routine played a beep. I tested with a schedule that called this routine once each minute. After my wife complained about the constant beeping (her desk is right next to mine), I decided to play a .WAV file instead. She later remarked that hearing tada.wav played every minute was probably worse than hearing the beeps.

Displaying a Pop-up Menu

One of the simplest routines in this program is shown in Listing 17.10. This routine displays a pop-up menu whenever the right mouse button is clicked.

Listing 17.10:   cSysTray1_MouseDown Event in Scheduler

```
Private Sub cSysTray1_MouseDown(Button As Integer, Id As Long)

If Button = 2 Then
    PopupMenu MenuTray
End If

End Sub
```

The fact that this routine is controlled by the cSysTray1 control isn't really important. You use the same code that you would use anywhere else in your program.

Accessing the Windows Registry

When Microsoft released Windows 95, it included a replacement for .INI files called the Windows Registry. All kinds of useful information is kept in the Registry, including your system's hardware configuration, operating system details, and information about your applications. It's a useful repository of information, but using it can be dangerous, so I'll begin this discussion with a warning.

If you really want to write a program that manipulates the Registry, don't do it on a production machine. All of the backups in the world may not be enough to allow you to completely recover your system. Always test your program on a machine that you can afford to destroy. If you can, link your computers together over a network and keep copies of your program and any other important information on the other computer. Only when you are satisfied that your program is stable should you think about testing it somewhere else. And even then, you should take all of the recommended precautions before trying your program.

Safety in Numbers

There are many ways to access the Registry. Probably the safest is to use standard Windows tools:

- Windows Explorer can manage all of the file type associations that make a function like ShellExecute so powerful.

- The Control Panel provides ways to configure your hardware.

- The Policy Editor is used establish rules and default values for your Desktop settings and system configuration options.

Using these tools ensures that the Registry is updated properly and helps to prevent problems.

Back Up Your Windows Registry

Remember those startup disks you didn't create when you installed Windows? Or perhaps you lost that envelope containing the emergency boot disks that came with your system. Find them now or create new ones. You will need them if you accidentally corrupt the Registry.

The safest way to ensure that you can recover from a Registry failure is to back up your entire system. The most common way is to back up your system to tape using a standard backup package. Just make sure that you understand how to recover your system from the backup tape.

TIP   **Emergency repair utility:** Your Windows 95 CD-ROM contains a program that you can use to create an backup copy of your critical files and restore those files from a DOS prompt. Check \Other\Misc\ERU on the CD-ROM for more details. Microsoft has improved how the Registry is managed in Windows 98. Select Start ➢ Accessories ➢ System Tools ➢ System Information and select the Registry Checker from the Tools menu. The Registry Checker program is run automatically each time the system is started, and it will automatically restore the Registry from a backup copy.

Another option is to back up your system to another disk drive. You can't just copy all of the files on your C: drive and expect it to work properly. However, there are several third-party tools that will create a backup copy of your disk drive on another disk drive.

While there is a great deal of information in common between the Windows 95/98 Registry and the Windows NT Registry, there is a lot of information that is unique to each operating system, and the structures to hold the information are different. These differences affect your backups.

Backing Up the Windows 95 or 98 Registry

Windows 95 and 98 store the Registry in two files, called SYSTEM.DAT and USER.DAT. These files are stored in the \Windows directory and marked as System, Hidden, and Read-Only. Each time Windows is started successfully, the current version of the Registry is copied to a backup file ending with .DA0. Even through Windows creates these backups, you should create your own backups. You can simply copy the DAT files to DA1, DA2, and so on to preserve the data.

WARNING **I lost all my settings:** Remember that if you need to restore a backup copy of the Registry, all your settings will revert to the values in that copy.

Using your DOS boot disk, you can rename the current Registry files with temporary names. Then you can rename your backup copies of the Registry using their proper names. Use the ATTRIB command to verify that the files are System, Hidden, and Read-Only. Then try to reboot your system. If all goes well, you can delete the old copies of the Registry.

Backing Up the Windows NT Registry

In Windows NT, the Registry is stored as a series of files called *hives*. Each hive represents a real root key in the Registry. Hives are stored in the \WinNT\System32\ Config directory as files without a file type. Information for a particular user is stored in the \WinNT\Profiles*User* directory where *User* is a valid user name.

Windows NT is a secure operating system, which means that you can't just go around copying Registry files as you can in Windows 95 or 98 and expect them to work properly. You could boot a DOS system and access the files if you have formatted the system drive as FAT, or you can use the Repair Disk Utility. This utility creates recovery information and a boot disk that you can use to try to recover your system.

Recovering Your Registry

Knowing how your backup and recovery process works is very important. You need to understand the risks when you change the Registry. I'm not trying to be all doom and gloom here, but unlike a database or a flat file, making a change to the Registry can affect your system's stability. Anyone who has had a corrupted Registry will acknowledge that. There's a big difference between knowing that you can recover and actually performing the recovery process.

You should test your recovery process at some point to make sure that it will work and that you know how it works. I've been in situations where a system I was responsible for became corrupted and I had to go through the recovery process. The recovery almost worked correctly. With a lot of hard work and even more luck, I was able to get the system running again, but I was cleaning up minor problems for weeks afterward. Once I modified the backup process slightly, I was able to recover without a glitch.

TIP   **Reinstalling Windows again and again and again:** After reinstalling Windows four times in four weeks while testing some beta code, I decided that there had to be a better way. On the average, it took about half a day to reinstall Windows with all of my usual applications. Using DriveImage from PowerQuest, I was able to create "standardized" Windows that included a complete Windows system, with all of the proper drivers, my usual applications, and my normal settings. It now takes me less than half an hour to restore my system from the backup file.

Understanding the Registry Structure

The Windows Registry contains a series of multiple-part keys that represents a hierarchical structure. Associated with each key are one or more values. Each value consists of a name and data pair. Every key always has a value with `Null` for the name. This is often displayed as (`Default`). This name may or may not have a value associated with it.

NOTE   **Null is not nothing:** There is a difference between a data value not having a value and a data value having a `Null` value.

Registry Data Types

Each data element associated with a name has a data type, as listed in Table 17.4. Windows NT supports all of the listed data types; only the first three types are supported by Windows 95 and 98. Also, Windows 95 and 98 Registry values are limited to 64KB bytes of storage. Windows NT data elements may be as large as 1MB.

TABLE 17.4: Windows Registry Data Types

Data Type	Size Limit	Description
String/REG_SZ	95/98: 64KB; NT: 1MB	A sequence of text characters
Binary/REQ_BINARY	95/98: 64KB; NT: 1MB	A string of binary characters
DWORD/REG_DWORD	32 bits	A **Long** integer
na/REG_EXPAND_SZ	1MB	An expandable string (NT only)
na/REG_MULTI_SZ	1MB	Multiple strings (NT only)

Registry Keys

The Registry contains a series of root keys that are used to reference information in the Registry:

- The HKEY_CLASSES_ROOT key is an alias of HKEY_LOCAL_MACHINE\Software\ Classes that refers to the associations between file types and programs.

- The HKEY_CURRENT_USER key is an alias of HKEY_USERS*username* that contains information about the current user specified by *username*.

- The HKEY_LOCAL_MACHINE key contains information about the machine's hardware and software configuration. I'll go into a bit more detail about this key in a moment.

- The HKEY_CURRENT_CONFIG key is an alias of HKEY_LOCAL_MACHINE\Config\ *config#* where *config#* represents 0001, 0002, and so on—the current configuration number.

- The HKEY_DYN_DATA key isn't a real key, nor is it an alias. It also doesn't exist in Windows NT. This is a temporary key that doesn't exist on disk and is used to hold information about the current Windows session.

- The HKEY_USERS key contains information about each user on your system. This is another key of interest, like HKEY_LOCAL_MACHINE, which I'll describe in more detail.

Note that not of these keys are available on both Windows 95/98 and Windows NT. Also, some the root keys provide shortcuts or aliases to other keys in the Registry.

Contents of HKEY_LOCAL_MACHINE

Only information that is common to all users will be stored here. While this key exists on both Windows 95/98 and Windows NT systems, much of the information stored here is different between the two machines. The HKEY_LOCAL_MACHINE key contains the following subkeys:

Config This subkey exists only on Windows 95/98 systems and contains a series of hardware configuration profiles. Each profile is a four-digit number beginning with 0001. Information is kept about the devices that are part of that configuration.

Enum This subkey also exists only on Windows 95/98 systems and contains information about every piece of hardware that has ever been installed on the system.

Hardware This subkey is used by Windows NT to describe the hardware configuration. This list is updated each time Windows NT is started. This subkey is also available in Windows 95/98, but not much information is stored here.

Network This is a Windows 95/98 subkey that contains information about the currently logged-on user.

SAM This subkey is found only on Windows NT. It contains security information about each user, group, and domain in Windows NT Server.

Security This subkey contains information about shared resources and open network connections on a Windows 95/98 system. On a Windows NT system, this subkey contains information about the local security policy. Note you will be prevented from accessing this key using the Registry Editor in Windows NT.

Software The subkey contains information about software installed on the system and that applies to all users. It contains information similar to that in \HKEY_USERS*username*\Software, except that the \HKEY_USERS key contains information that is specific to the user. This subkey is important to application developers, and I'll talk a bit more about it after the System subkey description.

System This subkey contains configuration information about which devices and operating system services are loaded and started. In Windows 95/98, information is stored only under the CurrentControlSet subkey. Windows NT stores the information in several different subkeys, including Clone, ControlSet001 to ControlSet003, CurrentControlSet, Select, and Setup.

You can use the Software subkey to store settings about your application that are independent of the particular user, such as paths to directories, installed features, and so on. The Software key is typically formatted as:

\HKEY_LOCAL_MACHINE\Software*Company**Product**Version*\

where *Company* is the name of the company that has released the software, *Product* is the name of the software product, and *Version* is the version number of the product. For example, the following key contains information about Microsoft Word:

\HKEY_LOCAL_MACHINE\Software\Microsoft\Office\8.0\Word\InstallRoot

Note that not all vendors (including Microsoft) always include Version as part of the key. Other types of information, such as file type associations (which are stored in Classes) and ODBC driver information, are also stored here.

Contents of HKEY_USERS In this subkey, a special user name called .Default contains the settings that will be used by the default user on your system. Within each user name is a set of subkeys that refer to various characteristics of a user:

AppEvents This subkey contains information about various events in the system and the sounds that should be played when events occur.

Console This is a Windows NT-only subkey that contains information about how to display character-based applications. It includes information such as window size, color, fonts, and so on.

Control Panel This subkey contains information about various settings that the user can change using the Control Panel. Subkeys include Accessibility, Appearance, Colors, Cursors, Desktop, International, and Mouse. Note that some of these subkeys may be present only if changes to the default value have been made through the Control Panel.

`Environment` This is a Windows NT-only subkey containing information about a user's environment variables.

`InstallLocationsMRU` This is a Windows 95/98-only subkey that contains path information that is used to install Windows and make subsequent changes to its configuration.

`Keyboard Layout` This subkey contains information about the keyboard.

`Network` This is a Windows 95/98-only subkey that contains information about mapped disk drives and network-attached disk drives that have been recently used.

`RemoteAccess` This is a Windows 95/98-only subkey that contains information about dial-up networking connections to other systems.

`Software` This subkey contains user-specific information about software packages installed on a system. This is similar in function to the \HKEY_LOCAL_MACHINE\Software key and follows the same suggested key-naming conventions. Of particular note is the `VB and VBA Program Settings` subkey, which contains the information from the `GetSetting` and `SaveSetting` routines. You can use the `Software` subkey to store settings about your application that apply only to a particular user, such as screen locations, color information, recently used files, and so on.

Using the Registry Editor

Microsoft supplies a tool called the Registry Editor (the RegEdit program) with Windows. This tool allows you to browse and edit items in the Registry. In Windows 95 and 98, there are essentially no restrictions on the changes you can make. If you are Administrator on a Windows NT system, you don't have as much freedom as you do under Windows 95/98 (which has no security restrictions), but you still can edit most of the entries in the Registry. Regular Windows NT users have even less freedom in the Registry than the Administrator user.

WARNING   **Use RegEdt32 on Windows NT:** Microsoft recommends that you use RegEdt32 on Windows NT rather then RegEdit. This is because RegEdit does not support the data types that are specific to Windows NT.

The Registry Editor presents a two-panel view of the Registry, as shown in Figure 17.7. On the left side is a list of Registry key values. A list of name and data pairs is on the right side.

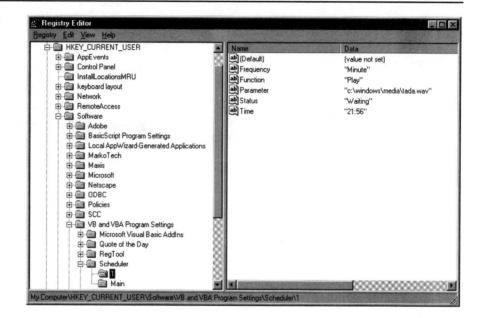

Reg Alert, Reg Alert, Reg Alert: The Registry Editor allows you direct access to the Registry. You can insert new keys and values, change existing values, and delete keys and their values. You can destroy your operating system. Use this program with extreme caution.

You can change the value of an existing value by clicking on its name. Figure 17.8 shows the Edit String dialog box that appears. Right-clicking on a value displays a pop-up menu that allows you to delete the value, rename it, or modify its contents. You can also use the regular menus to insert a new key or a new value with the specified data type. The only way to change the data type of a value is to delete the value and enter a new value.

FIGURE 17.8:

Editing a value in the
Registry Editor

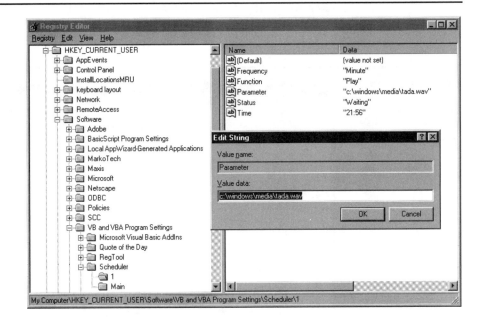

No need to write: Use the Registry Editor to look at entries in the Registry that were created with `SaveSetting`. This is the easiest way to verify that you wrote your data correctly.

Accessing the Registry from Visual Basic

After reading Chapter 16, you should have a good understanding of what it takes to use the Win32 API. Accessing the Registry is just as easy (or difficult) as using any of the routines you've seen so far. Listing 17.11 contains the header information you need in a program that accesses the Registry functions.

It's okay to be afraid: By now, I've probably scared you to the point where you are afraid to touch the Registry. This fear is good protection. It will prevent you from doing something stupid like deleting an item from your hardware configuration. Reading is the absolutely safest thing you can do with the Registry. Updating information is also safe when you're changing your own information.

Listing 17.11:   Windows Registry Access Header Information in RegTool

```
Option Explicit


' ============================================================
' = Windows Registry                                         =
' ============================================================

Public Const ERROR_SUCCESS = 0&
Public Const ERROR_NO_MORE_FILES = 18&
Public Const ERROR_MORE_DATA = 234

Public Const READ_CONTROL = &H20000
Public Const STANDARD_RIGHTS_ALL = &H1F0000
Public Const STANDARD_RIGHTS_EXECUTE = (READ_CONTROL)
Public Const STANDARD_RIGHTS_READ = (READ_CONTROL)
Public Const STANDARD_RIGHTS_REQUIRED = &HF0000
Public Const STANDARD_RIGHTS_WRITE = (READ_CONTROL)
Public Const SYNCHRONIZE = &H100000

Public Const HKEY_CLASSES_ROOT = &H80000000
Public Const HKEY_CURRENT_CONFIG = &H80000005
Public Const HKEY_CURRENT_USER = &H80000001
Public Const HKEY_DYN_DATA = &H80000006
Public Const HKEY_LOCAL_MACHINE = &H80000002
Public Const HKEY_PERFORMANCE_DATA = &H80000004
Public Const HKEY_USERS = &H80000003

Public Const KEY_CREATE_LINK = &H20
Public Const KEY_CREATE_SUB_KEY = &H4
Public Const KEY_ENUMERATE_SUB_KEYS = &H8
Public Const KEY_EVENT = &H1
Public Const KEY_NOTIFY = &H10
Public Const KEY_QUERY_VALUE = &H1
Public Const KEY_SET_VALUE = &H2
Public Const KEY_WRITE = ((STANDARD_RIGHTS_WRITE Or _
    KEY_SET_VALUE Or KEY_CREATE_SUB_KEY) And (Not SYNCHRONIZE))
Public Const KEY_ALL_ACCESS = ((STANDARD_RIGHTS_ALL Or _
    KEY_QUERY_VALUE Or KEY_SET_VALUE Or _
    KEY_CREATE_SUB_KEY Or KEY_ENUMERATE_SUB_KEYS Or _
    KEY_NOTIFY Or KEY_CREATE_LINK) And (Not SYNCHRONIZE))
```

```
Public Const KEY_READ = ((STANDARD_RIGHTS_READ Or _
    KEY_QUERY_VALUE Or KEY_ENUMERATE_SUB_KEYS Or KEY_NOTIFY) _
    And (Not SYNCHRONIZE))
Public Const KEY_EXECUTE = ((KEY_READ) And (Not SYNCHRONIZE))

Public Const REG_BINARY = 3
Public Const REG_CREATED_NEW_KEY = &H1
Public Const REG_DWORD = 4
Public Const REG_DWORD_BIG_ENDIAN = 5
Public Const REG_DWORD_LITTLE_ENDIAN = 4
Public Const REG_EXPAND_SZ = 2
Public Const REG_FULL_RESOURCE_DESCRIPTOR = 9
Public Const REG_LINK = 6
Public Const REG_MULTI_SZ = 7
Public Const REG_NONE = 0
Public Const REG_NOTIFY_CHANGE_ATTRIBUTES = &H2
Public Const REG_NOTIFY_CHANGE_LAST_SET = &H4
Public Const REG_NOTIFY_CHANGE_NAME = &H1
Public Const REG_NOTIFY_CHANGE_SECURITY = &H8
Public Const REG_OPENED_EXISTING_KEY = &H2
Public Const REG_OPTION_BACKUP_RESTORE = 4
Public Const REG_OPTION_CREATE_LINK = 2
Public Const REG_OPTION_NON_VOLATILE = 0
Public Const REG_OPTION_RESERVED = 0
Public Const REG_OPTION_VOLATILE = 1
Public Const REG_REFRESH_HIVE = &H2
Public Const REG_RESOURCE_LIST = 8
Public Const REG_RESOURCE_REQUIREMENTS_LIST = 10
Public Const REG_SZ = 1
Public Const REG_WHOLE_HIVE_VOLATILE = &H1
Public Const REG_LEGAL_CHANGE_FILTER = (REG_NOTIFY_CHANGE_NAME Or _
    REG_NOTIFY_CHANGE_ATTRIBUTES Or REG_NOTIFY_CHANGE_LAST_SET Or _
    REG_NOTIFY_CHANGE_SECURITY)
Public Const REG_LEGAL_OPTION = (REG_OPTION_RESERVED Or _
    REG_OPTION_NON_VOLATILE Or REG_OPTION_VOLATILE Or _
    REG_OPTION_CREATE_LINK Or REG_OPTION_BACKUP_RESTORE)

Public Type ACL
        AclRevision As Byte
        Sbz1 As Byte
        AclSize As Integer
        AceCount As Integer
```

```
        Sbz2 As Integer
End Type

Public Type FILETIME
        dwLowDateTime As Long
        dwHighDateTime As Long
End Type

Public Type SECURITY_ATTRIBUTES
        nLength As Long
        lpSecurityDescriptor As Long
        bInheritHandle As Long
End Type

Public Type SECURITY_DESCRIPTOR
        Revision As Byte
        Sbz1 As Byte
        Control As Long
        Owner As Long
        Group As Long
        Sacl As ACL
        Dacl As ACL
End Type

Public Declare Function RegCloseKey Lib "advapi32.dll" _
    (ByVal hkey As Long) As Long

Public Declare Function RegConnectRegistry Lib "advapi32.dll" _
    Alias "RegConnectRegistryA" (ByVal lpMachineName As String, _
    ByVal hkey As Long, phkResult As Long) As Long

Public Declare Function RegCreateKey Lib "advapi32.dll" _
    Alias "RegCreateKeyA" _
    (ByVal hkey As Long, ByVal lpSubKey As String, _
    phkResult As Long) As Long

Public Declare Function RegCreateKeyEx Lib "advapi32.dll" _
    Alias "RegCreateKeyExA" (ByVal hkey As Long, _
    ByVal lpSubKey As String, ByVal Reserved As Long, _
    ByVal lpClass As String, ByVal dwOptions As Long, _
    ByVal samDesired As Long, _
    lpSecurityAttributes As SECURITY_ATTRIBUTES, _
```

```
        phkResult As Long, lpdwDisposition As Long) As Long

Public Declare Function RegDeleteKey Lib "advapi32.dll" _
        Alias "RegDeleteKeyA" (ByVal hkey As Long, _
        ByVal lpSubKey As String) As Long

Public Declare Function RegDeleteValue Lib "advapi32.dll" _
        Alias "RegDeleteValueA" (ByVal hkey As Long, _
        ByVal lpValueName As String) As Long

Public Declare Function RegEnumKey Lib "advapi32.dll" _
        Alias "RegEnumKeyA" (ByVal hkey As Long, _
        ByVal dwIndex As Long, ByVal lpName As String, _
        ByVal cbName As Long) As Long

Public Declare Function RegEnumKeyEx Lib "advapi32.dll" _
        Alias "RegEnumKeyExA" (ByVal hkey As Long, _
        ByVal dwIndex As Long, ByVal lpName As String, _
        lpcbName As Long, ByVal lpReserved As Long, _
        ByVal lpClass As String, lpcbClass As Long, _
        lpftLastWriteTime As FILETIME) As Long

Public Declare Function RegEnumValue Lib "advapi32.dll" _
        Alias "RegEnumValueA" (ByVal hkey As Long, _
        ByVal dwIndex As Long, ByVal lpValueName As String, _
        lpcbValueName As Long, ByVal lpReserved As Long, _
        lpType As Long, lpData As Byte, lpcbData As Long) As Long

Public Declare Function RegFlushKey Lib "advapi32.dll" _
        (ByVal hkey As Long) As Long

Public Declare Function RegGetKeySecurity Lib "advapi32.dll" _
        (ByVal hkey As Long, ByVal SecurityInformation As Long, _
        pSecurityDescriptor As SECURITY_DESCRIPTOR, _
        lpcbSecurityDescriptor As Long) As Long

Public Declare Function RegLoadKey Lib "advapi32.dll" _
        Alias "RegLoadKeyA" (ByVal hkey As Long, _
        ByVal lpSubKey As String, ByVal lpFile As String) As Long

Public Declare Function RegNotifyChangeKeyValue Lib "advapi32.dll" _
        (ByVal hkey As Long, ByVal bWatchSubtree As Long, _
```

```
      ByVal dwNotifyFilter As Long, ByVal hEvent As Long, _
      ByVal fAsynchronus As Long) As Long

Public Declare Function RegOpenKey Lib "advapi32.dll" _
   Alias "RegOpenKeyA" (ByVal hkey As Long, _
   ByVal lpSubKey As String, phkResult As Long) As Long

Public Declare Function RegOpenKeyEx Lib "advapi32.dll" _
   Alias "RegOpenKeyExA" (ByVal hkey As Long, _
   ByVal lpSubKey As String, ByVal ulOptions As Long, _
   ByVal samDesired As Long, phkResult As Long) As Long

Public Declare Function RegQueryInfoKey Lib "advapi32.dll" _
   Alias "RegQueryInfoKeyA" (ByVal hkey As Long, _
   ByVal lpClass As String, lpcbClass As Long, _
   ByVal lpReserved As Long, lpcSubKeys As Long, _
   lpcbMaxSubKeyLen As Long, lpcbMaxClassLen As Long, _
   lpcValues As Long, lpcbMaxValueNameLen As Long, _
   lpcbMaxValueLen As Long, lpcbSecurityDescriptor As Long, _
   lpftLastWriteTime As FILETIME) As Long

Public Declare Function RegQueryValue Lib "advapi32.dll" _
   Alias "RegQueryValueA" (ByVal hkey As Long, _
   ByVal lpSubKey As String, ByVal lpValue As String, _
   lpcbValue As Long) As Long

Public Declare Function RegQueryValueEx Lib "advapi32.dll" _
   Alias "RegQueryValueExA" (ByVal hkey As Long, _
   ByVal lpValueName As String, ByVal lpReserved As Long, _
   lpType As Long, lpData As Any, lpcbData As Long) As Long

Public Declare Function RegQueryValueExString Lib "advapi32.dll" _
   Alias "RegQueryValueExA" (ByVal hkey As Long, _
   ByVal lpValueName As String, ByVal lpReserved As Long, _
   lpType As Long, ByVal lpData As String, lpcbData As Long) As Long

Public Declare Function RegReplaceKey Lib "advapi32.dll" _
   Alias "RegReplaceKeyA" (ByVal hkey As Long, _
   ByVal lpSubKey As String, ByVal lpNewFile As String, _
   ByVal lpOldFile As String) As Long

Public Declare Function RegRestoreKey Lib "advapi32.dll" _
```

```
        Alias "RegRestoreKeyA" (ByVal hkey As Long, _
        ByVal lpFile As String, ByVal dwFlags As Long) As Long

    Public Declare Function RegSaveKey Lib "advapi32.dll" _
        Alias "RegSaveKeyA" (ByVal hkey As Long, _
        ByVal lpFile As String, _
        lpSecurityAttributes As SECURITY_ATTRIBUTES) As Long

    Public Declare Function RegSetKeySecurity Lib "advapi32.dll" _
        (ByVal hkey As Long, ByVal SecurityInformation As Long, _
        pSecurityDescriptor As SECURITY_DESCRIPTOR) As Long

    Public Declare Function RegSetValue Lib "advapi32.dll" _
        Alias "RegSetValueA" (ByVal hkey As Long, _
        ByVal lpSubKey As String, ByVal dwType As Long, _
        ByVal lpData As String, ByVal cbData As Long) As Long

    Public Declare Function RegSetValueEx Lib "advapi32.dll" _
        Alias "RegSetValueExA" (ByVal hkey As Long, _
        ByVal lpValueName As String, ByVal Reserved As Long, _
        ByVal dwType As Long, lpData As Any, _
        ByVal cbData As Long) As Long

    Public Declare Function RegSetValueExString Lib "advapi32.dll" _
        Alias "RegSetValueExA" (ByVal hkey As Long, _
        ByVal lpValueName As String, ByVal Reserved As Long, _
        ByVal dwType As Long, ByVal lpData As String, _
        ByVal cbData As Long) As Long
```

Creating and Opening Keys

The RegCreateKey function creates a new key in the Registry and returns a handle to it. If the specified key value already exists, a handle to it is returned. The Reg-CreateKeyEx function works just like RegCreateKey, but it includes a few extra parameters that specify security attributes and object types.

The RegOpenKey function returns a handle to an existing key in the Registry. The RegOpenKeyEx function works like RegOpenKey, but it includes additional parameters that allow you to provide security and access information. You close the key using the RegCloseKey function.

Don't keep the handle open for too long: Handles should be closed as quickly as possible. You can always reopen a handle again later.

Getting, Setting, and Deleting Registry Information

The RegQueryInfoKey function returns a lot of information about a key and its subkeys. The ReqQueryValue function returns the data associated with a key's default value. The ReqQueryValueEx function returns the data for the specified value name. If there isn't sufficient space for the return value, ERROR_MORE_DATA will be returned.

Call me twice: You can determine the size of a value by passing a binary zero in place of the string reference (lpData) and passing a nonzero value for size of the return buffer (lpcbData). Then you can preallocate sufficient space for the return value and avoid the ERROR_MORE_DATA error.

The RegSetValue function is used to set the data part of a value with a Null name. The RegSetValueEx function will assign a value to the data part of a value for the specified name.

The RegDeleteKey function deletes a key and all of its subkeys and values from the Registry. The RegDeleteValue function deletes a value from the Registry. Both of these functions require an open key handle. Note that the handle still needs to be closed, even after the key has been deleted.

Iterating through the Registry

The RegEnumKeyEx function is used to iterate through a set of subkeys. The RegEnumKey function should not be used in a Visual Basic program. It exists for compatibility reasons and has been superceded by the RegEnumKeyEx function. To use this RegEnumKeyEx function, you should set the dwIndex parameter to zero for the first call, increment dwIndex, and repeat the call until the function returns ERROR_NO_MORE_ITEMS. You should not make any changes to any of the subkeys until you have finished the processing. The key handle must have been opened with the KEY_ENUMERATE_SUB_KEYS access option, which is included with the KEY_READ access option.

The RegEnumValue function is used to iterate through a set of values specified by the current key handle. You must have opened the key handle with the KEY_QUERY_VALUE access option. It works just like the RegEnumKeyEx function. You set dwIndex to zero for the first call and increment it each time afterwards until a response of ERROR_NO_MORE_ITEMS is received.

Getting Notice of Changes

The RegNotifyChangeKey value establishes a callback function that will be triggered whenever a change is made to the specified key or any of its subkeys. With this function, you need to use the AddressOf operator to pass the address of the function that will be called.

Closing Registry Keys

The RegCloseKey function closes the handle to a Registry key. A value of ERROR_SUCCESS will be returned if the call is successful. Use the RegFlushKey function to post any changes made to the Registry to disk when you need to be absolutely certain that the changes are written to disk. The RegCloseKey function posts the changes to disk using its lazy flusher.

WARNING   **Flush only when you need to:** Calling RegFlushKey can have a negative impact on your system's performance. You should call it only when you absolutely must have the most recent changes posted to disk.

Changing Key Security

The RegSetKeySecurity function will change the security of the specified key. This function requires the WRITE_OWNER permission or the SE_TAKE_OWNERSHIP_NAME privilege.

Loading, Replacing, and Saving Keys

The RegLoadKey function creates a new key in the Registry under the HKEY_USER or HKEY_LOCAL_MACHINE key and loads the contents of a hive file into that subkey. The RegReplaceKey function switches one file containing the Registry with another. The change takes place the next time the system is restarted.

The RegSaveKey creates a file containing the contents of the specified key and all of its subkeys. The RegRestoreKey replaces a key and subkeys with the contents of the specified file.

Accessing Remote Computers and Multiple Values

The RegConnectRegistry function returns a key handle that can be used to access a Registry on a remote computer.

The ReqQueryMultipleValues function returns information about one or more values of a key. However, it does not work in Visual Basic, because there is no way to pass an array of user-defined types to a function.

Writing Registry Programs

You can make your installation program look more professional by retrieving the user's name and organization from the Registry and asking the user if that information is correct. You can also use the Win32 API Registry calls to interact with the GetSetting, DeleteSetting, and SaveSetting routines in Visual Basic.

I wrote the RegTool program to demonstrate how to get and set Registry values with Visual Basic. Figure 17.9 shows its window.

FIGURE 17.9:

The RegTool program

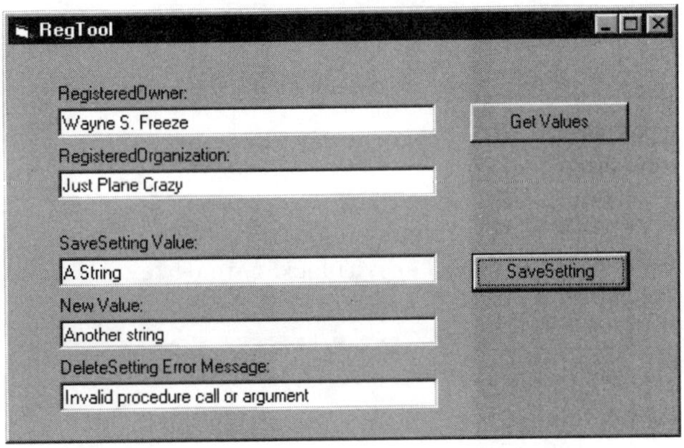

Retrieving Registry Information

Listing 17.12 shows how easy it is to retrieve that information from the Registry. You begin by getting a handle to the Registry key Software\Microsoft\Windows\CurrentVersion. This key holds a lot of interesting information about Windows. Note that this key works only for Windows 95/98. For Windows NT, use Software\Microsoft\Windows NT\CurrentVersion as the key.

Listing 17.12: **Command1_Click Event in RegTool**

```
Private Sub Command1_Click()

Dim hkey As Long
Dim c As Long
Dim r As Long
Dim s As String
Dim t As Long

r = RegOpenKeyEx(HKEY_LOCAL_MACHINE, _
    "Software\Microsoft\Windows\CurrentVersion", 0, KEY_READ, hkey)

If r = 0 Then
    c = 255
    s = String(c, Chr(0))
    r = RegQueryValueExString(hkey, "RegisteredOwner", 0, t, s, c)
    If r = 0 And c > 0 Then
        Text1.Text = Left(s, c - 1)
    End If

    c = 255
    s = String(c, Chr(0))
    r = RegQueryValueExString(hkey, "RegisteredOrganization", 0, t, s, c)
    If r = 0 And c > 0 Then
        Text2.Text = Left(s, c - 1)
    End If

End If

r = RegCloseKey(hkey)

End Sub
```

I begin by opening a handle to the key containing the information I want. I specify a value of KEY_READ since I don't plan to update any information. If I get a successful return code (= 0), then I pad a string with 255 Null characters and retrieve the data associated with the name "RegisteredOwner". If I get another successful return code and have at least one character in the return buffer, I display it in the Text3 text box. Note that the length returned in c includes the Null character at the end of the string, so the actual number of characters in s is one less. Then I repeat the same process over again to retrieve the information for "RegisteredOrganization" and display it in the Text2 text box.

Managing Information with the Win32 API

Listing 17.13 demonstrates that the information managed by the SaveSetting, GetSetting, and DeleteSetting routines can also be managed by the Win32 API routines.

Listing 17.13:   Command2_Click Event in RegTool

```
Private Sub Command2_Click()

Dim hkey As Long
Dim c As Long
Dim r As Long
Dim s As String
Dim t As Long

SaveSetting "RegTool", "Main", "TestValue1", "A String"

r = RegOpenKeyEx(HKEY_CURRENT_USER, _
    "Software\VB and VBA Program Settings\RegTool\Main", 0, _
      KEY_ALL_ACCESS, hkey)

If r = 0 Then
   c = 255
   s = String(c, Chr(0))
   r = RegQueryValueExString(hkey, "TestValue1", 0, t, s, c)
   If r = 0 And c > 0 Then
      Text3.Text = Left(s, c - 1)
   End If

   s = "Another string"
```

```
        r = RegSetValueExString(hkey, "TestValue1", 0, REG_SZ, s, Len(s) + 1)
        If r = 0 Then
            Text4.Text = GetSetting("RegTool", "Main", "TestValue1", "Error")
        End If

        r = RegDeleteValue(hkey, "TestValue1")
        If r = 0 Then
            On Error Resume Next
            DeleteSetting "RegTool", "Main", "TestValue1"
            If Err.Number <> 0 Then
                Text5.Text = Err.Description
            Else
                Text5.Text = "Value not deleted!"
            End If
        End If

    End If

    r = RegCloseKey(hkey)

End Sub
```

I begin by creating an entry under RegTool\Main in the Registry using the SaveSetting statement. Next, I open a key to the information by using the full key HKEY_CURRENT_USER\Software\VB and VBA Program Settings\RegTool\Main. I use this key to retrieve the value I inserted with the SaveSetting statement.

I continue by using the RegSetValueEx function to change the data associated with "TestValue1" to another string value. Then I use the GetSetting function to verify that it really worked.

Then I use the RegDeleteValue function to delete the value from the Registry and verify that is was deleted by using the DeleteSetting statement. Note that the DeleteSetting statement should fail, so an error message is actually okay. Finally I can close the handle to the Registry key and exit the routine.

Final Thoughts

Building a screen saver is a relatively easy process once you know the tricks. But I know people who have spent twenty dollars just to buy a screen saver that shows a series of images. After reading through the ten steps, you should be able to create your own slide show screen saver in the matter of a few hours.

In the case of the StarSX screen saver, drawing the same picture over and over again will get rather boring. However, it wouldn't be hard to rotate through some other pictures. You could modify the configuration form to save the set of parameters under a particular name in the Registry. Then you could use a combo box to display the list of parameter sets and to select the sets that should be shown. The picture part of the program could randomly select an entry and display that picture.

The Systray control serves a more useful purpose. Nearly any long-running program that doesn't often interact with a user could benefit from this control. For example, you might use it to track what is happening inside an ActiveX EXE program while the program is running as a server. Another idea is to use it to periodically check for mail using the Collaboration Data Objects and pop up a message when some arrives.

The Scheduler program I built is rather basic. You can specify when a function should start and how often it should be run after that, but you can't start something immediately unless you specify the time. When I load the schedule from the Registry, I don't allow you to immediately start processing those tasks that were in the schedule. It would be nice if I marked the time the various tasks completed. To do this, I would need to use a modified form of the `WaitProg` routine from the previous chapter, since I would like to track more than one task at a time. Maintaining a log file with the various events as they occur would also be beneficial. This would help the user look further back than the previous time the task executed.

Using the Win32 API Registry calls gives you the opportunity to get information about the system that Visual Basic doesn't provide. Although they also allow you to add and change information in the Registry, why bother? With the `SaveSetting` and `GetSetting` functions, you can save application-specific information without the potential risks.

You should note that there are many of Win32 API calls that will allow you to get information from the Registry without needing to search through it. For example, while all of the file type and associated program information is available in the Registry, the `FindExecutable` function performs the task without requiring you to build your own search logic.

One thing is clear—you should not assume that the material covered in this chapter is sufficient to teach you everything you need to know about the Registry and how to access it. There are several books available that cover the Registry in-depth, including how the information is arranged and how it should be accessed. You also can learn about other tools for performing Registry updates. These tools may offer a better alternative to using Visual Basic to update the Registry.

Dynamically Adding Controls at Runtime

- The Forms collection for tracking forms

- The traditional use of control arrays

- The Controls collection for handling controls

- The VBControlExtender object and ObjectEvent event for trapping control events

- Functions for working with dynamic controls

A new feature in Visual Basic 6.0 is the ability to add controls to your form at runtime. This is not merely adding controls defined in a control array, but creating brand new instances of controls that didn't exist when the program was created.

In this chapter, I'm going to explain how to create forms on the fly and then how to use the Forms collection to keep track of the forms you are using. Then I'll talk about several ways that you can add controls dynamically, including using the Controls collection. Finally, I'm going to cover a few support functions that are useful with dynamically created controls.

Creating Forms Dynamically

The most fundamental object in a Visual Basic 6 program is the Forms collection. This object contains one property, Count, and one method, Item. As you might guess, the Count property returns the number of forms in the collection, and the Item property returns an object reference to the specific form.

To demonstrate the techniques for using the Forms collection and creating forms dynamically, I built the Forms Collection Demo program, shown in Figure 18.1. This program performs three basic tasks:

- Create new forms.

- List all of the forms in the application.

- Delete all of the newly created forms.

FIGURE 18.1:

The Forms Collection
Demo program

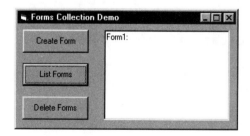

Creating a Form

Although the Forms collection provides some new methods to gather information about the forms in an application, you still need to create a new form dynamically. You can do this by defining a variable as Object or Form and using the New keyword in the Set statement, as shown in Listing 18.1. However, unlike previous versions of Visual Basic, you don't need to save the reference to the form, since you can get a reference to the new form any time you want.

Listing 18.1:   Command1_Click Event in Forms Collection Demo

```
Private Sub Command1_Click()

Dim f As Form

Set f = New Form2
f.Show

f.Tag = FormatNumber(FormCount, 0)
f.Left = Me.Left + Me.Width
f.Top = Me.Top + FormCount * 320
f.Caption = f.Caption & ": " & f.Tag
Set f = Nothing

FormCount = FormCount + 1

End Sub
```

After I create the form, I set the Tag property to a unique value that I will use later to identify the form. This isn't really necessary, because there is no requirement for a form's name to be unique in the collection. However, if the forms didn't have different Tag properties, the same name would be listed for every one. I also move each form to a slightly different location, as shown in Figure 18.2, simply to make it easier to see which forms have been created.

FIGURE 18.2:

Creating multiple forms

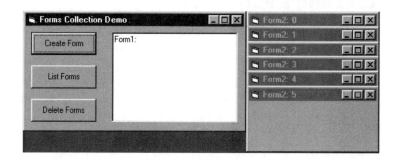

Listing Forms

When the user clicks the List Forms button, the demo program scans the Forms collection and adds each form's Name and Tag property values to the Text1 text box, as shown in Figure 18.3. I use Visual Basic's For Each statement to retrieve each form in the collection, as you can see in Listing 18.2.

FIGURE 18.3:

Finding forms in your program

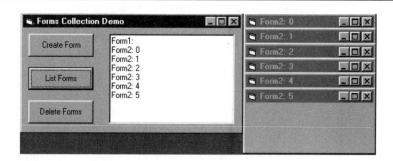

Listing 18.2:   **Command2_Click Event in Forms Collection Demo**

```
Private Sub Command2_Click()

Dim f As Form

Text1.Text = ""
```

```
For Each f In Forms
    Text1.Text = Text1.Text & f.Name & ": " & f.Tag & vbCrLf
Next f

End Sub
```

Deleting a Form

Deleting forms is just as easy as creating them, as long as you use the Forms collection. Listing 18.3 shows how I step through the forms in the Forms collection
and unload any form that does not have the same name as the current form.

Listing 18.3:   **Command3_Click Event in Forms Collection Demo**

```
Private Sub Command3_Click()

Dim f As Form

For Each f In Forms
    If f.Name <> Me.Name Then
        Unload f
    End If
Next f

End Sub
```

Adding New Controls Dynamically

Traditionally, the way that you create new instances of controls in Visual Basic is
to create a single control and make it the first element in a control array. Then you
can include additional elements on the form. The new controls are modeled after
the first control and inherit most of their property values.

Visual Basic 6 introduces the Controls collection, which represents a collection
of controls that currently populate a form. This collection includes controls that

were added at design time and new controls that have been added dynamically. The Controls collection also includes methods to create and delete controls that are not part of a control array.

To demonstrate the techniques for adding controls dynamically, I built the Dynamic Controls program, which performs the following tasks:

- Add a text box to a control array.

- Add a control listed in the combo box to the form without events.

- Add a CommandButton to the form with events.

- Add a control that uses ObjectEvents events.

- List all of the controls on the form.

- Demonstrate the CallByName function.

Of course, I could have built several smaller programs to accomplish the same things, but I felt it was important for you to see that all of these techniques can be used together in a single program.

Using Control Arrays

Control arrays have been around for a while. You use the Load statement to load additional elements of the control array. Any control that was loaded at runtime with the Load statement can be unloaded with the Unload statement.

Following the Traditional Approach

Newly created controls in a control array inherit all of the properties of the first control, except for Index, TabIndex, and Visible. The value for Index is set when the control is created. TabIndex is set to the next available value. Visible is set to False. After creating the control, you should adjust the Left and Top properties so they are different from the first control's values, and then set Visible to True to see the control.

In Listing 18.4, you see the traditional code to create a new element in the control array. I use a CtrlArray counter to track the index of the last control in the control array. I add one to this value and use the Load statement to create a new control. Then I set the Visible property to true, the Text property to the

Index value, and the Top property to a unique value so that you know which control you are looking at. Figure 18.4 shows the result.

Listing 18.4:   Command3_Click Event in Dynamic Controls

```
Private Sub Command3_Click()

CtrlArray = CtrlArray + 1
Load TBCtrlArray(CtrlArray)
TBCtrlArray(CtrlArray).Visible = True
TBCtrlArray(CtrlArray).Text = FormatNumber(CtrlArray, 0)
TBCtrlArray(CtrlArray).Top = CtrlArray * 400 + 100

End Sub
```

FIGURE 18.4:

Adding elements to a control array

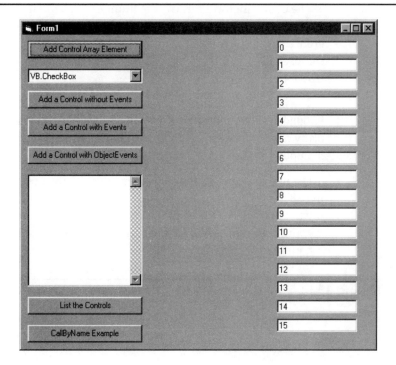

Creating an Element in a Control Array a New Way

Visual Basic 6 introduces some new methods to help you keep track of the elements in the control array. These methods are listed in Table 18.1.

TABLE 18.1: New Control Array Methods

Method	Description
Count	Returns the number of controls in the control array
Item	Returns a reference to the specified control in the control array
LBound	Returns the index of the first control in the control array
UBound	Returns the index of the last control in the control array

The Count method returns the number of elements in the control array. The Item method works like the Item method in a collection—it simply returns a reference to the specified control. Since the Item method is the default method, you can use either TBCtrlArray.Item(0) or TBCtrlArray(0) to refer to the first control in the collection.

The index of the first and last controls in the control array can be found in the LBound and UBound methods, respectively. Note that since elements in a control array need not be contiguous, the Count property may be smaller than UBound − LBound + 1.

Using these new methods, you can rewrite the Command3_Click event (in Listing 18.4), as shown in Listing 18.5. I don't need an independent variable (CtrlArray) to track the value of the last control in the control array, so I can simply compute the new value for the control's index and substitute that value everywhere CtrlArray was used in the previous version.

Listing 18.5: **Command3A_Click Event in Dynamic Controls**

```
Private Sub Command3A_Click()

Dim c As Integer

c = TBCtrlArray.UBound + 1
Load TBCtrlArray(c)
```

```
TBCtrlArray(c).Visible = True
TBCtrlArray(c).Text = FormatNumber(c, 0)
TBCtrlArray(c).Top = c * 400 + 100

End Sub
```

Using Events in a Control Array

A control array maps all of the controls into a single event routine for each event type and passes the Index property to uniquely identify the control that triggered the event. This allows newly created controls in the control array to use events also. Listing 18.6 shows a simple event where I turn the background color of the control to green whenever the control receives the focus. Note that I use the Index parameter to identify which control I want to change.

Listing 18.6:   **TBCtrlArray_GotFocus Event in Dynamic Controls**

```
Private Sub TBCtrlArray_GotFocus(Index As Integer)

TBCtrlArray(Index).BackColor = RGB(0, 255, 0)

End Sub
```

TIP   **Be lazy—use control arrays:** If you have a number of controls that perform similar functions, consider putting them in a control array. You can write your logic once and share it among all of the controls.

Deleting an Element in a Control Array

Using the Unload statement, you can delete an element of a control array that you added at runtime. You can't delete controls that were added at design time.

Listing 18.7 shows the code I wrote to demonstrate deleting control array elements. When a user double-clicks on a control, I remove it from the control array. Since I created only one copy of the control, I verify that Index is greater than zero before using the Unload statement. Figure 18.5 shows the results.

Listing 18.7:   **TBCtrlArray_DblClick Event in Dynamic Controls**

```
Private Sub TBCtrlArray_DblClick(Index As Integer)

If Index > 0 Then
    Unload TBCtrlArray(Index)
End If

End Sub
```

FIGURE 18.5:

Deleting elements in the
middle of a control array

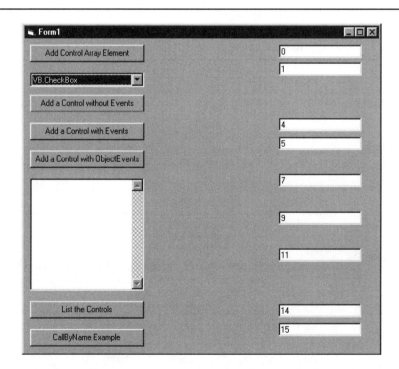

Creating Controls without Events

The new Controls collection allows you to easily add new controls. These controls need not be present on the form like control arrays. All you need to do is to specify the name of the control as a string when you use the Add method. Nearly any control can be added in this fashion.

The `Controls` collection is referenced by the `Controls` property of the `Form` object. This property provides access to the four properties and methods listed in Table 18.2.

TABLE 18.2:   Controls Collection Properties and Methods

Property/Method	Description
Add method	Inserts a new control to the `Controls` collection
Count property	Returns the number of controls in the `Controls` collection
Item method	Returns a reference to a control
Remove method	Deletes a control from the `Controls` collection

The `Add` method adds a new control to the form. The new control is placed on the form at location 0, 0 and has the `Visible` property set to `False`. To really use that control, move it to an empty location on the form.

The `Count` property simply returns the number of controls on the form. Each element of a control array is counted as a single control. The `Item` method merely returns a reference to the control. It is also the default method for the object, so you can omit the `Item` keyword and reference the control as `Me.Controls("Text1")`. The `Remove` method deletes a control from the form. However, you can't use this method on controls that were added at design time.

When you look at Listing 18.8, you'll notice that it is very similar to the code I used in Listing 18.4 to add a new element in a control array. The primary difference is that the `Load` statement was replaced with the `Controls.Add` method.

Listing 18.8:   **Command1_Click Event in Dynamic Controls**

```
Private Sub Command1_Click()

Dim c As Control

Set c = Me.Controls.Add(Combo1.Text, "x" & FormatNumber(CtrlNum, 0))

c.Visible = True
c.Left = 2880
c.Top = CtrlNum * 400 + 100

CtrlNum = CtrlNum + 1
```

```
Set c = Nothing

End Sub
```

The Add method has three parameters: a string containing the type of control you want to use, a string containing your local name for the control, and an object reference of the object that will contain the control. You can omit the object reference parameter if the control will reside directly on the form. If the control will reside in a Frame or Picture control, you must supply the appropriate reference.

If the Add method was successful and the control was created, an object reference to the new control will be returned. If you don't need this object reference, you can release it by assigning it a value of Nothing.

The drawback to creating controls this way is that you can't handle the control's events. For the most part, this shouldn't be a problem, but some controls, such as the CommandButton control, are pretty useless without events. Figure 18.6 shows a bunch of combo boxes that were added to the form with the code from Listing 18.8.

FIGURE 18.6:

A bunch of newly added combo boxes

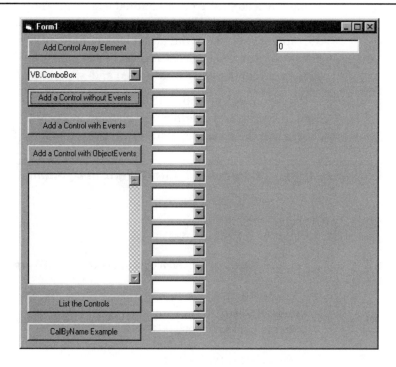

Finding Qualified Control Names

A qualified control name is usually formed by combining the name of the control plus the name of library that contains the control. For example, the Command-Button control resides in the VB library, so the qualified control name is VB .CommandButton. To determine the library name, look up the control using its common name with the Object Browser, as shown in Figure 18.7 (see Chapter 2 for more information about the Object Browser).

FIGURE 18.7:

Looking at the Command-Button control in the Object Viewer

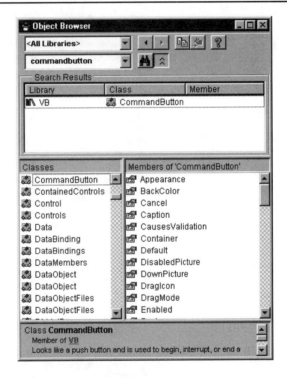

In some cases, the Object Browser doesn't give you the correct name. For instance, according to the Object Browser, you should use ComctlLib.Image-Combo for the ImageCombo control, as shown in Figure 18.8.

FIGURE 18.8:

Looking at the ImageCombo
control in the Object Viewer

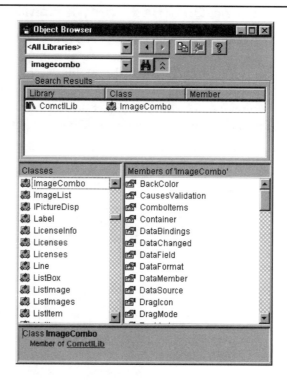

However, when you use that name, you will get the message shown here,
which gives you the correct name to use for the control:

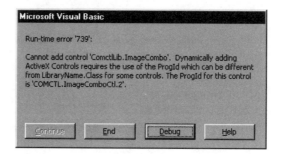

Adding Unused ActiveX Controls

Occasionally, you may get a runtime error 50153 when you try to add a control to your project:

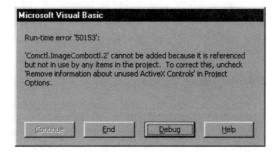

This happens when you have checked the option Remove Information about Unused ActiveX Controls in the project's properties, and then you try to create a control that was defined in the toolbox but not actively used in your program. Clearing the checkmark, as shown in Figure 18.9, will solve this problem.

FIGURE 18.9:

Clearing the Remove Information about Unused ActiveX Controls checkbox

Creating Controls with Normal Events

If you really need to dynamically add a control with events, you can do so with a little more work. The WithEvents keyword can be used when declaring an object variable to allow the object to trigger events. The problem is that the type of control must be defined at design time, and you can't create a control array. This means that you must define at design time each and every control you plan to use.

To define a control with events, you must insert a declaration statement like the following in the General section of your module:

```
Public WithEvents MyCommand As CommandButton
```

This statement defines MyCommand to be a CommandButton. It also allows you to define events for the object in your program. In this example, you would click on the Object drop-down box, select MyCommand, and browse the events in the Procedure drop-down box:

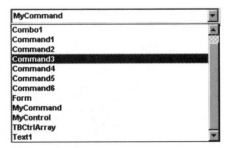

This process works exactly the same as if you had created the control at design time. Because Visual Basic has associated the exact type of control with the object variable, it can determine all of the events possible for the control. You then select the event you want to trap and add you code in the normal fashion, as shown in Listing 18.9.

Listing 18.9:   **MyCommand_Click Event in Dynamic Controls**

```
Private Sub MyCommand_Click()

MsgBox "MyCommand was pushed."

End Sub
```

I add the control to the form using the Controls.Add method, as shown in Listing 18.10. The only differences between this approach and the one I used previously are that I'm using a global variable and I don't set the object to Nothing at the end of the routine.

Listing 18.10:   Command4_Click Event in Dynamic Controls

```
Private Sub Command4_Click()

Set MyCommand = Me.Controls.Add("VB.CommandButton", "MyCommand")
MyCommand.Visible = True
MyCommand.Left = 2880
MyCommand.Top = 100
MyCommand.Caption = "MyCommand"

End Sub
```

Then at runtime, when the user clicks the Add a Control with Events button, the MyCommand button appears. Clicking the MyCommand button displays the message box, as shown in Figure 18.10.

FIGURE 18.10:

Clicking the MyCommand button triggers the MyCommand_Click event.

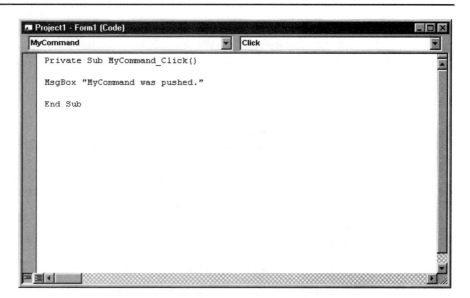

Creating Controls with ObjectEvent

One limitation of the `WithEvents` keyword with a specific type of control is that you can only use it with that control. You can't change the type of control on the fly and still be able to handle its events. As an alternative, Microsoft created a new object type called `VBControlExtender`, which allows you to trap events for any nonintrinsic control by combining most of them into one big event called an `ObjectEvent`.

To define a control that can use `ObjectEvent`, you must insert a declaration statement like the following in the General section of your module:

```
Public WithEvents MyControl As VBControlExtender
```

This statement defines the `MyControl` to be a `VBControlExtender` object. The `VBControlExtender` object contains many of the properties, methods, and events common to most controls. Although this technique can't be used with Visual Basic's intrinsic controls (controls with a qualified name that begins with VB), it can be used with nearly any other control.

TIP   **If in doubt, cheat:** If you really need to use `ObjectEvent` with one of the intrinsic controls, you can always wrap it in your own ActiveX control. Then your own ActiveX control will be supported by the `VBControlExtender` type.

Objects declared as type `VBControlExtender` have the events listed in Table 18.3. Most of these events are common to nearly every control, but `ObjectEvent` is unique. This event is a "super" event that will trap all other events that are generated for the control.

TABLE 18.3:   ObjectEvents Object Events

Event	Description
DragDrop	Occurs when a drag operation drops the item in the control
DragOver	Occurs while a drag operation is in process and the cursor is moved over the control
GotFocus	Occurs when the control gets the focus
LostFocus	Occurs when the control loses the focus
ObjectEvent	Occurs whenever an unlisted event occurs
Validate	Occurs when the focus is lost to a control that requires the data to be validated

There is one parameter associated with the `ObjectEvent` event, which is of type `EventInfo`. `EventInfo` contains the name of the event that was triggered and a reference to an object that holds the information that would normally be passed to the event. Table 18.4 lists the properties of the `EventInfo` object.

TABLE 18.4: EventInfo Object Properties

Property	Description
EventParameters	Contains a reference to the `EventParameters` collection that contains the set of parameters for the event specified by **Name**
Name	Contains the name of the event that would have been triggered

The `EventParameters` collection object contains the parameters that are passed to the event. Table 18.5 lists the `EventParameters` collection properties. The `Count` property contains the number of parameters. The `Item` property returns the parameter name and value as the `EventParameter` object.

TABLE 18.5: EventParameters Collection Properties

Property	Description
Count	Contains the number of items in the collection
Item	Contains a reference to an `EventParameter` object

The `EventParameter` object contains the information from a single parameter. Table 18.6 lists its properties. The `Name` property contains the name of the parameter, and the `Value` property contains the value of the parameter. Note that the `Value` property is a `Variant` and can contain any data type including yet another object.

TABLE 18.6: EventParameter Object Properties

Property	Description
Name	Contains the name of the event parameter
Value	Contains the value associated with **Name**

All this sounds a little complicated, so an example is in order. Listing 18.10 is a sample routine that can be used display the information related to each event as it is called. To use it, simply change the name from MyControl_ObjectEventA to MyControl_ObjectEvent. You will need to change the name of the existing MyControl _ObjectEvent routine (shown in Listing 18.11) before trying to rename the routine in Listing 18.10.

Listing 18.10: **MyControl_ObjectEventA Routine in Dynamic Controls**

```
Private Sub MyControl_ObjectEventA(Info As EventInfo)

Dim i As Integer

Debug.Print "-----------------"
Debug.Print Info.Name
Debug.Print Info.EventParameters.Count
For i = 0 To Info.EventParameters.Count - 1
   Debug.Print Info.EventParameters.Item(i).Name; "="; _
      Info.EventParameters.Item(i).Value
Next i

End Sub
```

Running the program and pressing the period key results in the following information being displayed in the Immediate window:

```
-----------------
KeyDown
 2
KeyCode= 46
Shift= 0
-----------------
Change
 0
-----------------
KeyUp
 2
KeyCode= 46
Shift= 0
```

The KeyDown event occurs first and contains two parameters: KeyCode, which is 46, and Shift, which is 0. Then the Change event is fired with no parameters. Finally, the KeyUp is fired with the same parameters that were passed to the Key-Down event.

A more realistic routine is shown in Listing 18.11. Well, it may not be that realistic, but it does show how you may want to code this event. You should trap each event you need by name with a Select statement and then process it as you would have processed each event as a separate routine.

Listing 18.11:   MyControl_ObjectEvent Event in Dynamic Controls

```
Private Sub MyControl_ObjectEvent(Info As EventInfo)

Select Case LCase(Info.Name)

Case "dropdown"
   MsgBox "Drop Down"

Case "change"
   MsgBox "Change: " & MyControl.Text

End Select

End Sub
```

Using Functions with Dynamically Created Controls

Adding controls to your form on the fly can make your life more complicated. To help you out, Microsoft includes a few functions that make it easier to deal with dynamically created controls:

- The CallByName function allows you to call a function, procedure, method, or property by specifying a string value.

- The TypeOf clause in an If statement allows you to determine the type of an object.

- The TypeName function is a more general-purpose version of the TypeOf clause that will return a string containing the name of the object's type.

Using the CallByName Function

The CallByName function is new in Visual Basic 6. It provides a way to call a routine, invoke a method, or access a property. The syntax of the function is:

```
value = CallByName(object, routine, calltype, arguments)
```

where:

- object is an object reference to the control.

- routine is a string containing the name of the routine, method, or property you wish to call.

- calltype is one of the following: vbGet (retrieves a value from a property), vbLet (assigns a value to a property), vbMethod (calls a method), or vbSet (assigns an object value to a property).

- arguments contains either a single value or an array of values used in the call.

Listing 18.12 contains a sample routine that creates a text box control and uses the CallByName function to set the value in the text property. Then I use the CallByName function to retrieve the contents of the text box and display it using MsgBox. Next, I move the text box to a different location before I prompt the user to delete the text box. Finally, I use the Remove method to delete the text box from the form.

Listing 18.12:   Command6_Click Event in Dynamic Controls

```
Private Sub Command6_Click()

Dim c As TextBox

Set c = Me.Controls.Add("VB.TextBox", "MyTextBox")

c.Visible = True
c.Left = 2880
```

```
    c.Top = 100

    Set c = Nothing

    CallByName Me.Controls("MyTextBox"), "Text", VbLet, "A text string"

    MsgBox CallByName(Me.Controls("MyTextBox"), "Text", VbGet)

    CallByName Me.Controls("MyTextBox"), "Move", VbMethod, 2880, 500, _
        1440, 240

    MsgBox "Press OK to delete MyTextBox"

    Me.Controls.Remove "MyTextBox"

End Sub
```

Determining Object Type with TypeOf

In an If statement, you can use the TypeOf clause to determine which type of object you are dealing with. For example, in the following code fragment, the TypeOf clause checks the variable myobject to see if it is a command button.

```
If TypeOf myobject Is CommandButton Then
```

The TypeOf clause is available only in the If statement and can't be used in a Select or Do statement or as part of a Boolean expression. If you need to known the type of a variable or expression, you should use the TypeName function, described next.

Getting Variable or Expression Type with TypeName

A new function in Visual Basic 6 is TypeName. This function returns a string containing the type of the variable or expression, which is useful for detecting the type of object you are dealing with. Table 18.7 lists the return values from the TypeName function.

TABLE 18.7:   Return Values from the TypeName Function

Value	Description
Specific object type	The name of a specific object (e.g., `CommandButton`, `Form`, `FileSystemObject`, etc.)
`Boolean`	A `Boolean` variable or expression
`Byte`	A `Byte` variable or expression
`Currency`	A `Currency` variable or expression
`Date`	A `Date` variable or expression
`Decimal`	A `Decimal` variable or expression
`Double`	A `Double` variable or expression
`Empty`	An uninitialized `Variant` variable or expression
`Error`	A `Variant` containing an `Error` expression
`Integer`	An `Integer` variable or expression
`Long`	A `Long` variable or expression
`Nothing`	An `Object` variable that doesn't refer to an object
`Null`	A `Variant` variable that doesn't contain any valid data
`Object`	An `Object` variable or expression
`Single`	A `Single` variable or expression
`String`	A `String` variable or expression
`Unknown`	An `Object` variable with an unknown type

In Listing 18.13, I use a `For Each` statement to loop through each element in the control collection. I call `IsControlArray` to determine if the object is a member of a control array. If it is a part of the control array, I display its name, subscript, and the type of its control. If it isn't, I just display the control's name and type, as shown in Figure 18.11.

Listing 18.13:   Command2_Click Event in Dynamic Controls

```
Private Sub Command2_Click()

Dim c As Control

On Error Resume Next

Text1.Text = ""

For Each c In Me.Controls
   If IsControlArray(c) Then
      Text1.Text = Text1.Text & c.Name & "(" & _
      FormatNumber(c.Index, 0) & "): " & TypeName(c) & vbCrLf
   Else
      Text1.Text = Text1.Text & c.Name & ": " & TypeName(c) & vbCrLf
   End If
Next c

End Sub
```

FIGURE 18.11:

Listing the controls in a form

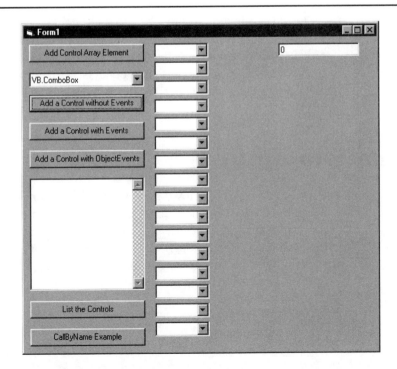

The `IsControlArray` function isn't part of Visual Basic—it's a little routine I hacked together to determine if an object is part of a control array Listing 18.14 shows this routine.

Listing 18.14:   IsControlArray Function in Dynamic Controls

```
Public Function IsControlArray(o As Object) As Boolean

' This routine sets the default return value to False. Then
' it attempts to see if the index property is numeric. If the
' object is a control array, then the index property should be
' numeric and the function will return True. If it isn't a
' control array, then the statement will fail leaving the
' default value of False unchanged.

On Error Resume Next

IsControlArray = False
IsControlArray = IsNumeric(o.Index)

End Function
```

This takes advantage of the facts that a statement is totally skipped when it has an error and that only the controls that are part of a control array have an `Index` property. The expression `IsNumeric(o.Index)` is always `True` when you have a control array and will always fail when it isn't a control array. Since a failing statement doesn't have any effect, the default value of `False` will not be changed.

Final Thoughts

Forms can be used in many different ways. I sometimes use forms as sort of a tear-off item. I'll create a generic form to display some information and then create a new copy of it each time I display it. The classic example is the multiple windows that a web browser has opened. The tear-off concept is also useful when writing MDI applications, where you want to create multiple forms inside the main window based on an existing model.

Perhaps the most useful aspect of the `Forms` collection is that you don't need to remember every form you opened when it comes time to close the application. Your exit logic merely closes every open form, except the main form, which is closed when the exit logic has finished.

Adding controls to your form at runtime may be more useful than you think. Suppose you have several database tables in your application and you need a utility program that can browse and update individual records in each table. You could build a generic Visual Basic form that allows you to select the name of the table and then automatically builds the form based on the parameters in the database. Controls that let you add, delete, and update records would already exist on the form, along with any other controls that would be common across all of the database tables. This approach would take a bit more time to develop than a stand-alone database editor program. However, I bet that it would save you time if you count the hours it would take to write a second or a third program, even if you used the first program as a model.

The best way to handle events for dynamic controls depends on your application. A database application may be able to perform any necessary edit checks before the information is inserted into the database, thus bypassing the need to check the individual field values. Control arrays allow you to perform the edit checks as you normally would, but are limited to a single type of control.

The type of control also has a big impact on how you handle events. While command buttons are useless without the ability to respond to events, you almost never use events with frames and labels.

Using `VBControlExtender` objects is perhaps the best way to handle events. Unfortunately, you can't use them with intrinsic controls like text boxes and command buttons, so they may not be as useful as you might think. I also wish that Microsoft would allow you to map multiple `VBControlExtender` objects into a single set of events, similar to a control array. This would let you manage a collection of unlike controls with a single set of events, which is what I think Microsoft was aiming at in the first place.

PART V

Application Optimization

CHAPTER

NINETEEN

19

Optimizing Your Application

- Application goals and constraints

- Tips for speeding up your code

- Tricks to make your user think your program is fast

- Memory conservation techniques

- Project type selection

- Optimization options

Optimizing your application involves looking at many factors and tweaking them to achieve one or more specific goals. One of the most classic optimization issues is the tradeoff between memory and CPU time. Some techniques to increase the performance of an application have a side effect of using more memory. Likewise, you can save memory by using a few more processor cycles.

If you don't believe me, trying reading a disk file one byte at a time, then try to read the file in one big chunk. Which one is faster? Reading the file in one big chunk. Which one uses less memory? Reading one byte at a time. Which method is more optimal? It depends. If you have enough memory, then reading the file in one big chunk is probably better. If you are already short on storage, then reading small chunks may actually result in better performance.

Many of the tricks and tips I'm going to discuss in this chapter fall into the category of good programming techniques. These techniques represent no real cost to implement and, in many cases, even improve the maintainability of your application.

As with any group of experts, not everyone will agree with the information here. My recommendation is to read through this material and try using the techniques with your own programs. Then you can judge how well the techniques really work.

Defining Your Goals and Constraints

Optimizing your application usually involves a series of trade-offs. To understand which trade-offs are acceptable and which are not, you need to understand what you are trying to accomplish. Without a clear goal, you can't determine if the change you made improved your application or made it worse.

Also, you need to understand any constraints placed on your application. If you make a change that violates any of the constraints, then no matter how much closer to your goal you get, the change is unacceptable.

Finally, you need know what the improvements are worth. Is it worth spending a hundred hours fine-tuning an application, only to improve its performance by less than one percent? In some cases, yes; in others, no. It really depends on the situation.

Setting Goals

A goal is usually a problem stated in a positive form. For example, "it's too slow" can be rewritten as "make it faster." It lets you know what you are seeking to accomplish.

The classic "make it faster" goal shouldn't be viewed as a single item. You should try to narrow the focus to something more specific like "make it load faster" or "process a transaction quicker." Without a relatively narrow goal, you can spend a lot of time addressing one specific area without actually solving the problem.

Defining Constraints

Constraints are limits that are placed on your application either by your equipment or your users. Sometimes, you will encounter a situation that will prevent you from taking advantage of a specific feature that could help you achieve your goal. For instance, you can't rely on FAT-32 disk drives to hold your application's files if you must support the original Windows 95.

Constraints can also be stated in terms of the hardware that will run your application. These are often specified as minimum memory size, processor speed, or amount of disk space. In some cases, it might be as simple as your application must fit on a single CD-ROM.

Understanding the Costs

I've known expert programmers who get carried away while optimizing a routine. Consider the case of a programmer spending a couple of weeks optimizing her application. For that effort, she was able to reduce the CPU time a particular function took from about a minute to only a couple of seconds—a 3000 percent improvement! However, this routine was called only once or twice a day. Another routine in the application ran for about two seconds, yet was called thousands of time a day. Improving this routine by only 10 percent would have made a much bigger difference. Optimizing the first routine would save 116 CPU seconds each day (based on 2 calls per day times a savings of 58 CPU seconds per call). Optimizing the other routine would save 1000 CPU seconds each day (based on 5000 calls per day times a savings of 0.2 CPU seconds per call).

What does this mean to you? Your time is valuable. Assuming that you could improve both functions in the same amount of time, it is obvious that improving the second function gives you better results. However, spending time on either function may be too expensive if you have a client waiting for new software. Likewise, adding another processor to the system might be cheaper than either optimization and would find another 36,000 CPU seconds over a ten-hour workday.

To decide where to spend your time, you can apply the old 80/20 rule (80 percent of the work is done by 20 percent of the program). Try to find the 20 percent and optimize that code before you worry about the other 80 percent. If you don't believe me, take a look at some of your own code. Separate it into two groups. Put it in the first group if any of the following is true:

- The code handles either initialization or termination.

- The code handles an error condition.

- The code represents an administrative function, such as creating new users or changing the permissions of existing users.

- The code provides a utility function that does not directly impact the main function of the application, such as displaying a message of the day or handling login and logout type of functions.

The rest of the code should go into the second group. You'll find that most of the code falls into the first group. Optimizing that code will not have nearly as large an impact as optimizing the code in the second group. The code in the second group represents the functions that are executed many times each day when compared with those in the first group. Of course, the code in the second group is probably harder to optimize, yet improvements here will yield the best results in the long run.

Following the General Rules

When I build my own applications, I follow a few general rules. They don't necessarily produce fully optimized applications by themselves, but they do help in the optimization process.

Getting It Right

My number one rule is get it right the first time. No matter how much you may work with some applications, you may not be able to improve their performance as much as you would by redesigning the application from scratch. It is important to choose the appropriate algorithms before you build the application. Changing them afterwards can be very expensive.

Consider the case of how to sort a series of values. A poorly written quick sort algorithm will almost always be faster than a heavily optimized bubble sort. However, a bubble sort of a handful of records may be faster than a quick sort, due to the quick sort's overhead.

Waiting Until Tomorrow

My second rule is always put off until tomorrow what you can do today, especially if it means you might not have to do it at all. The old saying "Never put off until tomorrow what you can do today" doesn't always hold with writing programs. In a program, you may spend resources performing a task whose results will never be used. This is typically found anywhere you need to initialize something.

Consider the case of the TreeView control. You can spend a lot of system resources to load everything into the control at one time or you could load just enough to satisfy the immediate need. As the user interacts with your program, you can load additional information on demand. Chances are you will never load everything, even if the application is used for several hours. And even if you did load everything a bit at a time, you would be no worse off than had you loaded everything at the start.

Building Modularly

My third rule is to build in a modular fashion. In other words, build your application as a series of components that can be replaced. In some ways, this contradicts my first rule, but you may not know the best way to optimize the application until after it has been built.

Building the application as a series of replaceable modules allows you to gain experience with the application and to narrow down where your bottlenecks are. Once you've isolated the area, you can then rewrite that module and not the entire program.

Consider the case of a data-access module. You may write the program to search for information in a series of text files. If you run into a problem where it takes too long to find your data, you could replace the data-access module with a new module that uses a database to hold the data. All you need to do is to duplicate the same interface, and your program can take advantage of the more efficient module.

TIP

Don't throw that code away—recycle it: Part of being a lazy programmer is never tossing out a useful piece of code away. If you're using the Enterprise edition of Visual Basic, you can save your code in SourceSafe or the Repository for later use. However, if you don't have these tools, you can do the same thing yourself by pasting the code into a file and saving it in a ZIP archive to conserve space.

Speeding Up Your Code

There are a lot of tricks you can use to make your application run faster. Many may be obvious, and a few may not be so obvious. All involve thinking through what you plan to accomplish with your program and choosing what tradeoffs are going to get you the most bang for the buck.

Using Integers and Longs

This is probably obvious, but it's definitely worth mentioning—calculations using Integer and Long values will run faster than calculations using Single, Double, or Currency values. Single values are more efficient than Double values, while Double values are more efficient than Currency variables.

If you have an application where you need to compute values to two or three decimal places, you can still use Integer or Long values. Simply assume that the variable has the appropriate number of decimal places. For instance, you can save the value $1.98 as a Long value of 198 as long as you remember to divide by 100 when you want the true value of the number. This is also known as an *implied decimal point*. Your calculations will be much faster using this technique. However, you need to be careful when using Visual Basic functions, since they won't know about the implied decimal point. Also, you need to take care when reading or saving values to make sure that you maintain the appropriate decimal point.

Avoiding Variants

Visual Basic includes a universal data type called `Variant`. A `Variant` variable can contain an `Integer` value, a `String` value, a `Date` value, or even an object reference. Unless you use a `Def` statement (`DefBool`, `DefByte`, `DefInteger`...) to assign a default data type other than `Variant`, any variable without a type is assumed to be a `Variant`.

While `Variant` variables are useful for beginning programmers and in situations where you're not sure what data type you're going use, this flexibility has a price. Visual Basic must determine which data type is needed and then convert the `Variant` into the appropriate data type at runtime. These conversions can significantly slow down your program, especially when performing simple mathematical operations.

Also, each `Variant` occupies 16 bytes of storage. Compare this to the 2 bytes required for an `Integer` or the 4 bytes for a `Long`. This can add up to a significant amount of storage when creating arrays or passing arguments to a subroutine or function.

Limiting Property Accesses

Accessing an object's property can be as much as 20 times slower than accessing a regular variable. So if you need to access a property several times in a row, you should save the property's value into a temporary variable and access the variable instead.

This is especially true if you want to append multiple blocks of text to the `Text` property of a text box. Each block of text takes longer to append than the previous block when the blocks are appended to the `Text` property directly. You can speed this up by declaring a temporary string variable and appending the text blocks to the string variable. Once all of the text blocks have been appended, you can assign the string variable to the `Text` property.

In the following code fragment, I initialize a multiple-line text box with the numbers 0 to 255. This can be a fairly expensive operation as the amount of text being retrieved from the property gets larger. Also adding to the expense is the extra overhead of using the property of a control.

```
Text1.Text = ""
For i = 0 To 255
    Text1.Text = Text1.Text & FormatNumber(i, 0) & vbCrLf
Next I
```

I rewrote the code fragment to replace the references to the text box with a temporary variable and then assigned the temporary variable to the text box after I created its new value:

```
t = ""
For i = 0 To 255
    t = t & FormatNumber(i, 0) & vbCrLf
Next i
Text1.Text = t
```

This routine is much faster. The first block took nearly two seconds on a Pentium 200; the second block was nearly instantaneous.

Setting AutoRedraw and ClipControls to False

Don't use AutoRedraw, or at least use it intelligently. Setting AutoRedraw to True means that Visual Basic keeps an invisible bitmap that shadows the control. Any changes to the control are first made in the bitmap and then the bitmap is copied to the screen. This takes extra memory and CPU cycles and slows down graphic methods such as Line, Circle, and PSet because of the extra work involved.

Note that setting AutoRedraw to False means that the graphics will be lost when another window is placed on top of your window and then removed. You need to place code in the Paint event to redraw the graphics or be willing to live with the lost graphics.

> **NOTE** **StarSX performance:** In both the StarSX program (discussed in Chapter 3) and screen saver (discussed in Chapter 17), I set AutoRedraw to False to improve performance. I didn't bother coding the Paint event, since I felt that the user could always redraw the graphic.

When using methods like Circle, Line, Print, and PSet, you should consider ClipControls to False for the Form object. Normally, using these methods will repaint the entire form. However, when you set ClipControls to False, only those parts of the form that have been changed will be repainted. This technique also applies if you use any of the drawing methods on frames or picture boxes.

Hiding Controls and Forms

One of the most expensive operations in Windows is repainting a display. Even appending a character to the end of a text box takes more resources than you would believe. In most cases, this isn't a problem. However, if you encounter a situation where a control flickers a lot while being updated, consider setting Visible to False. You can make your changes and then set Visible to True again.

Loading a form is a time-consuming task, especially if it has a lot of controls on it. Rather than unloading your form when you are done with it, consider hiding it. Then you can just make the hidden form visible when you need to show it again, rather than going through the initialization process a second time. Of course, the downside to this technique is that hidden forms still occupy a lot of memory, so you probably want to do this only for frequently used forms.

Using Collections

Arrays and collections both store information. The primary advantage of a collection over an array is that the collection can reference an element by specifying a key value rather than searching each individual object for a specific value. This makes it easier to write your programs when you need to reference objects by their key rather than their relative index. On the other hand, if you want to reference objects by their relative index value, using arrays will always be more efficient than a collection.

Consider the following code fragment:

```
Private Type myType
    myData As Variant
    myKey As Variant
End Type
Dim m(99) as myType

i = 1
Do While myKeyValue <> m(i).nyKey
    i = i + 1
Loop
MsgBox m(i).myData
```

To access an element in the m array, you need to search through the array looking for a match. This is an expensive process.

As an alternative, consider the code fragment below, which uses a `Collection` object to directly retrieve a data value. A `Collection` object has been optimized to retrieve data based on a particular key value, which is faster than a simple linear search.

```
Dim myCollection As New Collection

MsgBox myCollection(myKeyValue)
```

The following code fragment shows the fastest way to access a data value by key. It includes a series of constants that can be used as a direct subscript into an array. Of course, this approach isn't as flexible as the other approaches because you can't specify a string value for the key.

```
Dim m(99) as Variant

MsgBox m(myKeyValue22)
```

TIP   **For versus For Each:** With most collections, you can use either a simple **For** statement or a **For Each** statement to process each element of the collection. Besides being cleaner than a simple **For** statement, the **For Each** statement may also be more efficient. Each collection includes an iteration facility to determine the next object to be returned, which is used by the **For Each** statement. In the worst case, using the **For Each** statement is no different than using a simple **For** statement. Since you've got nothing to lose, why not use the **For Each** statement?

Using Lightweight Controls

Some of the intrinsic controls are not true controls; they are actually simulated by the Visual Basic runtime library. These lightweight controls are simpler and use fewer resources than their full-function cousins. They are also more limited than the real controls. You can easily identify a lightweight control by looking for the presence of an hWnd property. If it isn't present, then you have a lightweight control.

The classic lightweight control is the Image control. Compared to the Picture-Box control, the Image control uses less system resources while providing many of the same functions. Other lightweight controls include the Label, Line, Menu, and Shape controls.

Avoiding Anything Unnecessary

By limiting the number of controls, eliminating redundant code, and reducing the number and size of variables, you will use fewer systems resources, which can lead to better performance.

Each control on a form requires memory to hold its information and CPU time to perform routine functions, such as painting the control and handling initialization and termination issues. At a minimum, redundant code uses additional memory. However, if it is executed, it will use additional CPU time as well. Of course, fewer and smaller variables will occupy less memory, but there are some CPU savings here, because most of these variables will need initialization, which is done by using the CPU.

> **NOTE**   **Remember the trade-offs:** There will be some cases where the "less is more" approach is not your best choice. This is typically when you want to trade memory resources to save CPU resources or vice versa. But most of the time, this approach will result in making your applications more efficient.

For example, do you initialize a variable in one statement and then assign it a value two or three statements later without referencing it in between? Consider the following code fragment:

```
Dim i As Integer
Dim j As Integer
Dim s As String

i = 0
j = 0
s = " "

DoSomeStuff s
DoMoreStuff j

For i = 0 To 9
    DoSomething i
Next I
```

I declare three variables and make sure that they have initial values. Then I call three subroutines using these variables. The first two are simple calls, and the third one is inside a For Next loop. The initial values of the variables are used by the first two calls. However, the `For Next` loop reinitializes i to 0 when it starts. Thus, it wasn't necessary to initialize i in the first place.

WARNING

Trusting Visual Basic: If you are a trusting person, you don't need to initialize any of these values. Visual Basic will initialize all numeric variables to zero and all strings to empty when the routine is first called. However, I prefer to explicitly initialize my variables before I use them. You never know when some problem (like a block of code that changes values beyond the end of an array) is going to arise and cause these values to be changed before they're used.

You should also check to see if you still have various debugging statements built into your program. Statements using the `Debug` object like `Assert` and `Print` are not compiled when you compile your program into object code. However, if you use regular Visual Basic statements to aid you while debugging your program, leaving them in your code will negatively impact the program's performance.

Using Early Binding

Object references can be resolved at runtime (late binding) or compile-time (early binding). The data type of the object variable determines when the binding occurs. Declaring a variable as type `Variant` or `Object` will force late binding. Declaring a variable as type `ListItem` or `CommandButton` means that Visual Basic is able to do most of the work to bind the variable to the object when the program is compiled.

Early binding also helps type checking. With a variable declared to have a specific object type, Visual Basic can perform additional type checking to ensure that you didn't accidentally assign an improper value to the variable. It also lets IntelliSense assist you when coding properties and methods.

Unrolling Your Loops

Do you use a loop to perform the same calculation on all elements of an array? Do you use a loop to initialize the array? Consider unrolling the loop into a series of individual assignment statements. The individual statements will execute faster than the loop, but there is a cost of additional memory and code to maintain. This probably isn't practical if you have more than five or six elements in the array. However, if this code is buried deep inside a loop, the effect can be magnified many times.

Consider the following code fragment:

```
For i = 0 To 3
    x(i) = 0
Next i
```

This loop sets the four values of the x array to 0. Yet it involves an extra variable (i) and a bunch of arithmetic and comparison operations to support the For Next loop. The following statements perform the same function but avoid all the extra work:

```
x(0) = 0
x(1) = 0
x(2) = 0
x(3) = 0
```

Sending Multiple Requests to a Server

Since accessing objects in an ActiveX EXE server is more costly than accessing an ActiveX control, consider passing multiple requests with a single method. You can use an array or type structure to hold the parameters and receive the results.

Consider the following code fragment:

```
ActiveServer.FunctionA "parm1"
ActiveServer.FunctionC "parm2"
ActiveServer.FunctionE "parm3"
```

Compare it to this one:

```
Activeobject.FunctionABCDE "parm1", , "parm2", , "parm3"
```

The first block of code invokes the FunctionA, FunctionC, and FunctionE methods with three different parameters. The second block uses a method that performs multiple functions in a single call. If a missing value is passed to the method, then the function is not performed. Thus, I can perform the functions in one call and avoid all of the extra overhead that results from calling an ActiveX EXE.

Replacing Calls with Inline Code

Calling a subroutine or function is an expensive operation. In fact, if you have only one or two lines of code inside the routine, you may spend more CPU cycles on calling the subroutine than on running the code in the subroutine. You might want to consider replacing the call with the code inside the routine.

Consider the following subroutine:

```
Private Function Max(a As Variant, b As Variant) As Variant

If a < b Then
    Max = b
Else
    Max = a
End If

End Function
```

It returns the maximum of two values. You might use it like this to find the largest value in an array:

```
XMax = x(0)
For i = 1 to UBound(x)
    XMax = Max(x(i), XMax)
Next i
```

However the following block of code will be significantly faster:

```
For i = 0 to UBound(x)
    If x(i) > XMax Then
        XMax = x(i)
    End If
Next i
```

This code is faster for two reasons:

- You avoid the overhead of calling the function and getting the return value.

- You can discard some of the code from the general-purpose function that really isn't needed in this situation.

WARNING   **Think before you write:** It's important to use this technique only when you really need the speed or you're calling a trivial subroutine. You can easily end up with a subroutine that has 500 or even 1000 statements. While this might be more efficient, no one would want to maintain it.

Reducing the Dots in an Object Reference

Each dot you include in an object reference requires Visual Basic to perform an additional call to determine the referenced object. Using the With statement spreads this overhead over the statements inside. Note that you can also accomplish the same thing by setting an object variable to point to one of the lower-level objects to create a shortcut reference and then using the shortcut object instead of the fully qualified object.

In the following code fragment, you can see that I'm using a common prefix for each of several methods and properties:

```
MyAgent.Commands.Caption = "MyAgent Commands"
MyAgent.Commands.Visible = True
MyAgent.Commands.Add "Bye bye", "Bye bye", "... bye bye ...", True,
True
MyAgent.Commands.Add "Down", "Down", "... down ...", True, True
MyAgent.Commands.Add "Happy", "Happy", "... happy ...", True, True
```

It is more efficient to rewrite that code as:

```
With MyAgent.Commands
    .Caption = "MyAgent Commands"
    .Visible = True
    .Voice = "MyAgent Commands"
    .Add "Bye bye", "Bye bye", "... bye bye ...", True, True
    .Add "Down", "Down", "... down ...", True, True
    .Add "Happy", "Happy", "... happy ...", True, True
End With
```

This is fairly obvious when you remember that each object reference is really a call to a Property Get routine or a method subroutine. When you nest object references, these calls must be repeated to determine the correct object pointer for the final call. The With statement tells Visual Basic to remember this object reference, thus avoiding the overhead of the calls to get the same information it already has.

Testing for Empty Strings

If you need to determine if a string contains any data, use the Len function to see if the length of the string is zero rather than comparing it to the empty string. Using the Len function is significantly faster.

Typically, you would code an `If` statement like this:

```
If mystring = "" Then
```

However, here's a faster way:

```
If Len(mystring) = 0 Then
```

Remember that Visual Basic stores the current length of a string as a 16-bit integer at the front of the string. In the first case, Visual Basic will set up a comparison between `mystring` and an empty string that is kept as a constant. In the second case, Visual Basic merely returns the integer value at the front of the string. Although the difference is not significant in most cases, remember that this will be greatly magnified while inside a set of nested loops.

Moving Controls with Move

Repositioning a control with the `Move` method is faster than setting the individual location properties of a control. Setting the `Left`, `Width`, `Top`, and `Height` properties involves four different calls to the control, plus it repaints the control four different times. The `Move` method involves only one call and one repaint, which is significantly faster.

For example, consider the following block of code that repositions a form when it is displayed:

```
Me.Top = GetSetting(App.Title, Me.Name, "Top", 660)
Me.Left = GetSetting(App.Title, Me.Name, "Left", 660)
Me.Width = GetSetting(App.Title, Me.Name, "Width", 2880)
Me.Height = GetSetting(App.Title, Me.Name, "Height", 1440)
```

You can easily replace that code with the following code:

```
Me.Move GetSetting(App.Title, Me.Name, "Top", 660), _
        GetSetting(App.Title, Me.Name, "Left", 660), _
        GetSetting(App.Title, Me.Name, "Width", 2880), _
        GetSetting(App.Title, Me.Name, "Height", 1440)
```

This method performs only a single repaint rather than the four repaints required by the previous block of code.

Forgetting the Next Variable

When using a For Next loop, omit the variable in the Next statement. The Next statement will assume the closest For statement without a matching Next. This works extremely well in nested For Next loops.

In the following code fragment from the Charter program, you can see how I omitted the variable following each of the Next statements. The comments indicate which For statement is matched by each Next statement.

```
For i = 1 To MSFlexGrid1.Cols - 1
    For j = 1 To MSFlexGrid1.Rows - 1
        MSFlexGrid1.TextMatrix(j, i) = FormatNumber(Rnd * 100, 2)

    Next    ' Next j
Next        ' Next i
```

Tricking the User

In some cases, you can make a big difference in how fast your user believes your application runs without necessarily making the application any faster. These tricks involve shifting the work from times where the user finds waiting unacceptable to when the user may not even realize you're doing something besides handling their immediate activity.

Handling Long Tasks

One trick is to make a long task longer. Suppose you have a task that is going to take a while to run, such as printing a large report from the database. You may want to take advantage of the user's patience to perform a few other tasks, such as compressing the database file.

In other cases, you'll want to make a long task seem shorter. If you need to load a large file for the user to process, load just enough of the file to let the user start working. Then you can continue loading the file while the user works. You need to make sure that the user doesn't try to access the parts of the file that have yet to be loaded, but in general, the user is better off since he or she can access at least part of the data quickly.

Another technique I've talked about before is to include a `Me.Show` statement as the first statement in the `Form_Load` event of your form, followed by a `DoEvents` statement. This will display the form to the user before it is completely initialized. Normally, the form wouldn't be displayed until all of the code in the `Form_Load` event has finished. The user is happy because he or she sees immediate activity when your application starts, and you have time to perform all of your initialization logic.

Whenever possible, you should try to entertain the user during long tasks. Using a progress bar while performing a long-running task lets the user know that your program is still working:

If you are working your way through a file or database, consider displaying the page number or the key value from the database in the status bar every second or two. This also gives the user tangible feedback for estimating how much more time is required before the task is finished.

TIP

Learn from Microsoft: While installing the software, Microsoft often uses part of the display to show users new features in the application they are installing and advertise other products that the users might be interested in buying.

Performing Background Processing

Some applications perform lower-priority tasks with background processing. For example, Microsoft Excel recalculates the values in the spreadsheet as a background task.

You can do the same thing in your own programs. Just set the Timer control to trigger the `Timer` event every so often and then add some code to perform a little bit of your processing with each call. By performing a little bit of the work with each call, you don't slow down the user noticeably, but you can accomplish a lot of work over a relatively short span of time. A good example of this technique is in the StarSX program (discussed in Chapter 3). It draws only a single line each time the `Timer` event is fired.

Another approach to doing your work in the background is to start an ActiveX EXE program at a very low priority. Then you can feed work to this low-priority task and let it interrupt your main program when it's ready for more work. Because it is a low-priority task, it doesn't interfere with any other tasks running in your system. This approach is more efficient than using the Timer control because the program can use more idle time. Just be sure to include a lot of calls to DoEvents in the ActiveX EXE program to make sure that you don't block any other programs.

TIP   **Asynchronous ActiveX:** You can build an ActiveX EXE program that periodically checks an internal queue for work. Then you can add a method that adds work to the internal queue. When the work is finished, the program will raise an event in the calling program to return the results.

Displaying a Splash Panel

Another way to distract your users is to create a module, insert a subroutine called Main, and display a lightweight form that contains a nice picture plus your copyright information. This is called a *splash panel*. Figure 19.1 shows the splash panel for Car Collector (a shareware program I wrote a couple of years ago).

FIGURE 19.1:

The Car Collector splash panel

Then you can load your main form, preload some of your other forms, and perform your initialization logic. You can even put a timer in the splash panel to unload the form and let the user see your main form.

Loading Modules and Libraries

Visual Basic loads a module only when it is needed. You should put all of your global subroutines and functions into a single module, which Visual Basic will load when your program is first started. Then you should call functions in your global module or in your startup form module only when your application is first started. This will minimize the effort required to display your first form.

A Visual Basic program uses many different libraries at runtime, including the VB runtime library and the various ActiveX controls your application uses. If the libraries are not already loaded into memory, your application is going to wait until they are loaded. Consider running a simple Visual Basic program when the system starts that uses the same controls your main application uses. This means that you can load the libraries before the application is started, eliminating the load overhead

---

TIP

Hide it in plain sight: You might want to use the Systray control (described in Chapter 17) to anchor the program that loads your libraries at start time and not take up an entry in the Taskbar. You could also use the SysInfo control (described in Chapter 6) to detect system shutdowns and unload the libraries before the system shuts down.

Being Frugal with Memory

Memory—even virtual memory—is not an unlimited resource. You try to keep things in memory as an attempt to reduce disk accesses. However, with too much crammed into too little memory, you end up moving stuff into virtual memory on disk, which defeats the purpose of loading stuff into memory in the first place.

It's important to note that things like variable names, blank spaces, and comments do not take up memory in a compiled program. You can feel safe in the knowledge that you aren't penalized for making your program more readable and well documented.

Here are some ways that you can be frugal with memory:

- Keep in mind that complex forms need more memory. The more controls you put on a form, the more memory it will require when it becomes loaded into memory. Therefore, reducing the number of controls reduces the memory requirements. There is a limit of 254 control names on a form; however, a control array counts as only one name.

- You can reclaim space from strings. By setting a `String` variable to the empty string (`" "`), you can recover the space it was using.

- You can reclaim space from objects. Setting an `Object` variable to `Nothing` frees the space associated with the object if it is the last reference to the object. It also has the advantage of reducing the amount of cleanup work needed when your program terminates.

- By using dynamic arrays, you can reduce memory requirements by trimming the array to just the elements you need. Use the `ReDim` statement to change the dimensions of the array. You can use the `Erase` statement to free the memory associated with a dynamic array. You also can use the `Erase` statement on a fixed array; however, unless the elements are `Strings` or `Variant` variables containing strings or arrays, you will not reclaim any space.

- Use fewer graphics. Graphic images consume memory. The more graphics you have, the more memory you're going to use. The extra graphics not only put a burden on the amount of physical memory you have available, but also slow the time it takes to load forms and other objects from disk, whether they were included in the program file or not. You don't need a lot of graphics in most programs, and quite often they distract from what you're trying to accomplish anyway.

NOTE   **Don't confuse graphics with colors:** It is perfectly fine to make the background of your form and controls a bright pink or leave them button face gray (at least from a purely technical point of view). Both consume the same amount of memory.

- You can make your program more efficient by using constants. Constants are stored once in your program, not many times, thus reducing your program's memory requirements. You can use constants you define with the

Const statement or use predefined constants such as vbCrLf that can be found in the Object Browser.

- Use control arrays, because they consume fewer resources than the equivalent number of independent controls. Remember that you have only one event for all of the elements in a control array. So while a bit more code is needed to distinguish between the elements, less code is needed overall because the controls share the same event.

- Destroy your forms when you are finished with them. If you are finished with a form, you can use the Unload statement to remove the form from memory. This will free some memory resources. Note that this will not free all of the form's resources. To free them, you must set the form's object name to Nothing. (Set Form1 = Nothing).

> **NOTE**   **Not in plain sight:** A form can be loaded but not visible. This usually happens when you reference an object on the form, which in turn loads the form into memory.

- Look for unused routines and variables. I'm willing to bet that some complex programs—modified over a long period of time by several different people—include variables and routines that are not currently active. This often happens when you delete a control on the form without deleting the code from all of its events. Even though the code isn't referenced, it will still occupy memory.

Choosing the Optimal Program Type

When you build your program, you have a choice of several different types of projects. You can build a regular EXE program, an ActiveX control, an ActiveX DLL, and an ActiveX EXE. These projects vary in the types of components they can use, as shown in Table 19.1.

TABLE 19.1:   Object Types Available by Project Type

Object Type	Regular EXE	ActiveX Control	ActiveX EXE	ActiveX DLL
Public class	No	Yes	Yes	Yes
Form	Yes	Yes	Yes	Yes
MDI form	Yes	No	Yes	No
Module	Yes	Yes	Yes	Yes
Class module	Yes	Yes	Yes	Yes
User control	Yes	Yes	Yes	Yes
User document	No	No	Yes	Yes
Property Page	Yes	Yes	Yes	Yes
ActiveX Designer	Yes	Yes	Yes	Yes

Perhaps even more important, each type of project has different capabilities. Table 19.2 summarizes the capabilities available for each type.

TABLE 19.2:   Capabilities Available by Project Type

Capability	Regular EXE	ActiveX Control	ActiveX EXE	ActiveX DLL
File type	EXE	OCX	EXE	DLL
Public class	No	Yes	Yes	Yes
In-process server	No	Yes	No	Yes
Out-of-process server	No	No	Yes	No
Start stand-alone	Default	No	Yes	No
Start ActiveX component	No	No	Default	No

Here's the "short form" of which type of program you should use for what:

- Use an ActiveX control when you want a control you can put in your tool-box and add to any Visual Basic program you write.

- Use an ActiveX DLL when you have one or more common class libraries that you want to share with other programs and you want it to run in the same process as the client program.

- Use an ActiveX EXE when you have one or more common class libraries that you want to run in a different process from the client program, either on the same computer or on a different computer.

- Use a regular EXE when none of the above situations apply.

The regular EXE is the workhorse of Visual Basic, and most programs will be written using this project type. Unless you see a benefit to using one of the other program types, you should use this type. Let's take a closer look at when you might want to use another program type.

NOTE   **What about ActiveX documents?** An ActiveX document is not really a project type by itself. It is created as either an ActiveX DLL or an ActiveX EXE using the `User-Document` statement. Another program, most commonly Internet Explorer, must act as a container. Microsoft seems to make a big deal about ActiveX documents, pushing it as an important technology. Personally, I feel that ActiveX documents are a solution in search of a problem.

Using an ActiveX Control

You should be very familiar with the concept of ActiveX controls because you've used the ones in the Visual Basic toolbox. This type of project is used to build a visible object that is included in another program. It can't be by itself; it must be included in another program, such as a regular EXE program, Internet Explorer, or even another ActiveX control.

Although ActiveX controls usually have a visible component, this is not an absolute requirement. However, if what you have is really a set of class objects, then you should consider using an ActiveX DLL.

An ActiveX control runs as in in-process server, running inside the container program's address space. This type of ActiveX server is more efficient than an out-of-process server because it runs in the same address space. This means that you don't have any of the cross-process communications, which are fairly expensive to perform in Windows.

ActiveX controls must be registered before you can use them. Registering a control involves running the RegSvr32 program and specifying the name of the file that contains the control. This adds the information about the control to the Registry and lets other programs access the control simply by referencing it in their programs.

Using an ActiveX EXE

Programs like Microsoft Excel and Word are ActiveX EXE programs. They offer a combination of an executable program and a series of public classes. This type of project has the advantage of allowing other programs to access objects in your program.

An ActiveX EXE program runs as an out-of-process server. This means that when you access the objects in the ActiveX EXE from another program, they will be executed in a different process. Although the communications process adds a significant amount of overhead, you can exploit the abilities of a multiple-processor system. While your client program is running on one processor, the ActiveX EXE can be running on another. Of course, this requires a design where both programs can work cooperatively, but this is relatively easy to implement using methods that simply trigger a request and return. When the ActiveX EXE server has finished processing your request, it will trigger an event in the first program saying that the processing is complete.

The other advantage of ActiveX EXE programs is that they can run on a different system than the program that is accessing them. This is due to the magic of the Distributed Component Object Model (DCOM). As far as either program is concerned, they are running on the same system.

One drawback to an ActiveX EXE is that any global data can be overwritten if you have more than one client program accessing its facilities at the same time. This can be prevented if you are careful (or if you don't use global variables). You can use this to your advantage if you want to cache a lot of read-only data as global variables. Only one copy of the data would be stored, which would be shared among all of the client programs.

ActiveX EXE programs are self-registering. Simply run the program, and other programs can find your resources.

Using an ActiveX DLL

An ActiveX DLL contains a series of public classes that are made available to other programs. As with ActiveX controls, ActiveX DLLs are run in-process, meaning that they have less overhead than ActiveX EXE programs.

The primary advantage of using an ActiveX DLL over adding a class object to a regular program is that you can easily make the objects public. This simplifies programming if you have multiple applications that need to use these objects.

Another benefit of ActiveX DLLs over ActiveX EXEs is that the module-level variables are unique to each instance of the program using the DLL. Thus, there are no issues involving sharing data when multiple applications are using the single DLL file.

You may want to take advantage of the fact that an ActiveX DLL won't be loaded into memory unless you need it. This allows you to speed up the initial start-up time for your program by moving some objects to a separate file. However, if you reference any of the objects in the ActiveX DLL while starting your application, you will need to load the DLL as well, thus defeating the purpose of moving the code into a different file.

Using an ActiveX DLL is merely a matter of specifying the type library through the Project ➤ References menu item. The objects become available, and you can browse them with the Object Browser.

Choosing Optimizations

The Visual Basic compiler can compile a program into P-Code, as it did prior to Version 5, or it can compile it into your computer's native code for better performance. (The case for compiling into native code is so strong that I can't think of a single reason why you would want to compile your program into P-Code.) This choice is on the Compile tab of the Project Properties dialog box, as shown in Figure 19.2.

The Compile tab of the
Project Properties dialog box

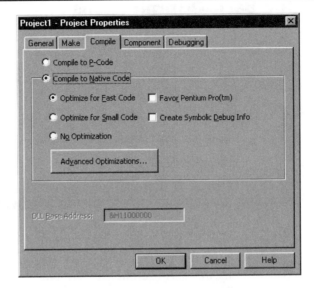

What Is P-Code?

Visual Basic takes each statement as it is entered and translates it into pseudocode, more commonly called P-Code. It is faster to interpret P-Code than trying to interpret each statement on the fly. This is the way that Visual Basic runs your program while you are using the IDE.

When you are ready to create an EXE file, you have two options:

- You can store the P-Code in the EXE file and continue to interpret it.

- You can compile the P-Code into the instruction set of the processor chip on your system. This is also known as native code.

Native code will usually run much faster than P-Code, depending on what your program is doing. Programs that use external processes like database calls may not see much of a difference, but a program that spends a lot of time performing calculations or string manipulations will see a significant improvement by using native code.

Setting Basic Optimizations

Once you check the Compile to Native Code box on the Compile tab, you can select some basic optimization parameters:

Optimize for Fast Code This will try to make your program run faster by making it a little larger.

Optimize for Small Code This will shrink the size of your program by trading CPU time for size.

No Optimization This means that the program is simply compiled and no analysis is done to determine how to improve your program.

Favor Pentium Pro This lets you favor the Pentium Pro instruction set over the normal Pentium instruction set. Since each different processor series (486, Pentium, and Pentium Pro) includes some different instructions, and the speed of each instruction varies in relation to other instructions, the optimizer must make some assumptions about the machine you will use. Choosing Favor Pentium Pro doesn't mean that your program won't run on a 486; it will just run a little slower than it would have had you not checked that box. However, your Pentium Pro and Pentium II users will love you for it!

Create Symbolic Debug Info This compiles the program with debugging information that can be used by the Visual C++ debugger. You probably don't want to enable this option unless you need the debugging information.

Setting Advanced Optimizations

The remaining optimization options are in a separate Advanced Optimizations dialog box, as shown in Figure 19.3. To get to this dialog box, click the Advanced Optimizations button in the Compile tab.

> **WARNING**   **It worked before:** Use extreme care when enabling any of the Advanced Optimizations options. Test your program thoroughly before you enable any of these options. If possible, capture some of the output with and without the optimization enabled and compare the results. If you are not 100 percent certain that the output is correct, don't use the optimization.

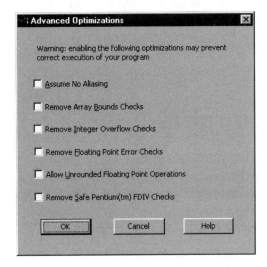

The Advanced Optimizations
dialog box

The Assume No Aliasing option means that none of the variables are known by different names. A variable can be known by different names if you pass a global variable by reference to a subroutine and then reference it by both its global name and its local parameter name. This can cause a problem if the optimizer chooses to take the contents of a variable and keep it in a register.

Enabling Assume No Aliasing can significantly speed up processing inside a loop, but it also can cause a problem if the contents of the variable are updated through a different variable name. This typically happens if you pass a module-level variable to a subroutine. You can access the contents by either the module-level name or by the routine's parameter name.

The Remove Array Bounds Checks, Remove Integer Overflow Checks, and Remove Floating Point Error Checks options all disable important checks in your program. Although removing these checks can improve performance (especially the array bounds check), errors could go undetected, and your program could return unpredictable (and just plain wrong) results.

The Allow Unrounded Floating Point Operations option allows the optimizer to perform floating-point operations much more efficiently. However, intermediate values may be kept at a higher precision, which could result in slightly different results. Also, comparisons may be affected when two values that you believe are equal may prove to be unequal when a higher degree of precision is used.

Remember the bug found on some early Pentium CPU chips where, under some conditions, using a floating-point divide (FDIV) instruction returned a bad result? Well, Microsoft checks the results of the FDIV instruction for errors. The Remove Safe Pentium FDIV Checks option takes this feature away.

Final Thoughts

A few years ago when I was writing a compiler, I realized that no matter how much optimization I did, there were limits to what I could do. I might be able to improve a program's performance by 10 or 20 percent. Occasionally, I might even do better, maybe reaching as high as a 50 percent improvement. But there were many situations where that isn't enough.

A user will generally not notice a change in response time, unless it cuts the time in half. Consider a program that takes 10 seconds to process a task. A 20 percent improvement will reduce it to 8 seconds. From a user's perspective, that's not a very noticeable change. Cut that time to 5 seconds, and the user will probably notice something is different. Cut that time to 1 second, and the user will be extremely happy.

When thinking about optimization, you should keep in mind that all of the optimization tricks you can use will not correct a slow design. Sometimes, you simply have to start over again. But don't believe for a moment that you are starting over from scratch. You already have a working program and a better understanding of what the program needs to accomplish. This information is invaluable when trying to build the next version of your program.

Another way to optimize your program's performance is to consider a hardware upgrade. Generally, you will improve your system's performance by either using a faster processor or adding more memory. Today's cost to go from 16MB of memory to 32MB is probably less than what an average programmer would make in an hour. If you are an expensive programmer, you might be able to jump all the way to 64MB for one hour's time.

However, there are times when you really need a faster processor. This is true if you're building graphic-intensive programs or compute-bound programs. Processors are also dropping in price at an alarming rate, while the speeds are increasing equally fast. For the last several years, I've noticed that the fastest computer in one year becomes a middle-of-the-pack performer in the second year; before the third year has passed, the machine has been dropped from the product line. With the speed increasing and the price dropping, you probably can get a new machine for a lot less money than you could in the past.

Choosing the right project type is usually a fairly easy job. Nine out of ten times, you're going to build a regular EXE file. ActiveX controls are useful when you want to have a common library of objects that have a visible component that you can use in another Visual Basic program. ActiveX DLLs are used mostly when you want to make public a series of class objects without a visual component. ActiveX EXEs are used when you need an out-of-process object server. The fact that you can build a program around these objects is almost secondary.

Having an ActiveX EXE on a different computer may be helpful when building client/server programs. You can use the ActiveX EXE to hold your application's business logic and then allow web-based applications and regular EXE-based programs to access this common set of logic without any special considerations. This also has the advantage of offloading work from your database and web server systems, which may help to improve their performance.

For every Visual Basic project, you can choose the optimization options that will be used when compiling your program. I strongly suggest that you not change any of the Advanced Optimization options. They expose your program to risks that are probably not worth the additional speed.

You also should leave the default value of Optimize for Fast Code alone. Unless you have a program with an enormous appetite for memory, your program probably will not run into a memory problem. If your target machine runs other applications like Word or Excel, you're probably going to be fine. Both of these applications use far more memory than a typical Visual Basic application.

Handling Errors in Visual Basic

- Visual Basic error-handling features

- Error trapping

- Generation of your own runtime errors

- Creation of your own help files

- The Microsoft Help Workshop

It's important to anticipate error conditions in your application and handle them properly. Nothing frustrates users more than seeing a message box announcing a runtime error in a language they don't understand. With some careful planning, you can prevent this from happening.

Not all error conditions are the result of problems. In some cases, Visual Basic is just letting you know that you've reached a particular state—such as a file doesn't exist or that you've reached the end of a database table. It's particularly important to trap these types of errors so that your program can respond properly to the condition.

Tied closely with trapping errors is displaying useful information to the user. One easy way to do this is through the use of help files.

In this chapter, I'll talk about handling errors and using help files. I'll show you how to display a help file from your Visual Basic program and how to create your own custom help files. You can even create your own runtime error that will reference information in your help file.

Using Visual Basic's Error-Handling Features

Visual Basic includes several tools to help you trap and handle any runtime errors in your program:

- The Err object contains information about the last error in your program.

- The On Error statement is useful for telling Visual Basic how to respond when an error occurs.

- The Resume statement is used to continue execution after an error has been trapped by the On Error statement.

These tools can be combined to implement robust error handling in your program.

Getting Error Information with the Err Object

You can find information about the most recent runtime error in the Err object. Table 20.1 lists the Err object properties and methods.

TABLE 20.1:   Err Object Properties and Methods

Property/Method	Description
Clear method	Clears any error information in the Err object
Description property	Contains a text description of the error message
HelpContext property	Contains the context ID of a more detailed description of the error
HelpFile property	Contains the name of the help file where the HelpContext can be found
LastDllError property	Contains the system error code from a call made to a DLL
Number property	Contains the error number
Raise method	Triggers an error condition
Source property	Contains a text description of the source of the error

The default property in this object is the Number property, which maintains compatibility with older programs that used the Err function. The Number property simply returns a Long value containing the error number. The Description property corresponds to the Error function and returns a string containing a short description of the error.

NOTE   **To Err (function) is human to Err (object) is divine:** In the 16-bit versions of Visual Basic, the Err function was used to return the current error number. You would then translate the error number into English by using the Error function, which would return the description of the specified error code (or of the last error that occurred if no parameter was specified). Both of these functions have been made obsolete by the Err object. However, since the Number property returns the same information and is the default property of the Err object, your 16-bit programs will continue to work without change.

The HelpFile and HelpContext properties contain sufficient information to use the CommonDialog control to display extended help information about the error. The Source property contains the name of the program or object class that caused the error. The LastDllError property contains the system code from a call to an external DLL file.

The Err object contains only two methods, Clear and Raise. The Clear method is used to erase the contents of all of the properties in the object. The Raise method allows you to trigger your own runtime errors.

TIP

Create your own errors: Error numbers in the range of `vbObjectError + 512` to `vbObjectError + 65535` are available for you to use in your applications. Simply use the `Err.Raise` method to trigger the error.

Handling Errors with the On Error Statement

There are three different forms of the `On Error` statement:

- The `On Error GoTo Line` statement will transfer control to the specified line number or line label when a runtime error occurs. The error logic at this location should take any corrective action necessary and then execute a `Resume` statement to continue processing or an `Exit Function` or `End Function` statement to leave the routine.

- The `On Error Resume Next` statement is the one I find most useful. This statement instructs Visual Basic to ignore the statement containing the error and continue processing with the next statement. Usually, the next statement should be an `If` statement to check the status of the `Err` object.

- The `On Error GoTo 0` statement cancels any previous `On Error` statements and allows Visual Basic to trap any runtime errors. Even if you have a statement number 0 in your routine, the error handler is still disabled.

All three operate within a single function or subroutine. Once the function or subroutine terminates, the error handler is cleared and error processing returns to normal.

WARNING

He's dead, Jim: Without an `On Error` statement, a runtime error is fatal. You program will be abruptly halted, files will be closed, and data will be lost. While you don't need to trap every error, you should try not to be the guy in the red shirt who beams down when an error is likely to occur.

Continuing with the Resume Statement

The `Resume` statement is used to continue execution after an error has been trapped by the `On Error` statement. It comes in three flavors:

- The `Resume` statement returns control back to the statement that failed and attempts to execute it again. You should use this option only if you were able to correct the problem that triggered the error. If you didn't correct the problem, you could potentially get into a loop where you will continue to trap the same error forever.

- The `Resume Next` statement returns control to the statement after the statement that failed. This is useful if you are performing several operations and you really don't care if they work or not (it's okay to fail when purging a file that doesn't exist). You just want to log the error and continue processing.

- The `Resume Line` statement will resume execution at the specified line number or line label. This is useful if you need to go back and process several statements to prepare to execute the statement again.

Programming Error Traps

There are really only two methods to trap errors in a Visual Basic program: using the `On Error GoTo` statement and using the `On Error Resume Next` statement. You also can generate your own runtime errors using the `Raise` method of the `Err` object. Each approach has its advantages and disadvantages. To demonstrate these techniques, I built the Make Errors program, shown in Figure 20.1.

FIGURE 20.1:

The Make Errors program

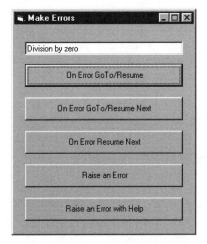

Using the On Error GoTo Statement

Clicking the On Error GoTo/Resume button in the Make Errors program triggers the Command1_Click event, shown in Listing 20.1. The code shows the traditional way to trap an error in Visual Basic. It uses the On Error GoTo label statement to trap the error and the Resume statement to rerun the statement that caused the error.

Listing 20.1:   Command1_Click Event in Make Errors

```
Private Sub Command1_Click()

Dim i As Integer
Dim j As Integer
Dim k As Integer

On Error GoTo ErrorLogic

i = 1
j = 0

k = i / j

Exit Sub

ErrorLogic:
    Text1.Text = Err.Description
    j = 1
    Resume

End Sub
```

I force an error by assigning i and j values of 1 and 0, respectively. Then I use these variables to force a divide-by-zero error (see Figure 20.1).

Immediately following the assignment statement, I put an Exit Sub statement to make sure that the program doesn't fall into the error-handling logic. This is important, because attempting to execute the error logic would generate an error when the Resume statement was executed. The error would be trapped by the On Error statement, and the program would start executing the statement immediately after the ErrorLogic label. When it reached the Resume statement again, it would generate an error again and go back to the ErrorLogic label. This process would loop forever, or at least until you killed the program.

The ErrorLogic label marks the beginning of the error logic. In this case, I display the error message in the Text1 text box and assign a new value to j that shouldn't generate an error. Then I use the Resume statement to take me back to the statement that triggered the error. The failed statement will be executed again (hopefully without errors) and then I'll exit the routine.

Clicking the On Error GoTo/Resume Next button in the Make Errors program triggers the event shown in Listing 20.2. This is very similar to Listing 20.1, but I use the Resume Next statement instead of the Resume statement. Since I don't execute the failed statement again, execution will resume with the Exit Sub statement.

Listing 20.2:　Command2_Click Event in Make Errors

```
Private Sub Command2_Click()

Dim i As Integer
Dim j As Integer
Dim k As Integer

On Error GoTo ErrorLogic

i = 1
j = 0

k = i / j

Exit Sub

ErrorLogic:
    Text1.Text = Err.Description
    Resume Next

End Sub
```

Using the On Error Resume Next Statement

Okay, how many people do you know that will admit to using the GoTo statement some time in their career? I admit that I have. After all, when I learned to program in BASIC many years ago, BASIC didn't include statements like If Then Else and Call. You couldn't even put a statement after the Then clause; you had to specify the line number of where you would continue executing.

After I found better ways to program than using the GoTo statement, I was happy to leave it behind. So when I started building Visual Basic programs and I looked at my choices, I immediately latched onto the On Error Resume Next statement.

Listing 20.3 shows the event triggered when the On Error Resume Next button in the Make Errors program is clicked. This is functionally identical to Listing 20.2; however, it is far more readable. The On Error Resume Next statement instructs Visual Basic to continue processing your program even though an error has occurred. If the statement is an assignment, then the target variable is assigned a Null value. Other failed statements are similarly ignored.

Listing 20.3:   **Command3_Click Event in Make Errors**

```
Private Sub Command3_Click()

Dim i As Integer
Dim j As Integer
Dim k As Integer

On Error Resume Next

i = 1
j = 0

k = i / j

If Err.Number <> 0 Then
    Text1.Text = Err.Description
End If

End Sub
```

The big advantage of the `On Error Resume Next` statement is that you can simply check the `Err` object immediately after the statement that might generate the error. You can take any corrective action you deem necessary without risking an infinite loop. In this case, I display the error on the screen and then leave the subroutine.

WARNING   **Many are called but few are errors:** Many statements will set the `Err` object when an error is encountered, but few (if any) statements will clear the `Err` object if they execute properly. To make sure that the statement that generated the error is the statement immediately before your `If` statement, use the `Err.Clear` method immediately before the statement in question.

Raising Your Own Errors

By using the `Raise` method of the `Err` object you can generate your own runtime errors. In the `Raise` statement, you can specify the error number, the source of the error, a text description of the error, the name of a help file, plus the help file context ID.

My `MakeAnError` subroutine is shown in Listing 20.4. Anytime I see an empty string, I raise my own error 1000. I include the name of a help file and a context reference for the help file.

Listing 20.4:   **MakeAnError Routine in Make Errors**

```
Private Sub MakeAnError(s As String)

If Len(s) = 0 Then
   Err.Raise vbObjectError + 1000, "MakeErrors", _
      "Empty string", App.Path & "\help.hlp", 1000
End If

End Sub
```

Displaying the Error Message

To show how this error is triggered, I wrote the Command4_Click routine, which is called by clicking the Raise an Error button in the Make Errors program. As shown in Listing 20.5, I set On Error Resume Next and then call the MakeAnError subroutine. After checking the Err object, I display the error number and the error message, as shown in Figure 20.2. Note that the absolute error number is rather large.

FIGURE 20.2:

Raising my own error

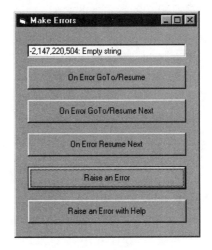

Listing 20.5:   **Command4_Click Event in Make Errors**

```
Private Sub Command4_Click()

On Error Resume Next

MakeAnError ""
If Err.Number <> 0 Then
    Text1.Text = FormatNumber(Err.Number, 0) & ": " & Err.Description
End If

End Sub
```

Displaying the Help Information

Since I return help file information in the MakeAnError routine, I decided to revise the error handling to display the help information. Listing 20.6 shows the event triggered when the Raise an Error with Help button in the Make Errors program is clicked.

Listing 20.6:   Command5_Click Event in Make Errors

```
Private Sub Command5_Click()

On Error Resume Next

MakeAnError ""
If Err.Number <> 0 Then
   Text1.Text = Err.Description
   If MsgBox("Display help?", vbYesNo) = vbYes Then
      CommonDialog1.HelpFile = Err.HelpFile
      CommonDialog1.HelpContext = Err.HelpContext
      CommonDialog1.HelpCommand = cdlHelpContext
      Err.Clear
      CommonDialog1.ShowHelp
   End If
End If

End Sub
```

After detecting the error, I ask the user if he or she wants to see help information. If the user clicks the Yes button, I save the HelpFile and HelpContext properties into the CommonDialog control and then set HelpCommand to display the help information for the specified context. Finally, I display the help information by using the ShowHelp method. Figure 20.3 shows the results.

Displaying help file information about an error

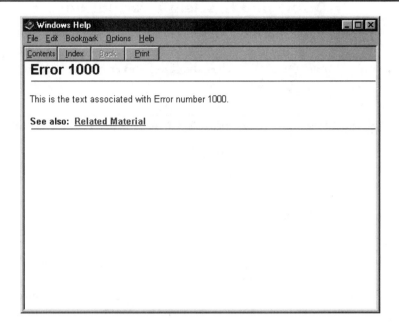

Adding Your Own Help File

Trapping errors is relatively simple compared to adding your own help file to your application. There are a number of steps that you need to follow, but the results are worth it. Your application will look more professional with a real Windows help file. Your two main tasks are to create the topic file and then build the help file.

> **WARNING** **I'm lost and I can't find the Help Workshop:** Don't despair, check in the \Common\Tools\VB\HCW directory. Simply run SETUP.EXE and wait for the setup process to finish. You don't even need to reboot your system.

Creating the Topic File

You start by creating a topic file, which contains the text that will be displayed when the help file is used. You can use any editor that can save a document in RTF format. In this case I used Microsoft Word 97, as shown in Figure 20.4.

FIGURE 20.4:

Creating the topic file as an RTF document

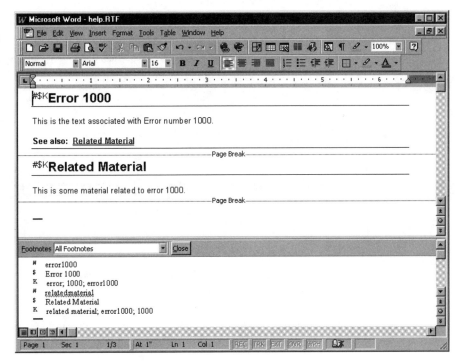

A topic file consists of a series of one or more topics with a hard (manual) page break separating each topic. Any text you can enter into an RTF document can be used in a help file. This means that you can use multiple character fonts, different colors, underlines, and more. When the topic is displayed, it will be automatically formatted as you specified.

TIP

Less is more: A topic is not limited to a single page of text. Even so, try to keep your topics short so that your users won't have to scroll through a long presentation to find the information they need.

Adding Footnotes

In my simple help file, I created two topics: Error 1000 and Related Material. Looking at Figure 20.4, the first thing you should notice is that each topic begins with several footnotes. These footnotes provide information about the topic to the help compiler. See Table 20.2 for a complete list of footnotes available.

TABLE 20.2: Footnotes Used in a Help File

Footnote	Parameter	Description
#	Topic ID	Contains a unique identifier that will be associated with this topic (required)
$	Title	Contains the title of the topic (optional)
K	Keyword	Contains a series of one or more keywords, which will be used when building an index (optional)
A	A-keyword	Contains a series of keywords for use with the ALink macro (optional)
+	Browse code	Contains the topic's place in a browse sequence (optional)
!	Entry macro	Contains the name of a macro to be run when the topic is displayed (optional)
*	Build tag	Identifies a topic for a conditional build (optional)
>	Window type	Contains the default window type for the topic (optional)

In my document, I used only three types of footnotes: Topic ID, Title, and Keyword. Here are their contents for the two topics:

Topic ID (#)	Title ($)	Keyword (K)
error1000	Error 1000	error, 1000, and error1000
relatedmaterial	Related Material	related, material, error1000, and 1000

> **TIP**
>
> **Unlock your topics with keywords:** Choose your keywords carefully, since they will be used to build the index. If you include the same keyword in every topic, the index will return too many entries for that keyword.

Linking to Another Topic

You also have the ability to jump from one topic to another using a link. A link contains two parts: the hotspot and a topic ID. The hotspot is the text that users will click on to take them to another topic. The topic ID is the same unique identifier I created with the # footnote. These two fields must be placed side by side with no spaces between them.

Then you mark the hotspot by formatting it with a double underline. The topic ID is formatted as hidden text. For example, in Word 97, you can add this formatting by selecting the appropriate characters, choosing Format ➢ Font, and selecting Double for Underline or Hidden for Effects, as shown in Figure 20.5.

FIGURE 20.5:

Formatting characters in Word 97

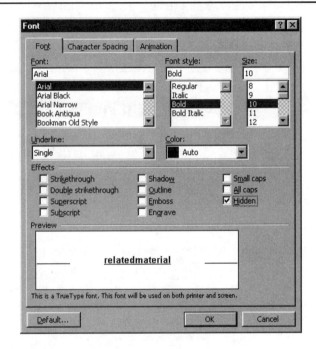

In Figure 20.5, I highlighted the text that should be hidden, since you can't see the hidden text in the book. When you open the file on the CD-ROM, you won't see the text, but if you select the characters from the end of the hotspot text to the end of the line and select Format ➢ Font, you'll see a checkmark in the Hidden checkbox (see Figure 20.5). If you remove the checkmark, you'll see the text in the document. Just remember that you need to hide the text before you build the help file; otherwise, the link will not work.

Building the Help File

Once you have a topic file, it's time to start the Help Workshop. This is a new facility in Visual Basic that helps you build help files by prompting you for the information.

With earlier versions of Visual Basic, you had to enter most of this information into a basic editor such as Notepad. The Help Workshop makes building help files much easier.

TIP

One step at a time: Don't try to build your entire help file before trying to compile it. Build a topic file with just a couple topics and compile it. Invariably, you will have some errors that will require fixing (I know I did). Resolving a few errors is much easier than resolving a whole lot of errors.

Creating a New Help File Project

Once you start the Help Workshop, select File ➤ New ➤ Help Project. In the dialog box that appears, shown in Figure 20.6, select the directory that you wish to use and enter a filename for your help file project. The Help Workshop will create an .HPJ file to contain the information you will enter and place some default values on the screen.

FIGURE 20.6:

A new help project

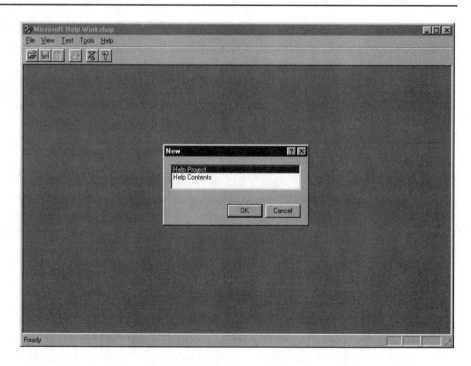

Adding the Topic File

Your next step is to add your topic file. Click the Files button on the right side of the Help Workshop window to display the Topic Files dialog box. Click the Add button on the right side of the dialog box to display a file open dialog box. Select your help topic file and click Open. Your topic file will be listed in the Topic Files dialog box, as shown in Figure 20.7. Click OK to accept the changes.

FIGURE 20.7:

Adding a topic file

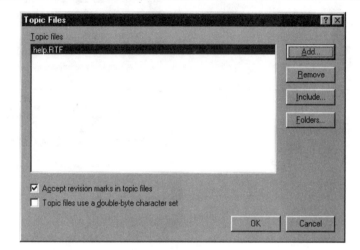

Mapping a Context ID to a Topic ID

The next step in this process is to map the context IDs used by your application to the topic IDs you defined in the topic file. Click the Map button on the right side of the Help Workshop window to display the Map dialog box and then click the Add button. In the Add Map Entry dialog box, enter the topic ID and the context ID. Since I have only one context ID, I specified error1000 for the topic ID and 1000 for the mapped numeric value, which is the context ID, as shown in Figure 20.8. Clicking OK accepts the new mapping and adds the mapping to the Map dialog box, as shown in Figure 20.9.

FIGURE 20.8:

Adding a new mapping

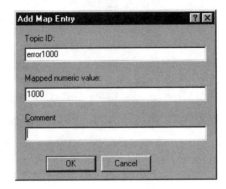

FIGURE 20.9:

Viewing the mappings

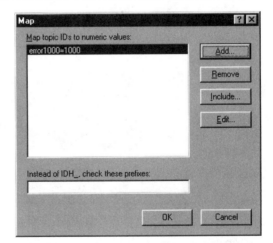

Setting Options

To set configuration options for your help file, click the Options button on the right side of the Help Workshop window. This displays the Options dialog box. Clicking on the FTS tab displays the options associated with a full text search. By default, a full text search index is not generated. However, I thought it would be nice to generate one for this file. Clicking on the Generate Full Text Search Index checkbox is all that it takes. Figure 20.10 shows this option selected on the FTS tab. Other options here allow you to increase the size of the index to allow more complete searching. For this example, a minimal search is all that's necessary.

FIGURE 20.10:

Generating a full text index

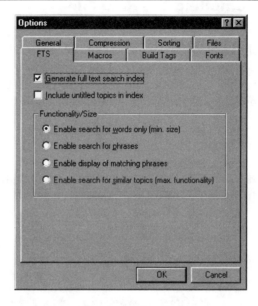

In order to use a full text search, it is necessary to create a compressed help file. Selecting the Compression tab of the Options dialog box displays information about compression. In this case, I selected Maximum compression, as shown in Figure 20.11.

FIGURE 20.11:

Selecting maximum compression

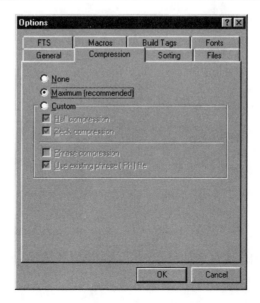

Compiling the Help File

Before compiling your help file, you can review the information selected for it in the main Help Workshop window, as shown in Figure 20.12. In this example, you can see that compression information is included (COMPRESS=) and that a full text search index should be generated (FTS=1). One topic file is selected (help.RTF), and one mapping is present (error1000=1000).

Once you are satisfied that everything is fine, click the Save and Compile button in the lower-right side of the Help Workshop window. The Help Workshop window will disappear for a moment and then reappear with the output from the help compiler, as shown in Figure 20.13. In this case, I have zero notes and warnings and a usable help file.

FIGURE 20.12:

Reviewing the help project file

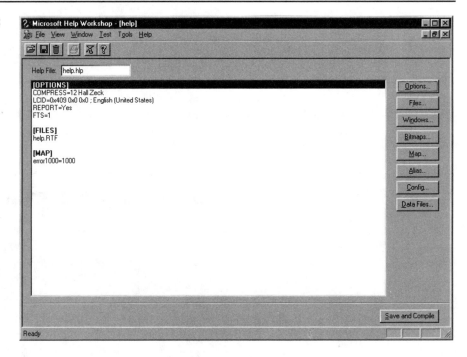

FIGURE 20.13:

After compiling the
help file

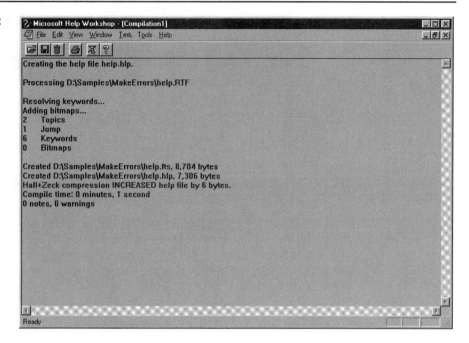

Trying It Out

You can run the WinHlp32 program to view your help file. Simply select Start ≻
Run and enter **WinHlp32**. Select the name of your help file from the Open dialog
box, as shown in Figure 20.14, and click Open to see your file.

Figure 20.15 shows the help file that I built. Since I didn't specify otherwise, the
Error 1000 topic is displayed because it is the first topic in the help file. Notice
that the footnote information is not displayed and that the Related Material
hotspot is now underlined with a single line rather than the double line I entered
in the RTF document.

FIGURE 20.14:

Running WinHlp32 to open a help file

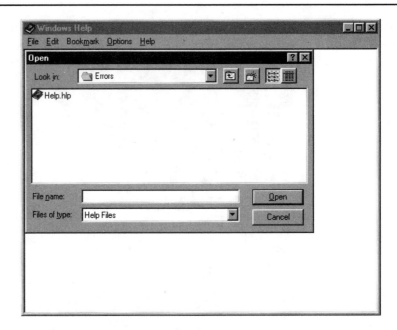

FIGURE 20.15:

The Error 1000 topic

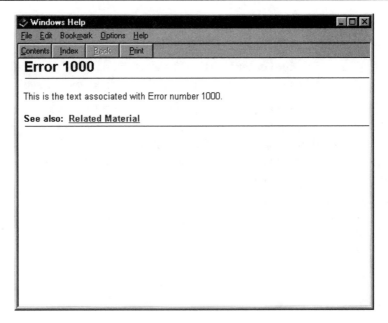

Clicking on the Related Material hotspot displays the Related Material topic, as shown in Figure 20.16. Again the footnote information is not visible. To get back to the original topic, simply click the Back button.

The Related Material topic

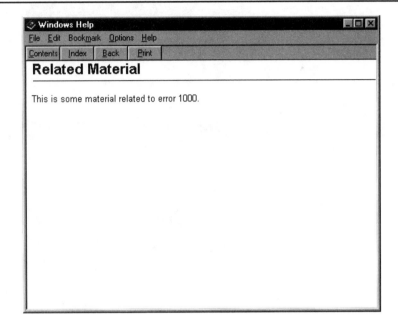

Clicking the Contents button displays the Error 1000 topic again. In your own help file, you should include a table of contents. The Help Workshop has a nice editor that will help you build your own table of contents.

Clicking the Index button displays the standard help file index, as shown in Figure 20.17. Notice that all of the keywords I defined are present.

FIGURE 20.17:

The help file's index

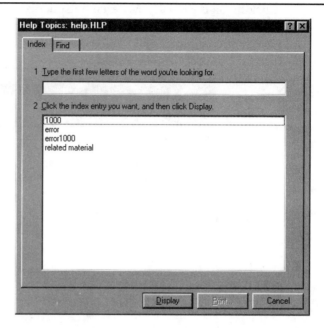

Selecting the Find tab allows you to access the full text search capability, as shown in Figure 20.18. Remember that I created this simply by checking a few checkboxes.

FIGURE 20.18:

The help file's full text search capabilities

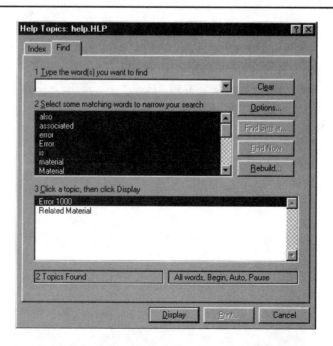

Final Thoughts

Visual Basic's error-handling capabilities are relatively good. You can trap your own runtime errors and then determine how you want to correct them. There are two approaches to detecting normal runtime errors. The first is to use the `On Error GoTo` statement, which redirects your program to a different location inside your subroutine. The second is the `On Error Resume Next` statement, which continues execution with the next statement.

After years of structured programming, I prefer not to go back to the bad old days of using `GoTo` statements. I've spent far too much time debugging other people's spaghetti logic that `GoTo` statements let them easily build. While you might not think this could happen in a Visual Basic program, I'm sure it could. In the samples I wrote for this chapter, there is only one possible source of a runtime error. This usually isn't true, especially when you need to handle a complex event. Imagine what would happen if you have a rather complex `Select` statement in a Toolbar control. You might not know where the error occurred, and if you have multiple error handlers in the same routine, you might not even be sure how the error was corrected.

I much prefer to use the `On Error Resume Next` statement, which allows you to handle error conditions in the same code fragment where the error occurred. This is much easier to understand for the person who wrote it and the three other people who may need to patch it over the program's lifetime.

Using help files is important in most applications. People who already use products like Microsoft Word or Excel are comfortable with using help information. The steps I went through in this chapter show the basics of creating a help file, but the real challenge is organizing the material. It can be difficult to create a comprehensive set of online documentation. The best teacher here is experience. You should try different techniques and listen to feedback from your users.

I just touched on some of the basic capabilities of the Help Workshop. You should take the time to go through its documentation. Some of its other features are the ability to include your own graphics in the file, a tool to help you build a good table of contents, and a facility to arrange your topics so you can browse them in sequence.

APPENDIX

A

Using Microsoft Transaction Server with Visual Basic

With the rise in popularity of multiple-tier client/server solutions, Microsoft Transaction Server (MTS) has become an integral part of any sophisticated multiple-tier solution using Microsoft technologies. MTS solves many of the problems faced by application developers by allowing them to focus on building application components that implement the business need rather than spending precious development time implementing distributed transaction and multi-user support.

This appendix provides an overview of the client/server architecture and explains how the Application Services model applies to that architecture. You will learn the basics of how MTS works and how to create Visual Basic ActiveX components that exploit MTS and the services that it provides. Finally, you will learn how to configure MTS to run application components on your network.

Understanding Distributed Application Architecture

It used to be that computers in the workplace existed in some sort of data vacuum. They were stand-alone machines that communicated with other machines only through some kind of removable medium such as a floppy diskette or an external hard drive. Application development in this environment focused on the creation of self-contained applications that did not rely on any external data sources or components. All data had to be imported to the local machine and used locally. Times have certainly changed!

Today, business applications that rely on data access are generally distributed throughout the enterprise. One or more computers on the network may host data that client applications throughout the network access. There may be yet another computer (or group of computers) that hosts components that provide business and data-access logic. All of these application components must work together perfectly for the application to function as intended.

Defining Client/Server Architecture

The driving concept in a client/server architecture is flexibility. A client/server architecture is often referred to as *multiple-tier* architecture because the execution of tasks is divided between applications and components.

A *tier* in client/server technology is a layer of software that accepts requests from and offers services to an application. For example, the client application represents the user services layer of the application (user and other services are discussed in the next section). This is a tier of the application. As a system architect, you can allocate tasks and processing to different tiers in the model. You can use a traditional two-tier model or increase application independence by moving to a multiple-tier model (multiple-tier architecture is discussed a bit later in this appendix). Within these models, you still have full control over the technology used to implement the solution and your chosen level of systems abstraction.

Figure A.1 illustrates some distinguishing characteristics of client/server design. You will notice immediately that the database engine has been moved from the client to the server. The server in this scenario is no longer a file server simply providing file services to the network. It is an application server hosting a process such as Microsoft SQL Server.

FIGURE A.1:

A basic client/server architecture

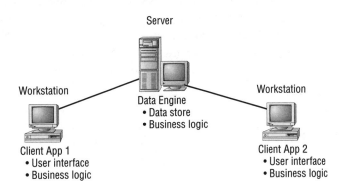

This transition is significant because it means that the client workstation is not responsible for all of the work involved in implementing the application. Tasks can be distributed between client and server, allowing each to participate in the process. In fact, you could say that the definition of client/server architecture is the intelligent distribution of tasks across tiers in the architecture.

The server is an active participant in the process of data reduction (minimizing the amount of data going across the network) and modification. This may leave many other activities, such as sorting and further data processing, to the client. Because of this design, a client/server database is not limited to small workgroup applications the way that file server applications are often limited.

Because client/server systems usually have much larger numbers of users, an increased load might be put on the network. Managing network resources becomes paramount in a client/server design.

Dividing Tasks into Services

When designing client/server solutions, you must make many choices concerning which pieces of the application will reside on which tiers of the architecture. With all of these choices, deciding exactly how to design your system can sometimes be difficult. However, some basic guidelines can help you choose.

The Application Services model can aid significantly in the client/server design process. This model divides application tasks into different services, which in turn can be applied to different tiers in the architecture.

The Application Services model defines three types of services: user, business, and data. Most client/server models implement user and data services at roughly the same points in the architecture; however, the business services layer is unique in its ability to work from various tiers, providing different advantages and creating different challenges. Figure A.2 illustrates the Application Services model and its possible mappings to physical architecture.

FIGURE A.2:

Client/server application services

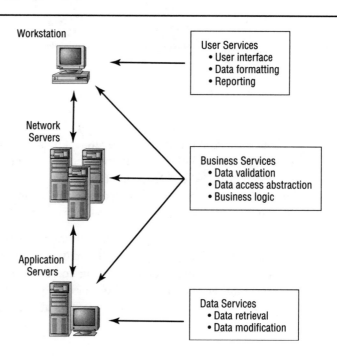

Workstation

User Services
• User interface
• Data formatting
• Reporting

Network Servers

Business Services
• Data validation
• Data access abstraction
• Business logic

Application Servers

Data Services
• Data retrieval
• Data modification

> **NOTE**
>
> **It's there even when it doesn't appear to be there:** User, business, and data services do not directly relate to the three "tiers" of the three-tier application environment. Even a single-tier application will contain user, business, and data services. In a single-tier architecture, all of these services simply reside on the same machine and usually in the same application.

User Services

User services deal with the interaction between the user and the application, as well as the preparation of data for user requirements. The following types of tasks usually fall into the category of user services:

- Receiving data input from users
- Packaging user input for further validation or server processing
- Data formatting
- Reporting
- Managing user preferences

User services define any and all client-side activities, no matter what the goals of those activities may be. For example, a single SQL Server database might actually be the data source for a number of different client applications. Some of these will perform standard business functions, such as inputting or extracting information; others may perform administrative duties, such as adding new users to the application or handling security concerns. All of these activities respond directly to the request of a user.

Developmental concerns for user services deal primarily with user interface design and user requirements. Application interfaces should be as intuitive as possible to their users. Users should have flexible approaches to working with data and application features. (Although an interface that limits user creativity may be more appealing to database managers, Microsoft's user interface design guidelines aim for flexibility.)

Other user services include data-formatting functions not used at the data services level. For example, if you want to have a result set sorted in a particular order, you can choose where that is to be done. Sorting can be done at the server or it can be done at the client. Because the server's primary role in data extraction is actually data reduction, operations that have no reductive effect (such as sorting) often are better implemented as part of the client application as a user service.

The implementation of client-side transactions is also a user services issue. Client transactions are used for logically organizing tasks and buffering data on the client so larger batches of data can be passed back to the server. For example, if you created a database application using the Microsoft Data Access Objects (DAO), you could use the workspace object to control transactions on the client side. This might provide an efficient data buffer on the client. You could even write your own logic to achieve similar functionality when using other models.

Data Services

Data services interact with the actual data source. The functionality of the data services layer is implemented at the database engine level, forcing data services to reside on the application server in the client/server scenario. Four functional areas are in the data services layer:

- Retrieving data and building result sets

- Inserting data

- Updating data

- Deleting data

The actual request for data interaction can come to the server in a variety of ways. It can come directly from the client application through the database server's proprietary API, through the Open Database Connectivity Application Programming Interface (ODBC API), or even from a business component through OLE DB. How the request gets to the server is irrelevant. Once there, it is handled in exactly the same way—through the database engine running on the server.

NOTE **If possible, move the work closer to the user:** Not all of the functionality implemented by the database server actually qualifies as a data service. For example, the sorting of data might better qualify as a data-formatting user service. The fact that the database server is able to implement a particular functionality does not mean that this is the best place in the architecture to put that implementation. Moving the work closer to the user reduces the workload on the machines where resources are typically scarce and takes advantage of the resources on the many user machines that are accessing the database server.

Transactions also play very important roles in data services implementation. True relational databases support *atomic edits*. This means that any group of changes made to a database can be marked as a transaction that will be guaranteed to commit in its entirety or roll back to a consistent state before the edits took place. In other words, when a transaction is issued to the server, either all of the transaction commits or none of it will commit. This is an atomic transaction. The database provides a transaction log that records all changes even before they physically occur to the data. If necessary, this log can be used to roll back or roll forward the transactions. I'll talk more about these concepts in the discussion of how MTS handles transactions, later in this appendix.

Business Services

Business services often make up the largest portion of the coding in a client/server application. The physical process of getting the client to talk to the server takes place at the business services layer. However, this layer also has many other tasks. Business services may include any of the following:

- Business rule and logic implementation

- Data validation

- Data access logic

- System administration logic

- Transaction support

Unlike user and data services, which are usually implemented as a monolithic client or server application residing entirely on one machine, the business services can be located in the client application, the server application, both, or neither. Let's take a closer look at the various approaches to implementing business services.

The Smart Client This approach stores business rules and logic in the client application. All data-access logic is also found at the client. The smart client approach uses all resources at the client level and frees precious resources at the server for data services, as shown in Figure A.3.

FIGURE A.3:

The smart client approach
to implementing business
services

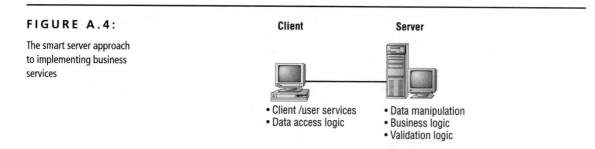

The primary disadvantage of this approach is that updating the business or data-access logic would require redeploying the entire client application, or at least the supporting dynamic link libraries (DLLs), on every client machine. As the developer, you also must be concerned with the hardware available on each of the clients. In this approach, it is critical that the hardware has the capacity to handle the load that is being placed on it.

The Smart Server   This approach consolidates all of the business and validation logic at a central server. In your server-side application, you would include all the necessary code to ensure that business rules were being followed. The advantage is obvious: By consolidating the logic in one location in the server application, you avoid the update/redeployment problem that can occur with the smart client approach. Instead of updating the logic on every client, you update the logic only once in the server. If the logic ever changes, you just need to make the modifications in the server application. Figure A.4 illustrates this approach.

FIGURE A.4:

The smart server approach
to implementing business
services

The primary disadvantage of this approach is that it places an enormous strain on the server. By shifting the logic to the server, you are forcing the server to perform all of those functions for every connected client. Whether or not this will have a performance impact on your application depends on how many users connect and the services provided by the server. If there are many users and many services, the effect can be significant. Another disadvantage might be that the server does not have the language elements to support robust business services layers, which would force the developer to implement some of these business rules on the client.

The Mixed Solution   Dividing the business and validation logic between the client and the server is possible. This approach allows each piece of the architecture to focus on its core strengths. The mixed solution approach is illustrated in Figure A.5.

FIGURE A.5:

The mixed solution approach to implementing business services

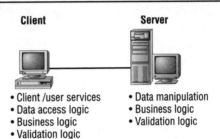

Client

Server

- Client /user services
- Data access logic
- Business logic
- Validation logic

- Data manipulation
- Business logic
- Validation logic

As you would expect, there are some disadvantages to this approach. Although you are making the most of the resources provided by every machine in the architecture, you still have the update/deployment problem characteristic of the smart client approach. In addition, your logic is distributed throughout your application at many levels, making it very difficult to maintain without excellent documentation. Even with excellent documentation, you probably will need to alter both client and server structures to upgrade the application.

Implementing a Multiple-Tier Architecture

The architectural examples discussed so far are all examples of traditional two-tier design, with two components participating in the process. This may be a very effective design under certain conditions. For example, if your application is not volatile (that is, it will not need significant updates in the future) and you have workstations that can handle more sophisticated applications, a two-tier smart client may be exactly what you need.

On the other hand, you may have a very powerful server machine. Even if the logic occasionally needs to be updated, as long as the user base does not overwhelm the capacity of the server, the smart server is an entirely viable option.

In other situations, the two-tier approach may not be satisfactory. An alternative is to use another tier. Not only can the business logic be located in a combination of the client and server applications, but it also may be independent of both the client and the server. This means that you can create components that are separate from both the client and the server and distribute them throughout the network. These components can define all business services. This approach is called *three-tier*, *n-tier*, or *multiple-tier* client/server architecture.

When implementing a multiple-tier solution, all business services are placed inside small components that provide services to both the client application and the server application. These components, created in a language such as Microsoft Visual Basic or Microsoft Visual C++, are implemented as Component Object Model (COM) objects. They may be accessed from the client application using the Distributed Component Object Model (DCOM). (See Chapter 15 for a discussion of how to access a separate ActiveX program using COM and DCOM.) Figure A.6 illustrates a basic multiple-tier architecture.

FIGURE A.6:

Multiple-tier client/server architecture

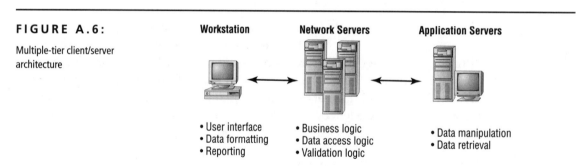

Workstation

Network Servers

Application Servers

- User interface
- Data formatting
- Reporting

- Business logic
- Data access logic
- Validation logic

- Data manipulation
- Data retrieval

These components can be distributed and run on multiple servers in the network, or they can be placed on the application server. This approach is also very modular, with each component object providing different services to the application. For example, one component may focus on the implementation of business logic and another might implement data-access logic.

Abstracting Data-Access Logic

As you may already know, databases can be accessed in many different ways. You can use the proprietary API of the database server, you can go through ODBC (Open Database Connectivity), or you can use one of many object models designed for simplifying the process of accessing database resources. To make matters more complicated, new approaches are being developed all the time. Your application may become obsolete if the method of data access you are using is no longer supported by its vendor.

One of the most useful elements of multiple-tier development is the ability to conceal from both the client and server any implementation details about how database connectivity is being made. Using components, you can place the actual implementation logic in the component and simply provide consistent public interfaces to the client and the server that access these components. This way, you can conceal the method of data access from the rest of the application.

For example, suppose that you are writing a client application in Visual Basic that will be accessing a Microsoft SQL Server database. The following options allow you to access the SQL Server data:

- Visual Basic allows you to use the Jet engine to access data from SQL Server through ODBC.

- If you are using Visual Basic Enterprise Edition, you can use the Remote Data Objects (RDO 2.0 or later).

- You can use the ActiveX Data Objects (ADO 1.5 or later) to access the data through the new OLE DB standard.

- You can write to the ODBC API directly using DLL calls from within Visual Basic or OLE DB calls from a C++ client.

Now let's assume that you decide to use RDO 2.0 to access your SQL Server database. Traditional two-tier design would require you to write the RDO data-access code in the client application. This client application would then connect to the SQL Server database directly. But what if Microsoft stops supporting RDO 2.0? You may want to upgrade your application to a new RDO version or even to go to another data-access model entirely, such as ADO. If you used the two-tier approach, you would need to redesign and redeploy the client application.

The alternative is to place the RDO code in a component object. This COM object would support properties and methods that would be visible through OLE automation to the client application. You could create methods such as `ConnectDB` or `InsertEmployee` that would be exposed through this COM object. Inside the component where the method is defined, the RDO code would be used to perform the task. Figure A.7 illustrates a scenario where this approach might be used.

FIGURE A.7:

Data access in a component object

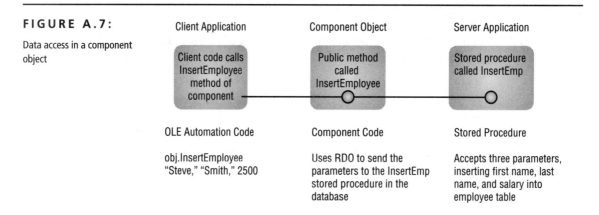

Client Application	Component Object	Server Application
Client code calls InsertEmployee method of component	Public method called InsertEmployee	Stored procedure called InsertEmp
OLE Automation Code	**Component Code**	**Stored Procedure**
obj.InsertEmployee "Steve," "Smith," 2500	Uses RDO to send the parameters to the InsertEmp stored procedure in the database	Accepts three parameters, inserting first name, last name, and salary into employee table

If the component object in this example supports a method called `Insert-Employee`, this method accepts values for all required fields as required parameters and accepts values for all optional fields as optional parameters. You can specify additional parameters for special types of inserts of other definable behavior. This method is a public interface of the component.

This component would be called from the client application using OLE automation. In a Visual Basic application, you would first create an object variable that referenced the component. Then you would call the `InsertEmployee` method through the object variable and pass all necessary parameters. Using RDO code, the component would accept these parameters and call the `InsertEmp` stored procedure on the server, passing the parameters received from the client application. SQL Server would make the actual data modifications to the employee table through the stored procedure. The insert can be created as a transaction in a stored procedure on the server, guaranteeing that the record is inserted in its entirety or not at all.

Now when Microsoft announces that it will no longer support RDO 2.0, no matter which approach to data access you chose, neither the client application nor the server application needs to be touched. As long as you don't alter the public interfaces and parameters that the component exposes, you can make the necessary data access changes by redesigning the component and then deploying the component in the network.

TIP

Isolate your programs from your data: When using this approach to abstracting data-access logic, you can add new properties and methods to access your data as the underlying database structures change. If possible, you should design your interface to be easily extendable to accommodate these changes. For more information about designing database-access applications, refer to *Visual Basic Developer's Handbook* (Petroutsos and Hough, published by Sybex, 1999).

Considering Multiple-Tier Design Performance Impacts

One advantage to implementing a multiple-tier design is that the modifiable components can be reused as libraries in a variety of applications. Another advantage is that deployment and updating are much simpler because the components need to be implemented in only one location (or just a few locations) on the network.

Notwithstanding these advantages, component architecture comes at a price, and that price is often performance. In the two-tier model, the entire application exists as two processes: one running on the client and the other running on the server. Multiple-tier architecture changes this structure significantly. Elements of the application run as at least three processes or more, depending on the way that the components are designed.

One problem is simply a matter of network traffic. Now instead of a single communication between client and server, you have communication between client and component, server and component, and perhaps component and component. This will increase network traffic and reduce network response time. Figure A.8 illustrates how dramatic this effect can be.

This is not the only problem, however. Remember that all clients will be working with the same components. When every client is interacting with the server directly, this usually does not pose much of a threat. After all, large database servers such as SQL Server and Oracle are designed to be *scalable* (able to handle greater traffic or volume). Unfortunately, the components usually are not scalable to the same degree that the database servers are. This means that if you plan to implement this design on a network with a large number of users, the components will almost certainly be a bottleneck in the application. Although it is possible to build objects that scale, this requires a significant amount of additional code. Scalable components can be quite complex to build.

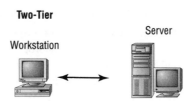

Two-Tier

Server

Workstation

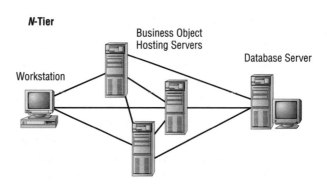

N-Tier

Business Object
Hosting Servers

Database Server

Workstation

Another problem is that while you are able to define true atomic transactions at the data services level, you may need to have the same functionality at the business services level. Suppose that you have a group of components that are designed to be used together. When any one component is used, it must be enlisted in a transaction with other components. Each component sends its own independent data-modification requests to the server, so these transactions cannot be enforced at the data services layer.

These problems can be resolved, as you will see in the next section; however, they must be considered in your multiple-tier designs. When selecting an appropriate multiple-tier design, you must consider things such as where in the network your objects will be implemented, the development system used to create the components, and other issues that may impact overall client/server application performance.

Scalability and the Internet

Scalability became an issue during the development of distributed processing architectures such as multiple-tier client/server systems. Because these systems could theoretically handle more users, it was imperative that all elements of the application be created to scale. This was easy for some elements. The database server, for example, has scalability as one of its central features. Products such as Oracle and Microsoft SQL Server can scale to unbelievable levels. It was the component, not the database server, that was the weak link in this chain.

The popularity of client/server architectures introduced the problem of scalable component architectures, but the Internet brought this problem to a whole new level. Although you can conceivably get by in a small to moderate client/server environment with objects that do not really scale, scalability issues can no longer be brushed aside if the application is exposed to the Internet.

Introducing Microsoft Transaction Server

Multiple-tier client/server design is much too good of an idea to scrap because of a few problems, especially if those problems can be overcome. In the previous section, I pointed out two primary complications in the multiple-tier scenario: the inability of objects to effectively scale and the inability of objects to enlist other objects in atomic transactions.

MTS was created to address these problems. First, MTS can be used to manage all multi-user considerations for a component architecture. In other words, you do not need to write sophisticated threading, security, and multi-user support into your components. MTS will provide that support for the components.

Second, MTS extends transaction support from the data services layer into the business services layer. This allows you to write components that focus on a core business function. MTS can enlist various components into transactions, providing reliable transaction support.

Providing Scalability

MTS provides all of the necessary services to manage multiple users, handle scaling resources, and take care of other issues central to scalability. Before MTS, to create an object that would truly scale, you needed to incorporate all of this functionality inside the component. With MTS, you only need to write a single-user object, which will be managed in a multi-user environment by MTS.

A major transition has been occurring at many businesses over the last year or two. This transition involves the seemingly infinite volume of Internet access. Taking an existing client/server application and putting it in the Internet so that remote employees, customers, suppliers, and the public can access the information in a database is problematic. Managing security and ensuring scalability for Internet applications also presents problems.

NOTE   **Designed for the Internet:** Microsoft created MTS with the Internet in mind. Due to scalability problems, traditional multiple-tier client/server applications would never survive if Internet traffic were allowed to access the applications' business objects. MTS provides the internal plumbing necessary to allow business objects to scale to the enterprise and beyond. For more details on how MTS works, see a book devoted to that topic, such as *Microsoft Transaction Server 2.0 (Roger Jennings' Database Workshop)* (published by Sams Publishing).

Figure A.9 illustrates how a client/server application may run over the Internet. Note that the internal client/server applications and the Internet application share some common elements, such as a data store and even components.

In this scenario, the component objects are required to handle Internet traffic as well as internal client/server traffic, creating a true scalability nightmare. The components are accessed from the web server through an Internet Service API (ISAPI) application such as Active Server Pages or possibly a Common Gateway Interface (CGI) application. The client to the component is actually the application running on the web server, not the web browser. Assuming that you choose to implement Active Server Pages, the ASP ISAPI application is responsible for collecting data from the data source and creating an HTML response that is sent back to the browser. Every time a browser makes a request for data in the database, an ISAPI routine will execute. Because data can be extracted from the database only by going through the component objects, this becomes a real scalability issue.

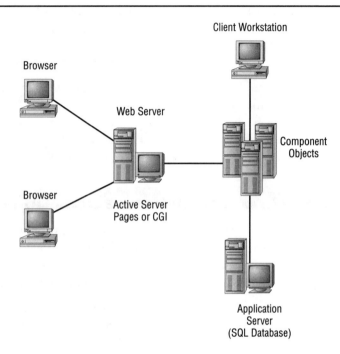

Now suppose that you install MTS on the same machine that hosts the components. By allowing the components to be managed by MTS, scalability is automatically provided, even if the objects are written as single-user components. MTS
does this by allowing the creation of objects called *packages*. Packages act as logical process containers for components. Components are installed into MTS packages, thus allowing MTS to control the resources used by the component.

Now the focus of scalability shifts. The component is no longer the bottleneck.
The bottleneck becomes the Windows NT operating system or the SQL Server
database. Windows NT clustering solves some of this problem, but the full solution lies in the next wave of products.

Adding Security

Another advantage of implementing MTS is security. MTS defines a security
model called *package security*. This approach to security allows you to assign a
user identity to packages, thus allowing the packages to act as a virtual user. In

some respects, the package can be thought of as a logical grouping of users, just like a network group. The package identity is given rights to perform any required activities on the underlying data sources. Then each network user or group is given access to the components in the package as needed.

The advantage of using this approach is tremendous. Instead of managing security at many tiers throughout the application, MTS manages the security at the package level. This unburdens the administrator significantly—database security is managed simply by granting access to the packages. The packages then act as a user filter to allow only qualified users into the database.

Supporting Transactions across Objects

In addition to supporting scalability, MTS supports transactions across objects at the business logic layer. This support allows you to focus the properties and methods of components on individual units of work. If larger tasks must be completed, these objects can be combined into transactions and used together.

Suppose that you are responsible for developing the accounts database application for a bank. Your application must support the functionality to deposit funds into an account as well as to withdraw funds from an account. You determine that the best way to do this is to use a multiple-tier solution so that it will be easier to update business and data-access logic in the future.

To support this functionality at the middle tier, you create one component called `Deposit` and another called `Withdrawal`. These components are used to encapsulate all the business and data-access logic needed to deposit or withdraw funds from an account.

Now suppose that the MIS director of the bank points out that the tellers must be able to transfer money from one account to another. This poses an interesting dilemma for you, because there are a few ways to accomplish this task.

One option is to create a stored procedure on the server that will perform the transfer as a single transaction and call that stored procedure from a component. This option would achieve the desired result, but it would require an additional stored procedure on the server that would need to be managed.

Another option is to create a component that calls the `Deposit` and `Withdrawal` components to perform the transfer. The new component would not need to do much more than call the other components. No additional modifications would need to be made to the server applications, which is advantageous. The problem with this solution is that the two called components actually would be individual transactions. This could cause a problem with data integrity.

The second solution is preferable except for the transaction problem. Fortunately, MTS can solve that problem. The three components (Deposit, Withdrawal, and Transfer) can be included in an MTS package. This will allow the three objects to work together under the context of a single transaction when necessary, but still let them work independently if required. This solution is illustrated in Figure A.10.

FIGURE A.10:

Component transaction support through MTS

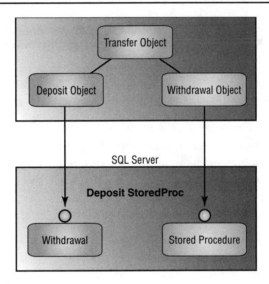

Using Context Objects

In reality, you should view transactions as a business rule. The purpose of the transaction is to ensure that the data remains in a consistent state. If transactions are actually business rules, then in your multiple-tier application model, you want those business rules moved from the data services layer to the business services layer, where they really belong.

To provide this type of transaction support through MTS, the components' code must be slightly modified. All of the components will recognize a special object called a *context object*. This context object will control the context of the transaction. By informing the context object about the success or failure to complete the work in the components, the context object can track the progress of the entire transaction.

Suppose that as a transfer is in progress, the `Withdrawal` component identifies three funds that are insufficient to perform the withdrawal. The `Withdrawal` object would inform the context object that the transaction cannot continue. When the context object reports to MTS that the transaction failed in at least one of its components, the entire transaction is forced to roll back.

Passing the ACID Test

Transactions managed by MTS are designed to pass the ACID test. An ACID transaction supports the attributes of atomicity, consistency, isolation, and durability.

Atomicity is the "all-or-nothing" property of a transaction. The transaction will either complete in its entirety or not at all. This is the basic concept of a transaction and must be strictly supported.

Consistency is the attribute of a transaction that defines its handling of states over time. In most transactions, the database will be in an inconsistent state at some point. For example, if you are implementing a transfer by performing a deposit and withdrawal, the state of the database is inconsistent at the point that the change has been made to one account but not the other. Every transaction must resolve its own inconsistency.

Isolation defines the level of exposure that data modifications in this transaction will have to other transactions. If you change data in a transaction, another transaction may be able to read that data immediately after your modification or you may need to commit your transaction before reading can take place. Data services enforce isolation through locking.

Durability is the ability of a database to recover if the data is left in an inconsistent state due to an unforeseen system failure. The transaction log provides the durability attribute in most relational database management systems. In Microsoft SQL Server, this transaction log is a *write-ahead log*, meaning that before any changes are made to the database tables, they are first written to the transaction log.

As an example of durability, suppose that you have just issued a transaction to SQL Server. In the middle of writing the committed changes to the server but before the transaction is actually committed, the power goes out, and as luck would have it, your power backup fails. No media damage has taken place because the transaction log stores all modifications before they are actually written to the database.

This log has a record of all of the data changes that were made to the database. Microsoft SQL Server will begin an auto-recovery process when the service is restarted. The transaction log can be used to roll back any changes made to the database by the uncommitted transaction.

Creating MTS-Enabled Components with Visual Basic

Visual Basic 6 was created with MTS in mind. It's simple to create a component in Visual Basic that fully exploits MTS and the services that it provides. Here, I'm going to explain how to create a component in Visual Basic that supports the apartment-threading model and can be implemented in MTS. Then I'll show you the additional code that would be required for a component to support transactions through MTS.

Creating the Services

To demonstrate creating an MTS-enabled component, I'm going to use an example of a simple program that accesses a table with author information in a publishing database and reports the number of authors there to the user. The client/server application uses the following elements:

- A stored procedure in Microsoft SQL Server that will select a count of the authors from the Authors table of the Pubs database.

- A component named Pubs that calls the stored procedure using the RDO 2.0 as the data-access model. This code is placed into the CountAuth property of the Authors class.

- A client application that instantiates the Pubs.Authors class and calls the CountAuth property. The resulting value from the property is returned to the user in the form of a message box.

Remember that Application Services model I talked about earlier in the chapter? Using that model, I start by defining the application in terms of services. Figure A.11 illustrates the relationship between tiers in the application.

FIGURE A.11:

Defining the application's
architecture

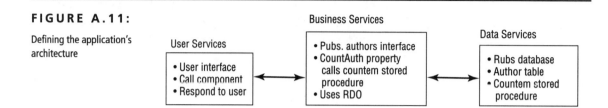

Setting Up Data Services

At the data services tier, I have the stored procedure. This procedure is called
countem, and it simply counts the number of records in the Authors table of the
Pubs database. This procedure can be created in many different ways, but I used
the SQL Server 6.5 ISQL/W utility, as shown in Figure A.12.

FIGURE A.12:

Creating the countem stored
procedure in ISQL/W

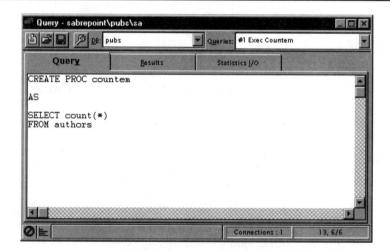

Setting Up Business Services

At the heart of the business services layer is the component created in Visual
Basic. I create this component as a single class module in an ActiveX DLL project.
The name of the class module is Authors. The component name is Pubs. The class

module contains one property called CountAuth. I used the following code to create this property.

```
Public Property Get CountAuth() As Integer

    Dim env As RDO.rdoEnvironment
    Dim cn As RDO.rdoConnection
    Dim rs As RDO.rdoResultset
    Dim strConn As String
    Dim iCount As Integer

    strConn = "DSN=Pubs;Database=Pubs;UID=sa;PWD=;"
    Set env = rdoEngine.rdoEnvironments(0)
    Set cn = env.OpenConnection("", rdDriverNoPrompt, False, strConn)
    Set rs = cn.OpenResultset("Exec Countem")
    iCount = rs(0).Value
    CountAuth = iCount

End Property()
```

> **NOTE**
>
> **Do what I say, not what I do:** Microsoft is actively pushing ADO. Since ADO offers all of the benefits of RDO 2.0 with the ability to access more types of databases, you should be using ADO for all new applications.

Among the properties set for the class object is the MTSTransactionMode property. This property alerts MTS that the installed components will interact with other components in a specified way. This object does not support transactions, so the property is set appropriately. You can set other values for the MTSTransactionMode property to specify that the class supports transactions, that the class requires transactions, or that the class is not even an MTS component. Figure A.13 illustrates these property values.

FIGURE A.13:

The MTSTransactionMode
property of a Visual Basic
class at design time

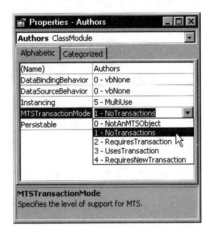

To complete the component, I compile it into an ActiveX DLL. Later, this DLL
will be installed into an MTS package and deployed through MTS.

Setting Up User Services

The role of user services is to provide an interface for the user and to call the services
of the component. MTS is transparent from the perspective of the client application.
The code to call a component is the same whether the developer chooses to deploy
the component through MTS or not. This allows the components to be highly exten-
sible. You can rewrite an existing component to use MTS, and you won't need to
make any changes in the client application code.

The sample application calls the ActiveX DLL by creating an object variable and
capturing the value of the CountAuth property of the component. The following
code shows how I did this:

```
'General Declarations
Option Explicit
Private PubsObj As Pubs.Authors

Private Sub Form_Load()

    Set PubsObj = CreateObject("Pubs.Authors")

End Sub
```

```
Private Sub cmdCount_Click()

    Dim iCount
    iCount = PubsObj.CountAuth
    MsgBox "There are " & FormatNumber(iCount, 0) & _
      " authors in the Pubs Database."

End Sub
```

Adding Transaction Support

As I mentioned earlier, in order for a component to support transactions, the MTSTransactionMode property must be set to allow or require transactions. However, this is not all that you need to do. The component must also communicate with MTS to provide information about the current state of the transaction.

The mechanism for providing this information to MTS is the context object. Whenever a new transaction begins in MTS, a context object is created to monitor the context of that transaction. MTS creates the context object automatically; you don't have to do anything to instantiate the object. However, you must write some additional code in your component to ensure that the context object is visible to your class. Then you can inform the context object concerning the status of the transaction.

Coding the Context Object

In Visual Basic, you usually create new object pointers by using the CreateObject method or the New keyword. When supporting transactions through MTS, this changes somewhat. First, you must capture the context object into your component. Then, if any other components are created, they are created within the context of the original transaction using the CreateInstance method of the context object.

Let's consider the example I used earlier to explain the concepts of transaction support and context objects. The hypothetical component contains Deposit, Withdrawal, and Transfer objects. The MTSTransactionMode property for the Deposit and Withdrawal objects would be set to UsesTransactions, because a transaction may be used but is not required. For the Transfer object, this property would be set to RequiresNewTransaction, because whenever this object is used, it requires the cooperation of the Deposit and Withdrawal objects.

The code inside the `Transfer` class would first access the context object and then use this context object to create the other objects needed for the transaction. This code would appear as follows:

```
Dim dep As Bank.Deposit
Dim wdl As Bank.Withdrawal
Dim CtxObject As ObjectContext
Set CtxObject = GetObjectContext
Set dep = CtxObject.CreateInstance("Bank.Deposit")
Set wdl = CvtxObject=CreateInstance("Bank.Withdrawal")
```

This code essentially passes the context object into each of the required supporting objects and envelops all three objects within the context of the same transaction.

The code inside the `Deposit` and `Withdrawal` classes would include the following:

```
Dim CtxObject as ObjectContext
Set CtxObject=GetObjectContext()
```

These statements capture the context of the transaction and allow the objects to report transaction status back to the context object.

Committing and Aborting Transactions

All the code inside each of the classes must complete successfully before the entire transaction can commit. The individual objects report either their success or failure to complete to the context object through methods called `SetComplete` and `SetAbort`. For example, the `Deposit` and `Withdrawal` objects might contain the following code to report this information to the context object:

```
Public Sub MethodA()
On Error GoTo err
' Do processing Here
CtxObject.SetComplete
Exit Sub
err:
ObjContext.SetAbort
End Sub
```

When the object calls the `SetComplete` method, the context object knows that the portion of the transaction for which the object is responsible has completed successfully. If the `SetAbort` method is used, then the entire transaction must abort, regardless of whether the other objects involved in the transaction were able to complete successfully. You would place similar code in the `Transfer` class, thus allowing each of the objects to report their transaction status.

Using the MSDTC

After the context object has received responses from all of the objects involved in the transaction, the transaction can then be formally committed or aborted. This service is provided by the Microsoft Distributed Transaction Coordinator (MDTC) and originally shipped with SQL Server 6.5. The MDTC can be considered the "traffic cop" of the transaction execution. Nothing commits until receiving approval from the MSDTC.

The MSDTC receives this directive from the Microsoft Transaction Server Executive (MTX). The MTX, although transparent to your clients, is actually involved every step of the way in creating this transaction. It handles the thread pooling for objects and the object instantiation needed to keep things running and scalable. When the MSDTC receives notice from the MTX that the transaction can commit or must abort, this action is executed without delay, thus reducing the potential contention for resources.

Deploying Components through MTS

Before you can deploy components through MTS, you must first create a package. MTS packages represent a group of components that execute in the same server process. This means that they share the same address space on the server as they execute. Packages contain components that are usually organized according to task. This means that components that are used together or support like behaviors are often included in the same package.

WARNING   **Plan before you pack:** Components can exist only in one package on any installation of MTS. For this reason, it is wise to plan your package deployment before creating the packages.

Creating an MTS Package

The easiest way to create packages in MTS is through the New Package Wizard. This wizard gives you two choices as to how you can create your packages: create a new package or import an existing package. Figure A.14 shows the Microsoft Management Console exploring MTS elements, where you can see the packages installed on the local computer.

FIGURE A.14:

Exploring MTS through the Microsoft Management Console

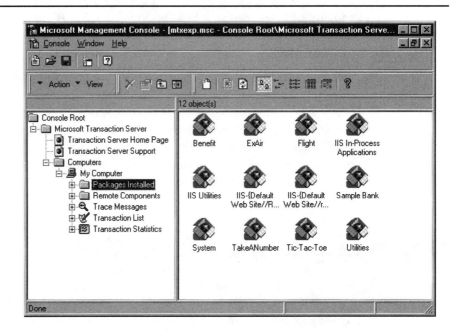

To access the New Package Wizard, right-click on the Packages Installed folder and select New from the pop-up menu. Figure A.15 shows the wizard's opening screen. When you click on the Create an Empty Package button, the wizard asks you to name the package, as shown in Figure A.16.

FIGURE A.15:

The New Package Wizard

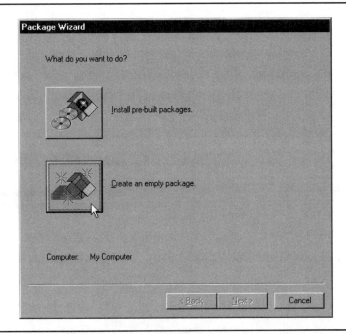

FIGURE A.16:

Naming the package

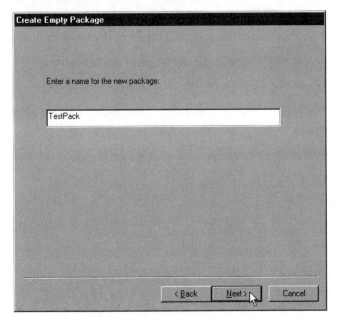

Next, the wizard allows you to specify security for your package. You have two choices, as shown in Figure A.17:

- You can allow each user to retain his or her interactive identity when using the component.

- You can assign a user identity to the component that will be used for all calls from that component.

FIGURE A.17:

Setting the component identity

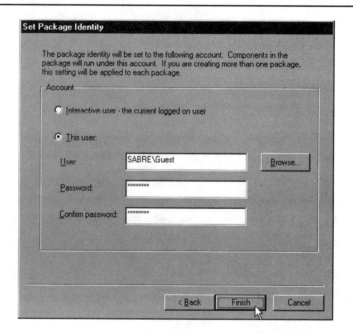

Your choice of security can make a significant difference in how your package is handled. If you choose to allow each user to retain his or her identity through the component, then all resources requested by that component must be authorized for the interactive user. If you set a single user for the component identity, then you only need to ensure that the assigned user identity has the needed rights for all other resources.

After you complete this window and click the Finish button, the wizard creates the package. Once you have created the package, you are ready to install your components. Figure A.18 shows a new package called `TestPack` with the Components and Roles folders underneath.

FIGURE A.18:

TestPack in the Microsoft
Management Console

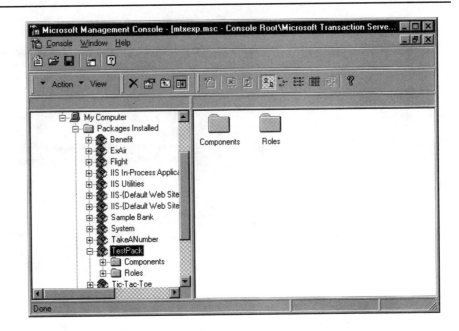

Rolling users together: Roles are collections of Windows NT users and groups that can be considered MTS groups. Rather than associating individual users and groups to MTS components, roles can be used to abstract a set of users and groups, thus providing additional flexibility when programming security through MTS.

Installing Components into a Package

To install a new component into an MTS package, drill down to the components folder in the package, right-click on that folder in the window, and select New from the pop-up menu. This runs the Component Wizard, as shown in Figure A.19.

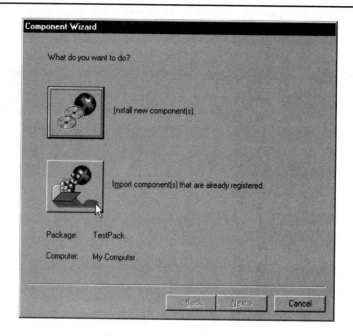

Like the New Package Wizard, this wizard also offers two choices: You can install a new component or components, or you can install components that are already registered on that machine. Since I compiled my Visual Basic component on my machine, the interfaces are already registered, so I select the second option.

Next, the wizard presents all of the available registered objects that can be installed as an MTS component, as shown in Figure A.20. Even though my Visual Basic component is called Pubs, it is listed here as Pubs.Authors. Every class that you create in Visual Basic registers a new interface. A single component may have many different classes. As long as those classes are public classes that can be created, they will appear in this list.

After you select objects and click on Finish, the wizard installs your MTS component. When installing the component into MTS, changes are made to the component's Registry entries. The LocalServer32 subkey under the CLSID for the object, which used to point to the DLL, now references the MTS Executive. Any calls to this component must go through MTS. Figure A.21 shows the Microsoft Management Console window after installing the Pubs.Authors component into the TestPack package.

FIGURE A.20:

Selecting objects to import

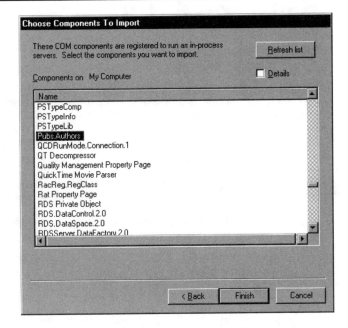

FIGURE A.21:

Pubs.Authors installed into
TestPack

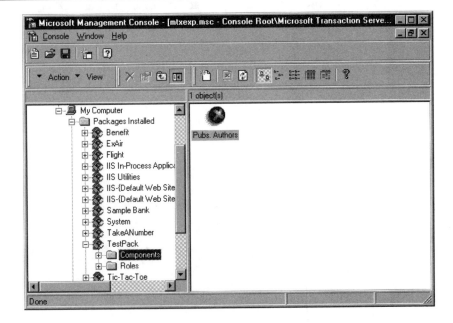

Looking to the Future

As you've learned in this appendix, the purpose of MTS is to help you create and deploy scalable, secure components for the enterprise and beyond. By allowing MTS to handle all of the threading through your objects, you can concentrate on the core business function of the component and not worry about writing thread support into the component.

You have also seen how MTS supports a more flexible security model. By allowing package identity and role association, both MTS declarative and programmatic security become much easier to maintain.

Finally, by allowing components to track their own transaction progress and report that progress back to the MTS Executive, you can complete the movement of business rules to the business services layer of the Application model. This allows a complete abstraction of one service from another. Each element of the application—whether it is a user, business, or data service—is completely separated from the implementation details of the application.

At this point, MTS is an independent service that installs onto a Windows NT platform, but the future is much brighter and more exciting. With the advent of Windows NT 5.0 and other technologies such as COM+, MTS will become increasingly integrated into the operating system and its services.

To say that MTS plays an important role in the future of distributed applications is an understatement. MTS is a critical element of enterprise scalability. Get comfortable with its architecture and implementation. The time you invest in learning about MTS now will definitely give you a big payback in the future.

APPENDIX

B

About the Sample Programs

One of the most important features of this book is that every program discussed in the text is included on the CD-ROM. A lot of code in these programs never made it into the book. It's worth the time to browse through some of these programs to see what you're missing.

To use these programs, simply find the appropriate directory on the CD-ROM and copy them to your hard drive. Then you can open the project with Visual Basic and run it, but first check the Notes section to make sure that the program doesn't have any special requirements.

This appendix provides a brief summary of each program included on the CD-ROM and notes the listings in this book that are from the program. The programs are presented in alphabetical order. For more information about each program, refer to the chapter (or chapters) that contain its listings.

Agent Demo

The Agent Demo program is a powerful tool for understanding how to implement speech recognition in Visual Basic. Its CD-ROM location is \Samples\ AgentDemo\Project1.vbp.

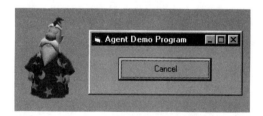

This program requires Microsoft Agent, which is installed as part of Visual Basic. You can find installation instructions in Chapter 14.

Excerpts from the code appear in the following listings:

Listing 14.4: Global Declarations for Agent Demo

Listing 14.5: Form_Load Event for Agent Demo

Listing 14.6: Agent1_Command Event for Agent Demo

Listing 14.7: Agent1_RequestComplete Event for Agent Demo

Listing 14.8: Command1_Click Event for Agent Demo

CDO Demo

The CDO Demo program shows you how to use the Collaboration Data Objects (CDO) to access the full capabilities of MAPI. You can use it to access your e-mail folders and other information stored in MAPI. Its CD-ROM location is \Samples\ CDO\Project1.vbp.

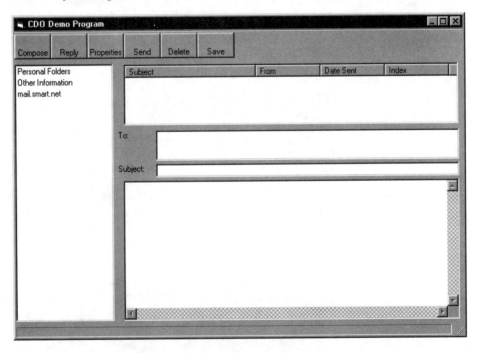

This program needs Outlook 98 in order to perform MAPI functions. The CDO library is not shipped with Visual Basic 6. Installing Outlook 98 also installs all of the necessary libraries to develop a CDO program.

Excerpts from the code appear in the following listings:

Listing 8.6: Form_Load Event in CDO Demo

Listing 8.7: LoadInfoStore Event in CDO Demo

Listing 8.8: LoadFolders Event in CDO Demo

Listing 8.9: TreeView1_NodeClick Event in CDO Demo

Listing 8.10: LoadMessages Routine in CDO Demo

Listing 8.11: ListView1_ItemClick Event in CDO Demo

Listing 8.12: Toolbar1_ButtonClick Event in CDO Demo

Charter

The Charter program demonstrates how to build a spreadsheet program using standard components from Microsoft like the MSFlexGrid, MSChart, and VBScript controls. Support is also included to for e-mailing documents via MAPI. Its CD-ROM location is \Samples\Charter\Project1.vbp.

This program appears in several different chapters where various new features are added. The program included in the CD-ROM contains all of the changes.

Excerpts from the code appear in the following listings:

Listing 7.7: NewChart Routine in Charter

Listing 7.8: StuffGrid Routine in Charter

Listing 7.9: StuffGridA Routine in Charter

Listing 7.10: MSFlexGrid1_KeyPress Event in Charter

Listing 7.11: MSFlexGrid1_KeyUp Event in Charter

Listing 7.12: Toolbar1_ButtonMenuClick Event in Charter

Listing 7.13: AlignCell Routine in Charter

Listing 7.14: SaveChart Routine in Charter

Listing 7.15: OpenChart Routine in Charter

Listing 7.16: ShowChart Routine in Charter

Listing 7.17: MenuChart_Click Routine in Charter

Listing 7.18: SetChartType Routine in Charter

Listing 7.19: Toolbar1_ButtonMenuClick Event in Charter

Listing 7.20: MSChart1_KeyPress Event in Charter

Listing 7.21: MSChart1_KeyUp Event in Charter

Listing 8.5: SendChart Routine in Charter

Listing 9.13: WritePage Routine in Charter

Listing 9.14: WriteEndDoc Routine in Charter

Listing 9.15: WritePicture Routine in Charter

Listing 9.16: WriteCenter Routine in Charter

Listing 9.17: PrintChart Routine in Charter

Listing 9.18: PrintGrid Routine in Charter

Listing 10.1: MenuChart_Click Routine in Charter

Listing 10.2: SetChartType Routine in Charter

Listing 10.3: MSChart1_MouseDown Event in Charter

Listing 13.15: Form_Load Event in Charter

Listing 13.16: MSFlexGrid_LeaveCell Event in Charter

Listing 13.17: Compute Function in Charter

Listing 13.18: Recalculate Routine in Charter

Control Tabs

The Control Tabs program demonstrates how to use tabs and access keys to help a user enter data in the form. It also shows you how to perform various edit checks and data validation on the different kinds of data a user may enter. Its CD-ROM location is \Samples\ControlTabs\Project1.vbp.

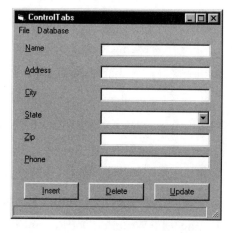

Excerpts from the code appear in the following listings:

Listing 6.7: Text6_KeyPress Event in Control Tabs

Listing 6.8: Text5_Change Event in Control Tabs

Listing 6.9: Text1_KeyPress Event in Control Tabs

Listing 6.10: Text3_Validate Event in Control Tabs

Listing 6.11: SmartType Routine in Control Tabs

Date/Time Demo

The Date/Time Demo Tool is used demonstrate how various date and time functions work, including CDate, Date, DateAdd, DateDiff, DatePart, Day, FormatDateTime, Hour, IsDate, Minute, Month, MonthName, Second, Time, TimePart, Timer, WeekDayName, and Year. Its CD-ROM location is \Samples\Date-TimeDemo\Project1.vbp.

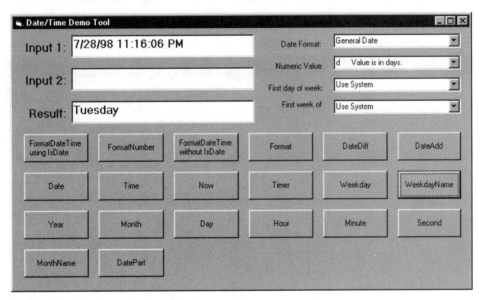

Excerpts from the code appear in the following listings:

Listing 5.1: Command1_Click Event in Date/Time Demo Tool

Listing 5.2: Command5_Click Event in Date/Time Demo Tool

Listing 5.3: Command6_Click Event in Date/Time Demo Tool

Listing 5.4: Command3_Click Event in Date/Time Demo Tool

Listing 5.5: Command9_Click Event in Date/Time Demo Tool

DateControl

The DateControl program demonstrates how to use the new the MonthView and DateTimePicker controls in your programs. Its CD-ROM location is \Samples\ DateControl\Project1.vbp.

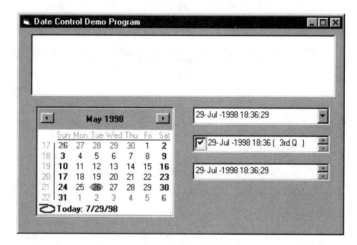

Excerpts from the code appear in the following listings:

Listing 10.13: MonthView1_DateClick Event in DateControl

Listing 10.14: MonthView1_SelChange Event in DateControl

Listing 10.15: MonthView1_GetDayBold Event in DateControl

Listing 10.16: DTPicker1_FormatSize Event in DateControl

Listing 10.17: DTPicker1_Format Event in DateControl

DoEvents

The DoEvents program demonstrates how to use a progress bar and other techniques to let the user know that your program is busy performing useful work. Its CD-ROM location is \Samples\DoEvents\Project1.vbp.

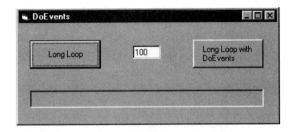

Excerpts from the code appear in the following listing:

Listing 6.12: DoIt Routine in DoEvents

Dynamic Controls

The Dynamic Controls program shows several different methods that are used to create and delete controls on the fly. These techniques include control arrays, controls without events, controls with events, and controls with `ObjectEvents`. This program also demonstrates how to use the `CallByName` routine and how to list the controls that are on a particular form using the `Controls` collection. Its CD-ROM location is \Samples\DynamicControls\Project1.vbp.

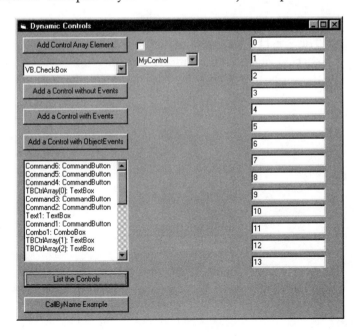

Excerpts from the code appear in the following listings:

Listing 18.4: Command3_Click Event in Dynamic Controls

Listing 18.5: Command3A_Click Event in Dynamic Controls

Listing 18.6: TBCtrlArray_GotFocus Event in Dynamic Control

Listing 18.7: TBCtrlArray_DblClick Event in Dynamic Control

Listing 18.8: Command1_Click Event in Dynamic Control

Listing 18.9: MyCommand_Click Event in Dynamic Control

Listing 18.10: Command4_Click Event in Dynamic Control

Listing 18.11: MyControl_ObjectEventA in Dynamic Control

Listing 18.12: MyControl_ObjectEvent in Dynamic Control

Listing 18.13: Command6_Click Event in Dynamic Control

Listing 18.14: Command2_Click Event in Dynamic Control

Listing 18.15: IsControlArray Function in Dynamic Control

Excel Demo

The Excel Demo program demonstrates using Excel objects to create a spreadsheet, using the information in the spreadsheet to create a chart, and then using the clipboard to copy the chart to the demo program. Its CD-ROM location is \Samples\ExcelDemoProgram\Project1.vbp.

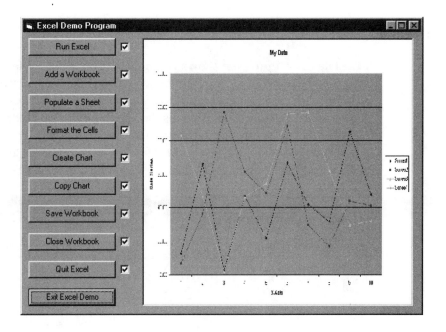

This program requires Excel 97 to be installed on the same computer as the application.

Excerpts from the code appear in the following listings:

Listing 15.4: Command1_Click Event in Excel Demo

Listing 15.5: Command2_Click Event in Excel Demo

Listing 15.6: Command3_Click Event in Excel Demo

Listing 15.7: Command4_Click Event in Excel Demo

Listing 15.8: Command5_Click Event in Excel Demo

Listing 15.9: Command6_Click Event in Excel Demo

Listing 15.10: Command7_Click Event in Excel Demo

Listing 15.11: Command8_Click Event in Excel Demo

Listing 15.12: Command9_Click Event in Excel Demo

File Viewer

The File Viewer program shows you how to use the File System Objects with the TreeView and ListView controls to build a program that can browse the files on your computer. It includes a pair of ActiveX controls called FileSelect and FileView. File-Select uses a TreeView control to display the computer's directory structure and a ListView control to display the files in a particular directory. The FileView control is used to display a file in a hexadecimal format, in an image file format, or as straight ASCII text. The program's CD-ROM location is \Samples\FileViewer\Group1.vbp.

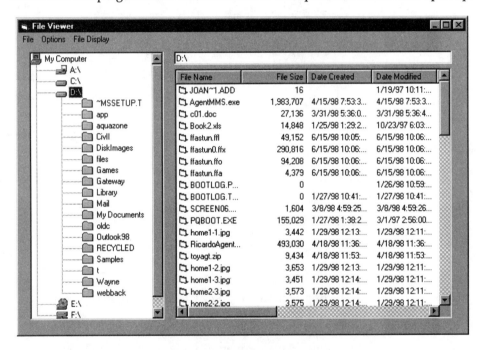

Excerpts from the code appear in the following listings:

Listing 4.14: Drive Information Retrieval in File Viewer

Listing 4.15: TreeView1_NodeClick Event in File Viewer

Listing 4.16: TreeView1_NodeClick Event in File Viewer (continued)

Listing 4.17: ShowHex Routine in File Viewer

Listing 7.1: AddNodes Routine in File Viewer

Listing 7.2: DeleteNodes Routine in File Viewer

Listing 7.3: TreeView1_DblClick Event in File Viewer

Listing 7.4: AddFiles Routine in File Viewer

Listing 7.5: ListView1_ColumnClick Event in File Viewer

Listing 7.6: ListView1_ItemClick Event in File Viewer

Financial Function Demo

The Financial Function Demo program demonstrates the use of the financial functions available in Visual Basic. You fill in the values in the text boxes and then click the desired command button. The parameters that were used in computing the value will be displayed with a blue background, and the answer will be displayed with a green background. Its CD-ROM location is \Samples\FinancialFunction\ Project1.vbp.

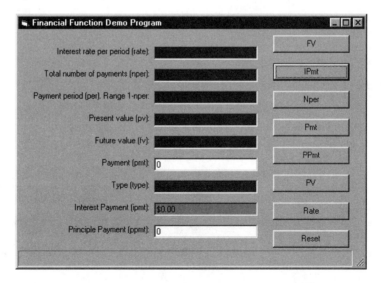

Excerpts from the code appear in the following listings:

Listing 5.6: Command4_Click Event in Financial Function Demo

Listing 10.4: CheckData Routine in Financial Function Demo

Forms Collection Demo

The Forms Collection Demo program demonstrates how to create and delete forms on the fly. Its CD-ROM location is \Samples\DynamicForms\Project1.vbp.

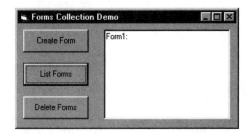

Excerpts from the code appear in the following listings:

Listing 18.1: Command1_Click Event in Forms Collection Demo

Listing 18.2: Command2_Click Event in Forms Collection Demo

Listing 18.3: Command3_Click Event in Forms Collection Demo

Hello Jill

The Hello Jill program is a simple MSAgent application that displays the selected Agent character and speaks specified text. Its CD-ROM location is \Samples\ HelloJill\Project.vbp.

This program requires the Microsoft Agent software, which comes with Visual Basic. You can find installation instructions in Chapter 14.

Excerpts from the code appear in the following listings:

Listing 14.1: Global Declarations for Hello Jill

Listing 14.2: Form_Load Event for Hello Jill

Listing 14.3: Command1_Click for Hello Jill

Honest Wayne's Used Airplane Lot

The Honest Wayne's Used Airplane Lot program has two parts. The client part (Project1.vbp) contains the user interface logic. The server part (Fleet.vbp) is an ActiveX server program that returns information about the aircraft that are available for sale. The CD-ROM locations are \Samples\AirplaneLot\Project1.vbp and \Samples\AirplaneLot\Fleet.vbp.

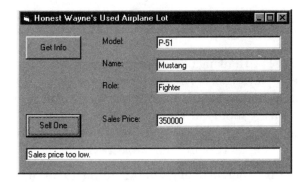

The server program must be running before you start the client program. I usually compile the server program to an EXE file and run it outside Visual Basic while I'm testing the other client program. However, sometimes it is desirable to run two copies of Visual Basic—one with the client and one with the server. That way, you can debug both at the same time.

Excerpts from the code appear in the following listings:

Listing 15.13: Airplane Object Definition for Wayne's Used Airplane Lot

Listing 15.14: Client's Form_Load Event for Wayne's Used Airplane Lot

Listing 15.15: Server's Class_Initialize Event for Wayne's Used
Airplane Lot

Listing 15.16: Server's AddOne Routine Event for Wayne's Used
Airplane Lot

Listing 15.17: Client's Command1_Click Event for Wayne's Used
Airplane Lot

Listing 15.18: Server's IsModel Function for Wayne's Used Airplane Lot

Listing 15.19: Server's FleetSize Function for Wayne's Used Airplane Lot

Listing 15.20: Client's Command2_Click Event for Wayne's Used
Airplane Lot

Listing 15.21: Server's SellOne Function for Wayne's Used Airplane Lot

Listing 15.22: Server's ErrorDescription Function for Wayne's Used
Airplane Lot

I'm Thinking of a Color

The I'm Thinking of a Color program is a computer game where a human contestant plays against two Microsoft Agent characters. A third character is the moderator. The moderator thinks of a color, and the three players try to guess it. The human's inputs are based on the speech recognition engine. This program is ideal for young children who can speak but aren't ready to type. Its CD-ROM location is \Samples\ColorGame\Project1.vbp.

This program requires the Microsoft Agent software, which comes with Visual Basic. You can find installation instructions in Chapter 14. A good computer microphone is highly recommended.

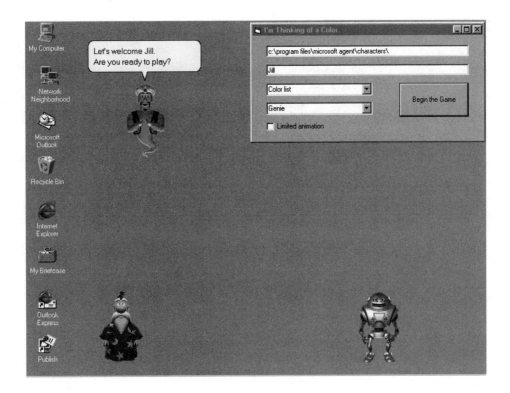

Excerpts from the code appear in the following listings:

Listing 14.9: Global Declarations for I'm Thinking of a Color

Listing 14.10: Form_Load Event for I'm Thinking of a Color

Listing 14.11: Command1_Click Event for I'm Thinking of a Color

Listing 14.12: PlayerInit Routine for I'm Thinking of a Color

Listing 14.13: AddCommands Routine for I'm Thinking of a Color

Listing 14.14: Agent1_Command Routine for I'm Thinking of a Color

Listing 14.15: PlayerWelcome Routine for I'm Thinking of a Color

Internet Updater

The Internet Updater program downloads a file over the Internet that contains information about each file that is part of an application. It then analyzes this information and determines which files should be downloaded to make the application current. Finally, it downloads the files and installs them into the application. Its CD-ROM location is \Samples\InternetUpdater\Project1.vbp.

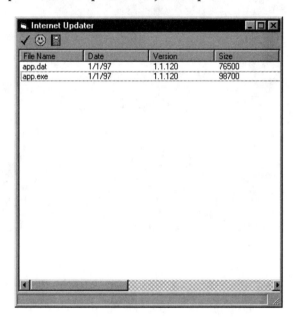

The Internet Updater needs either a web site or FTP site to check and download files. You can use the Personal Web Server, Internet Information Server, or any other web server on your machine to test the program locally.

Excerpts from the code appear in the following listings:

Listing 11.1: LoadRemoteInfo Routine in Internet Updater

Listing 11.2: AnalyzeInfo Routine in Internet Updater

Listing 11.3: UpdateInfo Routine in Internet Updater

Listing 11.4: GetFile Routine in Internet Updater

Listing 11.5: Inet1_StateChanged Event in Internet Updater

Listing 11.6: GetState Function in Internet Updater

Make Errors

The Make Errors program shows you how to trap and process various types of runtime errors. Its CD-ROM location is \Samples\MakeErrors\Project1.vbp.

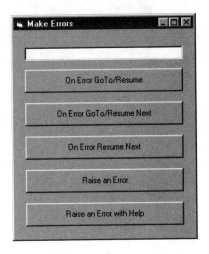

Excerpts from the code appear in the following listings:

Listing 20.1: Command1_Click Event in Make Errors

Listing 20.2: Command2_Click Event in Make Errors

Listing 20.3: Command3_Click Event in Make Errors

Listing 20.4: MakeAnError Routine in Make Errors

Listing 20.5: Command4_Click Event in Make Errors

Listing 20.6: Command5_Click Event in Make Errors

MAPI Demo

The MAPI Demo program shows you how to access the Simple MAPI controls (MAPISession and MAPIMessages) to send and receive e-mail. Its CD-ROM location is \Samples\MAPI\Project1.vbp.

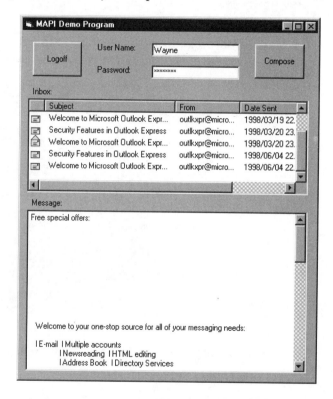

This program needs access to a MAPI-compliant mail system, such as Outlook Express or Outlook 98, in order to perform MAPI functions.

Excerpts from the code appear in the following listings:

Listing 8.1: Command1_Click Event in MAPI Demo

Listing 8.2: FetchMessages Routine in MAPI Demo

Listing 8.3: ListView1_ItemClick Event in MAPI Demo

Listing 8.4: Command2_Click Event in MAPI Demo

MSScript Demo

The MSScript Demo program shows you how to use the MSScript control to run simple VBScript programs. Its CD-ROM location is \Samples\MSScript\Project1.vbp.

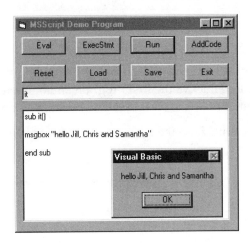

Excerpts from the code appear in the following listings:

Listing 13.1: Command7_Click Event in MSScript Demo

Listing 13.2: Command5_Click Event in MSScript Demo

Listing 13.3: Command4_Click Event in MSScript Demo

Listing 13.4: Command1_Click Event in MSScript Demo

Listing 13.5: ScriptControl1_Error Event in MSScript Demo

Notepad Writer

The Notepad Writer program demonstrates how to use `Shell`, `AppActivate`, and `SendKeys` to dynamically start and control another Windows program. It starts Notepad (or any program you specify in the Program text box) when you click the Start button. Its CD-ROM location is \Samples\Shell\Project1.vbp.

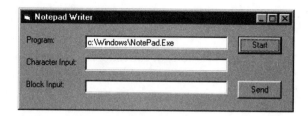

Notepad Writer can't control more than one program at a time. While it is possible to start a new program without ending the previous one, NotePad Writer will lose track of the first program and only interact with the new program. Also, although you can start a DOS program, you can't send any keystrokes to it.

Excerpts from the code appear in the following listings:

Listing 15.1: Command2_Click Event in Notepad Writer

Listing 15.2: Text2_KeyPress Event in Notepad Writer

Listing 15.3: Command1_Click Event in Notepad Writer

Package

The Package program is designed to show how to use Visual Basic's Package and Deployment Wizard. No code samples were included in the book. However, the complete information generated by the wizard is included on the CD-ROM in \Samples\Package\PlayIt.vbp.

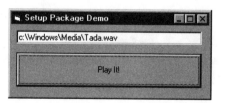

Print

The Print program shows how to perform various graphic and text functions on a printer. Its CD-ROM location is \Samples\Print\Project1.vbp.

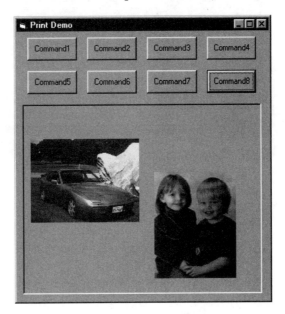

The program uses the Picture control to simulate a printer. If you want to try this with a real printer, simply replace `Picture1` with `Printer` throughout the program. Note that if you send output to your printer, you will need to stop the program after printing a single page.

Excerpts from the code appear in the following listings:

Listing 9.4: Command1_Click Event in Print

Listing 9.5: Command2_Click Event in Print

Listing 9.6: Command3_Click Event in Print

Listing 9.7: Command4_Click Event in Print

Listing 9.8: Command5_Click Event in Print

Listing 9.9: Command6_Click Event in Print

Listing 9.10: Command7_Click Event in Print

Listing 9.11: Command8_Click Event in Print

Listing 9.12: Sample01 Routine in Print

Printer

The Printer program demonstrates how to select and use the printers available on a computer. Its CD-ROM location is \Samples\Printer\Project1.vbp.

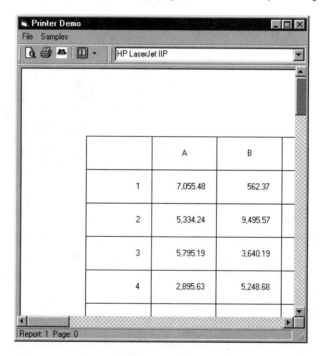

This program assumes that you have at least one printer available on your system.

Excerpts from the code appear in the following listings:

Listing 9.1: LoadPrinters Routine in Printer

Listing 9.2: Combo1_Click Event in Printer

Listing 9.3: MenuConfigure_Click Event in Printer

Quote of the Day

The Quote of the Day program uses the Winsock control to retrieve a quote from a Quote of the Day server. Its CD-ROM location is \Samples\Quote\Project1.vbp.

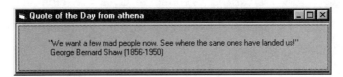

This program assumes that you have access to a Quote of the Day server. You can find this facility in Windows NT Server's Simple TCP/IP services package.

Excerpts from the code appear in the following listings:

Listing 12.1: Command1_Click Event in Quote

Listing 12.2: Winsock1_DataArrival Event in Quote

Random File Access

The Random File Access program shows how to read and write random-access files using the traditional Visual Basic file statements, functions, and controls. Its CD-ROM location is \Samples\SequentialFiles\Project1.vbp.

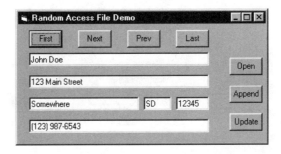

Excerpts from the code appear in the following listings:

Listing 4.8: Global Declarations in Random File Access

Listing 4.9: Command5_Click Event in Random File Access

Listing 4.10: Command1_Click Event in Random File Access

Listing 4.11: Command2_Click Event in Random File Access

Listing 4.12: Command6_Click Event in Random File Access

Listing 4.13: Command7_Click Event in Random File Access

Really Programmable Calculator

The Really Programmable Calculator program allows you to program your own calculator. You need to write code that handles all of the details, even down to what happens when you press the 1 key. Its CD-ROM location is \Samples\Calculator\Project1.vbp.

Excerpts from the code appear in the following listings:

Listing 13.6: KeyButton_Click Event in Programmable Calculator

Listing 13.7: Set_Click Event in Programmable Calculator

Listing 13.8: ScriptControl1_Error Event in Programmable Calculator

Listing 13.9: Form_Load Event in Programmable Calculator

Listing 13.10: LoadCode Script Routine in Programmable Calculator

Listing 13.11: Start of the Calc.MOD File

Listing 13.12: Press1 Script Routine in Programmable Calculator

Listing 13.13: PressAdd Script Routine in Programmable Calculator

Listing 13.14: PressEquals Script Routine in Programmable Calculator

RegTool

The RegTool program allows you to extract the registered owner and registered organization from the Windows Registry using Win32 API calls. It also demonstrates how the Win32 API Registry calls can be used to duplicate the GetSetting function and the SaveSetting statement in Visual Basic. Its CD-ROM location is \Samples\RegTool\Project1.vbp.

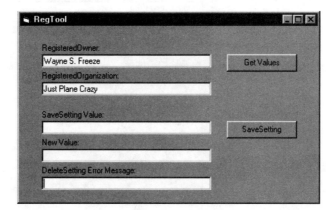

WARNING

Read before running: Using this program could potentially corrupt your Registry files. While I have tested it and believe it to be safe, please read and understand the Registry information discussed in Chapter 17 before using this program.

Excerpts from the code appear in the following listings:

Listing 17.11: Windows Registry Access Header Information for RegTool

Listing 17.12: Command1_Click Event in RegTool

Listing 17.13: Command2_Click Event in RegTool

Resource File Demo

The Resource File Demo utility shows how you can use a resource file in your application. You can specify a string number and click the Show button to display the string value. Alternatively, you can specify the bitmap, icon, or cursor number and type and click Show to see the graphic. Its CD-ROM location is \Samples\ResourceFile\Project1.vbp.

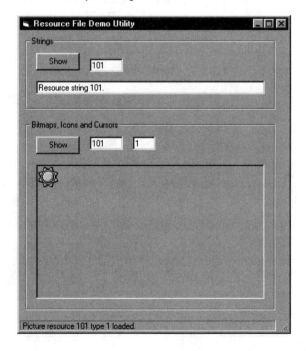

Excerpts from the code appear in the following listing:

Listing 5.9: Command1_Click Event in Resource File Demo

Scheduler

The Scheduler program is used to start various tasks at various intervals. This program shows you how to use the Systray ActiveX control to display an icon in the Taskbar. Its CD-ROM location is \Samples\Scheduler\Project1.vbp.

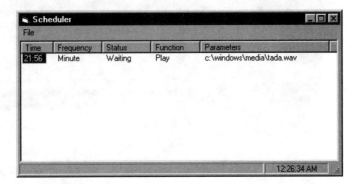

Excerpts from the code appear in the following listings:

Listing 17.7: Form_Load Event in Scheduler

Listing 17.8: Timer1_Event in Scheduler

Listing 17.9: RunMe Routine in Scheduler

Listing 17.10: cSysTray1_MouseDown Event in Scheduler

Screen Saver

The Screen Saver program is a major rewrite of the StarSX program to convert it to a screen saver. However, the basic algorithms remain unchanged, and the suggested parameters discussed in Chapter 17 apply equally to the Screen Saver and StarSX programs. Its CD-ROM location is \Samples\ScreenSaver\StarSx.vbp.

Excerpts from the code appear in the following listings:

Listing 17.1: Module-level Variables for Screen Saver's Pic Form

Listing 17.2: DrawArc Routine for Screen Saver's Pic Form

Listing 17.3: DrawStarSx Routine for Screen Saver's Pic Form

Listing 17.4: Form_Load Event for Screen Saver's Pic Form

Listing 17.5: Form_MouseMove Event for Screen Saver's Pic Form

Listing 17.6: Main Subroutine in Screen Saver

Sea Wars

The Sea Wars program implements a game similar to Battleship that you can play over the Internet. Its CD-ROM location is \Samples\SeaWar\Project1.vbp.

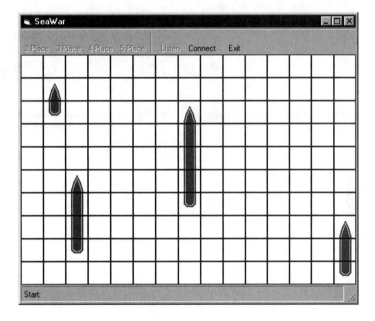

This program needs access to another computer over a TCP/IP network in order to play the game.

Excerpts from the code appear in the following listings:

Listing 12.8: Toolbar1_ButtonClick Event in Sea Wars

Listing 12.9: Winsock1_Connection Request in Sea Wars

Listing 12.10: Winsock1_DataArrival Event in Sea Wars

Listing 12.11: ProcessInput Routine in Sea Wars

Listing 12.12: DrawMyGrid Routine in Sea Wars

Listing 12.13: Water_Click Event in Sea Wars

Sequential File Access

The Sequential File Access program shows how to read and write sequential files using the traditional Visual Basic file statements, functions, and controls. Its CD-ROM location is \Samples\SequentialFiles\Project1.vbp.

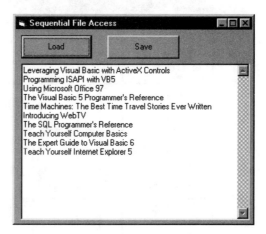

Excerpts from the code appear in the following listings:

Listing 4.6: Command1_Click Event in Sequential File Access

Listing 4.7: Command2_Click Event in Sequential File Access

Slide Show

The Slide Show program allows you to select a set of one or more images and then display them in sequence. Its CD-ROM location is \Samples\SlideShow\Project1.vbp. This program comes with three test .JPG images.

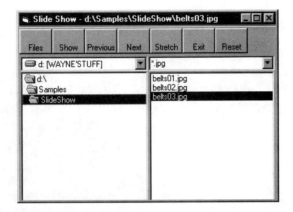

Excerpts from the code appear in the following listings:

 Listing 4.1: DriveList_Change Event in Slide Show

 Listing 4.2: DirList_Change Event in Slide Show

 Listing 4.3: FileTypes_Click Event in Slide Show

 Listing 4.4: Form_Load Event in Slide Show

 Listing 4.5: Toolbar1_ButtonClick Event in Slide Show

StarSX

The StarSX program draws interesting graphics based on parameters supplied to the program. See Chapter 17 and its discussion on screen savers for more information about useful parameters for this program. Its CD-ROM location is \Samples\StarSx\StarSx.vbp.

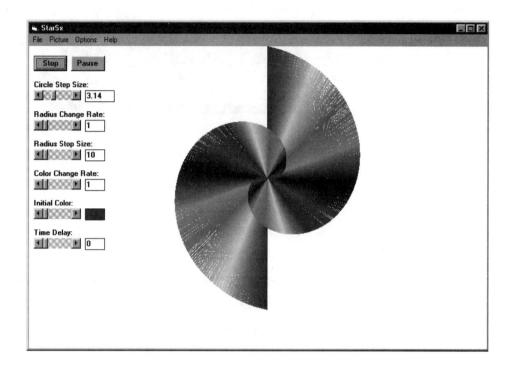

Excerpts from the code appear in the following listing:

Listing 3.1: DrawArc Routine in StarSX

String Demo

The String Demo program is used to demonstrate how various string functions work, including Filter, Format, FormatCurrency, FormatNumber, FormatPercent, InStr, InStrRev, Join, LCase, Left, Len, LTrim, Mid, Trim, Right, RTrim, Split, String, StrReverse, and UCase. Its CD-ROM location is \Samples\StringDemo\ Project1.vbp.

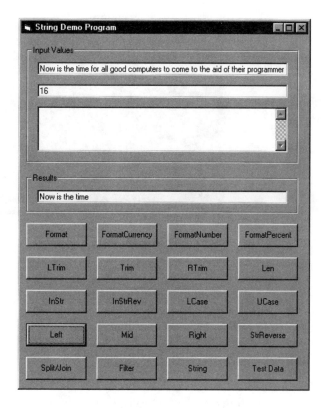

Excerpts from the code appear in the following listings:

Listing 5.7: Command17_Click Event in String Demo

Listing 5.8: Command18_Click Event in String Demo

System Information

The System Information program demonstrates how to use the SysInfo control to gather information about the operating system, the computer's battery (if it has one), and the screen. It also uses the App object to determine information about the application. Its CD-ROM location is \Samples\SysInfo\Project1.vbp.

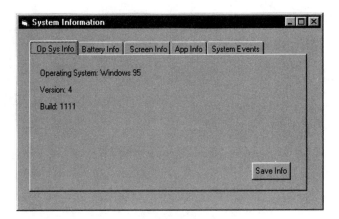

Excerpts from the code appear in the following listings:

Listing 6.13: GetSysInfo Routine in System Information

Listing 6.14: GetBatteryInfo Routine in System Information

Listing 6.15: GetScreenInfo Routine in System Information

Listing 6.16: GetAppInfo Routine in System Information

Listing 6.17: SysInfo1_DisplayChanged Event in System Information

Listing 6.18: Command1_Click Event in System Information

Telnet Server

The Telnet Server program demonstrates how to build an Internet server using a standard protocol such as Telnet. Its CD-ROM location is \Samples\Telnet-Server\Project1.vbp.

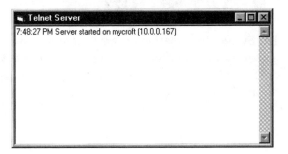

This program assumes that you have TCP/IP services installed on your machine.

Excerpts from the code appear in the following listings:

Listing 12.3: Form_Load Event in Telnet Server

Listing 12.4: PublicSocket_ConnectionRequest Event in Telnet Server

Listing 12.5: PrivateSocket_DataArrival Event in Telnet Server

Listing 12.6: ProcessInput Routine in Telnet Server

Listing 12.7: RunIt Routine in Telnet Server

Tips and Tricks Demo

The Tips and Tricks Demo program shows you how to center a form on the screen, how to remember where a form was placed on the screen, and how to resize a form with anchored and floating controls. Its CD-ROM location is \Samples\TipsDemo\TipsDemo.vbp.

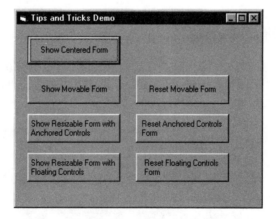

Excerpts from the code appear in the following listings:

Listing 6.1: Form_Load Event from Form2 in Tips and Tricks Demo

Listing 6.2: Form_Load Event from Form3 in Tips and Tricks Demo

Listing 6.3: Form_Unload Event from Form3 in Tips and Tricks Demo

Listing 6.4: Command3_Click Event from Form1 in Tips and Tricks Demo

Listing 6.5: Global Declarations from Form1 in Tips and Tricks Demo

Listing 6.6: Global Declarations from Form4 in Tips and Tricks Demo

VB4 Sample

The VB4 Sample program contains errors that you may encounter while converting a 16-bit Visual Basic 4.0 program to Visual Basic 6.0. This program is discussed in Chapter 1, in the section titled "Migration from Previous Versions of Visual Basic." Its CD-ROM location is \Samples\VB4Sample\Project1.vbp.

The program does not fix any of the problems it encounters. However, the .LOG files that are created when the program is loaded into Visual Basic 6 will contain details about the problems that need to be fixed before it will run in Visual Basic 6. An executable version is also supplied, but it requires the VB400016.DLL library to run.

Weather Maker

The Weather Maker program shows you how to do a number of different things with menus, toolbars, status bars, and CoolBars. Its CD-ROM location is \Samples\WeatherMaker\Project1.vbp.

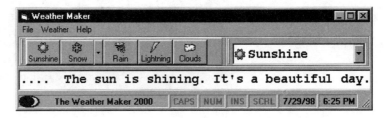

Excerpts from the code appear in the following listings:

Listing 10.5: Animating a Moon in Weather Maker

Listing 10.6: Toolbar1_ButtonClick Event in Weather Maker

Listing 10.7: Toolbar1_ButtonMenuClick Event in Weather Maker

Listing 10.8: The Toolbar1_Change Event in Weather Maker

Listing 10.9: SaveBandInfo Routine in Weather Maker

Listing 10.10: GetBandInfo Routine in Weather Maker

Listing 10.11: GetCoolBarInfo Routine in Weather Maker

Listing 10.12: CoolBar1_HeightChanged Event in Weather Maker

Listing 10.18: LoadImageCombo Routine in Weather Maker

Win32 API Demo

The Win32 API Demo program demonstrates many different Win32 API calls, including those related to time zones, general Windows information, environment information, and process information. It also shows how to delay execution of your program, change system colors, run programs and files, get icons, work with text and list boxes, and shut down Windows. Its CD-ROM location is \Samples\ Win32API\Project1.vbp.

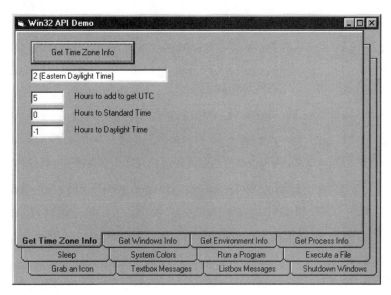

WARNING   **Be careful with Win32 API calls:** Read Chapter 16 carefully before trying this program. While I believe this program is safe, it may cause problems depending on your exact system configuration. Please exercise caution while trying it.

Excerpts from the code appear in the following listings:

Listing 16.1: Get Time Zone Header from Win32 API Demo

Listing 16.2: Command1_Click Event in Win32 API Demo

Listing 16.3: Get Windows Information Header from Win32 API Demo

Listing 16.4: Command2_Click Event in Win32 API Demo

Listing 16.5: Get Environment Information Header from Win32 API Demo

Listing 16.6: Command3_Click Event in Win32 API Demo

Listing 16.7: Command4_Click Event in Win32 API Demo

Listing 16.8: Get Process Information Header from Win32 API Demo

Listing 16.9: Command5_Click Event in Win32 API Demo

Listing 16.10: FileTimeToString Routine in Win32 API Demo

Listing 16.11: Sleep Header from Win32 API Demo

Listing 16.12: Command6_Event in Win32 API Demo

Listing 16.13: Command7_Event in Win32 API Demo

Listing 16.14: Get System Color Information Header from Win32 API Demo

Listing 16.15: Command8_Click Event in Win32 API Demo

Listing 16.16: Command9_Click Event in Win32 API Demo

Listing 16.17: Command10_Click Event in Win32 API Demo

Listing 16.18: Process Header Information from Win32 API Demo

Listing 16.19: RunProg Function in Win32 API Demo

Listing 16.20: WaitProg Routine in Win32 API Demo

Listing 16.21: Command11_Click Event in Win32 API Demo

Listing 16.22: Run a File Header Information from Win32 API Demo

Listing 16.23: StartMeUp Routine in Win32 API Demo

Listing 16.24: Command12_Click Event in Win32 API Demo

Listing 16.25: Get Icon Header Information from Win32 API Demo

Listing 16.26: Command13_Click Event in Win32 API Demo

Listing 16.27: Send Message Header Information from Win32 API Demo

Listing 16.28: Command14_Click Event in Win32 API Demo

Listing 16.29: Command15_Click Event in Win32 API Demo

Listing 16.30: Text21_KeyPress Event in Win32 API Demo

Listing 16.31: Shutdown Windows Header Information from Win32 API Demo

Listing 16.32: Command18_Click Event in Win32 API Demo

INDEX

Note to the Reader: Throughout this index **boldfaced** page numbers indicate primary discussions of a topic. *Italicized* page numbers indicate illustrations.

A

a characters
  for help file footnotes, 772
  as Mask characters, 383
A/P in date formats, 135
.AAF files, 520
aborting MTS transactions, **810–811**
About command, 335
Abs function, 471
Accept method, 426, 435
access keys, **174–175**, *175*
AccessType property, 401–402
ACE.EXE program, 509
.ACF files, 520
ACID test in MTS, **804–805**
Acknowledge animation, 524
ACL structure, 682–683
.ACS files, 520
ACStatus property, 188
ACTCNC.EXE program, 507
Activate method, 522, 526–527
ActivateInput events, 516, 518
Active Messaging, 259
Active Server Pages, 800
ActiveX controls, 18, **748–751**
  adding, **39–41**, *40*
  benefits of, 70
  unused, **711**
ActiveX Data Objects (ADO), 8, 27
ActiveX DLLs, 579, **748–750**, **752**

ActiveX documents, 18, 750
ActiveX EXEs, **579**, **748–751**
ActiveX programs, **578–579**. *See also* Honest Wayne's Used Airplane Lot program
Add Bitmap button, 155
Add Cursor button, 155
Add Custom Resource button, 155
Add File dialog box, 55, *55*
Add Icon button, 155
Add-In Manager, 51–52, *52*, 151
Add-Ins ➤ Add-In Manager command, 51
Add-Ins ➤ Package and Deployment Wizard command, 51
Add Map Entry dialog box, 775, *776*
Add method
  in AddressEntries, 276–277
  in Attachments, 272
  in Bands, 361, 364
  in Commands, 529–530
  in Controls, 707–708
  in Files, 114
  in Folders, 267
  in ListItems, 217
  in Messages, 268–269
  in Nodes, 210–211
  in Recipients, 274
Add Tab command, 41
Add Watch dialog box, 82–83, *83*
AddCode method, 467–468, 476, 480, 492
AddCommands routine, 548
AddFiles routine, 214, **216–218**
adding
  CoolBar band controls, **361–362**, *361*
  ListView items, **216–218**

random file records, **107**

Toolbar buttons, **352–354**, *352*

addition of dates, **139–140**

AddMultiple method, 274

AddNodes routine, 210–211, 214

AddObject method, 467, 489

AddOne routine, 583

address entries in CDO, **276–278**

address lists in CDO, **276**

Address property

in AddressEntry, 277

in Recipient, 274–275

AddressBook method, 265–266

AddressEntries collection, **276–277**

AddressEntries property, 276

AddressEntry objects, 270, **277–278**

AddressEntry property, 274–275

addresses

IP, **393–394**

for ports, **394–395**

for Winsock controls, 424

AddressList objects, 276

AddressLists collection, 276

AddressLists property, 264

Adjust Microphone button, 509, 512

ADO (ActiveX Data Objects), 8, 27

Advanced Optimizations dialog box, 754–756, *755*

Advanced Research Projects Agency (ARPA), 392–393

Advanced Settings button, 512

Advanced tab, **37–38**, *38*

Agent Demo program, **536–537**, *537*

global declarations in, **537**

initializing Commands collection in, **537–539**

spoken commands in, **539–541**

summary of, **822–823**

waiting for requests in, **541–542**

Agent1_Command routine

in Agent Demo, 539–541

in I'm Thinking of a Color, **549–550**

Agent1_RequestComplete routine, 542

Agents, **504–506**, *505*

controls for. *See* MSAgent controls

in games. *See* I'm Thinking of a Color program

installing, **509–510**

Airplane objects, 579–580

Airplanes objects, 579–580

Alert animation, 524

AlertReturn animation, 524

aliasing option, 755

Align property

in CoolBar, 360

in StatusBar, 340

in Toolbar, 350–351

AlignCell routine, **230–231**

alignment

in CoolBars, 360

in MSFlexGrid controls, **230–231**

in StatusBar panels, 342–343

in Toolbar controls, **350–351**

Alignment property, 342

Allow Unrounded Floating Point Operations option, 755

AllowCustomize property, 350, 357

AllowPrompt property, 381, 384

AllowSelections property, 243

AllowUI property, 465–466

Alt key

for access keys, 174

in SendKeys, 562

Alt1Confidence property, 517

Alt1Name property, 517

Alt1Voice property, 517

Alt2Confidence property, 517

Alt2Name property, 517

Alt2Voice property, 517

AM/PM in date formats, 135

AmbiguousNames property, 274–275

ampersands (&)

for access keys, 174

as Mask characters, 383

AMPM in date formats, 135

AnalyzeInfo routine, **411–414**

anchored controls, resizing, **168–171**, *168*

AniButton control, 23

animation

with Agents. *See* I'm Thinking of a Color program; Microsoft Agent; MSAgent controls

in StatusBar controls, **347–348**

annuity functions, **143–144**, *143*

anonymous FTP, 397

Ansi character set, 595

apartment threading model, 44

API Text Viewer, **601–602**, *602*

App object, **194–195**

AppActivate statement, **560**, 563–565

Appearance property, 350

Append file mode, 91

AppEvents key, 677

AppInfo tab, 195, *195*

Application property, 262

Application Title property, 661

applications

    deploying, **61**

    information about, **194–195**

    multiple copies of, **184**

    names for, 166

    printing from, **299**

Applications Services model, **788–789**, *788*

    business services in, **791–793**, *792–793*

    data services in, **790–791**

    user services in, **789–790**

Apply button, 485

arguments

    command-line, **47**

    in Win32 calls, 600

arithmetic with dates, **139–141**

ARPA (Advanced Research Projects Agency), 392–393

ARPANET, 393

Array function, 471

arrays

    bounds checking of, 755

    control. *See* control arrays

    debugging, **85**

    memory for, 747–748

    of menus, **336–338**

    speed of, **735–736**

arrow keys in SendKeys, 561–562

Asc/AscB/AscW functions, 471

ASCII characters

    in file displays, **121–123**, *122*

    groups of, 227

Assert statement, **78–79**, *78*

Assume No Aliasing option, 755

asterisks (*) for help file footnotes, 772

AsyncRead method, 10

AtEndOfLine property, 120

AtEndOfStream property, 120

Atn function, 471

atomicity in MTS transactions, 804

Attachment objects, **273**

AttachmentCount property, 256

Attachments collection, **272**

attachments in CDO, **272–273**

Attachments property, 269

attack statement, 446, 453

Attributes property

    in File, 117, 119

    in Folder, 114

AudioOutput objects, 533

AudioOutput property, 514–515

Auto Increment feature, 46

automating tasks. *See* ScriptControls; scripts

AutoRedraw, 734

AutoSize property, 342, 344

AutoTab property, 381

AvailableSpace property, 112

B

BackColor property, 531

background processing, **744–745**

backing up Registry, **672–674**

backslashes (\) as Mask characters, 383

Backspace key

    in Charter, 246

    in SendKeys, 561

Balloon objects, **531–532**

Balloon property, 520

BalloonHide events, 516

BalloonShow events, 516

Band controls in CoolBars, **358–359**, *358*

    adding, **364**

    adding controls to, **361–362**, *361*

Bands collection, 361

Bands property, 360

Bands tab, 361, *361*

.BAS file type, 19, 21

batch processing, ScriptControls for, 499

battery information, **188–191**, *189*

BatteryFullTime property, 188

BatteryInfo tab, 189, *189*

BatteryLifePercent property, 189

BatteryLifeTime property, 189

BatteryStatus property, 189

Battleship game. *See* Sea Wars program

BeginTrans method, 28

Bevel property, 343

Binary data type, 675

binary files, Loc function for, 93

Bind method, 426

binding, early and late, **738**

bitmaps, resource files for, 150, 155–156

Blink animation, 524

Bookmark events, 516

Boolean data type

    with TypeName, 720

    with Win32 API, 596–597

BorderColor property, 531

BorderStyle property, 350

braces ({}) in SendKeys, 561–562

brackets ([]) in SendKeys, 561–562

Break key in SendKeys, 561

Break When Value Changes option, 83–84

Break When Value is True option, 83–84

breakpoints, **79**

    hitting, **80–81**, *81*

    leaving, **81–82**, *81*

    with multiple-statement lines, 74

    setting, **80**, *80*

BSTR pointers, 598

bug prevention, **66**. *See also* debugging

    coding conventions for, **72–74**

    comments for, **70–72**

    KISS principle for, **68**

    Lazy Programmer techniques for, **74–75**

    object-oriented programming for, **69–70**

    Option Explicit statement for, **67–68**

    SMILE principle for, **68–69**

build levels of operating systems, 187

BuildPath method, 109

business applications, ScriptControls for, 499

business services

    in Applications Services model, **791–793**, *792–793*

    in MTS, **806–807**, *808*

ButtonClick events, 355

ButtonDropDown events, 355

ButtonMenuClick events, 355

buttons, Toolbar

    adding, **352–354**, *352*

    transparent, 351, *351*

Buttons tab, 352, *352*

ByRef parameters with strings, 598

Byte Arrays for Winsock data, 427

Byte data type

    in TypeName, 720

    in Win32 API, 596

BytesReceived property, 424

ByVal parameters with strings, 598

C

c characters

    in date formats, 135

    as Mask characters, 383

C language and Win32 API, 594

.ca domain, 393

.CAB files, 55

CAB Options window, 55, *56*

calculations, spreadsheet, **494–499**, *494*

calculators. *See* Really Programmable Calculator program

CalendarBackColor property, 373

CalendarForeColor property, 373

calendars

    in DateTimePicker controls, 372–373

    in MonthView controls, 367–370

CalendarTitleBackColor property, 373

CalendarTitleForeColor property, 373

CalendarTrailingForeColor property, 373

Call statement, 470

CallbackKeyDown method, 376

CallByName function, 10, **718–719**

calls for Win32 API, **599–600**

Cancel method, 402–403

CancelError property, 100

CapsLock key

    in SendKeys, 561

    in StatusBars, 343

Caption property and captions

    for access keys, 174

    in Band, 361–362

    in Command, 530, 538

    in Commands, 529

    for international editions, 158

    for Label controls, 175

    in Menu, 331

    in Toolbar buttons, 352

carets (^) in SendKeys, 560, 562

case-sensitivity

    in ImageCombo, 378–379

    in Win32 calls, 600

CaseSensitive property, 378–379

Categories property, 269–271

CauseValidation property, 180

Cbool function, 471

Cbyte function, 471

Ccur function, 471

CD command in FTP, 404, 406

Cdate function in VBScript, 471

CDate function in Visual Basic, 128, 133

CDbl function, 471

CDO (Collaboration Data Objects), **259**

    adding, **260–263**, *260–261*

    address entries, **276–278**

    address lists, **276**

    attachments, **272–273**

    folders, **267–268**

    InfoStores, **267**

    messages, **268–272**

    recipients, **274–275**

    Session object, **264–266**

CDO Demo program, **278**, *279*

    displaying folder contents in, **283–285**, *284*

    loading InfoStore information in, **280–281**, *280*

    loading MAPI folders in, **281–283**, *282*

    MAPI sessions in, **279–280**

    messages in

        composing, **289**

        deleting, **291**

        displaying, **286**, *286*

        processing, **287–291**, *290–291*

        properties of, **291**, *291*

        replying to, **290**

        saving, **291**

        sending, **289**, *290*

    summary of, **823–824**

CDO.DLL file, 260

CDUP command in FTP, 404, 406

CellAlignment property, 231

CellPicture property, 223

centering

    forms, **162–164**

    in StatusBar panels, 343

    text, **321–323**

centimeters in graphic methods, 314

CGI (Common Gateway Interface), 800

CGRAM.EXE program, 507

Change events

    in DirListBox, 96

    in DriveListBox, 96

    for Toolbars, 355

    for user-input checking, **178**

char data type, 596

Character method, 519

Character objects

    commands for, **517**

    methods for, **522–527**

    properties for, **520–521**

character processing in Notepad Writer, **564–565**

character sets, **595**

CharacterID property, 517

Characters collection, 514, **518–519**

    files for, **520**

    referencing characters in, **519**

CharsPerLine property, 531–532

ChartArea objects, 575

Charter program

  menu arrays in, **336–338**

  for MSChart controls

    chart titles, **243–246**, *244*

    chart types, **240–243**, *241*

    retrieving information in, **238–240**

  for MSFlexGrid controls

    aligning data in, **230–231**

    creating, **223–225**

    keyboard with, **226–229**

    loading data into, **225–226**, **234–237**

    saving data in, **231–234**

    selecting data in, **229–230**

  Print Preview window in, **318–325**

  spreadsheet equations in, **494–499**, *494*

  summary of, **824–826**

charts. *See also* MSChart controls

  copying, **575–576**, *576*

  titles of, **243–246**, *244*

  types of, **240–243**, *241*

  for worksheets, **574**, *575*

ChartStartCol property, 238

ChartStartRow property, 238

ChartStopCol property, 238

ChartStopRow property, 238

ChartType property, 240, 242

ChDir statement, 91–92

cheat command, 548

Check Names dialog box, 289, *290*

CheckBox property, 373–374

CheckData routine, 345–346

Checked property, 331

checking

  array bounds, 755

  user-input values, **176–177**

    Change events for, **178**

    ComboBoxes for, **180–183**

    Keypress events for, **177–178**

    LostFocus events for, **179**

    Validate events for, **180**

Child property, 358, 361

Children property, 214

Chr/ChrB/ChrW functions, 471

Chr speech tag, 526

Cint function, 471

Circle method, 297, 312–313

circles, generating, **312–313**, *313*

Class_Initialize events, 581–582

Class_Initialize routine, 582

Class objects, 581–582

Class property, **262–263**

Class_Terminate events, 581

Classes box in Object Browser, 49

Clear method

  in Err, 761, 767

  in Error, 469, 482

  in ListItems, 217

Click events

  in Menu, 331

  in MSAgent, 515–516

  in StatusBars, **346–348**

  in TreeView, 212

client/server applications. *See* Sea Wars program

client/server architecture, **786–788**, *787*

clients

  in business services, **791–792**, *792*

  for Internet, **428–432**, *429*

clipboard for Win32 API programs, 602

ClipControls, 734

ClipMode property, 382, 384

ClipText property, 382, 384

CLng function, 471

Close command

  on File menu, 333

  in FTP, 405–406

Close events, 427–428

Close method

  in Winsock, 426

  for workbooks, 577

Close property, 120

Close statement, 90–91

CloseHandle function, 606, 617, 630–632

CloseUp method, 376

closing
    FTP sessions, 406
    resource files, **156**, *156*
    Winsock, 428
    workbooks, **577**

.CLS file type, 19

Cls method, 305

cmdCount routine, 809

code
    inline, **739–740**
    native, **752–753**
    recycling, 732

code pages, 155

Code View tab, 483–486, *484*, 488

CodeObject property, 465–466

coding conventions, **72–74**

Col property, 226–227

Collaboration Data Objects. *See* CDO (Collaboration Data
    Objects); CDO Demo program

collections, speed of, **735–736**

colons (:)
    in date formats, 135
    as Mask characters, 383

colors
    guessing game. *See* I'm Thinking of a Color program
    in MonthView calendars, 369
    in Win32 API Demo program, **624–627**, *625*

ColSel property, 229

column headers in ListView controls, **215**, *216*

Column Headers tab, 215, *216*

Column property
    in Error, 469, 488
    in MSChart, 240
    in TextStream, 120

ColumnClick events, 219–220

ColumnHeader objects, 219

columns
    printing in, **306–307**, *306*
    in Sea Wars, 447

COM (Component Object Model), 794–796

.com domain, 393

Combo1_Click routine, 300

ComboBoxes
    in CoolBars, 358
    for data entry, **180–183**

ComboItem objects, 379–380

ComboItems property, 379

comma separated value (CSV) format, 234

Command and Control speech engine, 505, **507–509**, *508*

Command events, **516–517**

command-line arguments, **47**

Command method, 529

Command objects, 530

Command1_Click routine
    in Agent Demo, 542
    in Date/Time Demo, 133
    in Dynamic Controls, **707–708**
    in Excel Demo, **568–569**, *570*
    in Forms Collection Demo, 699
    in Hello Jill, 536
    in Honest Wayne's Used Airplane Lot, **583–584**
    in I'm Thinking of a Color, 546
    in Make Errors, **764–765**
    in MAPI Demo, 253–254
    in MSScript Demo program, 481
    in Notepad Writer, 565
    in Print, 304
    in Quote, **430–431**
    in Random Access File, 105–106
    in RegTool, **690–691**
    in Resource File Demo Utility, 158
    in Sequential File Access, 99–100
    in System Information, 200–201
    in Win32 API, **604–605**

Command2_Click routine
    in Dynamic Controls, 721
    in Excel Demo, 570
    in Forms Collection Demo, 700–701
    in Honest Wayne's Used Airplane Lot, 586
    in Make Errors, 765
    in MAPI Demo, 257
    in Notepad Writer, 564
    in Print, 305
    in Random Access File, 106–107
    in RegTool, **691–692**

in Sequential File Access, 101–102

in Win32 API Demo, **610–612**

Command3_Click routine

in Dynamic Controls, 703

in Excel Demo, 571–572

in Forms Collection Demo, 701

in Make Errors, **766–767**

in Print, 306

in Tips and Tricks Demo, 166

in Win32 API Demo, 613–614

Command3A_Click routine, 704–705

Command4_Click routine

in Dynamic Controls, 713

in Excel Demo, 573

in Financial Function Demo, 144

in Make Errors, 768

in MSScript Demo program, 480

in Printer, 307–308

in Win32 API Demo, 614

Command5_Click routine

in Date/Time Demo, 133

in Excel Demo, 574

in Make Errors, 769

in MSScript Demo program, 478

in Print, 309–310

in Random Access File, 105

in Win32 API Demo, 618–619

Command6_Click routine

in Date/Time Demo, 137

in Dynamic Controls, 718–719

in Excel Demo, 575–576

in Print, 311–312

in Random Access File, 107

in Win32 API Demo, 623

Command7_Click routine

in Excel Demo, 576–577

in MSScript Demo program, 476–477

in Print, 313

in Random Access File, 108

in Win32 API Demo, 623–624

Command8_Click routine

in Excel Demo, 577

in Print, 314

in Win32 API Demo, 626

Command9_Click routine

in Date/Time Demo, 140

in Excel Demo, 578

in Win32 API Demo, 627

Command10_Click routine, 627

Command11_Click routine, 633–634

Command12_Click routine, 637

Command13_Click routine, 640–641

Command14_Click routine, 645

Command15_Click routine, 645

Command17_Click routine, 149

Command18_Click routine

in String Demo, 150

in Win32 API Demo, 648

commands

in Agent Demo, **539–541**

in Telnet Server program, **440–442**, *441–442*

Commands collection, **527–530**, **537–539**

Commands property, 520

Commands window, 528, *528*

CommandsWindow objects, 533

CommandsWindow property, 514–515

commas (,)

as Mask characters, 383

in Print method, 306

in Win32 calls, 600

comments, **70–72**

committing MTS transactions, **810–811**

Common Gateway Interface (CGI), 800

CommonDialog control, 94

Communication between programs, **558**

with ActiveX programs. *See* Honest Wayne's Used Airplane Lot program

AppActivate for, **560**, 563–565

with Excel object. *See* Excel Demo program

SendKeys for, **560–565**

Shell for, **559**, 563–565

CompactDatabase method, 28

CompareIds method, 265

Compile tab, 752–753, *753*

Compile to Native Code option, 754

compilers, **17–18**

compiling
    conditional, **48**
    help files, **778**, *778–779*
    settings for, 752, *753*
Component Object Model (COM), 794–795
Component Wizard, **815–816**, *816–817*
Components dialog box, **39–41**, *40*
Compose method, 256, 259
composing CDO messages, **289**
compressed files, 558
Compression tab, 777, *777*
Compute function, **497–498**
ComputeControlSize method, 368–369
conditional compilation, **48**
Confidence property
    in Command, 530
    in UserInput, 517
ConfidenceText property, 530
Config key, 676
ConfigChangeCanceled events, 196
ConfigChanged events, 196
Configure option, 429
configuring
    Agent server, **510–513**, *511–513*
    CDO sessions, **266**
    Microsoft Agent, **506–509**, *508*
    screen savers, **661–663**, *664*
Confused animation, 524
ConfusedReturn animation, 524
Connect events, 427–428
Connect method, 426
Connected property, 515
ConnectionRequest events
    in Sea Wars, 448–449, 451
    in Winsock, 427
connections
    for Sea Wars, 443–444, **448–450**
    in Telnet Server program, **434–435**
    Winsock, 426, 428
consistency in MTS transactions, 804
Console key, 677
#CONST statement, 48
Const statement, 470

constants
    memory for, 747–748
    for Win32 API programs, **601**
constraints in optimizing, **728–730**
Contents and Index command, 335
context IDs, 775, *776*
context objects, **803–804**, **809–810**
control arrays, 435
    deleting elements in, **705–706**, *706*
    events in, 705
    new approach to, **704–705**
    traditional approach to, **702–703**, *703*
control characters, 227
Control Panel
    for dates, 132
    for locales, 151
    for Registry access, 672
Control Panel key, 677
Control Tabs program
    Change events in, **178**
    ComboBoxes in, **180–183**
    Keypress events in, **177–178**
    LostFocus events in, **179**
    summary of, **826**
    Validate events in, **180**
controls, 15
    access keys for, **174–175**, *175*
    ActiveX, 578, **748–751**
    arrays for. *See* control arrays
    for data entry, **366**
        DateTimePicker, **372–377**
        ImageCombo, **377–381**, *378*
        MaskedEdit, **381–385**
        MonthView, **367–371**
    dynamic, **701–706**, *703*, *706*
    without events, **706–711**, *708–711*
    hiding, **735**
    memory for, 747
    migration of, **22–27**
    moving, **742**
    new, **11–13**, *12–13*
    with normal events, **712–713**, *713*
    with ObjectEvents, **714–717**

qualified names for, **709–710**, *709–710*

resizing, **168–171**, *168*

speed of, 736–737

Controls collection, 701–702, 707

Controls directory, 25

Controls tab, 40–41, *40*

ConversationIndex property, 269, 271

ConversationTopic property, 269, 271

converting strings with dates, **132–134**

CoolBar controls, 11–12, *12*, **358–359**, *358*

adding bands to, **364**

adding controls to bands in, **361–362**, *361*

creating, **359–360**, *359*

loading, **365**

position of, **362–363**

resizing, **365–366**

CoolBar1_HeightChanged routine, 365–366

Copy command, 334

Copy method

in ChartArea, 575

in File, 117

in Folder, 114

CopyFile method, 109

CopyFolder method, 109

copying charts, **575–576**, *576*

copyright information, **45**, *46–47*

CopyTo method, 271–272

Cos function, 471

costs in optimizing, **729–730**

Count method, 704

Count property

in CDO objects, 262

in Commands, 529

in Controls, 707

in Drives, 111

in EventParameters, 715

in Files, 114, 117

in Forms, 698

in UserInput, 517

CountAuth property, 807–808

Create Empty Package dialog box, 812, *813*

Create Symbolic Debug Info option, 754

CreateConversationIndex method, 265–266

CreateDatabase method, 28

CreateFolder method, 110

CreateObject function, 567–568

enhancements to, 10

in FileSystemObject, 111

in VBScript, 471

CreateProcess function, 606, 630–632

CreateTextFile method

in FileSystemObject, 110

in Folder, 114

Crystal Reports, 24

Csng function, 472

CStr function, 145

CSV (comma separated value) format, 234

cSysTray1_MouseDown routine, 671

.CTL file type, 19

Ctrl key in SendKeys, 562

Ctrl+Break keys for debugging, **77**

.CTX file type, 19

Ctx speech tag, 526

CurDir statement, 91–92

curly braces ({}) in SendKeys, 561–562

Currency data type

speed of, 732

in TypeName, 720

with Win32 API, 597

Currency format, 148

CurrentUser property, 264

CurrentX property, 297, 307

CurrentY property, 297, 307

cursors

for long processing waits, 185

positioning in printing, **307–308**, *308*

resource files for, 150, 155–156

CustomFormat property, 373–374

Customize Toolbar dialog box, 357, *357*

Cut command, 334

D

d characters
  in date formats, 135–136
  in DateAdd and DateDiff, 140
  in DateTimePicker, 374
dashes (-)
  for menu separators, 331
  in SendKeys, 561
data-access
  for multiple-tier architecture, **795–797**, *796*
  new features for, 8
Data Access Objects (DAO), **27–29**
data entry controls, **366**
  DateTimePicker, **372–377**
  ImageCombo, **377–381**, *378*
  MaskedEdit, **381–385**
  MonthView, **367–371**
Data Environment, 8
Data Repeater control, 9
Data Report, 9
data services
  in Applications Services model, **790–791**
  in MTS, 806, *806*
data types
  in Registry, **675**
  speed of, **732**
  in VBScript, 470
  in Win32 API, **596–599**, *598*
DataArrival events, 427–428, 431–432, 435–436, 450
Database Designer, 9
database migration issues, **27–29**
DataGrid controls, 223, 240
Date command, 442
Date Control program
  DateTimePicker controls in, 376–377
  MonthView controls in, 370–371
  summary of, **828**
Date data type, 128
  in TypeName, 720
  and Year 2000 problem, 132

Date function
  in VBScript, 472
  in Visual Basic, 128, 138
Date statement, 138
Date/Time Demo program, 129, *130*
  data and time information in, **138–139**
  date arithmetic in, **139–141**
  formatting in, **133**, **137**, *137*
  summary of, **827**
DateAdd function, 128, **139–140**
DateClick events, 370
DateCreated property
  in File, 117
  in Folder, 114
DateDblClick events, 370
DateDiff function, 128, 132, **139–141**
DateLastAccessed property
  in File, 117
  in Folder, 115
DateLastModified property
  in File, 117
  in Folder, 115
DatePart function, 129
dates
  arithmetic with, **139–141**
  converting, **132–134**
  DateTimePicker for, **372–377**
  formats for, **134–138**, *137*
  formatting, **132–134**
  functions for, **128–129**, *130*
  information about, **138–139**
  MonthView for, **367–371**
  in StatusBars, 343
  year 2000 issues, **130–132**
DateSerial function
  in VBScript, 472
  in Visual Basic, 129, 134
DateTimePicker controls, 12, **372**
  adding, **372–375**
  programming, **376–377**
DateValue function
  in VBScript, 472

in Visual Basic, 129, 134

Day function, 129, 134

Day property

    in DateTimePicker, 373

    in MonthView, 368

DayBold property, 368

Daylight Savings Time, 198–199

DayOfWeek property

    in DateTimePicker, 373

    in MonthView, 368

days

    in date formats, 135–136

    in DateAdd and DateDiff, 140

    in DateTimePicker formats, 374

Daytime service, 395

DBCS (Double Byte Character Set), 595

DBEngine objects, 28

DblClick events

    in MSAgent, 515–516

    in StatusBars, 346

    in TreeView, 212–213

.DCA file type, 19

DCOM (Distributed Component Object Model), 751, 794

DDB function, 141–142

.DDF file type, 19

DeactivateInput events, 516, 518

Debug ➤ Add Watch command, 82

Debug.Assert statement, **78–79**, *78*

Debug ➤ Delete Watch command, 83

Debug ➤ Edit Watch command, 83

Debug.Print statement, **79**, *79*

debugging. *See also* bug prevention

    array problems, **85**

    bug isolation in, **75–79**, *76–79*

    Create Symbolic Debug Info option for, 754

    Error problems, **86**

    in interpreted languages, 17

    parameter ranges, **85**

    Visual Basic Debugger for, **79–84**, *80–81, 83–84*

decimal points (.)

    in domain names, 393

    implied, 732

    as Mask characters, 382

in object references, **741**

Decimal return value, 720

declarations, variable, **35–36**, **67–68**

Declare statement, **599–600**

.Default user name, 677

DefaultPassword property, 28

DefaultUser method, 28

/Delete argument, 47

Delete command

    on Edit menu, 334

    in FTP, 405

Delete key

    in Charter, 245

    in SendKeys, 561

Delete method

    in AddressEntries, 276–277

    in AddressEntry, 278

    in Attachment, 273

    in Attachments, 272

    in DAO, 29

    in File, 117

    in Folder, 115

    in Folders, 267

    in Message, 271–272, 291

    in Messages, 268–269

    in Recipient, 275

    in Recipients, 274

DeleteFile method, 110

DeleteFolder method, 110

DeleteNodes routine, 212

DeleteSetting statement, 692

deleting

    CDO messages, **291**

    control array elements, **705–706**, *706*

    forms, 701

    Nodes, **211–212**

    random file records, 103

    Registry information, 166

    Toolbar buttons, 352

    watch expressions, 83

DeliverNow method, 265–266

DeliveryReceipt property, 269, 271

demo programs information, **822–869**

.DEP file type, 19

Deploy option, 52

deploying

    applications, **61**

    components through MTS, **811**

        creating packages for, **812–815**, *812–815*

        installing components into packages for, **815–816**, *816–817*

depreciation functions, **142**

Description property

    in Character, 520–521

    in Err, 761

    in Error, 469

    in Request, 532

    in Toolbar buttons, 352

Designers tab, 41

designing menu structures, **331–335**, *332*

DestroyIcon function, 606, 639–640

Details method, 277–278

DeviceArrival events, 196

DeviceNames for Printers, 299–300

DeviceOtherEvent events, 196

DeviceQueryRemove events, 196

DeviceQueryRemoveFailed events, 196

DeviceRemoveComplete events, 196

DeviceRemovePending events, 196

DevModeChange events, 196

DHTML applications, 9–10, 19

Dictionary objects, 474

Dim statement, 470

DIR command in FTP, 405–406

Dir function, 92–93

directories for FTP files, 406

DirList_Change routine, 96

DirListBox control, 94–96

DisabledImageList property, 350

disk files. *See* files

display events, 198

Display Properties dialog box, 661–662, *662*

DisplayChanged events, 197

displaying

    Agents, **523**

    CDO messages, **286**, *286*

    file information, **94**, **121–123**, *122*

    folder contents, **283–285**, *284*

    icons in system tray, **664–671**, *666–667*

    StatusBar information, **345–346**

DisplayType property

    in AddressEntry, 277

    in Recipient, 275

distributed application architecture, **786**

    client/server architecture, **786–788**, *787*

    multiple-tier architecture, **793–799**, *794, 796, 798*

    services in, **788–793**, *788, 792–793*

Distributed Component Object Model (DCOM), 751, 794

.DLL file type, 19

DLLs

    ActiveX, 579, **748–750**, **752**

    for Win32 API, 594

DNS (Domain Name Servers), 394

Do/Loop statements, 470

.DOB file type, 19

Document property, 401–402

DoEvents program, 185–186, **828–829**

DoEvents routine, 123, 185

DoIt routine, 185–186

dollar signs ($) for help file footnotes, 772

Domain Name Servers (DNS), 394

domain names, **393–394**

Domain service, 395

DontRecognize animation, 524

DontRecognizeReturn animation, 524

dots (.)

    in domain names, 393

    as Mask characters, 382

    in object references, **741**

Double Byte Character Set (DBCS), 595

Double data types

    speed of, 732

    in TypeName, 720

    in Win32 API, 596

.DOX file type, 19

DragComplete events, 516, 518

DragDrop events, 714

DragOver events, 714

DragStart events, 516, 518

DrawArc routine
    in ScreenSaver, **654–655**
    in StarSX, **72**
DrawIcon function, 606, 639–640
DrawMyGrid routine, **455–456**
DrawStarSX routine, **655–656**
DrawStyle property, 297
DrawWidth property, 297
Drive objects
    in VBScript, 474
    in Visual Basic, **112–113**
Drive property
    in File, 118
    in Folder, 115
DriveExists method, 110
DriveImage program, 674
DriveLetter property, 112
DriveList_Change routine, 96
DriveListBox control, 94–96
Drives collection
    in VBScript, 474
    in Visual Basic, 111
Drives property, **110–111**
DriveType property, 112
drop-down menus on Toolbars, 348
.DSR file type, 20
.DSX file type, 20
DTPicker1_FormatEvent routine, 377
DTPicker1_FormatSize routine, 376
Duplicate command, 334
durability in MTS transactions, 804
DWORD data type
    in Registry, 675
    in Win32 API, 596
.DWS file type, 20
dynamic arrays, memory for, 747
Dynamic Controls program
    control arrays in
        deleting elements in, **705–706**, *706*
        events in, 705
        new approach to, **704–705**
        traditional approach to, **702–703**, *703*
    controls in
        without events, **706–711**, *708–711*

with normal events, **712–713**, *713*
    with ObjectEvents, **714–717**
functions for, **717–722**, *721*
summary of, **829–830**
dynamic forms, **698–701**, *698*, *700*
Dynasets, 28

E

e-mail messages. *See* CDO (Collaboration Data Objects); CDO Demo program; MAPI (Messaging Application Program Interface)
early binding, **738**
edges, printing to, **303–304**, *304–305*
Edit Code button, 485–486
Edit Icon Properties dialog box, 156, *156*
Edit Macro facility, 574
Edit menus, typical commands on, **334**
edit mode in Really Programmable Calculator, 485
Edit String dialog box, 679
Edit String Tables button, 153
editing
    forms, 27
    Registry, **678–680**, *679–680*
    strings, **149–150**
    watch expressions, 83
editions, **5–7**
Editor tab, 35–36, *35*
.edu domain, 393
80/20 rule, 730
ellipses (…) in menus, 333
#ELSE statement, 48
EM_CANUNDO messages, 645–646
EM_SETREADONLY messages, 644–645
EM_UNDO messages, 645–646
emergency repair utility, 672
emotions in Agents, 505
Emp speech tag, 526
Empty return value, 720
empty strings, testing for, **741–742**
Enabled property
    in Balloon, 531

in Command, 530, 539

in Menu, 331

in SpeechInput, 533

Encrypted property, 269, 271

End key in SendKeys, 561

EndDoc method, 298–299, 320

#ENDIF statement, 48

EnsureVisible property, 214

Enter key

in Charter, 246

in SendKeys, 561

Enterprise Edition, **5–7**

Enum key, 676

environment information, **612–614**, *612*

Environment key, 678

Environment tab, **36–37**, *37*

EOF function, 92

equations, scripts for, **494–499**, *494*

Erase statement

for dynamic arrays, 747

in VBScript, 470

Err function, 761

Err object, 767

error information in, **760–762**

in VBScript, 474

Error events

in MSScript Demo, 482

in Really Programmable Calculator, **487–489**

in ScriptControl, 468

in Winsock, 427–428

Error function, 761

Error objects

debugging, **86**

for ScriptControl, **468–469**

Error property, 465–466

Error return value, 720

ErrorDescription method, 580–581, 587–588

errors and error handling

Err for, **760–762**

On Error for, **762**

flagging, 178

help files for. *See* help files and information

in MSScript Demo, **481–482**, *482*

raising, **767–769**, *768*, *770*

in Really Programmable Calculator, **487–489**

Resume for, **762–763**

StatusBars for, 344

with Winsock, 428

Esc key in SendKeys, 561

Eval method, 467, 476, 478

evaluating expressions, **477–478**

EventInfo objects, 715

EventParameter objects, 715

EventParameters collection, 715

EventParameters property, 715

events, 16

information about, **196–200**, *199*

ListView, **220**

Toolbar, **354–356**

TreeView, **212–214**

Excel Demo program, **565–567**, *566*

charts in

copying, **575–576**, *576*

creating, **574**, *575*

creating and getting objects in, **567–569**, *570*

exiting Excel in, **577–578**

summary of, **830–831**

workbooks and worksheets in, 570, *571*

adding data to, 571–572, *572*

closing, **577**

creating, 570, *571*

formatting cells in, 572–573, *573*

saving, **576–577**

exclamation points (!) for help file footnotes, 772

.EXE file type, 20

Execute a File tab, 634

Execute method

in DAO, 29

in Internet Transfer, 402–403

ExecuteStatement method, 467, 476, 479–480, 492

Exit command, 333

Exit option, 430

exiting Excel, **577–578**

ExitWindowsEx function, 606, 646–648

Exp function, 472

Expanded property, 214

ExpandedImage property, 209

Explain animation, 525

ExplainReturn animation, 525

expressions

    evaluating, **477–478**

    watching, **82–84**, *83–84*

ExtractIcon function, 607, 639–641

ExtraData property, 520–521

F

factorials, 282

Favor Pentium Pro option, 754

Fetch method, 255

FetchMessages routine, **255–256**

Field property, 262

Fields collection, 29

Fields property, 262

FieldSize property, 29

File menus, typical commands on, **333**

File ➤ New ➤ Help Project command, 774

File objects

    in VBScript, 474

    in Visual Basic, **117–119**

File System Objects, 9, **108–111**, *109. See also* FileSystemObjects

File Transfer Protocol (FTP)

    with Internet Transfer controls, **397–399**, **404–406**

    port address for, 395

file types, **19–21**

File Types tab, 637, *638*

File Viewer program, 108

    adding ListView items in, **216–218**

    adding nodes in, **210–211**

    deleting nodes in, **211–212**

    drives in, **113**

    File objects in, **118–119**

    Folder objects in, 116

    hexadecimal displays in, **121–123**, *122*

    responding to ListView events in, **220**

    sorting ListView items in, **219–220**

    summary of, **832–833**

    TreeView events in, **212–214**

FileCopy statement, 91–92

FileDateTime function, 92

FileExists method, 110

FileLen function, 92–93

FileListBox control, 94–96

files, 90

    FileSystemObjects for. *See* FileSystemObjects

    functions for, **92–93**

    icons for, **637–641**, *638*

    information about, **94**, **117–118**

    random access to, **103–108**, *103*

    resource. *See* resource files

    running, **634–637**, *634*

    selecting, **94–99**, *95*

    sequential access to, **99–102**, *99–101*

    statements for, **90–92**

Files collection

    in VBScript, 474

    in Visual Basic, 114, 117

Files property, 115

FileSelect control, 108, 208, *209*

FileSystem property, 112

FileSystemObjects, **109–111**

    for drives, **111–113**

    for files, **117–119**

    for folders, **114–116**

    for sequential file access, **120–123**

    in VBScript, 474

FILETIME structure, 617

    converting data in, **619–620**

    in Windows Registry, 683

FileTimeToString routine, **619–620**

FileTimeToSystemTime function, 607, 616–617, 620

FileTypes_Click routine, 96

FileView control, **108–109**, *109*

FillColor property, 297

FillStyle property, 297

Filter function

    in VBScript, 472

    in Visual Basic, 145–146, 149–150

Financial Function Demo program, **143–144**, *143*

    StatusBar information in, **345–346**

    summary of, **833**

financial functions, **141–142**
  for annuities, **143–144**, *143*
  for depreciation and rate of return, **142**
Find command, 334
Find tab, 782, *782*
FindExecutable function, 607, 640
Finger service, 395
Finished window, 59, *60*
Fix function, 472
Fixed format, 148
FleetSize property, 580–581, 585–586
FleetValue property, 580–581
float data type in Win32 API, 596
floating controls, resizing, **171**
floating point error checking, 755
Folder objects, **114–116**
  in CDO, **267–268**
  in VBScript, 474
FolderExists method, 110
FolderID property
  in Folder, 268
  in Message, 269, 271
folders
  displaying contents of, **283–285**, *284*
  FileSystemObject for, **114–116**
  loading, **281–283**, *282*
  in Session, 266
Folders collection
  in CDO, **267–268**
  in VBScript, 474
Folders property, 267–268
Font property, 297
FontBold property, 531
FontCharSet property, 531
FontItalic property, 531
FontName property, 531
fonts for printing, **310–312**, *312*
Fonts property, 298
FontSize property, 531
FontStrikethru property, 531
FontUnderline property, 531
footers in printing, 317
footnotes in help topic files, **771–772**

For statement
  speed of, 736
  in VBScript, 470
For Each statement
  speed of, 736
  in VBScript, 470
Force exit option, 646
ForeColor property
  in Balloon, 531
  in Printer object and Picture control, 297
Form_Load routine
  in Agent Demo, 538
  in CDO Demo, 279–280
  in Charter, **495–496**
  in Hello Jill, **535–536**
  in Honest Wayne's Used Airplane Lot, **581–582**
  in I'm Thinking of a Color, 545
  in Really Programmable Calculator, 489
  in Scheduler, **667–669**
  in ScreenSaver, 656–657
  in SlideShow, 97
  in Telnet Server program, 433
  in Tips and Tricks Demo, 163, 165, 169–170
Form_MouseMove routine, 658
Form_Resize routine, 167–170
Form_Unload routine, 165–166
Format ➤ Font command, 773
Format function
  for dates, 129, **134–138**, *137*
  for strings, 145, **147–148**
Format method in DateTimePicker, 376
Format property
  in DateTimePicker, 373–374
  in MaskedEdit, 382
FormatCurrency function
  for strings, 145, 147–148, 159
  in VBScript, 472
FormatDateTime function
  for strings, 129, **132–133**, 145
  in VBScript, 472
FormatNumber function
  for strings, 145, 147–148, 159
  in VBScript, 472

FormatPercent function
>   for strings, 145, 147–148
>   in VBScript, 472
formats for dates
>   creating, **134–138**, *137*
>   in DateTimePicker, 374–375
FormatSize method, 376
FormattedText property, 382
FormatTimeDate function, 147–148, 159
formatting
>   dates, **132–134**
>   in MaskedEdit, **382–383**
>   string functions for, **147–148**
>   worksheet cells, 572–573, *573*
forms, 15
>   centering, **162–164**
>   deleting, 701
>   dynamic creation of, **698–701**, *698, 700*
>   editing, 27
>   hiding, **735**
>   listing, **700–701**, *700*
>   loading, **171–172**
>   memory for, 747–748
>   position of, **164–166**
>   resizing, **167–168**
>   tabs on, **172–174**, *173*
Forms collection, 698
Forms Collection Demo program, 698, *698*
>   creating forms in, **699**, *700*
>   deleting forms in, 701
>   listing forms in, **700–701**, *700*
>   summary of, **834**
Forward method, 271
FreeFile function, 90, 92
FreeSpace property, 112–113
.FRM file type, 20–21
.FRX file type, 20
fso variable, 111, 113
FTP (File Transfer Protocol)
>   with Internet Transfer controls, **397–399**, **404–406**
>   port address for, 395
FTS tab, 776, 777
full-screen mode in ScreenSaver, **657**

FullPath property, 210
FullSelect property, 220
Function/End Function statements, 470
function keys in SendKeys, 561–562
functions
>   date, **128–141**
>   financial, **141–144**
>   vs. inline code, **739–740**
>   naming conventions for, 73
>   for scripts, 475, *476*
>   string, **144–150**
>   in VBScript, **471–473**
>   in Win32 API programs, **606–608**
FV function, 141

G

game board for Sea Wars, **455–456**
games
>   guessing. *See* I'm Thinking of a Color program
>   ScriptControls for, 499
>   Sea Wars. *See* Sea Wars program
GameState variable, 457
Gauge control, 23
General Date format, 135
General Number format, 148
General tab
>   for CoolBars, 359, *359*
>   for license keys, **43–44**
>   in Project Properties, 43, *43*
>   for StatusBars, 341, *341*
>   for threading models, **44–45**
>   for Toolbars, 349, *349*, 353
Generate Full Text Search Index option, 776
Genie the Genie Agent, 504, *505*, 509
GestureAt method, 522, 524
GET command
>   in FTP, 405–406
>   in HTTP, 407
Get Environment Info tab, 612
Get Environment Information header, 613

Get Icon header, 639–640

Get method, 522, 527

Get Process Information header, **616–617**

Get Sleep Information header, 622

Get statement, 91–92, 105

Get System Color Information header, 625–626

Get Windows Info tab, 608

Get Windows Information header, **609–610**

GetAbsolutePathName method, 110

GetAddressEntry method, 265

GetAddressList method, 265–266

GetAppInfo routine, 195

GetArticle method, 265–266

GetAttr function, 92–93

GetBandInfo routine, 364

GetBaseName method, 110

GetBatteryInfo routine, 190–191

GetChunk method, 402–403, 406–407

GetComputerName function, 607, 609–611

GetCoolBarInfo routine, 365

GetCurrentProcess function, 607, 616–618

GetCurrentProcessId function, 607, 616–618

GetData routine
    in Financial Function Demo, 143
    in Winsock, 426–427, 432, 451

GetDayBold events, 370–371

GetDefaultFolder method, 265–266

GetDrive method, 110, 116

GetDriveName method, 110

GetEnvironmentVariable function, 607, 613

GetExtensionName method, 110

GetFile routine
    in FileSystemObject, 110, 123
    in Internet Updater, **415–416**

GetFileName method, 110

GetFirst method
    in AddressEntries, 276–277
    in Folders, 267
    in Messages, 268–269

GetFirstUnresolved method, 274

GetFirstVisible method, 379

GetFolder method
    in FileSystemObject, 110

in Session, 265–266

GetFolderName method, 110

GetFreeBusy method
    in AddressEntry, 277–278
    in Recipient, 275
    in Recipients, 274

GetHeader method, 402–403, 407

GetInfoStore method, 265–266

GetLast method
    in AddressEntries, 276–277
    in Folders, 267
    in Messages, 268–269

GetMessage method, 265–266

GetNext method
    in AddressEntries, 276–277
    in Folders, 267
    in Messages, 268–269

GetNextUnresolved method, 274

GetObject routine, 472, 567–568

GetOption method, 265–266

GetParentFolderName method, 110

GetPrevious method
    in AddressEntries, 276–277
    in Folders, 267
    in Messages, 268–269

GetPriorityClass function, 607, 616–617, 619

GetProcessTimes function, 607, 616–619

GetProcessWorkingSetSize function, 607, 616, 618–619

GetScreenInfo routine, **192–194**

GetSelectedPart method, 245

GetSetting function, 164–166, 653, 655, 692

GetSpecialFolder method, 110

GetState function, 416–417

GetSysColor function, 607, 624, 626

GetSysInfo routine, 188

GetSystemDirectory function, 607, 609–611

GetTempName method, 110, 123

GetTimeZoneInformation function, 602–607, *605*

GetUserName function, 607, 609–611

GetWindowsDirectory function, 607, 610–611

global declarations and variables
    in random files, **104**
    for scripts, 475, *476*

Global modules, 466

GMT time, 199

goals in optimizing, **728–730**

Gosub/Return statements, 74

GotFocus events, 714

GoTo statement

    avoiding, 74

    with On Error, 762, **764–765**

Grab an Icon tab, 638

Graph control, 23

graphics

    memory for, 747

    printing, **312–314**, *313*

greater than signs (>)

    for help file footnotes, 772

    as Mask characters, 383

Greet animation, 525

GreetReturn animation, 525

Grid control, 23

guessing games. *See* I'm Thinking of a Color program

H

h characters

    in date formats, 136

    in DateAdd and DateDiff, 140

    in DateTimePicker, 375

hard disk space for Microsoft Agent, 506

hardware configuration, events for, 197

Hardware key, 676

HasOtherClients property, 520–521

hDC property, 297

HEAD command, 407

headers

    in HTTP, **400**

    in printing, 317

Height property

    in Band, 361

    in Character, 520

    for controls, 171

    for forms, 167

in Printer object and Picture control, 297

    in Screen, 162–163

Hello Jill program, **534**, *534*

    global declarations in, **535**

    initializing controls in, **535–536**

    speaking in, **536**

    summary of, **834–835**

Help command, 442, *442*

help files and information, **13**, **770**

    compiling, **778**, *778–779*

    for error handling, **769**, *770*

    Internet Explorer 4 for, 8

    mapping context ID to topic ID for, 775, *776*

    new projects for, 774, *774*

    options for, **776–777**, *777*

    in Telnet Server program, 442, *442*

    testing, **779–782**, *780–782*

    topic files, **770–773**, *771, 773,* **775**, *775*

Help key in SendKeys, 562

Help menus, typical commands on, 335

Help Topics command, 335

Help Workshop, **773–774**

    compiling help files in, **778**, *778–779*

    mapping context ID to topic ID in, 775, *776*

    new projects in, 774, *774*

    options in, **776–777**, *777*

    setting up, 770

    topic files in, 775, *775*

HelpContext property

    in Err, 761, 769

    in Error, 469

HelpContextId property, 331

HelpFile property

    in Err, 761, 769

    in Error, 469

Hex function, 472

hexadecimal numbers in file displays, **121–123**, *122*

Hexify routine, 121, 123

HiddenMessages property, 267–268

Hide events, 516, 518

Hide method

    in Character, 522

    for forms, 171

hiding
    Agents, **523**
    controls and forms, **735**
    pop-up menus, 338
    Toolbar buttons, 358
Hierarchical FlexGrid control, 9
hInternet property, 401
hit statements, 446
hives in Registry, 673
HKEY_ keys in Registry, **675–676**
    HKEY_LOCAL_MACHINE, **676–677**
    HKEY_USERS, **677–678**
Home key in SendKeys, 562
Honest Wayne's Used Airplane Lot program, **579**
    airplane information in, **583–586**, *584*
    objects in, **579–581**
    placing orders in, **586–588**, *587*
    servers in, **581–583**, *582*
    summary of, **835–836**
hosts in URLs, 396
HotImageList property, 350
hotspots
    for help file links, 772–773
    for screen savers, 658
Hour function, 129, 134
Hour property, 373
hourglass cursor, 185
hours
    in date formats, 136
    in DateAdd and DateDiff, 140
    in DateTimePicker formats, 375
.HPJ files, 774
HTTP (HyperText Transfer Protocol), 395, **399–400**, **406–407**
hWnd parameter in SendMessage, 644
hWnd property for CoolBar controls, 360
HyperText Transfer Protocol (HTTP), 395, **399–400**, **406–407**

for international editions, 158
resource files for, 150, 155–156, *155*
in system tray, **664–671**, *666–667*
in Toolbar buttons, 353
in Toolbars, **351**
ID property
    in CDO objects, 262
    in InfoStore, 280, 283
IDE. *See* Integrated Development Environment (IDE)
Idle method, 28
IdleComplete events, 516
IdleOn property, 520–521
IdleStart events, 516
#IF THEN statements, 48
If/Then/Else/End If statements in VBScript, 470
IIS Applications, 9–10, 18–19
I'm Thinking of a Color program, **542–543**, *543*
    adding commands in, **548**
    beginning, **550–553**
    global declarations for, **544**
    initializing characters in, **547–548**
    receiving commands in, **549–550**
    running, **545–546**
    setting up, **544–545**
    summary of, **836–837**
Image controls, speed of, 736
Image property
    in ComboItem, 379–380
    in Node, 209
    in Toolbar buttons, 352
ImageCombo controls, 12, *13*, **377–378**, *378*
    adding, **378–380**
    programming, **380–381**
ImageList controls
    with ListView controls, 218
    for Toolbar controls, **351**
ImageList property, 350
images
    printing, **314**, *315*
    in StatusBars, 343
Immediate window, **77**, *77*
implied decimal points, 732
Importance property, 269, 271
Inbox property, 264

I

Icon view in ListView controls, 215
icons
    for files, **637–641**, *638*

inches in graphic methods, 314

Included Files window, 53, *54*

Indentation property

    in ComboItem, 379–380

    in ImageCombo, 378–379

Index property

    in Band, 361

    in CDO, 262

    in ColumnHeader, 219

    in ComboItem, 379–380

    in control arrays, 702–703, 705

    in Menu, 331

    in Panel, 343

    in Systray, 664–665

Indexes collection, 29

indexes for help files, 772, 776, 781, *782*

IndexFields collection, 29

Inet1_StateChanged routine, 416

infinite loops, 123, 466

InfoStore objects, 264, 266–267

InfoStores collection, 264, 267, **280–281**, *280*

InfoStores property, 264

IniPath property, 28

initializing

    Commands collection, **537–539**

    MAPI sessions, **279–280**

    ScriptControls, **495–496**

    variables, 737–738

inline code, **739–740**

Input file mode, 91

input formatting in MaskedEdit, **382–383**

Input function, 92–93

Input # statement, 91–92

InputBox function, 472

Insert Button button, 352

Insert key

    in SendKeys, 562

    in StatusBars, 343

Insert method, 529–530

Insert New String Table button, 155

Insert Panel button, 342

Insertable Objects tab, 41

Install Locations window, 58, *58*

Installation Title window, 56, *57*

installing

    Agents, **509–510**

    Microsoft Agent, **506–509**, *508*

    screen savers, **661–663**, *664*

InstallLocationsMRU key, 678

InStr function, 145

InStr/InStrB functions, 472

InStrRev function

    in VBScript, 472

    in Visual Basic, 145

Int function, 472

Integer data types

    speed of, 732

    in TypeName, 720

    in Win32 API, 596

Integrated Development Environment (IDE), **14**, *14*

    Object Browser, **48–50**, *49*

    objects and ActiveX controls in, **39–42**, *40*, *42*

    options for, **34–38**, *35*, *37–38*

    Package and Deployment Wizard, **50–62**, *51–60*

    project properties in, **42–48**, *43*, *46–47*

    templates for, **38–39**

interest rates in financial functions, 141

international programs

    character sets for, 595

    resource files for, **151**, **158–159**

Internet, **392–393**

    Agents on, 527

    client programs for, **428–432**, *429*

    client/server applications on. *See* Sea Wars program

    controls for. *See* Internet Transfer controls

    distributing shareware over, 61

    IP addresses and domain names for, **393–394**

    network service protocols for, **422–423**

    new features for, **9–10**

    port numbers and protocols for, **394–395**

    URLs for, **396**

    Winsock controls for, **423–428**

Internet Explorer 4, 7–8

Internet Information Server (IIS) applications, 9–10, 18–19

Internet server program, **432–433**

    multiple connection requests in, **434–435**

processing commands in, **440–442**, *441–442*

processing input lines in, **437–440**, *439*

running sessions in, **435–437**

starting server in, **433**, *434*

Internet Service API (ISAPI), 800

Internet Transfer controls

    adding, **400–402**

    FTP commands in, **404–406**

    HTTP commands in, **406–407**

    methods for, **402–404**

    programming, **407–417**

    protocols supported by, **397–400**

Internet Updater program, **407–408**

    analyzing remote file information in, **411–414**

    creating local and remote information files in, **408–409**

    loading remote file information in, **410–411**

    retrieving remote files in, **409–416**, *410*

    state information in, **416–417**

    summary of, **838–839**

    updating files in, **414–415**

InterNIC organization, 394

interpreted execution, 17

interpreters, **17**

Interrupt method, 522, 524, 527

intranets, 444

IP (Internet Protocol) addresses, **393–394**

IPmt FV function, 141

IRR FV function, 142

ISAPI (Internet Service API), 800

IsArray function, 472

IsControlArray function, 720–722

IsDate function

    in VBScript, 472

    in Visual Basic, 129, 133, 145

IsEmpty function, 472

IsModel method, 580, 584–585

IsNull function, 472

IsNumeric function

    in VBScript, 472

    in Visual Basic, 145

IsObject function, 472

isolation in MTS transactions, 804

IsReadOnly property, 276

IsReady property, 112–113

IsRole method, 581

IsRootFolder property, 115

IsSameAs method, 263

Item method

    in control arrays, 704

    in Controls, 707

Item property

    in CDO objects, 262

    in Characters, 519

    in Commands, 529

    in Drives, 111

    in EventParameters, 715

    in Files, 114, 117

ItemClick events, 220

J

.JNK files, 231–233

Join function

    in VBScript, 472

    in Visual Basic, 145–146, 149

K

K characters for help file footnotes, 772

Key property

    in Band, 361

    in ComboItem, 379

    in Node, 209–211

    in Panel, 343–344

    in Toolbar buttons, 353

keyboard for MSFlexGrid controls, **226–229**

Keyboard Layout key, 678

Keyboard View tab, 483, 485

KeyButton_Click routine, **485–486**

KeyButton events, **485–486**

KeyPress events

    in Charter, 245

    for MSFlexGrid controls, **227**

in Notepad Writer, 564
for user-input checking, **177–178**
keys, Registry, **674–678**
KeyState control, 23
KeyUp events
in Charter, **245–246**
for MSFlexGrid controls, **227–229**
keywords for help file footnotes, 772
Kill statement, 91–92
KillDoc method, 298–299
KISS principle, **68**

L

Label controls
captions for, 175
speed of, 736
Language property, 465–466
laptops, resume problems with, 197
LastDllError property, 761
late binding, **738**
Lazy Programmer techniques, **74–75**
LBound method, 704
Lcase function in VBScript, 472
LCase function in Visual Basic, 145
leap years, **131**
Learning Edition, **5–6**
left alignment in StatusBar panels, 343
Left function in Visual Basic, 145, 149
Left/LeftB functions in VBScript, 472
Left property
in Character, 520
in control arrays, 702
for forms, 164
Len= clause, 91
Len function in Visual Basic, 145, 741–742
Len/LenB functions in VBScript, 472
less than signs (<) as Mask characters, 383
libraries
loading, **746**
with Object Browser, 49

in Win32 calls, 599
license keys, **43–44**
lightweight controls, speed of, 736
Line controls, speed of, 736
Line Input # statement, 91–92, 99, 101
Line method, 297, 312
Line property
in Error, 469
in TextStream, 120
Linguistic Information Sound Editing Tool, 509
links in help topic files, **772–773**, *773*
LISET.EXE program, 509
List control, **208**
List view in ListView controls, 215
Listen method, 426
listeners, TCP, 423
listening tips with Agents, 512
listening with Winsock, 426
listing forms, **700–701**, *700*
ListItem objects, 215, 255–256
ListItems collection, 217–218
ListView controls, **215**
adding items to, **216–218**
column headers in, **215**, *216*
responding to events in, **220**
sorting items in, **219–220**
ListView1_ColumnClick routine, 219–220
ListView1_ItemClick routine
in CDO Demo, 286
in File Viewer, 220
in MAPI Demo, 256
Load_Code routine, **490–492**
Load method, 519
Loaded on Startup option, 151
Loaded/Unloaded option, 151
LoadFolders routine, **282–283**
LoadImageCombo routine, 380–381
LoadInfoStore routine, 281
loading
Agent characters, 519
CoolBar controls, **365**
forms, **171–172**
InfoStore information, **280–281**, *280*

MAPI folders, **281–283**, *282*

MSFlexGrid data, **225–226**, **234–237**

remote file information, **410–411**

speed of, 735, **746**

LoadMessages routine, **284–285**

LoadPicture function, 473

LoadPrinters routine, 300

LoadRemoteInfo routine, **410–411**, 415

LoadResData function, 150, 157

LoadResPicture function, 150, 157

LoadResString function, 150, **157–158**

Loc function, 93

local information files, **409**

locales

    code pages for, 155

    resource files for, **151**, **158–159**

LocalHostName property, 424

LocalIP property, 424

LocalPort property, 424, 435

locking modes, 91

LOF function, 93

.LOG file type, 20, 24

log files

    in migration, 24

    in MTS, **804–805**

    for system events, **199–200**, *199*

    for Telnet Server program, 433, *434*

Log function, 473

LogIt routine, 433, 435

Logoff exit option, 646

Logoff method, 265

logoffs in Telnet Server program, **441**, *441*

Logon method, **264–265**

logons in Telnet Server program, **437–440**, *439*

LogonUI property, 259

Long data types

    speed of, 732

    in TypeName, 720

    in Win32 API, 596

Long Date format, 135

long dates, 132, 135

long processing waits, handling, **184–186**, **743–744**

Long Time format, 135

loops

    infinite, 123

    in scripts, 466

    speed of, **738–739**

    spin, 553

LostFocus events

    for checking user-input values, **179**

    in ObjectEvents, 714

lParam parameter in SendMessage, 644

LPSTR data type, 596

LS command in FTP, **405–406**

Lst speech tag, 526

LTrim function

    in VBScript, 473

    in Visual Basic, 145, 149

M

m characters

    in date formats, 136

    in DateAdd and DateDiff, 140

    in DateTimePicker, 375

macros with Excel objects, 574

Main routine

    for loading forms, 171

    in ScreenSaver, **660**

.MAK file type, 20

Make Errors program, **763**, *763*

    On Error GoTo statement in, **764–765**

    On Error Resume Next statement in, **766–767**

    raising errors in, **767–769**, *768*, *770*

    summary of, **839**

Make tab

    for command-line arguments, **47**

    for conditional compilation, **48**

    for copyright and version information, **45–46**, *46–47*

MakeAnError routine, 767

Manage Scripts option, 52

Manager property, 277

Map dialog box, 775, *776*

Map speech tag, 526

MAPI (Messaging Application Program Interface), **252**, *253*.
    See also CDO (Collaboration Data Objects); CDO Demo
    program
  fetching messages in, 255–256
  initializing sessions, 279–280
  loading folders in, 281–283, *282*
  reading messages in, **256**
  sending messages in, **256–259**
  sessions for, **253–254**
MAPI Demo program
  fetching messages in, 255–256
  reading messages in, **256**
  sending messages in, 256–259
  sessions in, 253–254
  summary of, **840**
MAPIMessages controls, 255–256
MAPISession controls, **253–254**
mapping context ID to topic ID for help files, 775, *776*
Mark speech tag, 526
Mask property, 382
MaskEdBox1_ValidationError routine, 385
MaskedEdit controls, **381**
  adding, **381–384**
  programming, **384–385**
MaxDate property, 373–374
MaxLength property, 382
MaxSelCount property, 368–369
MDTC (Microsoft Distributed Transaction Coordinator), 811
Me name for active forms, 164
Medium Date format, 135
Medium Time format, 135
MeetingResponseStatus property, 275
Members property, 277
memory
  for Microsoft Agent, 506
  optimizing, 728, **746–748**
  requirements for, 7–8
Menu controls, **330–331**, 736
Menu Editor, 175, *176*
MenuChart_Click routine, **240–242**, *241*, 336–337
MenuConfigure_Click routine, 302
menus, **330–331**
  arrays of, **336–338**
  button, 354

pop-up, **338–340**, *339*, 671
  shortcut keys for, **175**, *176*
  structure for, **331–335**, *332*
  on Toolbars, 348
Merlin the Magician Agent, 504, *505*, 509–510
MerlinSfx Agent, 509–510, 536
Message objects, **268–270**
messages
  e-mail. *See* CDO (Collaboration Data Objects); CDO Demo
      program; MAPI (Messaging Application Program
      Interface)
  event, **15**
Messages collection, **268–269**
Messages property, 267–268
methods, 16
Microphone Wizard, 507–509, *508*, 512
Microsoft Agent, **504–506**, *505*
  Agent server for, **510–513**, *511–513*
  controls for. *See* MSAgent controls
  installing agents, **509–510**
  installing and configuring software, **506–509**, *508*
Microsoft Agent Character Editor, 505, 509
Microsoft Agent Linguistic Information Sound Editing Tool,
      505, 509
Microsoft Agent Properties dialog box, 509–510, *511*
Microsoft Developer's Network (MSDN), 5, 7–8, 13
Microsoft Distributed Transaction Coordinator (MDTC), 811
Microsoft Speech Recognizer Properties dialog box, 512–513, *512*
Microsoft Transaction Server (MTS), **786**, **799**
  installing components into packages for, **815–816**, *816–817*
  packages for, **812–815**, *812–815*
  scalability in, **800–801**, *801*
  security in, **801–802**
  services for, **805–809**, *806*, *808*
  transaction support for, **809–811**
  for transactions across objects, **802–803**, *803*
Microsoft Transaction Server Executive (MTX), 811
Mid function in Visual Basic, 146, 149
Mid/MidB functions in VBScript, 473
migration
  of controls, **22–27**
  of Data Access Objects, **27–29**
  issues in, **21–22**
  problems in, **24–27**

of Remote Data Objects, **29**

testing, **24**

MinDate property, 373–374

MinHeight property, 361

minus signs (-)

in menu separators, 331

in SendKeys, 561

Minute function, 129, 134

Minute property, 373

minutes

in date formats, 136

in DateAdd and DateDiff, 140

in DateTimePicker formats, 375

MinWidth property

in Band, 362

in Panel, 343–344

MIRR FV function, 142

miss statement, 446, 454

mixed solutions in business services, **793**, *793*

MixedState property, 353–354

MKDIR command in FTP, 405–406

MkDir statement in Visual Basic, 91–92

modes, file, 91

modularity in optimizing, **731–732**

modules, loading, **746**

Modules property, 465–466

Month function, 129, 134

Month property

in DateTimePicker, 373

in MonthView, 368

MonthBackColor property, 368

MonthBackProperty property, 370

MonthColumns property, 368–369

MonthName function, 129, 134

MonthRows property, 368–369

months

in date formats, 136

in DateAdd and DateDiff, 140

in DateTimePicker formats, 375

MonthView controls, 12, *12*, **367**

adding, **367–370**

programming, **370–371**

MonthView1_DateClick routine, 370

MonthView1_GetDayBold routine, 371

MonthView1_SelChange routine, 371

moon animation, **347–348**

MouseDblClick events, 665

MouseDown events, 665

MouseMove events, 666

MouseUp events, 666

Move events, 516

Move method

for controls, **742**

in File, 118

in Folder, 115

MoveCause property, 521

MoveFile method, 111

MoveFolder method, 111

MoveTo method

in Character, 522–523

in Message, 271–272

moving

Agents, **523**

controls, **742**

MSAgent controls, **513**, *514*

adding, **514–515**

balloons in, **531–532**

characters in, **518–527**

commands in, **527–530**

configuring server for, **510–513**, *511–513*

events for, **515–518**

example program, **534–536**, *534*

initializing, **535–536**

requests in, **532–533**

speech recognition engine for, **536–542**, *537*

MSAGENT.EXE program, 507

MSChart controls, **221–222**, *222*, **237–238**

chart titles in, **243–246**, *244*

chart types in, **240–243**, *241*

retrieving information from, **238–240**

MSChart1_KeyPress routine, 245

MSChart1_KeyUp routine, 246

MSChart1_MouseDown routine, 339–340

MSFlexGrid controls, **221–223**, *221*

aligning data in, **230–231**

creating, **223–225**

keyboard with, **226–229**

loading data into, **225–226, 234–237**

saving data in, **231–234**

selecting data in, **229–230**

MSFlexGrid1_KeyPress routine, 227

MSFlexGrid1_KeyUp routine, 228

MSFlexGrid1_LeaveCell routine, 496

MsgBox function in VBScript, 473

MsgBox statement for debugging, **76**, *76*

MsgDateReceived property, 256

MsgIndex property, 255–256

MsgNoteText property, 256

MsgOrigAddress property, 256

MsgSubject property, 256

MSHFlexGrid controls, 223

MSScript, 464–465

MSScript Demo program, **474–475**, *475*

adding code to, **475–477**, *476*

evaluating expressions in, **477–478**

executing statements in, **479–480**, *479*

handling errors in, **481–482**, *482*

running programs in, **480–481**, *480–481*

summary of, **841**

MTS. *See* Microsoft Transaction Server (MTS)

MTSTransactionMode property, 807, *808*, 809

MTX (Microsoft Transaction Server Executive), 811

Multimedia control, 656

multiple connection requests in Telnet Server program, **434–435**

multiple copies of applications, **184**

multiple languages, resource files for, **151, 158–159**

multiple statements on lines, 74

multiple-tier architecture, 786–787, **793–794**, *794*

data-access logic for, **795–797**, *796*

MTS for. *See* Microsoft Transaction Server (MTS)

performance in, **797–799**, *798*

MultiSelect property, 368–369

music in screen savers, 656

MyCommand_Click routine, 712

MyControl_ObjectEvent routine, 717

MyControl_ObjectEventA routine, **716–717**

N

n characters

in date formats, 136

in DateAdd and DateDiff, 140

n-tier client/server architecture, 794

Name method, 581

Name property

in CDO objects, 262

in Character, 521

in EventInfo, 715

in EventParameter, 715

in File, 118

in Folder, 115

in Menu, 331

in Systray, 664–665

in UserInput, 517

name statements, 446

names

for applications, 166

coding conventions for, **73**

for controls, **709–710**, *709–710*

for Internet computers, 393

in Registry, 674

for StatusBar panels, 344

used by Visual Basic, 144

in Win32 calls, 599

for Winsock controls, 424

native code, **752–753**

negative values in financial functions, 141

.net domain, 393

Network key

in HKEY_LOCAL_MACHINE, 676

in HKEY_USERS, 678

network service protocols, **422–423**

New command, 333, 699

New Package Wizard, **812–815**, *812–815*

new pages in Print Preview window, **319**

New Project window, 14, *14*

New String Table button, 153

NewChart routine, **223–225**

NewPage method, 298, 319

NewRow property, 362–364

Next statement, speed of, 743

9 characters in Mask, 383

nntp service, 395

No Optimization option, 754

Node objects, 209, 215

NodeClick events, 212

Nodes collection, 210–211

nonprintable ASCII characters, 227

normal mode in Really Programmable Calculator, 485

Notepad Writer program, **563**, *563*

    processing characters in, **564–565**

    starting, **563–564**

    summary of, **841–842**

Nothing keyword with Object, 747

Nothing return value in TypeName, 720

Now function, 129, 138

Nper function, 142

NPV function, 142

NSFNET, 393

Null values

    in Registry, 674

    in TypeName, 720

Number property

    in Err, 761

    in Error, 469

    in Request, 532

number signs (#)

    for help file footnotes, 772

    as Mask characters, 382

NumberOfLines property, 531

NumLock key

    in SendKeys, 562

    in StatusBars, 343

numrows statement, 446–447, 454

O

Object Browser, **48–50**, *49*

object-oriented programming, **69–70**

Object property, 664–665

Object return value in TypeName, 720

ObjectEvent events, 714

ObjectEvents objects, **714–717**

Objects

    late binding of, 738

    memory for, 747

    references to, 41–42, **741**

.OCA file type, 20

Oct function, 473

.OCX file type, 20

ODBC (Open Database Connectivity), 795

OLE Automation, 796

OLE Messaging, 259

OLEISAPI, 9

On Error statement, **762–763**

    with GoTo, **764–765**

    in MSScript Demo, 481–482

    with Resume Next, **766–767**

    in VBScript, 470

On/Off format, 148

Open command, 333

Open Database Connectivity (ODBC), 795

Open statement, 90–92

OpenAsTextStream method, 118, 123

OpenChart routine, **235–236**

OpenDatabase method, 29

opening

    random files, **104–105**

    resource files, **152**

OpenProcess function, 607, 630–631

OpenRecordset method, 28–29

OpenTextFile method, 111, 490

OpenTextStream method

    in File, 117, 120

    in FileSystemObject, 120

OpenURL method, 402–403, 410

operating system information, **187–188**, *187*

OperatingSystem property, 264

OpSysInfo tab, **187–188**, *187*

Optimize for Fast Code option, 754, 757

Optimize for Small Code option, 754

optimizing

    goals and constraints in, **728–730**

    memory, **746–748**

program types in, **748–752**

rules in, **730–731**

settings for, **752–756**, *753, 755*

speed. *See* speed

Option Explicit statement

in VBScript, 470

in Visual Basic, 35–36, **67–68**

optional parameters, 323

Options dialog box, *35*

for Help Workshop, 776–777, *777*

for icons, 637, *638*

for IDE, 34–35

for saving programs, **36–37**, *37*

for SDI environment, **37–38**, *38*

for variable declarations, **35–36**, **67–68**

Options method, 272

order of tabs, **173–174**

.org domain, 393

Orientation property

in CoolBar, 360

in Printer object, 298

OSBuild property, 187

OSPlatform property, 187

OSVersion property, 187

out-of-process servers, 751

Outbox property, 264

Outline control, 23

OutOfOffice property, 264

OutOfOfficeText property, 264

Output file mode, 91

Output tab, 510, *511*, 533

overflow checking, 755

packages in MTS, **801–802**

creating, **812–815**, *812–815*

installing components into, **815–816**, *816–817*

Packaging Report window, 59, *60*

.PAG file type, 20

Page property, 298

PageDown key in SendKeys, 562

PageUp key in SendKeys, 562

PaintPicture method, 297–298, 314

PanelClick events, 346

PanelDblClick events, 346

panels for StatusBar controls, **342–344**

Panels property, 340

Panels tab, 341–342, *342*

PaperSize property, 298

parameters

debugging, **85**

optional, 323

Parameters objects, 29

Parent objects, 262

Parent property

in CDO objects, 262

in Menu, 331

in Systray, 664–665

ParentFolder property

in File, 118

in Folder, 115

parentheses () in SendKeys, 561–562

Password property

in Internet Transfer, 401

in MAPISession, 254

passwords

for FTP, 397

for MAPI, 253–254, 258–259

in Telnet Server program, 438

in URLs, 396

Paste command, 334

Path property

in Drive, 112

in File, 118

in Folder, 115

paths

for Nodes, 210

P

P-code, **752–753**

Package and Deployment Wizard, 11, *11*, **50–62**, *51–60*

Package Folder window, 53, *54*

Package option, 52

Package program, **842**

Package Type window, 53, *53*

in URLs, 396

PathSeparator property, 210

Pau speech tag, 526

payments in financial functions, 141

PeekData method, 426–427

Percent format, 148

percent signs (%) in SendKeys, 560–562

periods (.)

    in domain names, 393

    as Mask characters, 382

    in object references, **741**

.PGX file type, 20

Picture controls, 296–298

Picture property

    in MSFlexGrid, 226

    in Panel, 343, 345

Pit speech tag, 526

Pitch property, 521

pixels, 314

Play method, 522, **524–526**

PlayerInit routine, 547–548

PlayerWelcome routine, **550–552**

Pleased animation, 525

PleasedReturn animation, 525

plus signs (+)

    for help file footnotes, 772

    in SendKeys, 561–562

Pmt function, 142

Policy Editor, 672

pop-up menus, **338–340**, *339*, 671

Pop3 service, 395

PopUp statement, 338

ports

    for Internet, **394–395**

    in URLs, 396

    for Winsock controls, 424–425

position

    of CoolBars, **362–363**

    of forms, **164–166**

    in printing

        of cursor, **307–308**, *308*

        of text, **308–310**, *310*

Position property

    in Attachment, 273

in Band, 362

POST command, 407

posted messages, 268

power

    events for, 197

    information about, **188–191**, *189*

PowerQuerySuspend events, 197

PowerResumeEvent events, 197

PowerStatusChanged events, 197

PowerSuspend events, 197

PPmt function, 142

prefixes in naming conventions, 73

Press1 routine, 492

PressAdd routine, 492–493

PressEquals routine, 493

PrevInstance property, 184

Print command, 333

Print Manager, 299

Print method, 297–298, 303

Print Preview command, 333

Print Preview window

    centering text in, **321–323**

    ending sessions in, **320**

    examples, **323–325**

    new pages in, **319**

    output for, **318–319**

    painting images in, **320**

Print program

    changing fonts in, **310–312**

    graphics in, **312–314**, *313*

    positioning cursor in, **307–308**, *308*

    summary of, **843–844**

    text in, **303–312**

Print Setup command, 333

Print # statement, 91–92, 99, 102

Print statement for debugging, **79**, *79*

print zones, 306

printable ASCII characters, 227

PrintChart routine, 324

Printer dialog box, **300–302**, *301*

Printer objects, **296–298**

Printer program

    positioning text in, **308–310**, *310*

    printing images in, **314**, *315*

printing spreadsheet pages in, **315–317**, *318*

selecting printers in, **299–302**, *301*

summary of, **844**

Printer Properties dialog box, **301–302**, *301*

PrinterDefault setting, 302

printers, selecting, **299–302**, *301*

Printers collection, 299–300

PrintGrid routine, **324–325**

printing, **296**. *See also* Print Preview window

from applications, **299**

in columns, **306–307**, *306*

cursor positioning in, **307–308**, *308*

to edges, **303–304**, *304–305*

fonts for, **310–312**, *312*

graphics, **312–314**, *313*

images, **314**, *315*

settings for, **300–302**, *301*

spreadsheet pages, **315–317**, *318*

text, **303–312**, *304–306, 308, 310, 312*

text positioning in, **308–310**, *310*

PrintQuality property, 298

priority classes, 617

Private statement, 470

PrivateSocket_DataArrival routine, **435–437**

Procedures property, 465–466

Process header, **629–630**

process information in Win32 API Demo, **614–620**, *615*

PROCESS_INFORMATION structure, 629–630

ProcessInput routine

in Sea Wars, **451–454**

in Telnet Server program, **437–440**

processor requirements

for Microsoft Agent, 506

for Visual Basic, 7–8

Professional Edition, **5–6**

program types, selecting, **748–752**

programmable calculators. *See* Really Programmable Calculator program

programs, saving, **36–37**, *37*

progress bars, 185, 744

progress tracking in Internet Transfer, 403–404

ProgressBar controls, 185

Project ➤ Components command, 40

Project ➤ New Resource File command, 152

Project Properties dialog box, **42–43**, *43*

for command-line arguments, **47**

for compiler settings, 752, *753*

for conditional compilation, **48**

for copyright and version information, **45–46**, *46–47*

for license keys, **43–44**

for threading models, **44–45**

Project ➤ References command, 41

Project window, 152, *153*

prompt characters in MaskedEdit, **384**

Prompt To Save Changes option, 37

PromptChar property, 382, 384

PromptInclude property, 382, 384

properties, 16

Properties dialog box for CDO messages, 291, *291*

property accesses, speed of, **733–734**

Property Pages dialog box

for CoolBars, 359–361, *359*

for StatusBars, 340–342, *341–342*

for Toolbars, 349, *349*, 352–354, *352*

PropertySheet objects, 533

PropertySheet property, 514–515

Protocol property

in Internet Transfer, 401–402

in Winsock, 424

protocol statements in Sea Wars, **451–454**

protocols

for Internet, 395

Internet Transfer support for, **397–400**

for Sea Wars, **445–448**

in URLs, 396

ProviderName property, 267

Proxy property, 401–402

proxy servers, 402

Pset method, 297, 312

Public statement, 470

PublicSocket_ConnectionRequest routine, **434–435**

PUT command

in FTP, 405–406

in HTTP, 407

Put statement, 91–92, 107–108

PV function, 142

PWD command in FTP, 405–406

Q

q characters
    in date formats, 136
    in DateAdd and DateDiff, 140
qualified names for controls, **709–710**, *709–710*
quarters
    in date formats, 136
    in DateAdd and DateDiff, 140
Query Designer, 9
QueryChangeConfig events, 197
QueryDefs collection, 29
question marks (?) as Mask characters, 383
QUIT command in FTP, 405–406
Quote of the Day program, **429–430**, *429*
    receiving quotes in, 431–432
    requesting quotes in, 430–431
    summary of, **845**
Quote of the Day server, **428–432**, *429*

R

Raise method, 761–762, **767–769**, *768, 770*
Random Access File program, **103**, *103*
    adding records in, **107**
    global declarations in, **104**
    opening files in, **104–105**
    reading files in, **105–107**
    summary of, **845–846**
    updating records in, **108**
random files, **103**
    adding records to, **107**
    global declarations in, **104**
    Loc function for, 93
    opening, **104–105**
    reading, **105–107**
    updating records in, **108**
Randomize statement, 470

Rate function, 142
rate of return functions, **142**
RDO (Remote Data Objects), 27, **29**, 796–797
Read animation, 525
Read file mode, 91
Read method, 120, 123
read-only text boxes, **644–646**
Read Write file mode, 91
ReadAll method, 121
ReadFromFile method, 273
reading
    MAPI messages, **256**
    random files, **105–107**
    sequential files, **99–101**, *100*, **120–123**, *122*
ReadLine method, 121
ReadReceipt property, 269, 271
ReadReturn animation, 525
Really Programmable Calculator program, **483–485**, *483–484*
    defining objects in, **489**
    KeyButton events in, **485–486**
    loading code in, **490–492**
    script program in, **492–493**
    summary of, **846–847**
    trapping errors in, **487–489**
    updating routines in, **486–487**
Reboot exit option, 646
Recalculate routine, **498**
receipts in financial functions, 141
receiving FTP files, 406
Recipient objects, **274–275**
Recipients collection, 274
Recipients property, 270
Record New Macro facility, 574
records in random files, 103
    adding, **107**
    updating, **108**
Recordset objects, 29
recovering Registry, **674**
recursive routines
    DeleteNodes, 212
    loading MAPI folders, **281–283**, *282*
RECV command in FTP, 405–406
recycling, code, 732

ReDim statement
    in VBScript, 471
    in Visual Basic, 142, 747
redrawing speed, **734**
redundant code, 737
references
    to objects, 41–42
    speed of, **741**
References dialog box, 41–42, *42*, 260
REG_ data types, 675
RegCloseKey function, 683, 686, 688
RegConnectRegistry function, 683, 689
RegCreateKey function, 683, 686
RegCreateKeyEx function, 683–684, 686
RegDeleteKey function, 684, 687
RegDeleteValue function, 684, 687, 692
RegEdt32 program, 678
RegEnumKey function, 684, 687
RegEnumKeyEx function, 684, 687–688
RegEnumValue function, 684, 688
RegFlushKey function, 684, 688
RegGetKeySecurity function, 684
Regional Settings
    for dates, 132
    for locales, 151
Register View tab, 484, *484*
Registry, **671–672**
    accessing from Visual Basic, **680–689**
    backing up, **672–674**
    command-line arguments for, 47
    editing, **678–680**, *679–680*
    for form position, 164–166
    for license keys, 44
    structure of, **674–678**
    writing programs for, **689–692**
Registry Checker program, 672
Registry Editor, **678–680**, *679–680*
RegLoadKey function, 684, 688
RegNotifyChangeKeyValue function, 684–685, 688
RegOpenKey function, 685–686
RegOpenKeyEx function, 685–686
RegQueryInfoKey function, 685, 687
RegQueryMultipleValues function, 689

RegQueryValue function, 685, 687
RegQueryValueEx function, 685, 687
RegQueryValueExString function, 685
RegReplaceKey function, 685, 688
RegRestoreKey function, 685–686, 689
RegSaveKey function, 686, 689
RegSetKeySecurity function, 686, 688
RegSetValue function, 686–687
RegSetValueEx function, 686–687
RegSetValueExString function, 686
RegSvr32 program, 751
RegTool program, **680–686**, 689, *689*
    accessing remote computers and multiple values in, 689
    keys in
        closing, 688
        creating and opening, **686–687**
        loading, replacing, and saving, 688–689
        security for, 688
    notices of changes in, 688
    Registry information in
        getting, setting, and deleting, **687**
        iterating through, **687–688**
        retrieving, **690–691**
    summary of, **847–848**
    Win32 API routines in, **691–692**
Remote Data Objects (RDO), 27, **29**, 796–797
remote information files for Internet Updater program, **408–416**
RemoteAccess key, 678
RemoteHost property, 401–402
RemoteHostIP property, 424
RemoteHostName property, 424
RemotePort property
    in Internet Transfer, 401–402
    in Winsock, 424
Remove Array Bounds Checks option, 755
Remove Button button, 352
Remove Floating Point Error Checks option, 755
Remove Information about Unused ActiveX Controls option, 711
Remove Integer Overflow Checks option, 755
Remove method
    in Commands, 529–530
    in Controls, 707
Remove Panel button, 342

Remove Safe Pentium FDIV Checks option, 756

RemoveAll method, 529–530

RENAME command in FTP, 405

Repeat command, 334

repetitive tasks. *See* ScriptControls; scripts

Replace command, 334

Replace function

in VBScript, 473

in Visual Basic, 146

Reply method, 272, 290

ReplyAll method, 272

replying to CDO messages, **290**

Report view in ListView controls, 215

Request objects, **532–533**

RequestComplete events, 516, 533

requests in Agent Demo, **541–542**

RequestStart events, 516, 533

RequestTimeout property, 401

RequestWait objects, 552

Require License Key option, 43

Require Variable Declaration option, 35, 68

requirements

for Microsoft Agent, 506

for Visual Basic, **7–8**

.RES file type, 20

/Reset argument, 47

Reset method in ScriptControl, 467

Reset option in Quote, 430

resizing

controls, **168–171**, *168*

CoolBars, **365–366**

forms, **167–168**

Resolve method

in Recipient, 275

in Recipients, 274, 289

Resource Editor

adding resources with, 155–156

enabling, 151, *152*

starting, **152–153**, *153*

Resource File Demo program

accessing resource files in, 157–158, *157*

summary of, **848**

resource files, **150**

accessing, **157–158**, *157*

adding resources to, **155–156**, *155–156*

adding strings to, **153–155**, *154–155*

closing, **156**, *156*

creating, **151–156**, *152–156*

for international editions, **151**, **158–159**

opening, **152**

resource IDs, 150, 154

response codes in Internet Transfer, 402

ResponseCode property, 401–402

ResponseInfo property, 401–402

Restart events, 516, 518

RestoreToolbar method, 357

Resume statement, **762–763**, **766–767**

revision information, **46**, *47*

RGB function, 473

RichTextBox controls, 123

right alignment in StatusBar panels, 343

Right function in Visual Basic, 146, 149

Right/RightB functions in VBScript, 473

RMDIR command in FTP, 405

RmDir statement, 91–92

Rnd function, 473

Robby the Robot Agent, 504, *505*, 509, 523, *523*

Role method, 581

roles, 815

Rollback method, 29

root folders, 114

RootFolder property

in Drive, 112

in InfoStore, 264, 267

Round function, 473

Row property

in MSChart, 240

in MSFlexGrid, 226–227

RowCount property, 360

rows in Sea Wars, 447

RowSel property, 229

Rst speech tag, 526

RTF format for help files, **770–771**, *771*, *773*

RTrim function

in VBScript, 473

in Visual basic, 146, 149

Run a File header, 635
Run a Program tab, 628
Run ➤ Break command, 77
Run ➤ Continue command, 81
Run method, 467, 476, 480–481
RunIt routine, **110–112**, *141–442*
RunMe routine, 669–670
running
    files, **634–637**, *634*
    MSScript Demo programs, **480–481**, *480–481*
RunProg function, **631–632**

S

s characters
    in date formats, 136
    in DateAdd and DateDiff, 140
    in DateTimePicker, 375
Sad animation, 525
SadReturn animation, 525
SAM key, 676
Sample01 routine, **315–317**
Save command, 333
Save As command, 333
SaveAs method, 576
SaveBandInfo routine, 363
SaveChart routine, **232–234**, 258
saved CDO messages, 268
SaveSetting function, 164, 166, 692
SaveToolbar method, 357
saving
    CDO messages, **291**
    CoolBar position, **362–363**
    form position, **164–166**
    MSFlexGrid data, **231–234**
    programs, **36–37**, *37*
    sequential files, **101–102**, *101*
    system information, **200–201**
    workbooks, **576–577**
scalability, **797–801**, *801*
Scale method, 297
ScaleHeight property, 297

ScaleLeft property, 297
ScaleMode property, 297, 314
ScaleTop property, 297
ScaleWidth property, 297
ScaleX method, 297
ScaleY method, 297
Scheduler program, **666–667**, *666–667*
    pop-up menus in, 671
    running, **669–670**
    starting, **667–669**
    summary of, **849**
Scientific format, 148
sck values, 425
.SCR files, 652
screen information, **191–194**, *192*
Screen object, 162–163, **191–194**
Screen Saver tab, 661–662, *662*
ScreenInfo tab, 192, *192*
ScreenSaver program, **652–653**
    configuration form for, **659**, *659*
    display portion of, **653–657**
    drawing star in, **654–656**
    full-screen mode in, **657**
    installing and configuring screen saver in, **661–663**, *664*
    loading forms in, 656–657
    Main routine in, **660**
    module-level variables in, **653–654**
    properties in, **661**
    summary of, **849–850**
    unloading forms in, **658**
ScriptControl1_Error routine
    in MSScript Demo, 482
    in Really Programmable Calculator, **488–489**
ScriptControls, **464–465**
    adding, **465–466**
    error information for, **468–469**
    events for, **468**
    initializing, **495–496**
    methods for, **466–468**
    MSScript Demo for, **474–482**, *475–482*
    uses for, **499**
scripts, **464**
    controls for. *See* ScriptControls
    MSScript Demo, **474–482**, *475–482*

programmable calculators. *See* Really Programmable Calculator program

for spreadsheet calculations, **494–499**, *494*

VBScript for, **469–474**

Scroll Lock key

with Agents, 512

in SendKeys, 562

in StatusBars, 343

Sea Wars program, **442–443**, *443*

attacking opponents in, **456–457**

connections in, **448–450**

game board for, **455–456**

playing, **443–444**, *445*

processing protocol statements in, **451–454**

protocols for, **445–448**

receiving data in, **450–451**

summary of, **851**

Search Results box in Object Browser, 49

searches

in help files, **776–777**, *777*, 782, *782*

in strings, **149**

seawars statement, 446, 454

Second function, 129, 134

Second property, 373

seconds

in date formats, 136

in DateAdd and DateDiff, 140

in DateTimePicker formats, 375

security

log on, 254

in MTS, **801–802**, 814

SECURITY_ATTRIBUTES structure, 683

SECURITY_DESCRIPTOR structure, 683

Security key, 676

Seek function, 93

Seek statement, 91–92

SelChange events, 370–371

Select Case/End Select statements, 471

Select method, 575

Selected property, 379

SelectedItem property

in ImageCombo, 379, 381

in TreeView, 212

selecting

files, **94–99**, *95*

MSFlexGrid data, **229–230**

printers, **299–302**, *301*

SelEnd property, 368–369

self-extracting .EXE files, 61

self-registering programs, 751

SelImage property, 380

SelLength property, 382, 488–489

SellOne method, 581, 586–587

SelStart property, 488–489

in MaskedEdit, 382

in MonthView, 368–369

SelText property, 382

semi-compiled programs, 18

semicolons (;)

in Print # statement, 102

in Print method, 303

SEND command in FTP, 405–406

Send Message header, 643–644

Send method

in MAPIMessages, 256, 259

in Message, 272

SendChart routine, **258–259**

SendComplete events, 427–428

SendData method, 426–427, 450

Sender property, 270

sending

CDO messages, **289**, *290*

FTP files, 406

MAPI messages, **256–259**

Winsock data, 427

SendKeys statement, **560–562**

SendMessage function, 607, 642, 644

SendProgress events, 427–428

Sensitivity property, 270–271

sent CDO messages, 268

Sent property, 270–271

separators

in date formats, 135

in menus, 331, 333

Sequential File Access program, **99**, *99*

reading files in, **99–101**, *100*

summary of, **852**

writing files in, **101–102**, *101*

sequential files, **99**, *99*

access to, **91–92**

FileSystemObject for, **120–123**

Loc function for, 93

reading, **99–101**, *100*, **120–123**, *122*

writing, **101–102**, *101*

SerialNumber property, 112

servers. *See also* Internet server program

in business services, **792–793**, *792*

in Honest Wayne's Used Airplane Lot, **581–583**, *582*

speed of, **739**

Session objects, 262

configuring, **266**

creating, 279–280

methods for, **265**

properties for, **264**

Session property, 262

SessionId property, 259, 354

sessions

CDO. *See* Session objects

MAPI, **253–254**, **279–280**

Telnet Server, **435–437**

Set_Click routine, **486–487**

Set New statement, 583, 699

Set Package Identity dialog box, 814, *814*

Set statement, 471

SetAbort method, 810

SetAttr statement, **91–92**

SetChartType routine, **242–243**, 337–338

SetComplete method, 810

SetEnvironmentVariable function, 607, 613–614

SetFirstVisible method, 379

SetFocus method, 179

SetLocaleIDs method, 265–266

SetOption method, 265–266

SetSysColors function, 607, 624, 626

SettingChanged events, 197

Setup Package Demo program, 51, *51*

setup programs, customizing, **61–62**

Sgn function, 473

Shape controls, speed of, 736

Shared file locking mode, 91

Shared Files window, 59, *59*

ShareName property, 112

Shell function, **559**, 563–565

ShellExecute function

for Registry access, 672

in Win32 API, 607, 634–636

Shift key in SendKeys, 562

short data type in Win32 API, 596

Short Date format, 135

short dates, 132, 135

Short Time format, 135

shortcut keys, **175**, *176*

ShortName property

in File, 118

in Folder, 115

ShortPath property

in File, 118

in Folder, 115

Show events, 516

Show Hidden Members command, 50

Show method

in Character, 522–523

for forms, 171

Show Ruler command, 335

ShowChart routine, **238–240**

ShowHex routine, **121–123**, *122*

ShowPrinter method, 300

ShowTips property, 350

ShowToday property, 368

ShowWeekNumber property, 368

Shutdown events, 516, 518

Shutdown exit option, 646

Shutdown Windows header, 647

Shutdown Windows tab, 646

shutting down Windows, **646–648**, *647*

Signed property, 270

SignOff method, 254

SignOn method, 253–254, 259

SimpleText property, 341

simplicity in bug prevention, **68–69**

Sin function, 473

Single data types
  speed of, 732
  in TypeName, 720
Single Document Interface (SDI) environment, **37–38**, *38*
single-threaded threading model, **44–45**
SitehWnd property, 465–466
16-bit controls, migration of, **23**
size
  of controls, **168–171**, *168*
  of CoolBars, **365–366**
  of forms, **167–168**
  of MonthView calendars, 368
  of MonthView controls, 369
  of StatusBar panels, **344**
  of subroutines, 68–69
SIZE command in FTP, 405
Size events in MSAgent, 516, 518
Size property
  in File, 118
  in Folder, 115
  in Message, 270–271
Skip method, 121
SkipLine method, 121
skipping form fields, 174
slashes (/)
  in date formats, 135
  as Mask characters, 383
Sleep function, 607, 620–621
Sleep routine, **621–624**
Sleep tab, 621
sleeping in Win32 API Demo, **620–624**, *621–622*
SlideShow program
  change events in, 96
  processing files in, **97–99**
  selecting files in, **94–95**, *95*
  summary of, **852–853**
SLN function, 142
Small Icon view in ListView controls, 215
smart clients, **791–792**, *792*
smart servers, **792–793**, *792*
SmartType routine, **181–183**
SMILE principle, **68–69**
Smtp service, 395

Snapshots, 28
social security numbers, 381
SocketHandle property, 424
Software key
  in HKEY_LOCAL_MACHINE, 676–677
  in HKEY_USERS, 678
Solitaire program, **628–634**, *628*
Sort method
  in AddressEntries, 276–277
  in Folders, 267
  in Messages, 268–269
Sorted property, 219
sorting ListView items, **219–220**
SortKey property, 219–220
SortOrder property, 219
sound cards for Microsoft Agent, 506
sound in screen savers, 656
SoundEffectsOn property, 521
Source property
  in Attachment, 273
  in Err, 761
  in Error, 469
Space function
  in VBScript, 473
  in Visual Basic, 146, 218
Spd speech tag, 526
Speak method, 522, **526**
speech engines and speech recognition, 505, **536–542**, *537*
Speech Input tab, 509–512, *511*
speech tags for Agents, 526
SpeechInput objects, 533
SpeechInput property, 514–515
SpeechInput tab, 533
speed, 728
  background processing in, **744–745**
  of collections, **735–736**
  of data types, **732**
  of early binding, **738**
  of empty string tests, **741–742**
  hiding controls and forms for, **735**
  of inline code, **739–740**
  of lightweight controls, 736
  of loading, **171–172**, **746**

of long tasks, **743–744**

of loops, **738–739**

of moving controls, **742**

of Next statements, 743

of object references, **741**

of property accesses, **733–734**

of redrawing, **734**

of server requests, **739**

splash panels for, **745–746**, *745*

unnecessary elements in, **737–738**

variants in, **733**

Speed property, 521

Spin control, 24

spin loops, 553

splash panels, **745–746**, *745*

Split function

   in VBScript, 473

   in Visual Basic, 102, 146, 149, 234, 236

spoken commands, 505, **536–542**, *537*

spool files, 299

spreadsheets. *See also* MSFlexGrid controls

   calculations in, **494–499**, *494*

   printing pages in, **315–317**, *318*

SQL Server data, 795

Sqr function, 473

square brackets ([]) in SendKeys, 561–562

SSTab controls, 483–484, *484*

Standard format, 148

Standard Setup Package option, 53

standard Windows applications, 18

StarSX program, **66–67**, *67*

   comments in, 71

   DrawArc routine in, **72**

   summary of, **853–854**

StarSx Settings dialog box, 659, *659*

Start Menu Item Properties window, 56, *58*

Start Menu Items window, 56, *57*

start statement in Sea Wars, 446, 454

StartMeUp routine, 636–637

StartOfWeek property, 368

STARTUPINFO structure, 629

state information in Internet Updater program, **416–417**

State property

   in ScriptControl, 465–466

   in Winsock, **424–425**

StateChanged event, 402–404, 416

Status property, **532–533**

StatusBar controls and status bars, **340–341**, *341–342*

   animation in, **347–348**

   click events in, **346–348**

   displaying information in, **345–346**

   panels for, **342–344**

   in Really Programmable Calculator, 485

Step Into option, 82

Step Out option, 82

Step Over option, 82

StillExecuting property, 401–402

stop command, 548, 550

Stop method, 522, 524, 527

Stop statement, 77

StopAll method, 522, 524, 527, 542

stopping Agent animation, 527

StoreID property, 270–271

Str function, 146, 148

StrComp function

   in VBScript, 473

   in Visual Basic, 146

StrConv function, 10, 146

String data type and strings

   converting with dates, **132–134**

   empty, **741–742**

   functions for, **144–146**, *147*

      for formatting, **147–148**

      for searching and editing, **149–150**

   memory for, 747

   in Registry, 675

   resource files for, 150

   in TypeName, 720

   with Win32 API, **597–599**, *598*

   for Winsock data, 427

String Demo program, 146, *147*

   searching and editing strings in, 149–150

   summary of, **854–855**

String function

   in VBScript, 473

in Visual Basic, 146
in Win32 API Demo, 611
String Table Editor, 153, *154*
StrReverse function
in VBScript, 473
in Visual Basic, 146
structures for Win32 API programs, **601**
StuffGrid routine, 225–226
StuffGridA routine, 226
Style property
in Band, 362
in Panel, 343, 345
in StatusBar, 341
in Toolbar, 350–351
in Toolbar buttons, 353
styles
for StatusBar panels, **343**
for Toolbar buttons, **353–354**
Sub statement, 471
SubFolders property, 114–115
SubItems collection, 218
Subject property, 270
Submitted property, 270–271
subroutines
naming conventions for, 73
size of, 68–69
Suggest animation, 525
SuggestReturn animation, 525
sunk statement, 446, 454
Surprised animation, 525
SurprisedReturn animation, 525
Suspended property, 515
SYD function, 142
synchronizing Agents, **526–527**
syntax checking, 17
SysColorsChanged events, 197
SysInfo control
for events, **196–200**, *199*
for operating system, **187–188**, *187*
for power and battery information, **188–191**, *189*
for screen, **191–192**, *192*
SysInfo1_DisplayChanged routine, 199–200
system colors, **624–627**, *625*
System Colors tab, 624

SYSTEM.DAT file, 673
System Information program
application information in, **194–195**
events in, **196–200**, *199*
operating system information in, **187–188**, *187*
power and battery information in, **188–191**, *189*
saving information in, **200–201**
screen information in, **191–194**, *192*
summary of, **855–856**
System key, 677
system requirements
for Microsoft Agent, 506
for Visual Basic, **7–8**
system tray, icons in, **664–671**, *666–667*
SYSTEMTIME structure, 601, 603, 617
Systray control, **664**
adding, **664–666**
programming, **666–671**, *666–667*
SysTray Demo dialog box, 666, *666–667*

T

t characters
in date formats, 136
in DateTimePicker, 375
Tab function, 307
Tab key, 172–173, 562
TabIndex property, 702
TableDefs collection, 29
Tables, 28
tables of contents for help files, 781
TabOrder property, 172–173
tabs
on forms, **172–174**, *173*
in toolboxes, 41
TabStop property, 172, 174–175
Tabstrip controls, 175
Tag property
in Menu, 331
in Systray, 664–665
Tan function, 473

TBCtrlArray_DblClick routine, 706

TBCtrlArray_GotFocus routine, 705

tbr styles, 353–354

TCP (Transmission Control Protocol), 422–423

TCP/IP connections, 443–444

Telnet Server program, **432–433**

   multiple connection requests in, **434–435**

   processing commands in, **440–442**, *441–442*

   processing input lines in, **437–440**, *439*

   running sessions in, **435–437**

   starting server in, **433**, *434*

   summary of, **856–857**

   Systray control for, 666

Telnet service, 395

templates, **38–39**

Testpack package, 815, *815*

text

   centering, **321–323**

   positioning, **308–310**, *310*

   printing, **303–312**, *304–306, 308, 310, 312*

text panel style, 343

Text property

   in ComboItem, 380

   in Error, 469

   in ImageCombo, 379

   in MaskedEdit, 382, 384

   in Message, 270–271

   in MSFlexGrid, 226–227

   in Node, 209–211

   in Panel, 343, 345

   speed of, **733–734**

text searches for help files, **776–777**, *777, 782, 782*

text-to-speech engines, 505, 526

text viewer, **601–602**, *602*

Text1_KeyPress routine, 179

Text2_KeyPress routine, 564

Text3_Validate routine, 180

Text5_Change routine, 178

Text6_KeyPress routine, 177

Text21_KeyPress routine, 645–646

TextAlignment property, 350

Textbox Messages tab, 642

textboxes

   in CoolBars, 358

   focus in, 175

   in Win32 API Demo, **641–646**, *642*

TextHeight method, 297, 309

TextMatrix property, 222–223, 225

TextStream objects

   in VBScript, 474

   in Visual basic, 117, **120–123**

TextWidth method, 298, 309

Think animation, 525

ThinkReturn animation, 525

32-bit controls, migration of, **23–24**

Thread per Object setting, 45

Thread Pool setting, 45

threading models, **44–45**

three-tier client/server architecture, 794

ThreeD control, 24

tiers in client/server architecture, 787

tildes (~t) in SendKeys, 561

time. *See also* dates

   in date formats, 136

   DateTimePicker for, **372–377**

   events for, 198–199

   in StatusBars, 343

Time command in Telnet Server program, 442

Time function

   in VBScript, 473

   in Visual Basic, 129, 138

Time service, 395

Time statement, 138

TIME_ZONE_ID_ constants, 604

TIME_ZONE_INFORMATION structure, 601, 603, 606

TimeChanged events, 197–198

TimeCreated property, 270–271

TimeExpired property, 270–271

TimeLastModified property, 270–271

Timeout events, 468

Timeout property, 465–466

Timer control, 668

Timer function, 129, 138

Timer1_Event routine, 669

TimeReceived property, 270–271

TimeSent property, 270–271

TimeSerial function

in VBScript, 473

in Visual Basic, 129, 134

TimeValue function

in VBScript, 473

in Visual Basic, 129, 134

Tips and Tricks Demo program

centering forms in, 163

position of forms in, **165–166**

resizing controls in, **168–171**

resizing forms prevention in, 167–168

summary of, **857–858**

TitleBackColor property, 368, 370

TitleForeColor property, 369–370

titles

for applications, 56, *57*

for MSChart controls, **243–246**, *244*

TitleText property, 245

.TLB file type, 20

Toolbar controls

adding buttons to, **352–354**, *352*

alignment and wrapping in, **350–351**

in CoolBars, 358

creating, **348–351**, *349, 351*

customizing, **357–358**, *357*

events for, **354–356**

ImageList controls for, **351**

in Really Programmable Calculator, 485

transparent buttons on, 351, *351*

Toolbar1_ButtonClick routine

in CDO Demo, **287–289**

in Sea Wars, 448–449

in SlideShow, 97–98

in Weather Maker, 355–356

Toolbar1_ButtonMenuClick routine

in Charter, 229, 244

in Weather Maker, 356

Toolbar1_Change routine, 357

tools, undocumented, 40

Tools ➢ Options command, 34

Tools ➢ Registry Checker command, 672

Tools ➢ Resource Editor command, 152

ToolTipText property

in Panel, 343–344

in Toolbar, 350

in Toolbar buttons, 353

Top property

in Character, 521

in control arrays, 702–703

for forms, 164

Topic Files dialog box, 775, *775*

topic files for help, **770–773**, *771, 773,* **775**, *775*

topic IDs, 775, *776*

TotalSize property, 112

TrackDefault property, 298

TrailingForeColor property, 369–370

Training button, 513

Training Wizard, 513, *513*

transactions. *See* Microsoft Transaction Server (MTS)

transfer time in Internet Transfer, 402

Transmission Control Protocol (TCP), 422–423

transparent Toolbar buttons, 351, *351*

trapping errors, **487–489**

TrayIcon property, 664–665

TrayTip property, 665

TreeView control, **208–214**, *209*

TreeView1_DblClick routine, 213

TreeView1_NodeClick routine

in CDO Demo, 284

in File Viewer, 116, 119

Trim function

in VBScript, 473

in Visual Basic, 146, 149

True/False format, 148

TruVoice text-to-speech engine, 505, 507

twips, 163, 314

TwipsPerPixel property, 163

TwipsPerPixelX routine, 191

TwipsPerPixelY routine, 191

Type property

in AddressEntry, 277

in Attachment, 273

in File, 118

in Folder, 115

in Message, 270

in Recipient, 275

Type statement, 92

Type structures, 103

TypeName function

     in VBScript, 473

     in Visual basic, **719–720**

TypeOf clause, **719**

U

UBound method, 704

Ucase function, 146

uchar data type, 596

UDP (User Datagram Protocol), 422–423

.uk domain, 393

Unattended Execution option, 45

underlining

     for access keys, 174

     for help file links, 773

underscore characters (_) with MaskedEdit, 384

undo buffers, **645–646**

Undo command, 334

undocumented tools, 40

Unicode character set, 595

UNIT data type, 596

Universal Resource Locators (URLs), **396**, **398–399**

Universal time, 199

Unknown return value, 720

Unload method, 519

unloading

     Agent characters, 519

     ScreenSaver forms, **658**

Unread property, 270

unrolling loops, **738–739**

unsigned data types, 597

unused routines and variables, 748

Update method

     in AddressEntry, 278

     in Message, 272

UpdateInfo routine, **414–415**

updating

     files in Internet Updater, **414–415**

     progress bars, 185

     random file records, **108**

UpDown property, 373

URL property, 401–402

URLs (Universal Resource Locators), **396**, **398–399**

.us domain, 393

USER.DAT file, 673

User Datagram Protocol (UDP), 422–423

user-input checking, **176–177**

     Change events for, **178**

     ComboBoxes for, **180–183**

     Keypress events for, **177–178**

     LostFocus events for, **179**

     Validate events for, **180**

user names

     in FTP, 397

     for MAPI, 253–254, 258–259

     in URLs, 396

user services

     in Applications Services model, **789–790**

     in MTS, **808–809**

UserInput objects, **517**

UserName property

     in Internet Transfer, 401–402

     in MAPISession, 254

UseSafeSubset property, 465–466

V

Validate events

     in ObjectEvents, 714

     for user-input checking, **180**

ValidLogon function, 438

Value property

     in DateTimePicker, 373

     in EventParameter, 715

     in MonthView, 369

     in Toolbar buttons, 353

values

     checking. *See* user-input checking

     in Registry, 674

variables
    coding conventions for, **73**
    declarations for, **35–36**, **67–68**
    initializing, 737–738
    memory for, 748
    naming conventions for, 74
Variant data type
    late binding of, 738
    for optional parameters, 323
    speed of, **733**
    in VBScript, 470
    in Win32 API, 596–597
VARIANTARG data type, 596
VariantHeight property, 360
VarType function, 473
VB folder, 40
vb WindowStyle parameters, 559
VB4 Sample program, **858**
VBA (Visual Basic for Applications), 464
VBControlExtender objects, 714
.VBD file type, 20
.VBG file type, 20
.VBL file type, 20, 44
.VBP file type, 20
.VBR file type, 20
VBScript, 464–465, **469**
    data types in, 470
    functions in, **471–473**
    objects in, **474**
    statements in, **470–471**
.VBW file type, 20
.VBX file type, 20
.VBZ file type, 20
Version property, 264
versions
    of operating systems, 187
    of projects, **46**, 47
View menus, typical commands on, 335
View ➤ Object Browser command, 48
views in ListView controls, 215
VisibilityCause property, 521
Visible property
    in Balloon, 531

    in Band, 362
    in Character, 521
    in Command, 530, 539
    in Commands, 529
    in control arrays, 702
    in Menu, 331
    for pop-up menus, 338
    in Toolbar buttons, 353, 358
VisibleDays property, 369
Visual Basic, evolution of, **4–5**
Visual Basic Debugger
    breakpoints in, **79–82**, *80–81*
    watching expressions in, **82–84**, *83–84*
Visual Basic for Applications (VBA), 464
Visual C++ language, 606
Visual Studio package, 5–6
Voice property
    in Command, 530, 538
    in Commands, 529
    in UserInput, 517
Vol speech tag, 526
VolumeName property, 112

W

w characters
    in date formats, 136
    in DateAdd and DateDiff, 140
Wait method, 522, 526–527, 552
WaitForIdleInput function, 608, 630–632
WaitForSingleObject function, 608, 630–633
WaitProg function, **632–633**
waits, handling, **184–186**, **743–744**
watch expressions, **82–84**, *83–84*
Water_Click routine, 451, **456–457**
Wave animation, 525
WaveReturn animation, 525
.WCT file type, 20
Weather Maker program
    for CoolBars
        adding bands to, 364

loading, 365

resizing, 365–366

saving position of, 363

MaskEdit controls in, 385

moon animation in, **347–348**

summary of, **858–859**

Toolbar events in, 355–356

Toolbars in, **357–358**, *357*

Week function, 134

Week property, 369

Weekday function, 129, 134

WeekdayName function, 129, 134

weekdays in DateAdd and DateDiff, 140

weeks in DateAdd and DateDiff, 140

well-known port addresses, **394–395**

While/Wend statements, 471

Who command, 442

Width property

in Band, 362, 364

in Character, 521

for controls, 171

for forms, 167

in Panel, 343–344

in Printer object and Picture control, 298

in Screen, 162–163

Win32 API Demo program

environment information in, **612–614**, *612*

file icons in, **637–641**, *638*

process information in, **614–620**, *615*

running files in, **634–637**, *634*

running programs in, **628–634**, *628*

shutting down Windows in, **646–648**, *647*

sleeping in, **620–624**, *621–622*

summary of, **859–861**

system colors in, **624–627**, *625*

text boxes in, **641–646**, *642*

time zone information in, **603–605**

windows information in, **608–612**, *609*

Win32 API programs, **594–595**

adding routines for, **602–606**, *605*

character sets in, **595**

data types in, **596–599**, *598*

declaring calls for, **599–600**

example. *See* Win32 API Demo program

functions in, **606–608**

structures and constants for, **601**

text viewer for, **601–602**, *602*

Window menus, typical commands on, 335

WindowList property, 331

windows

in programs, 15

retrieving information on, **608–612**, *609*

Windows program, shutting down, **646–648**, *647*

Windows Registry. *See* Registry

Windows Registry header, **681–686**

WindowState property, 657

WindowStyle parameter, 559

WinHlp32 program, **779–782**, *780–782*

Winsock controls

adding, **423–425**

events for, **427–428**

methods for, **426–427**

Winsock1_ConnectionRequest routine, 449–450

Winsock1_DataArrival routine

in Quote, **431–432**

in Sea Wars, 450

WinZip program, 61, 558

With statement, 741

WithEvents keyword, 712

Wizards, 11, *11*

WM_CHAR messages, 641

WM_CLEAR messages, 641

WM_QUERYENDSESSION messages, 646

WORD data type, 596

WorkAreaHeight property, 191

WorkAreaWidth property, 191

workbooks

closing, **577**

creating, 570, *571*

saving, **576–577**

worksheets

adding data to, 571–572, *572*

charting, **574**, *575*

creating, 570, *571*

formatting cells in, 572–573, *573*

Workspace objects, 28–29

wParam parameter in SendMessage, 644
Wrappable property, 350–351
wrapping in Toolbars, **350–351**
write-ahead logs in MTS, 804–805
Write animation, 525
Write file mode, 91
Write method, 121
Write # statement, 91–92
WriteBlankLines method, 121
WriteCenter routine, **321–323**
WriteEndDoc routine, 320, 325
WriteLeft routine, 321
WriteLine method, 121, 123
WriteNewPage routine, 319, 325
WritePicture routine, 320, 324
WriteReturn animation, 525
WriteRight routine, 321
WriteToFile method, 273
writing sequential files, **101–102**, *101*
www-http service, 395

in DateAdd and DateDiff, 140
in DateTimePicker, 375
year 2000 issues, **130**
    Date data type for, **132**
    extended date fields for, **131**
    leap years in, **131**
Year function, 129, 134
Year property
    in DateTimePicker, 373
    in MonthView, 369
years
    in date formats, 136
    in DateAdd and DateDiff, 140
    in DateTimePicker formats, 375
Yes/No format, 148
youwon statement, 446

X

x format character in DateTimePicker, 375

Y

y characters
    in date formats, 136

Z

zero-based array problems, **85**
.ZIP files, 558
Zoom In command, 335
Zoom Out command, 335
Zoom property, 298

Expert Guide to Visual Basic 6 Companion CD

 This book's autorun CD includes the convenient Sybex interface, which you can use to:

- Copy project files and examples created by the author to your hard disk.

- Install and try out new powerful software from TV Objects, InstallShield, Blue Sky, NuMega, LEADTools, and more.

Visual Basic Third-Party Software

This CD includes the most valuable software available for Visual Basic programmers. Use this software to speed development work, simplify debugging, create help files, and more.

Applet Designer 1.7 TV Objects' powerful Visual Basic–Java conversion tool. Write the applet in Visual Basic 6, then convert it to pure 100% Java.

Installshield Express Professional 2.1 A 30-day evaluation copy of the full custom-installation product for Visual Basic developers.

RoboHelp HTML 6 Enables you to create Microsoft's new HTML Help for Visual Basic applications running under Windows 98.

NuMega's Smartcheck Does more than detect errors—it explains why the errors occurred. This is the smart debugging program that is winning rave reviews.

LEADTools 10 Provides Active X controls for a wide range of imaging needs. Scanning, graphics editing, and conversion with more than 500 functions are available for you to try.

WinZip The number one compression software program. Don't surf the web without it!

Projects from the Author

This book contains numerous applications developed by the author to demonstrate features of the language, ActiveX controls, and power-user programming topics. You can use any of these projects in your work, royalty free. Here's a sampling of what you'll find on the CD:

I'm Thinking of a Color uses Microsoft Agent's speech recognition, speech synthesis, and animation technology to play the preschool children's game without a keyboard or mouse.

The Really Programmable Calculator shows you how to use the MSScript control to add VBScript macro processing to your own application.

Charter demonstrates how tools like MSFlexGrid, MSChart, MAPI, MSScript, and the Printer object can be combined to build a spreadsheet program.

Win32 API Demo demonstrates different Win32 API calls, including those related to getting time zone info, environment info, and process info; running other programs and files; delaying the execution of your program; changing system colors; and shutting down Windows.

Sea Wars implements a multiplayer game similar to Battleship, using Winsock to handle communications between programs.

Registry Tool allows you to extract the registered owner and registered organization from the Registry using Win32 API calls.

System Information demonstrates how to use the SysInfo control to gather information about the operating system, the computer's battery (if it has one), and the screen.

CDO Demo shows you how to use the Collaboration Data Objects (CDO) to access the full capabilities of MAPI. You can use it to send and receive e-mail, access mail folders, and get other information stored in Outlook 98.

File Viewer shows you how to use the TreeView and ListView controls by building a pair of ActiveX controls called FileSelect and FileView.

Agent Demo shows you how to use the speech recognition and animation features of Microsoft Agent in your own application.

Notepad Writer demonstrates how to use Shell, AppActivate, and SendKeys to dynamically start and control another Windows program.

DateControl demonstrates how to use the new date controls MonthView and DateTimePicker in your program.

Quote of the Day uses the Winsock control to retrieve a quote from a Quote of the Day server.

DoEvents demonstrates how to use a progress bar.

Hello Jill is a simple MSAgent application that displays the selected character and speaks specified text.